## Legal Theory in the Colonies

In colonial India and Mandatory Palestine, early twentieth-century legal scholars made important contributions to the study of the nature of law, particularly by analyzing Hindu and Jewish law – their ancient religious systems. This book reconstructs the lives and ideas of these scholars, revealing a forgotten global wave of jurisprudential innovation that appeared across many territories in the non-Western world. The book challenges the view that non-Western legal scholars working in the colonies were passive recipients of Western ideas. It argues that Indian and Jewish thinkers used Western historical and sociological approaches to law to reimagine Hindu and Jewish law, and to assert their relevance to modern legal and constitutional debates. Though historical in scope, the story this book tells is also relevant to contemporary tensions between Western liberal law and non-Western religious legal traditions. This title is available as open access on Cambridge Core.

Assaf Likhovski is the Danielle Rubinstein Professor of Comparative Law and Jurisprudence at Tel Aviv University. He is the author of *Law and Identity in Mandate Palestine* and *Tax Law and Social Norms in Mandatory Palestine and Israel*.

See the Studies in Legal History series website at
http://studiesinlegalhistory.org/

**Studies in Legal History**



## Other Books in the Series

Sonia Tycko, *Captured Consent: Contract Labor in English Charity, Colonization, and War, 1600–1700*
Jenny Huangfu Day, *Transborder Fugitives, Extradition, and Political Crimes in Modern China*
Maurits den Hollander, *Court, Credit, and Capital: Amsterdam's Insolvency Legislation in the Dutch Golden Age*
Zachary Herz, *The God and the Bureaucrat: Roman Law, Imperial Sovereignty, and Other Stories*
Kevin Arlyck, *The Nation at Sea: The Federal Courts and American Sovereignty, 1789–1825*
Ivan Lee, *Extradition and Empire: Sovereignty and Subjecthood in Hong Kong*
James Q. Whitman, *From Masters of Slaves to Lords of Lands: The Transformation of Ownership in the Western World*

Alastair McClure, *Trials of Sovereignty: Mercy, Violence, and the Making of Criminal Law in British India, 1857–1922*
Marie-Amélie George, *Family Matters: Queer Households and the Half-Century Struggle for Legal Recognition*
Simon Devereaux, *Execution, State and Society in England, 1660–1900*
Giuliana Perrone, *Nothing More than Freedom: The Failure of Abolition in American Law*
Christian G. Fritz, *Monitoring American Federalism: The History of State Legislative Resistance*
Ada Maria Kuskowski, *Vernacular Law: Writing and the Reinvention of Customary Law in Medieval France*
E. Claire Cage, *The Science of Proof: Forensic Medicine in Modern France*
Kristin A. Olbertson, *The Dreadful Word: Speech Crime and Polite Gentlemen in Massachusetts, 1690–1776*
Edgardo Pérez Morales, *Unraveling Abolition: Legal Culture and Slave Emancipation in Colombia*
Lyndsay Campbell, *Truth and Privilege: Libel Law in Massachusetts and Nova Scotia, 1820–1840*
Sara M. Butler, *Pain, Penance, and Protest: Peine Forte et Dure in Medieval England*
Michael Lobban, *Imperial Incarceration: Detention without Trial in the Making of British Colonial Africa*
Stefan Jurasinski and Lisi Oliver, *The Laws of Alfred: The Domboc and the Making of Anglo-Saxon Law*
Sascha Auerbach, *Armed with Sword and Scales: Law, Culture, and Local Courtrooms in London, 1860–1913*
Alejandro de La Fuente and Ariela J. Gross, *Becoming Free, Becoming Black: Race, Freedom, and the Law in Cuba, Virginia, and Louisiana*
Elizabeth Papp Kamali, *Felony and the Guilty Mind in Medieval England*
Jessica K. Lowe, *Murder in the Shenandoah: Making Law Sovereign in Revolutionary Virginia*
Michael A. Schoeppner, *Moral Contagion: Black Atlantic Sailors, Citizenship, and Diplomacy in Antebellum America*
Sam Erman, *Almost Citizens: Puerto Rico, the U.S. Constitution, and Empire*
Martha S. Jones, *Birthright Citizens: A History of Race and Rights in Antebellum America*
Julia Moses, *The First Modern Risk: Workplace Accidents and the Origins of European Social States*

Cynthia Nicoletti, *Secession on Trial: The Treason Prosecution of Jefferson Davis*

Edward James Kolla, *Sovereignty, International Law, and the French Revolution*

Assaf Likhovski, *Tax Law and Social Norms in Mandatory Palestine and Israel*

Robert W. Gordon, *Taming the Past: Essays on Law and History and History in Law*

Paul Garfinkel, *Criminal Law in Liberal and Fascist Italy*

Michelle A. McKinley, *Fractional Freedoms: Slavery, Intimacy, and Legal Mobilization in Colonial Lima, 1600–1700*

Karen M. Tani, *States of Dependency: Welfare, Rights, and American Governance, 1935–1972*

Stefan Jurasinski, *The Old English Penitentials and Anglo- Saxon Law*

Felice Batlan, *Women and Justice for the Poor: A History of Legal Aid, 1863–1945*

Sophia Z. Lee, *The Workplace Constitution from the New Deal to the New Right*

Mitra Sharafi, *Law and Identity in Colonial South Asia: Parsi Legal Culture, 1772–1947*

Michael A. Livingston, *The Fascists and the Jews of Italy: Mussolini's Race Laws, 1938–1943*

# Legal Theory in the Colonies

## *Hindu and Jewish Scholars under British Rule*

ASSAF LIKHOVSKI
*Tel Aviv University*

CAMBRIDGE
UNIVERSITY PRESS

**CAMBRIDGE**
**UNIVERSITY PRESS**

Shaftesbury Road, Cambridge CB2 8EA, United Kingdom

One Liberty Plaza, 20th Floor, New York, NY 10006, USA

477 Williamstown Road, Port Melbourne, VIC 3207, Australia

314–321, 3rd Floor, Plot 3, Splendor Forum, Jasola District Centre,
New Delhi – 110025, India

Cambridge University Press is part of Cambridge University Press & Assessment, a department of the University of Cambridge.

We share the University's mission to contribute to society through the pursuit of education, learning and research at the highest international levels of excellence.

www.cambridge.org
Information on this title: www.cambridge.org/9781009699884

DOI: 10.1017/9781009699877



First published 2026

*A catalogue record for this publication is available from the British Library*

*A Cataloging-in-Publication data record for this book is available from the Library of Congress*

ISBN 978-1-009-69988-4 Hardback
ISBN 978-1-009-69990-7 Paperback

*Dedicated to my late parents, Eliahu and Ruth Likhovski*

# Contents

# Figures

# Tables

# Acknowledgments

I began writing this book in 2018 and completed it during the *anni horribiles* of 2023–25. These three years were marked in Israel by the government's attempt to overhaul the judicial system, and later by the war sparked by Hamas' barbaric assault on Israel on October 7, 2023. During these difficult times, history offered a source of solace, reminding me that the dark present was not the only possibility, that there had been, and perhaps could be again, a time when religion was a source of shared hope and promise rather than of division and hatred. No less sustaining than history was the remarkable community of legal historians at Tel Aviv University and, more broadly, throughout Israel. I am grateful to Orna Alyagon-Darr, Leora Bilsky, Michael Birnhack, Ofra Bloch, Rivka Brot, Levy Cooper, Natalie Davidson, Talia Diskin, Arye Edrei, Rachel Friedman, Mary Haddad, Ron Harris, Roy Kreitner, Nomi Levenkron, Doreen Lustig, Maya Mark, Menny Mautner, Tamara Morsel-Eisenberg, Dina Moyal, Udi Neuman, Amihai Radzyner, Anat Rosenberg, Orit Rozin, Shani Schnitzer, David Schorr, Yoram Shachar, Ornit Shani, Rivi Weill, Melech Westreich, Shai Wozner, Neta Ziv, and many other friends and colleagues for their advice, assistance, comments, and camaraderie.

While working on this book, I was fortunate to spend short research leaves at two of Europe's leading legal history research institutes: the Centre Aquitain d'Histoire du Droit at the University of Bordeaux and the Max Planck Institute for Legal History and Legal Theory in Frankfurt. I would like to thank Nader Hakim, as well as Géraldine Cazals, Laetitia Guerlain, and Xavier Prévost in Bordeaux and Thomas Duve, Stefan Vogenauer, and Marietta Auer, as well as Ulrike Radden, in Frankfurt, for their warm hospitality and for the opportunity to present and discuss parts of this book during my time at their respective institutions.

For advice and feedback on drafts of some of the chapters of this book and other types of assistance I also thank Aya Bejermi, Yishai Blank, Tatiana Borisova, Luisa Brunori, William E. Butler, Li Chen, Raymond Cocks, Avihay Dorfman, Baudouin Dupret, Miriam Egbor, Magdalena Gebhart, Nishant Gokhale, Khinvraj Jangid, Oleksiy Kresin, Mitchel Lasser, James Loeffler, Nariaki Nakazato, Teemu Ruskola, Lena Salaymeh, Philippa Shimrat, Upasana Singh, Geetanjali Srikantan, Verena Steller, Shivprasad Swaminathan, Ragini Surana, Jin Wang, Zhiqiang Wang, and Mingzhe Zhu.

I am grateful for the feedback I received on earlier drafts of several chapters of this book when I presented them at Ben-Gurion University, the China University of Political Science and Law, Cornell University, the University of Haifa, the Israel Institute for Advanced Studies, Reichman University, Queen Mary University of London, and the Swiss Institute of Comparative Law, as well as at conferences of the American Society of Comparative Law, the American Society for Legal History, the Asian Legal History Association, the Australian and New Zealand Law and History Society, the European Society for Comparative Legal History, the Israeli Legal History Association, the British Legal History Conference, the Legal Histories of Empire Conference, and the TAU-Jindal Global University Conference.

My research assistants made the work on this book easier. I thank Reut Babai, Ido Ben Meir, Tamar Ben Ozer, Amit Berkovitz, Tanvi Bhargava, Neta Chehanovski, Katarzyna Czerwonogóra, Yoni Filc, Udita Ghosh, Nir Gonen, Matan Harel, Hazar Hasan, Ella Itkin, Julija Levin, Anna Lotan, Lama Obaid Zoabi, Diklah Shambadal, Rajbushan Shinde, and Noa Shmueli. I thank the staff at the libraries and archives I used, especially Lev Beingoltz, Niklaus Bütikofer, Giora Katz, Orly Levi, Hana Liashkevich, and Eran Tal. Special thanks are due to Amanda Dale for her excellent editorial work. Research for this book was supported by The Israel Science Foundation (grant nos. 405/15 and 1377/21), and The David Berg Foundation Institute for Law and History at Tel Aviv University.

Funding from Tel Aviv University and the Danielle Rubinstein Chair in Comparative Law and Jurisprudence, along with the assistance of Yossi Bar, Sharon Konforty, Liora Smurjik Cohen, and Eyal Zisser, made it possible for this book to be published open access, allowing the digital version to be freely read and reused under a Creative Commons license.

I am indebted to the American Society of Comparative Law and to Oxford University Press for their permission to use materials from my articles "A Colonial Legal Laboratory? Jurisprudential Innovation in British India," *American Journal of Comparative Law* 69 (2021): 44–91, and "Jurisprudence and Nationalism in the British Empire in the Early Twentieth Century: India, Egypt, and Palestine Compared," *English Historical Review* (forthcoming), in this book.

Working with Taisu Zhang, the book's academic editor, was a privilege. His steady guidance and expertise shaped every stage of the publication process, from submission to publication. The perceptive comments of the two anonymous reviewers substantially enriched the book's arguments. I thank Ruth Boyes, Cecelia Cancellaro, Victoria Phillips, and the rest of the editorial team at Cambridge University Press, for their valuable support throughout the publication process. At Integra Software Services I thank Sindhu Balasubramanian. Finally, I thank Sophie Rosinke for copy-editing this book, and Arc Indexing for the preparation of the index.

I am deeply grateful for the support of my extended family: my siblings Edo and Michal, and their partners, Sigale and Ben, as well as Amnon, Ahuva, Efrat, Gadi, Iris, and Elad. I am also thankful for the opportunity to have known the late Michal Wydra-Dangor, may her memory be a blessing. My children – Yotam, Hagar, and Daniel – and their partners, Carmel and Lior, bring immense joy and meaning to my life. Above all, I am profoundly thankful to my wife, Orly Erez-Likhovski, for her unwavering strength, wisdom, and love. She is, in every sense, a true woman of valor.

# Note on Transliteration and Terminology

I follow a simplified system of transliteration for Hebrew and Arabic. For place names, I follow historical usage, for example, Calcutta rather than Kolkata, or Odessa rather than Odesa. In rendering the names of individuals, I adopt the spelling they originally used in Latin script. All translations are my own, unless otherwise indicated.

# Introduction

In 1911, Samuel Eisenstadt, a young Russian-Jewish legal scholar, published an article calling for the revival of Jewish law. Addressing his Jewish readers, Eisenstadt proclaimed:

> Look at the shores of the Arabian Sea and the rivers of India! Great and ancient peoples of the Orient are awakening from their slumber, fighting for their freedom ... A new and enlightened society is emerging on the shores of Asia, and in its law and social customs, the spirit of religion is reflected in its pure oriental form. The Orient longs and yearns for the revelation of a strong and original oriental law, one that draws and nourishes itself from the source of oriental religion ... To this oriental society and its peoples, whose souls are close to our souls and whose feelings are close to our feelings, we must bring our advanced law, the law of the ancient Semitic people, the first and foremost of the enlightened peoples of Western Asia ... We must create an authentic Jewish society based on authentic Jewish law.[1]

This romantic passage reflects several ideas that may seem strange to modern readers, but were common among early twentieth-century Jewish intellectuals. The pan-Semitic and pan-Asian sentiments that Eisenstadt, a Zionist, expressed toward Arabs and Indians;[2] the

[1] Samuel Eisenstadt, "Le-Korot ha-Mishpat ha-'Ivri (Skirah Klalit)," *He-'Atid: Me'asef Sifruti Mada'i* 3 (1909–11): 194, 208.

[2] Racist discourse in the nineteenth and early twentieth centuries classified Jews as "Semites," in contrast to the so-called "Aryan" race, which was widely regarded as superior. Some Zionist Jews appropriated this framework to argue that Jews were historically and ethnically connected to other Asian peoples, particularly Arabs. For example, the early Zionist thinker Moshe Lilienblum wrote in 1881 that "we are strangers [in Europe], Semites [living] among Aryans, the sons of Shem among the sons of Japheth. A Palestinian

connection between "enlightened society," "law," and "the spirit of religion,"[3] and perhaps also the depiction of Jewish law as "oriental" rather than Western.[4]

tribe from Asia in European lands." See Hanan Harif, *Anashim Ahim Anahnu: Ha-Pniyah Mizrahah ba-Hagut ha-Tsiyonit* (Jerusalem: Shazar, 2019), 18, 27, 31. For additional discussions of Pan-Semitic and Pan-Asian sentiments in early Zionism, see, e.g., Paul Mendes-Flohr, *Divided Passions: Jewish Intellectuals and the Experience of Modernity* (Detroit, MI: Wayne State University Press, 1991), 77–132; Shimon Lev, *Nehirin lanu Shevilin de-Hodu: Ha-Mifgash beyn ha-'Olam ha-Yehudi-Tsiyoni le-Hodu ve-Tarbutah 'al Rek'a Tsmihat ha-Tnu'ot ha-Leumiyot* (Tel Aviv: Gama, 2018); Rephael G. Stern and Arie M. Dubnov, "A Part of Asia or Apart from Asia? Zionist Perceptions of Asia, 1947–1956," in *Unacknowledged Kinships: Postcolonial Studies and the Historiography of Zionism*, eds. Stefan Vogt, Derek Penslar, and Arieh Saposnik (Waltham, MA: Brandeis University Press, 2023), 233, 236–42; Avi-ram Tzoreff, *Kedmah Mizrahah: R. Binyamin, du-Le'umiyut ve-Tsiyonut sheke-Neged* (Jerusalem: Shazar, 2023), 103–53, 171–81; Amit Levy, *A New Orient: From German Scholarship to Middle Eastern Studies in Israel* (Waltham, MA: Brandeis University Press, 2024); Mostafa Hussein, *Hebrew Orientalism: Jewish Engagement with Arabo-Islamic Culture in Late Ottoman and British Palestine* (Princeton, NJ: Princeton University Press, 2026). On the many parallels between European Jews and the colonized populations of European empires (and also on the different ways in which Jewish history undermines the simplistic binary categories used by many historians of colonialism), see, e.g., Ethan Katz, Lisa Moses Leff, and Maud S. Mandel, "Introduction: Engaging Colonial History and Jewish History," in *Colonialism and the Jews*, eds. Ethan Katz, Lisa Moses Leff, and Maud S. Mandel (Bloomington, IN: Indiana University Press, 2017), 1.

3 The two normative systems that I will focus on in this book, Hindu and Jewish, as well as other systems I will mention such as Islamic law, do not easily fit into the Western categories of "law" and "religion." While these systems deal with issues that we would describe as legal, they also encompass topics that would be classified by Western observers as belonging to morality, theology, ritual, myth, history and literature. See, e.g., Hanina Ben-Menahem, "Is Talmudic Law a Religious Legal System? A Provisional Analysis," *Journal of Law and Religion* 24 (2008–09): 379; Timothy Lubin, Donald R. Davis, Jr., and Jayanth K. Krishnan, eds., "Introduction," in *Hinduism and Law: An Introduction* (Cambridge and New York: Cambridge University Press, 2010), 1, 6; Werner Menski, "Hindu Law in Modern Times: How Hindu Law Continues in Modern India," in *The Oxford History of Hinduism: Modern Hinduism*, ed. Torkel Brekke (Oxford: Oxford University Press, 2019), 244, 245, 254; Leora Batnitzky, "Between Ancestry and Belief: 'Judaism' and 'Hinduism' in the Nineteenth Century," *Modern Judaism* 41 (2021): 194; *Law as Religion, Religion as Law*, eds. David C. Flatto and Benjamin Porat (Cambridge: Cambridge University Press, 2022); Baudouin Dupret and Gianluca Parolin, "The Great Divide in Legal Discourse," in *State Law and Legal Positivism: The Global Rise of a New Paradigm*, eds. Baudouin Dupret and Jean-Louis Halpérin (Leiden: Brill, 2022), 5; Jean-Louis Halpérin, "Historical-Jurisprudential Methods," in *The Cambridge Handbook of Comparative Law*, eds. Mathias Siems and Po Jen Yap (New York: Cambridge University Press, 2024), 32, 37–8.

4 The leading comparative law scholar of the early twentieth century, Josef Kohler, classified Jewish law (both ancient and modern) as an "oriental" legal system, similar to Hindu, Islamic, Chinese, or Japanese law, distinguishing it from Greek and Roman

Eisenstadt published these words immediately after graduating from the Faculty of Law of the University of Bern, where he wrote a doctoral dissertation on the history of Jewish law.[5] In the following decades, which he first spent in Europe and then in Mandatory Palestine, he would work tirelessly to further his vision of a Jewish legal revival: the modernization of Jewish law in preparation for its use as the basis of the legal system of the future Jewish state. While this vision centered on what Eisenstadt defined as a non-Western legal system, it was inspired by Western legal theories, primarily the romantic–nationalist theory of the German Historical School but also, somewhat incongruously, Marxist legal theory.

Eisenstadt's utopian vision reflected a broader encounter between Western legal theories and non-Western law that occurred simultaneously in many territories during the first decades of the twentieth century. One could find this encounter in the ideas and works of several elite groups: politicians, administrators, historians writing on ancient law, and traditional religious experts.[6] This book focuses on another group: legal scholars teaching law in Western-style legal education institutions outside Europe. The book compares the ideas of these scholars in two territories that were part of the British Empire in the first half of the twentieth century: colonial India and Mandatory Palestine.

law. See Josef Kohler and Leopold Wenger, *Allgemeine Rechtsgeschichte*, Vol. 1: *Orientalisches Recht und Recht der Griechen und Römer* (Leipzig: Teubner, 1914), v–vi, 71–82. On the history of the contrast between "Aryan" and "Semitic" law, and its impact on nineteenth- and early twentieth-century comparative law scholarship, see Pier Giuseppe Monateri, "Black Gaius: A Quest for the Multicultural Origin of the Western Legal Tradition," *Hastings Law Journal* 51 (2000): 479, 490–6; Tomasz Giaro, "A Purely Western Tradition: The 100th Anniversary of the Orientalisation Debate," in *The Grand Strategy of Comparative Law: Themes, Methods, Developments*, eds. Luca Siliquini-Cinelli, Davide Gianti, and Mauro Balestrieri (New York: Routledge, 2024), 253. Of course, the fact that some non-Jewish and Jewish scholars in Europe saw the Jews (and Jewish law) as "Asian" or "Oriental" did not mean that Asians did so too. As one Israeli intellectual noted, "if Anti-Semitic Europe saw the Jews as 'Asians,' the Asians saw the Jews as completely European … not as an Asiatic nation … that is now returning to its homeland in Asia." See Efraim Broida, "Rashey Prakim 'al Hodu ve-Yisra'el," *Molad* 2(7) (October 1948): 10.

5 See Staatsarchiv des Kantons Bern, BB 8.2.466 (Fakultätsprotokoll, 1910 06–28).

6 See, e.g., Alexander Kaye, *The Invention of Jewish Theocracy: The Struggle for Legal Authority in Modern Israel* (New York: Oxford University Press, 2020).

The legal scholars of India and Palestine published textbooks, monographs, and academic and non-academic articles on law.[7] In the case of India, the publications were in English, the dominant language of law and legal scholarship in India.[8] In Mandatory Palestine, the works I discuss in this book were mainly written in Hebrew (or Arabic in the case of works by Palestinian-Arab lawyers). Some of these works were practical, designed to provide lawyers with knowledge about existing legal rules. Others were theoretical, intended to give their readers more abstract knowledge about the nature of law and its development. Such works dealt with legal philosophy, legal history, the sociology of law, and comparative law, all of which fall under the broad term "legal theory."[9] This book analyzes these theoretical works, asking how legal scholars in India and Palestine assimilated, critiqued, and modified Western ideas about the nature of law, its development, and its relationship with society.

Intellectual historians, legal historians, and even historians of some specific subfields of law, such as international law, have long been aware of the importance of writing histories of modern law that

[7] One legal genre this book does not explore is case law. This omission is due both to constraints of space and to the fact that English judicial conventions have traditionally discouraged the explicit citation of academic scholarship in judicial decisions. See, generally, Neil Duxbury, *Jurists and Judges: An Essay on Influence* (Oxford: Hart, 2001), 61–115.

[8] Since the University of Calcutta will be the primary institution examined in the sections of this book focused on India, a survey of Bengali-language works by the scholars under analysis was conducted, using the Hiteshranjan Sanyal Memorial Archive. While this extensive database includes writings by several of these scholars on literary, linguistic, and historical subjects, it does not contain works in Bengali by these scholars on legal topics.

[9] "Jurisprudence" is a term that was also used in the past to designate any non-practical legal work (hence scholars used terms such as "historical jurisprudence" and "sociological jurisprudence"). Today, "jurisprudence" is usually used in a narrower sense in the English-speaking world, referring only to the practice of asking philosophical questions about the nature of law. In this book, I will use the term "jurisprudence" in its older, broader, sense, as synonymous with legal theory. An additional term, "legal thought," is often used to describe both explicit as well as implicit assumptions that legal scholars and other jurists hold about the nature of law. See, generally, William Twining, *General Jurisprudence: Understanding Law from a Global Perspective* (Cambridge: Cambridge University Press, 2009), 8; Roger Cotterrell, *Sociological Jurisprudence: Juristic Thought and Social Inquiry* (Abingdon: Routledge, 2017); Brian Z. Tamanaha, "Sociological Jurisprudence Past and Present," *Law and Social Inquiry* 45 (2020): 493, 511–12; Marietta Auer, "What Is Legal Theory?" *Rg (Rechtsgeschichte)* 29 (2021): 30.

consider territories outside Europe and North America.[10] However, relatively few works examining the history of modern legal theory mention non-Western territories. The conventional assumption about this history is that non-Western legal scholars were merely passive recipients of ideas that had first appeared in the West. One can find this assumption in works written by legal historians.[11] Legal

[10] On the importance of studying the intellectual history of European peripheries, borderlands, and colonial territories, see, generally, Suzanne Marchand, "Has the History of the Disciplines Had Its Day?" in *Rethinking Modern European Intellectual History*, eds. Darrin M. McMahon and Samuel Moyn (New York: Oxford University Press, 2014), 130, 143–4; Stefan Nygård, Johan Strang, and Marja Jalava, "At the Periphery of European Intellectual Space," in *Decentering European Intellectual Space*, eds. Marja Jalava, Stefan Nygård, and Johan Strang (Leiden: Brill, 2018), 1, 2–8. On the need to write non-Eurocentric histories of jurisprudence, see, generally, Assaf Likhovski, "Czernowitz, Lincoln, Jerusalem, and the Comparative History of American Jurisprudence," *Theoretical Inquiries in Law* 4 (2003): 621; Werner Menski, *Comparative Law in a Global Context: The Legal Systems of Asia and Africa*, 2nd ed. (Cambridge: Cambridge University Press, 2006), 102–3, 119–28; Roger Cotterrell, "Ehrlich at the Edge of Empire: Centres and Peripheries in Legal Studies," in *Living Law: Reconsidering Eugen Ehrlich*, ed. Marc Hertogh (Oxford: Hart, 2008), 75, 77; Twining, *General Jurisprudence*, 10. On writing global histories of law, see, generally, Thomas Duve, ed., *Entanglements in Legal History: Conceptual Approaches* (Frankfurt am Main: Max Planck Institute for European Legal History, 2014); Thomas Duve, "What is Global Legal History?" *Comparative Legal History* 8 (2020): 73; Dupret and Halpérin, *State Law and Legal Positivism*. For discussions and examples of the non-Eurocentric histories of international law, see, e.g., Martti Koskenniemi, "Histories of International Law: Dealing with Eurocentrism," *Rechtsgeschichte* 19 (2011): 152; Arnulf Becker Lorca, *Mestizo International Law: A Global Intellectual History 1842–1933* (Cambridge: Cambridge University Press, 2014); Anthea Roberts, *Is International Law International?* (New York: Oxford University Press, 2017); Liliana Obregón, "Peripheral Histories of International Law," *Annual Review of Law and Social Science* 15 (2019): 437.

[11] See, e.g., Duncan Kennedy, "Three Globalizations of Law and Legal Thought: 1850–2000," in *The New Law and Economic Development: A Critical Appraisal*, eds. David M. Trubek and Alvaro Santos (New York: Cambridge University Press, 2006), 19, 29–30 (briefly mentioning local "resistance" to Western legal ideas); Jean-Louis Halpérin, *Profils des mondialisations du droit* (Paris: Dalloz, 2009); Jean-Louis Halpérin, *Five Legal Revolutions Since the 17th Century: An Analysis of a Global Legal History* (Cham: Springer, 2014). The institutional history of modern legal education in non-Western territories, too, is focused on the spread of Western models. See, e.g., Jean Portemer and Jean-Marie Carbasse, eds., "L'influence des Facultés françaises de droit Outre-Mer et à l'étranger," Numéro spécial, *Revue d'histoire des facultés de droit et de la science juridique* 15 (1994); Laetitia Guerlain et al., eds., "Enseigner le droit hors des frontières nationales (XIXe–XXe siècles)," Numéro spécial, *Cahiers Jean Moulin* 7 (2021), https://journals.openedition.org/cjm/1253; Catherine Fillon et al., eds., "Enseigner le droit

philosophers also express such views.[12] A similarly Eurocentric approach characterizes works dealing with the subfields of legal theory, such as comparative law.[13]

hors des frontières nationales (XIXe–XXe siècles): Deuxième partie," Numéro spécial, *Cahiers Jean Moulin* 9 (2023), https://journals.openedition.org/cjm/2051; Annamaria Monti, "Professeurs italiens enseignant à l'étranger (XIXe–XXe siècle): Pour une mise en perspective des trajectoires individuelles," *Cahiers Jean Moulin* 9 (2023), https://doi.org/10.4000/cjm.2233 (discussing French and Italian models); Susan Bartie and David Sandomierski, eds., *American Legal Education Abroad: Critical Histories* (New York: New York University Press, 2021) (discussing American models). See also Rogelio Pérez-Perdomo, *Legal Education in the Western World: A Cultural and Comparative History*, trans. Anapaula Pérez and Rosa Meléndez (Stanford, CA: Stanford University Press, 2024). A recent important, but broad-brush, description of the topic that includes several paragraphs on the history of modern legal education in some non-Western territories is Jean-Louis Halpérin, "Historical Landmarks in Mapping the Spread of Positive Law Teaching," in Dupret and Halpérin, *State Law and Legal Positivism*, 33.

12 In this vein, the impressive multi-volume *Treatise of Legal Philosophy and General Jurisprudence*, published between 2005 and 2016 by the Springer publishing company, which sought to provide a survey of the history of the philosophy of law from ancient times to the twentieth century, only contained very brief discussions of ancient Jewish and Islamic legal philosophy. The volumes in the series dealing with the twentieth century contained chapters devoted to Eastern European and Latin American legal philosophy, but they did not include any discussion of modern legal philosophy in the colonies of European Empires (or, indeed, in non-European countries such as China and Japan). See *A Treatise of Legal Philosophy and General Jurisprudence*, ed. Enrico Pattaro, 12 vols. (Dordrecht: Springer, 2005–16). It is interesting to note that older works, concerned with both pre-modern and modern legal philosophy, did include relatively extensive discussions of non-Western philosophies of law. See, e.g., Fritz Berolzheimer, *The World's Legal Philosophies*, trans. Rachel Szold Jastrow (Boston, MA: Boston Book Co., 1912) (discussing the philosophy of law of "Oriental civilization," i.e., the societies of the ancient Near East). For a general discussion, see also Halpérin, "Historical-Jurisprudential Methods."

13 For examples of some recent discussions of the history of comparative law, see Martti Koskenniemi and Ville Kari, "A More Elevated Patriotism: The Emergence of International and Comparative Law (Nineteenth Century)," in *The Oxford Handbook of European Legal History*, eds. Heikki Pihlajamäki et al. (Oxford: Oxford University Press, 2018): 974; George Mousourakis, *Comparative Law and Legal Traditions: Historical and Contemporary Perspectives* (Cham: Springer, 2019), 71–103; Oleksii V. Kresin, *Comparative Legal Studies 1750–1835: Approaches to Conceptualization*, ed. and trans. William E. Butler (London: Wildy, Simmonds and Hill, 2019); Balázs Fekete, *Paradigms in Modern European Comparative Law: A History* (Oxford: Hart, 2021). Cf. Annelise Riles, *Rethinking the Masters of Comparative Law* (Oxford: Hart, 2004) (a collection of essays which does include chapters on Japanese and Egyptian comparative law scholars). On the unexplored colonial roots of comparative law, see Helge Dedek, "The Tradition of Comparative Law: Comparison and Its Colonial Legacies," in *The Cambridge Handbook of*

Some of the institutions, thinkers, and works I examine in this book have previously been studied using national (that is, non-comparative) historiographical frameworks. Thus, there are many works that discuss how British colonial rulers viewed the normative systems of South Asia and reshaped them under the influence of Western jurisprudential theories.[14] However, the institutional history of Indian legal education remains relatively underexplored. Equally neglected is the study of how Indian jurists used Western legal concepts to examine their own religious legal traditions, particularly in the context of anti-colonial nationalist thought. As for Mandatory Palestine, some aspects of the institutional history of legal education and the history of the interaction between local legal scholars and Western jurisprudential ideas have been analyzed.[15] However, here, too, there has not been a thorough discussion of the topic, and there have certainly not been comparative works that seek to place the story of Mandatory Palestine within a broader framework.

By studying and comparing the history of legal theory in colonial India and Mandatory Palestine, this book seeks to provide a decentered, non-Eurocentric perspective on the global history of modern legal theory, adding a missing piece to existing accounts. It argues that the assumption underlying some leading works on the history of modern legal thought that no original development occurred outside the West is inaccurate.[16] Non-Western territories were not intellectual backwaters. The legal scholars working in these places were cosmopolitan and informed by the cutting-edge legal theories of their time. The works they produce were often insightful. Non-Western legal scholars had a distinctive vantage point because

*Comparative Law*, eds. Mathias Siems and Po Jen Yap (New York: Cambridge University Press, 2024), 387.

14 For recent summaries, see, e.g., Lubin et al., "Introduction," in *Hinduism and Law*, 1; Jean-Louis Halpérin, "Western Legal Transplants and India," *Jindal Global Law Review* 2 (2010): 14; Mitra Sharafi, "South Asian Legal History," *Annual Review of Law and Social Science* 11 (2015): 309.

15 See, e.g., Ronen Shamir, *The Colonies of Law: Colonialism, Zionism and Law in Early Mandate Palestine* (Cambridge: Cambridge University Press, 2000); Assaf Likhovski, *Law and Identity in Mandate Palestine* (Chapel Hill, NC: University of North Carolina Press, 2006); Amihai Radzyner, "Judaism and Jewish Law in Pre-State Palestine," in *The Cambridge Companion to Judaism and Law*, ed. Christine Hayes (New York: Cambridge University Press, 2017), 317.

16 See Kennedy, "Three Globalizations."

they taught law in areas where modern Western law and ancient normative traditions, such as customary and religious law, intermingled. These scholars were thus well-placed to question the theories produced by European thinkers, to revise Western conceptions of law with insights derived from non-Western legal systems, and even to argue, inspired by nationalist ideology, that one could not write the history of law without considering non-Western systems such as Hindu and Jewish law.

Another distinctive feature of the works examined in this book is the considerable effort scholars in colonial India and Mandatory Palestine devoted to demonstrating that the norms of their respective legal systems were not antiquated or regressive, but aligned with modern conceptions of society and politics. At the time, Western legal thought commonly regarded religious legal systems as occupying a lower rung on the ladder of evolutionary legal development, beneath modern Western law. As a result, such systems were often dismissed as irrelevant to contemporary legal, social, and political concerns.

In response, the scholars discussed here argued that their legal traditions shared meaningful affinities with modern Western law. A central focus of their work were norms dealing with personal status. In his influential 1861 book *Ancient Law*, Henry Maine, one of main advocates of the idea of legal evolution, famously asserted that "the movement of the progressive societies has hitherto been a movement from Status to Contract."[17] The scholars I study, whether explicitly or implicitly, rejected this claim. They challenged the notion that their ancient legal systems upheld rigid hierarchies of fixed status, and instead sought to justify norms found in them governing the most contested status categories: women, caste relations (in the context of Hindu law), and slavery.

Another area in which Western scholars saw a fundamental distinction between modern legal systems and religious ones was public law. Many Western thinkers maintained that democracy was a uniquely Western phenomenon, asserting that the modern liberal-democratic order had no parallel outside the West. In the Indian context, this belief manifested in the concept of "oriental despotism," which portrayed ancient Indian states as governed by absolute rulers.

[17] Henry Sumner Maine, *Ancient Law* (London: John Murray, 1861), 183.

Regarding Judaism, Jewish public law was seen as undeveloped because of the loss of Jewish political independence after the destruction of the Second Temple. Accordingly, the scholars of Hindu and Jewish law that I discuss devoted significant effort to identifying democratic principles within their respective legal traditions.

Underlying the discussions of status and democracy was a deeper concern with the role of individual will in the private and public spheres (in the private realm, in the relations between husband and wife or master and servant, and in the public realm between subjects and rulers). The works of the scholars I analyze reflected the early twentieth-century crisis of the liberal ideal of individualism which was centered around the notion that the role of law was to facilitate the expression on individual will. Some of the scholars I examine responded to this crisis by arguing that liberal individualism was now being replaced by socialist collectivism. From this perspective, they contended that religious legal systems, based as they were on collectivist assumptions about the nature of society, were not only compatible with this transition from individualism to collectivism (and from liberalism to socialism), but perhaps were even better suited to address its demands, and thus actually more "modern" than liberal Western law.[18]

The main protagonists of this book are local legal scholars working in two colonies of the British Empire, India and Palestine, but they were not free of European influences. The Indian scholars I discuss had hybrid scholarly identity, being members of a Westernized local elite. They studied in Western or Western-style legal institutions, so their legal thought combined Western and local ideas.[19] They reflected, in the legal realm, a broader attribute of non-Western nationalism which both resisted but also imitated the West.[20]

[18] The view that individualist law did not represent the ultimate "end of history" in the supposed evolution of legal systems was also found in the works of Paul Vinogradoff, one of Henry Maine's most prominent followers in the early twentieth century. See Paul Vinogradoff, *Outlines of Historical Jurisprudence*, Vol. 1: *Introduction – Tribal Law* (London: Oxford University Press, 1920), 158.

[19] For a general discussion of the hybrid identity of anti-colonial intellectuals, see, e.g., Cemil Aydin, *The Politics of Anti-Westernism in Asia: Visions of World Order in Pan-Islamic and Pan-Asian Thought* (New York: Columbia University Press, 2007).

[20] See, generally, Partha Chatterjee, *Nationalist Thought and the Colonial World: Derivative Discourse?* (London: Zed Books, 1993).

The Jewish legal scholars of Mandatory Palestine that I analyze and, more generally, early twentieth-century Zionist intellectuals, were also liminal figures on the borderline between West and East. Most of them were born in Europe. However, as I noted before, in the early part of the twentieth century, European Jews generally, and also Zionist Jews, were often considered foreigners by many non-Jewish Europeans. They were seen as Semitic aliens who had no place among the Aryans of Europe. As the passage with which I opened this introduction attests, this was also how many Jews, including many of the Jewish scholars I am interested in, viewed themselves.[21]

Although this book begins from the premise that the ideas of the scholars it examines merit serious attention, it is neither a celebratory account nor a hagiography. I do not set out to show that the scholars analyzed here were forgotten geniuses and that their works contained fundamental jurisprudential ideas. My goal is to reveal and analyze an overlooked chapter in the global history of modern legal theory; I make no claims suggesting that the missing piece discussed here should be considered the capstone of this history. The works I examine were interesting and innovative, but their impact on Western jurisprudential thought and on local legal communities was limited.[22]

[21] Zionists, and more generally Jews, are now often seen as privileged "whites," and Zionism is viewed as a European settler-colonial movement rather than as a movement of indigenous people returning (often after being ethnically cleansed from countries in Europe and the Middle East) to their ancient homeland. The view that identifies Jews as privileged "whites" is driven on occasion, I believe, by an age-old desire to frame Jews as the ultimate Other and attribute to them whatever evil (capitalism, communism, and now, colonialism) is currently fashionable. As historian David Nirenberg has argued in his book *Anti-Judaism*, the desire to frame the Jews as the ultimate Other has been a prominent and consistent feature of Western culture since antiquity. See David Nirenberg, *Anti-Judaism: The Western Tradition* (New York: Norton, 2013). For recent critical discussions of the view of Zionism as a settler-colonial movement, see, e.g., Yoav Gelber, "Is Zionism Colonialism?" in *The British Mandate in Palestine: A Centenary Volume, 1920–2020*, ed. Michael J. Cohen (New York: Routledge, 2020), 221; Stefan Vogt, Derek Penslar, and Arieh Saposnik, "Introduction: Unacknowledged Kinships," in *Unacknowledged Kinships*, 1. For an intermediate position, see also Derek J. Penslar, *Zionism: An Emotional State* (New Brunswick, NJ: Rutgers University Press, 2023), 67–98. Arguably, the very imposition of the indigenous-settler binary, appropriate for the study of countries such as the United States, Canada, Australia, or New Zealand, but ill-fitting in the case of Zionism, is itself a product of Western intellectual imperialism.

[22] The assessment of intellectual impact or "influence" is a tricky business. Citation practices are one possible approach, but influence can be exerted indirectly through

Some readers may experience moral ambivalence and unease when engaging with the ideas explored in this book. This reaction arises because the figures I study defy easy classification within today's fashionable yet reductive binary classification scheme, which splits the world into villainous oppressors and noble victims. On the one hand, the scholars I discuss challenged deeply problematic Western perceptions of non-Western religious law, perceptions which were often rooted in racist notions of European superiority. This might lead readers to view them as brave anti-colonial heroes. On the other hand, their attitudes toward their ancient religious legal systems were often (though not always) apologetic. They frequently justified or overlooked aspects of these legal systems that, from a modern liberal perspective, are highly problematic, for example, the inferior status accorded to women under such systems. My account seeks to describe the scholars I study as they were, complex individuals with both positive and negative ideas, not one-dimensional heroes or villains who can be easily placed into an anachronistic mold.

This book offers a comparative history of legal theory in India and Palestine.[23] Why compare these two specific territories? Colonial India and Mandatory Palestine were very different, not least in scale. India was a huge territory, both geographically and demographically. At the beginning of the interwar period, it was home to approximately a quarter of a billion people. Furthermore, important parts of India had been ruled by the British for centuries. In contrast, when the British assumed control of the territory they called Palestine at the end of the

channels that are often less visible, for example, through one's students. A classical discussion of the methodological pitfalls involved in the historical study of intellectual influence is provided by Quentin Skinner, "The Limits of Historical Explanation," *Philosophy* 41 (1966): 203. See also Gary Browning, "Agency and Influence in the History of Political Thought: The Agency of Influence and the Influence of Agency," *History of Political Thought* 31 (2010): 345.

[23] For a general discussion of some of the theoretical problems involved in writing comparative (or transnational, or entangled) histories, see, generally, Michael Werner and Bénédicte Zimmermann, "Beyond Comparison: *Histoire Croisée* and the Challenge of Reflexivity," *History and Theory* 45 (2006): 30. For recent surveys of comparative legal history scholarship, see Seán Patrick Donlan, "Comparative? Legal? History? Crossing Boundaries," in *Comparative Legal History*, eds. Olivier Moréteau, Aniceto Masferrer, and Kjell A. Modéer (Cheltenham: Edward Elgar, 2019), 78; Christopher Tomlins, "Literature Review Article: Comparative Legal History," in *Comparative Legal History*, eds. Christopher Tomlins and Elizabeth Josselyn Boalt (Cheltenham: Edward Elgar, 2021), 1.

First World War, this small territory had a population of fewer than 700,000. British rule in Palestine was also quite brief, lasting only three decades. Nevertheless, despite these differences, the two places shared some notable similarities. Specifically in the legal realm, the legal systems of both India and Palestine contained layers of secular and religious law. In India, imported British law existed alongside Hindu and Islamic law, which was applied by British courts in disputes involving family and inheritance matters. In Palestine, the legal system was based on Ottoman law, itself a mixture of Islamic and nineteenth-century French norms, together with English law imported by the British. Here, too, religious law (applied by Islamic, Jewish, and Christian courts) governed various personal law issues. In addition, another important aspect of the legal systems of India and Palestine, pertinent for the topic of this book, is that unlike many other British colonies, India and Palestine had a sophisticated system of academic legal education, which in turn led to the production of a sizeable body of works on legal theory in both places.[24]

There were also remarkable similarities in the politics and culture of colonial India and Mandatory Palestine. These similarities have already spawned a sizeable body of work comparing both places in the colonial and early postcolonial periods and discussing various forms of interaction between them.[25] Some of these works analyze

[24] In 1945, the territories controlled by the British Colonial Office, which at the time had a population of over 60 million people, had only four universities: the Royal University of Malta; Ceylon University College; the University of Hong Kong; and the Hebrew University of Jerusalem. Of these four universities, only the University of Malta had a law school. In Ceylon and Palestine, independent law schools established by the British (the Colombo Law College and the Jerusalem Law Classes) provided formal legal education. In addition, in Palestine, an independent Jewish law school, the Tel Aviv School of Law and Economics, existed. Thus, by the end of the Second World War, only three British law schools operated in all the territories administered by the Colonial Office. See The National Archives, London [TNA]: PRO CO 958/1, Minutes of the first meeting of the Commission on Higher Education in the Colonies, September 21, 1943, 1; TNA: PRO CO 958/3, "Report of the Commission on Higher Education in the Colonies," June 1945, 78; TNA, PRO CO 958/1, serial no. 25, Draft letter to the autonomous universities.

[25] Some examples are: Margaret Chatterjee, *Studies in Modern Jewish and Hindu Thought* (New York: St. Martin's Press, 1997); Yulia Egorova, *Jews and India: History, Image, Perceptions* (Milton Park: Routledge, 2006); Ayelet Harel-Shalev,

legal matters.[26] However, none of the existing works has focused on the institutional and intellectual history of legal education and legal scholarship, which this book discusses.

In the Indian case, the book will focus mainly on scholars writing on Hindu law. In the case of Mandatory Palestine, it will focus primarily on scholars writing on Jewish law. In both instances, some attention will also be devoted to theoretical works on Islamic law. My analysis of the history of legal theory in India and Palestine seeks to uncover differences between them, but it also reveals that many similar jurisprudential developments occurred in both. Chapter 7 expands the field of vision to two other non-Western territories, Egypt and China, in order to show that India and Mandatory Palestine were not isolated cases. Rather, they were part of a wider jurisprudential wave that appeared simultaneously in the first half of the twentieth century in many non-Western territories.

*The Challenge of Sustaining Democracy in Deeply Divided Societies: Citizenship, Rights, and Ethnic Conflicts in India and Israel* (Lanham, MD: Lexington Press, 2010); Faisal Devji, *Muslim Zion: Pakistan as a Political Idea* (Cambridge, MA: Harvard University Press, 2013); Michael Walzer, *The Paradox of Liberation: Secular Revolutions and Religious Counterrevolutions* (New Haven: Yale University Press, 2015); "Hodu/Yisrael," ed. Eitan Bar-Yosef, Special issue, *Teorya u-Vikoret* 44 (2015); Arie Dubnov, "Notes on the Zionist Passage to India, or: The Analogical Imagination and Its Boundaries," *Journal of Israeli History* 35 (2016): 177; Benjamin Siegel, "The Kibbutz and the Ashram: Sarvodaya Agriculture, Israeli Aid, and the Global Imaginaries of Indian Development," *American Historical Review* 125 (2020): 1175; Maria Birnbaum, "Entangled Empire: Religion and the Transnational History of Pakistan and Israel," *Millennium: Journal of International Studies* 50 (2022): 561; Stern and Dubnov, "A Part of Asia or Apart from Asia?"

26 See, e.g., Daphne Barak-Erez, "Symbolic Constitutionalism: On Sacred Cows and Abominable Pigs," *Law, Culture and the Humanities* 6 (2010): 420; Hanna Lerner, *Making Constitutions in Deeply Divided Societies* (Cambridge: Cambridge University Press, 2011); Yüksel Sezgin, *Human Rights under State-Enforced Religious Family Laws in Israel, Egypt, and India* (Cambridge: Cambridge University Press, 2013); Alexandre (Sandy) Kedar, "Expanding Legal Geographies: A Call for a Critical Comparative Approach," in *The Expanding Spaces of Law: A Timely Legal Geography*, eds. Irus Braverman et al. (Stanford, CA: Stanford University Press, 2014), 97; Rephael G. Stern, "Uncertain Comparisons: Zionist and Israeli Links to India and Pakistan in the Age of Partition and Decolonization," *Law and History Review* 39 (2021): 451; Gilad Abiri, "Intimate Rivals: The Freedom of Religious Nationalism," *Asian Journal of Law and Society* 8 (2021): 19; Yael Berda, *Colonial Bureaucracy and Contemporary Citizenship: Legacies of Race and Emergency in the Former British Empire* (Cambridge: Cambridge University Press, 2023).

I chose to focus on India and Palestine as the two detailed case studies in this book not only because of the striking parallels between them, but also due to the trajectory of my own academic journey. I began my scholarly career nearly three decades ago with a doctoral dissertation on the legal history of Mandatory Palestine. While working on a chapter on the history of legal education in that territory, I unexpectedly encountered a wealth of material on legal education in colonial India. At the time, however, I found almost no secondary literature on the subject. Back then, colonial legal history, including the history of law in colonial India, was still in its infancy, with relatively few scholars working in the field. In the decades since, the field has expanded significantly. Yet, curiously, the history of legal education and legal research in colonial India remains largely unwritten, as does the broader comparative history of legal education and scholarship within the British Empire. This book is, in part, the product of my long-standing desire to better understand this neglected history, and to place it in a comparative context.[27]

My choice of the two additional case studies used to illustrate the global jurisprudential wave discussed in Chapter 7 of this book, Egypt and China, was determined by practical considerations. A number of other territories could have served as compelling examples, including the French colonies in Africa and Asia, the Dutch East Indies, or independent states such as Imperial Japan.[28] I chose Egypt because

[27] For a recent discussion noting the lack of works on the history of Indian legal education (and also comparing the history of legal education in colonial India and French Indochina), see Sara Legrandjacques, "Inégaux en droit: approche comparée de l'enseignement juridique en Inde britannique et en Indochine française XIXe–XXe siècle," *Cahiers Jean Moulin* 7 (2021), https://doi.org/10.4000/cjm.1334.

[28] On French territories (and also French law schools in places such as Tehran and Tokyo), see, e.g., Laetitia Guerlain et al., "Pour une histoire de l'enseignement du droit hors des frontières nationales (XIXe–XXe siècle)," *Cahiers Jean Moulin* 7 (2021), https://doi.org/10.4000/cjm.1258. On the Dutch East Indies, see, e.g., Upik Djalins, "Re-Examining Subject Making in the Netherlands East Indies Legal Education: Pedagogy, Curriculum, and Colonial State Formation," *Itinerario* 37(2) (August 2013): 121. On Japan, see, e.g., Hitoshi Aoki, "Nobushige Hozumi: A Skillful Transplanter of Western Legal Thought into Japanese Soil," in *Rethinking the Masters of Comparative Law*, ed. Annelise Riles (Oxford: Hart, 2001), 129; Masayuki Murayama, "Kawashima and the Changing Focus on Japanese Legal Consciousness: A Selective History of the Sociology of Law in Japan," *International Journal of Law in Context* 9 (2013): 565; Colin Philip Charles Jones, "Living Law in Japan: Social Jurisprudence in the Interwar Period"

many of the relevant primary sources are in French and Arabic and are thus accessible to me. As for China, I was guided by the availability of a substantial body of English-language primary sources, and a relatively rich corpus of secondary literature in English.

This book seeks to correct and augment existing accounts in several scholarly domains: the intellectual history of law, legal philosophy, and the study of religion and politics. For intellectual historians of law, it challenges the West-centric narrative of the history of modern legal theory by foregrounding perspectives that originate outside the Western world. In doing so, it reorients the historiography of legal thought, pushing scholars to grapple with a broader, more inclusive intellectual landscape. This move is also relevant to scholars interested in specific subfields of legal theory, such as those concerned with writing a truly global history of comparative law in the early twentieth century.[29]

Legal philosophers will find that this book offers a critical re-examination of the basic assumptions of modern jurisprudence. It exposes the tension that existed (and continues to exist) between the claims of Western jurisprudence for universal applicability and the reality whereby certain non-Western normative systems do not entirely fit Western notions about the proper attributes of "law."[30] The ideas of the thinkers that I explore ought to inspire contemporary scholars of jurisprudence to pay more attention to non-Western legal systems in order to create comprehensive accounts of jurisprudence,

(PhD diss., Columbia University, 2017); Jason Morgan, *Law and Society in Imperial Japan: Suehiro Izutarō and the Search for Equity* (Amherst, NY: Cambria Press, 2020).

29 See, e.g., Günter Frankenberg, "Critical Histories of Comparative Law," in *The Oxford Handbook of Legal History*, eds. Markus Dubber and Christopher Tomlins (Oxford: Oxford University Press, 2018), 43.

30 An early example of this tension can be found in the works of the nineteenth-century English legal philosopher, John Austin, whose "general or universal jurisprudence" was intended to deal with "such subjects and ends of law as are common to all systems." See John Austin, *The Province of Jurisprudence Determined, and the Uses of the Study of Jurisprudence* (Indianapolis, IN: Hackett, 1998), 373. However, despite the claim to universality, Austin also stated that he was interested only in the "ampler and maturer systems of refined communities," adding that, because it is impossible to become familiar with all legal systems, "it is only the systems of two or three nations which deserve attention: the writings of the Roman Jurists; the decisions of English Judges in modern times; the provisions of French and Prussian Codes as to arrangement." Ibid., 367, 373.

accounts that benefit from the insights offered by non-Western legal systems and their history, principles, and legal institutions.[31]

Finally, this book is relevant to students of the contemporary relationship between religion and politics. It analyzes calls made in the first part of the twentieth century to adopt norms and values found in Hindu and Jewish law. Interest in such norms and values has not disappeared. Indeed, it is now widespread both in India and Israel. Some politicians and intellectuals in both places reject Western liberal law in the name of religious law and ancient national traditions. Similar observations can be made about scholars and politicians in the Muslim world. They are even relevant to jurists in the Far East who are interested in uniquely "Asian" culture, law, and legal philosophy or in subcategories of the term "Asia," such as Chinese law and culture.[32] Recovering the early twentieth-century history of the interaction between Western legal theories (and the liberal ideology upon which these theories were often based) and non-Western religious traditions is not simply an academic exercise. It is a critical task for anyone seeking a deeper understanding of the urgent legal and political questions that define our present. As global power structures shift, this book offers valuable insights into the enduring dynamics that shape the often contentious, yet sometimes collaborative, interplay between Western and non-Western legal systems and the values underlying them.

Part I of this book sets the scene by discussing the institutional context underlying the story I tell, focusing primarily, but not exclusively, on two specific institutions providing legal education: the University of Calcutta in India and the Tel Aviv School of Law and Economics in Mandatory Palestine. This part also analyzes textbooks on jurisprudence and other theoretical works written by British and local law teachers in colonial India and Mandatory Palestine.

[31] See Twining, *General Jurisprudence*, xi, 6–7, 269–92 (arguing that "the mainstream Western canon of jurisprudence needs to be critically reviewed and extended to take more account of other legal traditions and cultures").

[32] See, e.g., Ralf Michaels, "How Asian Should Asian Law Be?" in *Convergence and Divergence of Private Law in Asia*, ed. Gary Low (Cambridge: Cambridge University Press, 2022), 227; Samuli Seppänen, *Ideological Conflict and the Rule of Law in Contemporary China* (Cambridge: Cambridge University Press, 2016); Samuli Seppänen, "Anti-Formalism and the Preordained Birth of Chinese Jurisprudence," *China Perspectives* 2018(4) (2018): 31.

I begin Chapter 1 with an overview of the history of legal education in colonial India. Law schools appeared in India in the second half of the nineteenth century. By the beginning of the twentieth century, more institutions were providing legal education in India (and there were consequently more law students there) than in Britain. The chapter then turns to the history of the University of Calcutta, the leading university in India during the colonial period, and, even more specifically, the University of Calcutta College of Law, which opened in 1909. A discussion of jurisprudence textbooks produced in India follows. I first discuss works written by British professors in India in the late nineteenth century. I then explore works on jurisprudence written by Indian scholars. These include general works in which various Western jurisprudential approaches were summarized and theoretical works on Hindu legal philosophy published mainly by scholars associated with the University of Calcutta. The British textbooks and Indian works I examine were characterized by a more receptive approach to Continental legal theories than contemporaneous English works. Some works also criticized English jurisprudential theories using examples taken from local law and argued that Hindu legal ideas, norms, and institutions were preferable to Western ones. The unique nature of these works resulted from the need to teach jurisprudence in an environment where religious law coexisted alongside transplanted Western law. Another factor shaping the unique nature of the jurisprudential works written in colonial India was the anti-colonial nationalist ideology of their authors. Finally, I discuss theoretical works on Islamic law produced in India during the colonial period.

In Chapter 2, I turn to the history of the institutions providing legal education in Mandatory Palestine and then analyze the jurisprudence textbooks written by British and Jewish legal scholars working there. Just like the Indian textbooks, the works on jurisprudence produced in Palestine were characterized by their mixture of common-law and Continental legal theories, and their willingness to critique Western theories of law. They also viewed local religious law (Jewish law) not just as the source of family law but as a comprehensive alternative to Western law and jurisprudence. While focusing on Jewish scholars in Mandatory Palestine, the chapter also examines theoretical discussions of law found in works written by Palestinian-Arab lawyers.

Interlude 1, which follows Chapters 1 and 2, examines similarities and differences between the institutional history of legal education in India and Palestine. It also compares the jurisprudential works produced in both places. It then focuses on a specific topic: the goals that animated theoretical writings by Indian and Jewish scholars. I argue that one major difference between the two groups of scholars was the idea of legal revival, that is, the use of modernized religious law as a source of state law. This idea was the driving force of Jewish scholarship in Palestine but played only a minor role in the thought of scholars of Hindu law in India.

In Part II of the book, I provide parallel biographies of two legal scholars, Radhabinod Pal and Samuel Eisenstadt. These scholars were chosen because of the wealth of primary sources available, enabling a detailed reconstruction of their lives and ideas. Both scholars were born in the same year, 1886, and followed similar educational paths. Their academic careers were also similar in that both published works devoted to analyzing their respective religious legal systems using Western jurisprudential theories, attempting to show the superiority of religious law over Western law. The interest of both scholars in traditional religious law was combined, in their thought, with a commitment to radical politics – the rejection of Western liberal ideology in favor of Indian (and also Hindu) nationalism, in Pal's case; and Jewish nationalism, but also socialism and, later, communism, in Eisenstadt's case.

Chapter 3 examines the life and ideas of Radhabinod Pal, who published several books on Hindu jurisprudence. These books combined Aryan racial theories imported from Europe, Indian and Hindu nationalism, and pan-Asian sentiments. The chapter shows the influence of Henry Maine's evolutionary theory of law on Pal's thought and the impact of Roscoe Pound's sociological jurisprudence. It also examines some significant themes in Pal's writings: the attempt to show the antiquity and superiority of Hindu jurisprudence; the rejection of Western evolutionary schemes of law that placed Hindu law on a lower evolutionary rung; apologetic defenses of how Hindu law treated slaves, women, and members of the lower castes; an analysis of Hindu law as part of a large family of "Aryan legal systems"; and, finally, an emphasis on the collectivist nature of Hindu law, which Pal positively contrasted with Western individualism.

In Chapter 4, I discuss the life and ideas of Samuel Eisenstadt. Eisenstadt was a Jewish nationalist but also a socialist and, later, a communist, and his works reflected these ideological convictions. I introduce the jurisprudential influences that shaped Eisenstadt's view of law, showing how his works reflect the combined impact of the German Historical School and Marxist legal theory. I also discuss some of the ideas that animated his scholarship. Eisenstadt sought to show the superiority of Jewish law, for example, by arguing that Jewish legal education was better than Western legal education because of its non-elitist and non-materialist nature; he sought to prove that Jewish law did not represent a more primitive stage in legal evolution; and he was concerned with apologetically justifying more problematic aspects of Jewish law such as its attitude to slaves and women. Finally, like Pal, Eisenstadt highlighted the collectivist nature of Jewish law.

Interlude 2 draws insights from the similarities between the lives of Pal and Eisenstadt. In one sense, the two scholars were placed on opposite sides of the political spectrum since Pal espoused right-wing ideas, while Eisenstadt was a Marxist. However, ultimately, both were political radicals whose utopian political and legal ideas led them to seek alternatives to Western liberal law, blinding them to the problematic nature of these alternatives.

Part III of the book deals with works produced in India and Palestine on ancient Hindu and Jewish political thought, constitutional structures, and public law. Influenced by historicist jurisprudential approaches, Indian and Jewish scholars argued that notions such as the rule of law, democracy, elections, public opinion, personal liberty, and equality were not uniquely Western.

Chapter 5 discusses the Hindu polity literature, a body of works on ancient Indian political ideas, states, and constitutional and international law. The chapter shows how constitutional law and constitutional history (and related subjects such as international law) gradually emerged as topics of study in law schools in Britain and India in the late nineteenth and early twentieth centuries. It then paints a collective portrait of the scholars who produced the Hindu polity works and the ideas promoted therein. The authors of the Hindu polity literature argued that contrary to Western perceptions, ancient Indians were not only interested in spiritual matters. A significant corpus of practical treatises on statecraft emerged in ancient India. One can find in these treatises innovative ideas usually attributed to the West, such as the notion of the social contract or the idea of a system of norms governing interstate relations (that is, international law). The Hindu polity authors also invested much effort in countering the Western "Oriental despotism" image, according to which India was always governed by rulers whose power was considered divine and absolute, unconstrained by any system of checks and balances. These authors also attempted to show, contrary to the conventional view, that ancient Indian societies were not based on a rigid social hierarchy. The chapter then discusses the relationship of this literature to pan-Asianism and also mentions works on Islamic constitutional history that appeared in colonial India. Finally, the chapter explores some of the personal and political factors that led to the rise and decline of this body of works and the impact of this literature on actual demands for political and legal reforms during the colonial period and in the period immediately surrounding Indian independence in 1947.

Chapter 6 analyzes the equivalent scholarship on ancient Jewish public law created by scholars associated with the Tel Aviv School of Law and Economics. The chapter begins by discussing how constitutional law was taught in Mandatory Palestine. It then examines the life and works of some authors who wrote on Jewish public law in the first half of the twentieth century. An analysis of the main ideas that appeared in these works follows, including an examination of attempts to prove the existence of Jewish public law and its secular nature; arguments about the democratic nature of ancient Jewish states; efforts to show that seemingly modern notions, such as parliamentarism or civil rights, were to be found in ancient Jewish texts; and assertions about Jewish law as a source of foundational ideas of modern European constitutional and international law. I also examine the attitudes of Jewish law scholars to Christian political thought, and I briefly mention analogous discussions of Islamic public law found in works published by Palestinian-Arab authors. Finally, I analyze the causes leading to the appearance of this body of works, critiques of this oeuvre, and the impact of this literature on Jewish constitutional discourse in the period before and after Israeli independence in 1948.

Interlude 3 compares the Indian and Jewish works. Similar particularist and historicist jurisprudential assumptions drove the study of ancient constitutional history in both places. In the works produced in

India and Palestine, one also finds similar arguments about the existence and relevance of ancient Hindu and Jewish texts to modern public law and similar assertions about the resonance of the ancient Hindu and Jewish political institutions and values with Western democratic and liberal institutions and law. However, there were also differences between India and Mandatory Palestine in the comparative frameworks applied, the professional background of the authors, the sources used, the ideological motivations, and the role of law in the bodies of literature produced in both places. Finally, I ask about the possible interaction between Indian and Jewish scholars and note the similarity in the impact (or lack thereof) made by both bodies of scholarship on the constitutional law of the newly independent states of India and Israel.

In Chapter 7, I argue that the developments in India and Palestine also appeared elsewhere, thus highlighting the existence of an early twentieth-century non-Western jurisprudential wave present simultaneously in many territories. The chapter first briefly discusses the history of Egyptian legal education. It then analyzes jurisprudence textbooks produced by Egyptian scholars during the first decades of the twentieth century. Then follows an outline of the history of legal education institutions in early twentieth-century China and a discussion of themes found in theoretical works published by Chinese legal scholars during the same period. Finally, the chapter compares Egypt and China to India and Palestine and discusses whether the similarities between these places were due to mutual influence.

The Epilogue argues that the story told in the book is relevant to anyone interested in contemporary political and cultural conflicts over the relationship between Western and non-Western law and values. The legal scholars whose works I discuss in the book sought to reconcile West and East and to apply modern Western legal theories to the study of ancient religious law. They did not view Western and non-Western law, institutions, and values as irreconcilable. Instead, they sought to incorporate the history and ideas of their ancient legal systems into a global history of law, which would include both Western and non-Western law. At a time when democracy and liberal values are increasingly being questioned by politicians and thinkers outside the West (and also within it), the often-overlooked writings of early twentieth-century legal thinkers from colonial India and Mandatory Palestine still hold profound significance.

# PART I

# INSTITUTIONS AND WORKS

# 1

# Legal Education and Legal Theory in Colonial India

William Rattigan overcame humble origins to achieve great success. Born in British India in 1842 to an Irish father, Rattigan began his career in the lower ranks of the Indian civil service. He then studied law and practiced as a lawyer in Lahore, later moving to London, where he studied at King's College and was admitted to the English Bar. Returning to India, he served as a government advocate and judge of the Chief Court of the Punjab and a member of the Supreme Legislative Council of India. In 1885, Rattigan obtained a doctorate in law from the University of Göttingen in Germany. In 1887, he became the Vice-Chancellor of the University of the Punjab, serving until 1895. Rattigan was a polyglot conversant in five European languages, several vernacular Indian languages, and Persian. He published many books, including works on Hindu and Roman law, a textbook on private international law, and the leading digest of the customary law of the Punjab. In 1900, Rattigan returned to the United Kingdom and was elected as a Member of Parliament before his life was tragically cut short in a car accident.[1]

[1] F. H. Brown, "Rattigan, Sir William Henry," *Oxford Dictionary of National Biography*, https://doi.org/10.1093/ref:odnb/35680. Rattigan and his works were rarely mentioned in modern studies of nineteenth-century English jurisprudence. For example, in a lecture celebrating the work of the English jurisprudence scholar John Salmond, legal historian A. W. B. Simpson noted that, when Salmond's book *Jurisprudence* was first published in 1902, there were only four other comprehensive treatises on jurisprudence in print – by John Austin, William Markby, Thomas Erskine Holland, and Frederick Pollock. Simpson did not mention Rattigan's book, first published in 1888. See A. W. B. Simpson, "The Salmond Lecture," *Victoria*

In 1888, Rattigan published a textbook on jurisprudence written for his Indian law students.[2] Even though the book was, in many senses, more learned, sophisticated, and cosmopolitan than comparable works available in England at the time, it was far less influential.[3] This was primarily due to the fact that the book was written for Indian law students and was, therefore, seen as inferior to similar works published in the West. Such a view is evident, for example, in a review of Rattigan's book published in an American law journal in 1889. After noting Rattigan's "marked familiarity with the Roman and German jurists" and stating that "the whole work ... shows great research and diligence," the reviewer ended by condescendingly observing that "it is a learned and able work ... [that] shows a profundity of learning hardly to be looked for in India."[4] These dismissive words echo a broadly shared view that non-Western works on jurisprudence merely repeated Western ideas, a view held by Westerners and non-Westerners alike. For example, in 1958, when the Polish–Indian legal scholar C. H. Alexandrowicz published a bibliography of works on Indian law, he wrote (in the section of the bibliography devoted to jurisprudence) that, apart from some works on Hindu law, "Indian academic lawyers have made no

*University of Wellington Law Review* 38 (2007): 669, 670–1. Three works that do mention him are Michael Lobban, "Was There a Nineteenth Century 'English School of Jurisprudence'?" *Journal of Legal History* 16 (1995): 34, 51–2; Amanjit Kaur Sharanjit, "La colonisation et la transposition des concepts juridiques: L'exemple du droit coutumier au Punjab (Inde)," *Cahiers Jean Moulin* 6 (2020), https://doi.org/10.4000/cjm.1118; Faisal Chaudhry, *South Asia, the British Empire, and the Rise of Classical Legal Thought: Toward a Historical Ontology of the Law* (Oxford: Oxford University Press, 2024), 383, 391–7.

2 W. H. Rattigan, *The Science of Jurisprudence: Chiefly Intended for Indian Law Students* (Lahore: Civil and Military Gazette Press, 1888).

3 The scholarly consensus is that English jurisprudence in the period between the mid nineteenth century and the mid twentieth century was static and uninteresting, devoid of any major innovation, mostly repetitive, and generally "in a pretty sorry state." See Neil Duxbury, "English Jurisprudence between Austin and Hart," *Virginia Law Review* 91 (2005): 1, 2; William Cornish, Michael Lobban, and Keith Smith, "Theories of Law and Government," in *The Oxford History of the Laws of England*, ed. William Cornish et al., Vol. 11: *1820–1914 English Legal System* (Oxford: Oxford University Press, 2010), 72, 130; William Twining, *Jurist in Context: A Memoir* (Cambridge: Cambridge University Press, 2019), 29.

4 W. D. T. "Book Review," *American Law Review* 23 (1889): 461–2.

original contribution in this field."[5] Similarly, disparaging remarks about the unoriginality of Indian works can be found in later writings by Indian authors.[6]

In this chapter, I argue that this conventional view is wrong. Some theoretical works on law published in India in the late nineteenth and early twentieth centuries did not merely repeat ideas transplanted from England. During the colonial period, British legal scholars working in India, as well as Indian legal scholars, sometimes produced works on legal theory that were both interesting and original. The works produced were less insular and more cosmopolitan than English writings; they were critical of English legal theories claiming that these did not fit local reality; and, sometimes, the influence of nationalist ideology motivated local scholars to develop new theoretical insights derived from the study of local religious legal systems.[7] In order to understand that context out of which these works emerged, I will now briefly describe the history of legal education in England and British India in the nineteenth and early twentieth centuries.

## Legal Education in Nineteenth-Century England and British India

At the beginning of the nineteenth century, the education of English lawyers was a haphazard affair based on an unreliable apprenticeship system. In previous centuries, the Inns of Court had provided formal education for aspiring barristers, but after the English Civil War in the seventeenth century, studies at the Inns of Court atrophied. Academic courses on English law were first given in the late eighteenth and early

[5] Charles Henry Alexandrowicz, *A Bibliography of Indian Law* (Madras: Oxford University Press, 1958), 4. See also B. B. Misra, *The Indian Middle Classes: Their Growth in Modern Times* (London: Oxford University Press, 1961), 331.

[6] See G. S. Sharma, "Some Reflections on the Teaching of Jurisprudence in India," in *Studies in Law: An Anthology of Essays in Municipal and International Law*, ed. V. V. Deshpande (Bombay: Asia Publishing, 1961), 39; Rajkumari Agrawala, "Indian Legal Research: An Evolutionary and Perspective Analysis," *Journal of the Indian Law Institute* 24 (1982): 470, 470–5.

[7] On legal innovation in various sorts of peripheries, see, generally, Assaf Likhovski, "Czernowitz, Lincoln and Jerusalem and the Comparative History of American Jurisprudence," *Theoretical Inquiries in Law* 4 (2003): 621. For an autobiographical discussion of this phenomenon, see Twining, *Jurist in Context*, 39–77 (discussing Twining's experiences as a law teacher in Khartoum and Dar es Salaam in the late 1950s and early 1960s).

nineteenth centuries. William Blackstone lectured on common law in the mid eighteenth century at the University of Oxford. During the 1820s and 1830s, John Austin taught jurisprudence at University College in London, and Andrew Amos taught English law there. Courses on English law were also taught during this period at Cambridge University and King's College in London. However, compared to Continental and American legal education at the time, English legal education lagged far behind. Indeed, England's most advanced and comprehensive system of formal legal education in the first half of the nineteenth century was not connected to English law but to India. It was provided at Haileybury College, north of London, where the East India Company trained its administrators. The College, which existed between 1806 and 1858, offered a two-year course of studies, during which various legal topics were extensively covered.[8]

A Select Committee on Legal Education was established by the House of Commons in 1846, and, following the publication of its findings and a report by an 1852 Royal Commission, Oxford and Cambridge Universities expanded the teaching of English law, creating degree programs and various chairs on legal topics. In addition, a law faculty was created at King's College, and the Inns of Court appointed five Readers to deliver lectures on law. However, intending barristers or solicitors were not required to obtain a university law degree to practice; therefore, the number of practitioners holding such a degree was still relatively small. In the second half of the nineteenth century, there were attempts to create a "University of Law," or "General Law School," based on the Inns model, to provide broad legal education resembling German universities and other Continental institutions, but these attempts failed.[9]

[8] See, e.g., William Twining, *Blackstone's Tower: The English Law School* (London: Stevens, 1994), 24–6; Robin Morse, "Dower, Dogma and Grand Designs: Law at King's Nineteenth Century Style," in *King's College London: In the Service of Society*, ed. Christine Kenyon Jones (London: King's College, 2004), 60; Patrick Polden, "The Education of Lawyers," in *The Oxford History of the Laws of England*, ed. Cornish et al., Vol. 11, 1175; Andrew Watson, "The Legal Education Revolution that Failed: Attempts to Establish a Legal University in Victorian Britain," *Journal on European History of Law* 14 (2023): 28.

[9] See Polden, "The Education of Lawyers," 1181–201; Watson, "The Legal Education Revolution," 32–9; F. H. Lawson, *The Oxford Law School 1850–1965* (Oxford: Clarendon Press, 1968). Law was also taught in the second half of the nineteenth century at academic institutions in Birmingham, Manchester, and Liverpool.

Simultaneously with the changing nature of legal education, the nature of English law books also changed. Modern attempts to systematize English law using treatises began in the eighteenth century with Blackstone's *Commentaries on the Laws of England*. Law-treatise writing accelerated in the second half of the nineteenth century with the reforms in English legal education.[10] One specific subgenre of legal literature that evolved in the nineteenth century was that of books on jurisprudence. Unlike other kinds of legal treatises, the audience for these books mainly comprised law students.[11] Side-by-side with leading authors such as Jeremy Bentham, John Austin, and Henry Maine, writers such as Markby (1871), Holland (1880), and Salmond (1902) began to gain visibility. However, the underdeveloped state of legal education in England – limited in scope, relatively non-academic, and with little emphasis on research – was not conducive to creating a large and sophisticated body of works on jurisprudence.[12]

The history of Indian legal education in the nineteenth and early twentieth centuries mirrors that of England. The development of Indian legal education was connected to the gradual development of the modern Indian legal profession. Until the late eighteenth century, there was no regulation of the lawyers who appeared before the British courts operating in the Presidency towns of the East India Company (Calcutta, Bombay, and Madras), and the number of legal

[10] See, e.g., A. W. B. Simpson, "The Rise and Fall of the Legal Treatise: Legal Principles and the Forms of Legal Literature," *University of Chicago Law Review* 48 (1981): 632, 670–1; David Sugarman, "Legal Theory, the Common Law Mind and the Making of the Textbook Tradition," in *Legal Theory and Common Law*, ed. William Twinning (Oxford: Blackwell, 1986), 26; David Sugarman, "'A Hatred of Disorder': Legal Science, Liberalism and Imperialism," in *Dangerous Supplements: Resistance and Renewal in Jurisprudence*, ed. Peter Fitzpatrick (London: Pluto Press, 1991), 34; Steven Wilf, "Legal Treatise," in *The Oxford Handbook of Law and Humanities*, eds. Simon Stern et al. (New York: Oxford University Press, 2020), 687.

[11] For a history of English jurisprudence in the nineteenth and early twentieth centuries, see, generally, Lobban, "Was There a Nineteenth Century 'English School of Jurisprudence'?" For discussions on the history of English jurisprudence textbooks, see Simpson, "The Salmond Lecture," 670; Duxbury, "English Jurisprudence," 77–87; Cornish et al., "Theories of Law and Government," 123–31.

[12] Duxbury, "English Jurisprudence," 77–87. On the history of British comparative law scholarship during that period, see John W. Cairns, "Development of Comparative Law in Great Britain," in *The Oxford Handbook of Comparative Law*, eds. Mathias Reimann and Reinhard Zimmermann, 2nd ed. (Oxford: Oxford University Press, 2019), 111.

practitioners was exceedingly small. Over time, a nascent legal profession appeared, divided into several subcategories of lawyers; these were primarily British, to begin with, but a few local Indian lawyers later joined their ranks. However, even in the mid nineteenth century, the number of lawyers was still small.[13] The British also established courts in territories outside the three aforementioned Presidency towns, and here the lawyers (*vakils*) were Indian. These lawyers had to be familiar with Persian (the language of the courts until 1826) and to have been trained in Hindu or Islamic law.[14]

After the end of Company rule in 1858, the dual court system that had operated up to that point was replaced by a unified system of courts, at the apex of which stood the three High Courts of Calcutta, Bombay, and Madras. Additional High Courts later followed in cities such as Allahabad, Patna, and Lahore. Indian lawyers could plead before the High Courts, thus greatly expanding the scope and prestige of their work. In parallel, the requirements to practice as a *vakil* were expanded: these lawyers now had to acquire knowledge of English, study at a law college or university, and pass the High Court examination.[15] By the beginning of the twentieth century, a law degree had become an essential prerequisite for practicing law, at least in Bengal.[16]

[13] A detailed discussion of the regulation of the legal profession in nineteenth-century India can be found in M. P. Jain, *Outlines of Indian Legal and Constitutional History*, 7th ed. (Gurgaon: Lexis Nexis, 2016), 765–81. See also Samuel Schmitthener, "A Sketch of the Development of the Legal Profession in India," *Law and Society Review* 3 (1968/69): 337, 345; S. Dayal, "Legal Profession and Legal Education," in *The Indian Legal System*, ed. Joseph Minattur (New Delhi: Indian Law Institute, 1978), 148, 155; Agrawala, "Indian Legal Research," 470–5. On South India, specifically, see John J. Paul, *The Legal Profession in Colonial South India* (Bombay: Oxford University Press, 1991).

[14] Schmitthenner, "A Sketch," 349–55, 361–2; Dayal, "Legal Profession," 161.

[15] Schmitthenner, "A Sketch," 355–7.

[16] At that time, the legal profession in Bengal was divided into three distinct categories: advocates, *vakils*, and pleaders. Advocates were entitled to practice on both the original and appellate sides of the High Court and also subordinate courts. *Vakils* were entitled to practice on the appellate side of the High Court and also in subordinate courts. Pleaders were entitled to practice in subordinate courts only. University education in the United Kingdom or a law degree from one of the older Indian universities (Calcutta, Madras, Bombay, Allahabad, or Punjab) was required of advocates. *Vakils* were also required to hold a law degree from one of the older universities. Pleaders were required to hold a law degree from an Indian university. See Calcutta University Commission 1917–1919, *Report* (Calcutta: Superintendent of Government Printing, 1919), Vol. 3, 24–6.

Before the colonial period, Hindu law was taught by individual teachers (gurus) in Hindu temples and schools or, in the case of Islamic law, Islamic seminaries (*madrasas*). British colonial authorities created new institutions teaching traditional law, such as the Calcutta Madrasa (established in 1780) and the Benares Sanskrit College (established in 1791).[17] Gradually, institutions providing Western-style legal education also began to be established in India.[18] In Madras, the College of Fort St. George, established by the British in 1812, provided formal training for law officers and pleaders as early as 1816. While law classes in Madras were discontinued in the late 1830s, they were revived by George Norton, the Advocate General, in 1840, until Norton returned to England in 1853.[19] In 1855, law classes were established at Elphinstone College in Bombay, the Hindu College in Calcutta, and the Presidency College of Madras. In 1857, universities were established in the three Presidencies, and training in law was declared part of their functions.[20] Other universities followed (such

[17] See Vasudha Dalmia, "Sanskrit Scholars and Pandits of the Old School: The Benares Sanskrit College and the Constitution of Authority in the Late Nineteenth Century," *Journal of Indian Philosophy* 24 (1996): 321; Amit Kumar Suman, "Colonial State and Indigenous Islamic Learning: A Case Study of Calcutta *Madrasa*," *Paedagogica Historica* 58 (2022): 486.

[18] Here, I will discuss British India. On legal education in French India, see Laetitia Guerlain and Florence Renucci, "L'École de droit de Pondichéry (1838–1960): Étude exploratoire d'un établissement d'enseignement supérieur colonial," *Cahiers Jean Moulin* 7 (2021), https://doi.org/10.4000/cjm.1278. For a comparative history of legal education in colonial India and French Indochina, see Sara Legrandjacques, "Inégaux en droit: approche comparée de l'enseignement juridique en Inde britannique et en Indochine française XIXe–XXe siècle," *Cahiers Jean Moulin* 7 (2021), https://doi.org/10.4000/cjm.1334. A brief discussion of the history of legal education in colonial India is found in Jean-Louis Halpérin, "Historical Landmarks in Mapping the Spread of Positive Law Teaching," in *State Law and Legal Positivism: The Global Rise of a New Paradigm*, eds. Baudouin Dupret and Jean-Louis Halpérin (Leiden: Brill, 2022), 33, 52–4. I also discuss this topic in Assaf Likhovski, "Jurisprudence and Nationalism in the British Empire in the Early Twentieth Century: India, Egypt, and Palestine Compared," *English Historical Review* (forthcoming).

[19] Paul, *The Legal Profession*, 6, 31–3.

[20] Arjun P. Aggarwal, "Legal Education in India," *Journal of Legal Education* 12 (1959–60): 231, 232; Eric Ashby (with Mary Anderson), *Universities: British, Indian, African: A Study in the Ecology of Higher Education* (London: Weidenfeld and Nicolson, 1966), 54–64; Schmitthenner, "A Sketch," 362; Dayal, "Legal Profession," 161; Raymond Cocks, "'Sustaining the Character of a Judge': Conflict Within the Legal Thought of British India," *Journal of Legal History* 35 (2014): 44; Jain, *Outlines*, 794.

as the University of the Punjab, established in 1882, and the University of Allahabad, in 1887).

The actual role of these universities in the provision of legal education differed from place to place. In certain cities, such as Madras, legal education was concentrated in a single, dedicated law college operating under the affiliation of the local university. In others (such as Calcutta, which produced approximately half of all Indian law graduates in the late nineteenth century), there was no central law college until the beginning of the twentieth century. Instead, various colleges affiliated with the university taught law as just one subject area among others in the curriculum.[21] By the 1886 academic year, there were eighteen law schools in India and 1,716 law students. By 1896–1897, there were thirty-four such schools, teaching 3,020 students; and by 1939–1940, the number of law students had risen to 6,749. This compares to just 1,515 law students in the United Kingdom at that time.[22]

[21] [Indian Universities Commission], *Report of the Indian Universities Commission, 1902* (Simla: Government Central Printing Office, 1902), 34, 82; Misra, *Indian Middle Classes*, 326.

[22] Misra, *Indian Middle Classes*, 333; Schmitthenner, "A Sketch," 364, 366, 372; Dayal, "Legal Profession," 148, 155, 161–2, 164; Agrawala, "Indian Legal Research," 480–5; Legrandjacques, "Inégaux en droit," 7, 25. See also Aggarwal, "Legal Education," 232 (mentioning slightly different numbers for 1886–1887). The number of law students in the United Kingdom is for the academic year 1938–1939. See Duxbury, "English Jurisprudence," 79. Another indication of the difference in scale can be found by comparing the number of law teachers. In 1933–1934, there were only 109 teachers of law in England, while in the University of Calcutta alone there were 78. See Twining, *Blackstone's Tower*, 23–4; Calcutta University Commission 1917–1919, *Report*, 1:164. Beginning in the mid nineteenth century, South Asian students also traveled to England to train as barristers at the Inns of Court. Naturally, once they returned, many of these students came to occupy leading roles in their local legal system. Some of these London-trained barristers, such as Mohandas Gandhi (who studied law at the Inner Temple) or Muhammad Ali Jinnah (who trained at Lincoln's Inn), later became leading anti-colonial nationalist politicians. However, because of the costs involved in traveling and living in London, the number of South Asian students trained at the Inns of Court was relatively small compared to those studying law in British India. See Schmitthenner, "A Sketch," 365–7; Alan M. Guenther, "Syed Mahmood and the Transformation of Muslim Law in British India" (PhD diss., McGill University, 2004), 45–63; Mitra Sharafi, "A New History of Colonial Lawyering: Likhovski and Legal Identities in the British Empire," *Law and Social Inquiry* 32 (2007): 1059, 1060, 1082–3; Mitra Sharafi, *Law and Identity in Colonial South Asia: Parsi Legal Culture, 1772–1947* (New York: Cambridge University Press, 2014), 104–10; Verena Steller, "The 'Rule of Law' in British India, or a Rule of Lawyers? Indian Barristers vs the Colonial State," *Comparativ: Zeitschrift für Globalgeschichte und vergleichende Gesellschaftsforschung* 24(5) (2014): 78; Sara Legrandjacques, "Law of the

The gradual growth in the number of law students in nineteenth-century India did not change the nature of its legal education, and, generally speaking, "the study of law was not taken as a very serious exercise."[23] There was no standard legal education program, and the duration of studies varied from school to school. Part-time teachers taught law to part-time students. Courses were often delivered in the evening, attendance was non-mandatory, and law libraries were limited or non-existent. While jurisprudence was taught in Indian law schools (as well as other theoretical subjects, such as legal history and Roman law), the teaching was primarily technical and non-academic. Because legal education institutions in British India were geared to training lawyers rather than conducting legal scholarship, there was also little academic research or writing on law.[24]

However, the nature of legal education had evolved by the first decade of the twentieth century, at least at the University of Calcutta – the most important higher education institution in British India (see Figure 1.1). Established in 1857, it began, like other Indian universities of the period, as an examination-oriented entity modeled on the University of London, while the actual teaching was delivered by

Strongest? A Global Approach of Access to Law Studies and Its Social and Professional Impact in British India (1850s–1940s)," *Social Sciences* 10 (2021): 113; Mitra Sharafi, "South Asians at the Inns of Court: Empire, Expulsion, and Redemption circa 1900," in *In Between and Across: Legal History Without Boundaries*, eds. Kenneth W. Mack and Jacob Katz Cogan (New York: Oxford University Press, 2024), 179. On Indian law students in early twentieth-century Ireland see Conor Mulvagh, *Irish Days, Indian Memories: V. V. Giri and Indian Law Students at University College Dublin, 1913–1916* (Sallins: Irish Academic Press, 2016).

23 Jain, *Outlines*, 794.

24 Aggarwal, "Legal Education," 235, 237–9, 246–7; Schmitthenner, "A Sketch," 362; Agrawala, "Indian Legal Research," 496; Jain, *Outlines*, 794. A detailed list of the works that early twentieth-century Indian law students were expected to read can be found in "[Memorandum]," in Indian Universities Commission, *University of Bombay:* Part III*: Written Statements* (Calcutta: Office of the Superintendent of Government Printing, 1902), 1, 3–4 (suggesting that, for their first LL.B. exams, law students at the Government Law School in Bombay should be required to read excerpts from two books on jurisprudence (by Austin and Rattigan), as well as four additional books: on international law, the English Constitution, Roman Law, and Hindu law). See also William G. Rice, "A Quick Look at Legal Education in India and Pakistan," *Journal of Legal Education* 11 (1958): 364 (on Indian legal education in the early post-Independence period).

FIGURE 1.1 The University of Calcutta in the nineteenth century, view from College Square. On the left stands Senate House (demolished in 1960); on the right, Presidency College, one of the university's constituent colleges. Photograph from Getty Images.

the numerous colleges affiliated with it.[25] There were sixty such colleges at the beginning of the twentieth century, although less than a third of them taught law.[26]

In the first decade of the twentieth century, the University of Calcutta underwent significant reform. In 1904, the British enacted the Indian Universities Act. This sought to strengthen government control of Indian universities and thus undermine their independence. Indian nationalists vehemently opposed the Act. When the British decided to partition Bengal in 1905, Indian nationalists initiated a campaign involving various forms of protest – demonstrations, boycotts, labor unrest, acts of civil disobedience, and, ultimately, acts of terror – known as the Swadeshi Movement. The Movement reached

[25] For general histories of academic education in British India, see, e.g., Syed Nurullah and J. P. Paik, *History of Education in India during the British Period* (Bombay: Macmillan & Co., 1943); Syama Prasad Mookerjee, "Education in British India," *Annals of the American Academy of Political and Social Science* 233 (1944): 30; Sanjay Seth, *Subject Lessons: The Western Education of Colonial India* (Durham, NC: Duke University Press, 2007); Surja Datta, *A History of the Indian University System: Emerging from the Shadows of the Past* (London: Palgrave Macmillan, 2017).

[26] Calcutta University Commission 1917–1919, *Report*, 3:27–8; Presidency College Calcutta, *Centenary Volume, 1955* (Alipore: West Bengal Government Press, 1956), 12–13; P. N. Banerjee, "Foundation of the University Law College," *Calcutta University Law College Magazine* 27 (1959): ix–xi.

its zenith between 1905 and 1908. As part of the Movement, Bengali nationalists sought to promote self-sufficiency in the educational realm. One expression of this impulse was the creation of a National Council of Education in Bengal. The Council envisioned a system of education rooted in Indian culture and languages, in opposition to the Anglicized education promoted by the universities established by the British. This vision was manifested in the establishment of the Bengal National College in 1906. The College did not achieve the anticipated success. This was partly due to practical reasons involving the employment prospects of its graduates. It was also partly the result of the fact that the demand to de-Anglicize higher education in Bengal had spurred British officials to undertake significant reform in the nature of the education delivered at the University of Calcutta.[27]

In response to nationalist agitation, the British appointed Asutosh Mookerjee, a mathematician and jurist, as the Vice-Chancellor of the University of Calcutta in 1906 (see Figure 1.2). Mookerjee served in this post between 1906 and 1914 and again between 1921 and 1923. He was an academic entrepreneur who sought to emulate the German

FIGURE 1.2 Asutosh Mookerjee, c. 1920. Digital Library of India.

[27] Seth, *Subject Lessons*, 159–67; Sumit Sarkar, *The Swadeshi Movement in Bengal*, new ed. (Ranikhet: Permanent Black, 2010), 127–55.

university model and steer his institution toward academic research. He initiated a series of significant reforms that turned the university into the leading academic institution in India. He instigated the creation of a postgraduate teaching department, hired a host of talented Indian scholars, expanded the university library, and created a university press.[28]

Mookerjee was also a nationalist intellectual associated with the Swadeshi Movement, and his appointment as the university's Vice-Chancellor was a way for the British to calm nationalist agitation. However, in practice, Mookerjee used his position to further the nationalist goal of Indian cultural independence from Britain.[29] Like many Indian intellectuals, he opposed the view that "a single shelf of a good European library was worth the whole native literature of India and Arabia."[30] He appointed lecturers who were associated with radical nationalist politics, expanded the use of the vernacular Indian language at the university, and was keen to turn it into a center for studying and propagating Indian culture.[31]

[28] See University of Calcutta, *The Calendar 1931* (Calcutta: Calcutta University Press, 1931), 14, 16; *Hundred Years of the University of Calcutta: A History of the University Issued in Commemoration of the Centenary Celebration*, eds. Pramathanath Banerjee et al. ([Calcutta]: University of Calcutta [Press], 1957), 180–4, 217–28; Sarkar, *Swadeshi Movement*, 127–55; Nariaki Nakazato, *Neonationalist Mythology in Postwar Japan: Pal's Dissenting Judgment at the Tokyo War Crimes Tribunal* (Lanham, MD: Lexington Books, 2016), 85; Datta, *A History of the Indian University System*, 8, 43–6, 60–8.

[29] Kris Manjapra, "Knowledgeable Internationalism and the Swadeshi Movement, 1903–1921," *Economic and Political Weekly* 47(42) (October 2012): 53, 59–60. The establishment, in 1916, of Benares Hindu University is another example of the impact of Indian cultural nationalism (and Hindu nationalism) on Indian universities at the time. See Leah Renold, *A Hindu Education: Early Years of the Banaras Hindu University* (Delhi: Oxford University Press, 2005), 4–6.

[30] "Minute by the Hon'ble T. B. Macaulay dated the 2nd February 1835," in *Selections from the Educational Records*, ed. H. Sharp (Calcutta: Superintendent of Government Printing, 1920), 107, 109.

[31] University of Calcutta, *Calendar 1931*, 14, 16; *Hundred Years of the University of Calcutta*, 221; Narendra Krishna Sinha, *Asutosh Mookerjee: A Biographical Study* (Calcutta: Asutosh Mookerjee Centenary Committee, 1966), 56, 94–100, 114, 117, 140–4, 151; Sarkar, *Swadeshi Movement*, 127–55; Kris Manjapra, *Age of Entanglement: German and Indian Intellectuals Across Europe* (Cambridge, MA: Harvard University Press, 2014), 47–52; Kankan Bhattacharyya, "Sir Asutosh and Rise of Modern Science in India," *Indian Journal of History of Science* 50 (2015): 420, 424–33. It is interesting to note that Asutosh Mookerjee's son, Syama Prasad Mookerjee – who, like his father, also trained as a lawyer and

Specifically in the legal realm, Mookerjee, who had previously studied law and served as a judge in the Calcutta High Court, sought to reform legal education at the university, moving it in a more academic direction. Until his time, there was no college affiliated with the university that was entirely devoted to legal studies. A two-year postgraduate course of law lectures, with no mandatory attendance requirement, was all that was required to obtain a law degree.[32] In 1909, Mookerjee established the University of Calcutta College of Law, which was based on the idea that law was "neither a trade, nor a solemn jugglery, but a true and living science."[33] Law now became a three-year postgraduate degree. In addition to this Bachelor of Law program, the College offered students an advanced Master's degree and a doctorate in law. A dedicated library containing approximately 20,000 law books was also established.[34] Jurisprudence, Roman law, and Hindu law were taught at the College during its first academic year.[35] Hindu law, which Mookerjee once called a "monument of Asiatic genius," was studied not only at the College of Law but also at the Sanskrit College in Calcutta, established in 1824 and later affiliated with the University. It was also incorporated into the MA degree in

also served as Vice-Chancellor of the University of Calcutta (between 1934 and 1938) – was a leading right-wing Hindu nationalist politician. In 1939, Syama Prasad became the President of the Hindu nationalist Akhil Bharatiya Hindu Mahasabha Party, a forerunner of the Bharatiya Janata Party. See Christophe Jaffrelot, *The Hindu Nationalist Movement in India* (New York: Columbia University Press, 1996), 51.

32 Indian Universities Commission, *University of Calcutta:* Part II*: Written Statements Presented by Witnesses* (Calcutta: Office of the Superintendent of Government Printing, 1902), 80; Calcutta University Commission 1917–1919, *Report*, 3:34.

33 Asutosh Mukhopadhyay, *The Law of Perpetuities in British India* (Calcutta: Thacker, Spink and Co., 1902), 301. Mookerjee was quoting the English legal scholar Frederick Pollock, but he added the words "true and living," which did not appear in Pollock's original sentence. This was probably done under the impact of the state-of-the-art notion of "living law" that was fashionable at the time in Continental Europe. On this notion, see, e.g., Katharina Isabel Schmidt, "Law, Modernity, Crisis: German Free Lawyers, American Legal Realists, and the Transatlantic Turn to 'Life,' 1903–1933," *German Studies Review* 39 (2016): 121.

34 Calcutta University Commission 1917–1919, *Report*, 3:33–41. It should be noted that the creation of the Law College did not lead to a monopoly of the College on law teaching. A few other colleges affiliated to the university continued to offer law degrees. Ibid., 41–2.

35 University of Calcutta, *Calendar 1931*, 208–9.

Ancient Indian History and Culture, a program associated with the Carmichael Chair that Mookerjee established in 1912.[36]

Moving from legal education to legal research, throughout the nineteenth century, legal education in India was viewed as a technical matter involving the study of rules, not a science based on principles, and certainly not a discipline related in any way to the historical or social sciences. This was at least partly due to the acceptance of an understanding (associated with the works of the English legal philosopher John Austin) that defined law as a command imposed from above by the sovereign and as consisting mainly of statutes (in the Indian case, codes enacted by the British). As a result, the type of legal scholarship produced in India was narrow. In the early colonial period (until 1858), the primary genre of works created by English jurists in India comprised collections of regulations, rules, and case law and translations of Hindu and Islamic law books. In addition, digests and descriptive works attempting to summarize the rules on a given legal topic were also published.[37] Once the British embarked on the project of Indian codification, commentaries interpreting these codes also began to be published.[38]

One exception to the generally practical nature of Indian legal literature was that of the publications associated with the Tagore Law Lectures, an annual lecture series established in 1870. It was created by Prasanna Kumar Tagore, one of the members of the Tagore family, a family of Bengali intellectuals and nationalist activists. The annual lectures were given by leading non-Indian jurists (including, eventually, figures such as Holdsworth, Pollock, and Pound) and many Indian ones (most of them practicing judges and lawyers rather than law professors). The lectures were then published.[39] Most of the lectures published in the

[36] Calcutta University Commission 1917–1919, *Report*, 2:85–9, 102; Asutosh Mookerjee, "The Study of Law," in *The Judicial World of a Multi-Splendoured Genius: Sir Asutosh Mookerjee*, ed. Sudhish Pai (New Delhi: Universal Law Publishing 2014), 143, 146.

[37] Dayal, "Legal Profession," 162; Agrawala, "Indian Legal Research," 486–91.

[38] Agrawala, "Indian Legal Research," 497.

[39] On the series, see Calcutta University Commission 1917–1919, *Report*, 3:44; Agrawala, "Indian Legal Research," 497–8; Rajeev Dhavan, "Legal Research in India: The Role of the Indian Law Institute," *American Journal of Comparative Law* 34 (1986): 527, 529; Dolores F. Chew, "Of 'Unchaste' Widows and Tenants-for-Life: Legal Constructions of Gender and Property in Nineteenth Century Bengal" (PhD diss., University of Calcutta, 1994), 129, http://shodhganga.inflibnet.ac.in/handle/10603/164657; Shahbaz Ahmad

nineteenth century were descriptive surveys of the law of British India (such as the laws concerning mortgages, minors, marriage, inheritance, gifts, and agency). They were comprehensive and learned but formalist, non-contextual, and non-theoretical. They did not make use of history or the social sciences.[40] However, this changed in the early decades of the twentieth century when some of the lectures became more theoretical.

## British Jurisprudence Textbooks Written in India

English jurisprudence dominated Indian legal education during the colonial period. Why was it so dominant? Different scholars offered different reasons. Charles Lewis Tupper, the Vice-Chancellor of the University of the Punjab, argued in 1901 that, just as Greek art and philosophy had "fructified" Rome, and Greek and Roman literature had led to the transition from the Middle Ages to the Renaissance, so too was English culture playing the same role in "the Indian Renaissance now in progress." Specifically, in law studies, this role was to be played by English jurisprudence, which, claimed Tupper, "reigns alone" in this field (mentioning three thinkers, Bentham, Austin, and Maine).[41]

A different argument about the dominance of English jurisprudence in India – specifically, English analytical jurisprudence – was made after Indian Independence by S. N. Dhyani, a law professor at the University of Rajasthan in Jaipur. He wrote in 1985:

> ... during the heydays of British imperialism and absolute power no theory of law could fit in so eminently as Austin's analytical positivism which meant despotism, status quo, police state, anti-people government and alien laws and

Cheema, "Tagore Law Lecturer's [Sic] Contribution to Islamic Legal Scholarship in British India," *Al-Qalam* (December 2013): n.p.

40 See Agrawala, "Indian Legal Research," 497. One should note that some of the earlier lectures were broader in scope. See Nandini Chatterjee, "Law, Culture and History: Amir Ali's Interpretation of Islamic Tradition," in *Legal Histories of the British Empire: Laws, Engagements and Legacies*, eds. Shaunnagh Dorsett and John McLaren (London: Routledge, 2014), 45, 53–4 (discussing Ameer Ali's 1884 lectures on gifts in Islamic law). For a list of the topics of the Tagore Lectures, see University of Calcutta, *Hundred Years of the University of Calcutta*, 436–9.

41 C. L. Tupper, "English Jurisprudence and Indian Studies in Law," *Journal of the Society of Comparative Legislation* 3 (1901): 84, 86. See also Neeladri Bhattacharya, "Remaking Custom: The Discourse and Practice of Colonial Codification," in *Tradition, Dissent and Ideology: Essays in Honour of Romila Thapar*, eds. R. Champakalakshmi and S. Gopal (Delhi: Oxford University Press, 1996), 20.

judicial system – all rolled into one ... Austin was [the] god-father of [the Indian legal community before 1947] and his philosophy of law was their Bible which they capriciously worshiped by sacrificing the good of the people.[42]

Whether one agrees with Tupper or Dhyani, English jurisprudence was not *entirely* dominant. A relatively large number of books on jurisprudence were produced in India during the British period. At first, these works were written by British lawyers. Later, they were joined by Indian jurists. Most of the books produced in India were derivative, simply summarizing English ideas. Some, however, were unique in several senses.[43] First, some were more cosmopolitan than English works, relying more heavily on contemporary Continental and American legal theories compared to English works produced at the same time. Second, in some of the Indian works, the gap between English theories and Indian reality led the authors to critique prevailing English jurisprudential notions, which were supposed to be universal but were actually only applicable to modern Western law. Finally, in the first decades of the twentieth century, a new genre of jurisprudential works emerged in India: texts that employed Western jurisprudential notions to describe the principles and history of Hindu law (and, to a lesser extent, Islamic law), offering a different vision of the nature of law (and sometimes also of society) to the one provided by the British.[44] Such

[42] S. N. Dhyani, *Jurisprudence: A Study of Indian Legal Theory*, 2nd ed. (New Delhi: Metropolitan Book Co., 1985), 19–20. See also V. R. Krishna Iyer, "Towards a Third World Jurisprudence," in *Law versus Justice: Problems and Solutions* (New Delhi: Deep & Deep, 1981), 132–7. On Austinian jurisprudence and colonialism, see also Assaf Likhovski, *Law and Identity in Mandate Palestine* (Chapel Hill, NC: University of North Carolina Press, 2006), 114–16; G. Blaine Baker, "Popularizing the Rule of Law: Sheldon Amos and the International Scientific Series, 1874 to 1909," *Journal of Legal History* 33 (2012): 151, 165.

[43] On the role of India in the history of the law treatise, see Angela Fernandez and Markus Dubber, "Introduction: Putting the Legal Treatise in Its Place," in *Law Books in Action: Essays on the Anglo-American Legal Treatise*, eds. Markus Dubber and Angela Fernandez (Oxford: Hart, 2012), 1, 8–9. On the need for more studies of the history of the law book in South Asia, see, generally, Mitra Sharafi, "South Asian Legal History," *Annual Review of Law and Social Science* 11 (2015): 309, 323.

[44] The term "Hindu law" is used in this chapter to refer to what is sometimes called "traditional Hindu law" – the law found in ancient and medieval Indian texts – and not to the colonial descendent of this law, Anglo–Hindu law – the personal law of some non-Muslim communities in British India. Since the middle of the nineteenth century, the question of whether "Hindu law" actually existed before the British conquest has been hotly debated. On this, see the literature mentioned in note 99 below. For a recent discussion on the terminological problems associated with the term "Hindu law," see

works also illustrate the impact of nationalist ideology on jurisprudential thought in India.

The first comprehensive treatise on jurisprudence written in India was William Markby's *Elements of Law*.[45] This book was published in 1871, less than a decade after the publication of Austin's *Lectures on Jurisprudence*. Thus, it pioneered a long line of treatises that attempted to simplify Austin's lectures and render them more accessible to law students. Markby's book was based on a series of lectures he had given to a class of Indian students at the University of Calcutta in 1870.[46] Markby (see Figure 1.3) was related to John Austin's wife, Sarah, and he helped her prepare Austin's *Lectures on Jurisprudence* for publication in 1863. In 1866, he was appointed a judge at the Calcutta High Court, and he later served as the Vice-Chancellor of the University of Calcutta (1877–1878) before returning to England in 1878 and becoming the first Reader in Indian law at the University of Oxford.[47]

Markby's book seems to have been relatively influential (at least in the first decades after its publication), with six editions published between 1871 and 1905. It was published in the United Kingdom and was based

also Timothy Lubin, Donald R. Davis, Jr., and Jayanth K. Krishnan, "Introduction," in *Hinduism and Law: An Introduction*, eds. Timothy Lubin, Donald R. Davis, Jr., and Jayanth K. Krishnan (Cambridge and New York: Cambridge University Press, 2010), 1. For a general discussion on traditional Hindu law, see, e.g., Donald R. Davis, Jr., *The Spirit of Hindu Law* (Cambridge: Cambridge University Press, 2010). For a discussion on Anglo–Hindu law, see Donald R. Davis, Jr. and Timothy Lubin, "Hinduism and Colonial Law," in *Hinduism in the Modern World*, ed. Brian A. Hatcher (New York: Routledge, 2016), 96.

45 William Markby, *Elements of Law: Considered with Reference to Principles of General Jurisprudence* (Oxford: Clarendon Press, 1871). See also Duxbury, "English Jurisprudence," 7–8 (noting the Indian pedigree of Markby's book). For an earlier work, see John Bruce Norton, *Topics of Jurisprudence: Or Aids to the Office of the Indian Judge* (Madras: Higginbotham, 1862). Norton's book was essentially a collection of maxims on equity, accompanied by discussions of topics such as "mistake," "intention," and "agency." It was inspired by similar English works such as Herbert Broom, *A Selection of Legal Maxims* (London: A. Maxwell & Son, 1845). On Norton, see G. C. B., "John Bruce Norton (1815–1883)," in *Dictionary of National Biography*, ed. Sidney Lee (New York: Macmillan & Co., 1895), 41:216.

46 Markby, *Elements*, v.

47 T. G. Watkin, "Sir William Markby (1829–1914)," *Oxford Dictionary of National Biography* (Oxford: Oxford University Press, 2004), https://doi.org/10.1093/ref:odnb/50590. See also Lucy Taylor Markby, *Memories of Sir William Markby, K.C. I.E.: By His Wife* (Oxford: Clarendon Press, 1917).

FIGURE 1.3 Portrait of William Markby by Hubert von Herkomer. Photograph courtesy of Harvard Law School Library, Historical and Special Collections.

on a structure that later became a convention in late nineteenth- and early twentieth-century English jurisprudence textbooks.[48] Markby believed that the scientific study of law was universal, noting, for example, that his definition of law (based on Austin's definition) was not only relevant to English law. "No theory of religion, or of morals, or of politics, is involved in these views of law," he declared. "They are alike true for Hindoos, Mahommedans, and Christians."[49] Markby referred to India and its laws in many places in his book, which is unsurprising given its origins in a series of lectures at the University of Calcutta. Markby's Indian references were mostly used to illustrate his general arguments.[50]

48 The book was divided into twelve chapters discussing the following topics: general conception of law; sources of law; relations which arise out of law; primary duties and obligations; liability; grounds of non-liability; ownership; possession; servitudes or easements; prescription and limitation; sanctions and remedies; and procedure. The categories upon which this structure was based may perhaps be traced back to the structure of Blackstone's *Commentaries*, and even further back to Roman law.

49 Markby, *Elements*, 6.

50 Ibid., xii (Indian students and Roman law); ibid., 9 (the power of courts in India to review the acts of the Governor-General); ibid., 31 (comparing commentaries on English law to ones on Hindu law); ibid., 39 (the "Koran and the Shasters" were a source of law in India, just as "the precepts of the Bible have been applied to the

However, when he discussed the role of customary law in deciding cases, he argued – contrary to Austin – that custom was "not merely a branch of judge-made law" but an "independent source of law" and, indeed, "a notion older than law itself." In support of this argument, Markby mentioned ancient German village courts and "the village courts (punchayets) [sic] which exist to this day in Madras."[51] Indian examples provided to illustrate general jurisprudential points were also used in other works by Markby.[52]

In the final two decades of the nineteenth century, several works resembling Markby's were published in India.[53] The most ambitious of which was William Rattigan's *The Science of Jurisprudence*.[54] Rattigan modestly disclaimed "any intention" of presenting himself as "an original writer."[55] His book, he explained in the preface to the first edition, was written to "supply a want" for an accessible jurisprudence textbook for Indian students because Austin's book could not be understood even by English students, while Markby's and Holland's books were "not simple enough" for Indian ones.[56] However, the book *was* unique in some important senses. First, it was more "Indian" in focus than Markby's book, containing more mentions of topics related to India.[57] This Indian

institutions of daily life by ourselves ..."); ibid., 58 (Indian examples of juristic persons); ibid., 244 (imprisonment for debt in India).

51 Ibid., 33–4. On Markby's understanding of custom and Austinian jurisprudence, see also Michael Lobban, "Legal Theory and Judge-Made Law in England, 1850–1920," *Quaderni Fiorentini* 40 (2011): 553, 581–4.

52 See William Markby, "Analytical Jurisprudence," *The Law Magazine & Review and Quarterly Digest of All Reported Cases* 5th Ser. 1 (1876): 617, 625–7 (using the example of the recognition of interest by Muslim merchants in India, despite the Quranic prohibition on taking interest, to illustrate the Austinian notion of a tacit command). See also Wilfrid E. Rumble, *Doing Austin Justice: The Reception of John Austin's Philosophy of Law in Nineteenth-Century England* (London: Continuum, 2005), 161–2.

53 See R. B. Michell, *Jurisprudence: With Special Reference to the Law of India* (Madras: Higginbotham, 1883); Philip Morton, ed., *Outlines of Jurisprudence* (Allahabad: Pioneer Press, 1892); Philip Morton, *A Preliminary Manual of Jurisprudence for the Use of Students* (Lahore: The "News" Press, 1898).

54 The first edition of the book was published in India. The second and third editions were published in London. My discussion is based on the third edition. See William H. Rattigan, *The Science of Jurisprudence: Chiefly Intended for Indian Law Students*, 3rd ed. (London: Wildy, 1899).

55 Ibid., viii. 56 Ibid., vii.

57 Because of the "Indian" nature of Rattigan's book, it was recommended as the textbook on jurisprudence to be used in Indian law schools, rather than Markby's or Holland's books. See "[Memorandum]," in *Report of the Indian Universities Commission*, 3.

TABLE 1.1 The use of different keywords in Markby's and Rattigan's books

| Terms used in Markby's book | Number of instances | Terms used in Rattigan's book | Number of instances |
|---|---|---|---|
| English/England/ British | 272 | *India/Indian* | 382 |
| Roman/Rome | 103 | English/England/British | 287 |
| *India/Indian* | 97 | Roman/Romans/Rome | 184 |
| Austin/Austin's | 75 | *Hindu* | 54 |
| France/French | 47 | France/French | 33 |
| Savigny/Savigny's | 38 | *Allah* | 32 |
| *Hindoo/Hindoos* | 29 | Austin | 23 |
| America/American | 21 | America | 23 |
| Bentham | 16 | German/Germany | 20 |
| Maine | 15 | Justinian | 19 |
| *Mahommedans* | 14 | *Bengal* | 16 |
| German/Germany | 8 | *Madras* | 14 |
| *Bengal* | 7 | *Muhammadan* | 13 |
| Italian | 6 | Maine | 11 |

aspect becomes evident if we consider a quantitative analysis comparing the words used by Markby and Rattigan in their respective books. Table 1.1 lists the number of occurrences of specific keywords in both texts in descending order (the terms related to Indian law in both texts are italicized).[58]

As Table 1.2 shows, there is a marked difference in the prevalence of English-law-related terms versus Indian-law-related terms in the two works. Indian-law-related keywords (the "Indian cluster") comprised

[58] The table was created by comparing the first edition of Markby's book, published in 1871, with the third edition of Rattigan's book, published in 1899, using Wordclouds.com. While the two works are of different lengths, comparing the relative use of different keywords by the two authors reveals, I believe, the "Indian" orientation of Rattigan's book compared to Markby's. Such quantitative analysis is of limited value if one is only interested in the content of the jurisprudential arguments made by the two authors. However, it does illustrate the fact that Rattigan's book was more focused on Indian topics, and used more examples taken from Indian law and culture than Markby's book.

TABLE 1.2 A comparison of three clusters of law-related keywords in Markby's and Rattigan's books

| | Markby | Rattigan |
|---|---|---|
| English cluster | 399 (53%) | 350 (31%) |
| Continental cluster | 202 (27%) | 274 (24%) |
| Indian cluster | 142 (20%) | 511 (45%) |

just 20 percent of the keywords in Markby's book, compared to 45 percent in the case of Rattigan's book.

A second feature of Rattigan's book that can be considered unique was that, while Continental-law-related keywords appeared with similar frequency in both texts (27 percent of the words counted in Markby, compared to 24 percent in Rattigan), Rattigan's book contained more *in-depth* discussion of Continental legal theorists than Markby's book.[59] For example, Rattigan's exploration of the distinction between law and morality did not simply follow the conventional Austinian discussion. Instead, he devoted several pages to a survey of different Continental approaches to this distinction, mentioning both German legal thinkers (Krause, Jhering, Ahrens) and also Italian ones (Vico, Lioy), only then moving on to Austin's "narrower view" on the topic.[60] This Continental orientation was noted in a review of the second edition of the book published in the *Revue générale du droit* (July–August 1892).[61] Rattigan's educational trajectory, which included a doctorate from the University of

59 It should be noted that the source of inspiration for nineteenth-century English jurisprudential literature, Austin's *Lectures on Jurisprudence*, also relied heavily on Continental works (as indicated by the list of books provided at the beginning of Austin's book). See John Austin, *Lectures on Jurisprudence or the Philosophy of Positive Law*, 3rd ed. (London: John Murray, 1869), Vol. 1, ix–xiii. See also Stefan Vogenauer, "An Empire of Light? Learning and Lawmaking in the History of German Law," *Cambridge Law Journal* 64 (2005): 481. For a somewhat similar openness to non-English sources in another part of the British Empire, see, e.g., G. Blaine Baker, "The Reconstitution of Upper Canadian Legal Thought in the Late-Victorian Empire," *Law and History Review* 3 (1985): 219.

60 Rattigan, *Science*, 3rd ed., 5–10.

61 The review was cited on the opening page of the third edition of Rattigan's book. See Rattigan, *Science*, 3rd ed., "Press Opinions on the Second Edition."

Göttingen, may explain the more extensive references to Continental thinkers in his book.[62]

Finally, another significant aspect of Rattigan's book that set it apart was that it relied on Indian examples to refine or critique English theories of law. This is evident, for instance, in his discussion of the Austinian definition of law. The second chapter of the book began with a summary of the theory of "Austin and his followers" on the nature of law as the command of a sovereign. Rattigan then provided some conventional counter-examples to the Austinian theory (such as international law, which is conceived as "law" even though it is not created by a "sovereign"). He also criticized Austin's theory as relevant only to modern states where legislation was the main source of the law. As an example of law in other societies, he mentioned India, noting that Austin probably did not know that, in India, before the British conquest, life was governed by rules that were "as absolute as any" modern law but did not emanate from a political superior.[63] In this context, Rattigan mentioned examples such as the

[62] Roman and Continental legal ideas reached India through various channels. Non-English European merchants and settlers were one group of actors involved in importing Continental legal norms and ideas. In some localities in India, such as Goa (which was a Portuguese colony) or Pondicherry (which was French), these norms remained valid even after Indian Independence. See K. M. Sharma, "Civil Law in India," *Washington University Law Quarterly* 1 (1969): 1, 11–13, 17–38; Subhash C. Jain, "French Legal System in Pondicherry: An Introduction," *Journal of the Indian Law Institute* 12 (1970): 573. British lawyers trained in civil and canon law, British administrators influenced by their classical education, British judges using Roman and Continental texts in their judgments, and British law reformers emulating the Continental codification movement of the eighteenth and nineteenth centuries were other actors importing Roman and Continental law to India. For example, the first volume of Savigny's *System des heutigen romischen Rechts* was translated into English by a Madras judge, William Holloway, and Rattigan himself translated the second volume. On Holloway, and on the impact of Roman law in India more generally, see J. Duncan M. Derrett, "The Role of Roman Law and Continental Laws in India," *Zeitschrift für ausländisches und internationales Privatrecht* 24 (1959): 657, 670–82. See also Fernandez and Dubber, "Introduction," 12–13 (mentioning another Anglo-Indian translation of Savigny, Sir Erskine Perry's translation of Savigny's book on possession). Indian scholars such as Asutosh Mookerjee were also fascinated by Roman law and urged Indians to study it. See Sharma, "Civil Law," 5–11; Derrett, "Role of Roman Law."

[63] Rattigan, *Science*, 3rd ed., 16. For an earlier example of the same argument, see Gooroodass Banerjee, *The Hindu Law of Marriage and Stridhan* (Calcutta: Thacker, Spink and Co., 1879), 3–4. Interest in customs was also apparent in Markby's book. Markby mentioned Indian village courts as an example of courts basing their

customary rules that governed the life of village communities in the Punjab (customary law, it will be recalled, was a topic on which Rattigan wrote a digest). He also cited the example of Hindu laws, which were prescribed and reformed by Hindu sages (*rishis*), who had no temporal power. These sages, Rattigan continued, were able to introduce radical changes in the law using indirect methods. For example, "when they wished to abolish some prevailing practice or custom, they did not do so by an express injunction, but, by pretending to regulate the practice, they subjected it to so many conditions and ceremonial requirements as in reality to render its observance impossible," thus giving the Hindu codes "elasticity which has not rendered them obsolete despite the lapse of centuries."[64]

What is remarkable about this passage is that, using Indian examples, Rattigan managed in just a few pages not only to demonstrate the problematic nature of Austin's theory of law (as the command of a political sovereign) when applied to a non-modern legal system – a point made earlier in Maine's *Ancient Law* and other works by Maine – but also to attack the second dominant legal theory produced by nineteenth-century English jurisprudence, that of Maine himself (without naming him). In *Ancient Law* (first published in 1861), Maine described Hindu law as being based on outmoded codes that, because of the sanctity of religion, could not be reformed.[65] Rattigan argued that the conditions and requirements created by the *rishis* were *not* a mark of an outdated and problematic legal system but just the opposite: an indication of its elasticity and vitality.

decisions solely on customs. He also noted that the courts in India, when dealing with Hindus and Muslims, were directed by the legislature of British India to rule according to the "law and usages of Hindoos and Mahommedans, and not [according] to the law alone." See Markby, *Elements*, 34. However, Markby did not rely on these facts, as Rattigan did, to critique Austinian jurisprudence.

64 Rattigan, *Science*, 3rd ed., 13–18. On the role of customary law in the Punjab, see, generally, Bhattacharya, "Remaking Custom"; Andrew Sartori, "A Liberal Discourse of Custom in Colonial Bengal," *Past and Present* 212 (2011): 163.

65 For Maine's critique of Austin's command theory and for his view of Hindu law, see Henry Sumner Maine, *Ancient Law* (London: John Murray, 1861), 7–8, 16–20. See, generally, Raymond Cocks, *Sir Henry Maine: A Study in Victorian Jurisprudence* (Cambridge: Cambridge University Press, 2004); Enrico Pattaro, ed., *A Treatise of Legal Philosophy and General Jurisprudence*, Vol. 8: *A History of the Philosophy of Law in the Common Law World, 1600–1900* (Dordrecht: Springer, 2007), 198–9; David Rabban, *Law's History: American Legal Thought and the Transatlantic Turn to History* (New York: Cambridge University Press, 2013), 115–49.

The emphasis on the importance of custom was also evident in other parts of Rattigan's book. For example, in the chapter on the sources of law, Rattigan observed that one cannot "overstress ... [the] importance of giving due effect to custom," especially in the Punjab, where peasants were "extremely simple in their habits" and where, therefore, Hindu and Islamic laws were foreign. Indian law, Rattigan noted, was a "mosaic" in which "English, Muhammadan, and Hindu" law existed side-by-side with the customs of towns and villages. Austin's view that customary law was not "law" until the courts declared its existence was, therefore, "clearly erroneous," Rattigan contended.[66]

Customary law also played a significant part in another English jurisprudence book related to India: Carleton Kemp Allen's *Law in the Making*. Allen, who taught jurisprudence at Oxford, delivered the 1926 Tagore Law Lectures at the University of Calcutta, and his book was based on them.[67] The work focused on sources of law and discussed precedent, equity, and legislation, but the book's first and most sizeable part was devoted to custom. Allen explained this emphasis on custom by saying that, while French jurists could ignore custom because codes were their primary source of law, English lawyers – be they in India or the Privy Council – "cannot be unconscious of the part which custom has played and still plays in the legal development of civilizations even more complex than [their] own." Therefore, Allen argued, Indian customary law proved "the huge vitality of custom as a source of law and as a rule of conduct quite unrelated to any sovereign authority in the Austinian sense."[68]

Allen's book was reviewed in the *Calcutta Law Journal*. As we shall see in the next part of this chapter, by the 1920s, Indian scholars, too, were readily critiquing English jurisprudential approaches. The anonymous reviewer commended Allen for abandoning the Austinian model of law, but he also criticized him. One critique was that Allen's description of the attitude of ancient Hindu law to custom was based on outdated sources and did not take into account the latest theoretical works on the topic written by Indian scholars. A second critique was

66 Rattigan, *Science*, 3rd ed., 74–7.

67 Carleton Kemp Allen, *Law in the Making* (Oxford: Clarendon Press, 1927), v. On Allen, see E. T. Williams, "Allen, Sir Carleton Kemp," *Oxford Dictionary of National Biography*, https://doi.org/10.1093/ref:odnb/30383.

68 Allen, *Law in the Making*, 35–7.

that Allen viewed equity as a separate source of law – a view that was the result, said the reviewer, of English parochialism and formalism. In other legal systems, equity was not considered an independent source of law.[69]

The books I have discussed here illustrate one outcome of the transplantation of English jurisprudential ideas to India, namely their modification due to the gap between English theory and Indian reality. I will now discuss South Asian writers, whose works reflected the impact of Indian nationalist ideology. Nationalism led some Indian authors to be more receptive to non-English (Continental and American) jurisprudential theories. It led others to produce works that sought to tease out the jurisprudential notions underlying local (Hindu and Islamic) law and to portray these notions positively, in contrast with the negative image of non-Western law prevalent in English works at the time.

## Works on Jurisprudence Produced by Indian Authors

### *Works on Western Jurisprudence*

From the late nineteenth century onward, South Asian authors began publishing works on jurisprudence.[70] As these works were primarily

69 "Reviews," *Calcutta Law Journal* 48 (1928): 24n, 24n–25n.

70 The first jurisprudence book in English by a South Asian was authored by a young Burmese student studying in London. See Chan-Toon, *The Nature and Value of Jurisprudence, Roman Law and International Law* (London: W. Clowes & Sons, 1888). A second edition was published the following year. See Chan-Toon, *The Nature and Value of Jurisprudence*, 2nd enlarged ed. (London: Reeves and Turner, 1889), v–vii. For a somewhat unkind review of the second edition, see "Book Review," *Law Quarterly Review* 5 (1889): 322. On Chan-Toon (and his infamous wife), see "Chan-Toon, Mrs. M.: Mabel Mary Agnes Cosgrove," in *Edwardian Fiction: An Oxford Companion*, eds. Sandra Kemp, Charlotte Mitchell, and David Trotter (Oxford: Oxford University Press, 1997), 62; Gregory Mackie, "Forging Oscar Wilde: Mrs. Chan-Toon and for Love of the King," *English Literature in Transition, 1880–1920* 54 (2011): 267. It is interesting to note that Chan-Toon was also the author of one of the first books that attempted to summarize the principles of Buddhist law. See Chan-Toon, *The Principles of Buddhist Law: Also Containing a Translation of Important Portions of The Manu Thara Shwe Myin, with Notes* (Rangoon: Myles Standish, 1894). Additional works are P. C. Sen, *A Summary of Holland's Jurisprudence* (Konnagar near Calcutta: J. M. Sen & Co., 1896); Mohamed Kalandar Ally Khan, *A Summary of the Science of Jurisprudence with an Appendix Containing Leading Cases and Examination Questions* (Hyderabad:

meant to assist students in passing their exams, they adopted an uncritical approach to English jurisprudence. Thus, even when they mentioned Indian examples, these were not used to question the ideas of English thinkers.[71] However, there were also more original works. One such work was written by Karunamay Basu, the Chairman of the Board of Lecturers in Jurisprudence and Roman Law at the University Law College of Calcutta in the 1920s and 1930s.[72] Basu had a keen interest in contemporary American and Continental legal theories, which were more advanced and sophisticated than English ones, and these dominated his 1921 Tagore Lectures, which were published in two volumes in 1925 and 1929.[73]

One reason that Basu's lectures made copious use of Continental theories was practical: the fact that these theories were now easily accessible in English. Between 1909 and 1925, the Boston Book Company and its successor, the Macmillan Company, published a series of translations of major Continental jurisprudence books.[74]

Premier Steam Press, 1912); B. R. Agaskar and V. N. Vedak, *Summary Lecture Notes on Jurisprudence; Being a Student's Personal Book of Notes Covering the Matter Generally Required for the Paper on General Jurisprudence as Set at the First LL.B. Examination in Bombay* (Bombay: Vinaya Printing Press, 1917); M. Barkat Ali, *A Handbook of Jurisprudence* (Lahore: The Observer Press, 1919); "A Vakil," in *Principles of Jurisprudence: For the Use of Law Students*, 7th ed. (Calcutta: Das Gupta & Co., 1926); *A Hand-Book of Jurisprudence Incorporating Maine's Ancient Law* (Madras: V. Ramaswamy Sastrulu & Sons, 1929).

71 One exception is Syed Mohamad, the author of a summary of Holland's book, who advertised himself on the title page of his book as the "author of 'Mind and Molecular Theory', 'Science and Islam' etc." In his preface, he admitted that "I am yet a student myself." However, he continued, existing works summarizing the topic were of low quality, without explanation or critique, which "may have been useful to the rising sons of India in turning them out as Indian Jurists." While summarizing Holland's ideas, he therefore added notes to the text, in brackets, questioning some of them. See Syed Mohamad, *The Student's Holland: An Analytical Explanatory and Critical Commentary* (Allahabad: Ram Dayal Agarwala, 1912), i.

72 See University of Calcutta, *Calendar 1922* (Calcutta: Calcutta University Press, 1922), 9, 288; University of Calcutta, *Calendar 1931*, 208; Karunamay Basu, *The Modern Theories of Jurisprudence* (Calcutta: University of Calcutta, 1925), Vol. 1, iii.

73 Basu, *Modern Theories*, Vol. 1; Karunamay Basu, *The Modern Theories of Jurisprudence*, Vol. 2 (Calcutta: University of Calcutta, 1929) (this volume was subtitled *The Plea for a Synthetic Philosophy of Law*). See, generally, Nader Hakim and Fabrice Melleray, eds., *Le renouveau de la doctrine française: Les grands auteurs de la pensée juridique au tournant du XXe siècle* (Paris: Dalloz, 2009).

74 On the American translation project, see David S. Clark, "The Modern Development of American Comparative Law, 1904–1945," *American Journal of Comparative*

These books were heavily referenced by Basu in his book.[75] Basu's discussion of these works was rather unique. Other books and articles published in India during the same period also sometimes referred to Continental thinkers, but they did so in a far less comprehensive way.[76]

In addition to practical considerations, however, it seems that Basu's shift from a wholly English jurisprudential orientation to a more international one may have reflected a broader cultural trend associated with Indian nationalism. In the nineteenth century, Indian thinkers mostly turned to England for intellectual inspiration. This was certainly true for the mid nineteenth-century "Bengali Renaissance," which was associated with liberal thinkers such as Rammohun Roy and, later, with the Young Bengal movement, both influenced by English utilitarian thought.[77] It was even true when liberalism was

*Law* 55 (2007): 587, 599–600, 608. Another relevant American theoretical work was a three-volume collection of excerpts on the evolution of law. See *Evolution of Law: Select Readings on the Origin and Development of Legal Institutions*, eds. Albert Kocourek and John H. Wigmore eds., 3 vols. (Boston: Little, Brown and Co., 1915–1918). For discussions of the influence of American legal scholarship on Indian law in the later, post-Independence period, see Upendra Baxi, "Understanding the Traffic of Ideas in 'Law' between America and India," in *Traffic of Ideas between India and America*, ed. Robert M. Crunden (Delhi: Chanakya Press, 1985), 319; Rajeev Dhavan, "Borrowed Ideas: On the Impact of America Scholarship on Indian Law," *American Journal of Comparative Law* 33 (1985): 505; Jayanth K. Krishnan, "Professor Kingsfield Goes to Delhi: American Academics, the Ford Foundation, and the Development of Legal Education in India," *American Journal of Legal History* 47 (2003): 447; Jayanth K. Krishnan, "From the ALI to the ILI: The Efforts to Export an American Legal Institution," *Vanderbilt Journal of Transnational Law* 38 (2005): 1255.

[75] Basu's book mentioned the works of non-English legal theorists such as Berolzheimer, Gareis, Gray, Korkunov, Miraglia, and Pound.

[76] See, e.g., Sitaram Banerjee, "Philosophy and Law," *Calcutta Law Journal* 26 (1917): 5n (citing Jhering, Kohler, and Korkunov); "The Society and the Law (Psychical Theory of Society)," *Calcutta Law Journal* 28 (1918): 5n (mentioning Korkunov); B. K. Acharyya, "Scientific Study of Law," *Calcutta Law Journal* 27 (1918): 29n, 37n (mentioning Garies, Korkunov, and Pound, and also calling for the study of comparative law, following the example of Japanese legal education); K. Krishna Menon, *Outlines of Jurisprudence* (Madras: Huxley Press, 1929) (mentioning Savigny and Korkunov); Asoke Sen, "The Relation between Law and Morality," *Calcutta University Law College Magazine* 12 (1942): 75 (mentioning Korkunov, Pound, and Jellinek).

[77] See Andrew Sartori, *Bengal in Global Concept History: Culturalism in the Age of Capital* (Chicago, IL: University of Chicago Press, 2008), 68–108. On Indian liberal thought, see, generally, C. A. Bayly, *Recovering Liberties: Indian Thought in the Age of Liberalism and Empire* (Cambridge: Cambridge University Press, 2012).

replaced by neo-romantic Hindu revivalism in the late nineteenth century, best expressed in the works of writers such as Bankimchandra Chatterjee. Bankim's neo-Hinduism of the late nineteenth century may superficially be seen as a local reaction to English culture, but, in fact, it echoed contemporary English ideas about the nature of culture, nation, and religion. The late nineteenth-century Indian rejection of liberalism thus resonated with similar trends prevalent in England.[78]

However, as historian Kris Manjapra has shown, during the first two decades of the twentieth century (partly due to the Swadeshi Movement), and especially in the 1920s, Bengali intellectuals shifted their cultural outlook, replacing the Anglophilic tendencies of the previous generations of intellectuals with an international, multipolar, anti-colonial vision of the world, turning Calcutta into "the epicenter of anti-British intellectual politics."[79] For example, the shift from an English to an international orientation was evident in literature. While Bankim's late nineteenth-century literary magazine, *Bangadarshan*, still imagined the world through "the lenses of the British Empire" and the India–Britain axis, the equivalent literary magazine of the 1920s generation in Bengal, *Kallol*, offered its readers a multipolar internationalist perspective.[80] This move from an imperial to an international orientation was manifested in a rejection of the conventional English literary canon taught at the time at Indian universities, leading to the publication of literary works by non-English writers from places as diverse as the United States, Germany, Northern and Eastern Europe, Russia, and Japan. It also echoed other trends in Indian culture of the 1920s, such as a marked increase in the translation, publication, and trade of books in European languages other than English, the growing connections between the University of Calcutta and German and Japanese scholars, and the international literary tours of India's leading author, Rabindranath Tagore, during the interwar

78 Sartori, *Bengal*, 97, 120, 126–9.

79 Kris Manjapra, "From Imperial to International Horizons: A Hermeneutic Study of Bengali Modernism," *Modern Intellectual History* 8 (2011): 327; Manjapra, *Age of Entanglement*, 12, 41. On earlier, fin-de-siècle, French influences, see Sartori, *Bengal*, 136–42. On Indians studying at American universities in the early twentieth century (and on the politics of this move as an expression of Indian nationalism), see Manjapra, *Age of Entanglement*, 41, 52–4, 213; Sara Legrandjacques, "Global Students? The International Mobility and Identity of Students from Colonial India and Indochina, 1880s–1945," *Global Histories* 4(2) (October 2018): 46, 53–5.

80 Manjapra, "From Imperial to International Horizons," 337–9.

period.[81] Basu's lectures can be viewed as the jurisprudential manifestation of this broader movement away from English intellectual fashions, as discussed in detail by Manjapra.

In his first lecture of the series, Basu declared his independence from English jurisprudence and the analytical method, stating that his Tagore Law Lectures reflected "the new tendency" to study not only law but also "the science and philosophy of law." He also noted that this tendency had been adopted by the University of Calcutta, following the lead of the United States, where works by Continental jurists were being translated and studied. In recent years, he continued, the "limited" focus on the analytical school had changed. Americans were studying French and German legal theory, thus leading to the "rise of a new unified school of Sociological Jurisprudence," which was needed "for the better and more effective solution of the serious social and legal problems which can no longer be disposed of ... [by] ... superficial and pragmatic treatment." He observed:

> India cannot help sharing in these problems of the civilised world, and it is but meet and proper that the study of jurisprudence from the points of view of all the schools, should receive the same impetus and encouragement from the premier University of India as it is receiving in the continent of Europe and in the United States.[82]

Later in the book, Basu also noted the resistance of English jurisprudence to "sociological thought," adding that, unlike England, in the United States, "the sociological spirit ha[d] been awakened."[83] Basu's observation on the relative absence of Continental (and American) legal theories from contemporary English works was accurate.[84] For example,

[81] Ibid., 342, 345–6, 348; Manjapra, *Age of Entanglement*, 47–52, 98–102.

[82] Basu, *Modern Theories*, Vol. 1, xi–iii, liii.

[83] Ibid., Vol. 1, liii–iv. Other works written by Indian scholars of the time also showed an awareness of, and interest in, sociological jurisprudence. See Acharyya, "Scientific Study," 32n; Sures Chandra Chakravarti, *Studies in Jurisprudence and International Law* (Calcutta: Butterworth & Co., 1924); N. Srinivasan, "The Juristic and Political Ideas of Duguit," *Indian Journal of Political Science* 1 (1939): 1.

[84] See Duxbury, "English Jurisprudence," 37–8. Perhaps the closest English equivalent to Basu's book, both in terms of the period in which it was published and also its interest in non-English theories, was George Keeton's 1930 book. See George W. Keeton, *The Elementary Principles of Jurisprudence* (London: A. & C. Black, 1930). This book was based on lectures delivered in Hong Kong in 1924. On the influence of non-English legal theories on this book, see Duxbury, "English Jurisprudence," 9–13 (noting

in the 580 pages of the seventh edition of Salmond's *Jurisprudence*, published in 1924, sociological jurisprudence was not mentioned at all, and Roscoe Pound was mentioned only twice – once in a footnote mentioning an article of his that contained a general survey of schools of jurisprudence, and once in the bibliography.[85] In a similar vein, the newest edition of T. E. Holland's *Elements of Jurisprudence*, at the time of Basu's Tagore Lectures in 1921, was the twelfth edition of the textbook, published in 1917, from which the notion of "sociological jurisprudence" was absent.[86]

Another interesting point about Basu was his attitude to Hindu law. In the preface to the book, he mentioned a complaint he had received about the lack of attention to Hindu law in his lectures.[87] His somewhat puzzling answer to this criticism was that all the stages of the development of jurisprudence were already found in Hindu law: "My first impulse [in response to that criticism] naturally was to find some excuse in the fact that Hindu Jurisprudence is not 'modern.'" However, Basu continued, he had then realized that: "Hindu juristic theories had in fact passed through almost all the phases which characterised the various stage of the juristic history of Europe and Anglo-America since the dawn of civilisation; and moreover had reached in its most developed form a synthesis which has not yet been attained in the modern world."[88]

Keeton's awareness of American legal theories, such as legal realism, especially in the second edition of his book, published in 1949). One should also note the presence of Continental works by scholars such as Berolzheimer or Duguit in Keeton's book. See also Duxbury, "English Jurisprudence," 54–69 (discussing the impact of American legal realism on English works). For a general discussion of the relationship between English and American legal scholars, see David Sugarman, "A Special Relationship? American Influences on English Legal Education, c. 1870–1965," *International Journal of the Legal Profession* 18 (2011): 7.

85 John Salmond, *Jurisprudence*, 7th ed. (London: Sweet & Maxwell, 1924), 15, 564.

86 Thomas Erskine Holland, *Elements of Jurisprudence*, 12th ed. (New York: Oxford University Press, 1917).

87 Basu said in the preface to the first volume that "it was pointed out to me as a defect by a very high authority that my synopsis did not contain any reference to Hindu jurisprudence." In the preface to the second volume, he mentioned in this context "the great patron of learning, whose words [were] uttered while he was at the helm of our University," and noted that he was now dead, thus indicating that this person was Asutosh Mookerjee. Basu, *Modern Theories*, Vol. 1, vii; Vol. 2, vi.

88 Basu, *Modern Theories*, Vol. 1, vii. This might be seen as an echo of a more general theme in modern Western culture, the Orient as a source of ancient wisdom. See, e.g.,

Basu said in his book that the next step in the development of jurisprudence would be a synthesis of existing theories. In the preface, however, he argued that such a synthesis would not be novel. It would actually be "an adaptation of the synthetic philosophy and jurisprudence of the Hindus to modern conditions."[89] Basu repeated this point in his preface to the second volume, which was subtitled "A Plea for a Synthetic Philosophy of Law." He explained that the book was "only an expository study of the modern theories" and that "the proposed reconstruction of the Synthetic Philosophy of Law in the light and spirit of our ancient Oriental Philosophy should be, if at all ... taken up separately as an independent piece of work."[90]

Basu's lectures contained almost no references to Hindu or Islamic law. For example, the first lecture, which was a survey of legal theories between antiquity and the early modern period, was based on a view of jurisprudence as a Western creation. It began with the Greeks and Romans, moving directly on to the Middle Ages in Europe. There were no allusions to non-Western systems of law.[91]

While Basu argued in the preface to his book that Hindu jurisprudence was superior to its Western counterpart, in the book itself, Basu often

Harry Oldmeadow, "Ex Oriente Lux: Eastern Religions, Western Writers," *Literature & Aesthetics* 21 (2011): 23.

89 Basu, *Modern Theories*, Vol. 1, vii–viii. Another excuse Basu provided for not discussing Hindu legal theories was that "the comparative study of Hindu legal philosophy and jurisprudence in all its phases in the light of modern juristic theories is a fascinating subject for juristic research, and is further, bound to be immensely useful in the practical field of legal reform which is now-a-days so much in demand all over the civilised world." Nevertheless, he continued, "it is a vast subject, more comprehensive and arduous than even the whole course of my lectures, [ ... and, therefore,] I trust it may be selected as a future subject of the Tagore lectures and undertaken by some worthier devotee (than myself) alike of Hindu and the modern social and legal philosophy; or better still, considering that the subject is capable of infinite expansion and research, a more permanent chair or institution may be founded under suitable conditions to promote its culture." Ibid., Vol. 1, viii.

90 Basu, *Modern Theories*, Vol. 2, v–vi.

91 There were also only a few references to Indian terms. One example is the allusion to the Hindu notions of "atman" and "manas" as equivalents of Western notions of soul and mind. See Basu, *Modern Theories*, Vol. 1, 17, 323. Another example is the reference to yoga or darsana when explaining neo-platonism. See ibid., Vol. 1, 41, 42. Finally, in Basu's discussion of anarchism, a footnote said that "modern social anarchists of a religious or ethical type are represented by Tolstoy and Tucker, who do not advocate violence but passive resistance; cf. that advocated by Mr. Gandhi in leading the recent non-cooperation movement against the bureaucratic government in British India." Ibid., Vol. 1, 323.

repeated disparaging Western descriptions of non-Western law. For example, when discussing the critique of Austin's theory by what he called the "English Historical School" (specifically, Maine, Pollock, and Bryce), he noted that one of their objections to this theory was that:

> Austin's definition of law may be true with regard to the laws of advanced civilized states like the Roman Empire or the modern European states ... but can scarcely apply to the more backward states, past and present, e.g., the Oriental States, where the central power concerns itself only with the gathering of armies and levying of taxes and leaves the administration of law entirely to local courts and [village councils, i.e.,] *panchayaets* [sic].[92]

Basu then mentioned the response given by Austin's defenders (Holland, Markby, and Salmond), namely, that:

> ... the customary laws and rules of Oriental states ... are not positive laws at all in the Austinian sense. They may be yet regarded as mere rules or laws of morality – defective and deformed predecessors of the more perfected type that constitutes the positive laws of modern civilised states. You may historically trace the new modern type to the older as its source, as you can biologically trace the descent of man from the anthropoid ape; but the two logically belong to essentially separate species.[93]

Rather than question this equation of Oriental laws with apes, Basu repeated it, and this repetition seems to undermine his contention in the preface to the book that Hindu law and jurisprudence were actually more advanced than Western ones.[94]

The tendency to uncritically summarize Western works was also evident in other places in the book. For example, when discussing racial theories of law (based on thinkers such as Houston Stewart Chamberlain), Basu commented that "contact with superior foreign civilisations and legal systems develops the resources of a virile race and improves and reforms its indigenous social and legal fabric, as was the case with the Roman Republic; but similar influences would smother a weaker race and denationalise it."[95]

[92] Ibid., Vol. 1, 257–8. [93] Ibid., Vol. 1, 261.

[94] In a somewhat similar fashion, when Basu discussed Herbert Spencer's sociology, he talked about "European nations ... and of less civilised races, e.g., the Polynesians, the Africans, and some Asiatic people." Ibid., Vol. 1, 378.

[95] Ibid., Vol. 1, 429. See also his discussion of Chamberlain's pro-English racist sentiments. Ibid., Vol. 1, 432.

The unquestioning acceptance of Western theories sometimes led Basu to adopt contradictory positions. For example, in one place in the book, Basu criticized the classical economists of the early nineteenth century as if he were a Marxist. Thus, when describing the rise of the science of economics in the late eighteenth and early nineteenth centuries, he noted that economic theory (as well as jurisprudence) during that period were based on an individualistic ideology and the ideal of freedom of contract and, therefore, ignored class distinctions and the "debasement" of the proletariat. The abstract idea of "freedom of contract," he said, led only to the "freedom to perish."[96] Later in his book, he devoted several pages to a survey of socialist, communist, and anarchist social theories, including a summary of their critique of liberal law – a law that was designed, he said, to assist in the "economic enslavement of the masses."[97]

In another place in his book, however, Basu praised the Historical School for undermining the revolutionary spirit of the French Revolution, as if he were a conservative thinker, arguing that this school's portrayal of law as the "historic product of popular life slowly ... evolving ... and incapable of being suddenly and spasmodically changed" represented a "safe, healthy and orthodox line of thought," resisting the "tide of revolutionary ideas" of the eighteenth century "and their accompanying evil."[98] Basu may only have been attempting to accurately convey the main ideas of the schools of thought that he was describing, but the terms he used (such as "healthy") pointed to a contradictory espousal of both socialist and conservative ideas about the nature of law and society.

Basu was aware of the *need* to include non-Western law in his work (as is evident from the preface to his book). However, he did not actually do so. Other works written at the time were more critical of Western legal theories and more interested in non-Western law, specifically in Hindu law. I will now discuss such works, some of which were also based on Tagore Law Lectures, like Basu's book.

[96] Ibid., Vol. 1, 146–7.

[97] Ibid., Vol. 1, 311–27. It is interesting to note that contemporary English works, such as Holland's and Keeton's books, contained no such discussions of socialist legal theory.

[98] Ibid., Vol. 1, 174.

### *Theoretical Works on Hindu Law*

Interest in digesting and codifying "Hindu law" can be traced back to eighteenth-century British officials in India, such as William Jones. The English brought with them specific jurisprudential notions about the nature of law (and of "religion"), and these notions shaped how they constructed and represented local "law," whether Hindu or Islamic (and, later, also Buddhist law in colonial Burma).[99] In the following

[99] There is a large body of works discussing the extent to which the English invented the "law" of their South Asian subjects. Such discussions can be found in the nineteenth-century debate about the existence of "Hindu law" between James Henry Nelson and John D. Mayne. See J. H. Nelson, *A View of Hindu Law as Administered by the High Court of Judicature at Madras* (Madras: Higginbotham, 1877), i–iii, 1–16; J. H. Nelson, *A Prospectus of the Scientific Study of the Hindu Law* (London: C. Kegan Paul & Co., 1881), v–viii; John D. Mayne, "Hindu Law in Madras," *Law Quarterly Review* 3 (1887): 446; John D. Mayne, *A Treatise on Hindu Law and Usage*, 7th ed. (Madras: Higginbotham, 1906), ix–x, 2–5. On the Nelson vs. Mayne debate, including antecedents, and later discussions, see, e.g., Radhabinod Pal, *The History of Hindu Law in the Vedic Age and in Post-Vedic Times down the Institutes of Manu* (Calcutta: University of Calcutta Press, 1958), 1–2; J. D. M. Derrett, "J. H. Nelson: A Forgotten Administrator-Historian of India," in *Historians of India, Pakistan and Ceylon*, ed. C. H. Philips (London: Oxford University Press, 1961), 354; Lloyd I. Rudolph and Susanne Hoeber Rudolph, "Barristers and Brahmans in India: Legal Cultures and Social Change," *Comparative Studies in Society and History* 8 (1965): 24, 36–8; Nandini Bhattacharyya-Panda, *Appropriation and Invention of Tradition: The East India Company and Hindu Law in Early Colonial Bengal* (Oxford: Oxford University Press, 2008), 3–10, 30–2. Twentieth-century discussions of the topic include Marc Galanter, "The Displacement of Traditional Law in Modern India," *Journal of Social Issues* 24 (1968): 65, 69–76; Bernard S. Cohn, *Colonialism and Its Forms of Knowledge: The British in India* (Princeton: Princeton University Press, 1996), 57–75. For a relatively recent summary of the debate in the literature about the nature of British codification of Hindu Law, see Sharafi, "South Asian Legal History," 319. See also Jean-Louis Halpérin, "Western Legal Transplants and India," *Jindal Global Law Review* 2 (2010): 14; Davis and Lubin, "Hinduism and Colonial Law"; Axel Michaels, "The Practice of Classical Hindu Law," in Lubin et al., eds., *Hinduism and Law*, 58; Rachel Sturman, *The Government of Social Life in Colonial India: Liberalism, Religious Law and Women's Rights* (Cambridge: Cambridge University Press, 2012); Eleanor Newbigin, *The Hindu Family and the Emergence of Modern India: Law, Citizenship and Community* (Cambridge: Cambridge University Press, 2013); Geetanjali Srikantan, *Identifying and Regulating Religion in India: Law, History and the Place of Worship* (Cambridge: Cambridge University Press, 2020). For arguments that Hinduism itself was a modern construct, see, e.g., Gauri Vishwanathan, "Colonialism and the Construction of Hinduism," in *The Blackwell Companion to Hinduism*, ed. Gavin Flood (Oxford: Blackwell, 2003), 23, 26–27; Brian K. Pennington, *Was Hinduism Invented? Britons, Indians, and the Colonial Construction of Religion* (New York: Oxford University Press, 2005); Chaudhry, *South Asia*, 407–19. For a general discussion on the problem of designating

paragraphs, I will not discuss works dealing with the practical aspects of Anglo–Hindu law (that is, the personal law of most non-Muslims in India), whose primary audience comprised legal practitioners, nor will I discuss the way Hindu law was reflected in colonial case law.[100] Nor will I discuss works by Western and Indian Indologists such as Julius Jolly, Ganganatha Jha, or P. V. Kane.[101] Rather, I am interested here in texts on Hindu *jurisprudence* – that is, works (produced by Indian legal scholars) whose main concern was to discuss the more general aspects of Hindu law, whether its sources, the classification scheme used by Hindu jurists, significant concepts (such as ownership, contract, crime, and so on), or the history of Hindu law. This type of literature evolved at the beginning of the twentieth century and was associated with scholars linked to the University of Calcutta.[102]

The intellectual roots of this literature go back to pre-twentieth-century British missionary critiques of Hinduism, which portrayed it as idolatrous, superstitious, and morally degenerate.[103] These critiques provoked introspection and reform among Hindu intellectuals

ancient normative traditions as "legal systems," see Dupret and Halpérin, eds., *State Law and Legal Positivism.*

[100] See, e.g., William Hay Macnaghten, *Principles and Precedents of Hindu Law* (Calcutta: Baptist Mission Press, 1828–1829); Thomas Strange, *Hindu Law ...* (London: Parbury, Allen, 1830); Standish Grove Grady, *A Manual of Hindu Law for the Use of Students and Practitioners* (London: Wildy and Sons, 1871); Mayne, *A Treatise on Hindu Law and Usage*; Dinshah Fardunji Mulla, *Principles of Hindu Law* (Bombay: N. M. Tripathi, 1912). For a recent discussion of Hindu law in colonial case law, see, e.g., Tirthankar Roy and Anand V. Swamy, *Law and the Economy in Colonial India* (Chicago, IL: University of Chicago Press, 2016).

[101] See, e.g., Julius Jolly, *Hindu Law and Custom*, trans. Batakrishna Ghosh (Calcutta: Greater Indian Society, 1928); Ganganatha Jha, *Hindu Law in Its Sources*, 2 vols. (Allahabad: Indian Press, 1930–1933); P. V. Kane, *History of Dharmaśāstra*, 5 vols. (Poona: Bhandarkar Oriental Research Institute, 1930–1962). For works on specific subfields of Hindu law, see, e.g., Amareswar Thakur, *Hindu Law of Evidence: Or a Comparative Study of the Law of Evidence According to the Smrtis* (Calcutta: University of Calcutta Press, 1933).

[102] One can also find a few older works discussing some jurisprudential aspects of Hindu law – for example, whether the secular Austinian definition of law fitted the notion of law in Hindu law. See Chew, "Of 'Unchaste' Widows," 132–3, 148–50 (discussing books based on Tagore Lectures from the 1870s and 1880s, in which the Indian authors criticized the Western, secular definitions of law as inapplicable to Hindu law). See also Janaki Nath Pal Sastri, "Hindu Jurisprudence," *Calcutta Law Journal* 8–9 (1908–1909): 13n (an article on the topic published in several installments).

[103] See, generally, Geoffrey A. Oddie, *Imagined Hinduism: British Protestant Missionary Constructions of Hinduism, 1793–1900* (New Delhi: Sage, 2006).

influenced by the West who sought to reassert the philosophical richness and ethical foundations of Hinduism. Nineteenth-century religious and social reform movements like the Brahmo Samaj and Arya Samaj, also influenced by Western monotheism and rationalism, played pivotal roles in redefining Hindu identity.[104] The twentieth-century works dealing with legal theory that I will now discuss can be seen as another expression of the same mixture of Western ideas and Hindu traditions in colonial India.

I will discuss several books and articles on Hindu jurisprudence published in the first decades of the twentieth century. These were all based on Western jurisprudential theories, accepting some of its basic premises (for example, that there was, indeed, an entity that could be called "Hindu law" or that this entity could be described by using concepts taken from "universal" or "general" jurisprudence). However, these works were also critical of Western descriptions of Hindu law, especially those found in the writings of Henry Maine. I have selected these particular works even though they seem to have had little lasting influence in their own right, either in India or elsewhere.[105] However, they illustrate how Indian nationalist discourse shaped Indian jurisprudential works in the early twentieth century. Criticizing English jurisprudential theories was a way for these authors to indirectly criticize British colonial rule. Specifically, their writings sought to challenge two significant themes found in English jurisprudential works that tended to legitimize British colonial rule in India. First, the Austinian association of the term "law" exclusively with norms created by a sovereign in a top-down manner. Second, Maine's portrayal of Hindu law as "perverted" (and, therefore, in need of replacement by English law), an idea that was also associated with a broader theme – the view that Oriental societies were inherently despotic.[106]

104 See, e.g., Kenneth W. Jones, *Socio-Religious Reform Movements in British India* (Cambridge: Cambridge University Press, 1989).

105 For example, none of the works I will discuss is mentioned in modern works on Hindu law, such as Werner Menski, *Hindu Law: Beyond Tradition and Modernity* (New Delhi: Oxford University Press, 2003).

106 See, generally, Assaf Likhovski, "History of British Legal Education in Mandatory Palestine," in *Experimental Legal Education in a Globalized World: The Middle East and Beyond*, eds. Mutaz M. Qafisheh and Stephen A. Rosenbaum (Newcastle upon Tyne: Cambridge Scholars Publishing, 2016), 177, 189–97 (on the use of Austinian jurisprudence to legitimize British colonial rule). See also Karuna Mantena, *Alibis of*

Some aspects of the relationship between Indian nationalism and law have been explored in past literature – specifically, the fact that many of the leaders of the nationalist movement were lawyers by training. This feature was typical of many non-Western nationalist movements.[107] Another link between Indian nationalism and law can be found in the attempt, before and after Indian Independence, to replace the alien British legal system of the colonial period with a system based on adjudication by village councils (*panchayats*).[108] Here, I discuss one aspect of the links between law and Indian nationalism that, until now, has been overlooked – the attempt, during the colonial period, to use Hindu law to criticize Western jurisprudential notions.

The first scholar whose work I will discuss is Priyanath Sen. Sen was appointed Tagore Law Professor at the University of Calcutta in 1908 at the age of 35. He was due to deliver the 1909 Tagore Law Lectures but died that year. His lectures were published posthumously in 1918 in a book entitled *The General Principles of Hindu Jurisprudence* (see Figure 1.4).[109]

*Empire: Henry Maine and the Ends of Liberal Imperialism* (Princeton, NJ: Princeton University Press, 2010), 33–5 (on James Mill's argument that British colonial rule was meant to free Indians from their "stagnant" customs). On the image of Hindu law as frozen and "perverted," see Maine, *Ancient Law*, 20. See also Edward W. Said, *Orientalism* (New York: Vintage, 1979), 32–3, 102, 172, 208.

107 See, e.g., Schmitthenner, "A Sketch," 376–81; Mithi Mukherjee, *India in the Shadows of Empire: A Legal and Political History, 1774–1950* (Oxford: Oxford University Press, 2010), 105–49.

108 Marc Galanter, "The Aborted Restoration of 'Indigenous' Law in India," in *Law and Society in Modern India* (Delhi: Oxford University Press, 1997), 37. On the history of British and Nationalist attitudes to the Panchayats, see, generally, James Jaffe, *Ironies of Colonial Governance: Law, Custom and Justice in Colonial India* (Cambridge: Cambridge University Press, 2015); James Jaffe, "Gandhi, Lawyers, and the Courts' Boycott during the Non-Cooperation Movement," *Modern Asian Studies* 51 (2017): 1340. See also Deepa Das Acevedo, "Developments in Hindu Law from the Colonial to the Present," *Religion Compass* 7 (2013): 252, 257–8 (a brief discussion on the attempts by nationalists to reform specific aspects of Hindu law during the colonial period); Smita Narula, "Law and Hindu Nationalist Movements," in Lubin et al., eds., *Hinduism and Law*, 234 (a discussion of the relationship between Hindu nationalism and Hindu law after Indian Independence).

109 Priyanath Sen, *The General Principles of Hindu Law* (Calcutta: University of Calcutta Press, 1918). Sen came from an upper-caste family in Bengal and first studied Sanskrit with his father, who was a Sanskrit scholar. He was later trained as a Sanskrit scholar at the University of Calcutta. See "Dr. Priya Nath Sen," *Calcutta Law Journal* 10 (1909): 37n. See also Priya Nath Sen, *Philosophy of the*

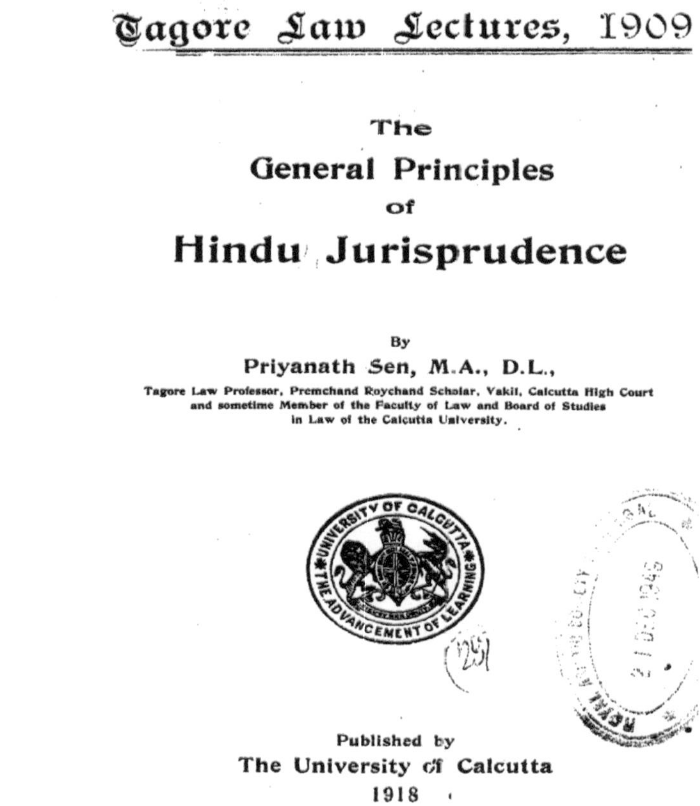
Tagore Law Lectures, 1909

The
General Principles
of
Hindu Jurisprudence

By
Priyanath Sen, M.A., D.L.,
Tagore Law Professor, Premchand Roychand Scholar, Vakil, Calcutta High Court
and sometime Member of the Faculty of Law and Board of Studies
in Law of the Calcutta University.

Published by
The University of Calcutta
1918

FIGURE 1.4 Title Page, Priyanath Sen, *The General Principles of Hindu Jurisprudence* (Calcutta: University of Calcutta Press, 1918). Digital Library of India.

The book discussed Hindu law using modern jurisprudential categories, thus combining Western and Indian ideas. The book was Western because Sen accepted the English definition of what jurisprudence was ("to analyse and systematise these essential

*Vedanta* (Calcutta: Oriental Publishing House, 1900). It is interesting to note that the lecture series delivered a year before, by Sripati Roy, was also more theoretical in comparison with previous years. See Sripati Roy, *Customs and Customary Law in British India* (Calcutta: Hare Press, 1911).

elements underlying the infinite variety of legal rules without special reference to the institutions of any particular country") and the Austinian division between general and particular jurisprudence.[110] Sen also accepted the notion that there are certain stages through which all legal systems must pass in their evolution.[111] He argued that his discussion of the general principles of Hindu law could serve to promote a more general understanding of the nature of law (in the same way that the study of Sanskrit contributed to the "science of philology").[112] He was convinced that Hindu law's "secular" parts could be disentangled (albeit with some difficulty) from the religious and moral parts. Thus, he focused on the parts that Western jurists saw as essential to law (property, family, contract, tort, criminal, procedural, and evidentiary law). Furthermore, in his book, he rejected the traditional classifications of Hindu law in favor of a new "scientific" classification scheme derived from the Roman tripartite division of law into things, persons, and actions, augmented by a special chapter on contractual obligations and another chapter on tort and crime.[113]

On the other hand, Sen showed how the Western, positivist, concept of law did not accord with Hindu law. Law, he said, was not the command of a sovereign accompanied by the threat of an earthly sanction (as John Austin argued). In Hindu jurisprudence, the king was subject to the law like all other human beings. The king did not legislate except in minor and temporary matters, and his role was merely that of enforcer of the law. Sanctions were not earthly punishments. Instead, disobedience led to misery, either in this life or in the life to come. Thus, unlike the "modern or Austinian view" of law, which argued that legal norms were "commands issuing from the King," the Hindu view was that law "issues from a source superior to the King, and the duty of enforcing [the law] is cast upon [the King] from above."[114] Sen also criticized the Western view that "Oriental

[110] Sen, *General Principles*, 2–3. [111] Ibid., 1–4. [112] Ibid., 5.

[113] Ibid., 6–7, 36. On the problematic distinction between "religious" and "secular" law, see Cohn, *Colonialism*, 71; Robert A. Yelle, "The Hindu Moses: Christian Polemics against Jewish Ritual and the Secularization of Hindu Law under Colonialism," *History of Religions* 49 (2011): 141.

[114] Sen, *General Principles*, 26–31. On sanctions in Hindu law, see also Jogendra Chunder Ghose, *The Principles of Hindu Law*, 3rd ed. (Calcutta: S. C. Auddy & Co., 1917), Vol. 1, 7. In Chapter 5 of this book, I discuss in more

Empires" lacked an interest in the rule of law, being merely concerned with raising taxes and armies. He argued that – at least as far as India was concerned – the primary duty of kings was to protect their subjects by enforcing the law.[115]

Sen also rejected the disparaging English approach to Hindu law found in Henry Maine's 1861 book, *Ancient Law*, where Maine described Hindu law as containing an "immense apparatus of cruel absurdities" and referred to a "feeble and perverted" Hindu civilization.[116] Sen's answer to this scathing depiction was to say that "the hostile aspersion" cast on Hindu law by "able but ill-informed critics" was the result of "ignorance and prejudice." Those critics, Sen asserted, "go into raptures at the bare mention of the [early Roman law code, the] Twelve Tables, but shake their heads at the mention of the name of Manu, and talk about 'feeble civilization' and 'cruel absurdities' without feeling the absurdity of criticising upon a subject which they had no opportunity to study."[117]

Hindu law was not perfect, Sen acknowledged, but it compared favorably with Roman law – and this comparison was objective, not a result of Sen's own "undue partiality towards [his] national system."[118] Sen directed these comments at Maine, although he did not mention him by name here. However, in another part of his book, when discussing the specific topic of the acquisition of property by conquest, Sen noted that the Hindu laws of war limited the rights of conquering kings more than Roman law did and that "we may be justly proud that Hindu law was less indulgent of the ferocity and cupidity of combatants [than Roman law,] and Sir Henry Maine, when he talked glibly of the 'feeble civilization' of the Hindus might well have taken notice of this."[119]

detail this argument as well as additional ones which appeared in works written in India in the first decades of the twentieth century on ancient Indian constitutional history.

115 Sen, *General Principles*, 30. 116 Maine, *Ancient Law*, 20.

117 Sen, *General Principles*, 37–8, 374. 118 Ibid.

119 Ibid, 61. Another work in which Maine's theories were criticized was Surendra Nath Sen, *An Essay on Hindu Jurisprudence* (Allahabad: Indian Press, 1911). While Maine portrayed Hindu law as inflexible and non-dynamic, unlike Roman and English law, Surendra Nath argued that this inflexibility was not "an unmixed evil" because it prevented the "adulteration" of the law, such as that witnessed in the case of Roman law after the Barbarian invasions. This inflexibility also ensured "uniformity, simplicity and certainty" (ibid., 7–8). Later in his book, Surendra Nath

There are several other places in the lectures where Sen sought, somewhat apologetically, to defend Hindu law relative to Western legal systems. For example, in his discussion of marital relationships, he defended the rules that prohibited widows from remarrying while allowing polygamy, noting that these rules "were due to social causes which I cannot here stop to discuss" and adding that, anyway, nowadays "monogamy is almost the rule and polygamy an exception."[120] His discussion of the Hindu law of slavery was opened by a remark on the existence of slavery in Roman law and a statement to the effect that, in ancient times, all legal systems recognized slavery.[121] When discussing the Hindu law of contractual obligations, Sen noted that, under Hindu law, there was no "distinct treatment of contracts in general," but he added that, while this might seem to be a shortcoming, the history of English law revealed this to be the case in England, too. Therefore, he reasoned, Hindu contract law was "as developed as most other systems of ancient law."[122]

Sen ended his lectures by stating again that Hindu law "would not compare unfavourably with even the most developed system of Ancient jurisprudence, the Roman," noting four "points of excellence" that characterized Hindu law: comprehensiveness, loftiness of ideal, logical consistency, and reasonableness.[123] Hindus should feel proud of their forefathers, he said, for their contribution to fields such as medicine, but also their contribution to jurisprudence. Like other Indian intellectuals who sought to show the glorious and progressive nature of Indian civilization, Sen, too, argued that India had a brilliant past.[124] This past, he said, included a system of jurisprudence that was as wise and old as that of the Romans. "The Sun," he concluded, "arose in the east and traveled

also discussed a large number of means by which the Brahmanical sages were able to repeal old laws, thus challenging the image of Hindu law as static (ibid., 38–41). In addition, the book also criticized the Austinian definition of law. Hindu law did not emanate from a sovereign human authority (the Hindu king being merely the enforcer of laws, not their creator), it was not necessarily a command (it included rules of conduct that Austin would not have considered law), and it was not related to the use of force (the sanctions being religious, not earthly) (ibid., 22–31). The identity of the author of this book is unclear; the British Library Catalog identifies the author as Surendra Nath Sen (1890–1962), who was a University of Calcutta historian. However, the title page of the book, published in Allahabad, states that the author is "a vakil, high court, nwp [North-Western Provinces]."

120 Sen, *General Principles*, 284. 121 Ibid., 293. 122 Ibid., 302–3.

123 Ibid., 374–77. 124 On this idea, see, generally Bayly, *Recovering Liberties*, 69.

towards the west, and it is the same light which illumines the whole world." He considered Kipling's words – "East is East and West is West and never the twain shall meet" – to be "supercilious," since "the same universal reason . . . permeates the universe, and its touch makes the whole world kin."[125] Here, it seems, Sen was echoing a central theme in Indian liberal and nationalist discourse: the idea that ancient Hindu civilization was on a par with, or even surpassed, that of Greece and Rome and that India had special, spiritual, universal lessons to teach the world.[126]

Turning to another Indian legal scholar whose work on Hindu jurisprudence is worthy of attention, Nares Chandra Sen Gupta was a Bengali legal scholar, writer, and political activist. He obtained his doctorate in law from the University of Calcutta in 1914 and was later a professor of law and Dean of the Faculty of Law of the University of Dacca, established in 1921. The curriculum at the University of Dacca emphasized both Islamic and Sanskrit studies and thus resonated with an interest in Hindu law.[127]

In 1914, Sen Gupta published a book based on his doctoral dissertation, *Sources of Law and Society in Ancient India*. The book relied not only on the existing English jurisprudential literature but also on leading works of Continental jurisprudence, such as Luigi Miraglia's *Comparative Legal Philosophy* and Nikolai M. Korkunov's *General Theory of Law*. It also showed an interest in "the sociological school of modern philosophical jurists."[128]

[125] Sen, *General Principles*, 376–8.

[126] See, generally, Bayly, *Recovering Liberties*, 156, 163. It is unclear how original some of Sen's arguments were, and to what extent he was merely repeating arguments made previously by others. For example, the rejection of Austinian positivism using the argument that Hindu law did not fit the Austinian model because its norms were not the commands of a political sovereign and were not accompanied by political sanctions was, as we saw, already present in earlier works, for example, in Rattigan's textbook. It was also present in works written by Indian lawyers. See Banerjee, *Hindu Law of Marriage*, 3; J. R. Ghorpure, *Hindu Law* (Bombay: Maruti Babaji, 1905), 1–2.

[127] For a brief biography, see Samaresh Devnath, "Sengupta, Naresh Chandra," in *Banglapedia: National Encyclopedia of Bangladesh* (Dhaka: Asiatic Society of Bangladesh, 2003), Vol. 9, 168. On the University of Dacca, see Ashby, *Universities*, 109–10, 134. On Sen Gupta's ongoing interest in the study of Hindu law, see N. C. Sengupta, "Hints on an Historical Study of Hindu Law," *Calcutta University Law College Magazine* 13 (1943): 7, 18.

[128] Nares Chandra Sen Gupta, *Sources of Law and Society in Ancient India* (Calcutta: Art Press, 1914), v–vii, 27.

In the introduction to his book, Sen Gupta claimed that his work contained "some advance on the existing knowledge" on ancient Indian law and society – an advance that, he said, "may possibly have a bearing" not only on the study of Hindu legal history but also "on general questions of jurisprudence."[129] One of the original arguments (according to Sen Gupta) made in the book was the argument that village communities were not, in fact, the most basic units of ancient Indian society but that each village was an aggregate of several small trans-village "ante-political" societies. A second significant point was the idea that, in Aryan societies, the law was based on agreement, and that this was one of the traits that distinguished these societies from those of the Semites, "with their autocratic judges, prophets and kings."[130] Another argument was that kingship was not the most primitive form of political organization. Instead, it only emerged gradually. According to Sen Gupta, Maine argued that kings were present at the dawn of society and were responsible for the administration of justice and the creation of law (and this view was supported by examples from the Bible and Homer). Sen Gupta, however, contended that Maine had ignored the fact that this was not necessarily the case in other civilizations. In some Aryan societies, unlike Semitic or Mongolian ones, kings were not the primary source of law and order. Instead of kings deciding disputes between members of society, arbitration was used "before judicial authority was centralized in the King."[131] This idea was also manifested in Rome and among the Germanic tribes, and it survives in the more modern concept of trial by one's peers.[132] Thus, instead of the typical "Oriental despotism" image of India and its laws, Sen Gupta's book suggested that there was a "constitution of ancient Indian society."[133]

This was not the only place in his book where Sen Gupta attempted to revise Maine's narrative. Later, when discussing the idea of kings as sources of law, he repeated the argument, stating that "the King as legislator is not an idea congenial to the Aryan mind." Quoting Miraglia, he argued that Aryans, unlike "Egypt[ians], Babylon[ians] ... Mussalmans [*sic*] and the Tartar tribes," never embraced "that all controlling despotism which blots out man," and that, in ancient India,

[129] Ibid., i–ii. [130] Ibid., i, ii, 8–20, 44. [131] Ibid., 22–3, 78. [132] Ibid., 22–3.

[133] Ibid., 8. On democracy in ancient India and on the idea of an "ancient Indian constitution" (two ideas which will be discussed in more detail in Chapter 5), see also Bayly, *Recovering Liberties*, 164, 267.

the idea that the king had legislative powers did not take root.[134] Maine was not the only English jurist whose work was attacked. Sen Gupta also criticized James Henry Nelson's argument in his book *A Prospectus of the Scientific Study of the Hindu Law* that Hindu law, per se, never existed, rejecting it using arguments made by earlier scholars.[135]

In 1925, by the time Sen Gupta was Dean of the Faculty of Law of Dacca University, he had published a second book, *The Evolution of Law*.[136] This book summarized the arguments of the English Historical Jurisprudence School and was mainly based on works by Maine and the British legal historian Paul Vinogradoff. However, as in his first book, here too Sen Gupta was not content with merely repeating English works, sometimes opting to criticize them. In the preface, he stated that "a long study of the history of ancient Indian law has revealed to me hitherto unrecognized truths" and that, therefore, "I have found myself unable to agree to many of the accepted notions on the history and character of [the] ancient legal institutions of India." The book, he continued, was meant to serve students, introducing them to "[h]istorico-comparative jurisprudence," but it was impossible to write it without "a certain measure of theorising ... and thinking on my own account, and diverging from favorite theories of the day."[137]

Sen Gupta's critique of Maine was sometimes based on earlier European theorists. One can see this, for example, in his remarks on the difference between Western and Oriental codes. Maine argued that Oriental codes (unlike Western ones) were problematic because of their association with religion. Sen Gupta contended that Maine was mistaken because *all* ancient laws were religious: "before the lawyer's law there always existed the law of the priest."[138] However, in arguing for the religious nature of ancient law, Sen Gupta based his argument on the work of the nineteenth-century French historian Fustel de Coulanges, not on Indian law.[139] Another example of this type of critique can be found in Sen Gupta's discussion of Maine's argument

[134] Sen Gupta, *Sources of Law and Society*, 80–1. The quote is taken from Luigi Miraglia, *Comparative Legal Philosophy: Applied to Legal Institutions*, trans. John Lisle (New York: Macmillan, 1921), 120.

[135] Sen Gupta, *Sources of Law and Society*, 5–6, 28–32, 50–51, 99–100.

[136] Nares Chandra Sen Gupta, *The Evolution of Law* (Calcutta: Calcutta University Press, 1925).

[137] Ibid., v–vi. [138] Ibid., 21. [139] Ibid., 18–19.

that adjudication preceded law. Sen Gupta rejected this argument based on the work of the German jurist B. W. Leist.[140]

However, in Sen Gupta's discussion of another stage in Maine's model of the evolution of law – the transition from the individual judgment of a king (*themis*) to rules found in customs administered by an aristocracy – he relied on Indian law to critique Maine. He asserted:

> Maine's theories about [the] transition ... to custom must also be corrected by the same qualification that it is not a universal law of evolution. Whatever may be said about the course of evolution in Greece or Rome it is perfectly clear that in India and, possibly, amongst the original Indo-Germanic race, there never was that absolute autocratic stage which would make the stage of Themis ... possible.[141]

Instead of kings, Sen Gupta claimed, ancient societies were governed by "a group of men ... devoted ... to the knowledge of superhuman things," such as the Magi of Persia, the Brahmins of India, or the Druids of Celtic lands.[142]

Another instance of the use of Indian examples to critique Western theories can be found in the chapter on "Family and Kindred." Here, Sen Gupta discussed debates about the nature of "the primitive family" (that is, whether ancient families were patriarchal or matriarchal). He mentioned both those thinkers who argued that the matriarchal family was the earlier type (McLennan, Morgan, Fustel de Coulanges, Kohler) and those (Maine) who argued that the earlier type was patriarchal. He declared the debate to be misconceived because "the form of social organisation everywhere is to some extent moulded by social and economic environments. The relative number of the two sexes, the physical and social surroundings of the community, the pressure of external enemies and such other circumstances make a particular form of social organisation the most suitable for the community."[143]

Thus, he explained, a paucity of females led to the adoption of polyandry. As an example to prove this point, he mentioned the Nambudiri Brahmins of Malabar and their matrilineal *Sambandham* system of marriage.[144] Similarly, when discussing forms of marriage, Sen Gupta argued that it was impossible to place various models of

[140] Ibid., 19–20. [141] Ibid., 22.
[142] Ibid., 22. See also ibid., 95–6 (an additional place in the book in which Maine was criticized).
[143] Ibid., 36. [144] Ibid., 34–7.

matrimony along a single linear line of evolution because there were "societies which have lapsed from a more advanced form of marriage to a more primitive one" due to changed environmental conditions.[145] As an example, he mentioned both Hindu marriage rules and those of the Romans. In India, he said, the most ancient form of marriage was based on consent between the bridegroom and the father of the bride, leading to a marriage based on "spiritual union" between husband and wife. Only in a later epoch did additional types of marriage start to form, based on the force of arms, purchase, theft or fraud, or the bride's consent. A similar process, he argued, occurred in Rome, the earliest form being *confarreatio* (a Roman form of marriage ceremony limited to patricians), which was later replaced by purchase and also by marriage upon consent of the bride alone. In both cases, the Indian and the Roman, the shift was due to environmental changes.[146] Sen Gupta also warned against assuming a "single universal course of evolution" when discussing the history of legal remedies and the administration of justice.[147]

Turning to other types of publications, Indian legal periodicals also published theoretical articles on Hindu law.[148] Here, I will briefly discuss two examples from the 1940s. The first was written by A. S. Panchapakesa Ayyar, an Indian jurist who studied law at Oxford and later served as a Justice of the Madras High Court.[149] Ayyar was a prolific writer, and his collected works include religious texts, plays, and novels. Many of these works deal with nationalist themes, including a 1941 article he wrote for the *Madras Law Journal* entitled "The Contribution of Hindu Law to World Jurisprudence."[150]

[145] Ibid., 55.

[146] Ibid., 56. It is not clear that he was depicting the development of Roman law correctly. See Blewett Lee, "A Sketch of Woman's Rights in Ancient Rome," *Northwestern Law Review* 2 (1894): 67, 69.

[147] Sen Gupta, *The Evolution of Law*, 68.

[148] See, e.g., Sastri, "Hindu Jurisprudence"; Nagendra Nath Mukerjee, "Indo-Aryan Penal Jurisprudence," *Calcutta Law Journal* 14 (1911): 29n; Atul Chandra Gupta, "The Spirit of Hindu Law," *Calcutta Law Journal* 42 (1925): 43n.

[149] Mohamed Elias, "A. S. Panchapakesa Ayyar," in *Encyclopedia of Post-Colonial Literatures in English*, eds. Eugene Benson and L. W. Conolly, 2nd ed. (London: Routledge, 2005), 1:91–2.

[150] A. S. Panchapakesa Ayyar, "The Contribution of Hindu Law to World Jurisprudence," Reprint from the *Madras Law Journal*, Golden Jubilee Number, 1941 [a copy of the reprint of this article can be found in the British Library].

Ayyar began his article with the argument that the Hindu contribution to jurisprudence had been obscured by the fact that "Hindu legal theories" have been "attack[ed]" and changed over time by "foreign ideas." Modern Hindu law, he continued, was not really Hindu law but an Anglo–Muslim creation because "centuries of Muslim and British rule" had "radically" altered Hindu law. Specifically, said Ayyar, these radical changes in Hindu law resulted from the fact that it had been applied by non-Hindu judges, "unacquainted with the basic Hindu ideals."[151]

The main argument of his article was that, just as the Hindus had made significant contributions to global science and culture (for example, the notion of "zero" in mathematics), they had also contributed to jurisprudence.[152] He then went on to list some of these contributions. Ayyar argued that they were to be found both in the realm of unique answers to questions such as "What is law?" and also in specific norms and institutions of public law (constitutional law, criminal law, or evidence law, as well as international law) and private law (property, tort, contract, and family law). For example, according to Ayyar, unlike Western legal systems, whose purpose was merely to ensure order, peace, and prosperity, the Hindus believed that the ultimate aim of the law was to realize righteousness and ensure the welfare of the universe and "every living thing." This meant, for example, that the Hindu kings were subject to the law just like their subjects and were seen as servants of the people, not *above* the law like English kings.[153]

A particular characteristic of Hindu law, according to Ayyar, was that law changed according to the times but also according to status: "[E]ach caste, asrama [stage in life], family, guild, and tract" had its own customs. This recognition of customary law, he argued, "saved India from stark oppression and drab uniformity, and enabled the roses, jasmines, champaks, lotuses and sunflowers to grow and develop in their own ways, with their peculiar colourings and perfumes."[154] Ayyar also claimed that Hindu law was one of the earliest legal systems to create both public and private international law.[155]

Some seemingly "primitive" characteristics of Hindu law, such as the idea of collective rather than individual responsibility for crimes,

[151] Ibid., 1. [152] Ibid., 1. [153] Ibid., 2–3, 5–6. [154] Ibid., 3. [155] Ibid., 8.

were described by Ayyar as desirable. He contended that they were "social and humane" in the sense of leading to a diminution in crime, unlike modern legal systems in which individual responsibility led to apathy regarding crimes committed by others. Another related argument was that Hindu law did not merely use sanctions to prevent crime but also used rewards for good conduct.[156] The article ended with the argument that "the unique beauty" of Hindu law was that it was developed by "sages, kings and caste heads, each group with unique gifts and capacities," rather than by a parliament, which Ayyar characterized as "an assembly elected on a haphazard system, and giving no sure guarantee of either wisdom or deliberation or even of public" well-being.[157]

A similar nationalist spirit inspired an article by Thakur Prasad Dubey, a provincial civil service judge in the United Provinces. In 1944, Dubey published a piece on "the beauties and comparative greatness" of Hindu law. In it, he argued that just as Roman law had influenced the laws of the West, Hindu law had influenced the laws of the East – those of China and Japan, for instance. In fact, he contended, Hindu law had also influenced the West (the Greeks, he claimed, borrowed their law of hypothecation from the Hindus).[158] The definitions provided by Hindu jurists for the basic abstract terms of jurisprudence (ownership, right, possession), said Dubey, were markedly superior to those offered by modern jurists such as Austin or Holland. The superiority of Hindu law, he continued, was also evident from the fact that the beneficiaries of its rules were "not only the human race" since Hindu law "aims at the protection and perpetuation of the whole sentient universe," including birds and beasts. The discussions of some specific topics in the article (gift, adverse possession, and the duties of judges) were all meant to prove the superiority of Hindu law.[159]

The article concluded by noting the "thrill of pleasure to find that our forefathers had a brilliant record in the domain of law" before the "pioneer nations of the West," such as Rome and Egypt, were even formed. While these Western civilizations were now dead, noted Dubey,

[156] Ibid., 8–10. [157] Ibid., 16.

[158] Thakur Prasad Dubey, "Hindu Jurisprudence: Its Beauties and Comparative Greatness," *Allahabad Law Journal* 42 (1944): 11.

[159] Ibid., 13.

"ours that started long before their birth yet exists." The West, he claimed, once argued that Indian culture was "absurd ... puerile ... uninspired ... grotesque ... [and] barbarous," only to ultimately discover that its own judgment had been erroneous. It was, therefore, a great irony, concluded Dubey, that some Indians, because of their general and legal education, still accepted this obsolete view of Hindu law, which, as a result, they had come to despise.[160]

Some Indian jurists, one can conclude, did not view Hindu law only as a source of examples to critique some of the specific details of English jurisprudential theories. Hindu law was also studied in order to create a sense of pride in Indian culture and to justify the claim that it was, in fact, superior to Western culture. Indeed, while some of the earlier writers of the 1910s and 1920s seem to have accepted the shrinkage of the scope of "living" Hindu law to the realm of personal law, arguing that the study of traditional Hindu law was justified only for the comparative jurisprudential insights it could yield, the 1940s authors I examined were implicitly critical of the fact that most of Hindu law was no longer applicable to contemporary India.[161] More explicitly, they extolled the "excellence" of Hindu law in areas such as criminal, evidence, and constitutional law.

### *Theoretical Works on Islamic Law*

Like other non-Western societies, Muslim societies in North Africa, the Middle East, and South Asia faced a flood of Western technologies,

[160] Ibid., 16–17. For similar sentiments, see S. Varadachariar, *The Hindu Judicial System* (Lucknow: Lucknow University, 1946), v.

[161] For the earlier approach, see Sen, *General Principles*, 5 (only parts of Hindu law were now applicable in the courts of British India because, "owing to altered conditions of the Hindu community, a considerable portion of [Hindu law] does not at all attract the attention of a practicing lawyer," and it had therefore "ceased ... to be living law"); Sen, *An Essay*, 117 ("the subject of Hindu Jurisprudence ... has hitherto been a virgin field ... [and] failed to attract more capable workers, presumably because the bulk of the Shastric laws ... [are] no longer the laws in force in British India, [and therefore] could not be expected to rouse a deep practical interest"). But see Sen Gupta, *Sources of Law and Society*, 6 (mentioning Nelson's argument that Hindu law never existed, and arguing that the similarity between "non-jural" customs of contemporary Hindu India and ancient Hindu law proved that it had existed, and still existed, and was not "affected by the political changes of history ... in spite of all aberrations and all subsequent influences").

scientific knowledge, and political ideologies in the nineteenth and twentieth centuries. Islamic law scholars, intellectuals, and politicians sought to reform Islamic law in order to deal with this influx.[162] Westernized lawyers interested in Islamic law also sought to use Western jurisprudential ideas to study and describe Islamic law. In Chapter 7, I will describe this phenomenon in Egypt. Here, I will analyze works on Islamic law written by lawyers in India.[163]

Islamic law was a significant component of the legal system of British India. This legal system – or, more accurately, Islamic personal law – as applied by the British (Anglo–Muhammadan law) governed the family life of the Muslims of India.[164] However, if we focus on the University of Calcutta, the intellectual epicenter of colonial India, it appears that there was less interest in the theoretical study of Islamic law than in the study of Hindu law there. Perhaps this was partly because there were relatively few Muslim law teachers and law students at the University. For example, in 1917, there was no Muslim among the staff members teaching law at the University: out of the seventy-eight lecturers teaching law at the College of Law and other

[162] See, e.g., Faisal Devji, "Apologetic Modernity," *Modern Intellectual History* 4 (2007): 61; Leor Halevi, *Modern Things on Trial: Islam's Global and Material Reformation in the Age of Rida, 1865–1935* (New York: Columbia University Press, 2019); Adeel Hussain, *Law and Muslim Political Thought in Late Colonial North India* (Oxford: Oxford University Press, 2022).

[163] Another major legal system in Colonial South Asia was Buddhist law. In Colonial Burma, the British created a body of Anglo–Buddhist personal law. In 1894, the Burmese author mentioned in n. 70 above, Chan-Toon, published a book summarizing the "principles" of this law. This was not a theoretical work, but one whose main audience was practitioners. See Chan-Toon, *Principles of Buddhist Law*. A similar work was Sisir Chandra Lahiri, *Principles of Modern Burmese Buddhist Law* (n.p.: Graduate Friends & Co., 1925). There were also historical works published in British India that dealt with the history of Buddhist law, written from a historical or a philological perspective, rather than attempting to critically engage with nineteenth- and early twentieth-century Western jurisprudence. See Durga N. Bhagvat, *Early Buddhist Jurisprudence* (Poona: Oriental Book Agency, 1939). On Buddhist law in colonial Burma, see also Andrew Huxley, "Positivists and Buddhists: The Rise and Fall of Anglo-Burmese Ecclesiastical Law," *Law and Social Inquiry* 26 (2001): 113; Sharafi, *Law and Identity*, 131–2.

[164] See, e.g., Iza R. Hussin, *The Politics of Islamic Law: Local Elites, Colonial Authority, and the Making of the Muslim State* (Chicago: University of Chicago Press, 2016); Julia Stephens, *Governing Islam: Law, Empire, and Secularism in South Asia* (Cambridge: Cambridge University Press, 2018). On the terminological problems of designating this system, see Stephens, *Governing Islam*, 8n19; Guenther, "Syed Mahmood," 11–13.

colleges, seventy-six were Hindus, two were European, and none was Muslim. In addition, while the Sanskrit College at Calcutta was affiliated with the University, the Calcutta Madrasah was not (although Arabic, Persian, and Islamic histories were taught, on a small scale, at the University, and it seems that there was some desire to turn it into a leading center of Islamic studies). Another indication of the same phenomenon is the fact that, in 1931, fewer than 11 percent (56 out of the 509) of graduates from the University of Calcutta College of Law were Muslims, while Muslims accounted for more than half of the population of undivided Bengal.[165]

Several comprehensive books on Anglo–Muhammadan law were published in India in the late nineteenth and early twentieth centuries.[166] These works relied on earlier translations and compilations on the topic, such as the *Hedaya*, a medieval commentary on Islamic law (first translated into English by Charles Hamilton in 1791), or William Macnaghten's 1825 compilation *Principles and Precedents of*

[165] Calcutta University Commission 1917–1919, *Report*, 1:164, 2:108–39; *University of Calcutta Convocation Addresses*, Vol. 6: *1924–34* (Calcutta: University of Calcutta Press, 1938), 240, 263; *Census of India, 1911*, Vol. 5, part II, *Bengal: Tables* (Calcutta: Bengal Secretariat Book Depot, 1913), 23–5. It is important to note that, in some areas of India, Muslim lawyers outnumbered Hindu ones. See Misra, *Indian Middle Classes*, 327–32 (noting that there were relatively few Muslim lawyers in Bengal, but that Muslim lawyers dominated the upper echelons of the bars of the United Provinces and Bihar).

[166] Michael Anderson mentioned nine such books written in the late nineteenth and early twentieth centuries. See Michael R. Anderson, "Islamic Law and the Colonial Encounter in British India," in *Institutions and Ideologies: A SOAS South Asian Reader*, eds. David Arnold and Peter Robb (London: Routledge, 1993), 165, 175–6. A more comprehensive list was recently compiled by Sohaira Siddiqui: see Sohaira Z. M. Siddiqui, *Islamic Law on Trial: Contesting Colonial Power in British India* (Oakland, CA: University of California Press, 2025), 161–2. See also Guenther, "Syed Mahmood," 28–30, 172–3 (another general discussion of works on Anglo–Muhammadan law in the late nineteenth and early twentieth centuries); Gregory C. Kozlowski, *Muslim Endowments and Society in British India* (Cambridge: Cambridge University Press, 1985), 130–1 (on the influence of English legal classification structures on texts on Islamic law published in India); John Strawson, "Revisiting Islamic Law: Marginal Notes from Colonial History," *Griffith Law Review* 12 (2003): 362, 369–70; John Strawson, "Islamic Law and English Texts," *Law and Critique* 6 (1995): 21; Scott Alan Kugle, "Framed, Blamed and Renamed: The Recasting of Islamic Jurisprudence in Colonial South Asia," *Modern Asian Studies* 35 (2001): 257; Elisa Giunchi, "The Reinvention of Sharia Under the British Raj: In Search of Authenticity and Certainty," *Journal of Asian Studies* 69 (2010): 1119.

*Moohummudan Law*.[167] Even when their titles proclaimed that they dealt with the more general aspects of Islamic law, these works were, in fact, surveys of contemporary law (and case law) on topics of personal law. Thus, they were primarily relevant to practicing lawyers rather than to legal scholars interested in the jurisprudential notions, or the legal history, of Islamic law.[168]

For example, Ameer Ali's *Student's Handbook of Mahommedan Law* (first published in 1891) contained only brief discussions of specific topics related to personal law, such as succession, marriage, dower, divorce, and gifts.[169] Personal law was also the topic of two other, more comprehensive and influential, books that Ameer Ali published in the 1880s.[170] His approach to Islamic law was more sophisticated than that of the English writers. He was more familiar with the sources of Islamic law and with the nineteenth-century European philological and ethnographic literature on this legal system. In addition, he often sought to place the rules that he was describing within their historical context (in order to show their relatively progressive nature).[171] However, unlike the works on Hindu law discussed in the previous subsection, the main goal of

167 *The Hedaya, or Guide: A Commentary on the Mussulman Laws*, trans. Charles Hamilton (London: T. Bensley, 1791); William Hay Macnaghten, *Principles and Precedents of Moohummudan Law* . . . (Calcutta: Mission Press, 1824). See, generally, Kugle, "Framed"; Strawson, "Revisiting Islamic Law," 375–6; Sohaira Siddiqui, "Navigating Colonial Power: Challenging Precedents and the Limitation of Local Elites," *Islamic Law and Society* 26 (2019): 272, 274–9.

168 In this subsection, I discuss books on Islamic law and jurisprudence. The interaction between English legal and jurisprudential ideas and Islamic law was not confined to such works. There were other, less direct, arenas of interaction, for example, in the decisions of Muslim judges in British India, such as Syed Mahmood. In addition, such interaction could be also found in other arenas, for example, in political writing. See Guenther, "Syed Mahmood," 54–5, 172–99. See also Siddiqui, "Navigating Colonial Power"; Siddiqui, *Islamic Law on Trial*.

169 See Ameer Ali, *Student's Handbook of Mahommedan Law*, 4th ed. (Calcutta: Thacker, Spink and Co., 1903).

170 Ameer Ali, *The Personal Law of the Mahommedans* (London: W. H. Allen, 1880); Ameer Ali, *The Law Relating to Gifts, Trusts and Testamentary Dispositions Among the Mahommedans* (Calcutta: Thacker, Spink and Co., 1885).

171 See Chatterjee, "Law, Culture and History," 45, 49–54. See also Cheema, "Tagore Law Lecturer's," 5–6. On Ali's knowledge of Arabic and of Islamic law, see Chatterjee, "Law, Culture and History," 48–9; *Muslims in India: A Biographical Dictionary*, ed. Naresh Kumar Jain (New Delhi: Manohar, 1979), Vol. 1, 85; *Memoirs and Other Writings of Syed Ameer Ali*, ed. Syed Razi Wasti (Lahore: People's Publishing House, 1968), 19.

Ameer Ali's books was to provide a more accurate picture of the specific fields of Islamic law that he dealt with, not to offer a general and theoretical overview of Islamic law as a way to contribute to the literature on general jurisprudence.

Other works published in the early twentieth century showed similar tendencies. In 1905, the Parsi lawyer, judge, and law professor Dinshah Fardunji Mulla published a book entitled *Principles of Mahomedan Law*. This book was "mainly designed for the use of students, as a guide to their study of Mahomedan law" and contained simple propositions on Islamic personal law.[172] It began with a few introductory pages describing Islamic legal history and the sources of Islamic law but then swiftly moved to an overview of the main topics of Anglo–Muhammadan personal law (such as succession, marriage, and divorce).[173]

Similarly, Faiz Badruddin Tyabji's *Principles of Muhammadan Law* sought to "state, in the form of a code, the principles of Muhammadan law, relating to subjects on which it is enforced in India."[174] Accordingly, the book included a thirty-four-page descriptive historical outline of the sources and schools of Islamic law, followed by approximately 1,000 pages devoted to a black-letter survey of Anglo–Muhammadan law dealing, again, with topics such as the scope of application of Islamic law in India, marriage, dower, divorce, and inheritance.[175]

[172] Dinshah Fardunji Mulla, *Principles of Mahomedan Law* (Bombay: Thacker and Co., 1905), iii.

[173] Ibid. For a critical assessment of Mulla's approach to Islamic law, see Shahbaz Ahmad Cheema, "Mulla's Principles of Mahomedan Law in Pakistani Courts: Undoing/Unraveling the Colonial Enterprise?" *Lahore University of Management Sciences Law Journal* 4 (2017): 56, 61–7. See also Shahbaz Ahmad Cheema and Samee Ozair Khan, "Genealogical Analysis of Islamic Law Books Relied on in the Courts of Pakistan," *Al-Adwa* 28(40) (2013): 23, 29–31. Mulla was a Parsi and, therefore, a religious "outsider" to Islamic law. A detailed discussion of his life can be found in Sharafi, *Law and Identity*, 113–15. On the role of native "outsiders" as mediators between local legal systems and the British, see Sharafi, "A New History of Colonial Lawyering," 1072–9.

[174] Faiz Badruddin Tyabji, *Principles of Muhammadan Law: An Essay at a Complete Statement of the Personal Law Applicable to Muslims in British India*, 2nd ed. (Calcutta: Butterworth, 1919), i.

[175] Ibid. Tyabji, the son of the first Muslim president of the Indian National Congress, studied at a modern Muslim school in Bombay, the Anjuman-I-Islam School

However, there was one book comparable to the Hindu jurisprudence works discussed in the previous subsection. This was *The Principles of Muhammadan Jurisprudence*, published in 1911 by Abdur Rahim, a Madras judge, based on his 1907 Tagore Lectures.[176] Books on Islamic law published before Abdur Rahim's book were focused on Muslim personal laws, and he regarded their treatment of jurisprudential topics as "introductory or insufficient."[177] This was also true of later works published in India.[178] The audience for Abdur Rahim's theoretical book on Islamic law comprised students and scholars rather than legal practitioners. His goal was to discuss "the general legal ideas and relations which form the proper province of jurisprudence" and to present Islamic law "as a scientific system instead of treating it, as is the habit ... of many lawyers in India, as

(founded by his father), and he turned to its Principal to translate the Arabic texts used in his book. See ibid., v–vi.

176 Abdur Rahim, *The Principles of Muhammadan Jurisprudence: According to the Hanafi, Maliki, Shafi'i and Hanbali Schools* (London: Luzac, 1911). The first chapter of the book, providing a historical overview of the legal history of Islam, was published in three installments in the *Columbia Law Review*. See Abdur Rahim, "Historical Sketch of Mohammedan Jurisprudence," *Columbia Law Review* 7 (1907): 101, 186, 255. Similar articles were published in Vols. 3 and 5 of the *Calcutta Law Journal* in 1906 and 1907. It is interesting to note that, while C. H. Alexandrowicz did mention a couple of works on Hindu jurisprudence in his 1958 bibliography of Indian law, he failed to mention Abdur Rahim's book. The only work on Islamic jurisprudence that he mentioned was a book by Columbia University Professor Joseph Schacht. See Alexandrowicz, *Bibliography*, 4, 6. But see Roscoe Pound, "Book Review," *Harvard Law Review* 29 (1916): 348 (noting the contribution of Abdur Rahim's book to the "science of law"). Abdur Rahim read Arabic, but the extent of his formal training in Islamic law is unclear (he studied in the government high school in the city of Midnapore in Bengal). Biographical information on him can be found in Jain, ed., *Muslims in India*, Vol. 1, 32–3; *Eminent Mussalmans* (Madras: G. A. Natesan & Co., 1926), 465, 467–9. In her recent book, Sohaira Siddiqui also discusses Abdur Rahim's book (as well as two additional works dealing with more specific theoretical issues, Syed Karamat Husein, *A Treatise on Right and Duty, Their Evolution, Definition, Analysis, and Classification According to Jurisprudence, Being a Portion of the Muhammadan Law of Gifts* (Allahabad: Indian Press, 1899) and Hamid Ali, *Custom and Law in Anglo-Muslim Jurisprudence* (Calcutta: Thacker, Spink and Co., 1938)). See Siddiqui, *Islamic Law on Trial*, 170–5.

177 See Cheema, "Tagore Law Lecturer's," 7.

178 See C. G. Weeramantry, *Islamic Jurisprudence: An International Perspective* (New York: St. Martin's Press, 1988), xi (Mohammad Hidayatullah, the Chief Justice, and later Vice President, of India, notes that "Abdur Rahim's book *Muslim Jurisprudence* has been for a long time the only book [on the topic] suitable for scholars").

an arbitrary collection of rules and dicta based on no intelligible data."[179] Indeed, Abdur Rahim declared in his preface that such a study of Islamic law may be relevant to "those who are interested in the science of jurisprudence" generally because Islamic law was an example of a system where law and religion met – and, therefore, Muslim jurists were attempting to create a legal system in which law was "an integral part of religion."[180]

The desire to describe Islamic law in a way that would benefit students of jurisprudence was manifested in the structure of the book. Unlike previous works, Abdur Rahim's book was not structured around the conventional divisions of Anglo–Muhammadan personal law. Instead, it partly echoed the structure of Salmond's book on jurisprudence.[181] It began with a chapter on the history of Islamic law, followed by chapters on the "sciences of law and classifications of law"; the sources of law; acts, rights, and obligations; legal capacity; ownership and possession; the acquisition of ownership; family law; torts; crimes; procedure and evidence; constitutional and administrative law; and international law. Family law, the major area that had practical importance for lawyers in colonial India, was relegated to a single chapter in the middle of the book.

In addition to structuring the book in a way that resonated with the structure of English jurisprudence textbooks of the period, Abdur Rahim also mentioned the resemblance between Islamic and Roman law, noting that such a resemblance might interest "students of comparative jurisprudence."[182] There were also many places in the book where he compared specific characteristics or rules of Islamic law to those of English law.[183]

Unlike the books on Hindu jurisprudence analyzed in the previous subsection, however, Abdur Rahim's book neither explicitly engaged with, nor criticized, Western jurisprudential theories, even when it could easily have done so. For example, when discussing the definition of law and the role of sanctions in Islamic law, Abdur Rahim noted that the term "law" was "not limited in the Muhammadan system to mandatory commands, far less to commands enforceable by the courts." Instead, it

179 Abdur Rahim, *Principles*, vi. 180 Ibid., vi–vii.
181 See Cheema, "Tagore Law Lecturer's," 8. 182 Abdur Rahim, *Principles*, 23.
183 Ibid., 35, 40, 55, 65, 97, 266, 271–2, 282, 305–7, 309, 382.

encompassed "all expressions of the lawgiver's will and wisdom, whether laying down what a man must do or must not do, what he may do, and what he ought to do or ought not to do, or merely making a declaration."[184] He then gave an example: the commandment "do not tell a lie, but tell the truth" was viewed in Islam as a law, he observed, even though there was no penalty for lying. In addition, sanctions in Islamic law were defined more broadly than in English law. Thus, obedience to the law was secured not just by the threat of penalty but also by the prospect of reward; and that penalty (and also the reward) could be delivered in the afterlife rather than this world.[185] This definition contradicted, of course, the Austinian view of what "law" and "sanction" were, but Abdur Rahim did not explicitly mention (or criticize) Austin's definition of the term "law" in his discussion.[186]

## Conclusion

Legal scholars in India produced works that were more than mere copies of English ones. First, the texts written in India were cosmopolitan; in addition to English legal theories, they were also receptive to state-of-the-art Continental ones. Second, Indian works were sometimes more critical of the ideas of major nineteenth-century English thinkers than English jurisprudential works. Finally, some of the texts produced in India were also unique because they were hybrid works that employed Western theories to describe non-Western legal systems: Hindu law and, to a lesser extent, Islamic law. The uniqueness of the Indian works derived from the need to teach non-English law students in an environment where religious law and customary law were important sources of legal norms. Some Indian works were also unique because of the influence of Indian nationalist ideology. Nationalism led some writers to espouse a broad range of jurisprudential theories, including non-English ones, to criticize Western jurisprudential notions (especially ones that seemed to place non-Western law on a lower evolutionary rung), and to create works that celebrated non-Western legal systems. Sometimes, Indian writers

[184] Ibid., 57. [185] Ibid., 57–9.

[186] The relative conservatism of the works on jurisprudence and Islamic law can be contrasted with the creative and critical engagement of Muslim scholars with Western liberal economic theory. See Stephens, *Governing Islam*, 155–67.

even offered alternative visions of the nature of law and its purpose, such as the argument made in both Ayyar's and Dubey's articles, according to which Hindu law sought to protect "every living thing" or "the whole sentient universe" and not just human beings, as was the case with Western law.

The works examined in this chapter were not influential in the sense of leaving a discernible long-term impact on scholars in either India or the West. Nevertheless, they are interesting partly because the characteristics of the jurisprudential literature that was explored in this chapter were also present in other places in the British Empire. The next chapter explores such works created in British-ruled Palestine.

2

# Legal Education and Legal Theory in Mandatory Palestine

Frederic Maurice Goadby studied law at the University of Oxford, graduating in 1901. Having worked for a few years in the City of London, in 1904 he became a lecturer at the Law Department of the University of Leeds. He then moved to Egypt, where he taught at the Khedivial Law School in Cairo. After the First World War, Goadby relocated to Palestine, serving as the Director of the newly established British law school there until 1933, when he retired and returned to England.[1]

In 1910, Goadby published a book entitled *Introduction to the Study of Law: A Handbook for the Use of Egyptian Law Students*. A second edition was published in 1914, and a third edition, revised for

[1] "University Intelligence. Oxford," *The Globe*, November 14, 1901; "University Intelligence," *The Times*, September 26, 1904; The University of Leeds, *First Report 1903–4* (Leeds: McCorquodale, 1905), 35; *Les sources du droit positif: Fascicule 1, Orient (Égypte, Palestine, Chine, Japon)*, ed. Elemér Balogh (Berlin: Hermann Sack, 1929); "Mesibah li-khvod Menahel Shi'urey ha-Mishpat," *Davar*, May 24, 1933; Dr. Norman Bentwich, "[Obituary] Dr. F. M. Goadby," *The Times*, August 18, 1956. On Goadby and his works, see also Assaf Likhovski, "Colonialism, Nationalism and Legal Education: The Case of Mandatory Palestine," in *The History of Law in a Multicultural Society: Israel 1917–1967*, eds. Ron Harris et al. (Dartmouth: Ashgate, 2002), 75; John Strawson, "Orientalism and Legal Education in the Middle East: Reading Frederic Goadby's Introduction to the Study of Law," *Legal Studies* 21 (2001): 663; John W. Cairns, "Development of Comparative Law in Great Britain," in *The Oxford Handbook of Comparative Law*, eds. Mathias Reimann and Reinhard Zimmermann, 2nd ed. (Oxford: Oxford University Press, 2019), 111, 125–6.

the benefit of Goadby's students in Mandatory Palestine, was published in 1921.[2] Goadby defined his book as an "elementary treatise on jurisprudence," but it was, in fact, more sophisticated. It was a jurisprudence textbook but also a work on comparative law, comprising extensive discussions of English and French law, legal institutions, and legal theories. The scope of Goadby's book was thus broader than that of contemporary jurisprudence textbooks published in England, and that of jurisprudence textbooks written in India, such as the book by Rattigan analyzed in Chapter 1. The legal systems of Egypt and Mandatory Palestine were greatly influenced by nineteenth-century French law. Therefore, Goadby had to devote more attention to detailed discussions of French legal theories than writers such as Rattigan, and, certainly, more attention than English textbook writers.[3]

Goadby's book was more learned and comprehensive than comparable works that appeared in England at the time; yet, just like Rattigan's Indian textbook, Goadby's book was not viewed this way by some Western scholars. The American legal scholar Roscoe Pound was enthusiastic, noting in his review of the first edition that the complexity of the legal system of Egypt, in which French, English, and Islamic law mingled, afforded sophisticated jurisprudential insights. Pound also praised the work because it summarized contemporary French legal theories that were inaccessible to many Anglo-American law professors.[4] However, the review of the first edition of Goadby's book in the leading English legal periodical of the time, the *Law Quarterly Review*, was lukewarm. The review of the second edition was simply mean, with the anonymous reviewer focusing on a few trivial typographical and substantive errors and

[2] Frederic M. Goadby, *Introduction to the Study of Law: A Handbook for the Use of Egyptian Law Students* (London: Butterworth, 1910); Frederic M. Goadby, *Introduction to the Study of Law: A Handbook for the Use of Law Students in Egypt and Palestine*, 3rd ed. (London: Butterworth, 1921).

[3] In the preface to the book, Goadby explained that English works that were used in Egypt, such as Holland's book, were written from a "dominantly English" point of view, which made them less useful for "students who know nothing and need to know nothing about English law." See Goadby, *Introduction to the Study of Law* (1910), v.

[4] R[oscoe] P[ound], "[Review] Introduction to the Study of Law: A Handbook for the Use of Egyptian Law Students by Frederic M. Goadby," *Harvard Law Review* 25 (1912): 397.

rhetorically wondering why the second edition was longer than the first one, containing lengthy discussions of the ideas of various legal scholars, given that the book was "intended for Egyptian students."[5]

This chapter explores works on jurisprudence written in Mandatory Palestine, such as Goadby's book. I show, just as I did in Chapter 1, that these works were interesting and original. Like Indian works, those written in Mandatory Palestine were cosmopolitan, revealing an awareness of both English and Continental legal theories. Their authors critiqued imported European approaches, and some also provided interesting insights into the jurisprudential lessons that local religious law could teach. I begin with a brief discussion of the history of institutions providing Western-style legal education in Palestine: the law school established by the British rulers of the country, whose first director was Goadby, and two Jewish academic institutions in which law was taught. I then discuss jurisprudence textbooks and other jurisprudential works written in the territory. First, I analyze Goadby's book and two Hebrew jurisprudence textbooks, and then I examine various works on the theoretical study of Jewish law. Finally, I explore legal works written by Arab scholars in Mandatory Palestine.

## Legal Education in Mandatory Palestine

The territory that became Mandatory Palestine was part of the Ottoman Empire until the end of the First World War when it was conquered by the British, who ruled it until 1948. It was, of course, much smaller in size and population than colonial India. When the British conquered Palestine, the territory had a population of less than 700,000. By 1948, when the British left, approximately 1.8 million inhabitants lived there.[6]

The relatively small size of the population was reflected in the limited number of lawyers practicing in late Ottoman Palestine.

5 M. S. A., "[Review] Introduction to the Study of the Law: A Handbook for the use of Egyptian Law Students," *Law Quarterly Review* 27 (1911): 121; "[Review] Introduction to the Study of the Law: A Handbook for the Use of Egyptian Law Students, 2nd edition, 1914," *Law Quarterly Review* 31 (1915): 123.

6 E. Mills, *Census of Palestine 1931* (Alexandria: Whitehead and Morris, 1933), Vol. 1, 44; United Nations Special Committee on Palestine, *Report to the General Assembly* (New York: n.p., 1947), Vol. 1, 11.

When the British took control of the territory, the number of lawyers "could be counted on the fingers of two hands."[7] During the late Ottoman period, there was no local law school in Palestine, and anyone seeking formal legal education had to travel to other parts of the Ottoman Empire to obtain it.[8] The Ottoman system of Western-style legal education dates back to the end of the nineteenth century. A law school was established in Istanbul in the 1870s, and law was also taught in other professional schools in Istanbul, such as the School for Civil Administration, the Imperial School, and the School for Shar'i Judges. By the beginning of the First World War, these schools had produced a few thousand graduates, several hundred of whom were Arabs, along with a few Jewish graduates. In 1908, the first Ottoman law school established in the Arab parts of the Empire opened in Baghdad. Another law school was established in Beirut in 1912.[9]

During the period of British rule, the number of lawyers in Palestine steadily grew. By the time the British withdrew from the country in 1948, there were more than a thousand lawyers.[10] Many of these were Jewish lawyers who received their legal education in Europe, the United Kingdom, or North America prior to moving to Palestine.[11]

7 Donald M. Reid, *Lawyers and Politics in the Arab World, 1880–1960* (Minneapolis, MN: Bibliotheca Islamica, 1981), 84; Norman de Mattos Bentwich and Helen Bentwich, *Mandate Memories, 1918–1948* (New York: Schocken, 1965), 212.

8 Israel State Archive [ISA], Record Group 3, LS 194/23 II, Note on the Jerusalem Law Classes; ISA, Record Group 3, CS 256, "Law Classes in Jerusalem," October 5, 1920; Gad Frumkin, *Derekh Shofet bi-Yerushalayim* (Tel Aviv: Dvir, 1954), 157.

9 Bernard Lewis, *The Emergence of Modern Turkey*, 2nd ed. (London: Oxford University Press, 1968), 181; Reid, *Lawyers*, 1–2, 76–9, 91–114, 303; Nathan Brun, *Shoftim u-Mishpetanim be-Erets Yisrael: Beyn Kushta li-Yerushalayim, 1900–1930* (Jerusalem: Magnes, 2008), 72–113; Mustafa Serdar Palabıyık, "International Law for Survival: Teaching International Law in the Late Ottoman Empire (1859–1922)," *Bulletin of SOAS* 78 (2015): 271, 275–6. On the Ottoman legal reforms of the nineteenth century, see, generally, Avi Rubin, *Ottoman Nizamiye Courts: Law and Modernity* (New York: Palgrave Macmillan, 2011). On Ottoman-educated intellectuals and bureaucrats in interwar Middle Eastern countries, see, generally, Michael Provence, *The Last Ottoman Generation and the Making of the Modern Middle East* (New York: Cambridge University Press, 2017).

10 Government of Palestine, *Report on Palestine Administration, July 1920–December 1921* (London: HMSO, 1922), 94–5; Reid, *Lawyers*, 313–14; Gabriel Strassman, *'Otey ha-Glimah: Toldot 'Arikhat ha-Din be-Erets Yisra'el* (Tel Aviv: Lishkat 'Orkhey ha-Din be-Yisra'el, 1984), 315–24.

11 Central Zionist Archives [CZA], A 255/706, Herbert Samuel, Speech at the Law Classes, 1924, 2; Bentwich and Bentwich, *Mandate Memories*, 212; Norman Bentwich, *My 77*

FIGURE 2.1 The Jerusalem Law Classes, 1920s. In the front row, Norman Bentwich, the Attorney General of Palestine, is seated fourth from the left, and Frederic Goadby, the director of the Law Classes, is seated fourth from the right. Reproduced by permission of Yad Izhak Ben-Zvi Photo Archives / Dr. Moshe Duchan Collection.

Others had studied law in neighboring Middle Eastern countries or were trained locally in Palestine.[12]

The leading institution providing legal education in Mandatory Palestine was a law school established by the British in 1920, the Jerusalem Law Classes (see Figure 2.1).

*Years: An Account of My Life and Times, 1883–1960* (Philadelphia, PA: Jewish Publication Society of America, 1961), 30–1.

[12] For a more detailed discussion of the history of legal education in Mandatory Palestine, see Likhovski, "Colonialism"; Assaf Likhovski, "Limudey ha-Mishpatim ba-Universitah ha-'Ivrit bi-Tkufat ha-Mandat" in *Toldot ha-Universitah ha-'Ivrit bi-Yerushalayim: Hitbasesut u-Tsmihah*, ed. Hagit Lavski (Jerusalem: Magnes Press, 2005), 543; Assaf Likhovski, *Law and Identity in Mandate Palestine* (Chapel Hill, NC: University of North Carolina Press, 2006), 106–26.

The five-year program of studies at the Law Classes was divided into two parts. The lectures in the first part were delivered in Hebrew or Arabic. Students who passed an examination at the end of this part were allowed to continue to the second part, in which lectures were delivered in English and dealt with more theoretical subjects such as jurisprudence and legal history.[13]

The Law Classes sought to provide legal education to court clerks and interpreters, as well as local lawyers and magistrates. It was, therefore, a vocational, not an academic, institution. Most lecturers were judges and other government officials. Civil servants who wanted to study there were often admitted even if they lacked the entry qualifications required of other students. The lectures took place in the evening so that these civil servants could attend.[14] The relatively practical nature of studies was also evident in the fact that most of the courses were merely descriptive surveys of various areas of law.[15]

The legal system of Mandatory Palestine contained a mixture of norms and institutions drawn from various legal systems: Islamic, Ottoman, French, and English law. In the realm of personal law, jurisdiction was given to religious courts that applied religious law. The Law Classes offered its students elective courses on Islamic and Jewish law. The elective course on Jewish law (called "rabbinical law" by the institution's administrators) focused on marriage and divorce, inheritance and guardianship, and the rules of procedure in rabbinical courts. The course included an introductory element on

13 "Beyt ha-Sefer le-Mishpatim," *Do'ar ha-Yom*, February 1, 1923; H. Kantrovitch, "The Jerusalem Law Classes," *Journal of the Society of Public Teachers of Law* 1937 (1937): 46, 46–7; ISA, Record Group 3, LS 194/23 II, Note on the Jerusalem Law Classes.

14 Regulations of the Jerusalem Law Classes, *Palestine Gazette*, May 25, 1933, sections 2, 5(4), 3, 8. In the 1920s, the British did contemplate the creation of a university in Palestine, to provide academic rather than vocational education. However, this idea never came to fruition. See Pinhas Ofer, "A Scheme for the Establishment of a British University in Jerusalem in the Late 1920s," *Middle Eastern Studies* 22 (1986): 274.

15 In addition to jurisprudence and legal history there were a few other courses that were more theoretical (political science, political economy, political history, and constitutional history). On the curriculum of the Law Classes, see Council of Legal Studies-Jerusalem, *Provisional Program of Studies and Examination Regulations, 1922* (n.p., Ha-Solel, n.d.); CZA, A 215/173, "Examinations, 1923"; Kantrovitch, "Jerusalem Law Classes"; Bentwich and Bentwich, *Mandate Memories*, 212–13.

the principles of Jewish law, but this part, too, focused on the fundamentals of family law.[16]

In addition to the Jerusalem Law Classes, two other non-governmental institutions in Mandatory Palestine taught law: the Hebrew University of Jerusalem and the Tel Aviv School of Law and Economics. The Hebrew University of Jerusalem was established in 1925.[17] It was a Zionist institution whose creation was inspired by the ideology of cultural Zionism, which sought to turn Palestine into a "spiritual center" of world Jewry. Initially, the university's founders planned a law school as part of the university. Accordingly, in 1919, the Zionist Department of Culture and Education asked Norman Bentwich, an Anglo-Zionist lawyer (who later served as the Attorney General of Palestine and was also the driving force behind the creation of the Jerusalem Law Classes), to prepare a detailed proposal for a faculty of law at the university.[18] Bentwich envisioned a faculty of law that would not merely be a vocational school for lawyers but an institution that would also train government officials and politicians. He proposed that students would study the principles of Jewish law as well as "English and American liberalism." Bentwich's proposed faculty of law would thus synthesize the study of ancient Jewish law with the study of modern Western law. It would offer courses on practical subjects but also courses on political economy, sociology, legal history, and the history of Roman law.[19]

Bentwich's proposal was not implemented.[20] A law faculty was only established at the Hebrew University in 1949, after Israeli independence. Nevertheless, two legal topics were taught at the Hebrew University during the British Mandate period: Jewish law and international law. The former was one of the topics taught at the Institute of Jewish Studies from its inception in 1925 by two professors, Simha Assaf and Asher

[16] Samuel Eisenstadt, "'Al Hora'at ha-Mishpat ha-'Ivri be-Veyt ha-Sefer shel Memshelet Erets Yisrael," *Ha-Mishpat* 2 (1927): 209. See also Paltiel Dikshtein, "Ha-Universitah veha-Mishpat," *Ha-'Olam*, August 18, 1931.

[17] For a detailed discussion, see Likhovski, "Limudey ha-Mishpatim," 543.

[18] Ha-Lishkah ha-Tsiyonit ha-Merkazit, "'Al Ve'idat ha-Universitah," *Ha-'Olam*, January 9, 1920, 12; Frumkin, *Derekh Shofet*, 231.

[19] CZA, A 255/826, Norman Bentwich, "Proposal for a Legal Faculty at the Jerusalem University."

[20] Likhovski, "Limudey ha-Mishpatim," 559.

Gulak.[21] In the 1940s, a small department devoted to Jewish law was also established. The goal of this department was to teach Jewish law "with special attention to the existing law in Palestine," that is, by focusing on Jewish family law.[22] With regard to international law at the Hebrew University, in the early 1930s, the institution received a donation from an English-Jewish industrialist, Sir Montague Burton, who was interested in international and industrial peace. Burton donated funds to establish chairs on these subjects at the Hebrew University and several English institutions. As Bentwich, who was appointed to this chair, was a lawyer by training, his courses had a legal orientation.[23] After the Second World War, Bentwich was joined by another international law scholar, Nathan Feinberg, and a Department of International Relations was established.[24] Another legal scholar hired by the Hebrew University in the 1940s was Guido (Gad) Tedeschi. Tedeschi was a young Italian-Jewish law professor appointed as a research fellow and later as a lecturer on jurisprudence at the Department of International Relations.[25]

The third institution providing legal education in Mandatory Palestine was the Tel Aviv Higher School for Law and Economics (see Figure 2.2). Like their counterparts at the Hebrew University, the founders of the Tel Aviv School were also influenced by the ideology of cultural Zionism. One expression of this influence, mirroring the practice at the Hebrew University, was the use of Hebrew as the language of instruction. Unlike the Hebrew University, however, the Tel Aviv School offered a complete course of legal studies.

The Tel Aviv School was one manifestation of the movement for the revival of Jewish law, which was active in the Jewish diaspora and Mandatory Palestine in the first decades of the twentieth century. This movement was inspired by the ideas of the nineteenth-century German Historical School, which saw law as an expression of the "national

[21] See CZA, A 212/37, Samuel Eisenstadt, "Ha-Universitah shel Tel Aviv: Beyt ha-Sefer le-Mishpat ve-le-Kalkalah," 4; David N. Myers, *Re-inventing the Jewish Past: European Jewish Intellectuals and the Zionist Return to History* (New York: Oxford University Press, 1995), 87–9.

[22] Hebrew University Archive, Jerusalem, Ha-Va'adah ha-Matmedet, Yeshivah Asirit, May 15, 1946.

[23] Bentwich, *My 77 Years*, 31, 98.

[24] Nathan Feinberg, *Pirkey Hayim ve-Zikhronot* (Jerusalem: Mabat, 1985), 139–42.

[25] Likhovski, "Limudey ha-Mishpatim," 554–7.

FIGURE 2.2 The Tel Nordau Primary School in Tel Aviv, where the classes of the Tel Aviv School of Law and Economics were held during the 1930s. Photograph courtesy of the Israel State Archive / Zoltan Kluger Photo Collection.

spirit" (*volksgeist*) of each nation and argued that the legal system of every nation should, therefore, be based on its own organic national legal traditions.[26] However, the legal system envisioned by the movement for the revival of Jewish law was not rooted in a fundamentalist application of all traditional halakhic norms.

[26] On this movement, see, generally Likhovski, *Law and Identity*; Ronen Shamir, *The Colonies of Law: Colonialism, Zionism and Law in Early Mandate Palestine* (Cambridge: Cambridge University Press, 2000); Amihai Radzyner, "Jewish Law in Palestine under Ottoman Rule and the Attitude toward Foreign Law," in *The Cambridge Companion to Judaism and Law*, ed. Christine Hayes (Cambridge: Cambridge University Press, 2017), 317; Nir Kedar, *Law and Identity in Israel: A Century of Debate* (Cambridge: Cambridge University Press, 2019). On pre-Zionist Jewish and non-Jewish scholarly interest in Jewish law, see, e.g., Shalom Albeck, "Ha-Mishpat ha-'Ivri u-Mada'ey ha-Yahadut," in *Heker ha-Torah shebe-'Alpeh be-Hamishim Shnot ha-Medinah*, ed. Zvi Arieh Steinfeld (Jerusalem: Orkhot, 2001/02), 15; Leora Batnitkzy, "From Politics to Law: Modern Jewish Thought and the Invention of Jewish Law," *Diné Israel* 26 (2008–10): 7. On some of the theoretical problems associated with the attempt to define the category "Jewish law," see, e.g., Rachel Rafael Neis, "The Seduction of Law: Rethinking Legal Studies in Jewish Studies," *Jewish Quarterly Review* 109 (2019): 119.

Scholars affiliated with the movement viewed norms concerned with topics such as dietary purity as irrelevant to their project. Instead, they focused primarily on those aspects of traditional Jewish law that addressed "secular" domains such as property and contract law.[27]

In 1917, Russian-Jewish law students, educated in Central European and Russian universities in the first decades of the twentieth century and inspired both by the ideas of the Historical School and also by cultural Zionism, established a scholarly society in Moscow for the study of Jewish Law (which they called *mishpat 'ivri*, literally "Hebrew Law").[28] In the early 1920s, growing restrictions on Zionist activities in the Soviet Union led many members of this Society to emigrate to Palestine, where the Jewish Law Society was re-established. In the 1920s and early 1930s, members of the Jewish Law Society were involved in several publishing ventures, including the publication of two legal journals, *Ha-Mishpat* and *Ha-Mishpat ha-'Ivri*. In addition, one of its members, Judah Junovitch, established a publishing house specializing in law and philosophy books. Members of the Society were also involved in the activities of an informal system of Zionist courts, which were active during the period of the Mandate, the Hebrew Courts of Arbitration (*mishpat ha-shalom ha-'ivri*). This system was staffed by lay judges who decided cases based on their own discretion, notions of justice and equity, and (sometimes) based on Jewish law.[29]

Members of the Jewish Law Society were also active in the realm of legal education. As early as 1918, they proposed the establishment of a Jewish law school in Palestine. They expected the Hebrew University to implement this proposal, and, when its leaders declined to do so, they harshly criticized them. During the 1920s and early 1930s, several proposals for creating a Jewish law school in Palestine were put

27 Assaf Likhovski, "The Invention of 'Hebrew Law' in Mandatory Palestine," *American Journal of Comparative Law* 46 (1998): 339, 348–50, 359–61; Likhovski, *Law and Identity*, 129–30.

28 "Hebrew law" is one of a group of terms (such as *halakhah*, the law of the Torah, rabbinical law, etc.) used to designate Jewish law. See, e.g., Likhovski, *Law and Identity*, 132–3. The Moscow Scholarly Society for the study of Jewish law had its roots in the Russian Jewish Historical and Ethnographic Society. See Jeffrey Veidlinger, *Jewish Public Culture in the Late Russian Empire* (Bloomington, IN: Indiana University Press, 2009), 229–60. See also Paltiel Dikshtein, "Ariyeh Karlin, ZL," *Ha-Praklit* 14 (1957): 380.

29 On this system, see, generally, Shamir, *Colonies of Law*; Likhovski, *Law and Identity*, 35–6, 130–2.

forward, none of which materialized. In the middle of the 1930s, however, conditions proved ripe as Jewish students and professors fleeing European anti-semitism flocked to Palestine. In 1934, a "World Conference of Jewish Law" was convened in Tel Aviv. Following the conference, four of the participants, three lawyers (Samuel Eisenstadt, Paltiel Dikshtein, and Max Laserson) and an economist (Benjamin Siew), resolved to establish a "Higher School of Law and Economics" in Tel Aviv. The resulting school, which accepted its first students in 1935, initially consisted of a department of law and a department of economics. Later, these were augmented by a business school, a political science department, and an accountancy institute.[30]

The Tel Aviv School was purposely designed to offer legal education that differed from that of the British-sponsored Jerusalem Law Classes. According to one of the founders of the Tel Aviv School, Dikshtein, the British officials who had established the Law Classes did not seek to train local lawyers who would see themselves as equal to the officials sent from the metropolis. Instead, he claimed, it would serve British goals if those taught at the Law Classes would see themselves, and would be seen by others, as inferior to British officials belonging to "the superior race, sent by the great British people to instill civilization in an underdeveloped and backward country." The Law Classes, argued Dikshtein, produced lawyers who had "narrow horizons" and viewed the existing political and legal framework of Mandatory Palestine as the optimal one, unable to imagine the "lofty ideals of proper [Jewish] national political revival."[31]

Legal education at the Tel Aviv School was characterized by its academic rather than vocational nature, by the influence of Continental rather than English law, and by the place given to Jewish law in the curriculum. About a third of its thirty-five lecturers previously held academic positions at various European universities, while the teaching staff at the Jerusalem Law Classes were mainly administrators or practicing lawyers.[32] The School's founders regarded the training of lawyers as a secondary aim. More important aims were providing the

[30] See Likhovski, "Colonialism," 82–3.

[31] Dikshtein, "Ha-Universitah veha-Mishpat," 633–4.

[32] Lecturers at the Tel Aviv School came from many European universities, having previously studied or taught law at London, Cambridge, Leeds, Bern, Rome, Modena, Florence, Brussels, Amsterdam, Paris, Heidelberg, Berlin, Leipzig, Vienna, Kaunas, Odessa, St. Petersburg, and New York. See CZA, A 212/2, Beyt

students "with a complete, university-level education in the social sciences, affairs of state, law, economics, and commerce," preparing future Jewish political and business leaders, and promoting the scientific research of law and the social sciences.[33] Because the training of lawyers was only a subsidiary aim, the curriculum was far more academically oriented than that of the Jerusalem Law Classes. At Tel Aviv, law students were required to take courses on the history of Jewish law, Roman law, comparative law, and one or two courses on philosophy. They were also required to take several social science courses, such as political economy, sociology, "colonial policy," "colonial criminology," and statistics. The legal courses they took were also more diverse. For example, the Tel Aviv School students took labor or administrative law courses, which were not offered at the Jerusalem Law Classes.[34]

Another characteristic of the Tel Aviv School was the impact of Continental law on its curriculum. Since most of its law lecturers were educated in the Continental legal tradition, Continental notions were more influential than in the Jerusalem Law Classes. For example, Roman law, the basis upon which all Continental legal systems are founded, was not taught in the Jerusalem Law Classes. At the Tel Aviv School, it was a compulsory subject.[35]

Finally, the Tel Aviv School was characterized by the relatively prominent role of Jewish law in the curriculum. One of the primary goals of the School was "to train jurists, lawyers, and judges who could fulfill the ideals of the [Jewish] nation in the field of legal revival, a revival that would be both Jewish and universal, absorbing the best

ha-Sefer ha-Gavohah le-Mishpat vele-Kalkalah, *Sefer ha-Shanah li-Shnat 1937/8*; CZA, A 212/2, Beyt ha-Sefer ha-Gavohah le-Mishpat vele-Kalkalah, *Sefer ha-Shanah li-Shnat 1947/8*, 35–40.

[33] CZA, A 212/32, *To the Friends of the Hebrew Science in the World* (1947); CZA, A 212/32, Paltiel Dikshtein, "'Al Beyt ha-Sefer ha-Gavohah le-Mishpat vele-Kalkalah be-Tel Aviv," 3.

[34] CZA, A 212/2, *Beyt ha-Sefer ha-Gavohah le-Mishpat ve-Kalkalah – Prospekt li-Shnat ha-Limudim 1937/8*; CZA, A 212/32, *To the Friends of the Hebrew Science in the World* (1947); CZA, A 212/32, Dikshtein, "'Al Beyt ha-Sefer ha-Gavohah le-Mishpat vele-Kalkalah be-Tel Aviv," 3.

[35] On the lack of a course on Roman law in the Law Classes, see also Dikshtein, "Ha-Universitah veha-Mishpat," 633. On the attitude of Jewish law scholars in Mandatory Palestine to Jewish law, see, generally, Assaf Likhovski, "The Eagle and the Dove: Jewish Law Scholars and Roman Law During the Interwar Period," in *Pensiero giuridico occidentale e giuristi romani: Eredità e genealogie*, eds. Pierre Bonin et al. (Turin: G. Giappichelli, 2019), 267.

spiritual achievements of the nations of the world, and imbued with the desires of justice and morality of Judaism."[36]

The School would thus offer a new type of legal education, one that would differ from both the Western education received by Jewish lawyers in Europe and the "colonial type legal education given by the Jerusalem law classes."[37] Consequently, the study of Jewish law permeated the curriculum of the Tel Aviv School, where students were obliged to take an extensive course on Jewish law and its history. One could also find sections dealing with Jewish law in courses devoted to other legal topics, such as criminal law, tort law, or international law.[38]

Given the Jewish nationalist agenda of the Tel Aviv School, it is unsurprising that it did not receive any support or recognition from the British authorities of Palestine, which feared that it "would be a center of radical anti-British sentiments." As a result, graduates of the Tel Aviv School could not take the Palestine Bar exams immediately after they had completed their studies. Instead, they had to obtain a permit to practice law in Palestine in a circuitous way. After graduating, they sought graduate law degrees abroad, in French or Italian universities.[39] These degrees enabled them to take the Palestine Bar exams for foreign-educated lawyers.[40]

36 Tel Aviv University Archive, Box 61.71, Beyt ha-Sefer ha-Gavohah le-Mishpat vele-Kalkalah, *Taktsir Yedi'ot li-Studentim li-Shnat 1945/6*, 3.

37 CZA, A 212/2, Beyt ha-Sefer ha-Gavohah le-Mishpat vele-Kalkalah, *Sefer ha-Shanah li-Shnat 1947/8*, 3; CZA, A 212/37, Samuel Eisenstadt, "Ha-Universitah shel Tel Aviv: Beyt ha-Sefer le-Mishpat ve-le-Kalkalah," 12.

38 Tel Aviv University Archive, Box 61.71, Beyt ha-Sefer ha-Gavohah le-Mishpat vele-Kalkalah, *Sidrey ha-Limudim ve-Tokhniyoteyhem 1944/45*, 7; Tel Aviv University Archive, Bar Shira Personal Archive, File 20, Hoda'ah 786, 2–4; Tel Aviv University Archive, Bar Shira Personal Archive, File 3, Hoda'ah 626, 12, 16; ibid., Hoda'ah 243, 6; Tel Aviv University Archive, Bar Shira Personal Archive, File 19, Beyt ha-Sefer ha-Gavohah le-Mishpat vele-Kalkalah, *Sefer ha-Shanah*, 1947/48, 19.

39 In 1944, the administrators of the School reached an agreement with French authorities that its graduates would be able to obtain a doctorate in law from the Beirut branch of the University of Lyon. Later, a similar arrangement was reached with the University of Florence. See CZA, A 212/37, Samuel Eisenstadt, *Ha-Universitah*, 12, 16–17, 72, 102; Yitzhak Orren, "Kenes Yovel ha-50 le-Veyt ha-Sefer le-Mishpat be-Tel Aviv: Divrey Ptihah," *'Iyuney Mishpat* 11 (1985/86): 5, 10, 14; Uri Cohen, "Ha-Mirdaf Ahar Legitimatsyah Akademit: Beyt ha-Sefer ha-Gavohah le-Mishpat vele-Kalkalah," *Mehkarey Mishpat* 25 (2009): 179, 198–9, 200–4.

40 Strassman, *'Otey ha-Glimah*, 74. Another factor that prevented British officials from recognizing the Tel Aviv School was their fears of Arab reactions. See CZA, A 212/37, Samuel Eisenstadt, *Ha-Universitah*, 102.

**British Jurisprudence in Palestine**

The leading jurisprudence textbook used in Mandatory Palestine was the third (expanded) edition of Frederic Goadby's book, first published in 1910 in Egypt when Goadby taught at the Khedivial Law School. Goadby stated in his preface to the first edition that he had written it because Egyptian students might find English textbooks, such as Holland's and Salmond's, "difficult."[41] We might recall that Rattigan's Indian textbook opened with a similar disclaimer, in which Rattigan renounced any intention of purporting to be an original writer and argued that the need for his book merely arose from the fact that Holland's book on jurisprudence, written for English students, was not simple enough for Indian students. However, like Rattigan's, Goadby's book was also far more than a mere summary of other works.

The book was a hybrid work, manifesting English and Continental legal influences. Its structure was semi-Continental (containing, following the Continental model, three consecutive chapters on persons, things, and acts). It featured many discussions and examples taken from non-English legal systems: Egyptian, Islamic, Roman, and French law. In addition, it used examples taken from the law of several modern non-Western systems: the Ottoman Empire, India, Siam, and Japan. Goadby's book also contained many references to nineteenth- and early twentieth-century Continental legal theorists, mostly French (for example, Capitant, Charmont, Esmein, Gény, Duguit, Planiol, and Saleilles) but also German (for example, Savigny and Jhering). The book even mentioned an Indian author (Syed Ameer Ali).[42] The ideas of Continental theorists appeared in the book side by side with discussions of English analytical and historical theories. This was true for more abstract issues, such as the role of precedent or of academic scholarship as sources of law in English and French law, but also for discussions of more technical problems, such as the criminal liability of corporations in the two legal systems.[43]

41 Goadby, *Introduction to the Study of Law* (1910), v.

42 See, e.g., ibid., xi–xii, 25, 51; Goadby, *Introduction to the Study of Law*, 3rd ed. (1921), 4, 182.

43 Goadby, *Introduction to the Study of Law* (1910), 24–5, 84–104, 112, 134, 142, 147, 150, 262.

TABLE 2.1 The use of different terms in Goadby's and Holland's books

| Terms | Number of mentions in Goadby's book | Number of mentions in Holland's book |
|---|---|---|
| England/English/Britain/British | 535 | 319 |
| France/French | 494 | 96 |
| Egypt/Egyptian | 253 | 0 |

The mixed, English–French orientation of the book is also evident from a quantitative analysis of Goadby's relative use of terms referring to England and France. Table 2.1 lists the number of occurrences of terms related to England, France, and Egypt in his book versus in the 12th edition of Holland's *Elements of Jurisprudence*, published at approximately the same time. We can observe that while, in Goadby's book, terms referring to England and France were used with roughly the same frequency, in Holland's book, the terms related to England were three times more prevalent.[44]

What was the role of Islamic law and modern Egyptian law in the book's first edition? Goadby envisioned a publication that would devote special attention to "three great systems" of law: Roman law (and its progeny, French law), English law, and finally "Mohammedan law." He, therefore, sometimes compared specific institutions of ancient Western law to their Muslim equivalents (the Roman jurisconsults and the medieval Muslim jurists). He also used examples taken from medieval Islamic philosophy or literature together with Western examples, for instance, when arguing that the Western historical and evolutionary concepts of law were also found in the thought of the medieval *Mu'tazilah* school.[45]

Goadby also sometimes used examples from modern Egyptian law to critique Western legal theories. Hence, the complex

[44] Table 2.1 was created using WordClouds.com. The lists are based on the first edition of Goadby's book and on Thomas Erskine Holland, *The Elements of Jurisprudence*, 12th ed. (New York: Oxford University Press, 1917).

[45] Goadby, *Introduction to the Study of Law* (1910), 8, 24, 46, 58, 104.

constitutional position of the Egyptian ruler, the Khedive, was mentioned as an example of the problematic nature of the Austinian concept of the sovereign. Austin defined the sovereign in a given state as the person, or persons, who had absolute, unlimited power (for example, the King-in-Parliament in England). However, the Egyptian Khedive received his powers from the Ottoman Sultan under coercion from European powers. This fact, argued Goadby, proved that Austin's concept was uniquely English and could not be generalized.[46] The book also included some references to Arabic legal terms, such as when comparing the terms "right" and "*droit*" to the Arabic term "*haq*."[47]

However, generally speaking, far less attention was devoted in the book to Islamic law (or Egyptian law) than to French and English law, except for a relatively extended discussion of the topic of *waqfs* (which were discussed in comparison to the English trusts).[48] As Goadby explained in his preface, "matters not governed in Egypt by European law have been dealt with very briefly."[49] The relatively limited scope of Goadby's discussion of Islamic law may have resulted from his limited knowledge of the topic. Much of the discussion relied on a single source, *Mahommedan Law* by the Indian author Syed Ameer Ali.[50]

The most interesting aspect of the role of Islamic law in the book was that Goadby sometimes used it to highlight deficiencies in Western jurisprudential theories (just like he used Egyptian law to critique the notion of sovereignty). Thus, when he discussed Austin's theory of law, Goadby noted several conventional critiques of this theory but then added that the "Mohammedan world furnishes us with a conception of law which cannot be honestly brought within Austin's definition." This was because, he reasoned, the authority of Islamic law and of the courts enforcing it was based on religion – that is, on a belief in the divine nature of the law and not the power of the state. Austin's theory, Goadby concluded, was not universal but Western, and did not explain religious legal systems such as Islamic, Jewish, or Hindu law. In another place in his book, Goadby noted that, unlike the modern

46 Ibid., 50–1. 47 Ibid., 58. 48 Ibid., 8–18, 241, 306, 320–2, 362–5.

49 Ibid., vi, 202, 313.

50 Goadby called the author "Amir Aly" and the work "Mohammedan Law." He did not mention the exact edition he was relying on.

Western sovereign who was seen as the source of all law, in Egypt, the notion of religion as the formal source of law "survive[d]."[51]

While Goadby used Islamic law to challenge some aspects of Western legal theories, his comparative insights did not lead him to question the general superiority of modern Western law – on the contrary. His discussion of customary and religious law was disparaging, quoting an author who compared the adherence to custom in "primitive society" to the "inherited habits of animals" and noting the conservative nature of both custom and religion. Goadby argued that adherence to these conservative sources of law was the mark of "arrested civilizations" in Africa and India, and he described the Quran as one example (together with the Laws of Hammurabi and the Laws of Moses) of a code that served a "primitive society." Goadby also claimed that "Mohammedan law" and Hindu law "retain[ed] the ideas of an earlier epoch," giving as an example the fact that they restricted freedom of inheritance.[52]

Goadby's book was based on an evolutionary understanding that distinguished between legal systems serving people "emerging from barbarism" and those who had "attained civilization."[53] It is unclear whether he regarded Islamic societies as the former type (Goadby may have been thinking of African societies here), but specifically regarding Islamic law, Goadby said that "in seeking to adapt law and state organization to European standards, the more progressive Mohammedan countries have introduced bodies of European law" to replace Islamic law.[54] Indeed, in his historical discussion, it is clear that Goadby saw both customary and religious law as representing two lower evolutionary stages of legal development and that he saw Western law, relying on the will of a human lawgiver (which allowed "radical and frequent" changes in the law), as representing "advanced civilization."[55] Goadby mentioned the reception of Western law in Egypt and other non-Western countries such as Turkey, India, Siam, and Japan and said that, in the future, Western law in these places would be "modified into greater conformity to national ideas." However, this would depend, he added, on

[51] Goadby, *Introduction to the Study of Law* (1910), 38–40, 68. The use of the example of religious law to show the limited nature of Austin's theory was not original. It can be traced back to Henry Maine. For Maine's critique of the Austinian theory of law, see, e.g., Henry Sumner Maine, *Ancient Law* (London: John Murray, 1861), 7–8.

[52] Goadby, *Introduction to the Study of Law* (1910), 69–72, 78, 121, 164.

[53] Ibid., 3. [54] Ibid., 18. [55] Ibid., 42.

the "formation ... of a school of independent thought," which did not exist yet in Egypt.[56]

The third edition of Goadby's book was published in 1921 after his relocation to Palestine. The title changed to *Introduction to the Study of Law: A Handbook for the Use of Law Students in Egypt and Palestine*. The legal system of Palestine was based on Ottoman law, with some new legislation based on English models. However, as Goadby acknowledged in the preface to the third edition, due to lack of time, he had done little to adapt the text to the needs of the students of Palestine, apart from adding a few references and remarks on the law of Palestine.[57] For example, there was no extended discussion of the Ottoman Civil Code, the *Mejelle*, which formed the basis of private law in Palestine in 1921.

Similarly, regarding Jewish law, which was more relevant in Palestine than in Egypt (because of the larger Jewish population in Palestine and also because the British were supposed to create a "national home for the Jewish people" there), the third edition of Goadby's book contained only two new remarks on Jewish law. First, Goadby criticized Savigny's view that early law developed only as customary law "by a process of silent adaptation to changing needs." To refute Savigny's depiction, Goadby mentioned Roman law (echoing an idea by Jhering), "Mohammedan law" (the result of "the mighty avalanche of conquest launched from Arabia"), and also Jewish law ("coming amid thunder and whirlwinds" from God on Mount Sinai).[58] A second, slightly longer, discussion of Jewish law appeared in the section dealing with juristic opinion as a source of law. After noting the role of legal scholars in English, French, Roman, and Islamic law, Goadby added a paragraph on Jewish law where he remarked that it was first based on "primitive custom," written down in the Bible, but then developed through rabbinical interpretation in the Mishnah and the Talmud, and later through the vehicles of rabbinical *responsa* and medieval and early modern codes created by the rabbis. He argued that this process was similar to the one in Islamic law. Goadby based his one-paragraph survey of Jewish legal history not on any written sources but on a conversation with Gad Frumkin, a leading Jewish judge in Palestine.[59]

[56] Ibid., 51. [57] Goadby, *Introduction to the Study of Law*, 3rd ed. (1921), v–vi.
[58] Ibid., 56. [59] Ibid., 136–7.

Another characteristic of the new third edition, it seems, was that Goadby now argued that the book was important because it could expose *English* students and scholars to Continental legal theories. In the preface, he wrote that "Continental writings upon legal theory are unduly neglected in English law schools, and it is my hope that this book, though primarily written for law students in Egypt, may perhaps induce some would-be English lawyers to read the works of such men as Charmont, Demogue, Gény, Saleilles, and Tarde."[60] References to Continental thinkers, however, were not limited to French scholars, and the book also mentioned other Continental works, such as the book by Russian scholar Nikolai Korkunov, *General Theory of Law*.[61]

## Works on Jurisprudence Produced by Jewish Authors in Palestine

### *Works on Western Jurisprudence*

The mixture of English and Continental legal theories in Egypt resulted from the French influence on the Egyptian legal system. In Palestine, too, French legal influence was significant because French law was the source of inspiration from the modernization of the Ottoman legal system in the nineteenth century. In addition, Continental legal and jurisprudential ideas were imported to Palestine by Jewish immigrants from Central and Eastern Europe. This avenue of influence could be seen, for example, in the reading materials of the jurisprudence course that Max Laserson, one of the founders of the Tel Aviv School, taught during the academic year 1938/39. The polyglot list of reference books that Laserson recommended to his students included two books by Laserson himself (one in Russian and the other in Hebrew), two English works (by Salmond and Pollock), the Hebrew translation of a book by the late-imperial Russian legal scholar Iosif Alekseevich Pokrovsky, and also a German jurisprudence textbook written, ironically, by Justus Hedemann, one of the leading legal scholars of Nazi Germany.[62]

Just as in India, in Palestine, too, local legal scholars produced cosmopolitan works on jurisprudence, in which analytical and historical English theories were mentioned alongside state-of-the-art

60 Ibid., v. 61 Ibid., 29–30, 101–3.

62 Tel Aviv University Archive, Yisrael Bar-Shira Personal Archive, File 3, "Hoda'ah 248: Tokhnit ha-Yediot le-Bhinot ha-Gmar: Kayits 1939," 4.

Continental anti-formalist theories of law.[63] One example of this phenomenon is a textbook entitled *Torat ha-Mishpat* (jurisprudence) written by Paltiel Dikshtein (Daykan). The first edition of this book was published in 1942/43, and the second in 1949/50, immediately after Israel's independence.[64] Dikshtein studied law at the University of Odessa and graduated in 1910. As a young lawyer and legal scholar, he was involved in the activity of the Jewish legal revival movement in Russia in the period before and immediately after the Russian Revolution. In 1921, he moved to Palestine, where he worked as a lawyer and a legal scholar. He was one of the founders of the Tel Aviv School of Law and Economics and a leading authority on criminal law in Palestine.[65]

Dikshtein's textbook was a stenographical summary of his lectures, divided into six chapters. The first two chapters were general and dealt with the nature of law, its sources, and the different types of legal rights. The other four chapters dealt with specific areas of civil law (property, obligations, family, and inheritance). The book included references to various legal theorists, such as the Russian legal scholar Iosif Pokrovsky and the Anglo-American scholars Oliver Wendell Holmes and John Salmond.[66]

Dikshtein also mentioned the ideas of the Free Law Movement. This movement, a precursor of the American legal realists, appeared in Central Europe in the first two decades of the twentieth century. The free law thinkers sought to overcome legal formalism by making law

[63] In addition to producing original works on jurisprudence, the Jews of Mandatory Palestine also translated textbooks and monographs on the subject authored by European scholars. See Iosif Pokrovsky, *Ha-Probleymot ha-Yesodiyot shel ha-Mishpat ha-Ezrahi*, trans. A. Litai (Jerusalem: Dfus ha-Po'alim, 1922/23). On this book, see Martin Avenarius, "Osnovnyia problemy grazhdanskago prava (Basic Problems of Private Law), 1917, Iosif Alekseevich Pokrovsky (1868–1920)," in *The Formation and Transmission of Western Legal Culture: 150 Books That Made the Law in the Age of Printing*, ed. Serge Dauchy et al. (Cham: Springer, 2016), 438. See also Rudolf von Jhering, *Ha-Ma'avak le-Mishpat*, trans. Baruch Krupnik (Tel Aviv: Mishpat u-Medinah, 1947).

[64] Paltiel Daykan (Dikshtein), *Torat ha-Mishpat: Taktsir ha-Hartsa'ot she-Nikre'u be-Veyt ha-Sefer ha-Gavohah le-Mishpat vele-Kalkalah be-Tel Aviv ba-Shanim 1942/3–1949/50* (Tel Aviv: Beyt ha-Sefer ha-Gavohah le-Mishpat vele-Kalkalah, 1949/50).

[65] David Tidhar, *Entsiklopedyah le-Halutsey ha-Yishuv u-Vonav* (Tel Aviv: Sifriyat Rishonim, 1949), Vol. 3, pp. 1433–4. Retrieved from http://www.tidhar.tourolib.org/tidhar/view/3/1433.

[66] Daykan (Dikshtein), *Torat ha-Mishpat*, 14, 38, 149.

adhere more closely to "life." They argued that instead of rigid rules and abstract concepts divorced from social reality and found only in state-produced codes, judges should base their judgments in individual cases on customs, traditions, and norms created by non-state actors, on facts discovered by the use of the new social sciences and, ultimately, also on their own personal discretion.[67] In his lectures, Dikshtein drew on the ideas of Free Law thinkers when discussing the tension between legal formalism and justice. He relied on a 1922 article of his where he argued that the apparent contradiction facing judges of the autonomous Zionist courts of Palestine, the Hebrew Courts of Arbitration between adhering to the formal rules of Jewish law and responding to the demands of justice, of modern society, and of the economy, was in fact a false dichotomy. Only those who read Jewish legal texts in a formalist way, Dikshtein contended – that is, as "dead" and "ossified" rules incapable of legal development – perceived such a contradiction. In fact, expert judges could use discretion to reconcile formal rules and informal justice by finding (within the formal rules) pathways to internal development and change that would lead to optimal results: decisions that would be both faithful to Jewish law and just.[68]

Dikshtein's book mentioned the ideas of Anglo-American, German, and Russian legal thinkers. It was also cosmopolitan because it included examples from many legal systems: Roman law, English law, and several modern legal systems such as French, German, and American law, as well as the law of Mandatory Palestine.[69] In a few

[67] On the Free Law Movement, see, e.g., James E. Herget and Stephen Wallace, "The German Free Law Movement as the Source of American Legal Realism," *Virginia Law Review* 73 (1987): 399; Assaf Likhovski, "Czernowitz, Lincoln and Jerusalem and the Comparative History of American Jurisprudence," *Theoretical Inquiries in Law* 4 (2003): 621; Katharina I. Schmidt, "Law, Modernity, Crisis: German Free Lawyers, American Legal Realists, and the Transatlantic Turn to 'Life,' 1903–1933," *German Studies Review* 39 (2016): 121.

[68] Daykan (Dikshtein), *Torat ha-Mishpat*, 13–14, 149; Paltiel Dikshtein, "Ha-Mishpat veha-Yosher be-Mishpat ha-Shalom ha-'Ivri," *Ha-Po'el ha-Tsa'ir* 15.33 (July 26, 1922), 5. In his textbook Dikshtein also mentioned Pokrovsky's book *Ha-Probleymot*, which contained a chapter on judicial discretion, including an extended discussion (and critique) of the ideas of both German and French Free Law thinkers. See Daykan (Dikshtein), *Torat ha-Mishpat*, 14; Pokrovsky, *Ha-Probleymot*, 53, 60–70. Another example of the influence of Free Law theory on Dikshtein's thought can be found in Paltiel Dikshtein, *Mishpat ha-Shalom Ha-'Ivri: She'elotav le-Halakhah ule-Ma'aseh* (Tel Aviv: Hotsa'at Mishpat ha-Shalom Ha-'Ivri ha-'Elyon, 1924/25), 14–19.

[69] Daykan (Dikshtein), *Torat ha-Mishpat*, 14, 38, 149.

instances in the book, Dikshtein referred to the sayings of ancient Jewish legal scholars, found in texts such as the Mishnah, side by side with similar sayings of Western thinkers such as Hobbes. In other places, examples from the Bible and Talmud were mentioned.[70] However, generally speaking, Jewish law did not play a significant role in Dikshtein's textbook.

Another example of the fact that, in Palestine, just like in India, one could find interest in state-of-the-art Continental non-formalist jurisprudential theories can be found in the work of Guido (Gad) Tedeschi. Tedeschi was born in 1907 in Rovigo in Northern Italy. His uncle, Giorgio Del Vecchio, was a leading philosopher of law and served as the Rector of the University of Rome. Tedeschi studied law in Rome and later taught in Cagliari and Perugia. In 1936, he was appointed a professor of law at the University of Siena but was dismissed two years later following the enactment of anti-semitic laws by the Italian Fascist regime.[71] Unlike many other Jewish scholars of his generation, Tedeschi had little affinity with, or interest in, Jewish law. This may have been partly the result of the fact that he was born into an assimilated family with a weak connection to Jewish traditions.[72]

In 1939, Tedeschi immigrated to Palestine. He initially lectured on admiralty law at the Tel Aviv School, but in 1941, he joined the Hebrew University of Jerusalem as a research fellow. He spent the 1940s working on several legal research projects. Most of these were practical and based on a formalist conception of law.[73] However, in

70 Ibid., 14, 15, 21.

71 Yosef Sagy, "Re'ayon 'im Profesor Gad Tedeschi," in *Sefer Zikaron le-Gad Tedeschi*, eds. Izhak Englard et al. (Jerusalem: Harry Sacher Institute, 1995), 23, 23–8. See also Likhovski, "Czernowitz," 652–6; Likhovski, "Limudey ha-Mishpatim," 554–7; Leslie Sebba, "Law and Society in Israel: An Emerging Agenda," *Israel Studies Forum* 17 (2001): 83, 102; Pablo Lerner, "Leaving Home, Transplanting Law: Guido Tedeschi and Other Jewish *Émigrés* from Europe," *Studi Senesi* 130 (2018): 229.

72 See *Mavo le-Torat ha-Mishpat 'alpi Hartsa'otav shel Professor G. Tedeschi*, ed. Aharon Barak (Jerusalem: Mif'al ha-Shikhpul, 1958), 50–1 (opposing the use of Jewish law as the basis of the Israeli legal system); Roberto Bachi, "Divrey Roberto Bachi," in *Le-Zikhro shel Gad Tedeschi: Davrim she-Ne'emru bi-Mlot Shloshim le-Moto* (Jerusalem: Ha-Akademyah ha-Yisre'elit le-Mada'im, 1995), 10.

73 The memoranda that Tedeschi wrote during this time are found in CZA, A 215/57/5, and CZA, A 215/57/6.

1944, Tedeschi wrote a project proposal entitled "On inductive research in legal life (with special reference to Palestine)." Here, he called on scholars of the law of Mandatory Palestine to adopt a socio-legal research agenda, to "study the life of the law, the law in action," following the ideas of Free Law thinkers such as Eugen Ehrlich, Ernst Fuchs, and Herman Kantorowicz. In his proposal, Tedeschi indicated that his socio-legal research in Palestine would focus on topics such as the prevalence of bigamy and divorce, standard clauses used in marriage contracts (*ktubot*); the division of estates among heirs (as well as the attempt to determine whether class or ethnic origin led to different property regimes); and the study of "legal life" in socialist communal agricultural settlements, the *kibbutzim*, with an emphasis on the way private law norms (regarding property, family, and inheritance) were applied in these settings.[74]

Tedeschi was familiar with state-of-the-art Continental jurisprudential theories before the 1940s.[75] However, his encounter with the colonial legal system of British-ruled Palestine certainly enhanced his interest in studying the relationship between law and society.[76] Socio-legal questions, noted Tedeschi in his research proposal, were especially acute in colonial legal systems. There were several reasons for this, he explained. One reason was the heterogeneous nature of colonial societies, such as Palestine, which were also immigrant societies. In such contexts, Tedeschi argued: "... the difference between the legal habits and attitudes of the various parts of the population, according to the countries of their origin, have not yet resolved themselves as a result of unified communal life, and given the prevailing pattern of immigration, are not likely to resolve themselves for a considerable time."[77]

[74] CZA, A 215/57/5, "On Inductive Study in Legal Life (Especially in Palestine)." The proposal was later published in Gad Tedeschi, *Mehkarim be-Mishpat Artsenu* (Jerusalem: Magnes, 1951/2), 1. It was also translated into English and published as Guido (Gad) Tedeschi, "On the Inductive Study of Law," in *Studies in Israel Law* (Jerusalem: Mif'al ha-Shikhpul, 1960), 1.

[75] See Guido Tedeschi, "Su lo Studio dell'applicazione del Diritto civile," *Annuario di diritto comparato e di studi legislativi* 7(1) (1932): 2. Tedeschi's 1944 research proposal was partly based on this article.

[76] See, e.g., Guido Tedeschi, "Preface to the Second Hebrew Edition," in *Studies in Israel Law*, vi.

[77] Tedeschi, "On the Inductive Study of Law," 4–5.

Second, in colonial societies, judges often applied laws without a deep understanding of the local culture. Tedeschi observed that British judges in Palestine were required to use certain norms of Jewish law, particularly in family matters, but frequently misapplied them. This, he explained, was because "they did not grasp the finer distinctions of that law, distinctions which it is difficult to discern if one does not actually 'live' the system: an outsider would just not understand them from a mere study of the abstract rules of the system."[78] A third reason for the relevance of socio-legal issues in colonial legal systems, also evident in the law of Palestine, was legal pluralism. In this context, Tedeschi observed that, in Palestine, there were certain "law-making centers" that competed with and, in a sense, undermined the authority of the state, such as the Jewish Agency, the General Federation of Jewish Labor, and the *kibbutzim*.[79]

## *Theoretical Works on Jewish Law*

In Palestine, just as in India, one could find theoretical works that mentioned or analyzed Jewish law.[80] One example of such works is a textbook published by Baruch (Boris) Gankin in 1949, immediately after the establishment of the State of Israel. Gankin was born in 1887

[78] Ibid., 6.

[79] Ibid., 18–19. Some of Tedeschi's later works showed the same interest in the study of law and society. See Gad Tedeschi, "Ha-Minhag be-Mishpatenu ha-Noheg veha-'Atiti," *Mishpatim* 5 (1973): 9, 56–7. See also Leslie Sebba, "Professor Tedeschi ve-'Torat ha-Hakikah' – Kol Kore ba-Midbar," in *Sefer Zikaron le-Gad Tedeschi*, eds. Izhak Englard et al. (Jerusalem: Harry Sacher Institute, 1995), 535, 551–7.

[80] In the following paragraphs, I discuss works that had jurisprudential aspects. There were also works published in Mandatory Palestine that were descriptive surveys of Jewish law or its history. These works will not be discussed here. See, e.g., Simha Assaf, *Ha-'Onshin aharey Hatimat ha-Talmud: Homer le-Toldot ha-Mishpat ha-'Ivri* (Jerusalem: n.p., 1921/22); Simha Assaf, *Batey ha-Din ve-Sidrehem aharey Hatimat ha-Talmud: Homer le-Toldot ha-Mishpat ha-'Ivri* (Jerusalem: Dfus ha-Po'alim, 1923/24); Asher Gulak, *Le-Heker Toldot ha-Mishpaṭ ha-'Ivri bi-Tekufat ha-Talmud* (Jerusalem: ha-Sefer, 1928/29); Asher Gulak, *Das Urkundenwesen im Talmud im Lichte der griechisch-aegyptischen Papyri und des griechischen und roemischen Rechts* (Jerusalem, R. Mass, 1935); Avraham Hayim Freimann, *Seder Kidushin ve-Nisu'in Ahare Hatimat ha-Talmud: Mehkar Histori-Dogmati be-Dine Yisra'el* (Jerusalem: Mosad ha-Rav Kook, 1944/45). Also noteworthy is a Hebrew-language monograph on the relationship of law and morality in Jewish law that was authored by a Jewish-American rabbi, Simon Federbusch. It was first published in New York in 1943 and republished in Mandatory Palestine in

in Shchedrin, a small town near Bobruysk, in what is today Belarus. He obtained a traditional religious Jewish education, studied law, and worked as a lawyer in Kiev. In 1925, Gankin became an attaché in the Soviet Embassy in Uruguay, relocating to Palestine in the 1930s. Gankin collaborated with Dikshtein, who taught jurisprudence at the Tel Aviv Law School, although he did not hold an official lecturing position there.[81]

Gankin published articles on the history of the Jews in Russia, as well as two short works of fiction. One of these latter works is *Shemhazai* (named after a fallen angel consumed by a lust for mortal women), which tells the story of a group of Jewish students studying for the external matriculation exams in late nineteenth-century Russia. The story ends with remarks about the impact of the secular Jewish enlightenment on Jewish culture and creativity. This process, the book's protagonist reflects, led Jews to become promoters of foreign works and ideas, rather than cultivating an "independent creative spirit [emanating from] the soul of the nation." The hero then compares modern Jewish and Russian cultures. Before the reign of Peter the Great, he notes, Russians were a "semi-ignorant and wild" nation. A century later, Russians started to excel in producing a unique, independent culture that reflected Russia's national spirit. The Russians had thus managed to absorb foreign influences while reshaping them to reflect their national character. The Jews, by contrast, a people once renowned for offering the world original ideas, had lost that creative vitality and now merely echoed the ideas and works of other nations.[82] The cultural nationalism that animated this story also informed Gankin's legal scholarship.

Gankin's main legal work was a two-volume textbook on jurisprudence. The first volume was completed in the fall of 1949, a year and a half after Israeli independence. It contained a preface by Dikshtein, the book's editor. Dikshtein noted therein that, during the period of the British Mandate, no book dealing with the general theory

1947. See Simon Federbusch, *Ha-Musar veha-Mishpat be-Yisrael* (Jerusalem: Mosad ha-Rav Kook, 1947).

[81] [Paltiel Dikshtein], [Obituary], National Library of Israel, Gankin Personal File (V 1630); ISA, Boris Gankin's Immigration File, ISA-MandatoryOrganizations-Naturalization-000zzga.

[82] Baruch Gankin, *Shemhazai: Sipur me-Hayey ha-Externim be-Russia mi-Kets ha-Me'ah She'avrah* (Jerusalem: Dfus Raphael Haim ha-Cohen, 1944/45), 92–4.

of law had been published in Hebrew and that law students used foreign texts expounding English jurisprudential theories (referring here to Goadby's book). Even the lectures on general jurisprudence at the Tel Aviv School (imparted by Dikshtein himself) were only published as "stenciled notes." In contrast, while Gankin's book did not presume to offer innovative ideas, it did provide a survey combining theories of Continental and English scholars with appropriate materials taken from the "thousands of years old" Jewish tradition.[83]

The first volume of Gankin's book contained an "introduction to the basic legal concepts," and the second volume, published in 1950, dealt with subfields of law (and was divided into four subsections dealing with private and public law, procedure, and interpretation). While the two volumes contained discussions of well-known topics that could be found in countless other jurisprudence textbooks, they also had some unique features. The first notable feature, much like Dikshtein's textbook, was its cosmopolitan character, reflecting a broad intellectual scope that included both English and Continental thinkers. Gankin cited nineteenth-century German scholars such as Savigny and Jhering, English legal theorists like Austin, as well as prominent Russian scholars. For instance, the opening chapter, which explored the "essence of law," examined the relationship between law and morality. After tracing the historical development of natural law theory, Gankin introduced the Russian legal scholar Leon Petrażycki, who created a unique, anti-formalist theory of law influenced by the new science of psychology. Gankin discussed, and critiqued, Petrażycki's attempt to distinguish law and morality by linking both to emotional experiences.[84] Later, within a discussion of sociological theories of law, Gankin included a brief outline of Marxist legal theory.[85]

A second interesting feature of the book was that Gankin attempted to apply the theories discussed to the particular legal setting of Mandatory Palestine. For example, he ended the first chapter, which contained a survey of major jurisprudential schools, by noting that all

[83] B. Gankin, *Torat ha-Mishpat*, Vol. 1: *Mavo la-Musagim ha-Mishpatiyim ha-Yesodiyim* (Jerusalem: n.p., 1949), Preface.

[84] Ibid., 8–11. See also 75–6 (discussing Petrażycki's theory about the difference between private and public law).

[85] Ibid., 14–15.

the theories he discussed about the nature of law and its sources applied only to ordinary times and not to extraordinary moments such as revolutions or periods of emergency when a minority imposed its will on a fearful and passive majority. He then provided another example of times when there was a gap between what the legal norms had to say and the actual circumstances experienced by the people subject to the law. The example he gave was "mandated territories," where "the English ... try to impose on the local inhabitants [English] law under the assumption that this law is universal, although it is [actually] foreign to the spirit of the inhabitants and their conditions of life."[86]

The third feature of Gankin's book was its use of Jewish law. The second chapter, entitled "The Study of Law," began with a brief paragraph that mentioned several possible approaches to the study of law (ethical, Marxist, economical, historical, comparative, and dogmatic) but then plunged into an extended discussion of the history of Jewish law.[87] Similarly, Gankin's exploration of the tension between law and equity began with a general overview of the topic but soon turned to a focused analysis of how this issue is addressed in the Talmud.[88] He also illustrated his discussions of other issues (such as the classification of types of norms or the question of the sources of law) with examples taken from both the Bible and the Talmud.[89]

Many other examples can be mentioned. In one place in the book, Gankin discussed the distinction between private and public law. This distinction, he said, could be traced back to Roman law. He then mentioned various theories that attempted to distinguish between the two types of law, ultimately referring to Hans Kelsen's approach, which rejected the distinction, arguing that all law, including private law, emanated from the state. This allowed Gankin to turn to Jewish law. Jewish law, he said, also rejected the distinction because it was based on the assumption that all norms ultimately emanated from God. The divine origins of all norms of Jewish law meant that all norms had the same sacred value and aimed to create a "perfect society based on social justice." Gankin then linked the private–public distinction to the ideological tension between individualism and collectivism. Unlike individualist Roman law, Gankin noted, in Jewish law, the individual was only a tiny link in the collective chain,

[86] Ibid., 17–18. [87] Ibid., 19–30. [88] Ibid., 36–8. [89] Ibid., 40–3, 70–2.

and the goal of law was to curb the individual's will for the collective's benefit in order to further social justice. The various categorization schemes used by Jewish law scholars throughout the ages, therefore, were not based on the distinction between private and public law and the individualist ideology that had inspired this distinction.[90]

Another example of the same kind of move can be found in Gankin's discussion of the notion of possession. This notion was first developed in Roman law, Gankin said, and was designed to mitigate acute disputes relating to the ownership of property. The protection granted by Roman law to the possessor against anyone threatening the latter's hold on the possessed object was meant to provide certainty and economic stability and prevent violence. The Roman notion of possession then spread to all European legal systems and also to Ottoman law. However, Gankin continued, this notion was not to be found in Jewish law because there was no need for it, given the "moral attitude of the [Jewish] people, who always avoided violence, fistfights, or bloodshed over property." Gankin was willing to see English law as somewhat similar to Jewish law in this regard, observing that, while medieval English law received the notion of possession from Roman law, the legal protection of possession gradually declined "as the [English] population acquired habits of peaceful living and moderation."[91]

The claim that Jewish law reflected a higher tier of social and legal development also appeared in Gankin's book in his discussion of the prohibition of excessive and compounded interest in Jewish law and in the argument that the legality principle (*nullum crimen sine lege* – no punishment without law) was already well developed in the Talmud but only appeared in Europe in the eighteenth century, during the French Revolution.[92]

Sometimes, Gankin's discussion of Jewish law contained apologetic undertones. For example, the age of legal capacity in Jewish law is

[90] Ibid., 77–81. Gankin's anti-individualist approach may have been related to his affinity to Soviet law. In the preface to a translation of his to the sections of the Soviet Civil Code dealing with inheritance law, he wrote that the Soviet law of inheritance was a "comprehensive, original and logical" system that "solve[d] many important problems in matters of inheritance that other legal systems" found difficult to resolve, and that, therefore, it could serve as "an instructive example" to other legal systems. See Baruch Gankin, *Mishpat ha-Yerushah shel Brit ha-Mo'etsot* (Jerusalem: Dfus Eretz Yisrael, n.d.). 3.

[91] Gankin, *Torat ha-Mishpat*, Vol. 1, 89–91. [92] Ibid., 105, 151.

relatively young compared to Western legal systems: twelve for girls and thirteen for boys. Gankin justified this fact by saying that the age of adulthood varied between different countries and depended on "customs, cultural state, and climate."[93] A similar apologetic tone was evident in his discussion of the attitude of Jewish law to the death penalty. Gankin saw the gradual abolition of the death penalty as a result of "cultural development." Jewish law imposed capital punishment on many types of offenses. However, said Gankin, because this law was "imbued with a special [spirit] of humaneness," it placed so many procedural obstacles in the way of actually implementing the death penalty that, in practice, it was abolished.[94] Gankin also favorably compared the cruel methods of execution found in many ancient legal systems with the limited number of methods of execution recognized in Jewish law, which, he argued, proved the progressiveness of ancient Jewish law.[95] Gankin, however, was not always apologetic. For example, when discussing the relationship between legislation and customary law, he equated the Palestinian Talmud (but not the Babylonian Talmud) with the Ottoman Civil Code, the *Mejelle*, and "other backward codes" because of the primacy they gave to custom over explicit rulemaking.[96]

A similar interest in the nexus between jurisprudence and Jewish law can be found in the works of Max Laserson (see Figure 2.3). Laserson was born in 1887 in the Latvian part of the Russian Empire. He studied law at St. Petersburg Imperial University under the leading late-imperial Russian legal philosopher, Leon Petrażycki. In 1921, Laserson moved to the newly independent state of Latvia, where he became a member of the Latvian Parliament and worked as a lawyer and a teacher in a private institution of higher education, the Riga Commercial College. In 1934, following an authoritarian coup d'état in Latvia, Laserson was imprisoned in a concentration camp for six months and then left for British-ruled Palestine. He became one of the four founders of the Tel Aviv School, teaching courses on constitutional law, public international

93 Ibid., 45–6.

94 Ibid., 152. On the impact of Jewish law on the (partial) abolition of the death penalty in post-1948 Israel, see Amihai Radzyner and Rivka Brot, "Masa' u-Masa le-Vitul 'Onesh ha-Mavet 'al 'Averat ha-Retsah," *'Iyuney Mishpat* 47 (2024): 475, 513–18.

95 Gankin, *Torat ha-Mishpat*, Vol. 1, 153.

96 Ibid., 60–1.

FIGURE 2.3 Max Laserson, c. 1934. Photograph courtesy of the National Library of Israel / Abraham Schwadron Collection.

law, and jurisprudence. In 1939, he moved to the United States, ultimately becoming a lecturer at Columbia University.[97]

Laserson was a polyglot, publishing works in seven languages: Russian, Yiddish, Latvian, German, Hebrew, French, and English. He wrote extensively on constitutional law, international law, and the philosophy of law.[98] One significant characteristic of Laserson's jurisprudential oeuvre was his interest in the Jewish contribution to jurisprudence, especially natural law theory.[99] A major topic of many

[97] For a more detailed discussion of Laserson's biography and his ideas, see Assaf Likhovski, "The Many Exiles of Max Laserson," *Clio@Themis* 22 (2022), http://journals.openedition.org/cliothemis/2087.

[98] See, generally, *Bibliography of the Chief Works of Max M. Laserson* (New York: n.p., 1947) (a copy is available at the Archive of the Association of Latvian and Estonian Jews in Israel, Shfayim, item number P49-15f); Likhovski, "The Many Exiles of Max Laserson."

[99] Laserson's interest in natural law was probably the result of the influence of Petrażycki's thought. On the important role that natural law played in Petrażycki's legal philosophy, see Andrzej Walicki, *Legal Philosophies of Russian Liberalism* (Notre Dame, IN: University of Notre Dame Press, 1992), 228–9, 263–4. On Laserson's original contribution to the development of a Petrażyckian perspective on the notion of natural law, see Elena V. Timoshina et al., "Other Russian or Polish Legal Realists," in *A Treatise of Legal Philosophy and General Jurisprudence*, eds. Enrico Pattaro and Corrado Roversi (Dordrecht: Springer, 2016), Vol. 12.2, 527, 539–42. On early twentieth-century varieties of natural law theory generally, see, e.g., Francesco Viola, "Introduction: Natural Law Theories in the Twentieth Century," in

of his works on natural law was the Jewish notion of the seven Noahide laws – a universal moral code binding all humanity established through a covenant between God and Noah after the flood. According to the Talmud, these laws included a prohibition on idolatry, murder, theft, and incest, and a duty to establish courts of law.[100]

One of Laserson's first articles, published in 1912 in the Moscow periodical *Voprosy Prava*, was devoted to natural law in ancient Jewish texts. This article manifested the influence of Marx's and Petrażycki's legal theories. The Marxist influence is evident, for example, in the emphasis that Laserson placed on the role of economic conditions in shaping law and in a class-based interpretation of biblical legal history, inspired by the work of the Marxist theoretician Karl Kautsky. Thus, Laserson argued, the fact that the Israelites were mainly nomadic herders and farmers, and not merchants and artisans, influenced their law, which was focused on land law rather than civil or commercial law. He called the prophets advocates of the people's rights, who stood by the "oppressed masses" and opposed the disparity between rich and poor in ancient Israel. He argued that biblical positive law served the interests of the powerful, while natural law reflected the interest of the lower classes; and he depicted the Second Temple Jewish sect, the Essenes, as "the first practical communists," and Jesus and his followers as constituting "a movement of the Jewish proletariat."[101] The Petrażyckian influence on Laserson's article is clear in his discussion of the relationship between psychology and law and his interest in the development of intuitive legal consciousness.[102]

*A Treatise of Legal Philosophy and General Jurisprudence*, eds. Enrico Pattaro and Corrado Roversi (Dordrecht: Springer, 2016), Vol. 12.2, 3; Nader Hakim, "Droit naturel et histoire chez François Gény," *Clio@Themis* 9 (2015), https://doi.org/10.35562/cliothemis.1534.

100 Interest in the Noahide laws was also expressed in the works of other legal scholars associated with the Tel Aviv School. See Samuel Eisenstadt, "Kadmoniyot ha-Mishpat ha-Yisre'eli," *Ha-'Am* Pt. 2 (May 18, 1917): 10, 11; Samuel Eisenstadt, "Le-Heker Mishpatenu ha-Pumbi," *Ha-Mishpat ha-'Ivri: Riv'on Mada'i* (1918): 8, 17–18. On the Noahide laws, see, e.g., Suzanne Last Stone, "Sinaitic and Noahide Law: Legal Pluralism in Jewish Law," *Cardozo Law Review* 12 (1991): 1157; Steven Robert Wilf, *The Law before the Law* (Lanham, MD: Lexington Books, 2008).

101 M. Ia. Lazerson, "Estestvennoe pravo v pamiatnikakh drevne-evreiskoi literatury i zakonodatelstva," *Voprosy Prava* 11 (1912): 108, 108–11, 116, 124, 126, 128, 129, 131.

102 Ibid., 109, 112–13, 118–19, 126–7, 129.

Unlike other Russian-Jewish scholars at the time, in this article, Laserson did not call in any way for a revival of Jewish law motivated by a Jewish-nationalist agenda. The article, written for a Russian audience, positioned Jewish legal history as a case study that could be used to illustrate broader theoretical concerns, whether Marxist or Petrażyckian. At this point, Laserson did not view Jewish law as a repository of norms and institutions that could be revived and used in the present; nor did he seek to prove the Jewish contribution to the global history of legal thought. However, in the second half of the 1930s, after moving to Palestine and starting to teach at the Tel Aviv School, a bastion of the Jewish legal revival movement, Laserson's use of Jewish law changed. Now, he sought to convince non-Jewish audiences that the history of Jewish law was relevant to the comparative history of global legal thought. He also worked to convince Jewish readers that Jewish law was not an archaic legal system but one based on modern values and, therefore, still relevant to the present.

These changes were evident in an article Laserson published in 1937 on the legal philosophy of the medieval Jewish scholar Maimonides. The article was first published in French in the journal of the International Institute for the Philosophy of Law and Legal Sociology, based in Paris. An expanded version of this article was later published in Hebrew as a short book.[103] The French article began with the statement that its purpose was to "fill a lacuna." The literature on the philosophy of law had ignored legal thinkers from the "non-Christian world," and Laserson sought to correct this omission by showing the influence of Maimonides on modern legal thinkers. Laserson argued that Maimonides' thought had influenced Baruch Spinoza and, via Spinoza, had made an impact on the ideas of Jean-Jacques Rousseau and, therefore, also on modern doctrines of international and constitutional law.[104]

In the Hebrew version of the article, Laserson sought to further a Jewish-nationalist jurisprudential agenda by arguing that Jewish

[103] Max Lazerson, "La philosophie du droit de Maïmonide," *Archives de philosophie du droit et de sociologie juridique* 7 (1937): 191; Max M. Laserson, *Ha-Filosofiyah ha-Mishpatit shel ha-Rambam* (Tel Aviv: Beyt ha-Sefer ha-Gavohah le-Mishpat vele-Kalkalah, 1939).

[104] Lazerson, "La philosophie du droit," 191, 201, 208–9, 216.

scholars should devote more attention to the study of Jewish legal thought and strive to prove that Jewish law was not an obsolete legal system but one that resonated with modern democratic values. Like the article in French, the Hebrew version began with a note on the importance of Jewish legal philosophers to the global history of law. After lamenting the fact that Jews had contributed to the development of Western legal philosophy but had neglected to tend "[their] own vineyard," Laserson argued that:

> ... we [Jewish law scholars] will mostly be able to permanently contribute to the global literature on law by analyzing Jewish legal philosophy and theory because our interpretative and dogmatic analysis is bound to remain, as any legal dogmatics, only on the national level ... the development of Jewish legal science demands that we discover the unique [contribution] of Jewish thought to the general treasure of human civilization.[105]

In particular, he claimed that the subject of his book, Maimonides, should be considered one of the foundational figures of the global science of law. Studying Jewish legal thought, Laserson continued, would also prove that commendable and modern notions such as natural rights, freedom, tolerance, and opposition to despotism were not modern Western inventions but had already appeared in ancient Jewish texts.[106]

Western jurisprudential literature claimed that the distinction between positive and natural law appeared only in the West and was related to the individualist nature of ancient Greek and Roman societies. This approach gave rise to the mistaken belief that Hugo Grotius was the originator of natural law theory. However, this was wrong, said Laserson. The critique of existing laws, leading to the appearance of the idea of natural law, was not a uniquely Western phenomenon since such a critique appeared in every society, including in ancient Jewish society.[107] Moreover, during the Middle Ages, Judaism – or, more specifically, Maimonides, in his treatise, *The Guide for the Perplexed* – developed the idea of natural law in a way that influenced early modern Western theorists. One major innovation that Laserson attributed to Maimonides was the notion of civil religion, that is, a narrow set of moral dogmas essential for the peace and stability of any state, such as the belief in God, in the afterlife, in

[105] Laserson, *Ha-Filosofiyah ha-Mishpatit*, 5. [106] Ibid., 6, 8. [107] Ibid., 10–12.

punishment for the wicked, and in reward for the good. The notion of civil religion, bolstering the state and guaranteeing its stability, can be found, said Laserson, in the works of Hobbes, Spinoza, and Rousseau. Laserson, however, argued that it could be traced back to Maimonides and specifically to chapter 28 of Part III of *The Guide for the Perplexed*.[108]

In arguing for the importance of Maimonides' thought, Laserson was motivated not only by cultural nationalism but also by a desire to show that Jewish legal thought constituted an important chapter in the history of global legal thought. He was also reacting to the events of the 1930s, attempting to use Maimonides' ideas to create a basis for a critique of both communist and Nazi ideology. Natural law (and civil religion) became such a basis, reflecting a broader effort evident in the works of liberal legal scholars in the 1930s to find some form of non-positivist theory of law that could serve as a foundation for the defense of the beleaguered democracies of the West.[109] Thus, after arguing that the idea of a civil religion first appeared in *The Guide for the Perplexed*, Laserson emphasized that this idea was now extremely important. The first modern democracies – Calvinist Geneva, England during the English Civil War, or France during the French Revolution – had civil religions, Laserson explained. This idea, however, was replaced in the nineteenth century by "ideological Manchesterism," that is, by the notion of ideological *laissez-faire*. Now, only anti-democratic states (the Soviet Union, Italy, and Germany) had obligatory political ideologies, Laserson said, and these were based on the denial of civic freedom.[110] Contemporary democratic states had long ignored the need to pay attention to the beliefs and opinions of their citizens, but they were now being forced (due to the threat of anti-democratic regimes) to create a "legal credo" for their subjects, a new civil religion. Laserson concluded his book by claiming that "they must rely not only on one of the last thinkers to

[108] Ibid., 40–1, 50, 56–62.

[109] Ibid., 58, citing Gustav Radbruch, "Le relativisme dans la philosophie de droit," *Archives de philosophie du droit et de sociologie juridique* 4 (1934): 105 (where Radbruch, the leading liberal German legal philosopher, argued that a parliamentary majority could not establish a permanent dictatorship, since it was an underlying principle of democracy that it could not permanently abolish itself).

[110] Laserson, *Ha-Filosofiyah ha-Mishpatit*, 58.

mention the idea of [civil religion], Rousseau," but also on one of the first thinkers who mentioned this idea: Maimonides.[111]

Laserson's interest in Jewish law continued after his move to the United States. For example, in 1948, he published a short piece on "the Hebrew Roots of International Law," in which he claimed that the Noahide laws had influenced early modern Christian pioneers of international law, such as Grotius and Selden.[112] Perhaps the most relevant article on Jewish law written during his American period, however, was published posthumously in 1953. In this article, Laserson compared Thomas Hobbes to the biblical figure of Job. He described the Book of Job as epitomizing a higher stage of moral and legal thought, the stage of natural law, compared to Hobbes' crass positivism, which ultimately led, he claimed, not just to the legal positivism of nineteenth-century thinkers such as John Austin but also, indirectly, to the legal theories prevalent in Nazi Germany.[113]

In Laserson's work, the interest in the nexus between jurisprudence and Jewish law was mainly expressed in an interest in the history of natural law theory. In articles published in Mandatory Palestine during the interwar period by other legal scholars, interest in this nexus found expression in works that compared Jewish law to Western law, particularly Roman law. I will now discuss these works, which can be placed on the borderline between comparative law and jurisprudence.[114]

Western thought since antiquity (and also Jewish thought) often used the "Rome versus Jerusalem" dichotomy to argue that Western/

111 Ibid., 62. In an earlier article, Laserson made a similar argument: contemporary democracies could no longer abandon the political education of the younger generations but had to return to the idea of civil religion and find a middle way between the anarchy of a total lack of ideological content in their schools, and the slavery (evident in totalitarian states) of an obligatory political religion. See Maxime Lazerson, "La réalité du droit et la politique juridique," in *IIe Annuaire de l'Institut International de Philosophie du Droit et de Sociologie Juridique: Travaux de la seconde session: Droit, Morale, Moeurs* (Paris: Sirey, 1935–36), 235, 245.

112 Max M. Laserson, "Hebrew Roots of International Law," *Menorah Journal* 36 (1948): 174. Another interesting discussion on the non-Christian roots of international law can be found in a typewritten essay in Hebrew that Laserson wrote in 1939, discussing international relations in the ancient Near East. See CZA, A 388/2, Max Laserson, "Ha-Yahasim ha-Beyn Leumiyim shel ha-Mizrah ha-Karov (1450 lifney ha-Sfirah)."

113 Max Laserson, "Power and Justice: Hobbes Versus Job," *Judaism: A Quarterly Journal of Jewish Life and Thought* 2 (1953): 52, 58.

114 For a more detailed discussion, see Likhovski, "The Eagle and the Dove."

Christian and Jewish culture and ideas were diametrically opposed.[115] Such notions also appeared in discussions of Jewish and Roman law. The difference between the two legal systems was a common topic of Jewish works written in the early twentieth century. One way to contrast these two systems was to argue that Roman law was based on authority and power while Jewish law was based on morality, implicitly echoing the positivism/natural law dichotomy. According to this approach, Jewish law was not just different from Roman law but also *better*: more moral and progressive.[116]

The distinction between the two legal systems was often based on comparing two concrete and related issues: individualism versus collectivism and subjectivism versus objectivism. For example, a 1927 article by a certain "B. Safra" from Russia (this was probably a pseudonym used to hide the identity of the author), which was published in the journal *Ha-Mishpat ha-'Ivri*, argued that Roman law prioritized individual liberty and the concept of absolute private property. Because of its religious nature, Jewish law regarded all property as ultimately belonging to God and did not view the right of property as paramount. Safra offered several examples to buttress this observation. For instance, he noted that Jewish law gave the poor a legal right to part of the produce of orchards and fields owned by the wealthy. Safra stated that Roman law was the source of many Western legal systems, but its influence was waning. In the future, he implied, modern legal systems would adopt the quasi-socialist notions upon which Jewish law was based.[117]

A related distinction to the individual/collective one was that between subjectivism and objectivism. Asher Gulak's 1925 inaugural lecture at the Hebrew University sought to compare "the spirit of the Jewish and Roman civil law."[118] In this lecture, Gulak argued that one principle that distinguished Jewish and Roman law and proved that the two systems were "derived from sources foreign to each other" was

[115] See, e.g., David Nirenberg, *Anti-Judaism: The Western Tradition* (New York: Norton, 2013). See also Yaacov Shavit, *Ha-Yahadut bi-Re'i ha-Yevanut* (Tel Aviv: 'Am 'Oved, 1992).

[116] See Likhovski, "The Eagle and the Dove," 286–9.

[117] B. Safra, "Ha-Kinyan ha-Prati ba-Mishpat ha-'Ivri," *Ha-Mishpat ha-'Ivri* 2 (1927): 25.

[118] Asher Gulak, "Hashva'ah Klalit beyn Ru'ah Diney Mamonot ha-'Ivriyim ve-Ru'ah Diney Mamonot ha-Roma'im," *Mad'ey ha-Yahadut* 1 (1925/26): 45.

related to the notion of will. Roman private and public law, said Gulak, were based on the exercise of will: the will of the individual, in the case of private law; and the sovereign's will in the case of public law. Both Roman private and public law were thus based on a devotion to the notion of sovereignty. The Jews, however, were devoted to justice, not sovereignty. As a result, their private law did not seek to empower the individual's will in creating legal relationships. Instead, such relationships were based on objective facts rather than subjective will.[119]

Gulak then noted that, in Roman law, the *pater familias* could adopt strangers (for example, as a method of forging political or military alliances between families). Adoption did not require any objective criteria. It was carried out merely by the exercise of will on the part of the adopter. In contrast, Jewish law did not recognize the possibility of adoption, and family relations were based purely on "objective" bloodlines. In addition, while Roman law mainly championed the notion of free testamentary dispositions, Jewish law, although it did recognize the possibility of creating wills, focused on creating rules in the case of intestacy. Gulak claimed that Roman civil law, sanctifying the will of the individual citizen, led to "tyranny and the oppression of the weak." In Jewish law, by contrast, the individual's exercising of their will was subject to "the demands of justice."[120]

Nineteenth-century legal thought, shaped by liberal ideology, would have viewed the absence of emphasis on individual free will in Jewish law as evidence of its inferiority. The fact that Jewish law did not give precedence to the free will of individuals would have been perceived as an indication that this legal system belonged to a low rung of the evolutionary legal ladder, at the top of which stood legal systems based on free will. However, by the 1920s, when Gulak gave his inaugural lecture, this fact would actually have led many legal scholars to classify Jewish law as more attuned to modern sensibilities than Roman law. Gulak himself was aware of this fact when he concluded that:

> ... the objective principles upon which our nation's private law is founded have many contact points with modern developments in legal science, in which, too, there is a tendency to weaken the power of the individual's will in his private relations with other individuals and to recognize the influence of social and

[119] Ibid., 45–7. [120] Ibid., 48–9.

objective principles in individual relations. The objective principles of Jewish private law and the moral principles they reveal prove the vitality of our nation's laws and the fertile influence they may have on modern legal ideas.[121]

## Jurisprudence and the Palestinian-Arab Community

In Chapter 1, I discussed theoretical works on Islamic law published in India, focusing specifically on the work of the Madras judge, Abdur Rahim. In Chapter 7, I will discuss Egypt, where there was a large community of legal scholars interested in applying Western legal theories to the study of Islamic legal history and jurisprudence. Such interest also existed among the Arab lawyers of Mandatory Palestine but on a smaller scale. In order to explain the relative difference in interest in legal theory between the Arab lawyers of Palestine and Egyptian lawyers, and also between the Arab and Jewish lawyers of Palestine, a short discussion of the history of book publishing in Palestine is required.

The Palestinian-Arab community in Mandatory Palestine was larger than the Jewish one. In 1931, Jews comprised only 17 percent of the population of approximately 1 million. By the end of British rule, the Jewish population comprised roughly 30 percent. However, while Mandatory Palestine was a major Jewish intellectual and cultural center, the centers of Arab and Islamic intellectual life were in places such as Egypt and Lebanon rather than in Palestine. The Jewish and Arab communities differed in literacy rates.[122] Another difference was that while there was an extensive Jewish autonomous school system in Palestine, which included many high schools and several higher

[121] Ibid., 50. But see Chaim Tchernowitz, "Reshimot ve-He'arot," *Ha-Mishpat* 2 (1927): 44 (an article devoted to criticizing Gulak's depictions of both Roman and Jewish law). On the rise of collectivism in early twentieth-century Western legal systems, see, generally, Duncan Kennedy, "Three Globalizations of Law and Legal Thought: 1850–2000," in *The New Law and Economic Development: A Critical Appraisal*, eds. David M. Trubek and Alvaro Santos (New York: Cambridge University Press, 2006), 19.

[122] According to the 1931 Census of Palestine, the literacy rate in the Jewish community was 86 percent. It was 58 percent among Christians (who were mainly Arabs), and 14 percent among Muslims. See Mills, *Census of Palestine 1931*, Vol. 1, 96, 206. For a general discussion of reading and literacy in late Ottoman and Mandatory Palestine, see Ami Ayalon, *Reading Palestine: Printing and Literacy, 1900–1948* (Austin, TX: University of Texas Press, 2004).

education institutions, there were very few Arab high schools and no Arab universities.[123] In the early 1930s, the political leader of the Palestinian-Arab community, Hajj Amin al-Husayni, attempted to establish an Islamic University (partly to be funded by Indian Muslims) that would compete with the Hebrew University, but this attempt failed. Al-Husayni was unable to secure enough funds, and events in the second half of the 1930s ultimately doomed the project, specifically the British repression of the Arab Revolt of 1936–39 and the fact that al-Husayni, who played a key role in the Revolt, fled the country in 1937.[124]

The difference in literacy and education rates was reflected in the number of publications in Arabic versus Hebrew in Palestine. The 1931 Census of Palestine reported that thirty-nine books in Arabic had been published in the territory between 1923 and 1931. During the same period, 1,120 books in Hebrew had been published there.[125] In the 1940s, Ishaq Musa al-Husayni, a Palestinian-Arab scholar, compiled a list of 209 Arabic books published in Palestine between 1919 and 1944, most of which were school textbooks. This number, stated Husayni, was less than the number of books published by the Jews of Palestine in a single year.[126] As for periodicals, according to the 1931 Census, thirty-nine periodicals were published in Arabic in Mandatory Palestine between 1923 and 1931, compared to 332 in Hebrew.[127]

The gap between Arabs and Jews was also evident in the legal realm. There were many learned Arab lawyers in Palestine, some of whom were

[123] Reid, *Lawyers*, 296–8.

[124] On the history of the failed attempt to create an Arab university in Palestine, see, generally, Ilan Pappé, "Why Only a Hebrew University? The Tale of the Arab University in Mandatory Jerusalem," *Jerusalem Quarterly* 92 (2022): 102, 110–14. On the secondary education system of Palestine, see, generally, Yoni Furas, *Educating Palestine: Teaching and Learning History under the Mandate* (Oxford: Oxford University Press, 2020), 218–31.

[125] Mills, *Census of Palestine 1931*, Vol. 1, 214, 219. The term "books" (as opposed to "pamphlets") was defined in the *Census* as pertaining to works of more than forty-eight pages. Note that the number of books written in Arabic may have been greater than reported because the relevant table in the *Census* stated that the figures for books in Arabic were "complete from 1927, [but] not necessarily complete prior to that year."

[126] See Ayalon, *Reading Palestine*, 67.

[127] Mills, *Census of Palestine 1931*, Vol. 1, 220. See also Mustafa Kabha, *Ha-'Itonut ha-'Aravit ha-Falastinit bi-Tkufat ha-Mandat ha-Briti 'al Erets-Yisrael* (Jerusalem: Yad Ben Zvi, 2004), 29.

involved in activities beyond the ordinary practice of law.[128] However, the institutional structures of the Arab legal community were less developed than those of the Jewish one. A voluntary national Jewish Bar Association was established in 1928. Arabs had local bar associations, but the National Arab Bar Association was only established in 1945 and remained inactive.[129] By the end of British rule in Palestine in 1948, there were 1,187 lawyers licensed to appear before the government courts of Palestine. Of these, 1,059 (90 percent) were Jews at a time when Jews comprised only a third of the population.[130] The dominance of Jews in the legal profession translated into a dominance in legal writing. Four Jewish legal periodicals appeared in Palestine during the period of the British Mandate, compared to just one Arabic legal periodical.[131] This discrepancy was also evident in the realm of law books. Very few law books in Arabic were written (or translated) in Palestine. According to the Census of 1931, only five of the thirty-nine books published in Arabic during the 1920s dealt with legal topics.[132]

128 See, e.g., Bayan Nuweihid al-Hout, "The Palestinian Political Elite During the Mandate Period," *Journal of Palestine Studies* 9 (1979): 85, 94–7; Reid, *Lawyers*, 295; Likhovski, *Law and Identity*, 173–210.

129 Reid, *Lawyers*, 312–13; Likhovski, *Law and Identity*, 25.

130 The numbers are based on the list of lawyers published in the *Palestine Gazette*, April 22, 1948, 309–20. See also Gal Amir and Na'ama Ben-Ze'ev, "Lawyers in Transition: Palestinian Arab Lawyers in the First Decade of the Jewish State," *Continuity and Change* 35 (2020): 371, 376 (noting that the 1946–47 Roll of Advocates listed only 110 Arab lawyers). It is possible to define the legal community in Palestine in a more capacious way to include, in addition to licensed lawyers, related professions such as petition writers, scholars of religious law, judges in the religious courts, and lay judges and arbitrators who were active in non-state forums of various sorts. See Yuval Ben Bassat, *Petitioning the Sultan: Protests and Justice in Late Ottoman Palestine* (London: I. B. Tauris, 2013) (on petition writers); Government of Palestine, *Report 1920–1921*, 91–3 (on the religious courts); Uri Kupferschmidt, *The Supreme Muslim Council: Islam under the British Mandate for Palestine* (Leiden: Brill, 1987), 78–84; Kamil al-'Asli, "Al-Fikr al-dini: al-'ulum al-islamiyyah fi Filastin," *al-Mawsu'ah al-filastiniyyah* (Beirut: n.p., 1990), Vol. 3, 443, 477–80 (discussing Islamic law experts).

131 Reid, *Lawyers*, 314–15. The Arab periodical was *al-Huquq*, which will be discussed below.

132 Mills, *Census of Palestine 1931*, Vol. 1, 219. The translators of Goadby's book on private international law into Arabic also complained in 1931 about the lack of law books in Arabic that law students at the Jerusalem Law Classes could use. See Hassan Sidqi al-Dajani and Salah al-Din al-'Abbasi, "kalimat al-mu'aribin," in Frederic M. Goadby, *Al-Qanun al-duwali wa-al-millali al-khass fi filastin wa-al-sharq*

One book in Arabic relevant, to some extent, to legal theory was a book on Bedouin customary law written by a leading Arab intellectual, ʻArif al-ʻArif, in the 1930s. However, ʻArif was neither a lawyer nor a legal scholar. Hence, his book did not provide a theoretical examination of the nature of Bedouin law nor even a history of this law. Instead, it was a descriptive survey of Bedouin society and customary norms.[133]

In the mid-1920s, Fahmi al-Husayni, an Arab lawyer, published a legal periodical, *al-Huquq*. This was a practitioner-oriented publication (unlike the Hebrew journal *Ha-Mishpat ha-ʻIvri*, which was published at around the same time and had an academic orientation). The articles in *al-Huquq* included reports on the decisions of courts in Palestine and abroad, police-related articles, and even poems. However, *al-Huquq* did carry some articles on the nature of law, comparative law surveys (for example, on ancient Egyptian, English, Jewish, Chinese, and Japanese law), and discussions of Islamic law and Islamic legal history. Many of these articles were translated from other languages or were written by non-Palestinian authors. For example, *al-Huquq* published a short translation of parts of Goadby's jurisprudence textbook or brief theoretical works written by Lebanese scholars ʻArif al-Nakdi and Issa Iskandar al-Maʻaluf. One could also find in it non-legal theoretical articles, such as excerpts from Karl Marx's *Communist Manifesto*.[134] The journal also contained reports exposing readers to Continental theories. For example, it published a report on the visit of the French anti-formalist legal scholar Léon Duguit to Egypt. This report briefly summarized Duguit's unique theory about the relationship between law and social solidarity.[135]

*al-adna* (Jerusalem: Matbaʻat bayt al-maqdas, 1931), 7. The books that *were* available were often summaries of lectures given at the Law Classes. See Francis Hayat, *Muhadarat fi al-qanun al-tijari* (Jerusalem: Dir al-rum, 1924); Abdel Latif Salah, *Sharh qanun al-muhakamat al-huquqiyyah* (Jerusalem: Madrasat dar al-aytam al-islamiyyah, 1924). See also Likhovski, *Law and Identity*, 173.

133 For a detailed discussion, see Likhovski, *Law and Identity*, 192–210.

134 For a discussion of the articles dealing with comparative and Islamic law, see Likhovski, *Law and Identity*, 179–83; Frederic Goadby, "Al-Qanun, al-haq, al-ʻadalah," *al-Huquq* 3 (1926): 7; ʻArif al-Nakdi, "Al-Qada' fi al-Islam," *al-Huquq* 3 (1926): 656, 850; Issa Iskandar al-Maʻaluf, "Al-Qada ʻind al-ʻArab," *al-Huquq* 3 (1926): 677; "Safhat min karl marx," *al-Huquq* 2(3) (1925): 1.

135 "Al-Ustaz dugi: ʻamid kulliyyat al-huquq al-jadid bil-qahirah," *al-Huquq* 2(10) (1925): 1, 5. Duguit was appointed the temporary Dean of the newly established

Few original theoretical works were published in *al-Huquq*. One example was an article by Husni ʻAbd al-Hadi, a lawyer from Nablus and a graduate of the Ottoman Law School in Istanbul, who wrote an article on the nature of obligations.[136] There were also some articles with a criminological focus, such as one written by Darwish Abu al-ʻAfiyah, which dealt with the economic and social factors causing crime and in which the Italian criminologist Cesare Lombroso was quoted, or an article about women as criminals that drew on the works of the French criminologist René Garraud.[137] In addition, in reviews published in the journal it is possible to find brief discussions about the progressive nature of Islamic law compared to European law and about the idea that the law of Muslim countries should reflect the "spirit" (*ruh*) of the Islamic nation.[138] There were also hints of a sentiment of pan-Asian solidarity in the journal, manifested in the publication of translated articles by Western writers on Chinese and Indian topics.[139]

## Conclusion

Despite its small size, Mandatory Palestine had a developed system of Western-style legal education. Law students in Palestine were exposed to English ideas about the nature of law and its development, but they

Faculty of Law of the Egyptian (now Cairo) University. See Léon Duguit, *Leçons de droit public général faites à la Faculté de droit de l'Université égyptienne* ... (Paris: Boccard, 1926), Preface; Leonard Wood, *Islamic Legal Revival: Reception of European Law and Transformations in Islamic Legal Thought in Egypt, 1875–1952* (Oxford: Oxford University Press, 2016), 153n1, 203–4.

136 Husni ʻAbd al-Hadi, "Muqayasat qawanin al-umam," *al-Huquq* 1 (1924): 227, 341.

137 Darwish Abu al-ʻAfiyah, "Al-ʻAwamil al-iqtisadiyyah wal-ijtimaʻiyyah min huduth al-jara'im," *al-Huquq* 1 (1924): 484, 670; "Al-Jins waal-jarimah," *al-Huquq* 2(2) (1925): 1, 2.

138 "Muqabalah bayn al-huquq al-romaniyyah waal-huquq al-islamiyyah waal-faransiyyah waal-inkliziyyah," *al-Huquq* 1 (1924): 909; "Al-Qada fi al-islam," *al-Huquq* 1 (1924): 911; "Durar al-hukkam fi al-suhuf waal-majalat," *al-Huquq* 2(7) (1925): 150, 151.

139 Gulilemo Frero, "al-Sharq waal-gharb," *al-Huquq* 2(8) (1925): 47; Kamil Samu'il Masiha, "Hayat al-ʻamilah bil-Sin," *al-Huquq* 1 (1924): 811. For a discussion of another example of the interest of a Palestinian-Arab lawyer in India during the period of the British Mandate, see Esmat Elhalaby, "Empire and Arab Indology," *Modern Intellectual History* 19 (2022): 1081 (discussing the works of the Lebanese-Palestinian lawyer and translator Wadiʻ Bustani).

were also exposed to state-of-the-art Continental anti-formalist theories. These were found in works written by English and Jewish legal scholars in Palestine about the philosophy and history of law. Like the Indian works discussed in Chapter 1, the writings produced in Palestine were characterized by cosmopolitanism and a willingness to critique English theories using examples taken from local law. Jewish scholars in Palestine were also interested in theoretical discussions on the nature and history of Jewish law, comparing it to Western law and using the comparison to make general claims about the nature of both systems. There were significant points of similarity between the institutional and intellectual histories of legal theory in colonial India and Mandatory Palestine. However, there were also substantial differences. Both will be explored now, in Interlude 1.

# *Interlude 1: Goals*

Colonial India and Mandatory Palestine both belonged to the British Empire, but they were very different territories. India was a core colony of the Empire. It was huge territorially, and it contained hundreds of millions of people. The British presence in India began in the seventeenth century as a commercial endeavor, later morphing into political rule. The centuries-long British presence made a profound impact on the politics and culture of India. In contrast, British rulers came to Palestine, a small territory with a tiny population, only at the end of the First World War and left after just a few decades, in 1948. While here, too, their presence had a long-lasting impact in certain respects, their legacy was certainly weaker compared to the case of India. The two territories and their respective populations were not only different in scale; the diversity and characteristics of the two societies, and the previous legal structures out of which the legal systems of the two territories were composed, also differed in myriad ways. However, the history of Western-style legal education in both places displayed similar traits.

In India and Palestine, the British established institutions that provided a formal legal education mainly based on imported English law and English legal theories. In both places, British – and, later, local – teachers used examples taken from local law to critique imported English theories. Colonial legal scholars in India and Palestine were also far more willing to refer to Continental jurisprudential theories in their works compared to contemporary English legal theorists. Some local legal scholars showed a keen interest in the jurisprudential analysis of their respective religious legal systems: Hindu law (and to some extent also Islamic law) in the case of India and Jewish law in the case of Mandatory Palestine. These scholars argued that these ancient systems, viewed by Western thinkers as being on a low rung of the legal evolutionary ladder, were not only the historical source of Western jurisprudential ideas but also contained notions and values that were more advanced and progressive than those found in Western law.

The interest that both Indian and Jewish law scholars displayed in the theoretical discussion of their ancient religious systems was born of the same ideology, nationalism – itself a Western transplant. Indian and Jewish nationalism, like nationalism in many other countries, Western and non-Western alike, went through a stage in which intellectuals sought to create a unified national identity by studying ancient national culture.[1] Specifically in the legal realm, the theoretical approach to the study of law that was identified with the German Historical School and with English historical jurisprudence motivated this interest in religious law. It was also motivated by a more fundamental human emotion: pride in one's long and resilient cultural heritage. For example, Jogendra Chunder Ghose, who taught law at the University of Calcutta, asserted in 1917 that:

> . . . the history of Hindu Law is the most wonderful chapter of the history of the world and of human institutions. Egypt and Babylon, Assyria and Persia . . . have passed away without a vestige remaining of their ancient institutions and religions . . . [they] have completely discarded their old religion, law and social institutions and adopted those of the Arabian prophet Mahomed . . .. The Brahmins of India however, maintained the old religion and the old law, through the many vicissitudes of two thousand years, and succeeded in

[1] See, e.g., Miroslav Hroch, *Social Preconditions of National Revival in Europe: A Comparative Analysis of the Social Composition of Patriotic Groups among the Smaller European Nations* (Cambridge: Cambridge University Press, 1985). It is interesting to note that the desire by colonial subjects to study and develop their own legal system in reaction to an engagement with the law of an empire is not necessarily a modern phenomenon. For an interesting argument about this sentiment in antiquity, see Yair Furstenberg, "Imperialism and the Creation of Local Law: The Case of Rabbinic Law," in *Legal Engagement: The Reception of Roman Law and Tribunals by Jews and Other Inhabitants of the Empire*, eds. Katell Bertholet et al. (Rome: École française de Rome, 2021), 271.

securing their ultimate victory ... [the] tenacity with which the [Hindus] have stuck to the old institutions and the old law is a wonderful phenomenon.[2]

Similarly, Rabbi Isaac Herzog, who served as a Chief Rabbi of Palestine in the 1930s and 1940s and had some affinity with the scholars of the Jewish legal revival movement, declared in 1936 that:

Rome, mistress of the ancient world, mighty in war and great in peace, destroyed the Jewish state and drove the Jewish people out of its magic land ... [Rome] has been admired throughout the centuries for her juristic genius. Her victim, Judaea, on the other hand, has not yet received due appreciation for her achievement in the field of law, an achievement which so strikingly attests [to] the intellectual powers of the Jewish race as well as its noble passion for righteousness.[3]

While the institutional and intellectual histories of legal theory in colonial India and Mandatory Palestine shared many similarities, there were also significant differences. In the institutional realm, the law schools of India were British creations. The most important institution that was examined in Chapter 1, the University of Calcutta College of Law, was created at the initiative of an Indian nationalist scholar, Asutosh Mookerjee. Nevertheless, it was part of a university that was ultimately governed by the British. In Palestine, too, British officials shaped the curriculum of one of the legal education institutions discussed earlier, the Jerusalem Law Classes (created as a vocational school rather than a university-affiliated academic institution). However, the two other institutions providing legal education, the Hebrew University and the Tel Aviv School, were both Zionist and they were created and operated independently of British rule – indeed, in the case of the Tel Aviv school, in opposition to it.

[2] Jogendra Chunder Ghose, *The Principles of Hindu Law*, 1st ed. (Calcutta: S. B. Chatterjee & Sons 1917), Vol. 2, i–ii. Some Westerners shared this sentiment: see Albert Swindlehurst, "Hindu Law and its Influence," *Yale Law Journal* 27 (1918): 857 ("when Britons roamed their forests clad in garments of skin and Teutonic tribes were concerned with little save war and tumult, the East had its legal systems, which were at once the product and the proof of a high civilization. Of these the most notable was that of the Brahmins, which regulated a vast territory and, with later additions, still governs the family relations of over two hundred millions of people").

[3] Isaac Herzog, *The Main Institutions of Jewish Law* (London: Soncino Press, 1936), Vol. 1, xv.

The colonial government's lack of involvement in law teaching at these two institutions had negative implications. The Hebrew University refrained from establishing a faculty of law, partly out of concern that doing so might antagonize the British authorities by competing with the Jerusalem Law Classes. The Tel Aviv School also suffered from the lack of government recognition. The law degree it conferred did not enable its graduates to take the Palestine Bar examinations, meaning they had to complete their studies abroad. However, the lack of British involvement also meant that the teaching of law at the Hebrew University and the Tel Aviv School placed a greater emphasis on studying Jewish law. This, together with many other factors, may have been one of the reasons that the effort to produce theoretical scholarship on the history and principles of (one of) the local religious legal systems seems to have been more sustained and broader in Mandatory Palestine than in colonial India, certainly relative to population size. In addition, unlike India, much of the scholarship in Palestine was produced by an unofficial organization, the Jewish Law Society, which had no Indian equivalent.

The institutional difference between law schools in India and Mandatory Palestine was related to a difference in the educational background and intellectual influences of the legal scholars in India and Palestine. In India, the authors I examined were mostly educated either in England or in the English-sponsored universities of India. Many were practicing lawyers who were in daily contact with India's court system, which applied anglicized Indian law. While some, such as Rattigan (who held a doctorate from a German university) and Basu (who wrote extensively on Continental legal theories), demonstrated an interest in Roman law and modern Continental jurisprudence, English legal theory remained the dominant influence in India.

This was not the case in Palestine. The legal system of Palestine and, more broadly, that of the Middle East was shaped by French law, which, in the nineteenth century, served as the primary European model for legal modernization in the Ottoman Empire and Egypt. As a result, even English authors such as Goadby had to be familiar with French law and French legal theories. In addition, most Jewish lawyers and legal scholars in Mandatory Palestine were immigrants who grew up and were educated in Central and Eastern Europe. Therefore, the primary source of influence on their ideas was not English thinkers such as Austin or Maine but the German Historical School, the Free Law Movement, and Russian scholars such as Petrażycki and Pokrovsky.

The different biographical trajectories of Indian and Jewish scholars also led to a difference in substantive ideas. Scholars in India rejected Austinian positivism and, more generally, nineteenth-century legal science, which saw the law as entirely autonomous. They also recognized the need to study law in anti-formalist ways, connecting legal research to society. However, because the leading anti-formalist jurisprudential theory they espoused was Maine's evolutionary approach, their scholarship on Hindu law was mainly historical and focused on the ancient history of this legal system. Their works were motivated by a desire to counter Western views of ancient Hindu law as backward and primitive and to show the past contribution of Indians to global jurisprudence.

Scholars in Palestine, too, espoused anti-formalism, but their version of it was more modern. It was sociological and sought to use a social sciences approach to study Jewish law. It was also more practical. While a historical perspective was undoubtedly present in works on Jewish law published in Palestine, these works also had a contemporary and applied edge. This, for example, was the case with Dikshtein's use of Free Law ideas to justify the anti-formalist approach that characterized judicial decision-making among the lay judges of the Hebrew Courts of Arbitration.

I would now like to focus on a comparison in the context of one specific topic: the goals of the theoretical scholarship in the two places. Here, too, one can point to both similarities and differences. In both India and Palestine, jurisprudential works shared the same pedagogical objective: to introduce students to the nature and history of law. In both places, works by local scholars also had an ideological, nationalist, goal: to foster pride in the national culture. However, in the case of Palestine only, another goal of the scholarship had to do with the idea of legal revival. The study of Jewish law was seen as a practical endeavor ultimately meant to lead to the use of the norms of Jewish law (belonging to legal fields such as contract or tort that could also be found in modern legal systems) as the basis of the legal system of the future independent state to be established once British colonial rule ended. In India, legal scholars did not argue that the anglicized contract law of India should be replaced by norms taken from Hindu contract law. Why was there a difference? The idea of Jewish legal revival originated in the scholarly and political program of the nineteenth-century German Historical School, which sought to use the national legal traditions of the German people as a source of norms of the new German civil code, the BGB. This program inspired the Jewish scholars but had less influence on the Indian ones. Jewish legal revival was also inspired by the successful revival of the Hebrew language, a major goal of cultural Zionism. In India, the desire to "revive" Sanskrit was far less influential.[4]

In colonial India, therefore, there were almost no calls to replace British-colonial law with Hindu law. This was not only the result of jurisprudential theories. Judaism, unlike Hinduism, has combined religious and national identity for three millennia, and Jewish law has been a central pillar of Jewish identity since antiquity. It was thus seen as amenable, despite the fact that it was a non-state legal system, to serve as the foundation of the legal system of a future Jewish nation-state, just like the revived Hebrew language. Hinduism is considerably more diverse than Judaism. Its numerous traditions, practices, and vast corpus of scriptures give rise to a broader spectrum of beliefs and practices compared to Judaism. Thus, Hindu law is more difficult to "revive" than Jewish law. The sources of Hindu law are also far less accessible to non-specialists than those of Jewish law. In addition, Hinduism generally, and Hindu law specifically, are also, in some sense, a modern British-colonial construct, which is not the case with Jewish law.

[4] On the revival of the Hebrew language see, e.g., Arieh B. Saposnik, *Becoming Hebrew: The Creation of a Jewish National Culture in Ottoman Palestine* (New York: Oxford University Press, 2008), 65–92. On Sanskrit, cf. Sheldon Pollock, "The Death of Sanskrit," *Comparative Studies in Society and History* 43 (2001): 392, 392–3; K. S. Kannan, ed., *Western Indology & Its Quest for Power: Proceedings of Swadeshi Indology Conference Series* (Chennai: Infinity Foundation India, 2017). See also Madhav M. Deshpande, "Efforts to Vernacularize Sanskrit: Degree of Success and Failure," in *Handbook of Languages and Ethnic Identity*, eds. Joshua A. Fishman and Ofelia García (Oxford: Oxford University Press, 2011), Vol. 2, 218. On the complexity to the notion of "revival" generally see, e.g., Tapan Raychaudhuri, *Europe Reconsidered: Perceptions of the West in Nineteenth-Century Bengal* (Delhi: Oxford University Press, 1988), 8–9 (discussing the problematic nature of using the term to "revival" to describe nineteenth-century Hindu revivalism in Bengal).

The idea of legal revival espoused by Jewish scholars was rooted in Continental notions of law being the product of the work of scholars rather than legislators or judges. While ancient Hindu law was also a product of scholars, modern English jurisprudential notions that connected the law to the state and its officials dominated Indian legal education during the colonial period and, it seems, also dominated the imagination of Indian scholars. The influence of English jurisprudential traditions made it more difficult for Indians to accept the idea of legal revival by actors unconnected to the state.

Differences in the nature of Hindu and Jewish religion and law were accompanied by differences in the social and political context in which Indian and Jewish scholars worked. Hindu law, and certainly its text-based, British-influenced colonial version, was associated with upper-caste, Brahmin, "high-culture," urban elites.[5] Unlike Jewish law, it was therefore identified only with specific segments of the society it was supposed to govern. The fact that Hindu law was based on and identified with the notion of caste division was anathema to the egalitarian promises of the Indian Nationalist Movement, especially once it moved to its mass mobilization phase. Furthermore, reviving those parts of Hindu law that were outside the realm of personal law would have undermined the vision that independent India would be a secular state based on Hindu–Muslim unity. Finally, the legal profession's power in India, committed as it was to anglicized Indian law, also impeded calls for the revival of Hindu law.[6]

[5] See, e.g., Upendra Baxi, "People's Law in India – the Hindu Society," in *Asian Indigenous Law: In Interaction with Received Law*, ed. Masaji Chiba (London: KPI, 1986), 216, 223–30.

[6] See, generally, Marc Galanter, "The Displacement of Traditional Law in Modern India," *Journal of Social Issues* 24 (1968): 65, 69–76; Marc Galanter, "The Aborted Restoration of 'Indigenous' Law in India," in *Law and Society in Modern India* (Delhi: Oxford University Press, 1997), 37. It is interesting to note that in his 1968 article Galanter compared the Indian experience with that of Israel, Pakistan, and Ireland. See Galanter, "Displacement," 35. See also Werner Menski, "Hindu Law in Modern Times: How Hindu Law Continues in Modern India," in *The Oxford History of Hinduism: Modern Hinduism*, ed. Torkel Brekke (Oxford: Oxford University Press, 2019), 244–5. Of course, it is possible to find, even in India, some exceptions. See, e.g., K. S. Ramaswami Sastri, "The Evolution of Law as a Science and as a Profession in India," *Hindu Law Journal* 5(10) (April 1923): 1, 16–18 (an article by a South Indian judge stating that it was the national duty of Indian lawyers "to incorporate in our substantive and adjective law the best elements of the ancient Indian system of jurisprudence," rather than applying Western law wholesale, since Hindu law was

The notion of Jewish legal revival faced political opposition from various quarters, too: conservative Orthodox rabbis unwilling to agree to any tampering with, or modernization of, Jewish law; secular Zionists who argued that, unlike the Hebrew language, which could be (and was indeed) secularized, Jewish law was too tightly bound to Jewish religion; and also anglicized lawyers who feared that Jewish law would undermine their livelihood, which was based on their familiarity with the British-colonial system. This combined opposition ultimately led to the failure of the movement for Jewish legal revival and to the adoption of the British-colonial law of Mandatory Palestine as the basis of the postcolonial Israeli State.[7] However, the relative robustness of the demands for legal revival in Mandatory Palestine, compared to colonial India, meant that the scholarly interest in the theoretical study of the jurisprudence and history of religious law was more substantial among Jewish scholars in Palestine than it was among Hindu scholars in India.

These differences, and others, between Indian and Jewish scholars will also be evident in the next part of the book, which is devoted to a description and comparison of the life and thought of two legal scholars, Radhabinod Pal and Samuel Eisenstadt, who were both significant actors in their respective scholarly communities.

"as enlightened and humane and refined as the Roman law and is nearer to our hearts and lives").

[7] On the failure of the Jewish legal revival movement, see, e.g., Assaf Likhovski, *Law and Identity in Mandate Palestine* (Chapel Hill, NC: University of North Carolina Press, 2006), 152–3. See also Ronen Shamir, *The Colonies of Law: Colonialism, Zionism and Law in Early Mandate Palestine* (Cambridge: Cambridge University Press, 2000).

PART II

# INDIVIDUAL SCHOLARS

3

# The Life and Jurisprudential Ideas of Radhabinod Pal

The Indian jurist Radhabinod Pal passed away in 1967, yet he has become an academic celebrity in recent years. Pal is famous in some quarters and notorious in others for his dissenting opinion in the Tokyo War Crimes Trial (1946–48), in which he sought to acquit twenty-five leaders of wartime Japan who were accused of crimes against peace, crimes against humanity, war crimes, and murder (see Figure 3.1).[1]

His lengthy opinion in that case, which was motivated by anti-colonial sentiments, has been lauded by some scholars as an early example of TWAIL (Third World Approaches to International Law) scholarship. It is, therefore, no wonder that most of the works written about him have been written by international law scholars.[2]

Pal also wrote extensively on the history and philosophy of Hindu law, but his works on these topics have received far less scholarly

[1] See Radhabinod Pal, *International Military Tribunal for the Far East: Dissentient Judgement of Justice Pal* (Tokyo: Kokusho Kankokai, 1999); Nariaki Nakazato, *Neonationalist Mythology in Postwar Japan: Pal's Dissenting Judgment at the Tokyo War Crimes Tribunal* (Lanham, MD: Lexington Books, 2016); Timothy Brook, "Radhabinod Pal on the Rape of Nanking: The Tokyo Judgment and the Guilt of History," in *The Nanking Atrocity 1937–38: Complicating the Picture*, ed. Bob Tadashi Wakabayashi, 2nd ed. (New York: Berghahn Books, 2017), 149; Gary J. Bass, *Judgment at Tokyo: World War II on Trial and the Making of Modern Asia* (New York: Knopf, 2023), 207–27, 585–9.

[2] See, e.g., Sujith Xavier, "Locating and Situating Justice Pal: TWAIL, International Criminal Tribunals, and Judicial Powers," *Asian Journal of International Law* 12 (2022): 292.

FIGURE 3.1 Radhabinod Pal, 1947. National Archives of the Netherlands.

attention. Some scholars have entirely ignored Pal's theoretical works. Others have mentioned them, but they are not the primary focus of the discussion. Pal's most detailed biography was written by the Japanese historian Nariaki Nakazato. Nakazato's book seeks to provide a nuanced (and somewhat unflattering portrait) of Pal in order to counter the "Pal cult" prevalent in Japanese right-wing revisionist circles.[3] Although Nakazato does discuss Pal's works on the philosophy and history of Hindu law, these are not central to the book.[4] Other authors exploring Pal's jurisprudential thought seek, like Nakazato, to provide a thicker context to Pal's Tokyo dissent.[5]

[3] Nakazato, *Neonationalist Mythology*, xxxii–xxxiii, 139–216. Nakazato mentions various connections between Hindu nationalists, with whom Pal was affiliated, and fascism and Nazism, and also notes some problematic aspects of Pal's own writings. See Nakazato, *Neonationalist Mythology*, 119, 133–4, 159–60.

[4] Nakazato, *Neonationalist Mythology*, 128–34.

[5] See Ashis Nandy, "The Other Within: The Strange Case of Radhabinod Pal's Judgment on Culpability," *New Literary History* 23 (1992): 45; Milinda Banerjee, "Does International Criminal Justice Require a Sovereign? Historicising Radhabinod Pal's Tokyo Judgment in Light of His 'Indian' Legal Philosophy," in *Historical Origins of International Criminal Law*, eds. Morten Bergsmo, Wui Ling Cheah, and Ping Yi (Brussels: Torkel Opsahl Academic EPublisher, 2014), Vol. 2, 67; Milinda Banerjee, *The Mortal God: Imagining the Sovereign in Colonial India* (Cambridge: Cambridge University Press, 2018), 261–2; Milinda Banerjee, "Sovereignty as a Motor of Global

None of these works examines Pal's jurisprudential ideas in their own right, unlike this chapter, whose focus is Pal's jurisprudential works rather than his Tokyo dissent.

## Life and Works

Pal was born in 1886 in a village in the Kushtia district of Bengal, now part of Bangladesh. He came from a family that belonged to an artisan (potters) caste.[6] His father disappeared when Pal was just three years old. However, his uneducated but ambitious mother pushed the child to excel in his studies, having as a model Sir Gooroodas Banerjee, a Bengali judge of the Calcutta High Court and the first Indian vice-chancellor of the University of Calcutta.[7] After studying at a series of provincial schools and at Rajshahi College in northern Bengal, Pal enrolled at the best Indian college of the time, Presidency College in Calcutta, where he acquired a master's degree in mathematics in 1907. In 1909, he obtained a law degree from Ripon College, another Calcutta institution. Between 1908 and 1911, Pal worked as a clerk in the Accountant-General's office in Allahabad. In 1911, he returned to Bengal and, until 1920, taught mathematics at Ananda Mohan College in the town of Mymensingh, north of Dacca, and also practiced law there. In 1920, Pal earned a master's degree in law from the University of Calcutta, and, at the suggestion of Sir Asutosh Mookerjee, the leading Bengali lawyer and educator, he resigned from his post at Mymensingh and moved to Calcutta.

In 1921, Pal started practicing as an advocate in the Calcutta High Court, and in 1923, he took up a teaching post at the Calcutta University College of Law. His doctorate, awarded in 1924, was

Conceptual Travel: Sanskritic Equivalents of 'Law' in Bengali Discursive Production," *Modern Intellectual History* 17 (2020): 487; Rohini Sen and Rashmi Raman, "Retelling Radha Binod Pal: The Outsider and the Native," in *The Dawn of a Discipline: International Criminal Justice and Its Early Exponents*, eds. Frédéric Mégret and Immi Tallgren (Cambridge: Cambridge University Press, 2020), 230.

6 See Nakazato, *Neonationalist Mythology*, 77–84. See also Somnath Pal, *Justice Dr. Radhabinod Pal: A Phenomenal & Inspirational Life's Journey*, trans. Asok Kumar Ray (New Delhi: Akansha Publishing House, 2020), 1–7.

7 Nakazato, *Neonationalist Mythology*, 84.

based on a dissertation on the Hindu philosophy of law.[8] Pal's interest in the topic may have been the result of the influence of his mentor, Mookerjee, or perhaps even the fact that his childhood model, Sir Gooroodas Banerjee, had also written on the topic.[9]

As a lawyer, Pal specialized in income tax litigation, serving as a legal advisor to the Government of India's Income Tax Department.[10] In the early 1940s, he was appointed to a temporary judicial position as an officiating judge of the Calcutta High Court. Between 1944 and 1946, Pal held the position of Vice-Chancellor of the University of Calcutta. On three occasions, he was invited to deliver the prestigious Tagore Law Lectures. Only one other lecturer in the history of this lecture series had this honor bestowed on them three times.[11]

In April 1946, Pal was appointed the Indian judge in the Tokyo Trial. Given his nationalist leanings, it is somewhat surprising that the British rulers of India nominated him – but this was probably due to a

8 Nakazato, *Neonationalist Mythology*, 95. The University of Calcutta awarded very few doctoral degrees in law. Pal was the fourteenth recipient of such a degree since the inception of the university. In the 1920s, only three such degrees were awarded. See *Hundred Years of the University of Calcutta: A History of the University Issued in Commemoration of the Centenary Celebration*, eds. Pramathanath Banerjee et al. (Calcutta: University of Calcutta Press, 1957), 446.

9 See Gooroodass Banerjee, *The Hindu Law of Marriage and Stridhan* (Calcutta: Thacker Spink and Co., 1879).

10 Pal wrote the leading commentary on the Indian Income Tax Act. See Radhabinod Pal, *The Law of Income Tax in British India: Being Act XI of 1922 as Amended by Act VII of 1939, with Explanatory Notes and Commentary* (Calcutta: Eastern Law House, 1940), Vol. 1. He also published a book on the law of limitations. See Radhabinod Pal, *The Law of Limitations in British India* (Calcutta: N. M. Raychowdhury & Co., 1933).

11 Pal gave the 1925 Tagore Law Lectures on the comparative history of the law of primogeniture (delivered in 1926), the 1930 Tagore Law Lectures on the Hindu philosophy of law (delivered in 1932), and the 1938 Tagore Law Lectures on crimes in international relations (delivered in 1951). See Radhabinod Pal, *The History of the Law of Primogeniture: With Special Reference to India, Ancient and Modern* [the Tagore Law Lectures, 1925] (Calcutta: University of Calcutta, 1929) [hereinafter "Pal, *Law of Primogeniture*"]. An earlier version of the 1929 book is Radha Binode Pal, *The History of the Law of Primogeniture: With Special Reference to India, Ancient and Modern (intended for Tagore Law Lectures, 1923)* (Calcutta: Oriental Press, 1922) (a copy is available at the British Library); Radhabinod Pal, *The History of Hindu Law in the Vedic Age and in Post-Vedic Times down to the Institutes of Manu* (Calcutta: University of Calcutta Press, 1958) [hereinafter "Pal, *History*," or "1958 book"]; Radhabinod Pal, *Crimes in International Relations* [the Tagore Law Lectures, 1938] (Calcutta: University of Calcutta Press, 1955). See also Nakazato, *Neonationalist Mythology*, 96, 133.

bureaucratic blunder by the British authorities. Pal was neither the first nor the second choice for the position. The initial nominee declined due to health issues, while the second failed to respond altogether. With the deadline for nominating an Indian judge rapidly approaching, British officials hastily turned to a pool of retired and serving Indian High Court judges. Although Pal was only a temporary judge at the time and did not strictly meet the qualifications, he applied and was ultimately selected. Owing to the urgency of the situation, no thorough evaluation of his political views was conducted.[12] Pal had already been involved in high-profile international legal activities before the Tokyo Trial. In 1937, for instance, he was appointed joint chairman of the International Academy of Comparative Law. However, it was Pal's dissent in Tokyo that made him famous the world over, especially in Japan, where his opinion was perceived in some circles as a sign of Asian solidarity against Western imperialism. After the Tokyo Trial, Pal served in a series of prominent positions. In 1952, he was elected to the UN-sponsored International Law Commission, becoming its chairman in 1958 and again in 1962. In 1957, he became a judge of the Permanent Court of Arbitration in The Hague, and in 1959, he was appointed National Professor of Jurisprudence by the Indian Government.

While Pal's political views and affiliations changed over the course of his life, generally speaking, he can be described as an anti-colonial thinker influenced by pan-Asian ideas, Indian nationalism, and (to a certain extent) also Hindu nationalism.[13] The sources of his Pan-Asian ideology go back to 1905. In the spring of that year, Japan won the Russo-Japanese War, providing a model for anti-colonial activists across the non-Western world. In Bengal, Japan's victory coincided with a political crisis that was the result of the partitioning of the province by the British, inspiring a nationalist awakening with which Pal came to identify.[14]

[12] Nakazato, *Neonationalist Mythology*, 7–9; Bass, *Judgment at Tokyo*, 224–7.

[13] See Nakazato, *Neonationalist Mythology*, xxii, 51, 65, 106, 117–28, 219; Banerjee, "Does International Criminal Justice Require a Sovereign?" 86–8.

[14] See, generally, Cemil Aydin, *The Politics of Anti-Westernism in Asia: Visions of World Order in Pan-Islamic and Pan-Asian Thought* (New York: Columbia University Press, 2007); Sumit Sarkar, *The Swadeshi Movement in Bengal*, new ed. (Ranikhet: Permanent Black, 2010); Carolien Stolte and Harald Fischer-Tiné,

Pal had several friends who were Indian nationalist activists. When he was a student at Presidency College he befriended Sarat Chandra Bose, the elder brother of Subhas Chandra Bose. Later, he would become an admirer of Bose's younger brother. The young Bose was the president of the Congress Party in the late 1930s. During the Second World War, he fled India to Nazi Germany. He was later appointed Commander of the Indian National Army, a military force that collaborated with the Japanese Army. Other acquaintances of Pal, too, or their relatives, were involved in radical Indian nationalist agitation and anti-British terrorism in Bengal.[15]

Pal was also connected with people associated with Hindu rather than Indian nationalism. In 1923, the Hindu nationalist activist V. D. Savarkar popularized the term *Hindutva* (Hinduness) to designate this ideology, which identified contemporary Hindus with the ancient Aryans and the Sanskrit language and argued that all Hindus shared a common race and a common culture. The notion of *Hindutva* was propounded by several radical right-wing political movements in India during the late-colonial period, movements that were somewhat inspired by, or had ties with, European fascism.[16] Pal was in close contact with Syama Prasad Mookerjee, the son of his University of Calcutta mentor, Asutosh Mookerjee. Syama Prasad, like his father, served as Vice-Chancellor of the University of Calcutta in the 1930s and then embarked on a Hindu nationalist political career. In 1943, Syama Prasad became president of the nationalist party Hindu Mahasabha. In 1951, he founded the right-wing Bharatiya Jana Sangh, a precursor to the Bharatiya Janata Party, one of the two major Indian political parties today. Like his father, Syama Prasad

"Imagining Asia in India: Nationalism and Internationalism (ca. 1905–1940)," *Comparative Studies in Society and History* 54 (2012): 65.

15 Nakazato, *Neonationalist Mythology*, 23, 88, 118, 218–19; Bass, *Judgment at Tokyo*, 222–3.

16 On early twentieth-century Hindu nationalism, see, e.g., Christophe Jaffrelot, *The Hindu Nationalist Movement in India* (New York: Columbia University Press, 1996); Chetan Bhatt, *Hindu Nationalism: Origins, Ideologies and Modern Myths* (Oxford: Berg, 2001); Manjari Katju, "The History of Hindu Nationalism in India," in *The Oxford History of Hinduism: Modern Hinduism*, ed. Torkel Brekke (Oxford: Oxford University Press, 2019), 203. On the relationship between Hindu nationalism, fascism, and Nazism during the colonial period, see, generally, Marzia Casolari, *In the Shadow of the Swastika: The Relationships between Indian Radical Nationalism, Italian Fascism and Nazism* (London: Routledge, 2020).

espoused a cultural-nationalist vision of Indian higher education.[17] Pal's relationship with Syama Prasad and his followers at the University of Calcutta was somewhat uneasy.[18] However, his main biographer, Nakazato, states that he was associated with the "periphery" of the Hindu Mahasabha party and "had many things in common with what is today called Hindu nationalism."[19]

During Pal's term as Vice-Chancellor of the University of Calcutta, he was involved in several nationalist incidents: In his 1945 convocation speech, Pal mentioned the need to serve the cause of Indian freedom, prompting the British Governor of Bengal to storm out of the hall. In the following year, Pal invited Jawaharlal Nehru, the future prime minister of India, newly released from a British prison, to give a convocation speech. Pal, together with Syama Prasad Mookerjee, was also present during violent student demonstrations that took place in Calcutta in November 1945 in protest at the trial of Indian National Army officers by the British.[20]

Pal published several books during his lifetime. This chapter will focus on his works on Hindu law. Modern specialists do not hold these works in high regard, and they are seldom cited.[21] However, my interest lies not in a "vertical" chronological discussion of the history of the modern scholarship on Hindu law, or Pal's influence (or lack thereof) on it, but in comparing some of the major themes found in

[17] On the Hindu Mahasabha Party, see Prabhu Bapu, *Hindu Mahasabha in Colonial North India,1915–1930: Constructing Nation and History* (New York: Routledge, 2013). For an example of Syama Prasad's vision, see, e.g., Syamaprasad Mookerjee, "Heritage of India [a lecture delivered in 1937 at Patna University]," in *Anthology of University College of Law Centenary Celebration 1909–2009* (Calcutta: Registrar of the University of Calcutta, 2010), 33, 38.

[18] See Bass, *Judgment at Tokyo*, 224, 637, 646.

[19] Nakazato, *Neonationalist Mythology*, 118–19, 219. But see Partha Chatterjee, *I Am the People: Reflections of Popular Sovereignty Today* (New York: Columbia University Press, 2020), 9 (claiming that Pal was not a Hindu nationalist).

[20] Nakazato, *Neonationalist Mythology*, 100–3; Somnath Pal, *Justice Dr. Radhabinod Pal*, 84–6; Bass, *Judgment at Tokyo*, 223–4; "Defiant I. N. A. Day Crowd in Calcutta: Police Open Fire, Congress Leaders' Appeal Unheeded," *The Times of India*, November 22, 1945; "Have a Vision of New India: Mr. Nehru's Call to Students," *Times of India*, March 11, 1946; Radhabinod Pal, "Convocation Address," *The Calcutta Review* (April 1946), 1. Pal's association with Syama Prasad Mookerjee and his brand of right-wing Hindu nationalism continued after Indian independence. See Nakazato, *Neonationalist Mythology*, 107–8.

[21] See Nakazato, *Neonationalist Mythology*, 136.

Pal's works with those found in the work of the other legal scholar whose thought I will examine in detail in the next chapter, on Samuel Eisenstadt.

Pal's doctoral dissertation served as the basis for his book *The Hindu Philosophy of Law in the Vedic and Post-Vedic Times Prior to the Institutes of Manu*. This book was published in Calcutta around the mid-1920s.[22] It was then used for Pal's 1930 Tagore Law Lectures, which he delivered in 1932.[23] The lectures were ultimately published in 1958 in a book entitled *The History of Hindu Law in the Vedic Age and in Post-Vedic Times Down to the Institutes of Manu*.[24]

The relatively short 1920s book was mainly based on Pal's reading of the Vedic hymns augmented by some references to works of Indologists such as Max Müller and the writings of Western political and legal philosophers – from Aristotle and Plato to Hobbes, Kant, John Austin, and Roscoe Pound. Pal began his book by discussing the importance of studying the "early Hindu fundamental conceptions of law" to reveal "the eternal glory of the old Hindu-philosophical-legal mind." This perspective was important, he argued, both because ancient Greece and Rome were "indebted to Vedic India," which had influenced their conception of law, and also because studying this history was "essential for a Hindu," since law reflects "the immutable soul of the races."[25] A brief overview of major Western theories of law followed. Pal then moved to a survey of the legal ideas embodied in specific Vedic hymns, attempting to attribute particular

[22] Radhabinod Pal, *The Hindu Philosophy of Law in the Vedic and Post-Vedic Times prior to the Institutes of Manu* ([Calcutta]: Biswabhandar press, n.d.) [hereinafter "Pal, *Philosophy*," or "1920s book"]. The British Library catalog entry states that the date of publication is 1927. The catalog of the library of the Max Planck Institute for Comparative Public Law states that the book was published c. 1925. Nakazato dates it to "circa 1926." See Nakazato, *Neonationalist Mythology*, 129. Two earlier related books were Radhabinod Pal, *History of Hindu Law During the Vedic and Post-Vedic Ages Down to the Age of Manusmriti: Introductory Lecture (Intended for Tagore Law Lectures 1918–1919)* (Calcutta: Lily Press, 1918) [hereinafter "Pal, *Introductory Lecture*"] and Radhabinod Pal, *The History of Hindu Law in the Vedic age and in the Post-Vedic Times down to the Institutes of Manu (Intended for Tagore Law Lectures 1928)* (Calcutta: Biswabhandar Press, [1927]) (which contained one complete chapter and several chapters in synopsis form only). On the dates of these books, see also Banerjee, "Does International Criminal Justice Require a Sovereign?," 73, n. 6.

[23] See Pal, *History*, title page and Preface. [24] Pal, *History*.

[25] Pal, *Philosophy*, ii, 2, 3.

legal (but also theological and cosmological) ideas to specific Vedic sages. Pal also discussed legal concepts common to all "early Aryans" during the Vedic period. His survey then turned to the Hindu philosophy of law during the Brahmana and Sutra periods, when Hindu thinkers came to emphasize the function of law as a method for preserving the status quo, including the caste system.[26] Major themes in Pal's analysis included the ends of the law, the social order, the Hindu doctrines of welfare and utility, the origin and role of the state, the sources of law, the place of custom as a source of law, and the role of reason in the creation of legal norms.

Pal's 1958 book, *The History of Hindu Law*, was far longer than his earlier *Hindu Philosophy of Law* and contained two parts. In the first part, Pal discussed Vedic society, political institutions, and the legal philosophy of the Vedic period, followed by developments in Hindu legal philosophy in the later Brahmana and Sutra periods. The second part of the book was devoted to an overview of the norms of Hindu law in the different epochs between the Vedic period and Manu's Code, each chapter discussing several categories of law (the law of persons, property, contract, crime, and procedure).

Another work related to Pal's interest in Hindu law was *The History of the Law of Primogeniture: With Special Reference to India, Ancient and Modern*, based on his 1925 Tagore Law Lectures, delivered in 1926. The 558-page book, published in 1929, was extremely ambitious. Unlike most other Tagore Lectures, it was not confined to India but dealt with the comparative history of primogeniture. The parts dealing with regions outside India were based on secondary literature, while those dealing with India were original.[27] About half of the book was devoted to the global history of primogeniture outside India, containing chapters addressing the ancient world (Egypt, Babylonia, Greece, and Rome), England and English-speaking territories, France, Germany, Russia, China, and Japan. The second half dealt with the history of primogeniture in India from antiquity to the present, beginning with Vedic and post-Vedic times, moving to the period of Islamic rule, and lastly, discussing

[26] Ibid., 109, 141.

[27] Pal, *Law of Primogeniture*, v (where Pal makes the distinction between the chapters dealing with the history of primogeniture "in Europe" (which also referred to other places outside India) and those dealing with India).

British India. The work was broad both in its geographical scope and also in its examination of a wide range of legal fields. It analyzed family law, the law of inheritance, property law, and various subfields of public law, such as constitutional, administrative, and tax law. The attempt to trace the global evolution of the concept of primogeniture led Pal to examine the history of this notion beyond private law, venturing into the rules regarding the inheritance of official positions, including those of kings or tax collectors.

## Ideas

### *Western Jurisprudential Influences*

Pal's works echoed themes found in nineteenth-century nationalist, evolutionary, and racial theories of law that appeared in Germany and England. It seems that Pal drew from the early nineteenth-century German Historical School the notion that law reflected the "spirit of the people" or, as he put it, "a people's individuality and originality ... finds expression notably in its law."[28] The mid nineteenth-century evolutionary version of the historical approach to law, embodied in the work of English scholar Henry Maine, also influenced Pal. One conspicuous influence of Maine's work was found in Pal's attitude to the type of sources that could be used to study ancient law and legal thought. A major source used by Pal in all his works was the Vedic hymns. Here, he followed Henry Maine's approach in his book *Ancient Law* of using poetry to reconstruct ancient law. Just as Maine turned to Homer to learn about the law of the ancient Greeks, so Pal turned to the ancient Vedic hymns, extracting from them "concepts of law."[29] Pal was also inspired by and accepted the idea that there were evolutionary stages through which every legal system was supposed to pass.[30]

While a major jurisprudential influence on Pal's scholarship was Henry Maine's evolutionary legal thought, Pal's works also showed an awareness of developments in early twentieth-century Western jurisprudence, especially the growing influence of sociology. His 1918 *Introductory Lecture* discussed the history of the Vedic Aryans

[28] Pal, *Philosophy*, 3. [29] Ibid., 13. [30] Pal, *Law of Primogeniture*, 1, 35, 170.

with reference to the works of the nineteenth-century sociologist Herbert Spencer.[31] In his 1920s book *The Hindu Philosophy of Law*, Pal mentioned the works of two pioneers of the field of legal sociology, the American scholar Roscoe Pound and the Austrian scholar Eugen Ehrlich. In this book, Pal wrote that historical jurisprudence was "discredited for the moment" and observed that "the fashion of the time calls for a sociological legal history" that is a study not merely of how legal doctrines evolved in the past but also "the social causes and social effects of legal doctrines" and the relationship of legal history to social and economic history. Given the lack of sources, it was impossible, Pal admitted, to offer a thorough sociological analysis of how the social circumstances of the ancient Aryans gave rise to their legal ideas.[32] Nevertheless, Pal's general understanding of the law was certainly influenced by the sociological approach, as is evident in his functionalist analysis of ancient Hindu law as a mechanism serving the "mundane" purpose of "the preservation of society" by providing stability.[33]

### *The Antiquity and Superiority of Ancient Hindu Law Compared to Western Law*

Nineteenth-century European representations of Hindu law, and of "Oriental law" more broadly, frequently cast it in a negative light, especially in contrast to Western legal traditions. Pal dedicated significant portions of his work to challenging these portrayals. His strategy, which mirrored that of many non-Western intellectuals of the era, can be described as a form of "triumphal apologetics," that is, an argumentative approach that not only sought to refute Western depictions but also asserted that Hindu law was in fact both more ancient and superior to its Western counterpart.[34]

[31] See Pal, *Introductory Lecture*, 17, 22, 41. Spencer inspired many of the intellectuals involved in the creation of Hindu nationalism. See Bhatt, *Hindu Nationalism*, 28–9, 52–4, 81–2, 90.

[32] See Pal, *Philosophy*, 3–10, 81.

[33] Pal, *Philosophy*, 175.

[34] On "triumphal apologetics," see, generally, Alexander Kaye, *The Invention of Jewish Theocracy: The Struggle for Legal Authority in Modern Israel* (New York: Oxford University Press, 2020), 54. See also Faisal Devji, "Apologetic Modernity," *Modern Intellectual History* 4 (2007): 61 (discussing apologetics in the India context, focusing on nineteenth-century India-Muslim thinkers).

Pal opened *The Hindu Philosophy of Law* with the argument, taken from the German legal philosopher Fritz Berolzheimer, that the legal and ethical conceptions of the Vedic Aryans influenced the ancient Greeks and Romans and, through them, all later European nations.[35] His 1929 book, *Law of Primogeniture*, too, praised non-Western law, generally, and Hindu law in particular. According to Pal, India, Babylonia, and China were "the three seats of archaic civilization," and "the ancient history of each is absolutely free from European influence."[36] In his 1958 book, Pal also made efforts to show the antiquity of Hindu law. In the Preface, Pal observed that "the history of Hindu law in the Vedic age really marks the dawn of law itself on this planet."[37] Relying again on the work of Berolzheimer, Pal argued that the Hindu concept of cosmic (and human) order, *rita*, as the basis of all law, influenced Greek, Roman, and Christian thinkers. Indian ideas were thus "antecedents of later legal and ethical developments among the Greeks and Romans."[38] At another point in his book, Pal criticized Western scholars who sought to "minimize … Vedic civilization" by dating the ancient collection of Sanskrit hymns, the *Rigveda*, to the year 1000 BC, thus implying that Hindu civilization appeared later than those of Egypt and Mesopotamia. Instead, Pal, relying on the works of previous scholars, argues that the beginning of Vedic culture dates back to about 6000 BC and, thus, predated "Babylon and Egypt."[39]

[35] Pal, *Philosophy*, 1–2, 10. See also Fritz Berolzheimer, *The World's Legal Philosophies*, trans. Rachel Szold Jastrow (Boston, MA: Boston Book Company, 1912), 37. This approach echoed European views of India as the cradle of civilization. See Edwin F. Bryant, *The Quest for the Origins of Vedic Culture: The Indo-Aryan Migration Debate* (New York: Oxford University Press, 2001), 18.

[36] Pal, *Law of Primogeniture*, 67, 87–8. [37] Pal, *History*, iii.

[38] Ibid., iv, 109–10. For earlier, similar, claims, see Janaki Nath Pal Sastri, "Hindu Jurisprudence," *Calcutta Law Journal* 8–9 (1908–09): 21n, 23n ("the deeper and more pervading spirit of Hindu philosophy had penetrated into the very depths of Plato's soul through Pythagoras … the doctrines of Pythagoras are oriental to the backbone, and even Brahmanical"); Nagendra Nath Mukerjee, "Indo-Aryan Penal Jurisprudence," *Calcutta Law Journal* 14 (1911): 29n (claiming that "India is the historical cradle of Jurisprudence. This Jurisprudence Hindu merchants and emigrants must have carried across the sea to the shores of more than one distant country," and also claiming that Egyptian, Greek, and Jewish law were all influenced by Hindu law).

[39] Pal, *History*, 7–9. He cited the eccentric works of Indian nationalist Bal Gangadhar Tilak on the topic, as well as the German Indologist, Hermann Jacobi.

Pal did not merely claim that Hindu law was older than Western law. He also claimed that it was better. In his 1920s book, he compared Hindu law to Roman law and "Semitic law" and sought to demonstrate the superiority of Hindu law and Hindu jurists, whom he described as pioneers in creating law and legal philosophy. It is not surprising, therefore, to find that Pal ended this book with a call to his readers to "admire and marvel how in the dim past, when the rest of the world was as yet steeped in darkness, these savants [the ancient Hindu jurists] reached at the light to light the path of future generations, how they struggled, with all their keenness of intellect, to harmonise the discordant and to evolve a cosmos out of a pervading chaos."[40]

Pal argued that the monotheistic notions of the "unity of God" and the "brotherhood of man" first appeared in India and that, unlike other cultures in which the ideas of the unity of God had led, ironically, to intolerance and persecution, the Vedic Aryans did not succumb to religious dogmatism. This noble tradition, Pal noted, continued in Buddhism, which alone, out of all great world religions, flourished without persecution, censorship, or inquisitions and, in this respect, was "enormously superior to Christianity." Pal characterized Christianity as a religion that is "wedded to militarism" and justifies its "bloodthirsty tendencies" by "an appeal to the savage Bronze-Age literature of the Old Testament." In contrast, Hindus and Buddhists, Pal argued, lived side by side in India in peace and were never "guilty ... of criminal lunacies [such] as the religious wars of the sixteenth and seventeenth centuries" in Europe.[41] Regarding earlier eras, Pal noted that the culture of the Vedic Aryans was "far in advance of the culture and civilization of the same period of the people of the countries from which it is said they migrated to India." In India, therefore, "there was no twilight before dawn" because "the great people which has led the van of Indian culture have left no record of slow and painful struggle onwards through lessening darkness of barbarism towards the light of civilization."[42]

[40] Pal, *Philosophy*, 175–6. [41] Pal, *History*, 244–6.

[42] Ibid., 36–8. In the footnote to this passage, Pal mentioned Lionel D. Barnett's book *The Heart of India* but, in fact, he was quoting another book by Barnett. See Lionel D. Barnett, *Antiquities of India* (London: Warner, 1913), 1.

*Evolutionary Schemes, Social Hierarchies, Democracy*

Moving to specific topics often found in Western works, negative portrayals of Hindu law mentioned its static nature, its lack of systematization, and its amorality. Western critiques of Hindu law also noted that the substance of Hindu law was problematic because of its inegalitarian and undemocratic nature.

In his 1958 book, Pal sought to subvert the idea, associated with Henry Maine, that Hindu law was "a stagnant system, always standing still" due to its religious nature. Pal argued that this was not the case: Hindu law was dynamic, capable of changing to accommodate new economic and social circumstances.[43] One indication of the continuously evolving nature of Hindu law was the appearance of Hindu philosophers of law. The philosophy of law, Pal said, arises when an existing legal norm, based on custom, seems inconvenient. In order to change the norm, philosophers turn to reason and nature to justify its replacement. Therefore, the fact that Hindu philosophers of law already appeared during the Vedic era was an indication that Hindu law was dynamic.[44] A further common Western critique of Hindu law as a legal system that Pal sought to challenge was that it lacked unity and was "disintegrated" (meaning that specific rules applied to particular castes). Pal's answer to this critique was to state that while Hindu law was personal rather than territorial, the notion of territorial law also appeared in Hindu law.[45] Finally, another Western critique was that ancient Hindu law was amoral because it lacked the concept of sin. In response, Pal argued that the Vedic hymns actually contain many examples of the belief in God, the perception of the difference between good and evil, and the notion that "God hates sin and loves virtue."[46]

Moving to the specific substance of Hindu law, a common Western critique was that Hindu law sought to preserve and glorify hierarchical social relations rather than being based on the notion of equality (a concept that is, of course, foreign to ancient religious legal systems in which various types of hierarchies between social groups are common). Specifically, there were three categories of persons that were treated as inferior by Hindu law: slaves, members of the lower

[43] Pal, *History*, 16–17. On the impact of religion on law in Maine's thought, see, e.g., Henry Sumner Maine, *Ancient Law* (London: John Murray, 1861), 15–18, 77.

[44] Pal, *History*, 16, 112. [45] Ibid., 21–3. [46] Ibid., 167.

castes, and women. Pal, it should be recalled, came from a family belonging to a caste of moderate social standing. He was also involved, later in his life, in encouraging female education (in 1948, he was appointed the president of the governing body of Bethune College, the first Asian institution of its kind for women).[47] Given these facts, it is understandable that the social hierarchies created by Hindu law would pose a problem for him.

Slavery was only briefly mentioned in Pal's 1918 book, *Introductory Lecture*, and was not discussed at all in his 1920s book.[48] It was also not a major topic in his 1958 book. Pal did note in this latter work that slavery existed in Vedic society, but he qualified this fact in two ways. First, he began his very brief discussion of slavery by stating that:

> ... from the earliest times in all nations the system by which the stronger enslave the weaker has prevailed. In early times it was usual to reduce to the status of slave all captives taken in war. This was really a step in advance of the earlier indiscriminate slaughter of the vanquished enemies.[49]

Second, while Pal noted that Vedic Aryans treated their slaves more like things than human beings, he nevertheless said that slaves could "improve their status and become almost equal to Aryans."[50]

As for the Hindu caste system, Pal used several arguments in its defense. First, he claimed that it did not exist in early Vedic society. "In the Rigveda," he argued, "there is no clear indication of the existence of caste in the proper Brahmanical sense of the word. This caste system was only introduced after the Brahmans had finally established their claims to the highest rank in the body politic."[51] Second, Pal acknowledged that, according to Hindu legal philosophy, the purpose of the law was "the preservation of the existing social institutions" – that is, the caste system. However, he argued that other ancient legal systems also regarded law as a method for preserving the social status quo. Specifically, he mentioned the Greeks, noting that the ancient Greek philosophers, too, were convinced that "in every society there must be grades, masters and servants, the

47 Nakazato, *Neonationalist Mythology*, 106. 48 Pal, *Introductory Lecture*, 26.

49 Pal, *History*, 299. 50 Ibid.

51 Pal, *History*, 70. This claim already appeared in his 1918 *Introductory Lecture*. See Pal, *Introductory Lecture*, 15. See also Banerjee, "Does International Criminal Justice Require a Sovereign?," 78. On the argument that the rigid notion of caste is, in some sense, a modern phenomenon, see Nicholas B. Dirks, *Castes of Mind: Colonialism and the Making of Modern India* (Princeton, NJ: Princeton University Press, 2001).

privileged and the unprivileged, the upper and lower classes," and that when the Greeks talked about equality, this was conceived as equality between members of the same class, not between all members of society.[52]

Another method of defending Hindu law from the charge of inequality was to question the desirability of equality itself. In his 1958 book, Pal referenced the anti-egalitarian and anti-democratic ideas of Friedrich Nietzsche.[53] Indeed, Pal devoted several pages of that work to a summary of Nietzsche's anti-egalitarian stance (based, it seems, on a chapter in a popular book, Will Durant's *The Story of Philosophy*), discussing Nietzsche's admiration for the Laws of Manu, and repeating Nietzsche's anti-democratic and anti-Christian ideas.[54] The allusion to Nietzsche's thought, it seems, was meant to imply that inequality was not merely a characteristic of ancient societies and ancient law.[55]

Finally, another strategy for downplaying the role of caste in Hindu law may have been to minimize the significance of purity and pollution in Indian social relations. For instance, in his discussion of Nietzsche's admiration for the Laws of Manu, Pal did acknowledge their "terrible" nature, and the way they were meant to reflect Brahmanical power. He even referenced specific provisions concerning social impurity. However, overall, the theme of purity and pollution was largely absent from his work.[56]

More generally, one might speculate that Pal's reluctance to directly criticize the caste-based nature of Hindu law might be seen as an academic variant of the concept of Sanskritization – that is, the process by which members of the lower castes seek social mobility by emulating the rituals or practices of the upper castes. Pal's apologetic attempt to defend Hindu law was, according to this approach, a way to obscure his relatively low social origin.[57]

[52] Pal, *History*, 209–10.

[53] On Nietzsche and Hindu law, see, e.g., Koenraad Elst, "Manu as a Weapon against Egalitarianism: Nietzsche and Hindu Political Philosophy," in *Nietzsche, Power and Politics: Rethinking Nietzsche's Legacy for Political Thought*, eds. Herman W. Siemens and Vasti Roodt (Berlin: Walter de Gruyter, 2008), 543.

[54] Pal, *History*, 261–9. It should be noted that Pal did not merely summarize Nietzsche's thought but also criticized it. See ibid., 265.

[55] See also Banerjee, "Does International Criminal Justice Require a Sovereign?," 78.

[56] Pal, *History*, 267–8.

[57] On Sanskritization, see, generally, Simon Charsley, "Sanskritization: The Career of an Anthropological Theory," *Contributions to Indian Sociology (n.s.)* 32 (1998): 527.

Regarding the attitude of early Hindu law to women, Pal claimed that they *were* treated as equal to men. After quoting some verses from the *Rigveda* that implied that women were treated like chattels, Pal pointed out that there was also evidence that "Aryan women," at least those belonging to the higher classes, "enjoyed equal freedom with men in all matters, social and religious," which indicated the "high state of culture" of Aryan society. Similarly, marriage in Vedic texts, noted Pal, was not coerced but based on choice for both husband and wife.[58] When discussing Hindu law in the Brahmana and Sutra periods, Pal said that modern legal systems were characterized by individualism (treating individual adults as independent of their families) and by seeing women as "self-sufficient units" independent of their husbands. He then commented that, "even under ancient and medieval conditions the legal sense of the Hindus was akin to and approached" that of modern law – for example, by recognizing that women could own property in their own right. This independence, he then noted, declined during the Brahmana and Sutra periods. For instance, in the case of marriage, while the consent of the woman was required during the Vedic age, this was not the case in later periods.[59]

Another aspect of Pal's perspective on the legal status of women was found in his discussion of matrimonial relations. Explaining the morality of Vedic society, Pal noted that it "differed vastly" from that of the original inhabitants of India, the Dravidians, and "still more from the unmixed barbarism of the other races of India." The matrimonial relations of Dravidian society were "rather loose" because it was a matriarchal society (unlike the "patriarchal and masculine" Vedic society). Vedic religion was "fairly right and respectable," in contrast to Dravidian religion, which was "dark and repulsive, obscene and bloody" (presumably because, in Vedic religion, masculine gods dominated the pantheon, while female gods dominated the Dravidian pantheon).[60]

[58] Pal, *History*, 292, 295. This claim already appeared in 1918. See Pal, *Introductory Lecture*, 15.

[59] Pal, *History*, 340, 344, 366, 393.

[60] Ibid., 36, 38, 45–6. Pal was quoting (and also misquoting) Barnett, *Antiquities of India*, 4. On the sources of the distinction between the Aryan and Dravidian "races," see, e.g., Thomas R. Trautmann, *Aryans in British India* (Berkeley, CA: University of California Press, 1997), 4.

Interestingly, in his book *Law of Primogeniture*, Pal went so far as to argue that ancient non-Western law had a more egalitarian attitude toward women than Western law. In his discussion of ancient Chinese and ancient Egyptian law and society, Pal approvingly quoted a book by nineteenth-century English author (and early feminist) Edith Jemima Simcox, who noted that, before the Semites and Aryans came to dominate the Old World, the first civilized states were established by "men of some other race – humane, industrious [... and] liberal in the treatment of women."[61]

Another strand of Western critique of the substance of Hindu law had to do with its alleged incompatibility with the notion of democracy.[62] In Pal's 1958 book, he described Vedic political institutions as advanced, relying on the works of scholars of ancient Indian constitutional history such as Kashi Prasad Jayaswal and Benoy Kumar Sarkar (whose works are discussed in detail in Chapter 5). Repeating the claims of these scholars, Pal argued that representative institutions such as parliaments were not an English notion imported to India – they existed in India before the period of the British conquest. Buddhist assemblies were one example of such institutions, Pal explained. However, he argued that "similar institutions" had existed even during the Vedic period, mentioning various types of Vedic assemblies in which "rudiments of the present-day parliamentary practice [were] discernible." Pal also mentioned republican political arrangements that arose in later periods of Hindu history and were somewhat similar to modern democratic assemblies.[63] While Pal was keen to show that Indians, too, had their own democratic institutions, he also qualified his comparison between Indian and Western ones, arguing that it would be wrong to equate the two. Quoting the Indian nationalist philosopher (and also revolutionary terrorist leader) Sri Aurobindo, Pal claimed that

[61] Pal, *Law of Primogeniture*, 188.

[62] Democracy is, of course, an ambiguous term encompassing a broad range of institutional arrangements, cultural expectations, and normative ideals. In Pal's work, as well as that of other scholars of Hindu law at the time, the most salient aspect of democracy was the fact that, using various mechanisms, it prevented absolute despotic power. For a modern discussion, see, e.g., David Stasavage, *The Decline and Rise of Democracy: A Global History from Antiquity to Today* (Princeton, NJ: Princeton University Press, 2020).

[63] Pal, *History*, 86–7, 89, 102, 107.

Indian political institutions were embedded in the "unique mentality" of the Indian race.[64]

## *Collectivism*

A major aspect of Pal's approach to the issue of law and hierarchical social relations was his rejection of liberal individualist notions of law and society. The interwar and post-war periods were a time when many intellectuals, including Pal, showed interest in alternatives to nineteenth-century liberalism, such as fascism, corporatism, socialism, and communism.[65] For example, when discussing the nature of law, Pal rebuffed the view that society was merely "an aggregate of isolated abstract individuals." He noted that the "Vedic Rishis [sages] scarcely ever consider man as 'a whole in himself' [...] The isolated individual of course is an absurd abstraction in the philosophy of such a people." According to the Vedic sages, law was a way of ensuring harmony – and harmony relied on "each individual's keeping within a predetermined groove."[66]

This was not merely a statement about ancient Hindu society. At one point in Pal's 1958 book, he embarked on a long digression chastising individualist Western civilization, which, he conceded, was "creative" but was also characterized by the evils of "disintegration and destruction" and "arrogant individualism." Vedic society was no less creative than Western modern society, he said, but its creativity was distinct in the sense that it sought "integration and balanced co-ordination" – in contrast to "the modern world" (the West), which sought "individual order" as opposed to "collective order." Western democracy created doubt and anxiety, undermining the communities that sustain the individual: "Freedom in the present-day life has lost its foundation in community and has become a torment; individualism of the present day strips the individual layer after layer of

64 Pal, *History*, 104–5. On Sri Aurobindo's nationalist ideas during the revolutionary phase of his life, see, e.g., Peter Heehs, "Aurobindo Ghose and Revolutionary Terrorism," *South Asia* 15 (1992): 47.

65 For an example of the attempt to argue that ancient Hindu political philosophy and modern socialism were based on similar values, see Hemchandra Ray[chaudhuri], "Was State-Socialism Known in Ancient India?" in *Sir Asutosh Mookerjee Silver Jubilee Volumes* (Calcutta: Calcutta University Press, 1922), Vol. 3.2, 429.

66 Pal, *History*, iii, 4, 159, 188.

protective tissue. We require individualism, but we require individualism which would not wall man off from community . . ."[67]

## Pal's Jurisprudential Contributions

Pal's works on Hindu jurisprudence were, in many senses, derivative. They repeated ideas that had first appeared in texts produced by Europeans or by other, earlier, Indian thinkers. However, since Pal was both a lawyer and a scholar of Indian history, he offered a unique perspective on Hindu jurisprudence, one that combined his ability to read the original Sanskrit texts with his familiarity with Western jurisprudential scholarship. Three specific (although not necessarily original) ideas that characterized Pal's works are outlined below.

### *The Aryan Framework*

One major aspect of Pal's 1920s works was the reliance on nineteenth-century Western linguistic, racial and legal theories that divided the world into races and assumed that all members of the same race shared similar legal ideas.[68] This perspective is reflected in the following statement by Pal:

> In passing from one nation to another, we observe shades of jural distinctions, which become material differences when the nations belong to different races. Race is indeed a dominant factor in the effort of the human activity to realise itself. Throughout the ages the diversity of race has influenced indelibly the generation of law. In law, as in other parts of life, the heart of the race is what we must seek to discover . . .[69]

[67] Ibid., 393, 395–8. It is interesting to note that some Indian nationalists actually argued that the opposite was true, that is, that Europeans were collectivists while Indians were individualists. See Ratan Lal, *Kashi Prasad Jayaswal: The Making of a "Nationalist" Historian* (Delhi: Aakar Books, 2018), 78.

[68] Note that the notion of "race" changed over the course of the nineteenth and twentieth centuries. It was not a stable notion and it was not always identified with biological markers such as skin color. See, generally, Trautmann, *Aryans*, 191. The shift to biology in nineteenth-century European race science is discussed in Ivan Hannaford, *Race: The History of an Idea in the West* (Washington, DC: Woodrow Wilson Center Press; Baltimore, MD: Johns Hopkins University Press, 1996), 235–76; Stefan Arvidsson, *Aryan Idols: Indo-European Mythology as Ideology and Science*, trans. Sonia Wichmann (Chicago: University of Chicago Press, 2006), 41–52.

[69] Pal, *Philosophy*, 3.

At the beginning of his 1920s book, Pal stated that comparative law was "a necessary preliminary" to the study of legal philosophy since comparative law would allow us to see, beyond the difference between different legal systems, the "organic unity" of the legal philosophy they share. Given the importance of the study of comparative law, nothing was more important, he said, than "a study of the ancient Hindu minds" and the early "Hindu fundamental conception of law" as a way to discover the shared legal concepts of the "Aryan races [sic]." The Aryans were divided into western and eastern branches, but they all shared the innate "Aryan love for systems," adding that "there is no world law, only racial laws."[70]

The theory about the existence of an "Aryan race" was a nineteenth-century European construct.[71] This theory is, now, of course, no longer in fashion. It was enthusiastically received in colonial India. It was used to prove the affinity between British colonial masters and their Indian subjects (especially upper-caste Indians). However, it could also be leveraged to support an argument for the antiquity and superiority of the Indian Aryans compared to European ones.[72] The infatuation of Europeans with ancient Indian ideas and symbols was also a feature that appealed to Indian intellectuals.[73] In Pal's works, Aryanism served as a tool for critiquing Western monotheistic religions (and, indirectly, Western law). It was also used as a foundation for the rejection of

[70] Ibid., i–iii, 3.

[71] See Trautmann, *Aryans*; Bryant, *Quest*. On the intellectual history of the term "Aryan," see also Kris Manjapra, *Age of Entanglement: German and Indian Intellectuals Across Europe* (Cambridge, MA: Harvard University Press, 2014), 75–85 (discussing twentieth-century phases in the history of the theory).

[72] Tapan Raychaudhuri, *Europe Reconsidered: Perceptions of the West in Nineteenth-Century Bengal* (Delhi: Oxford University Press, 1988), 8, 33–4; Trautmann, *Aryans*, 221–2; Bryant, *Quest*, 47; Romila Thapar, "The Theory of the Aryan Race and the Origins of the South Asian Civilisation," *Social Scientist* 24 (1996): 3. On the way European race science was transformed and replaced in mid twentieth-century Indian scientific discourse by the study of human blood group variation (seroanthropology) and other more "scientific" attempts to biologically classify the population of India, see Projit Bihari Mukharji, *Brown Skins, White Coats: Race Science in India, 1920–66* (Chicago, IL: University of Chicago Press, 2020).

[73] See, e.g., Arvidsson, *Aryan Idols*, 23–4, 28, 48 (discussing European Indomania and the notion of "Aryan brotherhood").

the concept of "oriental despotism" that nineteenth-century European thinkers often used when describing Indian civilization.[74]

Pal contrasted Aryans with the Semites, comparing the Vedic notion of law as a divine order governing the universe with the Semitic notion of God as "a personal and omnipotent Deity who gave the laws [commandments] just as He wills."[75] The distinction between the law of the Semites and "Aryan" law was not found in Henry Maine's work.[76] Pal may have taken this idea from the work of the nineteenth-century Bengali lawyer and intellectual Bankimchandra Chatterjee, who distinguished between the "Christian God," who was conceived as a despotic monarch constantly policing his subjects, and the Indian divinity who was immanent in all creatures.[77] Another possible source for this contrast may have been the works of late nineteenth-century German scholars such as the German Indologist Paul Deussen, who contrasted Hinduism with Judaism and Islam and their "unapproachable and sadistic God."[78] Of course, the fact that Islamic law was also a "Semitic" legal system was another advantage of the binary distinction between Aryan and Semitic law, at least for Hindu nationalists.

The distinction between Aryans and Semites also appeared in Pal's work in his discussion of the Aryan conception of the nature of the state. Relying on the works of the Italian legal philosopher Luigi Miraglia, Pal argued that the "individualistic" Semites never succeeded in creating political stability, alternating between anarchy,

[74] On the "oriental despotism" concept and Indian reactions to it, see Trautmann, *Aryans*, 103–4.

[75] Pal, *Philosophy*, ii, 3, 11–12.

[76] In his book *Ancient Law*, Maine did mention in one place Semites and people of "Indo-European" stock. See Maine, *Ancient Law*, 123. However, there was no attempt to compare their laws; and, in any event, in this early book, Maine paid very little attention to India, focusing mainly on Greece and Rome. On Maine's use of racial, linguistic, and evolutionary interpretative frameworks in this book and later ones, see Trautmann, *Aryans*, 203–6.

[77] See Banerjee, "Sovereignty," 494. Negative depictions of Judaism appeared in other works of Bengali intellectuals during the colonial period. See, generally, Yulia Egorova, *Jews and India: History, Image, Perceptions* (Milton Park and New York: Routledge, 2006).

[78] See M. Reza Pirbhai, "Demons in Hindutva: Writing a Theology for Hindu Nationalism," *Modern Intellectual History* 5 (2008): 27, 35–6.

despotism, and theocracy. In contrast, the Aryans created balanced governments composed of a king, a senate, and a general assembly.[79]

Interestingly, the emphasis in Pal's 1920s book on the "Aryan races" and the comparison between Semites and Aryans was toned down in his 1958 book. The term "Aryans" still appeared in the latter book. At one point, Pal still contrasted the Hindu gods with the "Semitic God" (whom he described as "whimsical and despotic").[80] In another place in this book Pal seemingly endorsed a comparison made by Nietzsche between the Laws of Manu and the Bible, quoting Nietzsche's characterization of the Bible as an "evil-smelling Jewish distillation of Rabbinism and superstition."[81] However, the explicit contrast found in the earlier work between "Aryan ideas" and "the Semitic-Hebraic faith" was no longer there. This change may have been the result of the association of the concept of Aryanism with Nazi thought, or perhaps it was due to the fact that, following the end of British rule in India in 1947, Pal no longer felt a strong need to contrast Hindu religion with Christianity or Islam, both of which were identified with this "Semitic God."

Nonetheless, while the notions of Aryan race and law were less prominent in Pal's 1958 book, the work still relied on a racial theory of Indian civilization, a theory first developed in late nineteenth-century Europe. According to this theory, the Aryans were light-skinned migrants from the North who invaded an India inhabited by a dark-skinned aborigine population.[82] Early in his 1958 book, Pal discussed this theory, observing that some Western scholars saw the Aryans as migrants or invaders, while also noting that the Indian scholar Abinas Chandra Das, a lecturer on ancient Indian history at the University of Calcutta, argued that the Aryans actually emerged in the Punjab.[83] Later in the book, however, Pal no longer qualified his discussion, talking about Aryan society as being, indeed, headed by a "foreign race of fairer skin and Indo-Germanic speech" and about the Aryans "streaming into" an India inhabited by Dravidian tribes who were of "blacker blood" and espoused a barbaric religion and manners.[84]

[79] Pal, *Philosophy*, 12. [80] Cf. Pal, *History*, 116; Pal, *Philosophy*, 11.
[81] Pal, *History*, 267. [82] Trautmann, *Aryans*, 206–11. [83] Pal, *History*, 35.
[84] Ibid., 44.

### *The Critique of Positivism*

A second, and related, theme evident in Pal's comparison of ancient Hindu and Western religion and law was the contrast he drew between the Hindu notion of law and modern Western positivist notions. In the work of the early nineteenth-century English legal philosopher John Austin, law was identified with the "command of the sovereign." According to such a definition, Hindu law could not be considered "law" since it did not originate in the commands of a human sovereign. In his 1920s *Philosophy*, Pal therefore compared the "Semitic-Hebraic" faith, which created a personal and omnipotent law-giving God, to the Vedic Aryan notion of law. Among the Vedic Aryans, Pal said, "there was never ... that all-controlling despotism which blot[s] out man." Instead, the Vedic Aryans saw ethics and law as part of an eternal, immutable, harmonious order that was not based on despotic godly will but was more powerful than even the gods themselves. The cosmic harmonious order to which these gods were subject was created "for human benefit," and they existed "for the purpose of maintaining the law."[85] This eternal law, some of the Vedic rishis argued, could be discerned by the sages who sought it within their own hearts.[86] Since law was not the product of a divine sovereign (and certainly not of a human sovereign), and it existed "above the sovereign," the Vedic rishis would not have believed "an Austin" if he were to have told them that "there is no law without a sovereign above the sovereign or besides the sovereign, law exists only through the sovereign."[87] The rishis also rejected the modern positivist notion of law as a tool for social change. The end goal of the law, according to Hindu legal philosophy, was to preserve the social status quo based on the division of society into four castes, thus ensuring peace in society.[88]

In his 1958 book, Pal repeated this rejection of the Austinian notion of law, suggesting that the source of law in ancient society was not the will of a political sovereign but "the light of Divine inspiration," prophetically influencing individual law.[89] In order to prove that the

[85] Pal, *Philosophy*, 11–12. 17, 20, 42, 65, 114–16, 162–3. The quote about Semitic despotism was taken from Luigi Miraglia, *Comparative Legal Philosophy: Applied to Legal Institutions*, trans. John Lisle (New York: Macmillan, 1921), 120.

[86] Pal, *Philosophy*, 35. [87] Ibid., 72. [88] Ibid., 108, 113, 134.

[89] Pal, *History*, 4.

ancient Hindu concept of law was not obsolete but was, in fact, also modern, Pal turned to a series of Western nineteenth- and twentieth-century jurisprudential thinkers who offered non-positivist definitions of law, the most important of which was Eugen Ehrlich. Quoting Ehrlich, Pal associated law not with the state and its institutions but with society, thus blurring the line between positive law and social norms.[90]

*The Law of Primogeniture* also contained lengthy jurisprudential digressions, for example, a discussion of the "Hindu theory of custom," allowing Pal to criticize the Austinian theory of law.[91] Indeed, Pal not only noted the difference between Western law and Hindu law in this respect but also used it to argue that Hindu law was superior:

> In those systems where law does not emanate from the sovereign political authority, the king's prerogative would not place him beyond the authority of law. Law that governs the subject would equally govern the king [...]. Our law is not the whimsical, wilful command of any god or man however powerful he be.[92]

Pal also indirectly criticized another element of Austin's definition of law: the notion of sanction. Since the ancient Hindu philosophers saw human nature as "essentially good and sociable," they did not see punishment as "a mere vulgar threat." Instead, punishment was seen as a "sublime purifier." Its existence was not due to the need for vengeance or the need to deter future offenders. Rather, it was "necessary for the welfare of the offender himself."[93]

Pal's attack on Austinian positivism was also meant to defend the very notion of Hindu law. The Austinian definition of law served as the basis of a famous nineteenth-century debate between two British officials, James Henry Nelson and John D. Mayne, about whether an entity called "Hindu law" actually existed.[94] Nelson defined law as commands by "political superiors" and, naturally, concluded that, on

90 Ibid., 4–6. 91 Pal, *Law of Primogeniture*, 368–77, 382–5, esp. 370, 373.

92 Ibid., 387. 93 Pal, *Philosophy*, 158. See also Pal, *History*, 211.

94 See Chapter 1. While Pal rejected the Austinian definition of law, he accepted different, equally problematic, Western notions. For example, he accepted the assumption that law and religion were different entities (and defined them according to Western definitions), and he sought to discover law in ancient written theological texts, rather than, for example, in customary practices. See, generally, Werner Menski, "Hindu

that basis, Hindu law could not be considered "law." As Pal noted, this definition was "narrow" in the sense of identifying law only with legislation, courts, and legal coercion. It was also associated, Pal explained, with a specific time and place – Europe after the rise of absolute monarchies in the early modern period. It did not fit the legal reality of ancient India.[95] Unlike modern Western law, Hindu law was always independent of the state, Pal argued. It did not emanate from it but was "above it and anterior to it," and, because of this quality, it allowed "the weaker to rule the stronger."[96]

Pal's depiction of Hindu law seems similar to the depiction of law by Western natural law thinkers. However, it is interesting to note that Pal also attempted to compare the Hindu notion of law to the ideas of the German Historical School, according to which law is not made by an individual human creator but reflects "the spirit of the people." Pal also compared the Hindu notion of law to the idea found in the "modern French legal theory" of social solidarity, according to which any act of legislation is not a "true creation of law, but a declaratory statement or mere evidence of the rule of law previously created by social solidarity."[97] French legal theory – specifically, the discussion of the relationship between instinct and reason in law by the French anti-formalist legal philosopher François Gény – was also used by Pal when discussing the sources of law according to the Hindu thinkers of the Sutra era.[98] Referring to the Manusmriti, Pal reasoned that "Manu may indeed be classed as a sociological jurist" (because he was concerned with the efficacy of the legal order rather than with its abstract validity).[99]

Law in Modern Times: How Hindu Law Continues in Modern India," in *The Oxford History of Hinduism: Modern Hinduism*, ed. Torkel Brekke (Oxford: Oxford University Press, 2019), 244, 251, 254; Geetanjali Srikantan, *Identifying and Regulating Religion in India: Law, History and the Place of Worship* (Cambridge: Cambridge University Press, 2020), 3, 14, 19–61. On the problematic view of both Hinduism and Judaism as "religions" in the Protestant sense, see Leora Batnitzky, "Between Ancestry and Belief: 'Judaism' and 'Hinduism' in the Nineteenth Century," *Modern Judaism* 41 (2021): 194.

95 Pal, *History*, 1–3. 96 Ibid., 259.

97 Ibid., 175–6. On the notion of social solidarity in French thought, see, e.g., J. E. S. Hayward, "Solidarity: The Social History of an Idea in Nineteenth Century France," *International Review of Social History* 4 (1959): 261.

98 Pal, *History*, 199–200. 99 Ibid., 227.

### *Hindu Law and Society as an Alternative to the West*

In his 1958 book, Pal criticized modern Western democracy at length. Recent events, he said (referring to the Second World War), had shown that common comparisons between the "strong, successful and progressive" European culture, based on democracy and industrialism, and the supposedly backward Indian culture were misplaced. "Perhaps the civilized world is no longer living in the delicious intoxication induced by the early success of science," reflected Pal, since science has been "put to evil use" and, thus, we are living in an age of "spiritual chaos, intellectual doubt and political decadence," one symptom of which has been the "acquisition of the atom bomb." Quoting Sri Aurobindo, Pal noted that, in contrast to Western society, which was now a "madhouse where delusions govern amid hopeless and needless suffering," the ideals of Indian society "were of the highest kind, its social order secured an inexpugnable basic stability, the strong life-force that worked in it was creative of an extraordinary energy, richness and interest, and the life organised remarkable in its opulence, variety in unity, beauty, productiveness, movement." Pal acknowledged Western economic superiority but argued that it was the result of Western imperialism. "Asia's billion people are made to keep on struggling against backwardness and starvation. Their struggle started more than a century and a half ago when these civilized lords of the West reached out aggressively for the wealth of the East."[100]

Pal distinguished between "the Western philosophy of life," which sought to transform the world, and the philosophy of ancient India, which saw the universe as static and asked humans to adapt themselves to the existing "cosmic order." Pal deemed the Western approach to be "creative" but simultaneously characterized by the evils of "disintegration and destruction." Vedic society, too, was creative, he claimed, in the sense that it sought "integration and balanced co-ordination," in contrast to modernity, which sought "subordination and domination" – the conquest of nature rather than "harmony with

[100] Pal, *History*, 86–9. On the intellectual history of the idea of a peaceful and spiritual Eastern or Asian civilization (juxtaposed with Western civilization portrayed as having the opposite qualities), see, e.g., Prasenjit Duara, "The Discourse of Civilization and Pan-Asianism," *Journal of World History* 12 (2001): 99, 108; Stolte and Fischer-Tiné, "Imagining Asia," 76.

nature." Western industrialism and democracy created doubt and anxiety, undermining the communities that sustain the individual. Pal thus called for a partial rejection of Western values, although he did acknowledge that it would be impossible to halt the industrialization of India if it were to protect itself from exploitation by the West.[101]

## Conclusion

Pal's works on Hindu law were not created in a vacuum. They reflected ideas prevalent in the first decades of the twentieth century in India and, more specifically, among Bengali intellectuals affiliated with the University of Calcutta. Pal's education, which combined familiarity with Hindu law and Western legal theories, and his political views, which were associated with Hindu cultural nationalism, naturally influenced his depiction of the philosophy and history of Hindu law. A similar relationship between life, politics, and legal thought is also found in the ideas of the person discussed in the next chapter, Samuel Eisenstadt.

[101] Pal, *History*, 393, 395–8. This perspective on Asian industrialization was partly a critique of Gandhi's views on the topic. See Nakazato, *Neonationalist Mythology*, 132.

4

# The Life and Jurisprudential Ideas of Samuel Eisenstadt

Samuel Eisenstadt was a prolific author and an active academic entrepreneur in various fields, including law, linguistics, and history. However, unlike Radhabinod Pal, he never achieved national, let alone international, fame. In 1950s Israel, he gained a degree of public notoriety for being a "red professor" – that is, a communist academic – but, generally speaking, he was a relatively obscure figure during his lifetime, and now he is almost totally forgotten.[1] A few scholars have mentioned his works, mainly because of his activity during the first decades of the twentieth century as one of the leaders

[1] It is interesting to note that Eisenstadt himself was involved throughout his life in several biographical projects. He wrote a biography of his father and edited collections devoted to the life of his wife and his son (who died prematurely). He wrote a book containing biographical portraits of various figures whom he admired, ranging from Lenin and Harriet Beecher Stowe to the Hassidic Rabbi Nachman of Breslov. He also edited a biography of Sarah Patt, a Jewish-American Yiddish theater actress. During the last years of his life, he worked on an extensive autobiography that was never published. After his death, his family commissioned a self-published hagiographic biography. See Samuel Eisenstadt, *Ha-Haluts ba-Ma'arakhah: Le-Zekher ha-Av veha-Moreh* (Tel Aviv: Likud, 1965); Samuel Eisenstadt, *Sefer Roza: Divrey Zikaron le-Re'ayah, le-Em, vele-Haverah* (Tel Aviv: n.p., 1959); Samuel Eisenstadt, *'Al 'Alumim she-Nikpedu* (Jerusalem: n.p., 1969/70); Samuel Eisenstadt, *Pionerishe Geshtaltn* (Tel Aviv: Oyfkum, 1970); Samuel Eisenstadt, ed., *Sarah Patt: Lebn un Shafn* (Tel Aviv: Oyfkum, 1970); Tehila Ofer, *Ish Hazon u-Ma'as: Hayav u-Fo'alo shel Prof. Shmuel Aizenshtadt* (Petah Tikvah: Dfus Havatselet, 1999). Chapters of his unpublished autobiography can be found in his personal archive. See Pinchas Lavon Institute for Labour Movement Research, Tel Aviv [Lavon Archive], IV-104–13. The bulk of his personal archive is located at the Lavon Archive. Another part is located at the Central Zionist Archives in Jerusalem. See Central Zionist Archives, A212.

of the movement for the revival of Jewish law, but there are no comprehensive studies of his life, which was far more eventful than Pal's, or of his thought.[2]

## Life and Works

Eisenstadt was born in 1886 in Borisov, a small provincial town in the western part of the Russian Empire (today's Belarus). He came from a wealthy family on his mother's side. His father, who ran a vocational school, was involved in socialist political activity as one of the founders of the Russian Zionist workers' party *Po'aley Tsiyon*. In 1903, the young Eisenstadt, too, joined this party. During the 1905 Russian Revolution, he took part in anti-government activities in Warsaw. He left Russia at the end of that year, moving to Switzerland to study law at the University of Bern.[3]

During the first decade of the twentieth century, this university, the largest in Switzerland, hosted approximately 700 Russian students, about 40 percent of its student population at the time. Of these, more than half were Jewish. Most of the Jewish-Russian students studied medicine or philosophy. Only a few of them studied law because, as foreigners, they could not stay and practice law in Switzerland after graduation and because there were restrictions on the practice of law by Jews in the Russian Empire. Russian students were attracted to Bern because admission requirements for foreign students were lax. They were not required to present a high school diploma and could instead gain admission by passing an entry exam. Russian-Jewish students were also attracted to Bern because two Jewish professors were teaching there. One was Ludwig Stein, a professor of philosophy,

[2] See Assaf Likhovski, *Law and Identity in Mandate Palestine* (Chapel Hill, NC: University of North Carolina Press, 2006), 129, 132–4, 140, 143–4, 149; Ronen Shamir, *The Colonies of Law: Colonialism, Zionism and Law in Early Mandate Palestine* (New York: Cambridge University Press, 2000), 71, 72, 170; Amihai Radzyner, "Judaism and Jewish Law in Pre-State Palestine," in *The Cambridge Companion to Judaism and Law*, ed. Christine Hayes (New York: Cambridge University Press, 2017), 317, 327–8.

[3] [Samuel Eisenstadt ], *Ta'arikhim Biyografim le-Yovel ha-70 shel ha-Professor Shmuel Aizenshtadt, 20 March 1956* (Tel Aviv: n.p., 1956) [a copy is available at the Beit Ariela Library, Tel Aviv]; "Shmuel Aizenshtadt," in *Entsiklopedyah le-Halutsey ha-Yishuv u-Vonav*, ed. David Tidhar (Tel Aviv: Sifriyat Rishonim, 1957), Vol. 8, 3075–9; Eisenstadt, *Ha-Haluts ba-Ma'arakhah*.

who counted among his former students future communist luminaries such as Rosa Luxemburg. The other Jewish professor, Naum Reichesberg, who taught statistics and economics, was active in socialist circles and was famous for his work on workers' rights.[4]

Eisenstadt spent four years in Bern, between 1906 and 1910. In 1908, while vacationing in Russia, he was arrested by the Tsarist police for revolutionary activities. Upon release from prison, he returned to Switzerland and, in 1910, graduated with a doctorate in law. The topic of his doctoral dissertation was the procedure of the Jewish courts in Palestine until the end of the Talmudic period.[5]

Following graduation, Eisenstadt returned to Russia, moving between various cities in the Empire. At first, he lived in Odessa, a hub of Zionist activities. There, he taught Jewish law at the Odessa Rabbinical Seminary, founded by a rabbi and scholar, Chaim Tchernowitz. Eisenstadt taught this subject using a "progressive socialist" approach, which appealed to his students but not to the conservative leaders of the Seminary, and this may have been the reason he only taught there for a brief period. During his time in Odessa, Eisenstadt also edited a short-lived Zionist student magazine.[6]

Between 1915 and 1925, Eisenstadt lived in Moscow. Until the First World War, Moscow was not a major Jewish cultural center. However, following the 1917 Bolshevik Revolution, the Jewish population of Moscow swelled, and the city became a focal point for Jewish and Zionist educational and cultural initiatives. Eisenstadt was involved in many of them, including establishing the scholarly society

4 Aline Masé, "Student Migration of Jews from Tsarist Russia to the Universities of Bern and Zürich, 1865–1914" (Master's thesis, Utrecht University, 2012), 27, 43–4, 51–7, 62, 66; "Ludwig Stein, Noted Political Observer and Philosopher, Dies," *Jewish Telegraph Agency* (July 16, 1930), www.jta.org/archive/ludwig-stein-noted-political-observer-and-philosopher-dies. On Jewish lawyers and Jewish cultural activity in the late Russian Empire, see, generally, Benjamin Nathans, *Beyond the Pale: The Jewish Encounter with Late Imperial Russia* (Berkeley, CA: University of California Press, 2004); Jeffrey Veidlinger, *Jewish Public Culture in the Late Russian Empire* (Bloomington, IN: Indiana University Press, 2009).

5 *Ta'arikhim Biyografim*, 2–3; Ofer, *Ish Hazon*, 26; Lavon Archive, IV-104–13–163, "Parashat Hayayi u-Fe'ulati," 1; Lavon Archive, IV-104–13–165. See also Staatsarchiv des Kantons Bern, BB 8.2.466 (Fakultätsprotokoll, 1910 06–28).

6 Lavon Archive, IV-104–13–165, [Autobiography], 1908–14; Ofer, *Ish Hazon*, 26–8; Eisenstadt, *Sefer Roza*; Samuel Eisenstadt, "Sifruto shel ha-Mishpat ha-'Ivri," in *Tsiyon be-Mishpat: 'Iyunim ba-Mishpat ha-'Ivri veha-Roma'i* (Tel Aviv: Ha-Mishpat, 1967), 130, 136 [hereinafter *Tsiyon*].

for the study of Jewish Law mentioned in Chapter 2. He also found work as the head of the Hebrew-Jewish Department in what is now the Russian State Library. Between 1923 and 1925, Eisenstadt also headed the National Minorities Department of the USSR Museum of the Revolution.[7] According to his unpublished autobiography, during his Moscow years, he was arrested twice for Zionist activity and was under constant surveillance by the Soviet State Security Service, the GPU.[8] Eisenstadt left the USSR in 1925, moving to Mandatory Palestine. His decision to immigrate may have been related to growing political harassment by the GPU.[9]

In Palestine, Eisenstadt served as the secretary of the Hebrew Language Committee (*va'ad ha-lashon ha-'ivrit*), an organization devoted to promoting the use of Hebrew by coining new words and publishing bulletins and dictionaries to assist in reviving Hebrew as a spoken language. Eisenstadt worked as the secretary of the Committee until it became an official government body (the Academy of the Hebrew Language) in 1953. Between 1933 and 1943, he was also the founder and director of the Labor Movement Archive and Museum (now the Lavon Institute for Labor Movement Research). His law-related activities during the period of the British Mandate in Palestine

[7] Lavon Archive, IV-104–13–165, [Autobiography], 1908–14; Ofer, *Ish Hazon*, 26–8; Eisenstadt, *Sefer Roza*; Samuel Eisenstadt, "Le-Toldot ha-Tsiburiyut veha-Tarbut ha-'Ivrit be-Rusyah bi-T'hilat ha-Me'ah ha-'Esrim," *He-'Avar* 16 (1968): 1, 2–10.

[8] Lavon Archive, IV-104–13-170b-1, Tazkir [undated Memo apparently addressed to Weizmann, Kisch, and Bentwich], 1. On his work at the Lenin Library, see Samuel Eisenstadt, "Mi Hetsil et ha-Sefer ha-'Ivri be-Moskvah," *Davar*, April 8, 1929; Lavon Archive, IV-104–13-123A. On Zionist activity in the USSR in the 1920s, see, generally, Ziva Galili, "The Soviet Experience of Zionism: Importing Soviet Political Culture to Palestine," *Journal of Israeli History* 24 (2005): 1, 9, 18–20. On Jewish culture during and after the Bolshevik Revolution, see, generally, Kenneth B. Moss, *Jewish Renaissance in the Russian Revolution* (Cambridge, MA: Harvard University Press, 2009).

[9] On the other hand, in an open letter addressed to Soviet readers that Eisenstadt wrote in 1966, he claimed that his immigration to Palestine had been approved by the Soviet authorities and that he intended to "actively work for the creation of a free and independent Jewish-Arab state, and for the elimination of the British mandatory regime." If true, this statement could imply that Soviet authorities may have seen him as some sort of an agent in Palestine. See Prof. Samuel Eisenstadt, "Ha-Mikhtav she-Lo Pursam," *Ma'ariv*, June 18, 1967, 14. It should also be noted that he was a friend of Semyon Dimanshtein, the head of the notorious Jewish Section of the Soviet Communist Party (*Evsektsiia*). See Samuel Eisenstadt, "Sodo shel Shim'on Dimanshtein," *He-'Avar* 15 (1968): 240.

included editing a legal periodical that appeared sporadically between 1927 and 1933 (*Ha-Mishpat*); teaching courses on Jewish law at the British-run legal education institution, the Jerusalem Law Classes; and co-founding the Tel Aviv School of Law and Economics. Here, Eisenstadt taught courses on Roman law and Jewish family law. In addition, although he was not a licensed lawyer, he worked as a consultant on Jewish family law.[10]

One particularly interesting aspect of Eisenstadt's life was his growing affiliation with communism. He was a lifelong socialist. His family history, one would assume, would preclude any sympathy for communism since his brother, who lived in the USSR, fell victim to the Stalinist terror wave of the late 1930s.[11] Despite this, Eisenstadt drifted further toward the Left during the early 1940s, following a spat with the leading Zionist-socialist party in Palestine, MAPAI, which led to his resignation from the position of the manager of the Labor Movement Archive. The path from a more centrist socialist political affiliation to communism was not uncommon at the time, often under the influence of the victory of the Red Army during the Second World War.[12] In Eisenstadt's case, the influence of his first wife, Roza, may have also played a role since she was described as "the real communist in the family."[13]

[10] *Ta'arikhim Biyografim*, 3–4; Ofer, *Ish Hazon*, 26–9. For a detailed description of the course that he taught in the 1920s in the Jerusalem Law Classes, see Samuel Eisenstadt, "'Al Hora'at ha-Mishpat ha-'Ivri be-Veyt ha-Sefer le-Mishpat shel Memshelet Eretz Yisrael," in *Tsiyon*, 120–9; Samuel Eisenstadt, "Munahey ha-Mishpat ha-'Ivriyim, Kinusam u-Mehkaram," in *Tsiyon*, 303.

[11] His brother, Baruch, was arrested in 1937, deported to Siberia, and never returned. Eisenstadt, *Ha-Haluts ba-Ma'arakhah*, 15, 166, 269–85. See also S. Oron, "Kibud Av," *He-'Avar* 13 (1966): 196, 197.

[12] The most well-known example is Moshe Sne, one of the leading Zionist politicians in the 1940s, who moved in the 1950s from liberal Zionism to anti-Zionist Communism. See Eli She'altiel, *Tamid be-Meri: Moshe Sne, Biyografyah, 1909–1948* (Tel Aviv: 'Am 'Oved, 2000).

[13] I. Remba, "Ha-Hogegim be-Veit Bodrov," *Herut*, November 7, 1958, 2. Roza was a committed communist and long-time activist for various progressive causes such as feminism and Jewish–Arab peace (including affiliation with the Jewish–Arab coexistence organization *Brit Shalom*). She was also a member of various communist-related associations in the 1940s and 1950s. See "Seminaryon le-Diney Mishpahah ba-Aretz," *Haaretz*, February 15, 1943, 3; Eisenstadt, *Sefer Roza*, 10–17; Samuel Eisenstadt, *Hayehah ha-Ruhaniyim shel Roza, li-Melot Arba' Shanim le-Motah* (Tel Aviv: n.p., 1961).

Beginning in the 1940s, Eisenstadt became involved in a variety of communist-affiliated political and educational activities in Palestine and, subsequently, the State of Israel. He became a member of the USSR Friendship League and, later, also a member of similar friendship associations with countries such as China and Cuba. He published a short-lived communist-affiliated magazine (*Likud*) in the late 1940s. He translated and published the constitutions of the USSR and East European states and other Soviet or Russian works, including a translation to Hebrew of Stalin's biography. In 1950, he began teaching a course on socialist law in the USSR and Eastern Europe at the Tel Aviv School. He established Marxist adult educational centers in both Tel Aviv ("The House of Science and Culture – A Center for Marxist Education," which operated from his apartment) and Haifa (the "Socialist University Classes"), where he delivered Marxist-influenced lectures on legal topics and Jewish history. He served as a member of the Israeli Central Committee of the communist-affiliated branch of the World Peace Movement and as a member of the Global Council of the World Peace Movement. He also served in various positions in communist-affiliated organizations such as the Israeli Union of Democratic Lawyers (and the International Association of Democratic Lawyers) and other Israeli fringe organizations of the 1950s, such as the Union for the Defense of Democratic Rights, the League of Human and Civil Rights, and the Central Committee for the Defense of the Arab Minority.[14]

Eisenstadt's status as a "red professor," and perhaps his blind infatuation with figures such as Lenin, whom he physically resembled

[14] *Ta'arikhim Biyografim*, 4–8; Lavon Archive, IV-104–13–214; Eisenstadt, *Sefer Roza*, 26–8; Ofer, *Ish Hazon*, 29–32, 100–1; G. F. Alexandrov et al., *Yosef Stalin: Korot Hayav*, trans. S. Eisenstadt (Merhavyah: Ha-Kibuts ha-Artsi, 1949). On the post-war communist peace movement, see, e.g., Geoffrey Roberts, "Averting Armageddon: The Communist Peace Movement, 1948–1956," in *The Oxford Handbook of the History of Communism*, ed. Stephen A. Smith (Oxford: Oxford University Press, 2014), 322. Eisenstadt's ideological commitment to communism may have been augmented by more personal reasons, such as the fact that his role in various communist-affiliated organizations allowed him to travel frequently to Europe at a time when most Israelis could not travel abroad. (Until 1961, Israelis who wanted to travel abroad had to obtain an exit permit in addition to a passport. Such a permit was relatively difficult to obtain. This policy was motivated by a desire to maintain foreign currency reserves and to prevent emigration, and also by the view that travel abroad was a bourgeois luxury that contradicted the egalitarian values of the new state. See

FIGURE 4.1 Samuel Eisenstadt. Reproduced by permission of the Lavon Institute for Labor Movement Research Photos Collection / Photographer: Benari.

(short, bald, and sporting a goatee, see Figure 4.1), aroused public resentment. Following the Suez Crisis, students at the Tel Aviv School published a petition condemning Eisenstadt's support for Nasser and for the Soviet repression of the 1956 Hungarian Revolution. They also criticized the course he taught on Soviet and East European law at the Tel Aviv School.[15]

In the early 1960s, perhaps due to the growing anti-Zionism of Soviet Bloc countries or perhaps because the influence of his first wife, Roza, was no longer keenly felt (she died in 1957), Eisenstadt

Orit Rozin, *A Home for All Jews: Citizenship, Rights and National Identity in the New Israeli State* (Waltham, MA: Brandeis University Press, 2016), 67–70, 88–95). On Eisenstadt's European journeys, see, e.g., Samuel Eisenstadt, *Rishmey Bikur be-Tsekhoslovakyah* (Tel Aviv: Likud, 1957); National Library of Israel, Israeli Communist Party Archive, Letters to the Central Committee, Eisenstadt to Mikunis, May 14, 1961; Eisenstadt, *Sefer Roza*, 31.

15 "Kruzim Neged Prof. Eisenstadt," *Ha-Boker*, November 23, 1956, 8; Avner Yehudah, "Te'anot – lo mi-T'hum ha-Politkah – el ha-Dr. Eisenstadt," *Avukah: Bit'on Agudat ha-Studentim leyad Beyt ha-Sefer ha-Gavohah le-Mishpat vele-Kalkalah Tel Aviv* 10 (1957): 11–12; "Ha-Studentim Hitsbiu be-Ragleyhem," *Herut*, March 19, 1957, 2; Ofer, *Ish Hazon*, 108–9.

gradually abandoned communism. In 1963, he left a meeting of the World Peace Council in protest because of an anti-Israeli decision. In 1964, he publicly condemned anti-semitic caricatures published in the Soviet press.[16] In 1965, the Israeli Communist Party split as the Soviet Union gradually aligned with the Arab side of the Arab–Israeli conflict, leading Eisenstadt to become more critical of the Soviet policies.[17] His final break with communism came following the Six-Day War, when, describing himself as an "old communist," he published a letter criticizing the Soviet Bloc for its anti-semitic approach and its support of the Arab cause.[18] Thus, while, in the 1950s, Eisenstadt had celebrated the victories of the Red Army during the Second World War, his 1967 book on the history of the revival of the Hebrew language was dedicated to "our victorious [Israeli] army."[19] Another late-life shift occurred in the linguistic realm. Eisenstadt was a lifelong champion of the Hebrew language, but during his later years, he published several works in Yiddish. One of his last major projects before he passed away in 1970 was to edit an autobiography, in Yiddish, of an obscure Jewish-American actress.[20]

Eisenstadt was a wide-ranging intellectual entrepreneur. He taught courses at many academic and non-academic venues. He established several legal and popular education institutions, including the Tel Aviv School of Law and Economics, which ultimately became Tel Aviv University.[21] He was a central player in the revival of the Hebrew

[16] "Gam Netsig MAKI 'Azav et Mo'etset Tnu'at ha-Shalom," *Ma'ariv*, December 5, 1963, 19; Lavon Archive, IV-104–13–186, "Le-Ma'arekhet Tel Aviv." In 1958, Eisenstadt claimed that he was "not a communist." See "Prof. Eisenstadt 'Lo Komunist,'" *Herut*, August 31, 1958, 4.

[17] In a letter that he claimed to have sent in late 1966 to the Soviet journal *Novoye Vremya*, he criticized Soviet foreign policy. The journal did not publish the letter, and it was ultimately published in Hebrew immediately following the June 1967 Six-Day War. See Prof. Samuel Eisenstadt, "Ha-Mikhtav she-Lo Pursam," *Ma'ariv*, June 18, 1967, 14.

[18] Samuel Eisenstadt, "Me'ha'ah ve-Kriah – Dvaro shel Komunist Vatik," *Ma'ariv*, October 1, 1967. See also Ofer, *Ish Hazon*, 94–6.

[19] Eisenstadt, *Sefer Roza*, 90–1; Samuel Eisenstadt, *Sfatenu ha-'Ivrit ha-Hayah* (Tel Aviv: Tkumah, 1967).

[20] Lavon Archive, IV-104–13–216; Eisenstadt, *Pionerishe Geshtaltn*; Samuel Eisenstadt, "Areynfir," in Eisenstadt, ed., *Sarah Patt*. On his positive attitude toward Yiddish, despite his work as a Hebrew linguist, see Ofer, *Ish Hazon*, 85.

[21] See, e.g., "Ha-Gimnasyah shel 'Erev," *Davar*, May 13, 1928.

language in Palestine, a prolific writer, editor, translator, and publisher of several (short-lived) journals.[22] He wrote works on Jewish law, the Hebrew language, the history of Jewish socialism in Hebrew and Yiddish, several biographical works, and even dabbled in children's stories.[23] Most of his works were written in Hebrew and Yiddish, although there were also publications in Russian, German, and English.[24]

In the legal realm, his *oeuvre* included a translation of one of the parts of the Justinian Code, a textbook on Roman law based on his lectures at the Tel Aviv School, as well as an extensive bibliography of works on Jewish law in several languages listing approximately 4,500 works.[25] He also published many law-related articles in various journals. Eisenstadt's estate included several additional unpublished works on law, such as a historical dictionary of Jewish legal terms and writings on family law, socialist law, and the history of workers in Greco-Roman Palestine.[26]

## Ideas

### *Western Jurisprudential Influences*

Eisenstadt wrote works on comparative law, Roman law, and Jewish law. He did not publish works dealing exclusively with jurisprudence.

[22] *Shaharit: 'Iton Mukdash le-'Inyeney ha-Tse'irim bi-Tfutsot ha-Golah* was a student journal published in Odessa in 1913. *Ha-Mishpat* was a legal journal published intermittently in Mandatory Palestine between 1927 and 1934. *Likud* was a communist-leaning cultural magazine published in Palestine in 1946–47.

[23] See, e.g., Lavon Archive, IV-104–13–216; Samuel Eisenstadt, *Prakim be-Toldot Tnu'at ha-Po'alim ha-Yehudit* (Merhavyah: Sifriyat Po'alim, 1944), Vol. 1; Alexander Radishchev, *Mas'a mi-Peterburg le-Moskvah*, trans. Samuel Eisenstadt (Tel Aviv: Likud, 1954); Eisenstadt, *Pionerishe Geshtaltn*; Eisenstadt, ed., *Sarah Patt*; Ha-Dod Shmuel [Samuel Eisenstadt], "Na'aley ha-Yeladim she-Heviu Shalom la-'Olam," *Kol ha-'Am*, August 17, 1962, 6; Ofer, *Ish Hazon*, 82.

[24] See, e.g., S. I. Eisenstadt, "Xarakter i istoricheskaia evoliutsiia evreiskogo prava," *Evreiski Student* 1(5) (1923): 11; Samuel Eisenstadt, "Early History and Principles of Jewish Family Law," *Juridical Review* 60(1) (1948): 48, reprinted in *Tsiyon*, iii; Samuel Eisenstadt, "Paralleleinblicke in das jüdische und römische Familien- und Erbrecht," *Klio* 40 (1962): 244, reprinted in *Tsiyon*, ix.

[25] Samuel Eisenstadt, *Ha-Institutsyot* (Jerusalem: Ha-Mishpat, 1929); Samuel Eisenstadt, *Ha-Mishpat ha-Roma'i: Toldotav ve-Torato* (Tel Aviv: Ha-Mishpat, 1953). A second edition was published in 1962. Samuel Eisenstadt, *'Ein Mishpat: Sefer Shimush Bibliyografi le-Sifrut ha-Mishpat ha-'Ivri* (Jerusalem: Ha-Mishpat, 1931).

[26] *Ta'arikhim Biyografim*, 9–10; Eisenstadt, *Tsiyon*, 7–8, 311–18.

However, jurisprudence was certainly an important aspect of his scholarship. There were two main jurisprudential sources of inspiration for his works: the German Historical School and Marxist legal theory. In addition, it seems that he was also influenced by the notion of living law that was popular in early twentieth-century Central European legal scholarship.

The ideas of the Historical School shaped Eisenstadt's views on law as a student and young legal scholar in the 1900s and 1910s.[27] Several key notions of this jurisprudential approach influenced Eisenstadt's work, including the premise that history is essential for the study of law and the idea that law is a reflection of national culture (or "the spirit of the people"). The agenda and activities of Historical School scholars also served Eisenstadt as a model for how modern Jewish law scholars should operate.

One example of the importance of history for Eisenstadt can be found in a 1914 book review that he wrote on a pioneering doctrinal work on Jewish law, *Principles of Jewish Law*, written by another Russian-Jewish legal scholar, Asher Gulak. Eisenstadt criticized Gulak for assuming that Jewish law was a timeless, static entity. Gulak, Eisenstadt argued, ignored the historical development of Jewish law. The specific rules of this legal system were not merely a reflection of some timeless essence but were influenced by the particular environments encountered by the Jews in their various diaspora communities.[28] A 1917 article by Eisenstadt repeated familiar Historical School themes, such as the idea that the origins of law are to be found in the ancient customs of the people. Legislation, said Eisenstadt, was always merely an articulation of the "hidden law" that previously existed as a "social truth."[29] Ancient Jewish national customs could be found in popular ballads, riddles, proverbs, and myths. They could also be discovered by comparing the law of

[27] By the 1920s, he was moving away from what he called a "religious, sentimental" approach to law toward a more "historical materialist" approach. However, throughout his life, he never entirely abandoned the ideas of the Historical School. See Samuel Eisenstadt, "Hakdamah," in *Tsiyon*, 7, 8.

[28] Samuel Eisenstadt, "Be-Sifruteynu ha-Mishpatit," *Ha-Schiloah* 31 (1914): 181. Eisenstadt also criticized Gulak for arguing that Jewish law seeks to enforce "individual justice" rather than, as Eisenstadt believed, social justice. See ibid., 188.

[29] Samuel Eisenstadt, "Kadmoniyot ha-Mishpat ha-Yisre'eli," *Ha-'Am* (March 9, 1917): 12–13.

ancient Israel to that of other ancient nations and to the laws of contemporary nomadic nations.[30]

The belief that law was a reflection of the spirit of the people was also central to Eisenstadt's description of the history of Jewish law.[31] Law, he said, mirrored the spirit of the race – and, in the case of Jewish law, the spirit of the "Semitic race."[32] The way Eisenstadt reconciled the static and the dynamic aspects of Jewish law was to say that, while the principles of the Torah of Moses were timeless, the specific details of the commandments of Jewish law changed with every generation; thus, adherence to the "spirit" of Jewish law could be reconciled with the fact that this law changed as history progressed.[33] Eisenstadt also sought to emulate the research agenda of the German scholars associated with the Historical School: the academic collection and study of historical legal materials, their systematization, and their subsequent use as the basis for national codification (the historical–dogmatic approach) inspired Eisenstadt's vision for the scholarly study of Jewish law.

Alongside the influence of the Historical School, Eisenstadt's thought also reflected Marxist legal ideas. Marxist legal theory had already appeared in his first law-related article, a Yiddish piece published in 1908 in a New York journal, while he was still a law student (see Figure 4.2).

The topic of this article was the history of labor relations and labor law in ancient Jewish society. Here, Eisenstadt offered a reading of biblical history using a class-struggle perspective (and also compared early biblical Jewish society, which he claimed was classless, to ancient Hindu society, which was divided into castes).[34]

In a 1923 article published in the USSR, Eisenstadt described Second Temple legal disputes between the Pharisees and the Sadducees, and between the Hillelite and the Shammaite schools of interpretation, as reflecting the nature of law as "an instrument of oppression in the hand of the ruling aristocracy."[35] Later, in 1926, he published a book in

[30] Ibid., 10, 11.

[31] Samuel Eisenstadt, "Le-Korot ha-Mishpat ha-'Ivri (Skirah Klalit)," *He-'Atid*: Me'asef Sifruti Mada'i 3 (1909–11): 194,199.

[32] Ibid., 195. [33] Ibid., 199–200.

[34] Samuel Eisenstadt, "Di Arbayter un di Arbayter-Frage in der Alter Yidisher Geshikhte," *Di Tsukunft* 8 (1908): 762, 763, 766–7.

[35] Eisenstadt, "Xarakter," 13.

די אַרבייטער און די אַרבייטער־פראַגע אין דער אַלטער אידישער געשיכטע

פון דר. שמואל א. אייזענשטאט

א.

FIGURE 4.2 Samuel Eisenstadt, “Di Arbayter un di Arbayter-Frage in der Alter Yidisher Geshikhte,” *Di Tsukunft* 8 (1908): 762.

Yiddish on the biblical prophets. In this book, he offered what many would see as an anachronistic, “secular” view of the prophets (admittedly quite common among Jewish and Zionist thinkers during that period), portraying them as “social activist[s] and political fighter[s],” who only used religious language because religion was the mode for social critique at the time, but were, in fact, “social thinkers,” "pioneering leaders and spokesmen for the village and city masses," "tribunes of the people," protesting at the corruption of the "ruling classes" or the "landowning class." According to Eisenstadt, the prophets sought to rally against the "poverty and destitution" of the "victimized masses," offering a "progressive" and "utopian" vision of "social justice and equality." The prophets, argued Eisenstadt, took this stance in the name of a "revolutionary social idea."[36]

Eisenstadt returned to the topic of ancient Jewish labor law in a 1937 article entitled "The Hebrew Worker During the Period of the Mishnah." Here, he provided a class-based Marxist-inspired history of the Jewish people. Eisenstadt described the biblical prophets as the ones "who first discovered the contradiction between the poverty and deprivation of the masses, and the luxurious life of the rulers." Such "exploitation" of the "popular masses," he said, also occurred during the period of Persian rule in Palestine. Later, the Sadducees, whom he described as a "conservative political party," blocked the development of "social legislation," found in embryonic form in Mosaic law, and the Pharisees, "party of the people," sought to "give a role to the working masses in the legislative process of the state." Some "urban intellectuals" also joined the "party of the artisans and peasants," seeking to "heal their moral consciousness, and purify their lives with hard work." During this period, laws to "safeguard the rights of the working community" were enacted, creating comprehensive labor legislation based on "social equity" – the first labor legislation ever created, according to Eisenstadt.[37] In a later lecture, delivered in 1948, Eisenstadt described the biblical prophets as defenders of "the rights of the working people, bearing the vision of world peace and the fraternity of nations," and again stated that the Pharisees fought to safeguard "the rights of the working masses."[38]

[36] Samuel Eisenstadt, *The Prophets: Their Times and Their Social Ideas*, trans. Max Rosenfeld (New York: YKUF, 1971), 5–8, 21, 22, 33, 45, 76, 111–17. The book was first published in Yiddish. See Samuel Eisenstadt, *Di Nevi'im: Zeyer tsayt un Zeyere Gezelshaftlekhe Ideyen* (Vilna: Klachkin, 1926). See also Samuel Eisenstadt, "'Al Ye'udo shel Tsibur ha-Sofrim be-Yemenu," *'Al ha-Mishmar*, July 9, 1948.

[37] Samuel Eisenstadt, "Ha-Po'el ha-'Ivri bi-Tkufat ha-Mishnah," *Ha-'Olam*, September 2, 1937, 1002–5.

[38] Eisenstadt, "'Al Ye'udo shel Tsibur."

In a popular lecture delivered in 1951, Eisenstadt told his listeners that, in regimes based on "class exploitation," law serves as a "weapon of the ruling class to oppress the exploited classes," but that socialist law is "a weapon of the working class ... to impose the dictatorship of the proletariat in order to vanquish capitalism and create a society free of exploitation."[39] In the 1950s, he also produced a fully fledged Marxist description of the history of Jewish family law, offering a "historical-sociological analysis" of the development of ancient Jewish family law based on the assumption that there was a defined sequence to the development of social–legal relationships and that no nation is free to circumvent any of the stages of that evolutionary scheme. In his analysis, he linked economic needs to family law rules regarding polygamy, dowry, family property, and inheritance. He noted the rise of a class-based society during the period of biblical judges and kings, discussing economic tensions, social ruptures, and the political subjugation of farmers by the kingly urban elite, and arguing, again, that class tensions led to the appearance of prophets – depicted by him as "social equality warriors and defenders of the rights of the farmers."[40] Another example of Eisenstadt's Marxist approach to the history of Jewish family law can be found in a 1962 article that he published in an East German history journal, in which he compared Jewish and Roman family and inheritance law.[41]

Marxist influence was also found in Eisenstadt's works on Roman law. One can see this influence in his 1953 textbook on the topic, which was based, he declared, on a social and historical approach to the study of Roman law – one that saw the development of this law as stemming from the conditions of the Roman economy and from a class struggle that stood at the basis of the Roman regime of slavery. In this book, Eisenstadt claimed, for example, that major changes in Roman law were the result of economic and political conditions: massive slave revolts that occurred in the territories ruled by Rome in the period between the first century BC and the first century AD.[42]

[39] "Mahzor Hartsaot 'Amamiyot 'al ha-Mishpat ha-Sotsyalisti," *Kol ha-'Am*, December 11, 1951.

[40] Samuel Eisenstadt, "Kavey Yesod be-Hitpathutam shel Diney-ha-Mishpahah ha-'Ivrit ha-Kdumim," in *Tsiyon*, 231, 238.

[41] Eisenstadt, "Paralleleinblicke," ix. [42] Eisenstadt, *Ha-Mishpat ha-Roma'i*, 11, 17.

Finally, Eisenstadt's works echoed the ideas of the German Free Law Movement.[43] In Chapter 2, I mentioned the impact of Free Law ideas on Dikshtein's thought. One can also see echoes of free law ideas, and especially the contrast between dry formal law and "living law," in Eisenstadt's works. In one of his first articles, written in Moscow in 1910, he said that Jewish law "should be filled up by the content of life and should nourish life with its spirit."[44] In another early article published in 1911, Eisenstadt provided a survey of Jewish legal history. Throughout the article, Eisenstadt talked about "life" or "social life" as determining the nature of law and modifying it. In this twenty-page article, the term "life" appeared in various permutations no less than forty times. Eisenstadt talked about Jewish law as being a "social science, a science of life," about oral Jewish law as a law that "flows and changes" with the flow of life. Here is how he poetically described the characteristics of legal discourse in the Talmud:

> The most sophisticated creation of Jewish law is the Talmud. It does not contain terse rules, dry paragraphs, or skeletal legal structures that do not speak to the heart or to logic. We see in the Talmud Jewish law at the time of its creation; we hear the debate as it bubbles and roars in the study hall, full of the storm of the senses and the exaltation of logic; every legal question is discussed passionately; the clear skies of the east are reflected in the debate, and it is adorned with the beautiful flowers of legend (*aggadah*). Before our eyes, a mighty battle unfolds; the sages fight with the tactics of developed logic and immense sharpness; they twist and turn, trespassing boundaries, soaring to the skies and descending to the depths of the idea they are debating, and finally, one of them appears with the crown of victory upon his head, his eyes shining. All the people see that his approach is true and just, and the matter is resolved.[45]

## *Apologetics: The Superiority of Jewish Law*

Eisenstadt claimed that, unlike previous scholars of Jewish law, he would not engage in an apologetic defense of this legal system. When

[43] On this movement, see, e.g., Katharina Isabel Schmidt, "Law, Modernity, Crisis: German Free Lawyers, American Legal Realists, and the Transatlantic Turn to 'Life,' 1903–1933," *German Studies Review* 39 (2016): 121.

[44] Samuel Eisenstadt, "Hevrah Mada'it le-Hakirat ha-Mishpat ha-'Ivri: Mikhtav Galuy," in *Tsiyon*, 31, 32.

[45] Eisenstadt, "Le-Korot," 194–5, 207.

surveying the literature on Jewish law in Europe from the Renaissance onward, he criticized eighteenth-century works for being apologetic and thus attempting to hide the "objective truth" regarding Jewish law.[46] However, in practice, Eisenstadt often actively sought to show the superiority of Jewish law. In his unpublished autobiography, he explicitly discussed this problem. Describing the very first courses he taught on Jewish law (at the Odessa Rabbinical Seminary), he noted that he was torn between his commitment to objective scientific critique and his "fervent love for our national heritage."[47]

Eisenstadt's urge to demonstrate the superiority of Jewish law was frequently found in those works of his in which he compared Jewish to Roman law. For example, in an article published in 1929, using a series of binary opposites, Eisenstadt claimed that Roman law was based primarily on power and the need to govern. In contrast, Jewish law was based on morality and the desire for absolute good. Roman law was based on action, and Jewish law was based on emotions. Roman law sought to serve the ruling citizens of Rome, many of whom were soldiers. At the center of Jewish law, in contrast, stood weak persons – the child, the orphan, the foreigner, the alien. Roman law was individualist, and Jewish law was collectivist. The purpose of Roman law was to protect the Roman conquerors, whereas the purpose of Jewish law was to maintain peace and justice. Roman law was based on external imposition and, therefore, did not require widespread learning of its rules. In contrast, Jewish law maintained itself through an extensive system of grassroots learning in Talmudic academies.[48]

[46] Eisenstadt, "Sifruto shel ha-Mishpat ha-'Ivri," in *Tsiyon*, 133. Another disavowal of Jewish apologetics can be found in Simon Federbusch, *Ha-Musar veha-Mishpat be-Yisrael* (Jerusalem: Mosad ha-Rav Kook, 1947), 8. For a general discussion of apologetics and Jewish Studies, see David Biale, "Between Polemics and Apologetics: Jewish Studies in the Age of Multiculturalism," *Jewish Studies Quarterly* 3 (1996): 174.

[47] Lavon Archive, IV-104–13–175, "Biyografiyah."

[48] Samuel Eisenstadt, "Yisrael ve-Romi be-Yetsiratam ha-Mishpatit," *Haaretz*, March 29, 1929. For a general discussion of the attitude of Jewish law scholars to Roman law during the interwar period, see Assaf Likhovski, "The Eagle and the Dove: Jewish Law Scholars and Roman Law During the Interwar Period," in *Pensiero giuridico occidentale e giuristi romani: Eredità e genealogie*, eds. Pierre Bonin et al. (Turin: G. Giappichelli, 2019), 267.

Eisenstadt repeated these dichotomies in a 1937 article. Jewish law, he said, was based on "justice, peace, and equality between all humans," while Roman law was based on the desire for "personal benefit, power, and control." Roman law, he explained, was modified by the morality of Jewish law following the Christianization of the Roman Empire; and, in subsequent centuries, there were repeated attempts to synthesize Jewish morality with Roman law. For example, Hugo Grotius undertook such an endeavor in the early modern period, with the creation of modern international law – whose goal, according to Eisenstadt, was to subdue the human urge to fight and dominate other persons. However, modern international law could not prevent global conflicts of the type that the world was witnessing in the 1930s. Only Jewish law could redeem the world from such conflicts.[49]

Finally, on the jurisprudential level, Eisenstadt argued for the superiority of Jewish law based on the nature of Jewish law texts and Jewish legal education. In a 1941 article, he contrasted the modern sovereign legislator, who "prevents freedom of opinion and silences opposing voices," with Jewish law, which he described as a "truly popular law." Because of its popular nature, Jewish law texts did not present a unitary façade: they contained evidence of the debates surrounding the rules of Jewish law. In the Talmud, for example, readers were exposed to the differing opinions of the rabbis and could decide for themselves if a certain rule was correct.[50] Eisenstadt also compared the Jewish model of legal education favorably with the model found in Western universities. In a 1913 article, Eisenstadt discussed the Jewish study hall (*beyt midrash*) and said that it represented a popular and non-hierarchical model of legal education that was not geared toward practical ends but toward pure learning. As such, it was superior to the Western model.[51]

[49] Samuel Eisenstadt, "Yotsrey ha-Mishpat be-Yisrael uve-Romi," *Haaretz*, December 23, 1937. See also Samuel Eisenstadt, "Musag ha-Ishiyut ha-Mishpatit ba-Mishpatim ha-'Ivri veha-Roma'i," in *Tsiyon*, 201.

[50] Samuel Eisenstadt, "Le-Hitpathuto shel ha-Klal be-Sifrutenu ha-Mishpatit," in *Tsiyon*, 156, 159.

[51] Samuel Eisenstadt, "Beyt ha-Midrash ha-'Ivri," *Shaharit* 1 (1913): 69–71. See also Eisenstadt, "Yisrael ve-Romi," 2.

### *Evolutionary Schemes, Social Hierarchies, Democracy*

Non-Western law was generally seen by nineteenth- and early twentieth-century Western legal thinkers as representing a lower rung on the evolutionary ladder of the development of law. One reason for this depiction was that non-Western law was understood as being closely tied to religion. Henry Maine, for example, described Hindu law in his book *Ancient Law* as a law based on ancient codes, which could not be reformed because of the sanctity of religion.[52]

Eisenstadt, both because of his apologetic approach to Jewish law and also because he was a lifelong secular socialist, sought to distance Jewish law from Jewish religion. He did acknowledge that, originally, law and religion were intermingled since law was seen as emanating from God.[53] He also conceded that Jewish law was based on the idea of heavenly justice.[54] However, the religious nature of Jewish law was not part of its essence. Jewish law, he proclaimed in an early article, was a secular law that was only "hidden" in religious texts because of the Jewish Exile.[55] In an article on the distinction between public and private Jewish law, he noted the religious nature of Jewish law but then explained that public law wore a "religious mask" during the Jewish Exile, Jewish religion merely being a "receptacle" for law. Because Jewish religion had a "social and national aspect," he claimed, it did not distort public law but, rather, preserved it until such time as its secular nature could be revealed.[56] Another aspect of Eisenstadt's ambivalent attitude to the religious nature of Jewish law can be found in his book on the biblical prophets. Here, he argued that the prophets were actually secular social reformers who used the language of religion only because that was the convention during biblical times.[57]

Just like Pal, Eisenstadt, too, devoted much effort to justifying the inegalitarian nature of the legal system he was studying. One major expression of this inegalitarianism was found in the existence of slavery. In a 1917 article, Eisenstadt observed that, while slaves did exist in ancient Israel and were treated as property, they were not seen

[52] See Henry Sumner Maine, *Ancient Law* (London: John Murray, 1861), 15–18, 77.

[53] Eisenstadt, "Le-Korot," 196. [54] Ibid., 203. [55] Ibid., 194–5.

[56] Samuel Eisenstadt, "Le-Heker Mishpatenu ha-Pumbi," *Ha-Mishpat ha-'Ivri: Riv'on Mada'i* (1918): 8, 11, 12, 20.

[57] Eisenstadt, *The Prophets*, 15, 16.

as similar to animals or movable property, as was the case in other ancient legal systems. Among nomadic peoples, such as the early Israelites, he said, the difference between slaves and masters was not great, and there was no chasm of class difference, such as that which existed in more economically advanced nations. Slaves and masters herded the flocks together, and slaves were not subjected to hard labor. For example, they were not involved in building city walls like slaves in urban societies. Slaves were considered members of the family and were able to inherit the property of a childless master.[58]

In a long article published in 1927, Eisenstadt compared the attitudes of Roman and Jewish law to slavery. He remarked that slavery existed in Roman law and was not initially regarded by Roman lawyers as problematic. However, with the rise of Christianity, Roman lawyers began to see slavery as opposed to natural law. All men, they came to believe, were born free; and, therefore, slavery became a problem to be justified. Jewish law did not have the same problem because, while Jewish law did recognize slavery, the recognition was "limited."[59] Roman law's initial attitude to slavery was the result of the fact that the Roman Empire was a huge state artificially composed of a conglomerate of occupied countries and nations, which could not survive without mass enslavement under harsh conditions. In contrast, the agrarian residents of Palestine had no opportunity or desire for conquest or the enslavement of war prisoners, and their main occupation – farming – was carried out by themselves or by tenants and hired hands. Jewish law recognized slavery, then, but the rules that governed it were far more lenient than those of Roman law. Thus, while Roman citizens could become slaves (and then lose their citizenship), Jews could not become lifelong slaves (and, if foreigners enslaved them, they had to be redeemed); slaves who were treated harshly by their owners were emancipated, unlike Roman slaves; and, although slaves could inherit the property of their childless master, the master could not inherit the property of the emancipated slave.[60]

One point on which Roman law was more liberal than Jewish law, to modern eyes, was that of the status of the children of slaves. Roman

58 Eisenstadt, "Kadmoniyot ha-Mishpat ha-Yisre'eli."

59 Samuel Eisenstadt, "He'arot le-Sefer ha-Institutsyot shel Yustinyanus Keysar," in *Tsiyon*, 75, 78–9.

60 Ibid., 80–4. See also Samuel Eisenstadt, "Ha-Mishpat ha-'Ivri veha-Mishpat Ha-Roma'i," *Ha-Boker*, February 19, 1942.

law declared that the child of a free man and a female slave was free, while Jewish law declared that this child was a slave. The harsher norms of Jewish law, explained Eisenstadt, were the result of the fact that foreign slaves were common in Rome, which thus became "an international nation." In contrast, Jews in Palestine waged constant wars against the influx of foreign slaves and, therefore, were less lenient toward the offspring of mixed couples.[61]

Eisenstadt also dealt extensively with the status of women in Jewish law. He taught family law at the Tel Aviv School of Law and Economics, and his wife was a member of various feminist organizations in 1950s Israel. Thus, it is not surprising that the topic concerned him, and his works on the legal status of women ranged widely. They included articles dealing with ancient Jewish family law, the legal position of women in the ancient city of Ugarit, and the status of women in contemporary Israel. However, Eisenstadt was not merely a scholar interested in describing family law. When the Israeli Parliament debated the Israeli Women's Equal Rights Law of 1951, Eisenstadt prepared a long memorandum criticizing the law for not being radical enough.[62] He also called for extensive reforms in Jewish family law, which the State of Israel applied in litigation between Jewish litigants and which tended to discriminate against women. Noting the conservative nature of this area of law, he advocated for creating a codification committee to reform it.[63]

When discussing the status of women in Jewish law, Eisenstadt often adopted a critical tone. For example, he said that polygamy, recognized by Jewish law in the biblical period but also later (for example, in the major sixteenth-century codification of Jewish law by Rabbi Joseph Karo), was a norm that was left over from the "primitive period" of Jewish law and that it should be formally abolished to ensure equal rights for women.[64] However, while, in some of his writings, Eisenstadt was critical of the attitude of Jewish law to

[61] Eisenstadt, "He'arot le-Sefer," 85–6.

[62] Eisenstadt, "Kavey Yesod," in *Tsiyon*, 231, 238; Samuel Eisenstadt, "Le-Matsavah ha-Mishpati shel ha-Ishah be-Ugarit," in *Tsiyon*, 247; Samuel Eisenstadt, "He'arot le-Hatsa'at Hok Shivuy Zkhuyot ha-Ishah," in *Tsiyon*, 184.

[63] Samuel Eisenstadt, "Beyn ha-Rashuyot: Ra'ayonot be-Diney Mishpahah be-Yisrael," in *Tsiyon*, 213.

[64] Samuel Eisenstadt, "Shiyarey ha-Poligamyah ba-Mishpat ha-'Ivri," in *Tsiyon*, 150–1.

women, one can also find evidence to the contrary. For example, in an article he published in English in 1948, Eisenstadt attempted to prove that Jewish law did not discriminate against women. In discussing law during the era of the biblical patriarchs, he noted that daughters and widows inherited an equal portion of the inheritance to that of men but that this rule did not apply when women married outside the family. This exception, he explained, was justified in order not to divide family property. He then stressed that, in this scenario, the women would be compensated for their lost share of the family property. Later, the protection of widows was guaranteed by a marriage contract containing provisions promising a minimum sum of fixed compensation for the wife in the case of divorce or the husband's death. In addition, daughters, too, were entitled to alimony upon the death of their father.[65]

A final aspect of Eisenstadt's apologetic attitude was found in his attempt to depict Jewish law as inherently democratic. Jewish law, he said, was not a product of rulers or kings. It was "popular [and] democratic ... the people were the creator of law" – or, more specifically, the prophets, who were the "tribunes of Israel" and personified the needs of the people.[66] Elsewhere, Eisenstadt discussed the history of the Council of Four Lands, a Jewish representative body that existed in early-modern Poland, describing it as being, in fact, a Jewish parliament.[67]

### *Collectivism*

In his 1953 textbook on Roman law, Eisenstadt devoted several pages to comparing Roman and Jewish law. Roman law, he said, was the law of a society of masters who owned both men and property, and their ownership was based on the notion that the individual right of private property had no limits. In contrast, the rules of property and inheritance in Jewish law were based on the idea of collective ownership, and the notion of individual property was undeveloped and limited.[68] The collectivist nature of Jewish law was also expressed

65 Eisenstadt, "Early History," in *Tsiyon*, vi. 66 Eisenstadt, "Le-Korot," 201.

67 Eisenstadt, "Le-Heker Mishpatenu ha-Pumbi," in *Tsiyon*, 48.

68 Eisenstadt, "Ha-Mishpat ha-'Ivri veha-Roma'i, " in *Tsiyon*, 260.

in specific legal doctrines such as the jubilee year rule, the seven-year agricultural sabbatical cycle, and in rules pertaining to labor law, charity, levirate marriage, and quasi-contract.[69]

In 1957, Eisenstadt published an article comparing the notion of the legal persons in Jewish and Roman law, claiming that this notion did not exist in ancient Roman law and only appeared later, in medieval and modern times. This, he claimed, was because the idea of a legal person required both a conception of property that did not focus solely on private property and also a recognition that abstract, bodiless entities can exist. Neither of these ideas, said Eisenstadt, was present in ancient Roman law, which was based on the premise of the absolute individual property rights of the head of the household, the *paterfamilias*, and on a polytheistic religion whose many gods took on bodily forms. In contrast, property in Jewish villages in Palestine until the end of the Second Temple period was held in common. Communal religious groups sharing their property, such as the Essenes, were also widespread. In addition, abstract thinking, which rejected corporeality, was also common among Jews, and this outlook was evident not solely in the theological realm but in the legal sphere too. Ancient manifestations of this approach included, for example, the collective liability of biblical towns and tribes, while later expressions were found in the appearance of local and central religious and charitable endowments.[70]

The individualism–collectivism contrast was also noted by Eisenstadt in an article in which he remarked that Roman law protected private property, unlike Jewish law (and other oriental legal systems), which saw individuals (and their property) as an indivisible part of the collective.[71] One qualification regarding the binary dichotomy between individualist Roman law and collectivist Jewish law that Eisenstadt did make, however, was that he noted how the Ten Commandments reflected a regime of private property.[72]

[69] Ibid., 267; Eisenstadt, *Ha-Mishpat ha-Roma'i*, 2nd ed. (1962), 30–1.

[70] Eisenstadt, "Musag ha-Ishiyut ha-Mishpatit," in *Tsiyon*, 201.

[71] Eisenstadt, "He'arot le-Sefer," in *Tsiyon*, 71, 72. See also Eisenstadt, "Ha-Mishpat ha-'Ivri veha-Roma'i," in *Tsiyon*, 266–7; Eisenstadt, "Early History," in iii–iv.

[72] Samuel Eisenstadt, "Kadmoniyot ha-Mishpat ha-'Ivri," in *Tsiyon*, 291, 294, 302.

## Eisenstadt's Unique Jurisprudential Ideas

Eisenstadt was not a deep jurisprudential thinker. Nevertheless, his scholarship contains several interesting ideas, three of which I will mention here.

### *Nationalist and Marxist Legal Theory Combined*

Eisenstadt saw no problem in combining the nationalist legal ideas of the Historical School with Marxist legal theory. This is less surprising than it perhaps seems. First, Marx himself was a student of Friedrich Carl von Savigny, the founder of the Historical School.[73] Marxist legal theory, therefore, may be seen as indebted to, and in part shaped by, the principles of this intellectual tradition. Second, 1920s Soviet policy, to which Eisenstadt was exposed while living in Moscow, encouraged and celebrated the creation and propagation of the national cultures of the nations that were living under Soviet rule rather than attempting to erase them. Lenin and Stalin, in particular, argued for national self-determination (within the confines of a unitary central Soviet state, of course). This policy led to the promotion of national languages (Yiddish, in the case of the Jews).[74] It also had implications in the legal sphere. In the early 1920s, for example, there were attempts to integrate Shari'a courts in Central Asia into the Soviet legal system and to "harmonize" Islamic law and Soviet legislation.[75] Thus, Eisenstadt's desire to study and use Jewish law would not have been seen by him as being in contradiction to his socialist and, later, communist beliefs.

### *A Non-Western Model of Legal Education*

In Jewish law, Eisenstadt found a unique concept of legal education that differed significantly from the Western concept. In an article

[73] See Norman Levine, "The German Historical School of Law and the Origins of Historical Materialism," *Journal of the History of Ideas* 48 (1987): 431, 443.

[74] See Yuri Slezkine, "The USSR as a Communal Apartment, or How a Socialist State Promoted Ethnic Particularism," *Slavic Review* 53 (1994): 414; Terry Martin, *The Affirmative Action Empire: Nations and Nationalism in the USSR, 1923–1939* (Ithaca, NY: Cornell University Press, 2001), 3, 49, 197–8.

[75] See, e.g., Paolo Sartori, "What Went Wrong? The Failure of Soviet Policy on Shari'a Courts in Turkestan, 1917–1923," *Die Welt des Islams* 50 (2010): 397.

published in 1913, Eisenstadt compared European universities to the "typically oriental" Jewish study hall. The Orient, he claimed, seeks spiritual development. It strives for harmony between religious and moral values and social needs, while the West seeks cultural conquest and technical development, and its universities are, therefore, places for the training of a professional and practical elite (medical doctors, lawyers, teachers, architects, and so on). Eisenstadt then contrasted Western universities with the Jewish study hall, which he characterized as a gathering place for those unsatisfied by mere territorial conquest or technical advancement. Unlike the Western university, he argued, the Jewish study hall is not a training ground for the sons of the upper classes of society – it is a popular institution open to all. There are no teachers and students, as everyone is both student and teacher simultaneously; everyone seeks an eternal living truth, where the boundaries between individuals blur in the noise of "enthusiastic debate." The Zionists of Palestine, he noted, had already established vocational schools. However, this was not enough. This oriental model of legal education embodied in the study hall should, he argued, be resurrected in Jerusalem, and "the great Hebrew worldview," frozen and enslaved in Europe to foreign cultures, should be revived, creating a new generation of Jewish youth imbued with both "tradition and life."[76] In his 1950s book on Roman law, Eisenstadt repeated these ideas about the unique nature of Jewish legal education. He observed that one of the major differences between Roman and Jewish law was that, unlike the Romans, the Jews did not view law as the exclusive domain of rulers and specialists only. Jewish law was a topic that all members of society were supposed to study.[77]

[76] Eisenstadt, "Beyt ha-Midrash ha-'Ivri," 69–71. See also Eisenstadt, "Yisrael ve-Romi," 2.

[77] Eisenstadt, *Ha-Mishpat ha-Roma'i*, 2nd ed. (1962), 30–1. The contrast that Eisenstadt drew between the Western and Jewish models of legal education reminds one of Robert Cover's distinction, made some seventy years later, in his landmark article "Nomos and Narrative." Here, Cover distinguished between the Jewish "paideic" or "pedagogic" approach to law, where law is created and maintained, bottom-up, by individual and communal study, and the Western "imperial" approach, in which norms are created and enforced, top-down, by formal institutions and where the obligation to study law was not seen as a universal duty incumbent on all members of society. See Robert C. Cover, "Foreword: The Supreme Court: 1982 Term [Nomos and Narrative]," *Harvard Law Review* 97 (1983): 1, 11–13.

## *A Non-Western Genealogy of International Law*

Finally, Eisenstadt offered an interesting argument about the antiquity of international law (echoing the ideas of other interwar Jewish law scholars who will be discussed in Chapter 6). As early as 1918, Eisenstadt argued that international law was not invented in the early modern period – one could already discern the rules of international law in the biblical period.[78] In 1926, he wrote an article attacking the common view that international law was created in Europe. The discovery of ancient Near Eastern texts by Western archaeologists, he said, revealed that international law was not born in Europe in the early modern era and should not only be associated with thinkers such as Hugo Grotius. The Bible and texts from Egypt, Babylonia, and the Hittite Empire indicated that international law existed in the ancient Near East. The generalization and abstraction that are hallmarks of modern international law were missing, but the idea itself could be found in literary myths, in diplomatic letters between ancient kings, and in specific treaties. Eisenstadt then offered an extended analysis of the Bible and the descriptions it contains of various international practices from the age of the Patriarchs and later biblical periods, identifying parallels with modern international law in areas such as international boundary-setting, negotiations, allegiances, treaties, the status of diplomatic envoys, and rules governing wars.[79] Eisenstadt also contrasted international treaties of the ancient Near East that were based on realist considerations – the need to show political strength and to accommodate the violence of the bigger powers of the region – with the ideas of the biblical prophetic movement, which, as it gained strength in ancient Israel, fostered a new approach to international law that was based on public morality.[80]

Another facet of Eisenstadt's argument about the antiquity of Jewish international law appeared in his book *The Prophets*, published in Yiddish in 1926. Eisenstadt described biblical prophets as "outspoken, principled opponents of war and bloodshed" who opposed the "reactionary" nature of war and were "internationalists"

[78] Eisenstadt, "Le-Heker Mishpatenu ha-Pumbi," 61–2.
[79] Samuel Eisenstadt, "Reshit Yihusav ha-Beyn Le'umim shel ha-'Am ha-Yisra'eli," in *Tsiyon*, 97.
[80] Ibid., 118.

in their outlook. According to his reading, the prophets "sharply criticized the never-ending militarization of the great powers [of the ancient biblical world] and sought to show the ineffectuality of physical power in international conflict," determined to expose "international injustice."[81]

In his discussions of international law, Eisenstadt voiced ideas that are somewhat comparable to the ideas of contemporary TWAIL (Third World Approaches to International Law) scholars. The proponents of TWAIL argue that international law is a system that was created by Europeans in the early modern period to legitimize and sustain the plunder and subjugation perpetrated by Western great powers on the Third World. TWAIL scholarship emerged in the late 1990s, but the scholars associated with it acknowledge that it had precursors. However, they place these precursors in the period of decolonization immediately after the Second World War.[82] Eisenstadt's discussion (as well as that of the scholars that will be discussed in Chapter 6) shows that similar ideas about the non-Western origins of international law antedated the end of the Second World War.

## Conclusion

Eisenstadt's life and thought were undeniably exceptional. No other thinker associated with the idea of reviving Jewish law combined a passion for cultural nationalism with a political commitment to communism. Nevertheless, in many other respects, Eisenstadt's views were similar to those of a larger cohort of early twentieth-century Zionist legal thinkers. The influence of the German Historical

[81] Eisenstadt, *The Prophets*, 30–2.

[82] See, e.g., Makau Mutua, "What Is TWAIL?" *Proceedings of the Annual Meeting (American Society of International Law)* 94 (2000): 31; David Armitage and Jennifer Pitts, "'This Modern Grotius': An Introduction to the Life and Thought of C.H. Alexandrowicz," in *The Law of Nations in Global History: C.H. Alexandrowicz*, eds. David Armitage and Jennifer Pitts (Oxford: Oxford University Press, 2017), 1, 10. For works that analyze the history of international law before the early modern era, see, e.g., Amnon Altman, *Tracing the Earliest Recorded Concepts of International Law: The Ancient Near East (2500–330 BCE)* (Leiden: Martinus Nijhoff, 2012); Jeremy I. Levitt, "The African Origins of International Law: Myth or Reality," *UCLA Journal of International Law and Foreign Affairs* 19 (2015): 113.

School, the assertion of Jewish law's superiority over Western legal systems, and the apologetic attempts to justify the more problematic aspects of this ancient legal system were all traits that were shared by many of Eisenstadt's fellow Jewish legal scholars working in the Diaspora, in Mandatory Palestine, and Israel. Can we also compare Eisenstadt to contemporary Indian legal scholars such as Pal? This is the question that I will now explore.

# *Interlude 2: Politics*

Radhabinod Pal and Samuel Eisenstadt were born in the same year, 1886, in two imperial territories, colonial India and imperial Russia. As young adults, both witnessed the momentous, revolutionary events of 1905. Russia's defeat in the Russo-Japanese War inspired young Indian nationalists such as Pal. It was also one of the factors that spurred a revolutionary wave of unrest across the Russian Empire during 1905, ultimately setting the stage for the downfall of the Empire twelve years later, in 1917, and shaping the lives of a generation of Russian socialist revolutionaries, including Eisenstadt.

Pal and Eisenstadt also shared many additional biographical traits: both followed similar educational trajectories, studying law in Western or Western-style academic institutions; both were influenced by a blend of Western historical and sociological theories of law; both sought to use the legal past in the service of a modern cause – namely, anti-colonial nationalism; both – perhaps because of a personal motivation to prove their academic worth as legal scholars, perhaps as a result of their shared resentment toward European culture, or perhaps as a result of heartfelt pride in their particular legal heritage – wrote apologetic works on their respective religious legal systems; both attempted to show that the conventional evolutionary Western view of non-Western legal systems was mistaken; both sought to show the superiority of these systems, for example, by favorably juxtaposing their alleged peace-loving nature with imperialistic Western society and law; and both sought to downplay the non-egalitarian aspects of their respective religious systems – for example, by arguing that persons deemed by these systems as socially inferior such as slaves and women were actually treated humanely, or that modern democratic institutions had their ancient counterparts in Hindu and Jewish law; both emphasized the collectivist nature of their respective legal systems and contrasted this collectivism favorably with Western individualism; and both held non-mainstream political views (Hindu, as opposed to Indian, nationalism in Pal's case and communism in Eisenstadt's case), which, perhaps, impeded the widespread reception of their legal ideas.

Pal's life and ideas represented a larger group of Indian scholars trained in law who were interested in Hindu legal history and Hindu jurisprudence. Most of these scholars were associated with the University of Calcutta. The ideas found in Pal's works on Hindu law echoed similar ideas found in other works produced in India in the late colonial period. However, unlike these scholars, who all remained obscure, Pal achieved lasting international recognition thanks to his Tokyo Trial dissent. Eisenstadt, too, was, in some senses, representative of a cohort of Jewish law scholars who were active in the early and middle decades of the twentieth century. Eisenstadt's affiliation with communism was unique, but apart from his idiosyncratic political views, his life and ideas mirrored those of many of his fellow Jewish law scholars: his Eastern European origins and the educational path that he followed, combining traditional religious studies with a law degree obtained from a European university, were two characteristics that many other scholars belonging to the early twentieth-century movement for the revival of Jewish law shared. His legal ideas were not unique either. One can find other works produced by Jewish law scholars at the time that show the influence of the Historical School. The arguments about the superiority of Jewish law over Roman law, the apologetic defense of some of the more unsavory aspects of Jewish law, and the interest in the collectivist elements of this legal system – all could be found in the writings of various scholars.

There were also significant biographical and jurisprudential differences between the two men. Pal began his academic career as a mathematics teacher, later focusing exclusively on law. Eisenstadt was far more versatile. He was a legal scholar, linguist, publisher, librarian, and political activist. His works spanned many genres and included academic articles, monographs, textbooks, and translations.

Pal published his works in English and thus wrote not just for an Indian audience but also for non-Indian readers. His intended audience was primarily academic, rather than the general public. Eisenstadt also produced academic works (for example, his bibliography of works on Jewish law), but some of his works (such as his book on the prophets) were intended for a broader, lay audience. Because Eisenstadt's works were written in Hebrew, his readership, by definition, was narrower.

Like other Indian scholars, Pal's discussion of Hindu law was heavily influenced by English law and by the ideas of English-speaking thinkers. Two major imaginary interlocutors of his were the nineteenth-century English legal scholars John Austin and Henry Maine, both of whom were criticized by Pal in his attempt to defend Hindu law. Eisenstadt's work was primarily influenced by Continental law scholarship and especially by the nineteenth-century German scholars of Roman law. Nineteenth-century historical approaches to the study of law influenced both men. However, Pal was also influenced by Continental anti-formalist legal theories, and by American sociological jurisprudence, while Eisenstadt blended the ideas of the Historical School with Marxist theory.

Pal and Eisenstadt were legal historians of ancient religious legal systems, but the historical approaches that informed their works differed. While Pal's works summarized and analyzed the history of Hindu law, the history he offered was not deeply embedded in the economic and social context of ancient Indian society. In contrast, Eisenstadt, inspired by Marxism, contextualized the history of Jewish law by linking it to economy and society.

The comparative legal taxonomies used by the two scholars were also different.[1] Pal sought to incorporate ancient Hindu law within a broader shared framework, that of the Aryan legal family. According to him, Hindu law was an early (and superior) Aryan legal system. Eisenstadt, meanwhile, focused not on similarity but on difference. He

[1] On the changing taxonomies used by comparative law scholars to classify both ancient and modern legal systems, see, generally, Mariana Pargendler, "The Rise and Decline of Legal Families," *American Journal of Comparative Law* 60 (2012): 1043; Balázs Fekete, *Paradigms in Modern European Comparative Law: A History* (Oxford: Hart, 2021).

sometimes referred to Jewish law as part of a larger, oriental, legal family.[2] However, perhaps because the two major legal systems he taught were Roman and Jewish law, Eisenstadt's comparative vision was often starkly binary. He talked about two major legal systems competing for dominance in global legal history: Roman and Jewish law, which represented different sets of values and jurisprudential ideas.

Like the scholars of Hindu and Jewish jurisprudence that I discussed in Part I of this book, the goals that underlay Pal's and Eisenstadt's interest in their respective ancient legal systems differed. Pal, like most other Indian scholars of his time, was largely interested in Hindu law not because he saw it as a possible source of norms for the future legal system of India but because he regarded its study as a way to bolster pride in the Hindu past. Eisenstadt, by contrast, like many other Jewish law scholars of his generation, was not interested in Jewish law merely for its historical significance. Rather, he approached it as a possible source for the law of the future Jewish State.

Pal was no proponent of the actual use of Hindu law to replace the legal system created by the British in India during the colonial era. When discussing the possible use of modern legal categories to analyze ancient law, he remarked that asking whether "an ancient institution was adequate for modern conditions" was misguided. Legal institutions should be judged with reference to the "peculiar social needs of their times" and not to the present, he reasoned.[3]

The fact that "legal revival" also meant, in the specific Indian context, modernization and unification of the law through codification may have led to Pal's rejection of this notion. This is evident in his reaction to the post-independence codification of Hindu personal law. In the

[2] For examples of the discussion of Jewish law within an "Oriental" legal family, see Samuel Eisenstadt, "Le-Korot ha-Mishpat ha-'Ivri (Skirah Klalit)," *He-'Atid: Me'asef Sifruti Mada'i* 3 (1909–11): 194, 207–8. Eisenstadt also attempted to compile a "Corpus Iuris Orientalis" that would compare the laws of ancient Near East societies. See Central Zionist Archives, A212/46. The "Oriental law" comparative framework informed the work of the German scholar Josef Kohler, and Eisenstadt may have borrowed this framework from him. See Josef Kohler and Leopold Wenger, *Allgemeine Rechtsgeschichte*, Vol. 1: *Orientalisches Recht und Recht der Griechen und Römer* (Leipzig: Teubner, 1914).

[3] Radhabinod Pal, *The History of Hindu Law in the Vedic Age and in Post-Vedic Times down to the Institutes of Manu* (Calcutta: University of Calcutta Press, 1958), 279 [hereinafter "Pal, *History*"].

mid-1950s, the newly independent Indian State enacted four Hindu Code Bills meant to reform and codify Hindu personal law (the Hindu Marriage Act, Hindu Succession Act, Hindu Minority and Guardianship Act, and Hindu Adoptions and Maintenance Act).[4] A month before the enactment of the Hindu Marriage Act of 1955, Pal participated in an all-India convention on the Hindu Code Bills, where he attacked both the reform of the Hindu law of succession and the Hindu law of marriage. Regarding the desire to introduce divorce in Hindu law, Pal said that the indissolubility of marriage "was the binding force that cemented it" and that "we must not shut our eyes to the evils of divorce." Other participants expressed similar sentiments, stating that "we should not blindly imitate the West."[5] One can conclude that Pal's works on Hindu law were not motivated by a desire for its actual use, because such use also entailed its modernization. Instead, Pal's works were meant to counter condescending Western portrayals of this legal system and to instill pride in ancient Indian history.

Pal's reluctance to use Hindu law was also applicable to Hindu jurisprudence. As we saw, a major characteristic of Hindu jurisprudence was its affinity with natural law theory. However, when the time came to apply the latter in practice, Pal could have easily based his Tokyo Trial opinion on natural law theory, but he declined to use the opportunity. Instead, Pal's dissent in Tokyo affirmed the positivist approach to international law.[6] In this context, it is interesting that

[4] See Rina Verma Williams, "Hindu Law as Personal Law: State and Identity in the Hindu Code Bills Debates, 1952–1956," in Timothy Lubin, Donald R. Davis Jr., and Jayanth K. Krishnan, *Hinduism and Law: An Introduction* (Cambridge and New York: Cambridge University Press, 2010), 105, 105–19; Werner Menski, "Hindu Law in Modern Times: How Hindu Law Continues in Modern India," in *The Oxford History of Hinduism: Modern Hinduism*, ed. Torkel Brekke (Oxford: Oxford University Press, 2019), 244, 255.

[5] See "Delhi Convention Attacks Hindu Code Changes," *Times of India*, April 11, 1955, 5. See also Nariaki Nakazato, *Neonationalist Mythology in Postwar Japan: Pal's Dissenting Judgment at the Tokyo War Crimes Tribunal* (Lanham, MD: Lexington Books, 2016), 105, 218.

[6] See, e.g., Nakazato, *Neonationalist Mythology*, xxvii; Gary J. Bass, *Judgment at Tokyo: World War II on Trial and the Making of Modern Asia* (New York: Knopf, 2023), 585–9. Milinda Banerjee argues that Pal's Tokyo Trial dissent was not positivist. While, in his jurisprudential writings, he embraced a conception of law similar to the Western conception of natural law, in Tokyo, Pal rejected natural law – but this rejection was the result of his regarding it as a pretext for Western imperialism. See

Pal's extremely lengthy Tokyo dissent does not mention Hindu law or Hindu jurisprudence.[7]

Meanwhile, the use of Jewish law as a foundational element of the legal system governing the lives of the Jews of Palestine (and later, the State of Israel) was a central concern for many early twentieth-century Jewish legal scholars, including Eisenstadt.[8] In Eisenstadt's view, the academic study of Jewish law was a prerequisite for the revival of Jewish law as the law of the Jewish community in Palestine and of the future Jewish State. In this, he was following the scholars of the German Historical School, who argued that the academic study of Roman and Germanic law should precede the creation of a civil code for Germany. The study of Jewish law, Eisenstadt believed, would thus serve to provide a basis for the law of a reborn Jewish polity.[9]

The difference between Pal's and Eisenstadt's attitudes to legal revival may have been partly the result of differences in their biographies. Eisenstadt studied law in a Central European university and was thus influenced by the idea (typical of Continental legal systems) that law professors play an important role in creating new legal norms. More specifically, the research agenda of the German Historical School, which gave legal scholars a major role in

Milinda Banerjee, "Does International Criminal Justice Require a Sovereign? Historicising Radhabinod Pal's Tokyo Judgment in Light of His 'Indian' Legal Philosophy," in *Historical Origins of International Criminal Law*, eds. Morten Bergsmo, Wui Ling Cheah, and Ping Yi (Brussels: Torkel Opsahl Academic EPublisher, 2014), Vol. 2, 69–70, 92–108; Milinda Banerjee, *The Mortal God: Imagining the Sovereign in Colonial India* (Cambridge: Cambridge University Press, 2018), 262; Milinda Banerjee, "Sovereignty as a Motor of Global Conceptual Travel: Sanskritic Equivalents of 'Law' in Bengali Discursive Production," *Modern Intellectual History* 17 (2020): 487, 501–2. See also Ashis Nandy, "The Other Within: The Strange Case of Radhabinod Pal's Judgment on Culpability," *New Literary History* 23 (1992): 45, 77–80; Partha Chatterjee, *I Am the People: Reflections of Popular Sovereignty Today* (New York: Columbia University Press, 2020), 154 n13 (arguing that Pal's Tokyo dissent echoed the idea found in the *Mahabharata* that war is the fault of both sides).

7 See Radhabinod Pal, *International Military Tribunal for the Far East: Dissentient Judgement of Justice Pal* (Tokyo: Kokusho Kankokai, 1999).

8 See, generally, Assaf Likhovski, *Law and Identity in Mandate Palestine* (Chapel Hill, NC: University of North Carolina Press, 2006), 127–53.

9 For some examples of his lifelong interest in legal revival, see Samuel Eisenstadt, "Le-Heker Mishpatenu ha-Pumbi," *Ha-Mishpat ha-'Ivri: Riv'on Mada'i* (1918): 8, 24–5; Samuel Eisenstadt, "Likrat ha-'Atsma'ut ha-Mishpatit [part I]," *Ha-'Olam*, April 14, 1938, 5; Samuel Eisenstadt, "Medinah u-Mishpat," *Ha-Praklit* 5 (1948): 113.

producing law codes based on historical materials they collected, inspired Eisenstadt's academic activities. In contrast, Pal, trained in an anglicized university in India, may have been less influenced by the Continental vision of the role of law professors (and, specifically, legal historians) as major producers of legal norms.[10] In addition, Pal was a legal scholar but also a practicing lawyer trained in anglicized Indian law. On the other hand, Eisenstadt was a scholar and law teacher, but not a legal practitioner. His legal training in Switzerland did not expose him to English law. When he moved to Palestine, he attempted to work as a consultant on Jewish family law, but he never formally practiced law, either in Mandatory Palestine or post-independence Israel. Thus, he was far less committed than Pal to the existing anglicized legal system within which he was working.

I would now like to focus on one specific topic, the political motivations of the two scholars. Both Pal and Eisenstadt espoused radical political ideologies. However, their political views were to be found at the two opposite ends of the spectrum. Pal was a right-wing nationalist, while Eisenstadt was a socialist and later a communist. How did their radical politics influence their scholarship?

The difference between right-wing and left-wing ideology led Pal and Eisenstadt to depict Hindu and Jewish law in different ways. Pal argued that the main goal of Hindu law was to preserve social stability. Law was supposed to reflect an immutable, harmonious cosmic order, and this order was reflected in a stable society characterized by integration and coordination, a society in which every person knew and accepted their place within the social hierarchy. On the other hand, Eisenstadt described Jewish law as a revolutionary rather than a conservative force, constantly striving toward social justice and endeavoring to protect the weak against the strong.

Despite being on both sides of the political spectrum, Pal and Eisenstadt's radical political views had a similar underlying utopian basis. They looked to their respective legal systems for alternative values to those of Western liberal law. Propelled by a utopian motivation, Pal and Eisenstadt mined the texts of their respective

[10] For a general discussion of the impact (or lack thereof) of English legal scholars on the creation of English legal norms in the nineteenth and twentieth centuries, see Neil Duxbury, *Jurists and Judges: An Essay on Influence* (Oxford: Hart, 2001), 61–115.

religious legal system to find a new legal and social vision that could replace the existing colonial order, and, more broadly, the liberal ideology that dominated their legal education. Yet their pursuit of an idealized past left them unable to confront the flaws within these systems. Pal, under the influence of pan-Asian, Indian, and perhaps also Hindu nationalism, could only see the dark side of the West: British colonial oppression in India and later (after the Second World War) American global imperialism, exemplified by the use of the atomic bomb against Japan. He downplayed the evils of his own inegalitarian caste-based legal system (as well as the evils of the heroes of his pan-Asian ideology, the Japanese). Eisenstadt, meanwhile, was tempted by a romantic infatuation with the biblical prophets and their modern-day emulators, communist intellectuals. He, therefore, sought to downplay the more problematic aspects of Jewish law (such as its attitude toward slaves and women) and also ignored the suffering and death of millions of persons killed by communism in the Soviet Union and elsewhere before, during, and after the reign of his hero, Joseph Stalin, whose biography, it will be recalled, he translated in the 1940s. This utopian romantic infatuation with the legal past was, it seems, a poor guide to the present and future, fostering idealized visions that provided enticing alternatives to the existing legal order but, ultimately, proved to be problematic.

Pal and Eisenstadt did not know of each other and knew little about each other's legal systems. Pal did not seem to know much about (post-biblical) Jewish law. This legal system was seldom mentioned in his scholarship, and in the few times he did mention it, he used secondary sources that portrayed it in an unflattering manner.[11] There were also

[11] See, e.g., Pal, *History*, 61 (citing Arnold Toynbee on rabbinical interpretation); ibid., 116 (on the "whimsical and despotic" Semitic God); ibid., 267 (citing Nietzsche's statement that the Manusmriti is "incomparably superior and more intellectual" than the Bible"). For another example from the same period of negative attitude to Jewish law, see Nagendra Nath Mukerjee, "Indo-Aryan Penal Jurisprudence," *Calcutta Law Journal* 14 (1911): 29n, 31n (claiming that Moses was influenced by Manu, but that Moses' penal laws were more barbaric than those of Manu because Egyptian slavery turned the Jews into "little better than wild, scalp-hunting savages, perpetually engaged in enacting among themselves ... duels or blood feuds"). A less radical comparison of ancient Hindu and Jewish criminal law is found in Sitaram Banerjee, "Principles of Criminology," *Calcutta Law Journal* 31 (1920): 1n.

hints of Holocaust denial in his works.[12] India and its laws were mentioned in some early articles by Eisenstadt.[13] However, apart from these brief allusions, there is no indication that he knew anything of any significance about Hindu law, let alone about Pal's scholarship.

There was one place in which Pal and Eisenstadt could have met but did not. In December 1954, an "Asian Conference of Lawyers" convened in Calcutta. This event was sponsored by the International Association of Democratic Lawyers (IADL), a progressive association that was, in fact, a Soviet-sponsored communist front organization.[14] Eisenstadt sent a telegram to the participants to support their struggle "for human rights, democratic freedoms, [and] coexistence in peace of free and sovereign nations."[15] Pal was an anti-communist.[16] However, curiously, he agreed to inaugurate this conference – perhaps the result of the anti-imperialist and anti-Western stance of the IADL.[17]

The communist ideology that lurked behind the IADL façade has long since lost its power, at least in most countries of the world. Now, with hindsight, we can see this ideology in all of its complexity: A movement

[12] See Radhabinod Pal, *Crimes in International Relations* [the Tagore Law Lectures, 1938] (Calcutta: University of Calcutta, 1955), 128–31 (where Pal juxtaposed a discussion of the Holocaust and a discussion of English anti-German propaganda during the First World War). It should be noted that, in the postwar era, Pal condemned Western racial theories. See Pal, *History*, 271–2. See also Nakazato, *Neonationalist Mythology*, 133; Bass, *Judgment at Tokyo*, 636–7.

[13] Samuel Eisenstadt, "Di Arbayter un di Arbayter-Frage in der Alter Yidisher Geshikhte," *Di Tsukunft* 8 (1908): 762, 763, 766–7; Eisenstadt, "Le-Korot," 208; Eisenstadt, "Le-Heker Mishpatenu ha-Pumbi," 17n1. Fleeting references to Hindu law are also found in the works of Eisenstadt's colleague Paltiel Dikshtein. See Paltiel Dikshtein, "Mehir Tsedek ve-Ona'ah," *Ha-Mishpat Ha-'Ivri* 1 (1925/26): 15, 20, 23 (mentioning examples of price regulation in ancient Indian law based on Kohler and Wenger, *Orientalisches Recht*).

[14] See Gene D. Overstreet and Marshall Windmiller, *Communism in India* (Berkeley, CA: University of California Press, 1959), 438. On the IADL, see, generally, International Commission of Jurists, *Under False Colours: A Report on the Character of the International Association of Democratic Lawyers* (The Hague: n.p., 1955); Howard B. Tolley Jr., *The International Commission of Jurists: Global Advocates for Human Rights* (Philadelphia, PA: University of Pennsylvania Press, 2010), 28–9.

[15] "Mahar be-Kalkuta – Ve'idat Anshey ha-Mishpat shel Artsot Asiah," *Kol Ha-'Am*, December 22, 1954.

[16] See Nakazato, *Neonationalist Mythology*, 51.

[17] Danial Latifi, "[Letter to the Editor]: Democratic Lawyers," *Times of India*, March 21, 1955.

born out of laudable concerns for the oppressed that morphed into a monstrous and evil dogma responsible for the murder of millions of people during the twentieth century. The same complexity is also the hallmark of nationalism, the ideology that inspired Pal and Eisenstadt. It, too, is emancipatory and oppressive, empowering and bloody simultaneously. The same ambivalence underlies any reflection on the life and ideas of Pal and Eisenstadt. The lives of both scholars are inspiring. Both came from oppressed groups and modest backgrounds. Both became highly educated legal scholars, producing an impressive array of interesting and sometimes even innovative works on their respective religious legal systems. However, both, in hindsight, made morally questionable political choices ultimately born out of their romantic infatuation with nationalist ideas and with their respective ancient religious legal systems.

Sometimes, however, romantic utopian infatuation with the past is not only negative but has a positive, hopeful side. In the next part of this book, I will focus on scholars writing not on law generally but on a specific legal subfield – public law. I will examine Indian and Jewish scholars belonging to the academic milieu that I described in Parts I and II of the book who wrote works on ancient Indian and Jewish public law under the influence of historicist jurisprudential theories. I will show how these scholars sought to prove that the institutions and values of ancient Indian and Jewish political thought and public law were compatible with modern Western democratic institutions and liberal values. This attempt had little impact on the actual constitutional law of post-independence India and Israel. However, as I shall ultimately argue in the Epilogue, it is relevant and important today because of its potential positive use in mitigating some of the anti-democratic and anti-liberal sentiments that have appeared in recent decades in Israel, India, and other countries.

# PART III

# ANCIENT PUBLIC LAW

# 5

# The Hindu Polity Literature

In 1946, Shriman Narayan Agarwal, a disciple of Mahatma Gandhi (and later the governor of Gujarat), wrote a proposal laying out the principles for a future Indian constitution.[1] In the introduction to his proposal, Agarwal argued that India should not base its constitution on Western models. Instead, it should create a "swadeshi" (that is, made in India) constitution, one which would reflect "our national genius, culture and traditions." India, he explained, "is a very ancient land." It experimented with various forms of government "at a time when Europe and the New World had not even come within the pale of civilization." It would be "a great insult to India" to create a constitution that would be based on a mixture of rules taken from the West. "Administrative systems cannot and should not be transplanted," he asserted. Each nation "has its unique culture and civilisation which may be called its 'Soul.' ... we have aped the West for long," he concluded, "let us now be proud of our Indian culture and institutions."[2]

[1] Shriman Narayan Agarwal, *Gandhian Constitution for Free India* (Allahabad: Kitabistan, 1946), 10–11. See also Granville Austin, *The Indian Constitution: Cornerstone of a Nation* (Oxford: Clarendon Press, 1966), 30–1; Tejas Parasher, *Radical Democracy in Modern Indian Political Thought* (Cambridge: Cambridge University Press, 2023), 108–19. For an earlier example of a "Gandhian constitution" (the 1939 constitution of the princely state of Aundh), see Apa Pant, *An Unusual Raja: Mahatma Gandhi and the Aundh Experiment* (Hyderabad: Sangam Books, 1989); Parasher, *Radical Democracy*, 99–101.

[2] Agarwal, *Gandhian Constitution*, 10–11.

Benegal Narsing Rau was one of India's leading jurists and diplomats in the early postcolonial period. He also served as an advisor to the Indian Constituent Assembly. In an article he wrote in 1949, Rau discussed the choice that faced the Indian Constituent Assembly between a presidential and parliamentary system of government. Rau chose to analyze this topic not by turning to Western constitutional models. Instead, he suggested that it would be profitable to "take a peep into the history of India ... and see how far her people have been accustomed to the theory and practice of parliamentary modes of government." Rau then remarked that while ancient Indian states were mostly monarchies, kings were expected to heed the advice of their ministers, who, in turn, were responsible to the people. He also noted that one can find ancient Indian texts dealing with procedures in assemblies, which "anticipate to an astonishing extent" the rules prevalent in modern parliaments. Therefore, he concluded, parliamentarism was a concept that was familiar to the ancient Indians.[3]

The particularist and historicist approach to constitution-making evident in both Agarwal's and Rau's works expressed, in the realm of public law, the Western historicist jurisprudential notions about the relationship between the "spirit" of a people and its laws that we encountered in the previous chapters. Montesquieu already argued, in the eighteenth century, that each nation had its own unique constitutional forms.[4] This idea later appeared in the works of the leader of the German Historical School, Friedrich Carl von Savigny, who declared that "in the earliest times to which authentic history extends, the law will be found to have already attained a fixed character, peculiar to the people, like their language, manners, and

[3] Benegal Narsing Rau, "The Parliamentary System of Government in India," *Washington Law Review and State Bar Journal* 24 (1949): 91, 91–3. For similar sentiments, see Austin, *Indian Constitution*, 325–6; Rohit De, "Constitutional Antecedents," in *The Oxford Handbook of the Indian Constitution*, eds. Sujit Choudhary, Madhav Khosla, and Pratap Bhanu Mehta (Oxford: Oxford University Press, 2016), 17, 18; Rohit De, *A People's Constitution: The Everyday Life of Law in the Indian Republic* (Princeton, NJ: Princeton University Press, 2018), 8–9. See also Rohit De and Ornit Shani, *Assembling India's Constitution: A New Democratic History* (Cambridge: Cambridge University Press, 2025), 172–3.

[4] See Otto Kahn-Freund, "On Uses and Misuses of Comparative Law," *Modern Law Review* 37 (1974): 1, 7.

constitution [*verfassung*]."[5] It was also common among nineteenth-century English political thinkers.[6] In India, these ideas can be traced back to a body of works that emerged in the early decades of the twentieth century in connection with the newly reformed University of Calcutta. These works – which can be collectively called the "Hindu polity" literature – analyzed the history of ancient Indian political ideas and institutions and also sometimes discussed ancient Indian public law, or more specifically, constitutional and international law.[7] Both Agarwal and Rau cited the Hindu polity literature.[8] In this chapter, I explore this literature.[9]

I begin with a brief description of how constitutional law and international law were taught in England and India in the late nineteenth century. I will then offer a group portrait of the authors who produced the Hindu polity literature. Next, I turn to several significant themes in these works, which stood at the intersection of history, political science, and constitutional law.[10] I conclude by

[5] F. C. von Savigny, *Of the Vocation of our Age for Legislation and Jurisprudence*, trans. Abraham Hayward (London: Littlewood, 1831), 24.

[6] See, e.g., John Stuart Mill, *Considerations on Representative Government* (London: Parker, 1861), 2–3.

[7] Modern "public law" encompasses additional subfields of law such as administrative, tax, and criminal law, which will not be discussed here.

[8] See Agarwal, *Gandhian Constitution*, 10–11 (citing the work of K. P. Jayaswal); Rau, "Parliamentary System," 93 (citing the works of K. P. Jayaswal and Beni Prasad).

[9] Some aspects of the Hindu polity literature have been analyzed in previous studies. See Ram Sharan Sharma, *Aspects of Political Ideas and Institutions in Ancient India*, 2nd rev. ed. (Delhi: Motilal Banarsidass, 1968), 1–13; Ronald B. Inden, *Imagining India* (Bloomington, IN: Indiana University Press, 2000), 188–98; Milinda Banerjee, *The Mortal God: Imagining the Sovereign in Colonial India* (Cambridge: Cambridge University Press, 2018), 228–38; Parasher, *Radical Democracy*, 71–92. See also C. A. Bayly, *Recovering Liberties: Indian Thought in the Age of Liberalism and Empire* (Cambridge: Cambridge University Press, 2012), 281–90 (focusing specifically on the thought of Benoy Kumar Sarkar and Radhakamal Mukerjee). There is also a study which is focused on the long-term use of one of the major sources of the Hindu polity literature, Kautilya's *Arthashastra*. See Maria Misra, "The Indian Machiavelli: Pragmatism versus Morality, and the Reception of the *Arthasastra* in India, 1905–2014," *Modern Asian Studies* 50 (2016): 310. For a general discussion on the importance of studying constitutional thought outside the West, see Philipp Dann, "Southern Turn, Northern Implications: Rethinking the Meaning of Colonial Legacies for Comparative Constitutional Studies," *Comparative Constitutional Studies* 1 (2023): 174.

[10] My main focus will be monographs or collections of lectures but I will also mention a few articles published in academic and non-academic journals. I will mostly discuss works published before Indian independence, and will make only scant reference to works published after 1947.

analyzing the general characteristics of this literature and the context which gave rise to it.

## The Study of Constitutional and International Law in England and India

Constitutional law gradually emerged as a distinct subject in English legal education only in the second half of the nineteenth century. Before that time, it was intertwined with other subjects. Thus, the first book of Blackstone's *Commentaries on the Laws of England*, published in 1765, which was based on lectures that Blackstone delivered at Oxford, dealt with subjects that we would now regard as belonging to constitutional law but also discussed administrative law, family law, labor law, and corporate law.[11]

The first professor of "English law and jurisprudence" at King's College, London, was John James Park, appointed in 1831. His book, *The Dogmas of the Constitution*, was published in 1832. However, shortly thereafter, in 1833, Park died, and subsequent professors of law at King's College had little interest in constitutional law.[12] Decades later, in the 1870s, Sheldon Amos served as the University of London examiner in constitutional law and history and wrote on the topic.[13] Constitutional law was also taught, beginning in 1850, at Queen's College, Birmingham and at Haileybury College, where the East India Company trained its administrators until 1858.[14]

11 William Blackstone, *Commentaries on the Laws of England* (Oxford: Clarendon Press, 1765), Vol. 1.

12 See Robin Morse, "Dower, Dogma and Grand Designs: Law at King's Nineteenth Century Style," in *King's College London: In the Service of Society*, ed. Christine Kenyon Jones (London: King's College, 2004), 60, 63, 65. On the teaching of law at the University of London in the nineteenth century, see also W. L. Twining, "Laws," in *The University of London and the World of Learning, 1836–1986*, ed. F. M. L. Thompson (London: Hambledon Press, 1990), 82, 86–96.

13 Sheldon Amos, *A Primer of the English Constitution and Government* (London: Longmans, 1877); G. Blaine Baker, "Popularizing the Rule of Law: Sheldon Amos and the International Scientific Series, 1874 to 1909," *Journal of Legal History* 33 (2012): 151, 156. For a general discussion of nineteenth-century English constitutional thought, see Jeffrey Goldsworthy, "Constitutional Theory and Thought," in *The Cambridge Constitutional History of the United Kingdom*, eds. Peter Cane and H. Kumarasingham (Cambridge: Cambridge University Press, 2023), 254, 277–81.

14 W. Wesley Pue, "Guild Training vs. Professional Education: The Committee on Legal Education and the Law Department of Queen's College, Birmingham in the 1850s,"

Five Readers teaching both constitutional law and legal history were appointed at the Inns of Court in 1852 – the same year that a Bachelor of Civil Law degree was introduced at the University of Oxford.[15] At Oxford, too, English constitutional law was first taught solely as part of the exam on the history of English law. It was only in 1886 that a paper on constitutional law per se was required of students.[16] During this period, English history professors such as William Stubbs and Edward Freeman published leading works on English constitutional history.[17] In the first decades of the twentieth century, the emphasis on history in the study of constitutional law at Oxford declined; administrative law was also added to the curriculum, and more attention was paid to the analysis of the case law relevant to modern constitutional law.[18]

The teaching of a topic related to constitutional law – international law – at English universities followed a similar trajectory of gradual growth. A Chair in International Law and Diplomacy was established at Oxford in 1859, and international law was one of the four examination topics at the Oxford School of Law and Modern History in the last decades of the century.[19] At King's College, international law was taught in the second half of the nineteenth

*American Journal of Legal History* 33 (1989): 241, 274; Andrew Watson, "The Legal Education Revolution that Failed: Attempts to Establish a Legal University in Victorian Britain," *Journal on European History of Law* 14 (2023): 28, 31.

15 Patrick Polden, "The Education of Lawyers," in *The Oxford History of the Laws of England*, ed. William Cornish et al., Vol. 11: *1820–1914 English Legal System* (Oxford: Oxford University Press, 2010), 1175, 1183. Later, at least at Lincoln's Inn, the lecturer who taught constitutional law did so together with public and private international law, legal history, and jurisprudence. Ibid., 1196.

16 Andrew Boon and Julian Webb, "Legal Education and Training in England and Wales: Back to the Future," *Journal of Legal Education* 58 (2008): 79, 85; F. H. Lawson, *The Oxford Law School 1850–1965* (Oxford: Clarendon Press, 1968), 39–40, 66.

17 See Edward A. Freeman, *The Growth of the English Constitution from the Earliest Times* (London: Macmillan, 1872); William Stubbs, *The Constitutional History of England: In Its Origins and Development*, 3 vols (Oxford: Clarendon Press, 1874–78). See, generally, Linda Colley, *The Gun, the Ship, and the Pen: Warfare, Constitutions, and the Making of the Modern World* (New York: Liveright, 2021), 415; Rocco Giurato, "Constitutional History Teaching in Britain (19th–20th Centuries)," *Giornale di Storia Costituzionale / Journal of Constitutional History* 47 (2024): 85.

18 Lawson, *Oxford Law School*, 77, 143. 19 Ibid., 25, 31, 36.

century by Leone Levi, who wrote mainly on commercial law but also published two books on international law in 1855 and 1887.[20]

In India, too, the teaching of constitutional law developed gradually. At the beginning of the twentieth century, constitutional law was not taught at any of the law colleges affiliated with the University of Calcutta, although Indian constitutional law was taught at the Madras Law College.[21] By the 1920s, however, constitutional law had become one of the four topics of the preliminary exams for bachelor of law students at the University of Calcutta.[22] Constitutional and administrative law also became part of the curriculum of the MA program in Political Philosophy and Political Economy.[23] In addition, the MA program in Ancient Indian History and Culture required extensive study of ancient Indian constitutional history. Several Tagore Law Lectures delivered during the first decades of the twentieth century dealt with various topics related to modern constitutional and administrative law.[24]

Public international law was not taught at the University of Calcutta College of Law in the early decades of the twentieth century, although private international law was a compulsory subject of the Master of Law degree.[25] However, public international law was mandatory for all postgraduate students in History and those studying Political Philosophy and Economics at the university. A Chair in International Law, held by Arthur Brown, was established in the 1920s. Foreign international law scholars such as Harvard University professors

[20] Morse, "Dower, Dogma and Grand Designs," 63, 65.

[21] "Mr. N. N. Ghosh, Principal, Metropolitan Institution," in Indian Universities Commission, *University of Calcutta:* Part II – *Written Statements Presented by Witnesses* (Calcutta: Office of the Superintendent of Government Printing, 1902), [80]; Indian Universities Commission, *Report of the Indian Universities Commission, 1902* (Simla: Government Central Printing Office, 1902), 34. See, generally, De, "Constitutional Antecedents," 26, 36–7.

[22] University of Calcutta, *The Calendar 1917* (Calcutta: Calcutta University, 1917), 503; University of Calcutta, *Regulations* (Calcutta: Calcutta University, 1927), 215, 217, 290. In the 1920s, Indian and English constitutional law were also the topic of one of the exams for a law degree at Benares Hindu University. See Benares Hindu University, *Calendar 1922–1925* (Benares: Benares Hindu University, n.d.), 322.

[23] University of Calcutta, *The Calendar 1931* (Calcutta: Calcutta University, 1931), 1004.

[24] See *Hundred Years of the University of Calcutta*, Pramathanath Banerjee et al. eds. (Calcutta: University of Calcutta, 1957), 438.

[25] See University of Calcutta, *Calendar 1931*, 100, 170–1.

Manley O. Hudson and George Grafton Wilson also lectured on the topic there in the 1920s.[26] International law, too, was the subject of several University of Calcutta lecture series.[27]

Some constitutional law teachers at the University of Calcutta focused mainly on the modern era – that is, on the constitutional arrangements of colonial India. For example, Naresh Chandra Roy, a professor of history and political science at City College Calcutta and a lecturer at the University of Calcutta, published several works on the constitutional and administrative structure of British India.[28] Jyoti Prasad Sarvadhikari, who taught constitutional law and Hindu law at the University of Calcutta College of Law, also published a book on modern constitutional law in the late 1920s.[29] However, there were many people affiliated with the University of Calcutta whose research was devoted to the study of ancient Indian constitutional history, often as part of a broader interest in the nature and institutions of ancient Indian states.

## Authors

This section offers a collective portrait of the authors of the Hindu polity works.[30] Unlike Pal and Eisenstadt, discussed in Part II of this book, there is less biographical information about most of the authors

[26] Ibid., 170–1, 182, 915, 935, 976–7, 1004.

[27] Ibid., 1070; *Hundred Years of the University of Calcutta*, 438.

[28] See Naresh Chandra Roy, *The Constitutional System of India* (Calcutta: University of Calcutta Press, 1937); Naresh Chandra Roy, *A Critical Study of Some Aspects of Public Administration in Bengal* (Calcutta: University of Calcutta Press, 1945). See also *Hundred Years of the University of Calcutta*, 385. After Indian independence, Roy did publish at least one work that also dealt with the pre-colonial period. See Naresh Chandra Roy, *Main Currents of Political Thinking in India: Two Lectures Delivered at the Federation Hall* (Calcutta: Bimal Ch. Ray, 1965). For a broader description of the scholarly literature on constitutional law produced in the British Empire during the colonial period, see H. Kumarasingham, "Written Differently: A Survey of Commonwealth Constitutional History in the Age of Decolonisation," *Journal of Imperial and Commonwealth History* 46 (2018): 874.

[29] Jyoti Prasad Sarvadhikari, *A Handbook of English Constitutional Law (with a Chapter on India)* (Calcutta: n.p., 1928). Another lawyer teaching at the University of Calcutta was Nagendranath Ghose, who delivered the 1918 Tagore Law Lectures on Comparative Administrative Law. See Nagendranath Ghose, *Comparative Administrative Law* (Calcutta: Butterworth, 1919); University of Calcutta, *Calendar 1931*, 104, 106.

[30] This discussion is not intended to be exhaustive. I will not deal with works published in the first decades after Indian independence, which were written by both Indian and non-Indian authors. See, e.g., A. S. Altekar, *State and Government in Ancient India:*

that I will discuss here. Nevertheless, they seem to have shared some similar traits. Many belonged to the same age group – born in or around the 1880s and coming of age in the first decade of the twentieth century. Most were educated in colleges affiliated with the University of Calcutta, and many later taught there or were associated in some other way with this institution. A few authors worked in other locations, but even in this case, they often had some link with the University of Calcutta.

Indian historians were already writing works on the history of India, inspired by Western models, in the nineteenth century.[31] Interest among Indian scholars in ancient Indian constitutional history became evident in the first decade of the twentieth century.[32] However, this interest received a significant boost with the discovery, in the South Indian city of Mysore, of the most important ancient Indian treatise on statecraft, the *Arthashastra* (translated as "the science of government" or "the science of wealth") in the first decade of the twentieth century. This treatise was traditionally attributed to the fourth-century BC Indian philosopher and statesman Chanakya (also called Kautilya), an advisor to the first Mauryan Emperor,

*From Earliest Times to c. 1200 A.D.* (Banaras: Motilal Banarsidass, 1949); D. Mackenzie Brown, *The White Umbrella: Indian Political Thought from Manu to Gandhi* (Berkeley, CA: University of California Press, 1953); Vishwanath Prasad Varma, *Studies in Hindu Political Thought and Its Metaphysical Foundations* (Delhi: Motilal Banarsidass, 1959); Sharma, *Aspects*; Upendra Nath Ghoshal, *A History of Indian Political Ideas: The Ancient Period and the Period of Transition to the Middle Ages* (Bombay: Oxford University Press, 1959); B. A. Saletore, *Ancient Indian Political Thought and Institutions* (Bombay: Asia Publishing, 1963); Radhakrishna Choudhary, *Kautilya's Political Ideas and Institutions* (Varanasi: Chowkhamba Sanskrit Series Office, 1971).

31 See, e.g., Ranajit Guha, *An Indian Historiography of India: A Nineteenth-Century Agenda and Its Implications* (Calcutta: K. P. Bagchi, 1988); Shamita Basu, *Religious Revivalism as Nationalist Discourse: Swami Vivekananda and New Hinduism in Nineteenth-Century Bengal* (New Delhi: Oxford University Press, 2002), 40–66.

32 In 1916, historian K. V. Rangaswami Aiyangar mentioned a "Mr. Puranam Nagabhushanam," who, as early as 1894, had written on the topic of "Kingship in Ancient India." I was unable to locate this source. See K. V. Rangaswami Aiyangar, *Considerations on Some Aspects of Ancient Indian Polity* (Madras: S. P. C. K. Press, 1916), 78. In his brief overview of the Hindu polity literature, Ram Sharan Sharma mentioned three articles published by *The Calcutta Review* and *The Modern Review* that appeared before 1900. These articles argued that the Western image of despotic Indian kings was misleading and that ancient Indian kings were not autocratic monarchs. Sharma described these articles as belonging to the "moderate," pre-national, phase of interest of Indian intellectuals in the topic. See Sharma, *Aspects*, 3.

Chandragupta. The manuscript of this treatise was discovered sometime before 1905 by Rudrapatna Shamasastry, the Chief Librarian of the Mysore Government Oriental Library. Shamasastry began publishing translations of sections of the *Arthashastra* in 1905, and an English translation of the entire work was published in 1915.[33]

The founding father of the Hindu polity literature was Kashi Prasad Jayaswal. Jayaswal, born in 1881, came from a low-caste (*kalwar*) but wealthy family. He studied history at Oxford and was also called to the English Bar. In England, he also came into contact with Indian nationalist revolutionaries and became a follower of the Hindu nationalist activist V. D. Savarkar. Jayaswal returned to India and settled in Calcutta in 1910, working there as a lawyer. He accepted the invitation of the Vice Chancellor of the University of Calcutta, Asutosh Mookerjee, to join its Department of Postgraduate Studies, but the British blocked his appointment because of his "seditionist" political views. Jayaswal moved to Patna in 1914, working there as a lawyer, journalist, and scholar.[34] Despite the move to Patna, Jayaswal's affiliation with the University of Calcutta continued even after his relocation, ultimately resulting in an invitation to deliver the Tagore Law Lectures in 1917.[35]

In 1913, Jayaswal published an article entitled "An Introduction to Hindu Polity" in the Calcutta nationalist magazine, *The Modern Review* (based on earlier articles published in 1911 and 1912). Here, he sought to show that, until the modern era, Indian governmental

[33] On the history of this text and its authorship, see, e.g., *King, Governance, and Law in Ancient India: Kautilya's Arthaśāstra*, trans. Patrick Olivelle (Oxford: Oxford University Press, 2012), 1; Misra, "The Indian Machiavelli," 314–18; Mark McClish, *The History of the Arthaśāstra: Sovereignty and Sacred Law in Ancient India* (Cambridge: Cambridge University Press, 2019).

[34] Gadadhar Prasad Ambastha, "Dr. K. P. Jayaswal: A Memoir," in K. P. Jayaswal, *Hindu Polity: A Constitutional History of India in Hindu Times*, 2nd enlarged ed. (Bangalore: Bangalore Printing & Publishing Co., 1943), xxiii, xxvi; J. S. Jha, ed., *K. P. Jayaswal Commemoration Volume* (Patna: K. P. Jayaswal Research Institute, 1981); Ratan Lal, *Kashi Prasad Jayaswal: The Making of a "Nationalist" Historian* (Delhi: Aakar Books, 2018), 1–56. After Jayaswal's move to Patna he seems to have moderated his political views. See ibid., 107–8.

[35] K. P. Jayaswal, *Manu and Yâjñavalkya – A Comparison and a Contrast: A Treatise on the Basic Hindu Law* (Calcutta: Butterworth, 1930); Lal, *Kashi Prasad Jayaswal*, 9–13, 21–2, 107–23, 161–71.

institutions had been "at par if not superior" to Western ones.[36] Such was the response to the publication that it prompted a trend of similar works.[37] Jayaswal continued working on the topic, publishing a two-volume book on Hindu polity in 1921.[38]

Other authors followed in Jayaswal's footsteps. Many of these were scholars who were educated and then taught at the University of Calcutta: Narendra Nath Law taught law, history, and philosophy at the university.[39] Pramathanath Bandyopadhyay (or Banerjee) also taught law and history. He was the Principal of the College of the Law in the late 1930s, and in 1946 he replaced Radhabinod Pal as the Vice-Chancellor of the university.[40] Pramatha Nath Banerjea, who studied at the Inns of Court, and also obtained a doctorate in economics from the University of London, was a professor of Economics.[41] Benoy Kumar Sarkar was a leading nationalist and pan-Asian intellectual in early

[36] K. P. Jayaswal, "An Introduction to Hindu Polity," *The Modern Review* 13 (1913): 535. See also K. P. Jayaswal, *Hindu Polity: A Constitutional History of India in Hindu Times* (Calcutta: Butterworth, 1924), v; Lal, *Kashi Prasad Jayaswal*, 155.

[37] On Jayaswal as a pioneer of the Hindu polity literature, see D. R. Bhandarkar, "Reminiscences," in *Professor K. V. Rangaswami Aiyangar Commemoration Volume* (Madras: G. S. Press, 1940), lvi. On Jayaswal's ideas, see also Inden, *Imagining India*, 188–9. For a survey of the literature from the period 1913–20, see Benoy Kumar Sarkar, *Positive Background of Hindu Sociology, Book II*, Part I: *Political* (Allahabad: Sudhindra Natha Vasu, 1921), 5–6. It should be noted that the term "Hindu polity" already appeared in the nineteenth century. See, e.g., *Hindu Polity (The Ordinances of Manu)*, trans. Edward W. Hopkins (London: Trubner, 1884).

[38] The first volume of this book dealt with ancient Indian assemblies and republics, and the second with monarchies and empires. The book was completed in 1918 but was only published in 1921. A later version, almost identical to the first version, was published in 1924 (this is the version which will be cited in this chapter). A second enlarged version was published in 1943 in Bangalore.

[39] See University of Calcutta, *Calendar 1931*, 7, 42, 48. His relevant works are Narendra Nath Law, *Studies in Ancient Hindu Polity: Based on the Arthaśâstra of Kautilya* (London: Longmans, 1914); Narendra Nath Law, *Inter-State Relations in Ancient India* (London: Luzac, 1920); Narendra Nath Law, *Aspects of Ancient Hindu Polity* (Oxford: Clarendon Press, 1921).

[40] *Hundred Years of the University of Calcutta*, 427; Pramathanath Bandyopadhyay, *International Law and Custom in Ancient India* (Calcutta: Calcutta University Press, 1920).

[41] "Bandyopadhyay" is the Sanskrit form of the Bengali surname "Banerjee." Note that there were two persons with similar names teaching at the University of Calcutta. Pramathanath Bandyopadhyay (or Banerjee), who was born in 1894 and died in 1976. He was a professor of law. Pramatha Nath Banerjea was born in 1879 and died in 1960. He was a professor of economics. The latter's relevant work is Pramathanath Banerjea, *Public Administration in Ancient India* (London: Macmillan, 1916). See also Inden, *Imagining India*, 192–3. On Banerjea's biography, see Dr. Dilip Mookherjee, "Acharya

twentieth-century Bengal. He became actively involved in the National Education Movement, the educational wing of the nationalist Swadeshi Movement which emerged in Bengal in 1905 in response to the British decision to partition the province. He later taught at the Department of Economics of the University of Calcutta, becoming head of the department in 1947.[42] Devadatta Ramakrishna Bhandarkar was the second Carmichael Chair of Ancient Indian History and Culture at the Department of History of the University of Calcutta, a chair established by Asutosh Mookerjee in 1912.[43] Bhandarkar's successor as the Carmichael Chair was Hemchandra Raychaudhuri.[44] Upendranath Ghoshal was a professor of history at Presidency College in Calcutta and a lecturer at the Departments of History and Politics at the University of Calcutta.[45] Narayan Chandra Bandyopadhyaya lectured at the University of Calcutta Departments of History and Anthropology.[46]

Pramatha Nath Banerjea, Oration at Federation Hall Society Auditorium," July 6, 2019, photocopy in the author's possession.

42 On his biography, see Suhrita Saha, "Benoy Kumar Sarkar (1887–1949): A Tryst with Destiny," *Sociological Bulletin* 62 (2013): 4, 5–6; Satadru Sen, *Benoy Kumar Sarkar: Restoring the Nation to the World* (New Delhi: Routledge, 2015); Martin J. Bayly, "Lineages of Indian International Relations: The Indian Council on World Affairs, the League of Nations, and the Pedagogy of Internationalism," *International History Review* 44 (2022): 819, 821. Relevant works of his are Benoy Kumar Sarkar, "Democratic Ideals and Republican Institutions in India," *American Political Science Review* 12 (1918): 581; Sarkar, *Positive Background*; Benoy Kumar Sarkar, *The Political Institutions and Theories of the Hindus* (Leipzig: von Markert, 1922).

43 B. C. Law, "The Late Professor Dr. Devadatta Ramkrishna Bhandarkar," *Annals of the Bhandarkar Oriental Research Institute* 30 (1949): 373, 373–4; University of Calcutta, *Calendar 1931*, 121. His works include D. R. Bhandarkar, *Lectures on the Ancient History of India on the Period from 650 to 325 B.C.* (Calcutta: University of Calcutta Press, 1919); D. R. Bhandarkar, *Some Aspects of Ancient Hindu Polity* (Benares: Benares Hindu University, 1929).

44 For his biography, see Ranabir Chakravarti, "Raychaudhuri, Hemchandra," in *Banglapedia: National Encyclopedia of Bengal*, https://en.banglapedia.org/index.php/Raychaudhuri,_Hemchandra. Relevant works are Hemchandra Ray[chaudhuri], "Was State-Socialism Known in Ancient India?" in *Sir Asutosh Mookerjee Silver Jubilee Volumes* (Calcutta: Calcutta University Press, 1922), Vol. 3.1, 429; Hemchandra Raychaudhuri, *Political History of Ancient India from the Accession of Parikshit to the Extinction of the Gupta Dynasty* (Calcutta: University of Calcutta Press, 1923).

45 See U. [N.] Ghoshal, *A History of Hindu Political Theories* (London: H. Milford, 1923). A later, somewhat similar, work is U. N. Ghoshal, *A History of Hindu Public Life* (Calcutta: Ramesh Ghoshal, 1945). See also U. N. Ghoshal, *Contributions to the History of the Hindu Revenue System* (Calcutta: University of Calcutta, 1929).

46 Narayan Chandra Bandyopadhaya, *Development of Hindu Polity and Political Theories* (Calcutta: Kerr, 1927). One review described this book as a "réchauffé"

Interest in ancient Indian political ideas and institutions was not limited to the law professors, economists, and historians teaching at the University of Calcutta. Scholars teaching at other Indian higher education institutions during the last decades of British rule in India were also interested in the topic. Often, these scholars were affiliated in some way with the University of Calcutta, either because they studied there during the heyday of interest in the subject in the 1910s or because they were invited to teach or lecture on the topic at Calcutta. This group included three scholars who completed their doctoral dissertations at the University of Calcutta during the 1910s. Radhakumud Mookerji earned his doctorate in 1915. He taught at the Bengal National College, a nationalist institute of education in Calcutta, moving in 1916 to Benares Hindu University, then to Mysore University, and finally to Lucknow University, where he served as the head of the History Department. He also served as a vice-president of a Hindu nationalist political party, the Hindu Mahasabha party.[47] Mookerji's younger brother, Radhakamal Mukerjee, taught economics and sociology at Lucknow University.[48] Ramesh Chandra Majumdar wrote a doctoral dissertation at the University of Calcutta,

of the works of Jayaswal and Sarkar. See A. B.-S. [probably Anantaprasad Banerji Sastri], "Reviews and Notes of Books," *Journal of the Bihar and Orissa Research Society* 14 (1928): 450; Narayan Chandra Bandyopadhyaya, *Kautilya: Or an Exposition of His Social Ideal and Political Theory* (Calcutta: Chuckervertty, 1927).

47 See "Biographical Sketch," in *Bharata-Kaumudi: Studies in Indology in Honour of Dr Radha Kumud Mookerji*, Pt. I, ed. N. K. Sidhanta (Allahabad: Indian Press, 1945), xii; Parasher, *Radical Democracy*, 73–83. Mookerji was one of the intellectuals associated with the Greater India Movement, which sought to explore and emphasize India's cultural and historical influence on Southeast Asia. On this movement, see, e.g., Susan Bayly, "Imagining 'Greater India': French and Indian Visions of Colonialism in the Indic Mode," *Modern Asian Studies* 38 (2004): 703; Jolita Zabarskaitė, *'Greater India' and the Indian Expansionist Imagination, c. 1885–1965: The Rise and Decline of the Idea of a Lost Hindu Empire* (Munich: De Gruyter, 2022). His works include Radhakumud Mookerji, "An Introductory Essay on the Age and Authenticity of the Arthaśâstra of Kautilya," in Law, *Studies*, ix; Radhakumud Mookerji, *Local Government in Ancient India* (Oxford: Clarendon Press, 1919).

48 His works include Radhakamal Mukerjee, *Democracies of the East: A Study in Comparative Politics* (London: P. S. King & Son, 1923), which compared ancient Indian political structures to those of China, Japan, and states of Southeast Asia. On this work, see Nazmul S. Sultan, "Between the Many and the One: Anticolonial Federalism and Popular Sovereignty," *Political Theory* 50 (2022): 247, 256–62; Parasher, *Radical Democracy*, 82–8.

published as a book in 1918. He was then appointed as the Dean of the Faculty of Arts at Dacca University.[49]

Three other scholars who wrote works on ancient Indian constitutional history had some affiliation with the University of Calcutta. As mentioned above, Rudrapatna Shamasastry was the person who discovered Kautilya's *Arthashastra*. He was a librarian and historian based in Mysore. In 1919, he was invited by Asutosh Mookerjee to deliver a ten-lecture series on subjects connected with the *Arthashastra* as part of the postgraduate lecture series at the University of Calcutta.[50] K. V. Rangaswami Aiyangar was a professor of history and economics at the Maharaja's College in Trivandrum in South India. In 1916, he published a book on ancient Hindu polity.[51] Aiyangar had various ties to the University of Calcutta. He served as an examiner on ethnology and anthropology there, and, in 1934, he delivered a series of lectures at the university on Indian cameralism.[52] Sivaswamy Aiyer was the Advocate-General of the Madras presidency and, later, Vice Chancellor of Madras University and Benares Hindu University.[53] In 1929, he delivered the Kamala Lectures at the University of Calcutta entitled "The Evolution of Moral Ideas in India."[54]

All the authors I have mentioned thus far had some affiliation with the University of Calcutta. There were other scholars not affiliated with the university whose works were also part of the corpus of works on Hindu polity. For example, Beni Prasad, who taught history, politics, and civics at the University of Allahabad, published two works in the

49 Ramesh Chandra Majumdar, *Corporate Life in Ancient India* (Calcutta: Surendra Nath Sen, 1918). A second edition was published in 1922. See Ramesh Chandra Majumdar, *Corporate Life in Ancient India*, 2nd ed. (Poona: Oriental Books, 1922). See also H. B. Sarkar, "Obituary Notices: Ramesh Chandra Majumdar," *Annals of the Bhandarkar Oriental Research Institute* 61 (1980): 361.

50 R. Shama Sastri, *Evolution of Indian Polity* (Calcutta: University of Calcutta, 1920), v, ix–xiv.

51 Aiyangar, *Considerations*.

52 *Professor K. V. Rangaswami Aiyangar Commemoration Volume*, xix, xxvi.

53 See, e.g., K. Chandrasekharan, *P. S. Sivaswami Aiyer*, 2nd reprint (New Delhi: Publication Division of the Government of India, 2000).

54 University of Calcutta, *Calendar 1931*, 178–80; P. S. Sivaswamy Aiyer, *Evolution of Hindu Moral Ideals* (Calcutta: Calcutta University, 1935). Aiyer was also interested in contemporary Indian constitutional law. See Sivaswamy Aiyer, *Indian Constitutional Problems* (Bombay: Taraporevala, 1928).

late 1920s on ancient Indian theories of government and ancient Indian political institutions.[55] V. R. Ramachandra Dikshitar was a professor of History and Archaeology at the University of Madras. He published a book on Hindu administrative institutions.[56] Anant Sadashiv Altekar, too, was a historian and archaeologist. He taught at Benares Hindu University and later at Patna University.[57] His works include a book on the position of women in ancient India, and an article about the lessons that ancient Indian constitutional history holds for the drafters of India's future constitution.[58] Finally, K. A. Nilakanta Sastri, who was trained at the University of Madras and ultimately became a professor of History there also displayed an interest in Kautilya's *Arthashastra*.[59]

### Themes

The authors of the Hindu polity literature saw the study of ancient Indian statecraft as a way to show "the genius of Hindu culture."[60] To do so, they sought to refute conventional negative Western images of ancient (and modern) India and, instead, to emphasize various positive aspects found (or purportedly found) in ancient Hindu texts. In the following paragraphs, I explore some common themes found in their works. My interest does not lie in asking whether the

[55] See Beni Prasad, *Theory of Government in Ancient India (Post-Vedic)* (Allahabad: Indian Press, 1927); Beni Prasad, *The State in Ancient India: A Study in the Structure and Practical Working of Political Institutions in North India in Ancient Times* (Allahabad: Indian Press, 1928). On Prasad, see Inden, *Imagining India*, 189–92; Parasher, *Radical Democracy*, 88–92.

[56] V. R. Ramachandra Dikshitar, *Hindu Administrative Institutions* (Madras: University of Madras, 1929).

[57] A. K. Narain, "Professor Anant Sadashiv Altekar," *Journal of the Numismatic Society of India* 22 (1960): xxvii, xxviii–xxx.

[58] A. S. Altekar, *The Position of Women in Hindu Civilization from Prehistoric Times to the Present Day* (Benares: Culture Publication House, 1938). For an earlier work on the topic, see Dwarka Nath Mitter, *The Position of Women in Hindu Law* (Calcutta: n.p., 1913); A. S. Altekar, "A Bird's-Eye View of the Hindu Polity: What It Teaches," *Proceedings of the Indian History Congress* 10 (1947): 56.

[59] See K. A. Nilakanta Sastri, "The Place of the Arthaśāstra in the Literature of Indian Polity," *Annals of the Bhandarkar Oriental Research Institute* 28 (1947): 84. On Nilakanta Sastri, see Kalyani Ramnath, "Intertwined Itineraries: Debt, Decolonization, and International Law in Post-World War II South Asia," *Law and History Review* 38 (2020): 1, 17.

[60] Ghoshal, *History of Hindu Political Theories*, ix–x.

early twentieth-century works accurately interpreted the authentic meaning of the ancient texts and correctly depicted the true nature of early Indian institutions. This is a question for historians of ancient South Asia. I am interested in how Indian scholars in the early twentieth century used the ancient texts to undermine negative Western images of India and to further their nationalist agendas.

### *Ancient Indian Political Theory: Practical, Secular, Innovative*

Western Indologists in the late nineteenth and early twentieth centuries often portrayed Indians as inherently spiritual and religious, suggesting they lacked aptitude for practical and secular pursuits. For example, the nineteenth-century German-English Indologist Max Müller argued that the Indians were "a nation of philosophers" and that "India has no place in the political history of the world."[61] Arthur Berriedale Keith, who taught Sanskrit and constitutional law at the University of Edinburgh in the first decades of the twentieth century, condescendingly acknowledged that one could find in India a "pedantic" and "intensive study of the practical aspect of government." Still, he also disparagingly noted that "the subtle and profound spirit of India ... is alien to the conception of man as a political organism, whose true end can be found only in and through membership of a social community. Hence, India offers nothing that can be regarded as a serious theory of politics in the wider sense of that term."[62] A related argument was that Indians, unlike Westerners, lacked a sense of nationalism and patriotism. Both arguments, said the Indian historian Sharma, were used to justify Western imperialism.[63]

The Hindu polity writers sought to show that India had its own pragmatic political tradition.[64] Narendra Nath Law, for instance,

[61] Ibid., 3–4 (quoting Müller's 1860 book, *A History of Ancient Sanskrit Literature*). See also Sarkar, *Positive Background*, 12; Georges Dumézil, *Mitra-Varuna: An Essay on Two Indo-European Representations of Sovereignty*, trans. Derek Coltman (New York: Zone Books, 1988), 34 (contrasting the "ritualist knowledge and philosophy" of India, with the Roman "art ... of human law").

[62] Arthur Berriedale Keith, "Foreword," in Law, *Aspects*, v. It is interesting to note in this context that Keith's monumental constitutional history of India begins only in the year 1600, with the establishment of the East India Company. See Arthur Berriedale Keith, *A Constitutional History of India 1600–1935* (London: Methuen, 1936).

[63] Sharma, *Aspects*, 1–2, 8. [64] Misra, "The Indian Machiavelli," 313, 318.

began his 1914 book with the statement that the *Arthashastra* proved the "secular and practical achievements of the ancient Hindus, as distinguished from the[ir] spiritual and intellectual [achievements]."[65] Ghoshal noted that the study of statecraft separated from the general Vedic culture at an early stage and became, in some sense, "an independent branch of knowledge which might be called a secular science." He, therefore, rejected Western images of the ancient Indians as uninterested in politics, arguing that they reflected a hollow "half-truth."[66] Banerjea turned the Western argument about the impractical nature of Indian thought on its head by comparing Kautilya to Machiavelli, noting that Kautilya "far surpassed his Italian rival" because, unlike Machiavelli, he was an active statesman and because his works were not merely abstract discussions of politics but were actually followed in practice.[67]

A related argument advanced by Western scholars was that the pervasive influence of religion in ancient India led to the uncritical acceptance of political ideas as dogma. This perception, argued Ghoshal, needed to be corrected because Buddhist political thought and the political theories found in the *Arthashastra* appealed to human reason rather than religious dogma. Ancient Indian political thinkers, said Ghoshal, were "earthy" and concerned with concrete problems of administration. They were not interested in speculative discussions of ideal polities.[68] Sarkar, too, argued that ancient Indian states were "thoroughly secular."[69]

Nationalist movements often claim that the national past was glorious. Jayaswal argued that "the constitutional progress made by

[65] Law, *Studies*, v.

[66] Ghoshal, *History of Hindu Political Theories*, ix, 3–4. This is not to say that ancient India political theory was portrayed as totally secular. In one of his articles, Law sought to enumerate various links between politics and religion in ancient India. See Narendra Nath Law, "The Religious Aspects of Ancient Hindu Polity," *The Modern Review* (December 1917): 620. Elsewhere, Ghoshal noted that Hindu thought did not recognize the clear separation of the religious and the secular and that ancient Indian political theory had both religious and secular aspects. See Upendranath Ghoshal, "The Brahminical Conception of the Science of Politics," in *Sir Asutosh Mookerjee Silver Jubilee Volumes* (Calcutta: Calcutta University Press, 1922), Vol. 3.1, 53; Ghoshal, *History of Hindu Political Theories*, 268–9.

[67] Banerjea, *Public Administration*, 10, 11n1.

[68] Ghoshal, *History of Hindu Political Theories*, 9–13, 114–15.

[69] Sarkar, *Positive Background*, 11; Sarkar, *Political Institutions*, 13.

the Hindu has probably not been equaled, much less surpassed, by any polity of antiquity." Jayaswal could not ignore the fact that, when he was writing these words, the British ruled India. The Golden Age of the Hindus, he therefore comforted his readers, "lies in the future" because "the [Hindu] race which evolved the greatest constitutional principles in antiquity" had now come into contact with "the greatest constitutional polity of modern times [i.e. Britain]," and this contact could "rejuvenate the race."[70]

The argument about the glorious nature of ancient Indian political theory was not only made abstractly. The Hindu polity authors also argued that certain major modern political concepts had an ancient Indian pedigree.[71] One such concept was the social contract theory. Thus, Bhandarkar noted that while Europeans believed that the social contract theory originated with Hobbes, one could already find it in the *Arthashastra*. Indeed, according to Bhandarkar, the Hindu version of the theory was superior to the European one. Hobbes' social contract transferred absolute power irrevocably from the people to the king, while, in the Indian version, the king did not enjoy unlimited power and was deemed a servant of the people. This was evident from the fact that taxes paid by the people to the king were seen as a wage that he received in return for providing security.[72]

Another claim about the originality of ancient Indian statecraft texts had to do with international law. Historians of international law are aware of the fact that international law's pedigree does not begin with Grotius in Europe in the early modern era but has non-European antecedents, including Indian ones.[73] However, when discussing the first scholars in the twentieth century who attempted to undermine the Eurocentric narrative about the history of international law, the existing scholarship ignores the works of early twentieth-century Indian scholars.[74]

70 Jayaswal, *Hindu Polity* (1924), Vol. 2, 209–10.

71 Sumit Sarkar, *The Swadeshi Movement in Bengal*, new ed. (Ranikhet: Permanent Black, 2010), 24.

72 Bhandarkar, *Lectures*, 119, 122.

73 See, e.g., Olga V. Butkevych, "History of Ancient International Law: Challenges and Prospects," *Journal of the History of International Law* 5 (2003): 189.

74 Thus, much scholarly attention has been devoted recently to the works of C. H. Alexandrowicz, a Polish scholar who taught at Madras in the 1950s. Alexandrowicz has been portrayed as a pioneer of the non-Eurocentric approach to

The main argument of Bandyopadhyay's 1920 book *International Law and Custom in Ancient India* was that contrary to Western claims that international law was a modern European invention, it had in fact existed in the ancient world. Specifically, Bandyopadhyay argued that ancient Indians created rules for the governance of interstate relations 2,000 years before Europe.[75] Based on sources such as the *Arthashastra* and the Code of Manu, Bandyopadhyay claimed that the religious norms governing interstate relations in ancient India could be defined as "laws" and were not just theoretical but were followed in practice. He admitted that certain topics (such as maritime warfare and blockades or rules about extradition and naturalization) were not dealt with by ancient Indian international law, but he insisted that the field itself did exist.[76] Bandyopadhyay's book went on to discuss the sources of international law, sovereignty, rules regarding ambassadors, rights, and duties of states, treaties, and

the history of international law, although Indian scholars preceded him. Alexandrowicz himself cited previous works of Indian authors such as Ghoshal and Altekar. See C. H. Alexandrowicz, "Kautilyan Principles and the Law of Nations," in *The Law of Nations in Global History*, eds. David Armitage and Jennifer Pitts (Oxford: Oxford University Press, 2017), 35, 36. Indian scholars working in the 1950s also acknowledged the earlier literature. See C. Joseph Chacko, "India's Contribution to the Field of International Law Concepts," *Recueil des Cours de l'Academie de Droit International* 93 (1958): 121, 121–43 (a discussion of ancient India mentioning the works of Banerjea, Nilakanta Sastri, and Altekar). However, the debt owed by Alexandrowicz, and other Indian authors writing in the period after Indian independence, to the early Indian authors is usually overlooked or only briefly mentioned. See David Armitage and Jennifer Pitts, "'This Modern Grotius': An Introduction to the Life and Thought of C. H. Alexandrowicz," in *The Law of Nations*, eds. Armitage and Pitts, 1–31; B. S. Chimni, "International Law Scholarship in Post-Colonial India: Coping with Dualism," *Leiden Journal of International Law* 23 (2010): 23, 28–9; Carl Landauer, "Passage from India: Nagendra Singh's India and International Law," *Indian Journal of International Law* 56 (2016): 265, 271, 282–4; Carl Landauer, "The Polish Rider: CH Alexandrowicz and the Reorientation of International Law, Part I: Madras Studies," *London Review of International Law* 7 (2019): 321, 330, 335–8; Ignacio de la Rasilla, "Looking Forward Through and Beyond the Western Classics of International Law," *Asian Journal of International Law* 13 (2023): 146, 162. But see, recently, Carl Landauer, "C. H. Alexandrowicz's India and the Kautilyan Moment," *Asian Journal of International Law* 15 (2025): 107, 111, 118–21; David Armitage and Ignacio de la Rasilla, "'The Most Neglected Province': British Historiography of International Law," in *The Cambridge History of International Law*, Vol. 1: *The Historiography of International Law*, eds. Randall Lesaffer and Anne Peters (Cambridge: Cambridge University Press, 2024), 293, 311 (acknowledge earlier Indian writers).

[75] Bandyopadhyay, *International Law and Custom*, 1–4. [76] Ibid., 6–13, 19–21.

alliances, the laws of war, norms regarding enemy persons and property, and the notion of neutrality.

Bandyopadhyay not only sought to show that the ancient Indians had created a body of international law rules. He also argued that "the rules of interstate relationships followed in ancient India were much more humane and much more elaborate than the rules followed by all nations of antiquity, and even by nations of modern Europe down perhaps to the time of the French Revolution."[77] Thus, while the ancient Greeks and Chinese (as well as modern Europeans) used the idea of "the family of civilized nations" to justify their mistreatment of the "barbarians," the ancient Indians saw even "wild tribes" and non-Aryans as deserving of the respect and protection of the law.[78]

A related theme found in the Hindu polity literature was the claim that ancient Indian states were, in some ways, similar to modern states in the scope of their intervention in the life of their subjects. Narendra Nath Law noted that the state described in the *Arthashastra* "anticipated" some of the functions of modern states by protecting "the disabled, the helpless and the infirm" and also "lower animals."[79] Radhakumud Mookerji argued that "socialism and communism (representing advanced democratic ideals of the modern age)" were to be found in ancient Indian self-governing organizations.[80] Hemchandra Raychaudhuri wrote an article claiming that "the ideal state depicted by Kautilya is far from one of laissez-faire, and the functions of such a state do not consist simply in protecting the personal freedom and property of the individual."[81]

An article by Dikshitar, published in 1939, argued that the goals of ancient Indian states were to "ensure the liberty of the citizens and to secure the general moral welfare." The Indian kings sought to protect the whole world, including all creatures, and their states were not despotic.

[77] Ibid., 6, 31–2.

[78] Ibid., 31–2. There were several additional works on ancient Indian international relations and international law that were published in the 1920s. See Law, *Inter-State Relations*; Kalidas Nag, *Les théories diplomatiques de L'Inde ancienne et l'Arthasastra* (Paris: Maisonneuve Frères, 1923); S. V. Viswanatha, *International Law in Ancient India* (Bombay: Longmans, 1925); Kalidas Nag and V. R. Ramachandra Dikshitar, "The Diplomatic Theories of Ancient India and the Arthashastra," *Journal of Indian History* 5 (1926): 235.

[79] Law, *Studies*, 3. [80] Mookerji, *Local Government*, 22–3.

[81] Ray[chaudhuri], "Was State-Socialism Known in Ancient India?," 429.

Unlike modern totalitarian states, whether communist or fascist, ancient Indian states were tolerant and did not crush the individual.[82] Another theme that Dikshitar emphasized – perhaps because it was significant in works on the nature of Hinduism, because of the growing political rift between Hindus and Muslims, or in response to the rise of racist states in Europe at the time – was that: "... tolerance was the corner-stone of the Hindu national state. It was a commonwealth composed of different groups, each allowed to develop its ideas and ideals and to follow its religious faith. Political rights were not denied to these groups, enabling their members to rise to their full stature in the discharge of their duties and the enjoyment of their rights."[83]

Altekar also argued (in 1947) that "the ancient Indian state was not merely a tax-gathering corporation, interested only in preserving law and order." The state in ancient India, he said, "interested itself in a number of ministrant activities of the nation-building type, which are being undertaken by the modern governments only in relatively recent times." The example he provided was in the realm of public education: state funding for "non-official colleges and universities."[84] Similarly, and at about the same time, the South Indian historian K. A. Nilakanta Sastri claimed that the administrative innovations discussed in Kautilya's *Arthashastra* proved that "under Kautilya's guidance the Mauryan Empire was attempting to evolve into a new type of state, more ubiquitous and far-reaching in its concern for the welfare of the people than anything known in India before, a state which we should now call the 'social-welfare State.'"[85]

While many Hindu polity authors uncritically sought to create an Indian pedigree to modern Western political ideas, others were more tentative in their claims. Like other Hindu polity writers, Upendranath Ghoshal argued that ancient Indian works introduced, for the first time, the idea of a social contract as the foundation of the political order.[86] However, generally speaking, Ghoshal was less infatuated with the ancient Indian texts; in the appendix to his book, in which

[82] V. R. Ramachandra Dikshitar, "The Social Order in Old India," *The Aryan Path* (April 1939): 182, 182–6.
[83] Ibid., 183. On Hinduism and tolerance, see, e.g., Basu, *Religious Revivalism*, 94–5.
[84] Altekar, "Bird's-Eye View," 61.
[85] Nilakanta Sastri, "Place of the Arthaśāstra," 94. See also Sharma, *Aspects*, 13.
[86] Ghoshal, *History of Hindu Political Theories*, 117–21.

he compared Indian and Western theories, he noted that Indian thinkers were less sophisticated than Western philosophers such as Hobbes, Grotius, Locke, or Rousseau. According to Ghoshal, the Indian works were unsystematic and were less rational than Western ones; and, while concepts such as the social contract were, indeed, found in ancient Indian works before they emerged in the West, the Indian writers fell "below the level attained by the [early modern] European exponents of these theories."[87]

### *Democracy, Republics, and Constitutional Limits on the Power of Monarchs*

The attempt to refute the Western notion of Oriental despotism was another central theme in the Hindu polity literature. The image that dominated modern European thought about politics in ancient India was that of states ruled by absolute kings, who were considered divine.[88] Western texts describing ancient Indian political theories often repeated Manu's statement that kings were "God[s] in human form."[89] As for Kautilya's *Arthashastra*, S. G. Vesey-FitzGerald, who taught Oriental law at Oxford and London, observed in 1923 that:

> Rome, or rather Byzantium, forgot her popular principles in a despotism ... [whereas] Hindu polity seems never to have had any popular principles to forget. If the *Arthashastra* ... can be accepted as giving a fair picture, the Maurya Empire rested on a system of ... espionage as paralysing as that of Tiberius or Domitian. For all that we mean by self-government, the world is indebted to the barbarians of the North, to the Frank, the Anglo-Saxon, and the Dane. To many of the best Hindu minds, even to-day, the idea of popular election to public office is an indecency.[90]

87 Ibid., 273–6.

88 See, e.g., Franco Venturi, "Oriental Despotism," *Journal of the History of Ideas* 24 (1963): 133; Inden, *Imagining India*, 51–4, 162–72; Bernard S. Cohn, *Colonialism and Its Forms of Knowledge: The British in India* (Princeton, NJ: Princeton University Press, 1996), 62–5; Jürgen Osterhammel, *Unfabling the East: The Enlightenment's Encounter with Asia*, trans. Robert Savage (Princeton, NJ: Princeton University Press, 2018), 334–83.

89 Sarkar, *Positive Background*, 10.

90 S. G. Vesey-FitzGerald, "The Place of Hindu Law in Comparative Jurisprudence," *Law Quarterly Review* 39 (1923): 357, 360. On the ambivalent attitude of some Indian nationalists toward the notion of democracy, see, generally, Nicholas Owen, "Democratisation and the British Empire," *Journal of Imperial and Commonwealth*

Already in the nineteenth century, liberal Indian thinkers sought to show that precolonial Indian governments had democratic aspects, such as the separation of powers.[91] Many Hindu polity works were animated by the same desire to refute the notion that Indian states were governed by despots and to prove the democratic credentials of these states.[92] Here, one can distinguish between two subthemes: the existence of republics in ancient India and the fact that Indian monarchs did not enjoy absolute power because institutional checks constrained them, or because they were constrained by law.

Some Hindu polity authors sought to show that non-monarchical states were not a Western invention. This argument was already present in Jayaswal's 1913 article, in which he asserted that monarchies were not the only form of government known in ancient India. Republics also existed.[93] Jayaswal was not the first to note the existence of such republics. The English Indologist T. W. Rhys Davids mentioned them in a 1903 book. However, Jayaswal certainly created a widespread interest in studying these republics.[94]

Jayaswal associated republics with the term *gana* (previously translated by European scholars as "corporation" or "tribe").[95] His book discussed the appearance of republics in Buddhist sources, in the *Arthashastra*, and in the works of ancient Greek writers on India.

*History* 47 (2019): 974, 981–5. But see Parasher, *Radical Democracy* (on the attempt of some Indian intellectuals to offer broader and more inclusive models to Western indirect representative democracy).

91 Bayly, *Recovering Liberties*, 51–4; De, "Constitutional Antecedents," 30–1 (discussing the argument about the democratic aspects of India's "ancient constitution" in the works of the early nineteenth-century Bengali reformer, Ram Mohan Roy). See also Karuna Mantena, *Alibis of Empire: Henry Maine and the Ends of Liberal Imperialism* (Princeton, NJ: Princeton University Press, 2010), 25; Christian R. Burset, *An Empire of Laws: Legal Pluralism in British Colonial Policy* (New Haven, CT: Yale University Press, 2023), 132–3 (on British notions of India's "ancient constitution" in eighteenth-century India).

92 Of course, the very term "democracy" is a multi-layered concept with various meanings, some of which are in conflict (e.g., the conflict between the idea that democracy means majority rule and the idea that democracy means the protection of minorities).

93 Jayaswal, "Introduction to Hindu Polity," 537.

94 T. W. Rhys Davids, *Buddhist India* (New York: Putnam, 1903), 2. See also Bhandarkar, *Lectures*, 140; David Stasavage, *The Decline and Rise of Democracy: A Global History from Antiquity to Today* (Princeton, NJ: Princeton University Press, 2020), 36–7.

95 Jayaswal, *Hindu Polity* (1924), Vol. 1, 27, 29.

Indian republics, Jayaswal argued, took various forms, some of them being democracies in which there were "parliaments," where every man could cast his vote to elect the state's leaders and where decisions were made by majority rule, based on procedures similar to those of modern parliamentary systems.[96] Jayaswal also claimed that at least some Hindu republics were based on the notion of political equality.[97] His book argued that Hindu republics were characterized by their morality, justice, discipline, efficient administration, and equality. They represented, he believed, a successful and long-standing governmental form.[98]

The same arguments can be found in Banerjea's 1916 book. Banerjea mentioned examples of republics that had existed during the Vedic era and noted that, as late as Alexander's invasion of India, some Indian states lived under democratic institutions, and the government of others was aristocratic rather than monarchical.[99] Through a detailed analysis of the sources, Bhandarkar, too, sought to provide a more granular discussion of the nature of ancient Indian republics, marshaling philological evidence to distinguish between different republican forms (oligarchy, aristocracy, and democracy).[100]

In 1919, Radhakumud Mookerji sought to challenge the image of Oriental despotism by highlighting the history of local organizations in ancient India. He argued that village communities and other local organizations, such as guilds, were "little republics," independent from state intervention, and thus able to preserve and develop Hindu culture even during the period of "alien" Islamic rule. Muslim rulers, Mookerji said, were unable to impose on the Hindus the "Semitic" model of a society governed by a single absolute ruler.[101] Conventional accounts of early Indian society depicted it as based on "respect for tradition and authority," but in fact, it was characterized by "the democratic principle," a principle which was manifested in the way village communities governed themselves and also in the existence of many "self-governing, 'kingless' states."[102] Shamasastry observed in

96 Ibid., Vol. 1, 81–5, 103. 97 Ibid., Vol. 1, 119, 170. 98 Ibid., Vol. 1, 174.

99 Banerjea, *Public Administration*, 42–5. 100 Bhandarkar, *Lectures*, 140–84.

101 Mookerji, *Local Government*, 2, 11–12, 15, 19, 23–4. See also Sarath Pillai, "German Lessons: Comparative Constitutionalism, States' Rights, and Federalist Imaginaries in Interwar India," *Comparative Studies in Society and History* 65 (2023): 801, 808–9 (on federalism and ancient Indian history).

his 1919 lectures (published in 1920) that the earliest Aryan societies in the West and the East had been democratic and that republics had existed in Vedic India.[103] Narendra Nath Law also argued in 1921 that some ancient Indian states were republics, and some of these republics were based on a democratic form of government.[104]

Unlike all these authors, Ghoshal cautioned in his 1923 book against the anachronism of "crediting the Hindus with notions of popular sovereignty and the like." However, he, too, was interested in countering the "Oriental despotism" notion. He stressed that "Indian states were not, contrary to the usual view, modeled after a uniform pattern, that of despotic monarchy." Instead, republics had existed in ancient India from the earliest periods until at least the fifth century AD. One could also find rival political theories in ancient India. The Brahmanical theory about the divine nature of kings existed side by side with the contractual Buddhist theory of society. Ghoshal did admit, though, that while republics existed, it was monarchies that "dominated the scene."[105]

According to Jayaswal, republics disappeared at a certain point in Hindu history, partly because they could only function well when states were small. As the territory of Indian states grew, republics were replaced by monarchies. However, Jayaswal assured his readers that Hindu monarchies also reflected laudable modern democratic notions. During Vedic times (and even later), monarchies were contractual, and kings, who were not considered divine, were elected by popular assemblies.[106] Such assemblies, said Jayaswal, were "national assembl[ies] of the whole people." They were tasked with electing kings (or re-electing them in the case of banishment), and everyone could participate in their work (unlike, for example, the folk assemblies of Western Europe).[107] Public opinion and the opinions of councils of ministers checked the power of kings – the

[102] Ibid., 22. [103] Shama Sastri, *Evolution*, 11–13, 24, 25–40.

[104] Law, *Aspects*, 4, 9–11, 37, 94.

[105] Ghoshal, *History of Hindu Political Theories*, viii, x, 1–3, 13, 27, 224.

[106] Jayaswal, *Hindu Polity* (1924), Vol. 2, 5, 7, 35, 114, 139, 152, 185, 199. Ghoshal, unlike Jayaswal, argued that the doctrine of the divinity of kings had its origins in the Vedic era. See Ghoshal, *History of Hindu Political Theories*, 27, 224.

[107] Jayaswal, *Hindu Polity* (1924), Vol. 2, 11, 14.

king was seen as a servant or slave of the state, shackled by strictly enforced limitations on his power.[108]

Banerjea, too, noted that, gradually, monarchies replaced other forms of government, mainly due to the growing size of Indian states, which made it difficult for popular assemblies to govern. He also argued that the king's power in these monarchies was limited. During Vedic times, kings were elected and deposed according to the will of the people. Later, kingship became hereditary. However, even then, the power of kings was constrained by the authority of their ministers and priests. Indian kings were, therefore, constitutional monarchs, and there were very few instances of Indian kings who could be described as despots. Another facet of absolute monarchy, the idea of the divinity of kings, was indeed present in India. However, unlike medieval European kings, who could do no wrong, in India, kings were considered divine only if they were righteous. Furthermore, kings were not owners of the territories of their state; the state existed for the well-being of the people, and the king was supposed to be the servant of his subjects and to further that well-being. Kingly power was never absolute (at least in theory).[109] Banerjea also discussed the history of popular assemblies and noted their gradual decline over time, again due to the growing size of states (as well as the increasing rigidity of caste structures).[110]

Shamasastry argued that, while there were already kings in Vedic India, sovereign power was not hereditary. Kings were elected and could be expelled.[111] Early Indian kingdoms were characterized by a unique institution – non-hereditary bachelor kings, who were required to consult with a "people's assembly" composed of representatives of all classes of society. The power of the early kings was kept in check by this assembly, which could banish or demote kings by majority vote. These constitutional checks were, he argued, employed against tyrannical kings in "a calm and peaceful" way, in contrast to the bloody revolutions against despotic kings "in other nations."[112] The king had a duty to consult frequently with the assembly and also with the members of the priestly aristocracy.[113]

[108] Ibid., Vol. 2, 5, 7, 35, 114, 139, 152, 185, 199.
[109] Banerjea, *Public Administration*, 50–1, 64–76. [110] Ibid., 97.
[111] Shama Sastri, *Evolution*, 11–13, 24, 25–40.
[112] Ibid., ix–xiv, 78–9, 82, 84–5, 163–5. [113] Ibid., 91, 96, 98.

According to Shamasastry, Dravidian kingdoms were first established in the Middle Ages in reaction to Jainism and Buddhism. Their rise was accompanied by a new model of kingship: theocratic monarchies. The deification of kings freed them from popular checks. However, while these types of kings have usually been viewed as despotic, Shamasastry argued that they, too, were restrained: their power was reined in by religion and priestly power. The Islamic conquest, Shamasastry said, had stopped the further evolution of Indian polities. Had the Indians been able to continue their political evolution, Shamasastry assured his readers, they would have developed "a limited monarchy subject to popular will," just as Britain had done.[114] Despotism was, thus, according to Shamasastry, only a mark of one (late) period in the history of Indian political institutions; and, even during this period, it was checked by religion and by priestly power.

Narendra Nath Law repeated the theme of the elective rather than hereditary nature of ancient kings and noted the fact that the people could sometimes expel kings. He also said that the king's power was curbed by an assembly or state council, which, at least during the Vedic era, was "more or less of a democratic character." Monarchies rather than republics were the standard form of government in India. However, this resulted from the fact that the Aryans in India were surrounded by hostile races.[115]

Bhandarkar noted that while kings were considered divine, they were also seen as servants of the people, and their power was not absolute. There were many checks on the king's power – for example, the fact that society was made up of various self-governing communities whose rules and regulations the king did not have the luxury of ignoring.[116]

Again, a more critical approach was found in Ghoshal's 1923 book. Ghoshal did note that, during the Vedic period, tribal assemblies checked the king's power.[117] He also observed that Hindu thinkers

114 Ibid., ix–xiv, 137, 146–7, 162.

115 Law, *Aspects*, 4, 9–11, 37, 94. Law may have taken this idea from the works of the English Indologist Arthur Anthony Macdonell. See also Banerjea, *Public Administration*, 42.

116 Bhandarkar, *Lectures*, 134.

117 Ghoshal, *History of Hindu Political Theories*, 23.

developed principles and maxims limiting the king's arbitrary exercise of power and regarding his role as being that of servant of the people. However, while some scholars have viewed this idea of the king as the people's servant as an indication of the development of notions of popular sovereignty in India, Ghoshal was not willing to go so far. He believed that while there were "germs of the idea of the sovereignty of the people in Hindu [political] theory, these were never worked out into an independent and logically complete system."[118]

Law as a constraint on the power of monarchs was also a major theme in the Hindu polity works. According to Jayaswal, kings were seen as protectors of the law. The rituals undertaken during their coronation ceremony portrayed them as being not above the law but under the law. The law was thus "the king of kings," and it, rather than the king, reigned supreme.[119]

Ghoshal quoted the Brihadaranyaka Upanishad, which said that "the Brahman created law which is the Kshattra of the Kshattra. Therefore, there is nothing higher than the Law. Thenceforth, even a weak man rules stronger with the help of the Law ..."[120] Ghoshal also commented that, while the king in ancient India was entrusted with "the highest executive function," the concept of sacred law, interpreted by the Brahmans, was wholly separate from the power of the king. The king was tasked with duties such as protecting the traditional rights of individuals and groups – rights that were enshrined in sacred law. Thus, kingship, even when the doctrine of the divine nature of kings was dominant, was perceived as "an office and not a lordship," and the king was viewed as subject to law, like any other person.[121]

Not all scholars accepted this natural law version of ancient Hindu jurisprudence. In the works of Banerjea, we find an argument about the gradual growth in the power of kings to legislate. According to him, the law was first viewed as being higher than society and of divine origin. Kings had to abide by the laws and the customs of the country and were not seen as above the law but as its servants.[122] However, bodies of priests, as well as the king, subsequently began to create new norms

[118] Ibid., 15–16, 270–2. [119] Jayaswal, *Hindu Polity* (1924), Vol. 2, 6, 152, 185.
[120] Ghoshal, *History of Hindu Political Theories*, 54. [121] Ibid., 15–16, 270–2.
[122] Banerjea, *Public Administration*, 50–1, 76.

indirectly, in a way somewhat similar to modern legislation.[123] Similarly, Nilakanta Sastri argued in 1947 that, at least in Kautilya's *Arthashastra*, monarchical legislation was placed above all other sources of law: royal decrees were seen as superior to the three other sources of norms: Dharma, contract, and custom.[124]

### Equality

When discussing legal procedures, Banerjea noted that one feature of the legal system of ancient Indian states that was "not ... very pleasing to note" was that "the idea of equality before the law was not fully developed in Ancient India ... The law was not the same for all but depended upon the status of the person concerned." Thus, people belonging to one of the higher castes were immune from some of the punishments imposed on lower-caste criminals.[125]

How did Indian authors deal with the problem of caste? Sometimes, the tactic regarding castes was to argue that Western observers misunderstood the ideals of Hindu society. S. S. Setlur, a judge and Professor of Law at the Government Law College in Bombay, explained in 1907 that because "the oriental and the occidental are as poles asunder in their mental outfit," Westerners misunderstand Hindu society. In this society, duty instead of right governs social life, and the higher one is on the social scale, the more restrictions and duties one has.[126]

Other authors argued that ancient Indian political theory actually contained egalitarian notions. For example, Shamasastry argued that the modern Western principles of "equality, fraternity, and liberty" had counterparts in ancient India's Jain and Buddhist states.[127] The rise of Jainism and Buddhism, calling for the equality and fraternity of men (and also "charity to man and beast alike"), was accomplished

[123] Ibid., 131, 138–40. [124] Nilakanta Sastri, "Place of the Arthaśāstra," 89–90.

[125] Banerjea, *Public Administration*, 170–1. But see Kiron Kumar Roy Chaudhury, "Hindoo Penal Law," *Calcutta University Law College Magazine* 12 (1942): 61, 64 (claiming that lower-caste individuals were punished more lightly than Brahmins).

[126] S. S. Setlur, "Origin and Development of the Bengal School of Hindu Law," *Law Quarterly Review* 23 (1907): 202, 207–8. On Setlur, see *Indian Biographical Dictionary*, ed. C. Hayavadana Rao (Madras: Pillar & Co., 1915), 389.

[127] Shama Sastri, *Evolution*, x, xiv.

with neither violence nor destruction. Jainism and Buddhism sought to reform India's religious and social order, creating an order without distinctions between persons and classes and with no priestly oligarchy. Unlike similar social revolutions in the West, which were accompanied by much loss of life, the social revolutions of Jainism and Buddhism occurred "with no trace of bloodshed" – due, perhaps, to the uniquely peaceful temperament of the ancient Indians.[128]

A chapter of Aiyer's 1935 book on Hindu moral ideas discussed slavery. Aiyer began the chapter by pointing out that slavery was a common phenomenon in most countries including civilized ones, and then went on to discuss in detail various rules which mitigated the lot of slaves in ancient Hindu law. For example, masters had a duty to treat their slaves kindly, and slaves could inherit and acquire property and also redeem themselves. During Buddhist times, the position of slaves further improved, and in any event, the slaves of "oriental countries" were "generally free from the cruelty and inhumanity which attended the treatment of negro slaves by the Christian nations of Europe." Indeed, specifically speaking of the British, "the system of slavery which prevailed in the British colonies and in the slave states of North America surpassed in cruelty the slavery of any pagan country, ancient or modern."[129]

Another problematic issue was the way ancient Hindu law treated women. Sarkar devoted a part of his book, *The Political Institutions and Theories of the Hindus*, to "the Hindu Constitution." In this part, he discussed, among other topics, women's rights, arguing that ancient Hindu law reflected views on women comparable to those in modern legal systems. In ancient Hindu law, Sarkar said, one could discern two important attributes associated with modern law: that individuals were treated as independent of collective entities such as the family; and that women were seen as self-standing individuals whose rights were not dependent on their husbands' will. Sarkar compared the rules regarding marital property in modern European states with the Hindu rules and concluded that modern European rules would have fallen short of the rules protecting women's rights in ancient India. For

[128] Ibid., x, 112–16.

[129] Aiyer, *Evolution*, 88–91. On various forms of slavery prevalent in fact in colonial India, see Indrani Chatterjee, *Gender, Slavery and Law in Colonial India* (New Delhi: Oxford University Press, 1999).

example, in ancient Hindu law, the husband had no right to his wife's property. Similarly, discussing ancient Hindu criminal law, Sarkar argued that, in contrast to the criminal legislation of the Maurya Empire (which was extremely severe), that of the Gupta and Vardhana Empires was extremely mild. Indeed, the fact that there was no use of judicial torture and that capital punishment was extremely rare meant that "the modern world is still behind the conscience of the Hindu world of the fifth century." Sarkar also claimed that one of the most significant Western institutions fostering liberty, the jury, was not a uniquely European concept because juries were also found in ancient Hindu law.[130]

Dikshitar argued in a 1939 article that the Western critique of the ancient Indian society as unequal was wrong. A conventional image of Hindu society was that Hindu women were treated as slaves – but, in fact, they were honored and could possess wealth and own property. As for the role of castes in Hindu society, Dikshitar contended that the modern argument that all were equal was purely theoretical. In ancient Indian society, "there was nothing too high, nothing too low, in that social organisation. Each individual rose to his full mental vigour in his own sphere and made his mark." Indeed, "the cry of equal rights for all men would confuse the social relationship. We can speak only in theory of the equal worth of persons." In practice, argued Dikshitar, "persons are not equally worthy." Furthermore, he observed that Hindu society was similar to the ideal Platonic society, which was divided into three classes according to their respective social functions.[131]

[130] Sarkar, *Political Institutions*, 27–9, 79–83. On women, see also Satish Chandra Banerji, "The Woman in Hindu Law," *Allahabad Law Journal* 11 (1913): 25; Altekar, *Position of Women*. It should be noted that when actual reforms promoting gender equality were suggested in the 1940s, some Hindu law scholars were quick to reject them. See, e.g., J. Majumdar, "A Criticism of the Draft Hindu Code," *Calcutta University Law College Magazine* 14 (1944): 3. On ancient Indian criminal law, see also Ramaprasad Das Gupta, *Crime and Punishment in Ancient India* (Calcutta: Book Company, 1930).

[131] Dikshitar, "Social Order," 184–6. Another example of the claim that Hindu law treated women better than Western law is found in Atul Chatterjee, "Roman Law and Hindu Law: A Comparative Study," *Calcutta University Law College Magazine* 10 (1939): 37, 40.

## *Pan-Asianism and Islam*

The discovery of Kautilya's *Arthashastra* in 1905 coincided with Japan's victory in the Russo-Japanese War. Some Indian intellectuals linked the two events, seeing the discovery as yet more proof of the fact that Asia could compete with the West.[132] One manifestation of this idea is evident in Sarkar's works.[133] In his article "Democratic Ideals and Republican Institutions in India," published in 1918 in *American Political Science Review*, Sarkar offered a comparative study of political institutions in Asia. He argued that the democratic conception of the equality of all men, which in the West was rooted in the Bible, had its equivalent in Hindu, Chinese, and Muslim works.[134] Another aspect of democracy that Sarkar found in both the West and Asia was the non-absolutist concept of kingship. According to Chinese political theory, a king was subject to deposition if he misbehaved. In India, too, kings were not regarded as divine and were subject to fines or expulsion if they violated the law.[135] While these two aspects of the ideal of democracy surfaced, according to Sarkar, in both China and India, other features (the existence of republics, popular assemblies, councils of ministers, village assemblies, and decentralization) were only to be found, it seems, in ancient India. Therefore, most of Sarkar's article focused on these institutions in India during the Vedic and later periods, relying on earlier works by Jayaswal and Law.[136]

Like Sarkar, Ghoshal argued that the one reason for the study of the ancient Indian literature was that it could serve as a contribution to the creation of a truly global study of politics by furnishing "the data, from an Eastern point of view, of a true science of Comparative Politics, a science taking cognisance of distinct types of institutions and theories conceived to be rooted in different conditions of existence and forms of race-consciousness, and involving the fullest recognition of the multilinear evolution of human social organisations."[137]

[132] Misra, "The Indian Machiavelli," 319–20.
[133] An earlier expression of Sarkar's ideas is found in the works of the Indian philosopher Brajendra Nath Seal. See Parasher, *Radical Democracy*, 43–8. Later, similar ideas were found in the work of Radhakamal Mukerjee. See Mukerjee, *Democracies of the East*.
[134] Sarkar, "Democratic Ideals," 581–3. See also Sarkar, *Positive Background*, 39.
[135] Sarkar, "Democratic Ideals," 583–4. [136] Ibid., 584–606.
[137] Ghoshal, *History of Hindu Political Theories*, ix–x.

However, pan-Asian notions of solidarity were not shared by all the scholars I mentioned. As I noted before, Radhakumud Mookerji identified "alien" Islamic rule with the "Semitic" model of a society governed by a single absolute ruler, and Shamasastry argued that the Islamic conquest of India stopped the evolution of Indian political institutions toward constitutional monarchy and popular government.

The relationship between Islamic law and political theory and notions such as popular sovereignty, republicanism, liberal values, and other topics that I explored in this chapter was, of course, also of concern across the Muslim world in the nineteenth and twentieth centuries, and Islamic religious scholars, intellectuals, and politicians devoted much attention to them.[138] It is not surprising, therefore, that simultaneously with the appearance of the Hindu polity literature, one could find Indian Muslim legal scholars exploring the nexus between Islam and Western political ideas, and that these scholars, like the Hindu compatriots, argued that the notion of the rule of law, constitutional constraints on executive power, popular sovereignty, and republicanism were compatible with Islamic law.[139]

For example, the Madras judge, Abdur Rahim, devoted a chapter of his 1911 book on Islamic jurisprudence to a discussion of Islamic constitutional, administrative, and international law. He noted that the supreme executive head of the Islamic state, the Caliph, Imam, or Sultan, was bound by the law and by the decisions of the courts like any other citizen. The "true Islamic idea" (though, unfortunately, not the practice) was of a "vast Muslim republic": the Caliph was supposed to be elected by the notables of the community, and he could be deposed if he did not follow the law. Abdur Rahim did not claim that Islamic

[138] For some recent discussions, see, e.g., Faiz Ahmed, *Afghanistan Rising: Islamic Law and Statecraft between the Ottoman and British Empires* (Cambridge, MA: Harvard University Press, 2017); Andrew F. March, *The Caliphate of Men: Popular Sovereignty in Modern Islamic Thought* (Cambridge, MA: Harvard University Press, 2019); Adeel Hussain, *Law and Muslim Political Thought in Late Colonial North India* (Oxford: Oxford University Press, 2022). For a theoretical discussion arguing that Islam and the modern Western conception of the state are incompatible, see Wael B. Hallaq, *The Impossible State: Islam, Politics, and Modernity's Moral Predicament* (New York: Columbia University Press, 2013).

[139] See, generally, Banerjee, *Mortal God*, 224–5, 238–40. On works on Islamic legal history written in India during the colonial period, see also Sohaira Z. M. Siddiqui, *Islamic Law on Trial: Contesting Colonial Power in British India* (Oakland, CA: University of California Press, 2025), 167, 179.

societies were based on egalitarian notions, but he did mention examples of egalitarian norms regarding women – for example, the fact that according to Islamic law, women could be appointed as judges (although they could not adjudicate criminal law matters). As for international law, the Islamic law of war allowed Muslims to kill or enslave prisoners of war, but women, children, the aged, and the diseased were not to be killed or maltreated. International treaties between Muslim and non-Muslim states were respected (in most circumstances).[140]

Salahuddin Khuda Bukhsh, an Oxford-educated barrister and lecturer on the history of Islam at the University of Calcutta, translated several German works on the political history of Islam. Khuda Bukhsh described Islamic law as "second only to Roman law in breadth of view, in refinement, in humanity, and wisdom" and argued that Arab political discourse was more impressive than that of "Hobbes or Locke or the revolutionary scribes of France and Germany."[141] In an essay on the notion of sovereignty in Islam, Khuda Bukhsh discussed at length the idea of elected rather than hereditary rule in Islam, attempting to prove the dominance of this notion based on early Islamic history but also based on the writing of medieval Muslim philosophers such as al-Mawardi, who, he claimed, espoused an early version of the social contract theory.[142]

140 Abdur Rahim, *The Principles of Muhammadan Jurisprudence: According to the Hanafi, Maliki, Shafi'i and Hanbali Schools* (London: Luzac, 1911), 383–5, 389, 393–4. The description of early Islamic law as "republican" rather than despotic was also found in the work of the Indian judge Syed Mahmood. See Alan M. Guenther, "Syed Mahmood and the Transformation of Muslim Law in British India" (PhD diss., McGill University, 2004), 173–6. A slightly later manifestation of the interest in the Islamic Caliphate in India is found in the short-lived Khilafat Movement (1919–24), which was a pan-Islamic political campaign by Indian Muslims to pressure the British government to preserve the authority of the Ottoman Caliphate after the First World War. However, Abdur Rahim and the other Muslim authors I explore here were elite Westernized intellectuals and thus their politics were quite different than the populist and more traditionalist agenda of the Khilafat Movement. On this movement, see, generally, Gail Minault, *The Khilafat Movement: Religious Symbolism and Political Mobilization in India* (New York: Columbia University Press, 1982); M. Naeem Qureshi, *Pan-Islam in British Indian Politics: A Study of the Khilafat Movement, 1918–1924* (Leiden: Brill, 1999).

141 S. Khuda Bukhsh, preface to *The Orient under the Caliphs by Alfred Kremer*, trans. S. Khuda Bukhsh (Calcutta: University of Calcutta Press, 1920), xi.

142 S. Khuda Bukhsh, "The Islamic Conception of Sovereignty," in *Essays: Indian and Islamic* (London: Probsthain, 1912), 25, 25–46.

There were also works dealing specifically with Islam and international law. For example, in 1912, Syed H. R. Abdul Majid, an English-trained barrister, published an article on Islamic international law. In it, he claimed that the Muslim laws of war were humane and "compared favourably" with those of other nations of antiquity, and with those of the medieval West. Muslim warriors were forbidden from destroying enemy property or killing prisoners of war, and the Christian and Jewish residents of towns conquered by the Muslims were granted religious freedom.[143]

## Characteristics

### *The Rise and Decline of the Hindu Polity Literature*

As we have seen, among the factors that led to the appearance of the Hindu polity literature was the discovery of Kautilya's *Arthashastra* by Shamasastry. However, interest in the topic was not merely the result of the scholarly opportunities afforded by the discovery of a new historical source. The emergence of the Hindu polity literature was also spurred by personal and political factors at work in early twentieth-century Bengal.

The first factor was the personal influence of Asutosh Mookerjee, who, in many respects, was the instigator of the academic interest in studying ancient Indian history and society, including ancient Hindu constitutional history and law, at the University of Calcutta. Jayaswal, it should be recalled, moved to Calcutta from the United Kingdom in 1910, and it was there that he wrote his pioneering 1913 article. He did so while in close contact with Asutosh Mookerjee, who asked him to join the University of Calcutta Department of Postgraduate Studies. The manuscript of the book that Jayaswal published on the topic was deposited with Mookerjee and was supposed to be published by Calcutta University Press. Due to an attempt to plagiarize the book,

[143] Syed H. R. Abdul Majid, "Moslem International Law," *Law Quarterly Review* 28 (1912): 89. See also Guenther, "Syed Mahmood," 30, 173. For modern discussions, see, e.g., Ignacio de la Rasilla and Ayesha Shahid, eds., *International Law and Islam: Historical Explorations* (Leiden: Brill, 2019); Mohammad Fadel, "Sovereignty, Territoriality, and Private International Law in Classical Muslim International Law," *American Journal of Comparative Law* 71 (2023): 853.

Jayaswal ultimately published it in Patna. Nevertheless, he retained his links with the University of Calcutta and Mookerjee, even after leaving the city in 1914.[144] The books written by Bhandarkar, Shamasastry, Majumdar, and Ghoshal contained dedications to Mookerjee or lavish praise of Mookerjee's support and contributions to the study of the history of ancient India.[145]

Mookerjee himself, in his 1922 convocation address, mentioned the attempts of "narrow-minded and unsympathetic" Western scholars to disparage Indian cultural achievements. Specifically, he mentioned the claim by the Oxford historian Vincent Smith that India was unfit for self-government because representative institutions did not exist in ancient India and then mentioned the works of Bhandarkar, Jayaswal, Radhakumud Mookerji, Majumdar, and Law, who he said "demolished" this argument.[146]

A second factor leading to the appearance of the Hindu polity literature was related to political trends in Bengal and in India, more generally, during the first decade of the twentieth century. As Aiyangar noted in an article published in the late 1920s, the study of ancient Indian political forms has blossomed "mainly as the result of national feeling, and the natural desire to seek in our past history the justification for current political reforms and ideals."[147]

In Chapter 1, I discussed several factors that led to changes in the nature of education at the University of Calcutta in the first decade of the twentieth century: the 1904 Indian Universities Act, which sought to strengthen government control of Indian universities and thus undermine their independence and was vehemently opposed by Indian nationalists; the British decision in 1905 to partition Bengal, resulting in the Swadeshi Movement leading to the creation of the National Council of Education in Bengal; and the appointment in 1907 of Asutosh Mookerjee as the Vice Chancellor of the University of Calcutta.

144 Jayaswal, *Hindu Polity* (1924), vi; Ambastha, "Dr. K. P. Jayaswal," xxv.

145 Bhandarkar, *Lectures*, dedication page; Shama Sastri, *Evolution*, dedication page; Majumdar, *Corporate Life in Ancient India*, 2nd ed., dedication page, viii; Ghoshal, *History of Hindu Political Theories*, xi.

146 *University of Calcutta Convocation Addresses*, Vol. 5: *1915–23* (Calcutta: University of Calcutta Press, 1925), 456, 474–5.

147 K. V. Rangaswami Aiyangar, "The Evolution of Ancient Indian Polities," in *Sir Asutosh Memorial Volume*, ed. J. N. Samaddar (Patna: J. N. Samaddar, 1928), 164.

The emergence of the Hindu polity literature, associated chiefly with scholars affiliated with the University of Calcutta, can be viewed as one specific manifestation of the more general idea that animated the Swadeshi Movement, the concept of Indian self-building.[148] This link between politics and the Hindu polity literature did not go unnoticed. A review of Jayaswal's book by Arthur Berriedale Keith, published in 1925, noted the "large number" of works recently published on the history of Indian political thought and organization and stated that the appearance of this literature was a result of "the growth of interest in India in political reform."[149] Keith's words here may have referred to Indian demands for self-government, of which the Swadeshi Movement was just one manifestation, or he may have been thinking of the various constitutional changes that the British embarked on in response to these demands in the first decades of the twentieth century. Specifically, two such major changes were the 1909 Morley–Minto Reforms (the Indian Councils Act of 1909), which increased the participation of Indians in the executive and legislative branches of the government of India, and the Montagu–Chelmsford Reforms (the Government of India Act of 1919), which sought to promote "self-governing" institutions and introduced a system of dyarchy in India, with some areas of government at the provincial level transferred from British control to the control of Indians elected through an expanded system of voting.[150] Indeed, as historian Milinda Banerjee has noted, in the debates regarding the Government of India Act of 1919, the Hindu polity literature was cited by the only Indian member of the Viceroy's Executive Council, C. Sankaran Nair.[151]

The peak of interest in the topic of Hindu polity came in the second half of the 1920s and was followed by a sharp decline. This can be observed in Figure 5.1, which shows a Google Ngram Viewer chart of the frequency of the appearance of the term "Hindu Polity" in books written in English between 1800 and 2020.[152]

148 Sharma, *Aspects*, 4–6; Misra, "The Indian Machiavelli," 320.

149 Arthur Berriedale Keith, "Hindu Constitutional Law," *Journal of Comparative Legislation and International Law* 7 (1925): 265.

150 See, e.g., Barbara D. Metcalf and Thomas R. Metcalf, *A Concise History of Modern India*, 2nd ed. (New York: Cambridge University Press, 2006), 160–8.

151 Banerjee, *Mortal God*, 230–1.

152 See also Sharma, *Aspects*, 5, 10, 12; Misra, "The Indian Machiavelli," 313.

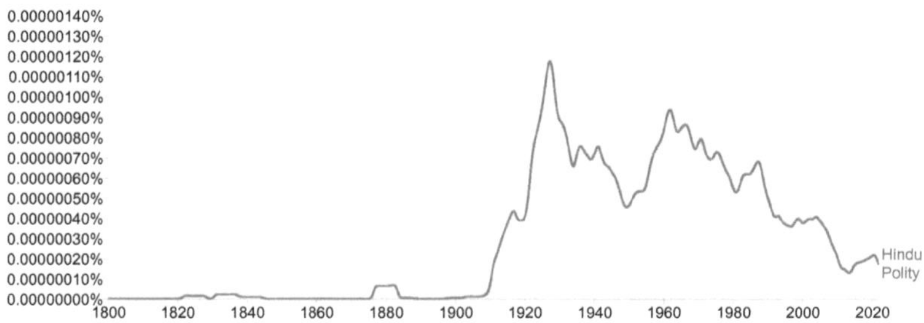


FIGURE 5.1 The frequency of the appearance of the term "Hindu Polity" in books in English. Source: Google Ngram Viewer, https://books.google.com/ngrams.

What can explain this decline? One reason may have been the death of Asutosh Mookerjee in 1924. Other, broader, reasons were mentioned by historians Ram Sharan Sharma and Maria Misra. Sharma noted the restricted social appeal of the Hindu polity literature. These works mainly attracted the educated middle classes and members of the upper castes; they could not appeal to members of the lower castes or Muslims.[153] According to Misra, the social values associated with a major source of the Hindu polity tradition, Kautilya's *Arthashastra*, did not accord with the ideas of two important groups of Indian nationalists: Hindu revivalists such as Bal Gangadhar Tilak disliked the secular and amoral nature of the *Arthashastra*, its lax attitude toward the Hindu caste-based social hierarchy and Brahmin dominance, and its relatively pro-female values. Nationalist politicians such as Gandhi and Nehru disliked its cynical and unethical tone.[154] Interest in ancient Indian political theory, Misra concludes, thus reflected one specific phase in the history of pre-independence Indian nationalism, the phase associated with the Swadeshi Movement and Hindu activists in Bengal.

[153] Sharma, *Aspects*, 12–13.

[154] Misra, "The Indian Machiavelli," 321–31. While Gandhi may not have liked Kautilya's *Arthashastra*, he was portrayed in Agarwal's 1946 constitutional proposal as the only Indian leader interested in the study of ancient Indian constitutional history. See Agarwal, *Gandhian Constitution*, 13. See also Partha Chatterjee, *Nationalist Thought and the Colonial World: Derivative Discourse?* (London: Zed Books, 1993), 85–166 (comparing Gandhi's and Nehru's attitudes to Indian traditions).

*Apologetics*

Within the Hindu polity literature, one can identify two opposite trends. Many works were driven by an anachronistic and apologetic desire to counter Western images of ancient India and to instill pride in the Hindu past by highlighting the similarities between ancient India and the modern West. However, some scholars looked askance at this apologetic motivation. The critique came from Western scholars but also from Indian ones. One example of the former can be found in Keith's review of Jayaswal's book, in which he argued that Jayaswal's desire to find indications of democracy in ancient India was unsupported by the evidence. Keith said that the claim that republics existed during the Vedic period was based on a mistranslation. Republics did exist during later periods but they were aristocratic rather than democratic. The description of kings as elected, subject to law, and bound by the advice of their ministers was not the actual reality, Keith added, but merely "Brahmanical speculation."[155]

However, critique was not limited to Western scholars. In his 1921 book, Sarkar expressed the view that much of the existing literature did not clearly distinguish between actual institutions and "pious wishes or ideals of [political] theorizers."[156] Echoing this skepticism, Bhandarkar remarked that Jayaswal's work was "unfortunately vitiated by the patriotic bias" and by the fact that he was known "not only for misquotations but also experiments at translation."[157] Ghoshal's work, too, was far less celebratory than other Hindu polity works. Rejecting the anachronism embedded in the attempt to trace the origins of modern Western institutions back to ancient India, Ghoshal was willing to compare ancient Indian political notions unfavorably with early modern Western ones and also keen to reject apologetic theories such as the elected rather than divine nature of Vedic kings, the popular and democratic nature of Vedic assemblies, the existence of republics in the Vedic era, or the contractual nature of the state described in ancient Indian texts.[158]

[155] Keith, "Hindu Constitutional Law," 265.

[156] Sarkar, *Positive Background*, 7–8. [157] Bhandarkar, "Reminiscences," lvi.

[158] See, in this context, his critique of Jayaswal in U. N. Ghoshal, *The Beginnings of Indian Historiography and Other Essays* (Calcutta: Ramesh Ghoshal, 1944), 105, 107, 109, 111, 144.

Nevertheless, Ghoshal did emphasize the originality of certain aspects of Hindu statecraft literature, such as the fact that Buddhist texts contained perhaps the earliest version of the social contract theory (albeit in a less systematic and developed form than in early modern European political theories). In an article entitled "The Genius of Indian Polity," Ghoshal first identified two contradictory approaches to the history of Indian political thought. He associated one of these approaches with Western scholars (such as Vincent Smith, the author of *The Oxford History of India*, or Henry Herbert Dowell, the editor of *The Cambridge History of India*). These scholars regarded Indian political thought as uninteresting because, they claimed, it did not evolve and because autocracy was the dominant form of government. In contrast, scholars like Jayaswal, Radhakumud Mookerji, Altekar, and Majumdar advanced the opposing view that the Indian king was "virtually a constitutional slave" and ancient India a "vast rural democracy." Ghoshal adopted an intermediate position, rejecting the argument that the ultimate disappearance of republics in ancient India meant that democratic institutions were somehow alien to its culture (Ghoshal reminded his readers that, in Europe, too, republican forms of government were not universal and that, for most of European history, monarchical forms had dominated the continent). While self-governing institutions existed during Vedic times, said Ghoshal, they tended to be replaced by centralized bureaucracies. Therefore, the picture of India as a "vast rural democracy" was inaccurate. It would also be wrong to conceptualize Dharma rules regarding the duties of kings as equivalent to modern constitutional law since these rules were not based on popular consent, and there was no human mechanism to enforce them. More generally, Ghoshal argued, it would be wrong to claim that ancient Indian states had a system of checks and balances to limit monarchical power.[159]

[159] U. N. Ghoshal, "The Genius of Hindu Polity," in *Studies in Indian History and Culture*, 2nd rev. ed. (Calcutta: Orient Longmans, 1965), 195. This was an enlarged edition of the original 1944 edition entitled *Beginnings of Indian Historiography*. The enlarged edition was first published in 1957 and a second revised edition was published in 1965.

*The Role of Law*

The Hindu polity literature was the product of lawyers, historians (and archaeologists), and social scientists. However, several of the historians and social scientists also possessed legal training. For example, Pramatha Nath Banerjea was a professor of Economics but was also called to the English Bar. Several chapters of his 1916 book *Public Administration in Ancient India* were devoted to legal matters, such as the structure, procedure, and rules of evidence of ancient Indian courts.[160] He also discussed various sources of law in ancient India, including custom and legislation.[161]

Nevertheless, naturally, each professional group approached the topic of Hindu polity with its own emphasis. Historians such as Bhandarkar invested much intellectual effort in philological questions about the exact meaning of specific Sanskrit terms.[162] Social scientists like Sarkar were drawn to the ancient Hindu polity texts as sources for creating a non-Eurocentric (or, as Sarkar put it, non-"Eur-American" [sic]) science of comparative politics.[163] Lawyers were keen to examine specific rules governing ancient Indian institutions, and one can sometimes find in their works arguments that the topic was important because of its relevance to the constitutional law of modern India.

Jayaswal's 1921 book can be seen as an example of an effort to extract norms relevant to modern constitutional law from ancient sources, even when this was problematic because of the lack of sources and the anachronism involved. The book included a chapter dealing with what might be called parliamentary procedures in the assemblies of ancient Hindu republics. Jayaswal could locate only one historical reference to this topic, a story about members of the sixth century BC Shakya republic deciding by majority vote whether to surrender to the Kingdom of Kosala. Jayaswal, therefore, suggested an "indirect" way of reconstructing parliamentary procedures in ancient

160 See Mookherjee, "Acharya Pramatha Nath Banerjea"; Banerjea, *Public Administration*, 141–72.

161 Banerjea, *Public Administration*, 131–40.

162 See, e.g., Bhandarkar's extensive discussion on the meaning of the terms *Samgha* and *Gana* in the fourth lecture of his 1918 Carmichael Lectures Series. Bhandarkar, *Lectures*, 140–84.

163 See, e.g., Sarkar, *Political Institutions*, vii–ix.

Indian republics. The rules for making decisions in Buddhist monastic assemblies (*samgha* or *sangha*), he argued, were copied from the rules of decision-making in political communities. Hence, by studying the rules of these monastic assemblies, one could arrive at an idea of the rules of political ones. Jayaswal then embarked on a highly detailed discussion of the procedural rules dealing with decision-making in Buddhist monasteries, which he took from works such as the collection of Buddhist texts edited in the late nineteenth century by T. W. Rhys-Davids and Hermann Oldenberg.[164] Topics analyzed by Jayaswal included the exact language of the motions that started deliberations in the assembly, requirements regarding quorum, the existence of an assembly "whip," rules regarding votes of members present in the assembly and absentee members, the use of ballots, delegations of decisions to ad-hoc committees, *res judicata*, censuring members of the assembly, the role of clerks and recorders of the House, and the use of referenda.[165]

A similar interest in reconstructing the detailed rules of ancient Hindu law is found in Narendra Nath Law's 1914 book. This book was divided into two halves. The first half was devoted to non-legal topics discussed in Kautilya's *Arthashastra* (mining, irrigation, livestock, communications, and public utilities). The second half dealt directly with legal matters, beginning with courts and their procedure (including rules related to evidence). Law then turned to a long and detailed examination of various aspects of ancient Indian contract law based on the *Arthashastra* and many other sources. Contract law, a private law topic, was not discussed by other Hindu polity authors, and it is not clear what prompted Law to devote a sizeable portion of the book to it. The discussion included topics such as the requisites of a valid contract (dealing with norms regarding the parties, the role and use of witnesses, the time, the place, and the identity of the contracting parties, rules regarding undue influences, and consideration). Additional issues discussed were contracts for the sale of immovable property, the antiquity of the right of pre-emption,

164 T. W. Rhys Davids and Hermann Oldenberg, trans., *The Sacred Books of the East*, Vol. 13: *Vinaya Texts* – Part 1 (Oxford: Clarendon Press, 1881).

165 Jayaswal, *Hindu Polity* (1924), Vol. 1, 103–17.

the sale of moveable property, loans, deposits, pledges, mortgages, bills of exchange, contracts of service, and partnerships.[166]

*Outcome*

In discussing the impact of the Hindu polity literature, one can distinguish between, on the one hand, its academic impact in the West (that is, how Western Indologists and other Western scholars viewed it) and, on the other, its practical impact in India. Reactions to the Hindu polity literature in the West were mixed. Jayaswal's pioneering 1913 article – which was based on a historical approach to Hindu law characterized by viewing this legal system as dynamic and comprehensive, not confined to personal law only – was praised by the German comparative lawyer Josef Kohler, who was perhaps the most important comparative law scholar in the first decades of the twentieth century.[167]

However, many Western scholars in the early twentieth century continued to view ancient Indian states through the conventional nineteenth-century Western lens, associating them with despotism.[168] Accordingly, the nationalist tone of the Hindu polity literature was received with suspicion.[169] In a 1925 review of the Hindu polity literature, the Indologist Julius Jolly argued that it was not scientific enough. The nationalist tendencies and desire for Indian independence had led Indian scholars to mix history and politics, and, therefore, their conclusions were to be received with caution, he claimed.[170] Similarly, Arthur Berriedale Keith stated in 1927 that "the interest and value of the theme [of Hindu polity] have suffered unhappily from the unwise enthusiasm of some writers who have attempted to prove that India made notable contributions to the theory of politics, and that constitutional monarchy was early recognised."[171]

166 Law, *Studies*, 136–95. 167 See Ambastha, "Dr. K. P. Jayaswal."
168 See, e.g., Inden, *Imagining India*, 183. 169 Lal, *Kashi Prasad Jayaswal*, 160–1.
170 Julius Jolly, "Über die alte politische Literatur Indiens und ihre Bearbeiter," *Zeitschrift für vergleichende Rechtswissenschaft* 41 (1925): 305, 318. See also Benoy Kumar Sarkar, "The German Translation of the Kautilyan Arthasastra," *Indian Historical Quarterly* 4 (1928): 348, 382–3.
171 Arthur Berriedale Keith, "Foreword," in Prasad, *Theory of Government*, v, vi.

The same attitude can be found in Western discussions of Indian works that dealt with ancient Hindu international law. In a 1922 article, a British lawyer, W. S. Armour, criticized those Indian authors who argued that "there was a complete system of international law in ancient India." The use of a term such as "international law," said Armour, "with a history wholly modern" was inappropriate because:

> ... the territories of Indian Rajas could scarcely be called states at all in the modern sense of the term. Non-Indian peoples do not come within the scope of the Hindu religion or social system, and the rules I have cited could scarcely be called laws. It is doubtful whether some were even customs, as the evidence does not show that they were observed.[172]

Western scholars adopted a critical attitude toward the Hindu polity literature. Within India, one could distinguish between those scholars who were focused only on the historical significance of the ancient Indian texts and those who were keen to explore their practical application to modern constitutional debates. Some Hindu polity works were based on a "scientific" or antiquarian approach, with no explicit call to apply their lessons to the present. However, other works, such as those by Radhakumud Mookerji, called for applying Indian constitutional history to modern constitutional debates. In his 1919 book, Mookerji stated that studying the history of ancient Indian institutions would be useful not just for teaching the people "national self-respect" but also for more practical reasons. Such study would enable the government to "shape" new governmental institutions "upon the lines of the old."[173]

Non-academic writers echoed this approach. In 1934, an Indian lawyer, Achintya Mukherjee, published an article that urged the makers of the future constitution of India to study ancient Indian constitutional history. "Every nation," Mukherjee explained, "builds up a polity of its own, which reflects its own distinctive type of culture." Constitutional changes, if introduced, "should be congenial to the nature of the political evolution of the nation." He then went on

[172] W. S. Armour, "Customs of Warfare in Ancient India," *Transactions of the Grotius Society* 8 (1922): 71, 83. See also Chimni, "International Law Scholarship," 23, 29.

[173] Mookerji, *Local Government*, 21. See also Sharma, *Aspects*, 9; Parasher, *Radical Democracy*, 73.

to briefly discuss some significant themes found in the Hindu polity literature: kings were elected; the *Danda Neeti* – that is, "the Constitutional Law of the land" – was placed above the kings, who had a duty to protect their subjects; there was an "Aryan Constitution," according to which kings did not have absolute power but had to fulfill the instructions of their assemblies and councils, in which all segments of society were represented; and, generally speaking, the ancient Indian monarchy was a constitutional rather than an absolute monarchy.[174]

The 1940s saw additional calls to use the Hindu polity literature as a source of inspiration for the Indian Constitution. At the beginning of this chapter, I mentioned Agarwal's and Rau's works, but there were other examples. An article by Anant Sadashiv Altekar of Benares Hindu University published in 1947 stated that: "India is at present engaged in framing a new constitution. It will, therefore be not uninteresting to survey ancient Indian polity and its achievements. If we take an impartial survey of it we may learn some important lessons for the present and the future."[175]

What lessons were offered by Altekar? First, he noted the existence of republics in ancient India and argued that they disappeared because they were only appropriate in smaller states united by tribal loyalty. However, he argued, modern India could become a democratic republic despite its massive size because "distances have been annihilated now," and the idea of representative government could replace the need for tribal loyalty. A further reason for the decline of republics was internal strife within their assemblies. This should be a lesson to the future Indian Parliament, Altekar contended.[176]

Moving on to Indian kings, Altekar noted that ancient Indian monarchs were seen as trustees and were celebrated only if they promoted the well-being of their subjects. Modern Indian monarchs could continue to rule Indian (princely) states, but only if they were virtuous, he reasoned. One of the problems with ancient Indian kings was that the mechanisms designed to restrict tyrannical tendencies were weak. Popular assemblies were one such mechanism, but they

174 Achintya Mukherjee, "The Science of Hindu Polity: Some Old Ideas for the Present Situation," *The Aryan Path* (September 1934): 572.

175 Altekar, "Bird's-Eye View," 56.

176 Ibid., 56–8.

disappeared after the Vedic era, leaving mainly the fear of divine punishment as a constraint on tyranny. Modern India, he said, should, therefore, develop secular, practical remedies to control the actions of tyrannical rulers.[177] Another mechanism to constrain tyranny in ancient India was decentralization, as evident in the need to obtain the consent of town and village councils for many governmental actions. The complexity of modern life, Altekar observed, made the reliance on village councils more problematic. Nevertheless, he did recommend using them in some instances.[178]

Altekar discussed the fact that ancient Indian states accepted and promoted the caste system and that, therefore, the idea of the equality of all citizens before the law did not exist in ancient India. However, he assured his readers that "inequalities existed in all civilisations, eastern and western, and have not completely disappeared even in modern times." In this sense, India was not unique.[179] Finally, Altekar noted that ancient Indian empires were based on a model of a central government that also permitted the existence of local governments enjoying relative autonomy. This idea of a strong and united India that also granted full autonomy to its provinces should be followed now, he urged.[180]

[177] Ibid., 58. [178] Ibid., 59–60. [179] Ibid., 62.

[180] Ibid., 63–5. While the Hindu polity literature influenced the ideas of some of the people involved in debates about the Indian Constitution in the period before and after Indian independence, the impact of this literature on actual Indian constitutional arrangements seems to have been rather negligible. One indication of this is the fact that in the debates of the Indian Constituent Assembly there seems to have been almost no direct or indirect references to the Hindu polity literature. However, one could find non-constitutional examples of the impact of the Hindu polity literature (or, more accurately, of Kautilya's *Arthashastra*) in the period immediately after Indian independence. For example, a curious, but interesting, suggestion that was made immediately after Indian independence came from Professor Hari Charan Ghosh, who taught economics at Bangabasi College and Calcutta University and was associated with the nationalist Hindu Mahasabha Party. Ghosh argued that Western economics was created for an industrialized civilization, not an agricultural one like India. It led to wars and to impoverished masses. Western economics only focused on the material side of human life, ignoring other aspects such as the moral realm, he observed, bringing stability but not peace and happiness. Economists, Ghosh argued, should seek to prevent merchants and industrialists from concentrating wealth in their own hands, by implementing ideas such as the just price theory. Now that India was independent, reasoned Ghosh, its people should decide whether to render India an "eastern

## Conclusion

The Hindu polity literature was a result of a specific time and place: Calcutta in the 1910s and 1920s. This body of works had a close affinity with the Swadeshi Movement in Bengal. Many of the Hindu polity authors were lawyers by training, but their writings were not taught at the College of Law of the University of Calcutta. Instead, their works became part of the curriculum in related fields such as History, Political Science, and Economics. While historians were naturally interested in this literature, it also had some contemporary relevance. It echoed Indian nationalist themes prevalent in the first decades of the twentieth century, and it was also mentioned in (although it had little impact on) Indian constitutional discourse in the period leading up to and immediately following Indian independence in 1947.

The depictions of ancient Indian political theory and institutions found in the Hindu polity works may have been anachronistic, and, as more critical observers already noted in the 1920s, the nationalist ideology of the authors may have led them to describe the nature of

district of New York and London, or develop India on her own lines." Ghosh concluded: "Kautilyan Economy, besides being the most scientific Economics, both applied and theoretical, successfully survived the onslaught of several devastating Wars, [e]specially during the thousand years of Muslim Rule. Besides conferring full material benefits, it had a religious significance. In [a] society [based on its principles], one gained primarily not only economic well-being, but a right life, a clear conscience and a spiritual perfection." See "Notes: Kautilyan Studies in Calcutta University," *The Modern Review* 84 (1948): 259, 260. On Ghosh, see Indranil Chattopadhyay, "Quit India Movement in Northern Bengal: A Study of Socio-Economic Perspective" (PhD diss., University of North Bengal University, 2009), 171. The journal issue in which these arguments appeared stated that the proposal to teach "Kautilyan Economics" was adopted by the Board of Studies in Economics at the University of Calcutta in 1948. However, I was unable to verify that this suggestion was indeed adopted. Another interesting example of the influence of the *Arthashastra* on Indian legal discourse immediately after independence is the fact that B. R. Ambedkar, the leading Indian jurist and politician, relied on Kautilya in debates over his draft of the Hindu Code Bill of 1949–50, which sought to reform Hindu law to improve women's rights over their property, to allow divorce, and to prevent polygamy. Ambedkar argued that traditional Hindu marriage law was a Brahminical distortion of the old Hindu law of marriage, echoes of which could be found in the *Arthashastra*. See Misra, "The Indian Machiavelli," 327–9.

ancient Indian states inaccurately. Nevertheless, the Hindu polity literature is interesting as an expression of Indian and Hindu cultural nationalism during the first decades of the twentieth century. Similar things can be said about works dealing with Jewish public law that appeared during the same period in Europe, North America, and Mandatory Palestine. These works will be discussed in the next chapter.

# 6

# The Study of Ancient Jewish Public Law

In 1944, Ya'acov Berman, a Religious Zionist rabbi living in Mandatory Palestine, published a book in Hebrew on Jewish political thought. In this book, Berman urged his readers to adopt a historicist approach to constitutional law. Quoting the nineteenth-century German legal scholar Rudolf von Jhering on the "national spirit" that underlies the legal system of every nation, Berman argued that ancient Jewish traditions could serve as the basis of the constitutional law of the future Jewish state. Jewish law, he claimed, had an answer to all the problems facing modern constitutional and international lawyers. "We are standing on the threshold of great and decisive events," he explained, and the Jews of Palestine would soon need to create a constitution for themselves. When the time came, Berman proclaimed, secular Zionists would turn to "Assyria and Egypt" – or, more accurately, to their modern equivalents, "Switzerland and Albania." They would thus seek to create a borrowed constitution, he warned, that would not include any trace of Jewish heritage, despite the fact that the greatest non-Jewish constitutional thinkers had borrowed their ideas from the Jews.[1]

Despite Berman's suggestion that secular Zionists were uninterested in Jewish constitutional traditions, some secular Zionist intellectuals also embraced the historicist approach that Berman advocated. For instance, in 1946, Eliezer Livneh, a secular socialist Zionist journalist,

[1] Ya'acov Berman, *Torat ha-Medinah be-Yisrael* (Jerusalem: Mosad ha-Rav Kook, 1944), 12–15.

argued that the future Jewish state should draw on Jewish political thought rather than Western models, contending that the Jewish nation was fundamentally distinct from all others. He further maintained that key features of modern Western states, such as democracy and the protection of social rights, had their origins in Jewish political tradition.[2]

The State of Israel was established four years after Berman published his book. The months before and after Israel's declaration of independence, on May 14, 1948, saw intensive constitution-making efforts (although, ultimately, these efforts would fail, rendering Israel one of the few countries in the world that, to this day, does not have a comprehensive single-document constitution). The official drafter of the Israeli constitution was a German-Jewish Zionist lawyer called Leo Kohn, who prepared three consecutive drafts.[3] Kohn was an observant Jew, and his commentaries on these drafts included references to the influence of Jewish constitutional traditions. In a commentary Kohn wrote on the final draft of his proposed constitution, published in January 1949, he stated – in words that echo those of S. N. Agarwal and B. N. Rau, with which I opened Chapter 5 – that "if a Constitution is to command the enduring loyalty of a people, it must be rooted in its moral and political traditions."[4]

Some Jewish constitution-makers, it seems, espoused historicist ideas about constitutional law similar to those we saw Indian scholars using in Chapter 5. In this chapter I explore these ideas. I examine works on Jewish public law, focusing mainly, but not exclusively, on scholars working in Mandatory Palestine during the period of the British Mandate. I begin by describing how constitutional law and international law were taught in the academic institutions of Palestine and then briefly introduce the scholars writing on Jewish constitutional history. The next part of the chapter summarizes some of the major ideas found in the texts produced by those authors.

2 Eliezer Liebenstein (Livneh), "Be-Fetah ha-Sefer," in *Ha-Medinah ha-'Ivrit: Yalkut Mekorot u-Firkey Mahshavah*, ed. S. Levi (Tel Aviv: Be-Terem, 1946/47), 9–15.

3 On Kohn and his constitutional drafts, see Amihai Radzyner, "A Constitution for Israel: The Design of the Leo Kohn Proposal, 1948," *Israel Studies* 15 (2010): 1; Aviram Shahal, "Ha-Hukah she-Nishkehah: Hatsa'at ha-Hukah shel Leo Kohn veha-Be'ayah ha-'Arvit" (LLM thesis: Tel Aviv University, 2014).

4 Leo Kohn, "Observations on the Constitution," *Jewish Frontier* (January 1949): 10, 10–11.

Finally, I analyze the general characteristics of the works discussed in this chapter and the context which gave rise to them. Like the previous chapter, my interest does not lie in debating whether the early twentieth-century Jewish works accurately interpreted the authentic meaning of the ancient texts they examined and correctly depicted the true nature of Jewish political institutions and law. Instead, my goal is to understand how the nationalist ideology of some Jewish scholars in the early twentieth century influenced their writings on Jewish public law.

## The Study of Constitutional and International Law in Mandatory Palestine

The three institutions that offered modern legal education in Mandatory Palestine taught various aspects of constitutional and international law. In the 1920s, students at the Jerusalem Law Classes were required to take a course entitled Constitutional History, a course on political science, and another on public international law.[5] In the 1930s, the course title was changed to Constitutional Law, and it was restructured, now containing three parts. Students first studied "the law and custom of the English constitution," including a discussion of constitutional rights such as personal freedom and freedom of speech. They then learned the constitutional law of the British Empire, focusing on the Dominions and British India. In the third part, they studied the constitutional law of Mandatory Palestine. Additional relevant topics (the League of Nations and the mandates system) were taught as part of the course on public international law.[6] The lecturer teaching the course on Constitutional Law, Ephraim Salant, was the author of one of the

[5] See Israel State Archive [ISA], 0006zh6, Law Classes, Council of Legal Studies, [Schedule of Examinations], [518], [552], [608]. See also Assaf Likhovski and Aviram Shahal, "Israeli Pre-State Constitutionalism," in *The Oxford Handbook of the Israeli Constitution*, eds. Aharon Barak, Barak Medina, and Yaniv Roznai (Oxford: Oxford University Press, forthcoming).

[6] *Palestine Gazette*, October 29, 1936, 1177–78, 1182–83; H. Kantrovitch, "The Jerusalem Law Classes," *Journal of the Society of Public Teachers of Law* 1937 (1937): 46. On the emergence of the constitutional law of the British Empire as a scholarly subject in the interwar period, see Donal K. Coffey, "Constitutional Law and Empire in Interwar Britain: Universities, Liberty, Nationality and Parliamentary Supremacy," *Northern Ireland Legal Quarterly* 71 (2020): 193.

first books on the constitutional law of the British Empire.[7] While Jewish students at the Law Classes also studied a course on Jewish law, it seems that this course focused only on the specific area of Jewish law that had practical application in Mandatory Palestine: Jewish family law.[8]

Students at the Tel Aviv School of Law and Economics were required to take two constitutional law courses, one on the constitutional law of Great Britain and the British Empire and another on the constitutional law of Palestine. They were also offered a course on the mandates systems and a course on international law.[9] Constitutional law was taught by Shmuel Ussishkin, who had studied law at the Universities of Odessa and Cambridge.[10] During the Mandatory period, Ussishkin published three books on the topic in Hebrew.[11] He had a strong affinity to English constitutional traditions. Readers of his books were told that "England and its [political] regime have served as the epitome of democracy ... a classic example of an ideal regime which promises the citizen freedom and security, unafraid of the tyranny of government officials ... a country where the ideals of popular rule and civic freedom have been realized."[12] Beyond Ussishkin's books, students at Tel Aviv were also assigned English textbooks dealing with constitutional law (such as Dicey, Ridges, and Chalmers).[13]

International law was also taught at the Tel Aviv School of Law and Economics. The compulsory course on international law there included a discussion of the Jewish contribution to international law, focusing on the biblical period. Thus, the first part of the course on the

[7] E. Salant, *An Outline of the Constitutional Laws of the British Empire* (London: Sweet & Maxwell, 1934).

[8] See H. Kantrovitch, "Ha-Shi'urim le-Mishpat," *Ha-Mishpat ha-'Ivri* 1 (1925/26): 145, 146.

[9] Tel Aviv University [TAU] Archive, Box 61.71, Beyt ha-Sefer ha-Gavohah le-Mishpat vele-Kalkalah, *Tokhniyot ha-Limudim vi-Yediot* 1938/39, 12–15; TAU Archive, Box 61.71, Beyt ha-Sefer ha-Gavohah le-Mishpat vele-Kalkalah, *Sidrey ha-Limudim ve-Tokhniyoteyhem* 1944/45, 5, 8–9.

[10] "Shmuel Ussishkin," in *Entsiklopediyah le-Halutzey ha-Yishuv u-Vonav*, ed. David Tidhar (Tel Aviv: Sifriyat Rishonim, 1950), Vol. 4, 1731.

[11] Shmuel Ussishkin, *Prakim ba-Mishpat ha-Konstitutsyoni ha-Angli* (Jerusalem: Dfus ha-Po'alim, 1927); Shmuel Ussishkin, *Shitat ha-Shilton ba-Keysarut ha-Britit* (Tel Aviv: Mitzpeh, 1937); Shmuel Ussishkin, *Ha-Mishtar ha-Medini be-Britanyah* (Tel Aviv: Umah u-Moledet, 1945/46).

[12] Ussishkin, *Ha-Mishtar ha-Medini*, 5.

[13] TAU University Archive, Bar Shira Personal Archive, File 3, Hoda'ah 626.

topic, taught in 1939 by Max Laserson, dealt with themes such as international relations between the countries of the ancient Near East: Egypt, Babylon, Assyria, and Canaan; the Israelite notions of agreement, treaty, and covenant; elements of international relations in the relationship between the tribes of Israel during the periods of the biblical judges, and the period of the first Israelite kings, David and Solomon.[14]

In addition to these courses, an extensive course on Jewish law and its history was offered at the Tel Aviv School of Law and Economics. This course was divided into three sections dealing with Jewish private law, Jewish family law, and Jewish public law. The latter section on Jewish public law included topics such as biblical kings and their wars, the Jewish courts during the Second Temple period, and the institutions of Jewish communities in the medieval and early-modern periods.[15] Another required course at the Tel Aviv School dealt with political science (*torat ha-medinah*). Most of this course was devoted to studying universal political concepts such as the social contract, sovereignty, imperialism, and the separation of powers, but it seems that there was also some effort to relate these topics to Jewish constitutional history. Thus, topics covered in this course included biblical pre-monarchical society and the nature of Jewish theocracy in the Bible, the Talmud, and the works of the medieval Jewish scholar Maimonides.[16]

[14] TAU University Archive, Bar Shira Personal Archive, File 19, Beyt ha-Sefer ha-Gavohah le-Mishpat vele-Kalkalah, *Sefer ha-Shanah*, 1947/48, 19; TAU University Archive, Bar Shira Personal Archive, File 3, Hoda'ah 243, 6.

[15] TAU University Archive, Box 61.71, Beyt ha-Sefer ha-Gavohah le-Mishpat vele-Kalkalah, *Sidrey ha-Limudim ve-Tokhniyoteyhem* 1944/45, 7; TAU University Archive, Bar Shira Personal Archive, File 20, Hoda'ah 786, 2–4.

[16] TAU University Archive, Bar Shira Personal Archive, File 19, Beyt ha-Sefer ha-Gavohah le-Mishpat vele-Kalkalah, *Sefer ha-Shanah*, 1947/48, 17. In the 1940s, the main lecturer on political philosophy and political science at the Tel Aviv School of Law and Economics was an Italian-Jewish professor, Yitzhak (Isacco) Sciaky. Sciaky, a Revisionist Zionist and a disciple of the fascist philosopher Giovanni Gentile, taught philosophy and political science at the Universities of Florence and Urbino, before fleeing Italy for Palestine in 1939. He wrote extensively in Italian and Hebrew on topics related to politics, jurisprudence, and constitutional law, but not on Jewish law. Indeed, in the introduction to a textbook that Sciaky published in the early 1950s on political science, he said that one of the main weaknesses of Jewish national culture was the fact that it was unable to create substantive theories of jurisprudence and political philosophy. See Yitzhak Sciaky, *Pirkey Mavo le-Mada' ha-Medinah*

Finally, while the Faculty of Law of the Hebrew University of Jerusalem was only established in 1949, some courses dealing with international law had already been taught at the university during the Mandatory period. In the early 1930s, the university received a donation from an English Jewish industrialist, Sir Montague Burton, who was interested in "the causes of international and industrial peace" and donated funds to establish Chairs on these subjects at the Hebrew University and several English universities. At the Hebrew University, the Chair was devoted to "the international law of peace" and was held by the former Attorney General of Palestine, Norman Bentwich.[17] Bentwich had been involved in the activities of the Jewish Law Society in Palestine in the 1920s, and was interested in the nexus between religion and international law. His course of lectures on the topic, later published as a book, included discussions on the impact of Jewish law (as well as Christianity, Islam, Hinduism, and Far Eastern religions) on international law.[18]

(Tel Aviv: Mishpat u-Medinah, 1951/52), 11. On Sciaky, see, generally, Vincenzo Pinto, "Between Imago and Res: The Revisionist-Zionist Movement's Relationship with Fascist Italy, 1922–1938," *Israel Affairs* 10 (2004): 90.

[17] Norman Bentwich, *My 77 Years: An Account of My Life and Times, 1883–1960* (Philadelphia, PA: Jewish Publication Society of America, 1961), 98–9; Assaf Likhovski, "Limudey ha-Mishpatim ba-Universitah ha-'Ivrit bi-Tkufat ha-Mandat," in *Toldot ha-Universitah ha-'Ivrit bi-Yerushalayim: Hitbasesut u-Tsmihah*, ed. Hagit Lavsky (Jerusalem: Magnes Press, 2005), 543, 553. On the history of the social sciences, including political science and international relations, at the Hebrew University during the mandatory period, see, generally, Nahum Gross, "Mada'i ha-Hevrah ba-Universitah ha-'Ivrit 'ad 1948/9: Tokhniyot ve-Hathalot," in *Toldot ha-Universitah ha-'Ivrit: Hitbasesut u-Tsmihah*, ed. Hagit Lavsky (Jerusalem: Magnes Press, 2005): 503.

[18] See Norman Bentwich, *The Religious Foundations of Internationalism: A Study in International Relations through the Ages* (London: Allen & Unwin, 1933). For the titles and topics of the courses that Bentwich taught at the Hebrew University, see Likhovski, "Limudey ha-Mishpatim ba-Universitah ha-'Ivrit," 553–4. See also Norman Bentwich, *Ha-Mishpat ha-Beyn Leumi*, trans. Joseph Nedava (Jerusalem: Aharonson, 1945), 6–7. Other relevant teachers included Nathan Feinberg and Leon Roth. Feinberg began teaching international relations and international law at the university in 1945 and was the first Dean of the Faculty of Law. Jewish law did not play a role in his teachings. On Feinberg, see, e.g., Rotem Giladi, *Jews, Sovereignty, and International Law: Ideology, Identity, and Ambivalence in Early Israeli Diplomacy* (Oxford: Oxford University Press, 2021). Leon Roth, an observant Jew, taught political philosophy at the Hebrew University beginning in 1928. He published several works on political philosophy, political science, and democracy. Despite Roth's interest in Judaism and in religion generally, he did not explore the nexus between political science and Jewish law in his works. On Roth, see "Zikhron

A major aspect of teaching and research at the Hebrew University was the study of Jewish history, undertaken by members of the Institute of Jewish Studies, one of the three original research institutes of the University.[19] Shortly before his appointment as a lecturer at the Institute, Simha Assaf, a Russian-Jewish scholar, had published two books dealing with topics related to public law: Jewish criminal law and Jewish courts and their procedures.[20] However, Assaf did not pursue these topics later. Another Jewish Studies scholar who taught at the Hebrew University was Asher Gulak. Unlike Assaf, who had no legal training, Gulak studied law at the University of Dorpat (now Tartu) during the final years of the Russian Empire, graduating in 1911. Gulak was one of the founders of the Jewish Law Society established in Moscow in 1917. One of Gulak's earliest articles, published in several installments, focused on Jewish public law.[21] However, in his landmark four-volume *Principles of Jewish Law*, published between 1913 and 1922, he focused on private law and only briefly mentioned Jewish public law.[22] Later, while teaching at the Hebrew University in the 1920s and 1930s, Gulak also focused on the study of Jewish private rather than public law.[23]

le-Rishonim: Hayim Yehudah Roth," *Katarsis* 11 (2009): 196. (It should be noted, however, that a collection of lectures that Roth edited immediately after the establishment of the State of Israel, in 1949, included a lecture by Ephraim Urbach, later a professor of Talmud at the Hebrew University, entitled "Using our Traditional Literature to Educate the Citizen." In this lecture Urbach argued that one could find in traditional Jewish sources discussions of topics such as personal liberty, the rule of law, and democracy. See Ephraim Urbach, "Ha-Shimush be-Sifrutenu ha-Masortit le-Hinukho shel ha-Ezrah," in *'Al Hinukh ha-Ezrah*, ed. H. Y. Roth (Jerusalem: Magnes Press, 1949/50), 91.)

19 See David N. Myers, *Re-inventing the Jewish Past: European Jewish Intellectuals and the Zionist Return to History* (New York: Oxford University Press, 1995).

20 Simha Assaf, *Ha-'Onshin aharey Hatimat ha-Talmud: Homer le-Toldot ha-Mishpat ha-'Ivri* (Jerusalem: n.p., 1921/22); Simha Assaf, *Batey ha-Din ve-Sidrehem aharey Hatimat ha-Talmud: Homer le-Toldot ha-Mishpat ha-'Ivri* (Jerusalem: Dfus ha-Po'alim, 1923/24). See also Myers, *Re-inventing*, 86–7.

21 Asher Gulak, "Ha-Probleymot ha-Mamlakhtiyot be-Divrey Yemey 'Amenu," *Ha-'Am*, December 30, 1916, 20; January 13, 1917, 14; February 3, 1917, 15; February 10, 1916, 13.

22 Asher Gulak, *Yesodey ha-Mishpat ha-'Ivri* (Berlin: Dvir, 1922), Vol. 1, 7–8, 11.

23 See Assaf Likhovski, *Law and Identity in Mandate Palestine* (Chapel Hill, NC: University of North Carolina Press, 2006), 162–3. See also Myers, *Re-inventing*, 88–9.

The interest that some of the lecturers in constitutional and international law in Mandatory Palestine showed toward teaching and studying Jewish law was part of a broader scholarly interest in the topic, manifested in works by Jews and non-Jews alike in Palestine and abroad. I will now describe some of these scholars.

## Authors

My discussion of the Hindu polity literature in Chapter 5 focused on Calcutta in the first decades of the twentieth century. Such a geographical and temporal focus is not possible in the Jewish case. The Jewish community in Palestine was merely one of several centers of Jewish intellectual and cultural life during the interwar period. Some scholars interested in Jewish public law lived in Palestine, but many did not. Any discussion of the literature produced in Palestine must therefore take into account parallel works emerging from major Jewish intellectual centers in Europe and North America. Moreover, interest in Jewish public law did not appear in the twentieth century. Given the Jewish roots of Christianity, it is not surprising that Christian scholars were interested in Jewish political institutions and public law. Thus, early-modern Christian Humanists, influenced by the ideas of the Reformation, wrote about the rules of Jewish law regarding kings, courts, the poor, women, slaves, and converts. These scholars published works on Jewish law in Latin, often utilizing Roman law concepts to describe Jewish law. Later, the American Founding Fathers showed a similar interest in Jewish political thought, and this interest continued into the nineteenth and early twentieth centuries.[24] As for traditional Jewish religious scholars,

[24] See, e.g., Samuel Eisenstadt, "Sifruto shel ha-Mishpat ha-'Ivri," in *Tsiyon be-Mishpat: 'Iyunim ba-Mishpat ha-'Ivri veha-Roma'i* (Tel Aviv: Ha-Mishpat, 1967), 130, 132. A bibliography of the works of the early-modern Humanists on this topic can be found in Samuel Eisenstadt, *'Ein Mishpat: Sefer Shimush Bibliyografi le-Sifrut ha-Mishpat ha-'Ivri* (Jerusalem: Ha-Mishpat, 1931), 101–52. See also Gordon Schochet, Fania Oz-Salzberger, and Meirav Jones, eds., *Political Hebraism: Judaic Sources in Early Modern Political Thought* (Jerusalem: Shalem Press, 2008); Eric Nelson, *The Hebrew Republic: Jewish Sources and the Transformation of European Political Thought* (Cambridge, MA: Harvard University Press, 2010); R. Charles Weller, *Moses, Muhammad and Nature's God in Early American Religious-Legal History, 1640–1830: A Global Crosscultural Perspective* (Cham: Palgrave Macmillan, 2024). For specific examples of nineteenth- and early twentieth-century works, see, e.g., E. W. Edersheim, *The Law*

despite the loss of Jewish political independence and the destruction of the Second Jewish Temple (70 AD), Jews in later periods lived in autonomous communities governed by their own rules. Jewish law, therefore, developed an extensive body of norms to deal with the collective aspects of Jewish life, and generations of rabbis studied, discussed, and developed these rules (as well as studying the rules that would govern the ideal Jewish polity of the future).[25]

Beginning in the seventeenth century with the works of Baruch Spinoza, efforts were made to turn Judaism into a "religion" in the Protestant sense – a private affair divorced from political life and law – thus allowing individual Jews to fit into the new European political framework of secular nation-states. These attempts continued in the works of eighteenth- and nineteenth-century German-Jewish scholars. However, following the appearance of Zionism in the late nineteenth century, some Zionist (and non-Zionist) thinkers started questioning the view that Judaism was merely a matter of individual religious choice and emphasized the collective, national aspects of Judaism, thus gradually leading to a renewed interest in the Jewish political institutions and the norms governing them.[26]

*and Polity of the Jews* (London: Religious Tract Society, 1883) (Edersheim was a Jewish convert to Christianity); Albert Bailey and Charles Foster Kent, *History of the Hebrew Commonwealth* (New York: Scribner, 1920).

25 See, e.g., Michael Walzer, Menachem Lorberbaum, and Noam J. Zohar, eds., *The Jewish Political Tradition*, 3 vols (New Haven, CT: Yale University Press, 2000–2018); Moshe Hellinger, ed., *Ha-Masoret ha-Politit ha-Yehudit le-Dorotehah* (Ramat Gan: Bar Ilan University Press, 2010); Leora Batnitzky and Yonatan Brafman, eds., *Jewish Legal Theories: Writings on State, Religion, and Morality* (Waltham, MA: Brandeis University Press, 2018); Yehuda Brandes, *Yahadut ve-Zkhuyot Ezrah: Ha-Masoret ha-Ezrahit be-Yisrael* (Jerusalem: IDI Press, 2019). For examples of extensive medieval discussions, see, e.g., Gerald J. Blidstein, *'Ekronot Mediniyim be-Mishnat ha-Rambam: 'Iyunim be-Mishnato ha-Hilkhatit* (Ramat Gan: Bar Ilan University Press, 1983); Menachem Lorberbaum, *Politics and the Limits of Law: Secularizing the Political in Medieval Jewish Thought* (Stanford, CA: Stanford University Press, 2001). For a collection of modern sources and essays, see, e.g., Beni Porat, ed., *Mahshavot 'al Demokratyah Yehudit* (Jerusalem: IDI Press, 2010). For a discussion of the various contemporary organizations involved in the study of the Jewish political tradition, see Asaf Yedidya, *Halakha and the Challenge of Israeli Sovereignty* (Lanham, MD: Lexington Books, 2019), 191–3.

26 See, e.g., Leora Batnitzky, *How Judaism Became a Religion* (Princeton, NJ: Princeton University Press, 2011). For an example of interest in Jewish political thought and public law (including international law) among pre-Zionist German-Jewish nineteenth-century scholars, see, e.g., Joseph Levin Saalschütz, *Das mosaische Recht: mit Berücksichtigung des spätern jüdischen* (Berlin: Heymann, 1846–48).

In the early decades of the twentieth century, at least three distinct groups were writing on the topic of Jewish public law: (i) Orthodox rabbis using traditional *halakhic* idioms and genres; (ii) Jewish scholars working in the Diaspora, writing Western languages; and (iii) Cultural Zionists (both observant and secular), writing mainly in Hebrew. These Cultural Zionists were often associated with the movement for the revival of Jewish law and the Tel Aviv School of Law and Economics, and they sought to use the ancient materials as a source of inspiration for the law governing future Jewish political entities in the Diaspora and Palestine. Let us now turn to each of these groups.

### *Orthodox Rabbis Using Traditional Halakhic Idioms*

In the early decades of the twentieth century, several Diaspora rabbis wrote significant works on Jewish public law. Among the most prominent was Rabbi Haim Hirschensohn, who was born in Palestine in the mid nineteenth century, and immigrated to the United States in 1903.[27] Influenced by the democratic culture of the United States (which, he argued, was influenced by the Bible), Hirschensohn envisioned a future democratic Jewish state based on Jewish law. In works such as his multi-volume collection of *responsa*, *Malki ba-Kodesh*, published between 1919 and 1928, Hirschensohn argued that democracy was in complete accord with the commandments of Jewish law, demonstrating his argument by reference to the biblical idea of the covenant between God and his people, and the legislative role given to laymen in post-biblical Diaspora Jewish communities. Hirschensohn rejected claims that Jewish law required a monarchical regime. He also argued that the conventional view that Jewish law prevented women from voting or

[27] Hirschensohn was just one of a group of rabbis living in the Jewish Diaspora and interested in the topic. See Reuven Margaliot, *Tal T'hiyah* (Lwow: Margulies, 1921/22). See also Yehudah Gershoni, *Sefer Mishpat ha-Melukhah: 'al Hilkhot Melakhim leha-Rambam, Z"L* (New York: n.p., 1949/50); Yedidya, *Halakha*, 72–5; Alexander Kaye, *The Invention of Jewish Theocracy: The Struggle for Legal Authority in Modern Israel* (New York: Oxford University Press, 2020), 34–7.

holding public office was incorrect.[28] Hirschensohn's works also included discussions of topics related to international law.[29]

Rabbis active in Mandatory Palestine produced similar works devoted to applying Jewish law to address the challenges and needs of a modern society and state. This literature, which was also mostly written in traditional *halakhic* idioms, dealt with many concrete practical problems, such as how to adjust the rules of Jewish law to the needs of modern agriculture. The rabbis also dealt with more abstract questions, including the possibility of reviving ancient Jewish political institutions such as the central Jewish judicial institution of the Second Temple period, the *Sanhedrin*. Prominent rabbinical figures such as Ben-Zion Meir Hai Uziel, the Sephardi Chief Rabbi of Palestine, and Isaac Herzog, the Ashkenazi Chief Rabbi, played key roles in shaping this body of literature. Neither Uziel nor Herzog had formal legal training. However, the rabbinic discourse on Jewish public law in Mandatory Palestine also included legally trained contributors, such as Rabbi Isaac Breuer, a Hungarian-German Jew, who studied law in Frankfurt and practiced there until immigrating to Palestine in 1936.[30]

As historian Alexander Kaye has argued, by the 1940s, some of these rabbis had gradually come to embrace a radical take on the role of Jewish law in a future Jewish state: the idea of a Jewish theocracy. Jewish law, they believed, would not merely constitute one historical

[28] See Eliezer Schweid, *Democracy and Halakhah* (Lanham, MD: University Press of America, 1994), xvii–xxi, 47–76; Asher Cohen, *Ha-Talit veha-Degel: Ha-Tsiyonut ha-Datit ve-Hazon Medinat ha-Torah bi-Yemey Reshit ha-Medinah* (Jerusalem: Yad Ben-Zvi, 1998), 21; David Zohar, *Mehuyavut Yehudit be-'Olam Moderni: Ha-Rav Hayim Hirshenzon ve-Yahaso el ha-Modernah* (Tel Aviv: Ha-Kibuts ha-Me'uhad, 2003), 19–30, 163–217; Yedidya, *Halakha*, 61–72.

[29] See Haim Hirschensohn, *Malki ba-Kodesh: She'elot u-Tshuvot be-Hanhagat ha-Mamlakhah be-Yisrael 'al-pi Darkey ha-Halakhah* (St. Louis, MO: Moineshter, 1918/19), 1:11–12. See also Amos Israel-Vleeschhouwer, "Yahas ha-Halakhah la-Mishpat ha-Beyn Leumi: Nitu'ah ha-Psikah ve-Nituah Tahalikhi" (PhD diss., Tel Aviv University Faculty of Law, 2012), 79–91.

[30] For more detailed discussions of this body of works, see Cohen, *Ha-Talit veha-Degel*; Yedidya, *Halakha*; Ofer Chen, *Hemshekhiyut u-Mifneh: Mi-Germanyah le-Eretz Yisrael: Ha-Ortodoxyah ha-Modernit le-Nokhah ha-Etgar ha-Tsiyoni* (Tel Aviv: Ha-Kibuts ha-Meuhad, 2015), 293–312; Kaye, *Invention*; Arye Edrei, "Halom ha-Mishpat: Ha-Rav Herzog veha-Rav Goren 'al Yahasey Mishpat ve-Halakhah be-Yisrael," *Diné Israel* 35–36 (2022): 31; Arye Edrei, "A Religious Zionist Dream: Rabbi Herzog's Vision of Israeli Law," *Jewish Quarterly Review* 112 (2022): 620.

source of institutions and norms of the future Jewish state, nor would the legal system of this state be a pluralist one, in which Jewish law and courts would coexist alongside courts using secular law. Instead, swayed by the profoundly modern and novel notion of Jewish theocracy – one with no real precedent in Jewish history – these rabbis were convinced that the future Jewish state would be governed by a single centralized legal system based on Jewish law, which would be declared in the future Israeli constitution as the fundamental law of the state.[31]

## *Jewish Scholars in the Diaspora Writing in Western Languages*

Jewish scholars in the Diaspora also wrote extensively on Jewish public law with the intention of addressing broader audiences, Jews but perhaps also Gentiles. One example of such works, from Germany, is a 1914 volume that was part of a series called *Monumenta Talmudica*. The volumes of this series contained digests of passages translated from the Talmud. The volume dealing with law, edited by a young historian, Salomon Gandz, dealt with Jewish public law and included passages on kings, courts, priests, and the rules pertaining to the administration of Jewish communities.[32]

Jewish-American authors writing in English also belonged to this group. Mayer Sulzberger, a Philadelphia judge, published two relevant books in the early 1910s, one on biblical parliamentarism and the other on "the polity of the ancient Hebrews."[33] Israel Friedlaender, a professor at the Jewish Theological Seminary of America in New York, wrote an essay on the political ideals of the prophets. Another essay of his sought to refute the notion, common among "Aryan" scholars, and also some Jewish ones, that Jews (specifically) and Semites (generally) were incapable of self-government and that the

[31] Kaye, *Invention*, 14, 25.

[32] Salomon Gandz, ed., *Monumenta Talmudica*, Vol. 2: *Recht* (Vienna: Orion, 1914). See also Amihai Radzyner, "Talmid Haham shelo Nispad Ka-Halakhah: Yaacov Shmuel Zuri u-Mehkarav ba-Mishpat ha-'Ivri 'al Reka Toldot Mehkar T'hum Ze," *Shenaton ha-Mishpat ha-'Ivri* 23 (2004/05): 253, 290–1.

[33] Mayer Sulzberger, *The Am Ha-Aretz: The Ancient Hebrew Parliament: A Chapter in the Constitutional History of Ancient Israel* (Philadelphia, PA: Greenstone, 1910); Mayer Sulzberger, *The Polity of the Ancient Hebrews* (Philadelphia, PA: Greenstone, 1912).

biblical Jewish states were characterized by "bad government, tyranny, and oppression," just like every other "little oriental state."[34] Nathan Isaacs, a law professor at Harvard University, published a book chapter devoted to the "Legacy of Israel," in which he analyzed the influence of Judaism on various aspects of public and private Western law. Here, Isaacs argued, for example, that Judaism was the source of the Christian idea of the separation of Church and State.[35]

A 1928 book by Abba Hillel Silver, an American Reform Rabbi and Zionist leader, provided a detailed discussion of Jewish democracy. In this book, Silver argued that ancient biblical Jews, as well as post-biblical ones, were animated by a democratic spirit: when the Jews wandered in the Sinai Desert, they were not governed by kings; nor were kings present during the initial period of Israelite settlement in Canaan. Later in biblical history, kings did appear, explained Silver, but, unlike kings in other ancient monarchies, they were not deified. Silver claimed that the Bible generally displayed a critical approach to the idea of monarchy, as is evident by the stories about the prophets and their critique of both kings and the priestly class. Once Jewish independence was lost, Silver said, kings and temples were replaced by democratic institutions: the synagogue, led by lay leaders, and the religious school, open to all Jews and based on the notion of popular rather than elite education. During later periods of Jewish history, an aristocracy of legal scholars emerged, but the Jewish masses rebelled time and again against this aristocracy, as is evident by the appearance of movements such as medieval Karaism or early-modern Hasidism.[36] A later work by Silver contained an extensive discussion of Jewish attitudes to the notion of equality based on the Bible and on post-biblical sources such as the Talmud. In this work, Silver claimed that Judaism was characterized by its egalitarian nature, unlike religions such as Hinduism, with its caste

34 Israel Friedlaender, "The Political Ideal of the Prophets," in *Past and Present: A Collection of Jewish Essays* (Cincinnati, OH: Ark, 1919), 1; Israel Friedlaender, "Were Our Ancestors Capable of Self-Government?" in *Past and Present*, 39, 40.

35 Nathan Isaacs, "The Influence of Judaism on Western Law," in *The Legacy of Israel*, ed. George Adam Smith et al. (Oxford: Clarendon Press, 1927), 377. On Isaacs, see, generally, Samuel Flaks, "Law, Religion, and Pluralism: The Thought and Experiences of Nathan Isaacs (1886–1941)," *Touro Law Review* 29 (2013): 307.

36 Abba Hillel Silver, *The Democratic Impulse in Jewish History* (New York: Bloch, 1928).

system. More generally, Silver argued that the notion of social hierarchy was "an Aryan concept."[37]

In the middle decades of the twentieth century, an American law professor, Helen Silving, wrote several articles on Jewish public law. Silving was born in the Galician part of the Austro-Hungarian Empire to an orthodox Jewish family. She studied law at the University of Vienna, becoming one of the first female students associated with the intellectual circle which formed around the leading Austrian legal theorist, Hans Kelsen. With the rise of Nazism, she fled to the United States, later earning a law degree from Columbia University. In 1956, she became a professor of law at the University of Puerto Rico and, thus, one of the first female law professors in the United States. An expert in criminal law, Silving also taught in South Korea, where her husband, Paul K. Ryu, who was a prominent legal scholar, served as President of Seoul National University.[38]

In her articles on Jewish law, Silving argued that the Old Testament was a political document containing various fundamental concepts that had shaped modern Western democracy. In particular, she pointed to the belief that legal rules should be based on the consent of the governed; the notion of the rule of law; the concept of the social contract; the idea of constitutional constraints on monarchical power; the principle of equality of all citizens before the law; the claim that laws should be accessible to all the members of the polity and should be studied by all its members; freedom of thought; due process; equal protection; and respect for popular will (but not respect for popular will embodied in the notion of majority rule).[39]

[37] Abba Hillel Silver, *Where Judaism Differed: An Inquiry into the Distinctiveness of Judaism* (New York: Macmillan, 1956), 224, 225–7.

[38] See Helen Silving, *Helen Silving: Memoirs* (New York: Vantage, 1988); Reut Yael Paz, "A Forgotten Kelsenian? The Story of Helen Silving-Ryu (1906–1993)," *European Journal of International Law* 25 (2014): 1123; Miriam Gassner, "The Distaff Side? Hans Kelsen's Viennese Female Students," *Journal on European History of Law* 15(1) (2024): 2, 8.

[39] Helen Silving, "The State Contract in the Old Testament," *Journal of Religion* 24 (1944): 17; Helen Silving, "The Jurisprudence of the Old Testament," *New York University Law Review* 28 (1953): 1129; Helen Silving, "The Origins of the Magnae Cartae," *Harvard Journal on Legislation* 3 (1965): 117. A Hebrew version of the second article was published as Helen Silving, "Torat ha-Mishpat sheba-Tanakh," *Ha-Praklit* 13 (1956/57): 49.

### *Cultural Zionists*

The final group of authors that will be the focus of this chapter comprised Cultural Zionists working in both the Diaspora and Mandatory Palestine. Unlike the first group of authors, orthodox rabbis, this group of scholars analyzed Jewish public law using Western historical and legal concepts. Unlike the writers belonging to the second group of authors, the works of the Cultural Zionist authors were mainly written in Hebrew. In addition, Cultural Zionist authors sought to convince their readers not only that Jewish law was a *source* of modern political institutions and law but also that it could be *used* in the present.

Several Polish-born Zionist scholars working in the Diaspora belonged to this group. They included Jacob Zuri who studied philosophy, linguistics, history, sociology, and law in France, Germany, and Switzerland, immigrated to Palestine in 1912 and taught at the Jerusalem Law Classes and the Hebrew University, but returned to Europe in the late 1920s, where he remained active until his death in 1943.[40] Jacob Mikliszanski studied law in France and obtained a doctoral degree from the Sorbonne in 1935. During the Second World War, he fled to the United States, where he taught at Dropsie College in Philadelphia and at Hebrew College in Massachusetts.[41] Mikliszanski published several works on Jewish law and international criminal law and the law of war.[42] Simon

[40] On Zuri, see J. K. Mikliszanski, "J. S. Zuri," in *'Ishim u-Dmuyot be-Hohmat Yisrael be-Eropah ha-Mizrahit lifney Shki'atah*, ed. Samuel K. Misrky (New York: Ha-'Ogen, 1959), 338; Radzyner, "Talmid"; Amihai Radzyner, "Jewish Law in London: Between Two Societies," *Jewish Law Annual* 18 (2010): 81. His works on Jewish public law include J. S. Zuri-Rzezak, *Mishpat ha-Talmud*, Vol. 8: *Mishpat ha-Medinah* (Warsaw: Merkaz, 1922); Jacob Zuri, *Toldot ha-Mishpat ha-Tsiburi ha-'Ivri*, 6 vols (Paris, London, Tel Aviv: Voltaire, Urim, Mitspeh, 1930/31–1938); Radzyner, "Talmid," 294–304, 346–7.

[41] See Kopek Mikliszanski, *Le droit pénal international d'après la législation polonaise* (Paris: Recueil Sirey, 1935); Daniel Judson, "A Home for Jewish Learning in 'The City on the Hill': The History of Hebrew College," in *Hiddushim: Celebrating Hebrew College's Centennial*, eds. Jonathan D. Sarna, Arthur Green, and Michael Fishbane (Boston, MA: Academic Studies Press, 2022), 11.

[42] J. K. Mikliszanski, "Ha-Mishpat ha-Plili ha-Beyn Le'umi 'al-pi ha-Mishpat ha-'Ivri," in *Gvilin: Le-Mahshevet ha-Torah veha-'Avodah*, eds. Yehudah Yefet and Moshe Krone (Warsaw: Jabne, 1937), 58. This article was later republished as a separate pamphlet; see J. K. Mikliszanski, *Ha-Mishpat ha-Plili ha-Beyn Le'umi 'al-pi ha-Mishpat ha-'Ivri* (Warsaw: Haohela, 1938). See also J. K. Mikliszanski,

Federbusch was ordained in Poland as a rabbi and later studied at the Universities of Krakow, Lwow, and Vienna, where he obtained a doctorate in law. Federbusch was a member of the Polish Parliament in the 1920s and served as the president of the Religious Zionist Party, Mizrahi, in Galicia. In 1931, he moved to Finland, serving as the Chief Rabbi there until 1940, when he immigrated to the United States.[43] In 1952, inspired by the establishment of the State of Israel, Federbusch published a book in Hebrew containing a comprehensive discussion of Jewish public law.[44]

Moving to scholars based mainly in Palestine, three of the four founders of the Tel Aviv School of Law and Economics, Samuel Eisenstadt, Paltiel Dikshtein, and Max Laserson, wrote on Jewish public law.[45] Another notable figure associated with this school was Shimshon Rosenbaum. A Russian Jew, Rosenbaum studied law in

"Yesodot Beyn-Leumiyim ba-Mishpat ha-'Ivri," in *'Arakhim ve-Ha'arakhot* (Jerusalem: Neuman, 1975), 11; J. K. Mikliszanski, "Mishpat ha-Milhamah," in *'Arakhim ve-Ha'arakhot*, 80; Jacques K. Mikliszanski, "Military Life among the Ancient Hebrews," *Jewish Review* 1 (1943): 169; J. K. Mikliszanski, "Hukat Shalom," *Ha-Do'ar* 28 (1949): 718. On the renewed interest in the Jewish law of war in the twentieth century, see, generally, Ayre Edrei, "Law, Interpretation, and Ideology: The Renewal of the Jewish Laws of War in the State of Israel," *Cardozo Law Review* 28 (2006): 187; Arye Edrei and Anver M. Emon, "Sovereignty, Law, and the Pedagogy of Historical Fantasy: On the *Halakha* on the Laws of War and the *Fiqh* on *Dhimmis*," in *Islamic and Jewish Legal Reasoning: Encountering Our Legal Other*, ed. Anver M. Emon (London: Oneworld, 2016), 155.

43 On Federbusch, see "Simon Federbush [*sic*], Rabbi Here, Dead," *New York Times* (August 21, 1969); "Federbusch, Simon," *Universal Jewish Encyclopedia* (New York: Ktav, 1969), Vol. 4, 622; Alan Mittleman, "*Mishpat Hamelukhah* and the Jewish Political Tradition in the Thought of R. Shimon Federbush," *Jewish Political Studies Review* 10 (1998): 67.

44 Simon Federbusch, *Mishpat ha-Melukhah be-Yisrael* (Jerusalem: Mosad ha-Rav Kook, 1952). See also Yedidya, *Halakha*, 133–9 (discussing Federbusch and other American rabbis writing in Hebrew on the topic).

45 Samuel Eisenstadt, "Le-Heker Mishpatenu ha-Pumbi," *Ha-Mishpat ha-'Ivri: Riv'on Mada'i* (1918): 8; Samuel Eisenstadt, "Reshit Yihusav ha-Beyn Le'umim shel ha-'Am ha-Yisra'eli," in *Tsiyon*, 97; Samuel Eisenstadt, *Di Nevi'im: Zeyer tsayt un Zeyere Gezelshaftlekhe Ideyen* (Vilna: Klachkin, 1926). This book was translated to English. See Samuel Eisenstadt, *The Prophets: Their Times and Their Social Ideas*, trans. Max Rosenfeld (New York: YKUF, 1971); Paltiel Dikshtein, "Mishpat u-Medinah be-Yisrael [part I]," *Ha-Tekufah* 28 (1935): 363; Paltiel Dikshtein, "Mishpat u-Medinah be-Yisrael [part II]," *Ha-Tekufah* 29 (1936): 245; Paltiel Dikshtein, "Mishpat u-Medinah be-Yisrael [part III]," *Ha-Tekufah* 34–5 (1950): 664. The first two parts were reprinted in *Professor Paltiel Daykan (Dikshtein): Mivhar Monografyot, Mehkarim u-Ma'amarim*, ed. Yitzhak Orren (Tel Aviv: Yavneh, 1975), 179; Max M. Laserson, "Hebrew Roots of International Law," *Menorah Journal* 36 (1948): 174. See also

Vienna and Odessa during the 1880s before establishing a legal practice in Minsk. He played a significant political role in early twentieth-century Russia, serving as a member of the country's first elected parliament, the State Duma, formed after the 1905 Revolution. After the First World War, he was an important figure in the political development of the newly independent Lithuanian state. His roles included Deputy Foreign Minister, member of the Lithuanian Constituent Assembly, Member of Parliament, and Minister for Jewish Affairs. In 1924, Rosenbaum moved to Palestine. There he led the Tel Aviv Branch of the Jewish Law Society, served as President of the Jewish Courts of Arbitration, and was involved in the early stages of the creation of the Tel Aviv School of Law and Economics.[46] While mainly a lawyer and politician, Rosenbaum was also a legal scholar. He wrote about the impact of Jewish law on international law, and on the secular, non-theocratic nature of ancient Jewish states.[47]

Two other persons connected to the Jewish Law Society were Rabbi Arye L. Grajewsky and Rabbi Ya'acov Berman. Grajewsky, born in Poland, immigrated to Palestine as a child. He pursued legal studies in Egypt, at the Cairo Law School, and later completed his legal education in the Sorbonne in Paris, where he also studied philosophy. In 1935, he returned to Palestine and worked as both a teacher and a lawyer.[48] Berman studied law at Saint Petersburg University and later taught, like Eisenstadt, at the

Assaf Likhovski, "The Many Exiles of Max Laserson," *Clio@Themis* 22 (2022), http://journals.openedition.org/cliothemis/2087.

46 See P. Dikshtein, "Birkat Yovel: Shimshon Rosenbaum," *Ha-Mishpat ha-'Ivri* 4 (1932/33): 205; "Shimshon Rosenbaum Z"L," *Ha-Mishpat* 5(5) (1935): 1; Paltiel Dikshtein, "Shimshon Rosenbaum," *Ha-Mishpat Ha-'Ivri* 5 (1936/37): 278; Eglė Bendikaitė, "Intermediary between Worlds: Shimshon Rosenbaum: Lawyer, Zionist, and Politician," *Osteuropa: Impulses for Europe* 2008(8–10) (2008): 171; Eglė Bendikaitė, "One Man's Struggle: The Politics of Shimshon Rosenbaum," *Jahrbuch des Simon-Dubnow-Instituts* 13 (2014): 87; Eglė Bendikaitė, "Interwar Lithuania as a Laboratory of International Law," *Jus Gentium* 2 (2017): 555, 561–4.

47 See "'Orekh ha-Din S. Rosenbaum: Ha-Mishpat ha-Beyn Leumi be-Yisrael bi-Yemey Kedem," *Ha-Mishpat Ha-'Ivri* 1 (1925/26): 204; Shimshon Rosenbaum, "Shgi'ot Mekubalot," *Ha-Mishpat ha-'Ivri* 4 (1932/33): 113.

48 "Avraham Arye Leib Grajewsky," *Entsiklopediyah le-Halutzey ha-Yishuv u-Vonav* (Tel Aviv: Sifriyat Rishonim, 1949), ed. David Tidhar, Vol. 3, 1465–6; Arye L. Grajewsky, "Ha-Medinah veha-Knesiyah, ha-Mishpat veha-Dat," in *Sugyot ba-Mishpat uva-Historyah*, ed. Yosef Kariv (Jerusalem: Jerusalem Post, 1971/72), 60.

Odessa Rabbinical Seminary. In 1921, he moved to Palestine, where he served as a General Inspector in the school system affiliated with the Religious Zionist Mizrahi movement. In 1944, he published the book on Jewish political theory cited at the beginning of this chapter.[49] Finally, interest in ancient Jewish political institutions and law was also evident in a 1946 collection of Jewish sources titled *The Hebrew State*, published in Mandatory Palestine.[50] This book contained a long introduction by Eliezer Liebenstein (Livneh), a secular journalist associated with the Zionist Socialist MAPAI political party, whose historicist approach to constitutional law closely paralleled Berman's.[51]

## Themes

### *Jewish Public Law: Developed, Secular, Innovative*

A preliminary challenge that scholars of Jewish public law had to address before discussing specific topics was that most of the development of Jewish law had occurred *after* the Jews lost their political independence following the destruction of the Second Temple by the Romans in 70 AD. While Jewish communities in the Diaspora did have communal institutions, these never resembled those

49 "Ha-Rav Ya'acov Berman," in Tidhar, ed., *Entsiklopediyah* (1950), Vol. 4, 1757–8; Amihai Radzyner, "Ha-Mishpat ha-'Ivri beyn Leumi le-Dati: Ha-Dilemah shel ha-Tnu'ah ha-Datit Leumit," *Mekhkarey Mishpat* 26 (2010): 91, 150; Berman, *Torat ha-Medinah*.

50 This collection was part of a group of works published in Mandatory Palestine on political theory. See Jacob Ben-Amittay, *Torat ha-Medinah ha-Klalit* (Tel Aviv: Tkufah, 1935); J. J. Rousseau, *'Al ha-Amanah ha-Hevrutit [sic]: O 'Ekronot ha-Mishpat ha-Medini*, trans. Yosef Or (Jerusalem: Hotsa'at Sfarim al-yad ha-Universitah ha-'Ivrit, 1931/32); Plato, *Ha-Medinah*, trans. Zevi Diesendruck (Tel Aviv: Mitzpeh, 1935/36); Aristotle, *Ha-Politikah*, trans. L. Roth (Jerusalem: Hotsa'at Sfarim 'al-yad ha-Universitah ha-'Ivrit, 1935/36); Chenmelech Merchavia, ed., *Herut u-Mishtar: Adam-'Am-Medinah-Ma'amad: Otsar Te'udot Historiyot u-Folitiyot* (Jerusalem: Goren, 1945); Meir Hillel Ben-Shamai, ed., *Sefer ha-Adam veha-Medinah* (Tel Aviv: Neuman, 1947/48).

51 Livneh, "Be-Fetah ha-Sefer," 9–32. See also Kalman Kahana, "Li-Ve'ayat Ha-Thukah ha-Toratit 'Avur ha-Medinah," *She'arim*, December 11, 1947, 2 (an interesting review and critique of this "leftist" collection by a religious politician). On Livneh, see "Eliezer Livneh," in Tidhar, ed., *Entsiklopediyah* (1949), Vol. 3, 1417; Moshe Shamir, "Met Eliezer Livneh," *Ma'ariv*, March 2, 1975, 4; Meir Bareli, "Eliezer Livneh (Liebenstein)," *Davar*, March 7, 1975, 11.

of a modern state. Therefore, it was perfectly feasible to claim that Jewish public law did not exist.[52]

In an article published in Moscow in the inaugural 1918 volume of the journal *Ha-Mishpat ha-'Ivri*, Samuel Eisenstadt traced the development of Jewish public law from the biblical period onward. He argued that it had already existed, in embryonic form, in the periods of the biblical patriarchs and that it had continued to develop until the end of the Second Temple period. Even after the Jews lost their political independence, Eisenstadt added, Jewish public law did not disappear because Jewish communities in the Diaspora enjoyed a certain level of autonomy and, thus, rules were created by individual Jewish communities, as well as by supra-community organizations such as the Council of Four Lands (the central body representing Jewish communities in the early-modern Polish–Lithuanian Commonwealth).[53]

Jewish law was often compared to another ancient legal system, Roman law. The common view of Roman law was that the private law part of Roman law was far more developed than its public law dimension. In his article, Eisenstadt noted this common view of Roman law and referred to the work of Theodor Mommsen, the nineteenth-century German historian. Mommsen had rediscovered Roman public law, which had long remained obscured within the great sixth-century Roman law text, the *Corpus Iuris Civilis*, in the interstices of private law. Referring to Mommsen's approach, Eisenstadt declared that the same task awaited scholars of Jewish law, who, like the German Romanists, should endeavor to rediscover the original rules of Jewish public law.[54] The study of Jewish public law, he said, was important not only for scholarly reasons but also because it would serve a practical goal, assisting in the creation of a new Jewish political life that would not be reliant on foreign sources but based on Jewish ones.[55]

Eisenstadt's article also addressed a second major objection to the existence of Jewish public law – namely, the claim that Jewish law, being inherently religious, could not serve as the basis for public legal

[52] See, e.g., Kaye, *Invention*, 10.

[53] Eisenstadt, "Le-Heker Mishpatenu ha-Pumbi," 8–9, 13–14, 19–20.

[54] Ibid., 8, 22–4. [55] Ibid., 24.

norms. In the modern Western context, religion is typically confined to the private sphere, while law, especially public law, is seen as belonging to the public sphere and is expected to operate independently of religious influence. This separation is seen as essential to the functioning of the modern secular state.[56] In response to this objection Eisenstadt argued that Jewish law was not really religious. Religion was merely a "mask" hiding its secular nature.[57]

A connected idea, whose origins date back to the works of the Roman-Jewish historian Josephus, was that ancient Jewish kingdoms were theocracies. Asher Gulak spent most of his career writing on private law. In his monumental book *Principles of Jewish Law*, published in the period immediately before and after the First World War, Gulak stated that, unlike other legal systems, Jewish law developed independently of the existence of a state. Moreover, he claimed that even when the Jews enjoyed political independence, the goal of Jewish law was not to enable governance but to further just relationships between individuals. Once Jewish independence was lost, constitutional, administrative, and criminal law became defunct, and only private law continued to develop.[58] However, in 1917, Gulak published a four-part article in a Jewish-Russian newspaper on the history of ancient Jewish politics. In this article, he argued that the conventional view of ancient Jewish kingdoms as theocracies was wrong: the Israelite and Jewish kingdoms of the First and Second Temple periods were secular. One could find two forces contending within these kingdoms – kings implementing ordinary secular policies; and religious prophets, independent and critical of the kings, who were animated by a vision of ethical politics based on justice. This division also appeared in the

[56] Indeed, Nathan Isaacs claimed that the modern idea of the separation of Church and State actually had a Jewish origin. While politics and religion were initially fused together in ancient Jewish states, the Jews ultimately developed the idea of a cleavage between ordinary civil law and ecclesiastical law. This Jewish notion, explained Isaacs, influenced the creation of Christian canon law dealing with certain topics such as marriage and divorce, and separate from the law of the state. See Isaacs, "Influence of Judaism," 387–91.

[57] Eisenstadt, "Le-Heker Mishpatenu ha-Pumbi," 11–12, 20. For the opposite view – that the separation of religion and state was not possible in the Jewish case because Jewish nationalism was connected to Jewish religion, and because Jewish religion was political in nature – see Rav Tsa'ir [Chaim Tchernowitz], "Ha-Dat veha-Medinah," in *Sha'arey Tsiyon* (New York: n.p., 1936), 162.

[58] Gulak, *Yesodey*, Vol. 1, 7–8, 11 (this volume was first published in 1913).

realm of legislation, according to Gulak. Kings legislated, just as those in other ancient Near Eastern kingdoms did, but the prophets criticized royal legislation because they saw it as unjust and oppressive.[59]

Another scholar, Shimshon Rosenbaum, wrote in a 1930s article entitled "Common Errors" that the Christian tradition erroneously argued that Jewish polities were theocracies. Initially, Rosenbaum said, Jewish priests did have some influence on politics, as was the case with all other peoples in their early history, but this influence waned. Between the second century BC and the first century AD, the Hasmonean dynasty ruled Judea. While the Hasmoneans were a priestly family, they ruled the Jewish state not because of their priestly lineage but because they were associated with the fight for Jewish independence. The assumption that Jewish polities were theocracies, said Rosenbaum, was echoed in the belief that Jewish law was religious, but upon examining the content of Jewish law, it would become clear that it was secular.[60]

Another aspect of the debate over the religious nature of Jewish law can be found in discussions of legal dualism – the notion that secular and religious courts and secular and religious law should exist side by side. Simon Federbusch devoted a chapter of his 1952 book to a distinction between "the law of the Torah" and "the law of the kingdom" (*mishpat ha-melukhah*). Federbusch argued that Jewish law recognized the king's power to create rules to deal with myriad public matters in the realms of administrative, civil, and criminal law as long as these rules were not in direct contravention of the rules of the Torah. He traced this idea to the era of Moses and the period of the biblical kings and argued that this distinction also legitimized communal enactments in Jewish communities in the Diaspora (*takanot ha-kahal*). One could also use this distinction, Federbusch said, to provide *halakhic* legitimacy to the norms created by the secular legislature and the secular courts of the new State of Israel.[61]

59 Gulak, "Ha-Probleymot,"December 30, 1916, 20; January 13, 1917, 14; February 3, 1917, 15; February 10, 1917, 13.

60 Rosenbaum, "Shgi'ot Mekubalot," 113–14.

61 Federbusch, *Mishpat ha-Melukhah*, 42–54. See also Kahana, "Li-Ve'ayat Ha-Thukah ha-Toratit." Federbusch's approach stood in direct contrast to the idea of a Jewish theocracy that some Religious Zionist rabbis in Palestine began to champion at approximately the same time. See, generally, Kaye, *Invention*, 30–1, 41–4.

The argument that Jewish public law was irrelevant to a modern Jewish state was also based on the image of Jewish law as an inferior, and perhaps also barbaric, legal system. There were two facets associated with this image. One facet was the argument, found in the works of German non-Jewish biblical scholars in the nineteenth and twentieth centuries, that biblical laws (as well as biblical theological and moral concepts such as monotheism or social justice) were copied from the laws of more developed Near Eastern nations. Yerucham (Philip) Korngruen, a teacher at the Tel Aviv School of Law and Economics (who also served as a District Judge in Mandatory Palestine), wrote a book comparing Mosaic law with the laws of Babylonia, Assyria, and the Hittite Empire to refute this argument.[62]

The second facet of the image of Jewish law as inferior stemmed not from comparisons with other ancient legal systems, but with modern ones, based on the claim that Jewish law was antiquated and, thus, irrelevant to modern needs. In the works of the scholars discussed here, a common response to this claim was to show that Jewish law was *not* antiquated but dynamic and innovative and, therefore, on par with modern legal systems. Specifically, it was argued that two major legal fields often regarded as "modern" were already present in ancient Jewish law: social law, meant to protect the rights of the weakest groups in society; and international law.

Early Zionist political leaders, when discussing their vision of a future Jewish state in Palestine, sometimes mentioned biblical rules that had a socio-economic dimension. For example, the rules regarding land redemption, slave emancipation, and debt forgiveness during the Jubilee year, or the idea of the Sabbath as a model for the protection of workers' rights. Zionist leaders pointed to these laws as models for legislation in the future Jewish state, a state that they envisioned as founded on the principles of social justice.[63]

Similarly, the Jewish legal scholars I analyze in this chapter also turned to the biblical prophets and their notions of social justice. For example, in his book on the prophets, Eisenstadt, whose political views were on the spectrum between socialism and communism, explained

[62] P. Korngruen, *Hukey ha-Mizrah ha-Kadmon: Mehkar Hashva'ah be-Mishpetey Yisrael, Bavel, Ashur ve-Het* (Tel Aviv: Yavneh, 1944), 288.

[63] Yedidya, *Halakha*, 17–21.

that they were actually secular social reformers. The prophets, he claimed, saw God as a source of "social truth and justice" and as the "defender of the poor and of the weak, the punisher of every brute and oppressor," furthering a "humanist, universal worldview."[64] Jewish law was thus a revolutionary law, which contained, even in ancient times, ideas commonly believed to have appeared only in the modern era.

A detailed discussion of Jewish social and labor laws is found in Federbusch's book. He argued that the social legislation that characterizes modern progressive states can be traced back to ancient Jewish law. Jewish law imposed various duties designed to assist the poorest and weakest members of society, such as the duty of universal education. It created the notion of progressive taxation, and developed various regulations designed to protect the health and safety of workers and all other persons. Jewish law sought to limit the right of private property, and ancient Jewish social movements (such as the Essenes) embraced notions of *communal* property. Furthermore, Federbusch noted that Jewish law prohibited usury, celebrated the dignity of manual labor and laborers, pioneered the concept of social insurance, and recognized the right of workers to strike and unionize.[65]

International law, often seen as a distinctly modern legal field, was also viewed by some early twentieth-century scholars as having roots in the principles of ancient Jewish law. This claim appeared in the works of both non-Jewish and Jewish scholars. One non-Jewish scholar who argued that Jewish law in antiquity (as well as other ancient legal systems) contained rules dealing with international law was the German comparative law scholar Josef Kohler. In 1918, Kohler published a book that included a discussion of the history of ancient international law. Kohler devoted several pages of his book to describing biblical international law. Much of this discussion dealt with the laws of war, which Kohler analyzed in all their rather gory detail (killing of male captives, distribution of captive women and children as the spoils of war, and so on). Kohler also mentioned the vision of universal peace found in the Book of Isaiah but argued that

64 Eisenstadt, *The Prophets*, 15, 16.

65 Federbusch, *Mishpat ha-Melukhah*, 100–11, 124–84. See also Benjamin Manasseh Lewin, *Masekhet Po'alim: Talmud Katan* (Jerusalem: Mosad ha-Rav Kook, 1942/43) (a digest of *halakhic* labor law).

such a vision could not be seen as part of international law because it was a utopian messianic idea divorced from earthly politics.[66]

In contrast to Kohler's relatively objective approach, Jewish authors often claimed that the Jews *invented* international law and that the international law norms they created were more humane and, therefore, more "modern" than those of other nations in antiquity.[67] For example, in 1917, Gulak wrote an article tracing the notion of universally just law applicable to all nations to the biblical prophets. Gulak also noted that the biblical prophets created the ideal of perpetual peace and contrasted this ideal favorably with modern pacifism, which, he said, was based on the notion that peace would only result from legal coercion by an alliance of powerful nations.[68] Eisenstadt, too, published an article in the 1920s discussing in detail the Jewish (and, more generally, ancient Near Eastern) roots of international law.[69] The same volume in which Eisenstadt's article appeared also contained a brief report on a lecture delivered in 1925 at the Tel Aviv branch of the Jewish Law Society by Shimshon Rosenbaum, in which Rosenbaum had argued that international law first appeared in the Bible.[70]

International law was taught at the Hebrew University in the 1930s by Norman Bentwich. In his 1932 inaugural lecture, Bentwich claimed that the ideas of universal peace and one universal law applicable to all nations – principles upon which modern international law and its institutions (the League of Nations) were based – had their roots in the prophecies of the biblical prophets.[71] In an article published during the same year, Bentwich discussed the Bible as the source of the international laws of war. The Bible, he said, was one of the major fonts of international law in the early modern period. Christian legal scholars such as the early-modern English jurist John Selden were

[66] Josef Kohler, *Grundlagen des völkerrechts: Vergangenheit, gegenwart, zukunft* (Stuttgart: Enke, 1918), 21–3.

[67] For a brief discussion of the interwar literature on this topic, see Israel-Vleeschhouwer, *Yahas ha-Halakhah*, 23–4.

[68] Gulak, "Ha-Probleymot," *Ha-'Am*, December 30, 1916, 20; *Ha-'Am*, February 10, 1916, 13, 14–15.

[69] Eisenstadt, "Reshit Yihusav," reprinted in *Tsiyon*, 97.

[70] "'Orekh ha-Din S. Rosenbaum," 204–5.

[71] Norman Bentwich, *Yerushalayim: 'Ir ha-Shalom* (Jerusalem: Hebrew University Press, 1932). See also Bentwich, *Religious Foundations*.

inspired by the Bible (and also by medieval Jewish scholars such as Maimonides and Nachmanides) when distinguishing between just and unjust wars. According to Bentwich, Jewish law was also the source of inspiration for the Muslim laws of war – for example, the idea that Muslims should fight infidels but should protect the "people of the book" (Jews and Christians), provided they submit to Muslim rule.[72]

The Jewish-Polish-French-American scholar Jacob Mikliszanski published detailed discussions of two subfields of international law: international criminal law; and the laws of war. In a 1937 article, Mikliszanski claimed that, unlike all other ancient legal systems, Jewish law was able to create a just and moral system of international criminal law. This general claim was not original. It was based on an observation made in a 1922 book by the French international law professor Henri Donnedieu de Vabres, who had supervised Mikliszanski's doctoral dissertation.[73] However, the discussion that Mikliszanski offered in his article regarding Jewish rules dealing with international crimes was far more detailed than that presented in Donnedieu's book.[74]

In articles published in the 1940s, Mikliszanski dealt with the Jewish laws of war. He claimed that, while the ancient Jews were a peace-loving people, the need to defend themselves, coupled with their love of legality and justice, led them to create the first international law rules governing war. These rules dealt with topics such as the declaration of war, siege, prisoners of war, conquest, treatment of enemy women, ceasefires, and the cession of war.[75]

Mikliszanski repeatedly stressed the humanitarian and progressive nature of the Jewish laws of war. One notable (and problematic) example that he offered to illustrate this claim was his discussion of

72 Norman Bentwich, "Ha-Tanakh ke-Makor le-Diney ha-Milhamah shel he-'Amim," *Ha-Mishpat ha-'Ivri* 4 (1932/33): 147, 149–50. See also Bentwich, *Religious Foundations*, 169. On Selden and Jewish law, see also Mark Somos, "Political Thought and the Historiography of International Law," in *The Cambridge History of International Law*, Vol. 1: *The Historiography of International Law*, eds. Randall Lesaffer and Anne Peters (Cambridge: Cambridge University Press, 2024), 107, 119–20.

73 Henri Donnedieu de Vabres, *Introduction à l'étude du droit pénal international* (Paris: Sirey, 1922), 18–19; Mikliszanski, *Le droit pénal international*, title page. See also Mikliszanski, *Ha-Mishpat*, 4.

74 Mikliszanski, *Ha-Mishpat*, 11.

75 Mikliszanski, "Mishpat ha-Milhamah," 80.

the biblical rule dealing with the treatment of captured enemy women. The rule on the topic stated that:

> ... when you take the field against your enemies, and the Lord your God delivers them into your power and you take some of them captive, and you see among the captives a beautiful woman and you desire her and would take her to wife, you shall bring her into your house, and she shall trim her hair, pare her nails, and discard her captive's garb. She shall spend a month's time in your house lamenting her father and mother; after that you may come to her and possess her, and she shall be your wife. Then, should you no longer want her, you must release her outright. You must not sell her for money: since you had your will of her, you must not enslave her.[76]

Most modern readers would view this rule with horror. However, Mikliszanski claimed that this was actually a progressive rule. Captive women were not to be immediately raped and enslaved (as they would have been if caught by non-Jewish nations in antiquity). Instead, they were to be treated in what Mikliszanski apologetically argued was a (comparatively) humane manner: they would be given time for mourning and would be married to their captor.[77]

Ya'acov Berman also argued that the roots of modern international law could be found in the Bible. These roots included the general biblical notion that justice and mercy constitute the basis of law, as well as specific biblical norms regarding foreigners, international alliances, and the laws of war. Some observers, said Berman, would argue that biblical rules were not "legal" because they were not backed by sanctions. However, Berman insisted that they should be seen as "law" because the mutual interests of nations necessitated them, despite the fact that they were more similar to the norms of morality than to law. In any event, there could be no doubt, claimed Berman, that early-modern Western international law scholars publicly acknowledged their debt to Judaism.[78]

Max Laserson, too, argued that international law had Jewish roots. In an article published in 1948, he stated that the two founding figures of modern international law, Hugo Grotius and John Selden, both acknowledged "the importance of Jewish religio-juridical teachings." Grotius was influenced by the natural law ideas found in the Old

[76] Deuteronomy 21:10–14. [77] Mikliszanski, "Mishpat ha-Milhamah," 116–20.
[78] Berman, *Torat ha-Medinah*, 28, 83–4.

Testament. Selden was also influenced by the Bible but he was also inspired by the Talmud. Both Grotius and Selden referred to the Jewish notion of a universal law applicable to all human beings as embodied in the concept of the seven Noahide laws.[79]

Finally, Federbusch argued that Judaism was unique among ancient religions in its pursuit of the idea of universal peace and that the original idea of the need for rules constraining war was a Jewish one. He justified his stance by alluding to the fact that the Jewish God was not seen as a national God but as a universal one, giving birth, in turn, to the concept of the fraternity of all God's creatures. Federbusch then discussed various Jewish rules dealing with the declaration of war and its pursuit (prohibition on total war, protection of and compassion toward enemy civilians, siege, prisoners of war, the annexation of enemy territory, treaties, and neutrality).[80] Like Mikliszanski, Federbusch, too, discussed the biblical rule regarding the treatment of captured enemy women, and he too argued that the fact that women captives were not killed and that their captors were instructed to deal with them in a (relatively) honorable manner was an indication of the moral superiority of Jewish law. Like Mikliszanski, then, Federbusch positioned Jewish law favorably compared to the laws of war of other ancient nations, which sanctioned the outright "murder, without compunction, of all prisoners of war."[81]

### *Democracy, Constitutional Limits on the Power of Monarchs, and Republics*

Indian authors devoted considerable effort to challenging the Western portrayal of ancient Indian states as ruled by Oriental despots, seeking instead to highlight parallels between Indian political structures and modern democratic institutions. In the Jewish case, the "Oriental despotism" trope was not overly problematic because, for most of their history, Jews had not had a state of their own and, thus, by definition, were not governed by despotic rulers. However, the question did arise in relation to the biblical period during which independent Jewish states did exist. Many Jewish scholars working

[79] Laserson, "Hebrew Roots of International Law."
[80] Federbusch, *Mishpat ha-Melukhah*, 184–220. [81] Ibid., 213–15.

during the first decades of the twentieth century were keen to emphasize that Judaism and democracy *were* compatible or, indeed, that Judaism was, in fact, one of the very sources of the modern concept of democracy. This topic figured prominently in the works of American rabbis Hirschensohn and Silver, but it also appeared in works published in Mandatory Palestine and Israel. Eliezer Livneh argued in 1946 that a permanent attribute of Jewish political thought was its resistance to autocracy, whether by a dictator or by a monarch.[82] While Western democracy was considered a major achievement of European nations, Livneh observed, the historical sources of European democracies were found in the Protestant Reformation; and the essence of Protestantism was an attempt to return to the Bible. Without the Bible, he reasoned, democracy would not have been established in countries such as England or Switzerland.[83]

In his 1950s book, Federbusch argued that the democratic nature of the Jewish state was, somewhat paradoxically, related to its theocratic nature. The Jewish state was not a theocracy, Federbusch said, if that term was used to designate a state where the priests ruled and their followers enjoyed special privileges. Indeed, the Jewish state was one in which all people, no matter their religion or ethnicity, were perceived as equal and in which rulers and priests, Church and State, had always been kept separate from the earliest days of Moses and Aaron until the days of the last King of Judea. The Jewish state was a theocracy, argued Federbusch, only in the sense that it was based on the notion that God ruled all the people in the world; in practice, however, it was a democracy in which all people were equal. The despotic idea was foreign to Jews because it implied a *human* ruler and, thus, a rejection of the power of God.[84] A concrete manifestation of this principle was found in the fact that no *halakhic* punishments even existed for the crimes of *lèse majesté* and treason. Jewish law sought to punish persons for rejecting God or the Torah but not for opposing a human ruler.[85]

Jewish democracy, argued Federbusch, was the result of the fact that Israelite society began as a non-hierarchical democratic tribal society. The biblical idea of a covenant between God and his people – which,

[82] Livneh, "Be-Fetah ha-Sefer," 9–15. [83] Ibid., 12–13.
[84] Federbusch, *Mishpat ha-Melukhah*, 25–32. [85] Ibid., 79–90.

according to Federbusch, was the source of the modern social contract concept – was an additional source of the democratic idea because it was based on the consent of the people. Similar democratic notions, Federbusch continued, could be found in the Talmud and in Maimonides, for example, in the Talmudic rule that "we make no decree upon the community unless the majority are able to abide by it." In addition, the assent of the community was required for the appointment of Israelite kings and, later, for the appointment of leaders of Jewish communities in the post-biblical period.[86]

Discussions of democracy were often accompanied by discussions of the limitations placed on the power of rulers through the mechanisms of the rule of law, separation of powers, and constitutional monarchy. One author, located in Russia and using what seems to have been a pseudonym, Y. Yehoshafat, published an article in the late 1920s in the journal of the Jewish Law Society in Palestine, *Ha-Mishpat ha-'Ivri*, on the rule of law in non-Jewish and Jewish law. Yehoshafat noted that unlike other ancient Oriental nations, the Jews did not see their kings as divine and did not believe that God spoke to his people through their kings. Monarchs were limited and bound by law. This idea was preserved in the period after the return from the Babylonian exile. In the post-exilic Jewish state, the priests, together with the members of the Supreme Court (Great *Sanhederin*), limited the power of rulers in the name of the law, thus strengthening the democratic inclination of the Jews, based on their respect for the humanity of each individual.[87]

Grajewsky depicted Jewish kings as devoid of any legislative power. Although the king was regarded as responsible for *applying* the law, the legislative power per se was in the hands of the guardians of the Torah, which could, therefore, be understood as a "constitution." The king himself was subject to the rules of the Torah, and if he "betrayed" these rules, the prophet would dethrone him and pass the monarchical power to another person. It was time, Grajewsky urged, that humanity freed itself from the rules of Roman law – a system that only imposed

[86] Ibid., 32–7. On democracy and Jewish law, see also Arye Edrei, "Menachem Elon veha-Mishpat ha-'Ivri: Tsiyuney Derekh," in *Halakhah u-Mishpat: Sefer ha-Zikaron le-Menachem Elon*, ed. Arye Edrei (Tsafririm: Nevo, 2018), 13, 17–18 (on the mid-twentieth-century scholarly interest in rulemaking by "the people" in medieval and early modern Jewish communities).

[87] Y. Yehoshafat, "Shilton ha-Hok," *Ha-Mishpat ha-'Ivri* 3 (1928/29): 1, 5–7.

order using overwhelming force – and adopted instead Jewish law, the law of justice and equity, imbued with superior moral and social concepts.[88]

Ya'acov Berman's 1944 book used the biblical story of Naboth's vineyard to argue that the notions of the rule of law, generally, and of laws constraining the power of kings, specifically, were prevalent in biblical times. Unlike other Near Eastern kings and even modern ones, King Ahab was powerless to confiscate Naboth's vineyard, which was protected by the concept of private property. The only way that King Ahab could obtain the vineyard he so desired was by hiring two witnesses to falsely accuse Naboth of being a blasphemer. Furthermore, Berman argued, in the ancient world, including Greece and Rome, the monarch was usually a military leader and, therefore, often a tyrant with unlimited legislative power. Modern European nations inherited Roman law and thus followed the same tradition, the only exception being England, where the king's power was limited by law. Biblical kings, like English ones, were not free to legislate, their role being to implement the law rather than create it. The biblical priests, prophets, elders, and people had the power to remove kings, Berman explained. Indeed, he argued that the terms "the people" and "priests and elders" might actually have been used to designate various types of assemblies whose decisions the kings had to follow. In addition, monarchical power was limited by prophets exercising the right of free speech to criticize kings when they deviated from the laws of the Torah, thus inspiring the modern English notion of free speech and, indeed, other modern English and American constitutional notions.[89]

Eliezer Livneh, too, discussed in detail how Jewish political traditions constrained the power of kings and argued that the notion of the separation of powers was not an early-modern idea that

[88] Grajewsky, "Ha-Medinah veha-Knesiyah," 60, 63–4, 68–9. An interesting aspect of this topic, appearing both in works on Hindu law and ones of Jewish law, was the argument that even God was subject to the rules of religious law. For this argument in the Jewish context, see Chaim Tchernowitz, "'Al ha-Historiyah shel ha- Ha-Mishpat Ha-'Ivri," *Ha-Mishpat Ha-'Ivri* 1 (1925/26): 1, 9–10.

[89] Berman, *Torat ha-Medinah*, 21, 28–37, 54, 65–9. On the protection of individual property in Jewish law, see also Hillel Zeitlin, "Kdushat ha-Kinyan be-Mamlakhah Toratit," in *Gvilin: Le-Mahshevet ha-Torah veha-'Avodah*, eds. Yehudah Yefet and Moshe Krone (Warsaw: Jabne, 1937), 13.

originated with Montesquieu or the American Founding Fathers (or even ancient Greece and Rome) but, rather, had its origins in the Bible. Livneh found evidence supporting this claim in the biblical story of Judge Abimelech's despotic rule and Jotham's fable. He also cited provisions taken from the Book of Deuteronomy that commanded that the future King of the Israelites should not "consider himself better than his fellow Israelites and turn from the law to the right or to the left." In addition, said Livneh, according to the Bible, priests and prophets were supposed to constrain kings – kings were not seen as divine and were expected to further the causes of justice and law.[90]

In 1946, the same year Livneh published his work, Zeev Falk, a young law student at the Jerusalem Law Classes, published an article comparing the rule of law in English and Jewish law. Falk began his article by noting that one of the marks of a nation's development was the appearance of the notion of the rule of law. In primitive nations (and modern dictatorships), autocratic rulers have absolute power. In contrast, in developed countries, political leaders are subject to the law. English law, observed Falk, was an example of a legal system in which the notion of the rule of law was most fully developed; but, even in English law, there was a rule according to which "the king can do no wrong" because kings were seen – following the positivist approach to law – as the source of the law. Judges were merely the servants of kings. In Jewish law, an equivalent rule, discussed in the Babylonian Talmud in Tractate Sanhedrin, was that "a king can neither act as a judge nor can he be judged." According to the Talmud, this rule originated in the Hasmonean period, when King Yannai refused to be judged by the Supreme Court (Great *Sanhedrin*). However, kings of the Davidic line, traditionally perceived as the only true and lawful kings of Israel, *were* subject to the law. Jewish law, Falk added, was based on the natural law notion according to which the king does not create law. Instead, the law embodies eternal godly justice, to which the king, like any other person, was subject.[91]

90 Livneh, "Be-Fetah ha-Sefer," 9–15.

91 Z. Falk, "Shilton ha-Mishpat," *'Alon Agudat ha-Talmidim ha-'Ivriyim be-Veyt ha-Sefer le-Mishpatim bi-Yerushalayim* (June 1946): 3 (a copy is available at the National Library of Israel, Jerusalem). See also Berman, *Torat ha-Medinah*, 57–8.

Finally, Federbusch, summarizing the ideas mentioned above, argued that, in the Jewish state, kings were not perceived as divine, did not enjoy special privileges, and were viewed as equal to all other citizens. They were subject to law, enjoyed no legal immunity, and could not confiscate the property of ordinary citizens.[92] State and religion were separated in the history of the Israelite states, beginning with the time of Moses who, according to Federbusch, appointed Joshua as the head of a civil court system, and Aaron as the head of a religious court system. This separation continued later. The Talmud and Maimonides recognized the legislative power invested in the Israelite kings – and, later, in the democratic bodies of the Jewish communities in the Diaspora – to create norms in all areas of law. However, the norms they enacted could not violate what Federbusch saw as the basic norm of Jewish law: equality between all citizens.[93]

Indian scholars devoted much effort to proving that some ancient Indian states were republics rather than monarchies. There were fewer references to republican forms of government in the works of Jewish scholars, but such references could sometimes be found. In 1927, discussing the origins of the notion of the separation of powers, Grajewsky referred to it as "the basis of the modern republic." The fact that the biblical kings were subject to the laws of the Torah and that they could be removed if they transgressed these laws meant that the biblical kingdom was "a quasi-republic, subject to divine guidance, not based on power and servitude [to the king] but on justice and equity."[94]

Livneh's 1946 work also connected the notion of the separation of powers with the republican mode of government. According to him, "out of a general disdain for the monarchy," some Jewish political thinkers embraced republican notions. In this context, he referred to two examples: first, the fact that the Hasmonean leader (*nasi*) was not an absolute ruler but merely the head of a body called "the Jewish assembly" (*hever ha-yehudim*); and, second, the argument by the fifteenth-century Jewish leader and scholar Don Isaac Abarbanel that

[92] Federbusch, *Mishpat ha-Melukhah*, 21–3.

[93] Ibid., 43–54. On constitutional monarchy, see also Kaye, *Invention*, 80 (discussing the idea in Rabbi Herzog's works).

[94] Grajewsky, "Ha-Medinah veha-Knesiyah," 68.

"if leaders are good, we better have many rather than one, and if they are bad, the one is more dangerous than the many."[95]

A more developed discussion of the attitude of Jewish law to republics is found in Federbusch's 1952 book. Federbusch argued, based on the biblical story about the reluctance of the prophet Samuel to anoint Saul as the King of Israel, that monarchy was incompatible with Judaism, because it contradicted one of its core tenets, the inherent equality of all individuals. The Torah, Federbusch said, taught believers to hate despotism and condemn monarchical rule because of its potential to hinder personal freedom. Drawing on the pro-republican sayings of Don Isaac Abarbanel, Federbusch argued that monarchy was not a necessary attribute of Judaism and that Judaism also envisioned other types of government: by judges and prophets.[96] Federbusch also claimed that Jewish law prevented the appointment of a king as the head of the recently established State of Israel. According to Maimonides, a king could only be appointed by a court of seventy ordained elders and a prophet. As rabbinical ordination and prophets no longer existed, the State of Israel could not become a monarchy according to Jewish law.[97]

### *Equality*

Works of scholars in the Diaspora and Mandatory Palestine often argued that equality was a basic characteristic of Jewish law.[98] For example, in 1946, Livneh argued that the notions of equality and dignity were to be found in the Bible and that these were the source of various social laws protecting slaves, salaried workers, and the poor. Livneh also argued that the Bible was the source of the notion of liberty, which emerged out of the story of the liberation of the Jews from Egyptian bondage, as well as out of the words of the prophets.[99]

[95] Livneh, "Be-Fetah ha-Sefer," 15.

[96] Federbusch, *Mishpat ha-Melukhah*, 37–9, 41.

[97] Ibid., 41. On republicanism in Federbusch's thought, see also Mittleman, "*Mishpat Hamelukhah*," 77–8.

[98] I will not discuss the attempts by orthodox rabbis using traditional *halakhic* idioms to grapple with the notion of equality. For a detailed discussion, see, e.g., Edrei, "Halom ha-Mishpat," 40–6. For an additional discussion (focusing on American thinkers), see Martin Sicker, "Democracy and Judaism: The Question of Equality," *Jewish Political Studies Review* 5 (1993): 57, 61–2.

[99] Livneh, "Be-Fetah ha-Sefer," 16–22.

Similarly, Federbusch claimed in his 1952 book that the ancient Jewish state was unique because it was based on the idea that the goal of the state was not conquest and power but the furtherance of morality. One consequence was that the Jewish state was founded on the concept of social justice: it was the first to treat all its inhabitants – poor and rich, master and slave, citizen and foreigner – equally, and this idea inspired both the eighteenth-century French revolutionaries and the American Founding Fathers.[100]

In a 1950s article that compared Mosaic laws and those of the Babylonian King Hammurabi, Paltiel Dikshtein argued that the laws of Moses were morally advanced compared to those of other ancient Near Eastern nations. Absolute equality, he said, did not exist even in the contemporary world, but if one compared the Jews to other nations of the ancient Near East, one would find that the Jews treated slaves and foreigners better than other nations. Israelite society was not class-based like ancient Indian or Egyptian society; and while the laws of Hammurabi were based on distinctions between various categories of persons, Mosaic law emphasized the notion of equality.[101]

Moving from general principles to specific topics, discussions of the attitude of Jewish law toward slaves, women, and foreigners echoed the arguments made about equality generally. Let me turn first to the topic of slaves in Jewish law. One type of argument about slavery found in the works of Jewish scholars was the claim that, since early Israelite society was an undeveloped, un-hierarchical, nomadic, shepherd society, slaves were treated less harshly by their masters than slaves in the developed urban societies of the ancient world. The slaves of the early Israelites shared the living quarters and the food of their masters. They were unshackled because their work required freedom of movement, and they were treated no more harshly by the head of the family than by his own sons. This argument was made in 1917 by Eisenstadt. It was repeated in a book on the comparative laws of the nations of the ancient Near East, written by another Tel Aviv School teacher, Yerucham Korngruen, which was published in 1944.[102]

100 Federbusch, *Mishpat ha-Melukhah*, 13, 15, 18–20.

101 Paltiel Dikshtein, "Hukey Moshe ve-Hukey Hammurabi," in Orren, ed., *Professor Paltiel Daykan (Dikshtein)*, 150, 153–4.

102 See Samuel Eisenstadt, "Kadmoniyot ha-Mishpat ha-Yisre'eli," *Ha-'Am* (May 18, 1917): 10, 12; Korngruen, *Hukey ha-Mizrah ha-Kadmon*, 30–1.

In 1944, Ya'acov Berman argued that the most important innovations of biblical law were the twin notions of liberty and equality. Many biblical commandments, he said, were based on the "memory of Egypt" – that is, on the fact that the Israelites were slaves in Egypt. The Egyptian experience led the Israelites to reject the idea of a hierarchical society. Jews, he claimed, were the only nation in antiquity that did not recognize the special privileges of classes or tribes, and even the Israelite kings were urged not to see themselves as more privileged than "ordinary" people since the only master of the Israelites was God. Slavery, Berman said, was actually abolished by biblical law since Jewish slaves were indentured servants who had to be freed after six years, and non-Jewish slaves were protected from abuse by their masters. This led Berman to assert that, in fact, "the Torah seeks to abolish slavery completely."[103]

Federbusch also discussed slavery in his book. He took an apologetic stance, conceding that Jewish law did recognize slavery but arguing that this was because total abolition was impossible, given that slavery had existed in the ancient world (and also, until recently, even in modern states like the United States). He then listed the various rules meant to protect slaves from abuse in Jewish law and also claimed that the Talmud envisioned the abolition of slavery as a desirable goal.[104]

Moving to women, Jacob Teplicki, a lawyer based in Saint Petersburg, claimed in an article published in 1918 that there were almost no differences in the legal capacities of men versus women in post-biblical Jewish law.[105] In a 1920s article about the right of women to serve as guardians of minors or invalids, Simha Assaf argued – against the conventional view of the majority of Jewish law

103 Berman also argued, quoting biblical rules regarding debt forgiveness and the prohibition on interest, that the Bible sought to avoid the creation of unequal classes and of a "destitute" and "nomadic" proletariat. In addition, Berman claimed that the Bible sought to prevent the creation of a class of experts with a monopoly on knowledge. In Egypt, the scribes monopolized learning and science, but Judaism created a general duty of education, which was the best guarantee of the protection of progress and freedom, justice, and law. See Berman, *Torat ha-Medinah*, 24–8.

104 Federbusch, *Mishpat ha-Melukhah*, 157–64. For additional discussions of slavery, see, e.g. Moshe Findling, *T'hukat ha-'Avodah* (Jerusalem: Schreiber, 1944/45), 8–11; S. B. Feldman, *Hok ha-'Avodah ha-Kadum ba-'Olam* (Jerusalem: Ha-Ya'adah le-Torah ve-Sifrut shel ha-Mo'atsah le-Ma'an ha-Shabat, 1947/48).

105 J. Teplicki, "Diney Mamonot," *Ha-Mishpat ha-'Ivri: Riv'on Mada'i* (1918): 77, 79.

scholars – that, according to Jewish law, a court *could* appoint women as guardians.[106]

In 1950, Paltiel Dikshtein published a pamphlet on behalf of the main feminist organization in Israel at the time, the Jewish Women's Equal Rights Association. This was a practical work meant to inform lay readers about women's legal rights. However, in the introduction, Dikshtein argued that, while "in some details," women were undeniably considered inferior to men in Jewish law, these details were "secondary." In principle, he contended, Jewish law viewed men and women as equals, citing passages in which women were described as equal to men – for example, in their respective relationships with their children.[107]

Federbusch discussed women's rights in a chapter of his book dealing with the appointment of public officers such as kings and judges. The conventional *halakhic* rule was that women could not be appointed to public office, but Federbusch questioned this rule, noting that there were biblical counter-examples (the prophetess and judge Deborah, for instance). In addition, some rabbinical commentators argued that women could be appointed to public office and could also (again, contrary to conventional *halakhic* opinion) serve as witnesses. Federbusch also stated that, according to Jewish law, women were obliged to serve in the army during defensive wars.[108]

Jewish law scholars invested much effort in showing that Jewish law treated "foreigners" – that is, non-Jews – equitably. The legal status of foreigners was not a major concern of the Indian scholars discussed in Chapter 5, but it played a major role in Jewish apologetics.[109] Mikliszanski, whose works focused on Jewish international law,

[106] Simha Assaf, "Minuy Nashim le-Apotropsut," *Ha-Mishpat ha-'Ivri* 2 (1926/27): 75.

[107] Paltiel Daykan (Dikshtein), *Ha-Matsav ha-Mishpati shel ha-Ishah be-Yisrael* (Tel Aviv: Tversky, 1949/50), 12–13. For a similar pamphlet from the 1930s, see Bernard Joseph, *Zkhuyot ha-Ishah 'al pi Hukey Eretz Yisrael* (Jerusalem: Hit'ahdut Nashim 'Ivriyot, 1929/30).

[108] Federbusch, *Mishpat ha-Melukhah*, 67–9, 192. Just like Indian scholars, such as Pal, claimed that castes did not exist in early Hindu law, and that they only appeared later, so some Jewish law scholars argued that a regression in the rights of Jewish women only occurred during the Talmudic period as the result of the influence of Greek law. See Tchernowitz, "'Al ha-Historiyah shel ha- Ha-Mishpat Ha-'Ivri," 12.

[109] For a general discussion of the history of Jewish attitudes to Gentiles, see Adi Ophir and Ishay Rosen-Zvi, *Goy: Israel's Multiple Others and the Birth of the Gentile* (Oxford: Oxford University Press, 2018).

naturally devoted attention to the question of how foreigners were treated by Jewish law, an issue that touched on both international criminal law and also private international law. He listed various terms used to designate foreigners in Hebrew. He then noted that the laws of other ancient nations did not treat foreigners as equal to natives: legal duties were imposed more strictly on foreigners, and they did not enjoy the same rights granted to persons belonging to the nation. Unlike the laws of other ancient Near Eastern nations, however, biblical Jewish law declared that "the same laws and regulations will apply both to you and to the foreigner residing among you."[110]

Mikliszanski also rejected a claim made by his doctoral supervisor, Henri Donnedieu de Vabres, that in contrast to biblical law, Talmudic law diverged from the principle of equality between Jews and non-Jews. The Talmud, said Mikliszanski, also followed the spirit of biblical law. As an example, he cited the Jewish notion of universal law enshrined in the seven Noahide laws. In addition, Mikliszanski noted that, according to the Talmud, foreigners were protected by Jewish criminal law almost like Jews. In Jewish civil law of the Talmudic period, there were certain contractual and tort rules that only applied to Jews. However, Mikliszanski justified this difference, citing Maimonides, by saying that these rules did not apply in inter-Gentile transactions and, therefore, Jewish law was justified in not using them in civil cases involving Jewish–Gentile transactions.[111]

### *Pan-Asianism and Islam*

Some of the Indian authors that I discussed in the previous chapter, such as Benoy Kumar Sarkar, sought to place the study of ancient Indian history within a wider comparative context that would lead to the creation of a non-Western, pan-Asian (Hindu, Chinese, and Muslim) history of democratic institutions. Another broader comparative framework used by Indian authors was the "Aryan legal family" notion employed to contrast democratic Aryan political

[110] Numbers 15, 16.

[111] Mikliszanski, *Ha-Mishpat*, 6, 10–14. Federbusch also discussed the protection of foreigners by Jewish law. In his book, he analyzed in detail the various categories of non-Jews classified by Jewish law, using the modern language of "minority rights" to discuss them. Federbusch, *Mishpat ha-Melukhah*, 54–60.

institutions with what was claimed to be the Semitic approach to government, characterized as top-down and despotic.

As we saw in the Introduction, pan-Asian notions appeared in the early works of Samuel Eisenstadt. Generally speaking, however, pan-Asian ideas played only a very minor role in Zionist thought and, consequently, also in the works of the authors that I analyze in this chapter. As for the Aryan–Semitic contrast, it was mentioned in the works of two Jewish-American scholars that I examined in this chapter, but in the opposite sense to that of the Indian works. Israel Friedlaender argued that absolutism and tyranny were neither Jewish nor general Semitic traits, and Abba Hillel Silver argued that the notion of social hierarchy was an Aryan rather than a Jewish notion.[112]

In the case of Jewish public law, the broader comparative context was provided not by pan-Asianism or the linguistic/racial Aryan-Semitic binary contrast but by Christianity. Christianity grew out of Judaism, and Jewish authors, therefore, claimed that legal doctrines – and, indeed, entire legal fields – identified with the modern Christian West (the notion of the separation of Church and State, the idea of limits on monarchical power, or the field of international law) originated in Jewish sources, first and foremost in the Bible. In this sense, the Jewish scholars were more ambitious than their Indian contemporaries. Indian scholars only sought to underscore the similarity of their ancient political institutions to those of the West (and perhaps also prove their greater antiquity compared to the West). The Jewish scholars, on the other hand, made a bolder claim, arguing that Judaism influenced the very creation of modern Western political institutions and law.

As for Islam, while it sometimes figured (negatively) in the Hindu polity literature as the force arresting the development of Indian political thought, there was almost no mention of it in the Jewish works, and when it did appear, it was depicted in a way similar to the way Christianity was portrayed, that is, as an inheritor of ideas that first appeared in Judaism. This is what was claimed by Norman Bentwich when he discussed Judaism as the source of inspiration for the Muslim laws of war.[113]

112 Friedlaender, "Were Our Ancestors," 39–40; Silver, *Where Judaism Differed*, 227.

113 Bentwich, "Ha-Tanakh ke-Makor le-Diney ha-Milhamah," 149–50; Bentwich, *Religious Foundations*, 169.

Finally, one can ask whether the Arabs of Mandatory Palestine produced works on Islamic public law comparable to the works on Jewish public law that were analyzed here. As I noted in Chapter 2, the Arabs of Mandatory Palestine did not create a formal system of academic legal education similar to the one that the Jews of Palestine did, and the scholarly output of works on law written by Arab lawyers and intellectuals in Palestine was far smaller than that of the Jews. However, some of the ideas I discussed here also appeared in works in Arabic. First, there were several articles published in the Arabic periodical *al-Huquq* devoted to constitutional law, focusing specifically on civil rights such as freedom of expression and freedom of the press in modern law.[114] One could also find articles arguing against applying the rules of international law only to the supposedly "civilized" European nations since, for example, Chinese civilization was older than European civilization.[115]

*Al-Huquq* also published articles discussing the relationship between religion (in this case, Islam) and modern institutions and values. One article published in the journal was a translation from Turkish to Arabic of an excerpt from a 1913 book by the Ottoman politician and constitutional law scholar Babanzade İsmail Hakkı. This excerpt discussed the concept of the Islamic Caliphate. It rejected the European view that the Caliphate was a despotic state, noting (just like Salahuddin Khuda Bukhsh did in India) that, at first, the office of the caliph was not hereditary and that the first caliphs were elected.[116] One could also find in *al-Huquq* articles in which it was argued that Islam espoused liberal values, for example, religious freedom, or articles that apologetically defended Islam from the accusation that it saw women as inferior.[117] Such arguments also appeared in non-legal works. A primary school textbook written by Palestinian educator 'Izzat Darwaza and used in the *an-Najah* school in Nablus, where Darwaza served as a principal, noted that, unlike

[114] See "Hurriyyat al-sahafah," *al-Huquq* 1 (1924): 664; "Hurriyyat al-fikr," *al-Huquq* 2(5) (1925): 1; "Al-Din wa-hurriyyat al-raay," *al-Huquq* 2(8) (1925): 66.

[115] "Al-Huquq al-dawliyyah," *al-Huquq* 1 (1924): 436, 442.

[116] Babanzade İsmail Hakkı, "al-Hakimiyyah al-siyasiyyah waal-ahkam al-islamiyyah," *al-Huquq* 1 (1924): 540, 542.

[117] See "Hurriyyat al-adyan," *al-Huquq* 2(1) (1925): 7, 11–12; "Al-Talaq waal-zawaj wa-ikhtilaf al-nazr fi-hima' bayn al-sharq waal-gharb," *al-Huquq* 2(4) (1925): 21 (an article translated from the Egyptian journal *al-Hilal*).

medieval Christianity, Islam promoted religious freedom. An Egyptian textbook used for religious instruction in the secondary school classes at *an-Najah* discussed the Islamic notion of consultation (*shura*) as a proof that early Islamic societies were not autocratic.[118]

## Characteristics

### *Causes Leading to the Appearance of the Jewish Public Law Scholarship*

Works on Jewish public law were far more varied than the Indian works. For example, they were dispersed geographically between Europe, North America, and Mandatory Palestine; there was greater ideological diversity among the authors writing them; and they were written in more than one language. Nevertheless, it is still possible to inquire into the causes leading to the appearance of these writings.

As in the Indian case, one factor leading to the publication of the Jewish works may have been the personal biography of the authors involved. For example, it would seem natural to expect Jewish lawyer-politicians, possessing both traditional *halakhic* knowledge and also experience serving in interwar European parliaments, to engage with and write about Jewish public law. Such was the case of Shimshon Rosenbaum (who was a Member of the Lithuanian Parliament and a Minister of the Lithuanian Government during the interwar period), Max Laserson (who was a Member of the Latvian Parliament), and Simon Federbusch (who was a Member of the Polish Parliament). Other authors had less formal political credentials but were nevertheless highly involved in politics, as was the case with rabbi Isaac Breuer, one of the leaders of the ultra-Orthodox political party *Agudath Yisrael*. Unlike Breuer, Rabbi Isaac Herzog was not a member of any political party. However, he was exposed to constitutional politics when, before immigrating to Palestine, he served as Chief Rabbi of the Irish Free Republic. In that role, he befriended Ireland's Prime Minister, Éamon de Valera, and was

118 See Suzanne Schneider, *Mandatory Separation: Religion, Education, and Mass Politics in Palestine* (Stanford, CA: Stanford University Press, 2018), 156, 158.

involved in drafting the Irish Constitution of 1937.[119] Finally, more prosaic personal factors may also have played a role. For example, Jacob Mikliszanski wrote a doctoral dissertation on international law as a student in France. It is, therefore, unsurprising that he would follow this dissertation with articles discussing international law and Jewish law.

Apart from personal factors, political events also played a role in the appearance of the works on Jewish public law. It seems that there were minor peaks in interest in the topic of Jewish public law, peaks that were associated with changing political prospects for the establishment of a Jewish state in Palestine. One event that may have prompted a heightened interest was the Balfour Declaration of 1917, in which the British declared their support for the creation of a Jewish "national home" in Palestine. The Balfour Declaration, a major milestone in the process leading to the establishment of the State of Israel in 1948, was mentioned in the lectures delivered at the founding conference of the Jewish Law Society in Moscow. In the introduction to the first issue of the journal of that society, published in Moscow in September 1918, the editors explained that the study of Jewish law was of academic but also practical importance because:

> ... in recent days, our nation is slowly acquiring political freedoms and the right of self-determination in some aspects of its public life in the Diaspora while simultaneously creating a free national center in our country [Palestine] ... and both the autonomy in the Diaspora and the center in Palestine require rules that will define the outward forms of the life of the nation.[120]

A second peak of interest in the topic was associated with the decade preceding the establishment of a Jewish state in Palestine in 1948. One early manifestation of this interest was a memorandum on the constitution of a future Jewish state written by Isaac Breuer, following the recommendations of Britain's Peel Commission in

[119] See Amihai Radzyner, "The Irish Influence on the Israeli Constitution Proposal, 1948," in *The Irish Constitution: Perspectives and Prospects*, ed. Eoin Carolan (Haywards Heath: Bloomsbury, 2012), 59, 82–3.

[120] "Te'udatenu," *Ha-Mishpat ha-'Ivri: Riv'on Mada'i* (1918): 3–4. See also See Mordechai Zalkin, "The 'Hebrew Law Society' and the Emergence of Hebrew-Nationalism in the Early 20th-Century Russian Empire," *Diné Israel* 33 (2019): 137*, 147*n72.

1937 to partition Palestine into two states, Jewish and Arab.[121] Later that decade, increased interest in such questions was evident in the writings of observant Orthodox rabbis and scholars such as Herzog.[122] The late 1940s also saw secular authors such as Eliezer Livneh writing on Jewish public law. A 1949 newspaper article reviewing recently published works in Hebrew on political science noted the surge in publications on the subject.[123] Arguably, works by American authors such as Federbusch and Silving in the early 1950s, immediately after Israeli independence, were also part of the same trend.

### *Apologetics*

Most of the works I have discussed in this chapter sought to demonstrate that Jewish political institutions and norms were compatible with modern Western democratic and liberal values, thus defending Jewish law from its detractors and also bolstering Jewish self-pride.[124] In the Indian case, the critique of this literature took the form of arguments questioning its historical accuracy. In the Jewish case, it seems the critique was mainly ideological. One can identify three different types of critique associated with three different ideologies: secular liberalism, secular right-wing anti-liberalism, and religious anti-liberalism.

An example of the first type of critique can be found in an article written by Haim Cohn, a German-Jewish lawyer in Palestine. Cohn, who would later become Israel's Attorney General and a leading Supreme Court Justice, came from an orthodox Jewish family. However, in the 1940s, he gradually renounced his religious convictions in favor of liberal secularism. In 1946, as a young lawyer, Cohn wrote an article attacking

[121] The memorandum was reprinted in 1949. See Yitzhak Breuer, "Tokhnit le-Hukah ba-Medinah ha-Yehudit," *Yavneh* 3 (1949): 33. See, generally, Shuki Friedman and Amihai Radzyner, *Hukah shelo Ktuvah ba-Torah* (Jerusalem: IDI Press, 2006).

[122] Cohen, *Ha-Talit veha-Degel*, 6, 30–2 (noting that the period of the transition towards Israeli independence led to an increased interest in *halakhic* discussions related to issues of public law).

[123] "Kamah ve-Notseret Sifrut 'al Mahut ha-Medinah," *Ma'ariv*, April 29, 1949.

[124] For an interesting theoretical discussion of the nature of presentist, ahistorical, discussions of Jewish law, see Yemima Ben-Menahem, "Havnayah Ratsyonalit," *Diné Yisrael* 35–6 (2022): 13.

the idea of using Jewish law (both private and public) as the law of the future Jewish state. In this article, he rhetorically asked whether it would be right to adopt the rules of Jewish law, which had been created in the medieval Jewish ghettos of Europe by oppressed communities separated from their neighbors by "dark and tall walls." The supposed "judicial independence" of Jewish communities in the Diaspora was not genuine sovereign independence, he said, but more reminiscent of the "wretched" independence of a prisoner sitting in his prison cell, with no present or future, just a past.[125]

The second type of critique was tied to secular right-wing non-liberal ideology. Here are three examples of such sentiments. The first example of such a non-liberal critique of Jewish apologetics can be found in a report by an anonymous author on a 1925 lecture delivered by Shimshon Rosenbaum to the Tel Aviv Branch of the Jewish Law Society. According to this report, Rosenbaum claimed that, unlike all other ancient nations, the ancient Israelites recognized the rights of other nations and those of foreigners, thus creating, in effect, international law. The report then noted that some of the audience at Rosenbaum's lecture objected to his apologetic approach and argued that it was easy to find biblical passages attesting to feelings of hatred and revenge that the ancient Israelites harbored toward their enemies – feelings that these anonymous commentators praised because they saw them as natural and common in any "healthy nation." Our Torah, said these commentators, did not create laws based on "abstract morality that can only exist in a utopia."[126]

A far more radical critique of Jewish apologetics was evident in the reactions of right-wing fascist Jewish students to Norman Bentwich's 1932 inaugural lecture at the Hebrew University, entitled "Jerusalem: City of Peace." In this lecture, it will be recalled, Bentwich claimed that the vision of peace and the idea of one universal law applicable to all nations, upon which modern international law and its institutions (the League of Nations) were based, had their roots in the words of the biblical prophets.[127]

[125] Haim Cohn, "De'agah le-Yom Mahar," *Ha-Praklit* 3 (1946): 38, 42–3.
[126] "'Orekh ha-Din S. Rosenbaum," 204–5.
[127] Bentwich, *Yerushalayim: 'Ir ha-Shalom.*

During the lecture, young radical right-wing Zionist activists, some of them students at the university, rioted. Catcalls were shouted, stink bombs were thrown, physical violence ensued, and twelve rioters were arrested.[128] The leader of the rioters was Abba Ahimeir, a member of the Jewish clandestine fascist organization *Brit ha-Biryonim* (the Alliance of Hoodlums).[129] In a viciously worded article published after the event in the newspaper with which the rioters were affiliated, Ahimeir attacked Bentwich for espousing universalist messages and for his praise of Islam and Christianity, calling him a radical assimilationist and Christian propagandist. An anonymous editorial published in the same newspaper called the new Chair "a work of the devil himself" and argued that, instead of a Chair devoted to world peace, the Hebrew University should have established a military academy.[130] In the trial of the twelve rioters, one of their lawyers, in reaction to the argument of the prosecutor that the deeds of his clients reminded one of the behavior of the Nazis in Germany, retorted that, had the Nazis abandoned the anti-Jewish plank of their program, he would have supported them, since "Hitler saved Germany."[131]

The third example of critiques tied to non-liberal ideology is found in an article on Jewish public law published by Paltiel Dikshtein.[132] Dikshtein began this piece with a jurisprudential discussion of the

[128] "Ha-Katedrah le-Ma'an ha-Shalom Nehefekhet li-Sde Krav," *Do'ar ha-Yom*, February 11, 1932, 1; Bentwich, *My 77 Years*, 98–100.

[129] See, generally, Dan Tamir, *Hebrew Fascism in Palestine, 1922–1942* (Cham: Palgrave Macmillan, 2018).

[130] Abba Sikra [Abba Ahimeir], "Bentwich ha-Mitbolel veha-Misyoner," *Hazit ha-'Am*, February 19, 1932, 2; "El ha-Tsiyonim veha-No'ar ha-Yisre'eli," *Hazit ha-'Am*, February 12, 1932, 1.

[131] "Yerushalayim 'Ir ha-Shalom be-'Ulam Beyt ha-Din," *Do'ar ha-Yom*, May 3, 1932, 1, 4. It is interesting to note that one of the right-wing rioters involved in attempting to disrupt Bentwich's lecture was Benzion Netanyahu, the father of the Israeli prime-minister, Benjamin Netanyahu. It was during this event that Benzion first met his future wife, Cela, leaving one to wonder whether the course of Israeli (and indeed Middle Eastern) history might have been totally different had Bentwich chosen a less controversial subject as the topic of his inaugural lecture. See Ari Shavit, "Be-Tsel ha-Historyah," *Haaretz*, May 1, 2012; Adi 'Armon, "Ha-Ma'avakim ha-Leumiyim she-'Itsvu et 'Olamo shel Benzion Netanyahu," *Haaretz*, August 5, 2016.

[132] The article was published in three instalments. See Dikshtein, "Mishpat u-Medinah be-Yisrael," pts I, II, and III. The first two parts were reprinted in Orren, ed., *Professor Paltiel Daykan (Dikshtein)*, 179.

relationship between law and the state. Law, he said, was Janus-faced. It strives for order, government, discipline, stability, security, and public needs, but it also seeks peace, justice, equity, morality, and virtue, based on respect for the needs of individuals. The former goals rely, Dikshtein said, on the existence of a strong state that could utilize its means of coercion to achieve them. Dikshtein then used this observation to distinguish between Roman and Jewish law. The Roman state, he explained, was the strongest in the world. Its conquests were due to the discipline of the Roman Army, and this discipline was transferred to the civic realm, generating obedience among Roman citizens to a legal system that ensured a stable and secure order of life. Jewish law, on the other hand, was the exact opposite of Roman law because it preferred justice, equity, and morality over stability and security.[133]

These attributes of Jewish law, Dikshtein reasoned, were not something that should be praised. They represented a major *weakness* of Jewish law as a system divorced from the needs of the state. Unlike the Romans, the Jews never managed to create a strong state. Their states were not only weak militarily but also structurally. Truly independent and successful Jewish states, such as David's and Solomon's kingdom or the Hasmonean kingdom, were short-lived. These states could not create a strong internal order that unified all members of the nation around a common discipline, which led to internal quarrels. One reason for these quarrels, Dikshtein said, was institutional. Thousands of years before Montesquieu had discussed the notion of separation of powers, it existed in the Hasmonean kingdom, where the two institutions at the head of the state, the king and the Supreme Court (the Great *Sanhedrin*), fought each other, but this separation did not lead to a better functioning state, quite the opposite.[134]

Dikshtein asserted that because of the weakness of the Jewish states and, later, the complete loss of Jewish independence, Jewish law could

133 Dikshtein, "Mishpat u-Medinah [part I]," 368–72. On comparisons of Roman and Jewish law by Jewish law scholars in the interwar period, see, generally, Assaf Likhovski, "The Eagle and the Dove: Jewish Law Scholars and Roman Law During the Interwar Period," in *Pensiero giuridico occidentale e giuristi romani: Eredità e genealogie*, eds. Pierre Bonin et al. (Turin: G. Giappichelli, 2019), 267.

134 Dikshtein, "Mishpat u-Medinah [part I]," 372–4.

not rely on state coercion and, therefore, had to resort to other means of pressure, such as moral and religious persuasion, social ostracism, and the coercive power of the non-Jewish states in which the Jews of the Diaspora lived. As a result of the political weakness of the Jews, major parts of Jewish public law (constitutional law, international law, administrative law, and tax law) remained in a rudimentary and underdeveloped state. Other areas of public law (criminal law and civil and criminal procedure) that are on the borderline between public and private law did develop, although they, too, were affected by the lack of Jewish political independence.[135]

Finally, the third type of critique appeared in the works of ultra-Orthodox thinkers. This critique was based on the rejection of democracy and the liberal notion of equality. Following the Peel Commission's 1937 partition plan for Palestine, Rabbi Isaac Breuer wrote a memorandum on the constitutional arrangements of a future Jewish state, which envisioned a state governed by Jewish law and categorically stated that "the applicability of Jewish law, as the law of the Israeli nation, is not dependent upon its acceptance or non-acceptance by the Israeli people."[136]

Breuer also rejected the assumption that Jewish law shared modern law's commitment to the idea of equality. In one of his early articles, written while he was still living in Germany in 1910, Breuer argued that the very structure of Jewish law was based on a distinction between various categories of persons (Jews and non-Jews, men and women, masters and slaves) with unequal duties and, therefore, also unequal rights. Being an ultra-Orthodox Jew, Breuer did not criticize this fact but saw it as justified because the animating principle of Jewish law was not humanism but the duty to serve God.[137] It is,

[135] Ibid., 376. On the use of social norms and taxation in Jewish communities in the Diaspora, see Assaf Likhovski, *Tax Law and Social Norms in Mandatory Palestine and Israel* (New York: Cambridge University Press, 2017), 25–34.

[136] Breuer, "Tokhnit," 33. See also Yedidya, *Halakha*, 109–10. For a theoretical discussion of Breuer's changing views on the relationship between the state and Jewish law, see, generally, Arye Edrei, "Rav-Tarbutiyut be-Girsah Haredit Mukdement: Yitzhak Breuer mi-Medinat ha-Torah le-Kehilat ha-Torah," *Diné Israel* 32 (2018): 187.

[137] Isaac Breuer, "The Philosophical Foundations of Jewish and of Modern Law," reprinted in Batnitzky and Brafman, eds., *Jewish Legal Theories*, 125; Yedidya, *Halakha*, 103–6.

therefore, no wonder that, in his final work, *Nahali'el*, published posthumously in 1951, Breuer envisioned a utopian state based on the Torah, in which slavery was permitted and non-Jews were discriminated against.[138]

A similar endorsement of slavery could be found in a 1947 newspaper article by another leader of the ultra-Orthodox community in Palestine, Kalman Kahana. In this article, Kahana claimed that the institution of (Jewish) slavery was actually a required aspect of the law of the ideal Torah state. Slavery was not merely a matter of a "chance agreement" between master and slave. Its existence was required since enslavement was one of the punishments used by ancient Jewish criminal law. Kahana explained that it was also needed, relying here on Maimonides – to set in motion the redemption clauses of the Jubilee year. When there were no slaves to emancipate during a Jubilee year, land could not be restored to its original owner. Kahana, therefore, concluded that since the commandment of the Jubilee year was an important feature of the economic legislation of the Torah, the existence of Jewish slavery was required in the ideal *halakhic* state.[139]

### *The Role of Law*

The authors of the works discussed in this chapter had different educational backgrounds. Some, such as Rabbis Hirschensohn or Herzog, had no formal legal training (other rabbis, including Berman, Breuer, and Grajewsky, did). Another group of authors – among them

[138] Isaac Breuer, *Nahali'el: Yesodot ha-Hinukh le-Mitsvot ha-Torah* (Jerusalem: Mosad ha-Rav Kook, 1982), 353–5; Yedidya, *Halakha*, 112–13. On the utopian nature of some of Breuer's later writings, see also Edrei, "Rav-Tarbutiyut," 203–4, 207–9.

[139] Kahana, "Li-Ve'ayat Ha-Thukah ha-Toratit." Another example of a religiously inspired rejection of democracy is found in the work of an obscure Religious Zionist author, Haim Rambani, who was a high school teacher in the city of Safed in the north of Mandatory Palestine. In the 1940s, Rambani published a Kabbalah-influenced work in which he outlined a utopian proposal for economic and social relations in the "age of redemption." Citing sources such as Plato and Lenin, Rambani argued that relying on the opinions of the majority was an incorrect method for resolving conflicts of interest among the groups comprising society. He offered instead what seems to have been a corporatist model of political government at the head of which was a single ruler. See Haim Rambani, *Dat u-Medinah: Shitat Mahshavah be-Torat ha-Hevrah* (Jerusalem: Reuven Mass, 1942/43), 312–18.

Gulak, Zuri, Federbusch, and Mikliszanski – had *some* legal training or even formal law degrees but were not active lawyers or law professors. Some, such as Rosenbaum, were trained lawyers and practiced law but were also politicians. Others were law professors: Bentwich, Eisenstadt, Dikshtein, and Silving.

Whether the Jewish law authors had legal training or not, the discussions in the works examined in this chapter were often legal because the Jewish law sources were rule-oriented. The ancient Indian sources that served the Hindu polity literature discussed in the previous chapter were often government manuals, meaning that detailed legal rules could only be extracted from them indirectly and with some difficulty (as was the case, for example, with Jayaswal's discussion of ancient Indian "parliamentary procedures"). In contrast, although the Bible includes a mix of different genres (law codes, but also historical narratives, poetry, prophecy, and so on), later Jewish texts were mostly legal, and these later texts easily lent themselves to discussions that focused not only on describing Jewish political ideas and institutions but also on describing the rules governing them.

### *Outcome*

Just as in the Indian case discussed in the previous chapter, in the Jewish case, too, references to the works on Jewish constitutional history appeared in the writing of Israel's would-be constitution-makers in the period leading to Israeli independence in 1948. Major examples of such references are found in the writing of the official drafter of the Israeli constitution, Leo Kohn. At the beginning of this chapter, I mentioned the 1949 commentary that Kohn wrote on his draft constitution, in which he stated that "if a Constitution is to command the enduring loyalty of a people, it must be rooted in its moral and political traditions." What were these traditions? As Kohn explained:

> From its early beginnings, Judaism aimed not merely at individual perfection, but at the shaping of a social order. [Judaism's] aim was the evolution of a "Kingdom of Priests and a Holy People" ruled … by the Deity itself, [… thus embodying] justice to be accorded equally to the rich and to the poor; the sanctity of the Sabbath, but no less so the holiness of the working day; freedom of contract, but, above that, the greater freedom of the Sabbatical and the Jubilee Years

which restore liberty to the slave and give back to the poor man his lost heritage ... [These] timeless ideals [should be reflected in Israel's constitution, which must be based on] ... the spiritual order of the ancient Hebrew theocracy under which the divinely granted rights of man were immune from royal interference, under which prophets defied kings and governors, under which the holiness of life and the rights of the orphan and the widow were protected by the authority of the Invisible King.[140]

In the Hebrew version of his commentary, Kohn added a quote from an essay entitled *Moses* by the nineteenth-century American political economist Henry George, which argued that human rights were a Jewish invention: "from between the paws of the rock-hewn Sphinx [the Egyptian despotic state] rises the genius of human liberty, and the trumpets of the Exodus throb with the defiant proclamation of the rights of humanity."[141]

In February 1950, Prime Minister David Ben-Gurion delivered a speech before the Israeli Parliament in which he opposed the creation of a rigid, comprehensive constitution for Israel. In an attempt to rescue his constitutional project, Kohn wrote a letter to Ben-Gurion in which he sought to connect the future Israeli constitution with Jewish constitutional history. Knowing that Ben-Gurion admired the Bible, Kohn attempted to convince him to continue with the constitution-drafting project by stating that the source of modern Western constitutionalism was the biblical notion of a covenant between God and his people. The authors of modern constitutions in America and Europe, Kohn wrote, sought to prevent arbitrary government. They were "greatly inspired by the limits placed on the power of the king in the ancient Israelite kingdom, and by the bold attitude of the prophets of Israel which declared the sovereignty of moral law,

140 Kohn, "Observations," 10–11. See also Carl J. Friedrich, "The Israeli Covenant," *Jewish Frontier* (January 1949): 24, 25 (the Israeli Constitution "clearly expresses a matter of profound symbolic significance: the ancient Hebrew tradition of government under the law which influenced all of Western political thought ... the challenges of the prophets, and ageless stories like that of Naboth's vineyard").

141 Yehuda Pinchas (Leo) Kohn, *Hukah le-Yisrael: Hatsa'ah ve-Divrey Hesber* (Ha-Kiryah [Tel Aviv]: Mo'etset ha-Medinah, 1949), 23, quoting Henry George, *Moses* (Capon Springs, WV: Anti-Poverty Club, n.d.), 6. On the complex relationship between religious thought and human rights discourse in the middle of the twentieth century, see James Loeffler, "The Religions of Human Rights," *Harvard Theological Review* 116 (2023): 147.

standing above kings and ministers." Citing Mayer Sulzberger's 1910 book on ancient Jewish parliamentarism, Kohn argued that a body similar to a parliament existed in the Bible side by side with the authority of the king.[142]

In 1952, the *Jerusalem Post* reported on the establishment of a collaborative comparative law project jointly undertaken by the Israeli Ministry of Justice and Harvard Law School. This project was meant to provide Israeli legislators with comparative information about legal arrangements in different countries that could be used in drafting future Israeli enactments.[143] When Kohn read about this project, he was furious. He wrote a long letter to the Israeli Minister of Justice, Bernard (Dov) Joseph. The newspaper article, he said, had caused him "real pain." Jews were not "some backward tribe in Central Africa" that had "suddenly emerged from a primitive existence into the full glare of twentieth-century statehood." Jews had an ancient, highly developed, and unparalleled legal tradition, one that:

> . . . embodied the bold concept of a social order utterly repugnant to that of the Ancient East – an order under which rich and poor, kings and priests, were subject to one law, under which the rights of the common man were immune from royal interference, where prophets upbraided and defied arbitrary rulers and a misguided populace, and the holiness of life and the rights of the orphan and widow were protected by the authority of an Invisible king.[144]

This unique heritage was preserved after the loss of Jewish independence, continued Kohn, because the Jews had maintained a "state in exile" in their communities in the Diaspora, upholding but also developing their law, and their legal traditions immensely influenced Western law (quoting here Nathan Isaacs' work). Now that "we have again a state of our own," Kohn argued, we (the Jewish people) should go "back to our own sources, trying to evolve the law of the State in accordance with our own moral and legal

142 Israel State Archive [ISA], Het-Tsadi 2392/15, Leo Kohn to David Ben-Gurion, February 24, 1950.

143 Richard Weiss, "Research at Harvard Helps Untangle Israeli Law," *Jerusalem Post*, April 14, 1952; Assaf Likhovski, "Argonauts of the Eastern Mediterranean: Legal Transplants and Signaling," *Theoretical Inquiries in Law* 10 (2009): 619.

144 ISA, File Het-Tsadi 2393/13, Kohn to Joseph, April 18, 1952. I would like to thank Rivka Brot for bringing this letter to my attention.

traditions," and not abandon "our own vineyards" by ignoring Jewish legal history and blindly mimicking foreign law.[145]

Despite the lip service paid to Jewish constitutional traditions, the main sources of inspiration for Kohn's drafts were modern constitutions. As legal historian Amihai Radzyner has noted, regarding Kohn's ongoing work on a proposed constitution, the actual impact of Jewish traditions on the drafting process was relatively limited and mostly symbolic. Indeed, although Kohn responded to criticisms from rabbis and politicians by amending his later drafts to link his proposed constitution more closely to Jewish traditions, his various modifications were mainly symbolic.[146]

In any event, Kohn's work had little lasting impact. Israel never promulgated a comprehensive single-document constitution, not least because politicians were unable to reach a consensus on its content. Their disagreements partly derived from religious–secular tensions in Israel's first Parliament (which was also its constituent assembly). In June 1950, after two years of work on the drafts prepared by Kohn, the Israeli Parliament decided to abandon the project and instead declared that a series of "basic laws" would be gradually enacted, each dealing with a different part of the future Israeli constitution.[147]

## Conclusion

Just as the premises of the Hindu polity literature were in some sense anachronistic and therefore problematic, so, too, were the attempts to gloss over the differences between Jewish law and modern democracy and liberalism. While Jewish traditions certainly had an impact on Christianity and, more generally, Western civilization, including an influence on Western liberal and democratic thought in the early modern and modern periods, one can find Jewish texts that conveyed contrary messages. For example, if one seeks to counter the argument that Judaism and republicanism are compatible, one can easily find

145 Ibid. 146 Radzyner, "A Constitution," 8–16.

147 There is a relatively large body of literature on the topic. For a list of sources, see Assaf Likhovski, "The Rise and Demise of Constitutional Duties in Israel," *American Journal of Legal History* 61 (2021): 90, 95n17.

sources implying that monarchy is actually the only possible Jewish mode of government.[148] Nevertheless, the attempt to study Jewish public law is interesting for various reasons. One of them is the uncanny resemblance between the Indian and Jewish works published during the first half of the twentieth century. This resemblance will now be discussed.

[148] Deuteronomy 17:14–15.

# *Interlude 3: Impact*

Indian and Jewish works on ancient public law shared many similar traits. The works produced in India and Palestine were based on the assumption that political institutions and public law were not universal but were particular to each nation and that history should be used in their study. Constitutional structures and constitutional law, both Indian and Jewish scholars believed, were a reflection of the "spirit" of the people.

The similarity was not confined to the particularist and historicist approach that Indians and Jews adopted to study their ancient constitutional laws. The two groups made similar claims about their respective systems: that they were characterized by ancient, sophisticated, and secular political institutions and law; that fundamental concepts associated with modern Western political thought (the social contract theory, the separation of powers, the idea of international law) had Indian or Jewish antecedents; and that one could find in these ancient systems the notions of democracy, republicanism, constitutional monarchy (where the power of the ruler to govern and legislate at will was limited), and the idea of the rule of law. Despite evidence to the contrary, both groups of scholars argued that legal and social equality was not a modern invention but could be found (admittedly, with some effort) in Hindu and Jewish law. In both the Indian and Jewish case, one could also find more critical voices: Benoy Kumar Sarkar, Devadatta Ramakrishna Bhandarkar, and, above all, Upendranath Ghoshal adopted a more critical and less celebratory attitude. In Mandatory Palestine, Haim Cohn and Paltiel Dikshtein were similarly skeptical about some of the claims made by their Jewish counterparts.

There were, of course, also differences between Hindu and Jewish authors. The Hindu polity literature was mostly the product of a specific time and place. It was created by scholars mainly affiliated with the University of Calcutta in the first decades of the twentieth century. The Jewish public law literature, in contrast, was more diverse. Temporally, the roots of this literature go back to traditional medieval Jewish thinkers and to the early-modern Humanists. Its geographical scope in the early twentieth century was also broader as it was produced in multiple locations and written by Jewish authors based in Europe, North America, and Palestine.

Professionally, the Hindu polity authors were academics affiliated with law, history, archaeology, and the social sciences departments. The Jewish authors belonged to a more heterogeneous group. Some were linked to Jewish higher education institutions such as the Hebrew University in Jerusalem or the Tel Aviv School of Law and Economics, but many had other non-academic occupations: rabbis, practicing lawyers, and politicians. As a result of their university affiliation, the ideas of the Hindu polity scholars mostly appeared in academic monographs. In the Jewish case, academic works were accompanied by popular books and articles aimed at lay readers (for example, Berman's 1944 book) and halakhic texts.

Linguistically, the Jewish works were also more diverse. While the Indian works were written in English, the Jewish works were written in a variety of languages, including English, German, and Hebrew.[1] The linguistic differences also reflected the different audiences that the Indian and Jewish authors were endeavoring to address. In the case of Jewish scholars, the works written in Hebrew were meant to convince skeptical Jewish readers that the study of Jewish legal institutions could inspire and contribute to modern constitutional

[1] The Hindu polity authors also published works in other languages. For example, Kashi Prasad Jayaswal had a sizeable body of works in Hindi. See Ratan Lal, *Kashi Prasad Jayaswal: The Making of a "Nationalist" Historian* (Delhi: Aakar Books, 2018), 57–101. However, based on bibliographies that are available on many of the Indian scholars, it seems that their works on constitutional history were primarily or exclusively written in English.

law. When writing in other languages, the audience that Jewish scholars were addressing was not necessarily Jewish. Therefore, the contemporary relevance of Jewish public law (whether it was fit for revival or not) was not necessarily one of the main goals of the non-Hebrew works.

The comparative framework used by the authors of the Hindu polity literature was based on the notion of an "Aryan legal family" or, in a few cases, on pan-Asianism. These comparative frameworks did not play an important role in the Jewish case. Instead, Jewish scholars sometimes compared Jewish public law to Roman law and sometimes argued that Jewish law shaped major public law notions found in Christianity.

The Indian and Jewish works were based on different primary sources. In the Indian case, the use of ancient texts was sometimes augmented by including archaeological evidence. For example, Radhakumud Mookerji's book on local government referred to ancient coins, seals, and inscriptions. The Jewish works relied only on manuscripts and published texts. Another difference was found in the periods examined. In the Indian case, the major turning point in the history of Hindu political independence only occurred in the Middle Ages when Islamic states were established in India. In the Jewish case, the pivotal shift occurred earlier with the Roman conquest of Palestine, followed by the Second Temple's destruction in 70 AD. Consequently, the Indian sources used were often connected to the actual political reality of the time in which they were created, while the post-Biblical Jewish sources were divorced from practical political concerns, and were describing ideal rather than actual polities. The difference in the periods examined was related to a substantive difference. At least for some of the Hindu polity authors, Islam, representing, according to Radhakumud Mookerji, the "Semitic" model of a society governed by a single absolute ruler, was the "other" against which they defined themselves. In the Jewish case, Islam was almost totally absent from the discussion.

It is not always clear what the exact political affiliations of the Hindu polity authors were, although some of them certainly had links with Hindu nationalism. A few scholars, such as Radhakumud Mookerji and Hemchandra Raychaudhuri, also expressed some affinity to socialist ideas, but socialism was not a major factor influencing the Hindu polity works per se. In the case of the Jewish writers, as we have seen, three groups could be distinguished based on their commitment to religion and nationalism (Orthodox rabbis, Jewish scholars in the Diaspora writing in Western languages, and Cultural Zionists). Another possible way to subdivide the Jewish authors would have been to distinguish between anti-nationalists (such as the anti-Zionist Breuer) and Zionists of different sorts: Religious Zionists (such as Federbusch), socialists (such as Livneh), and even communists (such as Eisenstadt). Thus, while the main Western ideology that shaped the Indian works was nationalism, in the Jewish case, nationalism was certainly the main ideology but Marxism, too, played a role.

Regarding motivation, both Indians and Jews sought to prove that Western images of their political institutions and thought were erroneous. However, in the Indian case, the motivation of the authors seems to have been mainly to foster pride in a national past (although one can also sometimes find calls for the practical application of ancient Indian constitutional history in the design of contemporary constitutional arrangements). In the Jewish case, too, one can discern a desire to refute Western images of Judaism and its political institutions, implicitly driven by a wish to drum up pride in the past. Arguably, though, the vision of reviving Jewish public law was an even stronger motivation. Such motivation can be found in the works of Religious Zionist scholars, including Berman and Federbusch, and secular scholars, such as Eisenstadt. As a consequence, while the Hindu polity literature was not part of the law school curriculum in colonial India, Jewish students, at least at the Tel Aviv School, were required to study not only modern constitutional and international law but also ancient Jewish public law.

Turning to the details of the substantive content of the Indian and Jewish works, it seems that, while similar themes appeared throughout these works, there were also some differences in emphasis. For example, the Indians were greatly concerned with the "Oriental despotism" image. This image also appeared in Jewish works (in Israel Friedlaender's writings, for instance), but the main problem that concerned Jewish authors was not that of strong despotic political institutions but the opposite: how to refute the image of weak Jewish states and institutions, and the image of Jewish public law as antiquated and therefore irrelevant. Similarly, while Indians invested much effort in discussing democracy and the existence of republics to counter Western views of ancient Indian states as absolute monarchies, the Jews, though sometimes discussing these topics, were less concerned with them.

There were other substantive differences in emphasis. In discussions of equality, Indian scholars devoted effort to the problematic category of caste, which had no parallel in Jewish society. Jewish scholars, meanwhile, endeavored to prove that Gentiles were not subject to discrimination, while the topic of the legal rights of foreigners was of little concern to Indian scholars. Another difference between Indian and Jewish authors had to do with economic equality. Perhaps because of the greater influence of socialist ideology on certain Jewish scholars, they took great pains to prove that Jewish law sought to further workers' rights and economic equality. In the Indian writings, economic equality was a minor theme.

Finally, there seems to have been a difference in how law was presented in the works of the two groups. While many of the Indian scholars were lawyers by training, the Hindu polity works were primarily historical and devoted to describing political ideas and institutions rather than detailing the rules governing them. In the Jewish case, legal topics were more prominent. This, perhaps, resulted from the different nature of the sources used. In the Indian case, the sources used (such as the *Arthashastra*) were government manuals, not legal codes. In the Jewish case, the oldest source used, the Bible, was also not primarily a legal code. However, later sources were mainly legal (the Talmud, or the section of Maimonides' code dealing with the rules about kings and wars (*hilkhot melakhim*)). Another reason for the more legal orientation of the Jewish works had to do with the motivation of the authors. As noted earlier, the Indian works were mostly driven by the desire to instill pride in the national past. In the Jewish case, this motivation existed side by side with the vision of harnessing the ideas and institutions found in Jewish constitutional history as building blocks for the constitutional law of the future Jewish state.

Was there any interaction between the scholars of Mandatory Palestine and India? The authors of the Hindu polity literature did not mention Jewish political traditions (apart, perhaps, from a reference found in Sarkar's work to the biblical roots of Western conceptions of equality). Jewish authors seem to have been equally oblivious to the

Indian works. They did not allude to India except, perhaps, for passing references contrasting Jewish egalitarianism and the "Aryan" hierarchical concept of society expressed in the Indian caste system.[2]

Although there was no direct dialogue between the Indian and Jewish scholars, there are subtle indications of an indirect and circuitous constitutional exchange between them. At the beginning of Chapter 5, I mentioned a 1949 article by B. N. Rau, one of the leading drafters of the Indian Constitution, in which he turned to the Hindu polity literature to bolster an argument about the choice between a presidential and a parliamentary system in the future constitution of India. Rau then published a subsequent article that same year on the future of the Indian constitution. This later article appeared in the journal of the Indian Council of World Affairs, *India Quarterly*.[3]

In 1953, another article dealing with the constitution of a newly established postcolonial state, Israel, appeared in the same journal, *India Quarterly*. This piece was written by the drafter of Israel's would-be constitution, Leo Kohn, and it described the constitution-making efforts of the State of Israel after independence in 1948.[4] At one point in the article, Kohn described his draft constitution and

[2] Abba Hillel Silver, *Where Judaism Differed: An Inquiry into the Distinctiveness of Judaism* (New York: Macmillan, 1956), 224, 225–7; Paltiel Dikshtein, "Hukey Moshe ve-Hukey Hammurabi," in *Professor Paltiel Daykan (Dikshtein): Mivhar Monografyot, Mehkarim u- Ma'amarim*, ed. Yitzhak Orren (Tel Aviv: Yavneh, 1975), 150, 153–4. The only citation of Indian scholarship by a Jewish scholar writing on Jewish public law that I found was in Norman Bentwich's work. See Norman Bentwich, *The Religious Foundations of Internationalism: A Study in International Relations through the Ages* (London: Allen & Unwin, 1933), 181–203, 160n1, 184n2, 287 (discussing Hinduism, Buddhism, and the religions of China and Japan, and citing S. V. Viswanatha 's book, *International Law in Ancient India* (Bombay: Longmans, 1925), and Ameer Ali 's book, *The Spirit of Islam* (Calcutta: S. K. Lahiri & Co., 1902)).

[3] B. N. Rau, "The Indian Constitution," *India Quarterly* 5 (1949): 293.

[4] Leo Kohn, "The Constitution of Israel," *India Quarterly* 9 (1953): 78, 80. It is interesting to note that the issue in which this article was published (which only contained four articles) was opened by another article written by a Zionist author, Joseph B. Schechtman. Schechtman was a right-wing Revisionist Zionist political activist. He was also a leading expert on the topic of forced population transfers. He published many works on the topic, including one on the India–Pakistan population transfer which followed the partition of India. This, perhaps, is the reason the editors of the *India Quarterly* were interested in his work. On Schechtman, see, generally, Antonio Ferrara, "Eugene Kulischer, Joseph Schechtman and the Historiography of European Forced Migrations," *Journal of Contemporary History* 46 (2011): 715.

noted that, in the chapter dealing with human rights, "an effort was made to embody some of the characteristic spiritual traditions of the Jewish people."[5] Kohn then affirmed that "the sanctity of human life and the dignity of man were postulated as major objects of the State's solicitude. The death penalty was to be abolished." This remark, perhaps, did indeed indicate the influence of Jewish traditions on the draft Israeli constitution since one can find post-biblical Jewish sources expressing a hostile attitude to capital punishment.[6] However, following these words, Kohn continued to list many other constitutional rights that seem to have stemmed from modern constitutional and human rights discourse rather than from Jewish law (habeas corpus, prohibition of preventive detention and military courts, right to form trade unions, and so on). As Kohn himself later noted, "Western parliamentary democracy" was the actual model he had followed in drafting the Israeli Constitution; and, while Kohn himself was well aware of the literature on Jewish constitutional traditions, his Indian readers could learn little from his article about them, or about their potential influence on Israeli constitutional drafting, because Kohn did not describe these traditions in detail.[7]

Both Rau's and Kohn's articles paid lip service to the literature analyzed in Chapters 5 and 6. Yet, when the moment came to actually use constitutional traditions, the mid-century drafters of the (successful) Indian constitution and the (failed) Israeli constitution opted not to use them. As a result, the actual impact of the scholarly works discussed here proved more limited than it might have otherwise been, and in this respect, too, India and Israel were similar.

[5] Kohn, "Constitution of Israel," 80.

[6] See, e.g., Nathan J. Diament, "Judaism and the Death penalty: Of Two Minds but One Heart," *Tradition: A Journal of Orthodox Jewish Thought* 38 (2004): 76. The death penalty, except in rare cases such as those of former Nazis, was indeed abolished by the Israeli Parliament in 1954. See Amihai Radzyner and Rivka Brot, "Masa' u-Masa le-Vitul 'Onesh ha-Mavet 'al 'Averat ha-Retsah," *'Iyuney Mishpat* 47 (2024): 475.

[7] Kohn, "Constitution of Israel," 81.

# 7

# Legal Education and Legal Theory in Egypt and China

This chapter describes the development of legal education and legal theory in Egypt and China during the first decades of the twentieth century. Egypt was under indirect British rule during this period, while China was an independent state (although its sovereignty was compromised due to the intervention of foreign powers in its affairs in various ways). Despite these differing political circumstances, both countries experienced comparable trends in the development of legal education and legal theory. These developments also reflected the patterns that I discussed in the previous chapters when analyzing India and Palestine.

I do not aim to provide an exhaustive analysis of the history of legal education and legal theory during the early twentieth century in Egypt and China. Rather, I seek to demonstrate that the history of legal theory in India and Palestine was not unique. These two territories were part of a broader global jurisprudential wave that emerged more or less simultaneously in many different parts of the world, including Egypt and China.

## Egypt

The origins of European-inspired legal education in Egypt can be traced back to the nineteenth century. Early and mid nineteenth-century Egypt was formally a province of the Ottoman Empire but was, de facto, ruled by a local dynasty established by the Ottoman

Governor, Muhammad Ali. In 1882, the British occupied Egypt in response to a local revolt; and, between 1914 and 1922, Egypt was a British protectorate. In 1922, Egypt became nominally independent, but British presence (and influence) continued until the Suez Crisis of 1956. Against this backdrop, Egypt developed one of the most advanced systems of modern legal education in the British Empire.

Beginning in 1868, students could enroll in law courses at the Cairo School of Languages and Administration. Later, a fully fledged public institution, the Khedivial Law School, was established. The name of this school and its institutional status changed several times until it became Cairo University Law Faculty. Here, I will call it "The Cairo Faculty."[1] French professors and French law dominated the curriculum at the Cairo Faculty due to the strong French influence on modern Egyptian law. In 1907, the British managed to dismiss the French dean of the school, Édouard Lambert. Courses were subsequently taught in English by British professors, although the British could never fully eliminate the French influence. English dominance waned toward the mid-1920s when the school became part of the Egyptian University (later called King Fuad I University and now Cairo University), an institution inspired by Egyptian nationalist ideology (see Figure 7.1). In 1890, another Cairo-based law school, run by French missionaries and supported by the French government, provided Egyptian students with an alternative venue for legal education. There were also institutions teaching Islamic law. These included Al-Azhar University, established in the tenth century, but also new institutions such as Dar al-ʿUlum, a teacher-training school, whose judicial section was established in 1887, and the School for Shariʿa Judges, which operated between 1907 and 1930, when it was integrated into Al-Azhar University.[2]

1 The most comprehensive work on the topic is Leonard Wood's excellent book, *Islamic Legal Revival: Reception of European Law and Transformations in Islamic Legal Thought in Egypt, 1875–1952* (New York: Oxford University Press, 2016). Wood discusses the various names of the Cairo Faculty in ibid., 153n1. See also Amr Shalakany, *Izdihar wa-inhiyar al-nukhbah al-qanuniyyah al-misriyyah, 1805–2005* (Cairo: Dar al-shuruq, 2013), 150–1 (also discussing the pre-1868 period).

2 On the history of legal education and legal research in Egypt, see Farhat Jacob Ziadeh, *Lawyers, the Rule of Law and Liberalism in Modern Egypt* (Stanford, CA: Stanford University Press, 1968), 19–20; Byron D. Cannon, "Social Tensions and the Teaching of European Law in Egypt before 1900," *History of Education Quarterly* 15 (1975): 299; Donald M. Reid, *Lawyers and Politics in the Arab World, 1880–1960* (Minneapolis, MN: Bibliotheca Islamica, 1981), 17–24, 121–2, 297–8; Catherine Fillon, "L'enseignement du droit, instrument et enjeu de la diplomatie

FIGURE 7.1 Cairo University, 1940 (the law school building is visible on the right-hand side). Photograph from Getty Images.

culturelle française: L'exemple de l'Égypte au début du XXe siècle," *Mil neuf cent. Revue d'histoire intellectuelle* 29 (2011): 123; Samera Esmeir, *Juridical Humanity: A Colonial History* (Stanford, CA: Stanford University Press, 2012); Shalakany, *Izdihar*, 147–69; Götz Nordbruch, "Arab Scholars at the Institut de Droit Comparé in Lyon: Rereading the History of Arab-European Intellectual Encounters in the Interwar Period," in *Transnational Islam in Interwar Europe: Muslim Activists and Thinkers*, eds. Götz Nordbruch and Umar Ryad (New York: Palgrave Macmillan, 2014), 89; Wood, *Islamic Legal Revival*, 153–99; Jean-Louis Halpérin, "Historical Landmarks in Mapping the Spread of Positive Law Teaching," in *State Law and Legal Positivism: The Global Rise of a New Paradigm*, eds. Baudouin Dupret and Jean-Louis Halpérin (Leiden: Brill, 2022), 33, 55–6. The history of legal theory in early twentieth-century Egypt is also discussed in studies devoted to the life and ideas of the leading Egyptian legal scholar of the time, 'Abd al-Razzaq al-Sanhuri. See Enid Hill, *Al-Sanhuri and Islamic Law: The Place and Significance of Islamic Law in the Life and Work of 'Abd al-Razzaq Ahmad al-Sanhuri, Egyptian Jurist and Scholar, 1895–1971* (Cairo: American University in Cairo Press, 1987); Amr Shalakany, "Sanhuri, and the Historical Origins of Comparative Law in the Arab World (Or How Sometimes Losing your *Asalah* Can Be Good for You)," in *Rethinking the Masters of Comparative Law*, ed. Annelise Riles (Oxford: Hart, 2001), 152; Guy Bechor, *The Sanhuri Code, and the Emergence of Modern Arab Civil Law (1932 to 1949)* (Leiden: Brill, 2007). On the history of Egyptian higher education institutions, see, generally, Haggai Erlich, *Students and University in 20th Century Egyptian Politics* (London: F. Cass, 1989); Donald Malcolm Reid, *Cairo University and the Making of Modern Egypt* (Cambridge: Cambridge University Press, 1990); Hilary Kalmbach, *Islamic Knowledge and the Making of Modern Egypt* (Cambridge: Cambridge University Press, 2020).

In Chapter 2, I discussed the jurisprudence textbook that Frederic Goadby wrote while teaching in Cairo. Goadby was just one of several theoretically minded European law professors who taught at the Cairo Faculty, such as Maurice Amos or Léon Duguit. Just as in the case of Palestine, alongside the works of European law teachers, jurisprudence textbooks written by local law scholars began to be published. Two such Egyptian books, both written in Arabic, will be mentioned here. The first was a textbook by Muhammad Kamil Mursi and Sayyid Mustafa, published in 1923.[3] After studying law in Egypt, Mursi obtained a doctorate in law from the University of Dijon in France in 1914. In 1920, he began teaching at the Cairo Faculty (delivering his lectures in Arabic rather than English). Later, he became the Egyptian Minister of Justice, the Head of Egypt's Supreme Administrative Court, and the President of Cairo University.[4] His co-author, Sayyid Mustafa, was an Egyptian judge who eventually became the President of the Egyptian Court of Cassation.[5]

The second textbook was published by ʻAbd al-Razzaq al-Sanhuri and Ahmad Hishmat Abu Sittit in 1941.[6] Sanhuri was the most important Arab legal scholar of the first part of the twentieth century. He graduated from the Cairo Faculty in 1917 and later studied in France at the University of Lyon. He subsequently taught at the Cairo Faculty and served in various judicial positions, ultimately being appointed the Head of the Egyptian State Council. He was associated with Egyptian

[3] Muhammad Kamil Mursi and Sayyid Mustafa, *Usul al-qawanin: maʻa tatbiqat min al-qanun al-misri wa-baʻad al-qawanin al-ukhra* (Cairo: al-Matbaʻah al-rahmaniyyah, 1923). On the Continental antecedents of such works, see Wood, *Islamic Legal Revival*, 126–7, 188, 210–11. For the argument that the genre was also based on earlier Islamic works, see Esmeir, *Juridical Humanity*, 48. Lists of books written in this genre can be found in Wood, *Islamic Legal Revival*, 209–12; Esmeir, *Juridical Humanity*, 46–53. See also Samera Esmeir, "On the Coloniality of Modern Law," *Critical Analysis of Law* 2 (2015): 19, 32–3.

[4] Khayr al-Din al-Zirikli, *al-Aʻlam: qamus tarajim li-ashhar al-rijal wa-al-nisa min al-ʻArab wa-al-mustaʻribin wa-al-mustashriqin*, 15th ed. (Beirut: Dar al-ʻilm lil-malayin, 2002), Vol. 7, 13.

[5] Ibid., Vol. 3, 148.

[6] ʻAbd al-Razzaq al-Sanhuri and Ahmad Hishmat Abu Sittit, *Usul al-qanun* (Cairo: Matbaʻat lajnat al-ta'lif wa-al-tarjamah wa-al-nashr, 1941). I use the short form "Sanhuri" (without the definite article) rather than "al-Sanhuri" in this chapter. In addition, I transliterated Sanhuri's co-author's surname as Abu Sittit, following Enid Hill's rendering, although the name also appears in English sources as Abu Sutayt and Abu Steit.

nationalist politics and, specifically, with the Sa'adist party, an offshoot of the nationalist *Wafd* party, representing middle-class, educated professionals. He also showed an affinity with socialist ideology.[7]

Beginning in the early 1930s, Sanhuri called for replacing the nineteenth-century Egyptian Civil Codes, which were mainly based on French law, with a new code based on Islamic law and inspired by French jurisprudential ideas. The new code, which was ultimately enacted in 1948 and entered into force in 1949, later served as the model for the civil codes of many other Arab countries.[8] Sanhuri's works were influenced both by a nationalist desire to see Islamic law used as the basis of modern Egyptian law and also by his socialist commitment to promoting distributive justice in Egyptian society.[9]

The jurisprudential cosmopolitanism that characterized Egypt at the time was related to the fact that the country, including its legal system, was a battleground between French and English influences. The English saw the French – whose culture was espoused by young Egyptian nationalists as an antidote to British rule – as their main rivals. This French–English cultural tension had multiple manifestations, including the aforementioned competition over control of the Cairo Faculty.[10]

[7] Bechor, *Sanhuri Code*, 39–41, 103, 109–10. For examples of his socialist affinity, see also 'Abd al-Razzaq al-Sanhuri, *'Abd al-Razzaq al-Sanhuri min khilal awraqihi al-shakhsiyyah*, eds. Nadiyah al-Sanhuri and Tawfiq al-Shawi (Cairo: al-Zahrah, 1988), 93, 105, 312.

[8] See Hill, *Al-Sanhuri and Islamic Law*, 84–90; Bechor, *Sanhuri Code*. On the nineteenth-century codes, which combined French, Italian, Belgian, and Islamic law, see Richard A. Debs, *Islamic Law and Civil Code: The Law of Property in Egypt* (New York: Columbia University Press, 2010), 69–71. On the question of the extent to which the new Sanhuri code was, indeed, "Islamic," see Enid Hill, "Islamic Law as a Source for the Development of a Comparative Jurisprudence, the 'Modern Science of Codification': Theory and Practice in the Life and Work of 'Abd al-Razzaq Ahmad al-Sanhuri (1895–1971)," in *Islamic Law: Social and Historical Contexts*, ed. Aziz al-Azmeh (London: Routledge, 1988), 146, 171–7.

[9] See Amr Shalakany, "Between Identity and Redistribution: Sanhuri, Genealogy and the Will to Islamise," *Islamic Law and Society* 8 (2001): 201, 217–19; Bechor, *Sanhuri Code*, 319.

[10] Cannon, "Social Tensions," 308–11; Wood, *Islamic Legal Revival*, 129; Shalakany, *Izdihar*, 159. Competition between French and English law and lawyers also occurred in Mandatory Palestine. See Assaf Likhovski, "Le droit comme objet de conflit culturel anglo-français dans la Palestine mandataire," in *De Balfour à Ben Gourion: Les puissances européennes et la Palestine 1917–1948*, eds. Dominique Trimbur and Ran Aaronsohn (Paris: CNRS, 2008), 201.

Traces of the battle between English and Continental legal influences can be found in Egyptian jurisprudence textbooks. Mursi and Mustafa's textbook used leading English jurisprudence works (by T. E. Holland, John Salmond, and the aforementioned book by Goadby). However, it also relied on French authors, including anti-formalist thinkers such as François Gény, and German and other Continental writers – for example, the Russian legal scholar Nikolai Korkonuv.[11] Mursi and Mustafa compared how nineteenth-century English and German scholars defined law, focusing specifically on the difference between the definition offered by the English analytical scholar John Austin (law as the "command of a human sovereign") and that adopted by the German Historical School (law as a reflection of the "spirit of the people.") They declared the definition of the Historical School to be superior to Austin's definition because it allowed one to see Islamic law as a legal system, whereas Austin's understanding was incompatible with the existence of Islamic law (and other "Eastern" legal systems such as Hindu law) since Islamic law was not created by the commands of a human sovereign.[12]

French legal thinkers such as Léon Duguit (who visited the Cairo Faculty in 1925–26) developed the notion that the law was related to social solidarity.[13] Such ideas also appeared in Mursi and Mustafa's book – for example, when discussing the argument that legislators should strive to further distributive justice and social solidarity by "protecting the weak, assisting the poor, spreading education, defending minorities such as workers … [and] seeking to further the welfare of the nation even if this comes at the expense of some individuals."[14]

[11] Mursi and Mustafa, *Usul al-qawanin*, 3.

[12] Ibid., 30, 33–5. See also Esmeir, *Juridical Humanity*, 300n115.

[13] On the notion of solidarity in early twentieth-century French legal thought and its impact on Egypt, see Paul Babie and Jessica Viven-Wilksch, eds., *Léon Duguit and the Social Obligation Norm of Property: A Translation and Global Exploration* (Singapore: Springer, 2019); Wood, *Islamic Legal Revival*, 119–20. On Duguit's term in Cairo, see Léon Duguit, *Leçons de droit public général faites à la Faculté de droit de l'Université égyptienne* … (Paris: E. de Boccard, 1926), preface; Shalakany, "Sanhuri," 170n52; Wood, *Islamic Legal Revival*, 203–4. On Egyptian social justice discourse, see, generally, Relli Shechter, *The Egyptian Social Contract: A History of State–Middle Class Relations* (Edinburgh: Edinburgh University Press, 2023).

[14] Mursi and Mustafa, *Usul al-qawanin*, 54–5, 65–6.

The textbook written by Sanhuri and Abu Sittit also included a survey of various European approaches to jurisprudence, providing readers with a broad account of both English and Continental theories. Here, too, one could find discussions of John Austin's approach to the definition of law, side by side with surveys of the different approaches of nineteenth-century Continental schools, such as the French *école de l'exégèse*, the German Historical School, or the purpose theory of law developed by German jurist Rudolf von Jhering. References to equivalent Islamic approaches often accompanied such theoretical discussions. For example, the discussion by Sanhuri and Abu Sittit of natural law theories included a note on natural law in the thought of the medieval *Mu'tazilah* school, and Austinian positivism was equated to the approach of the medieval *Ash'ari* school.[15] As with Mursi and Mustafa's book, modern French approaches were dominant in Sanhuri and Abu Sittit's book. In particular, the authors emphasized figures such as Gény and Duguit, who represented then-fashionable anti-formalist, sociological approaches to law. Sanhuri and Abu Sittit also devoted special attention to favorably describing Duguit's notion of social solidarity as the foundation of society and law.[16]

Just as Indian and Jewish scholars sought to compare their religious legal systems with Western ones in their jurisprudence textbooks, so did their Egyptian counterparts. Mursi and Mustafa claimed in their book that there were just three fundamental legal systems in the world – Islamic, Roman, and English law – and that these could be considered the source of all modern positive law. They added that Islamic law was, through conquest, the source of the laws of many countries (Egypt, Syria, Persia, Turkey, Central Asia, North Africa, Spain, and India). Surprisingly, they also included China in the list of countries influenced by Islamic law.[17]

Sanhuri and Abu Sittit's book also contained an argument about the pioneering nature of Islamic law. One of the first topics discussed by these authors was the attitude of various legal systems toward jurisprudence. After mentioning different modern legal systems (English, American, and French), the book moved to Roman law, noting its technical superiority but also remarking on the fact that

[15] Sanhuri and Abu Sittit, *Usul al-qanun*, 43. [16] Ibid., 60–7.
[17] Mursi and Mustafa, *Usul al-qawanin*, 111.

Roman jurists did not display any great interest in legal philosophy. Sanhuri and Abu Sittit then noted that Islamic jurists, just like their Roman counterparts, excelled in the precision and logic of their technical discussions of law. Islamic jurists, they then added, "surpassed the Romans – and also non-Romans ... in creating a science similar to [modern] jurisprudence." This science (*usul al-fiqh*) was devoted to "the study of the sources of the shari'a and the ways in which detailed rulings could be extrapolated from these sources."[18] Thus, Islamic scholars, Sanhuri and Abu Sittit claimed – not Roman scholars – were the forerunners of modern jurisprudence.[19]

Western depictions of non-Western religious legal systems described them as outdated and static. Mursi and Mustafa counter-argued that the antiquity of Islamic law did not impede its modern application. Contrary to common Western depictions of Islamic law, this was *not* a fixed system, unmalleable and inapplicable to modern society. Islamic law, Mursi and Mustafa explained, could be legitimately applied to any time and any place because Islamic rulers could create norms to deal with new conditions and, more generally, because it contained rules dealing with topics that modern legal systems also addressed (such as contract law, family law, property law, criminal law, procedural law, and so on). Thanks to this comprehensiveness, the authors reasoned, Islamic law, unlike other religious legal systems, was "legal" in the modern, positivist, sense.[20]

Given their favorable stance toward Islam, it is not surprising that Sanhuri and Abu Sittit's book also portrayed it positively when discussing the role of religion as a source of law. Religion, the authors said, adopts customary norms but discards those elements of customs that are "corrupt, upholding what is good, violently shaking what is old, tearing down what cannot hold, and [thus] moving humanity forward." Religion was, therefore, a progressive force.[21] Islamic scholars could collaborate with professional jurists, explained Sanhuri and Abu Sittit, and use the consensus of the community (*ijma'*) as a fertile source for the revival of Islamic law in a way that would bring its rulings in line with contemporary needs and new

[18] Sanhuri and Abu Sittit, *Usul al-qanun*, 10–11, 122–3.
[19] See also Wood, *Islamic Legal Revival*, 261–2.
[20] Mursi and Mustafa, *Usul al-qawanin*, 37–8, 62, 180–1.
[21] Sanhuri and Abu Sittit, *Usul al-qanun*, 95.

circumstances. Such a revival was to be desired because Islamic law contained some of the "most modern and finest" legal principles.[22]

Sanhuri and Abu Sittit lamented the fact that both modern Egyptian legal scholars and, to a lesser degree, Egyptian judges were still heavily influenced by French law and that Egyptian law, therefore, lacked a unique Egyptian character. This, they continued, was true not only of the judges belonging to the civil and mixed courts of Egypt but also the judges of the Islamic courts, who were only "imitators and not independent interpreters." Given that shar'i judges were mere imitators, it was not surprising that they could not advance the Shari'a and assist in its evolution to enable it to meet the requirements of the current age. Similarly, Islamic legal scholars were depicted in Sanhuri and Abu Sittit's book as imitators, too, unwilling to adapt the Shari'a to the spirit of the times.[23]

However, Islamic law was not merely seen by these authors as a resource that could be used for practical legal reforms. Sanhuri and Abu Sittit also believed in its global jurisprudential impact. After discussing the contemporary state of Egyptian jurisprudence, they cited, in a footnote, a passage from Sanhuri's book *General Theory of Obligations*, in which he said:

We must first "Egyptianize" jurisprudence (*fiqh*) ... see in it our national imprint, and feel in it the impact of our mentality. Our jurisprudence remains occupied today by the French foreign occupation ... [and we] still seek guidance in French jurisprudence and barely deviate from its course, as if [we] were its shadow and loyal minion. If we are destined to have our own independent jurisprudence ... we must take one final step; we must move beyond the national bounds into the global ones in order to pay some of what is due to humanity ... to advance global jurisprudence or what jurists call comparative law ... and the most important means to help us reach this goal is to be concerned with Islamic law, the law of the East, God's revelation, and the product of the minds of its intellectuals grown in its desert, its plains and valleys, for it is a flame of the soul of the East, and a lantern of Islamic light,

[22] Ibid., 98. When arguing that Islamic law was dynamic, it seems that Sanhuri's main opponent was not Henry Maine (as was the case in India) but, rather, European scholars of Islam such as Christiaan Snouck Hurgronje and Ignác Goldziher. See Abd-el-Razzak Ah. el-Sanhoury, "Le droit musulman comme élément de refonte du Code civil égyptien," in *Introduction à l'étude du droit comparé: recueil d'études en l'honneur d'Edouard Lambert* (Paris: Sirey, 1938), Vol. 3, 621, 622.

[23] Sanhuri and Abu Sittit, *Usul al-qanun*, 138–40.

where the East meets Islam, the former is bathed in the light of the latter, and the soul of the latter is breathed into the former until they fuse to become one. This is Islamic law, and should it spread its wings ... we would be able to use this [Islamic] legacy to infuse the spirit of independence into our jurisprudence, and our judiciary, and our legislation, and then we would be able to share this new light with the world to enlighten one facet of the global culture of law.[24]

Moving to works dealing specifically with Islamic public law, one can find an interest in this topic in the works of Sanhuri, who, despite his reputation as primarily a private law scholar, also contributed to the study of Islamic public law. This was evident, for example, in one of his two doctoral theses that he wrote in France. In this work, which dealt with both Islamic international law and constitutional law, Sanhuri examined the past and future of the Islamic caliphate.[25] The rules of Islamic law regarding the caliph and the caliphate, Sanhuri argued, proved the democratic nature of Islam: Islamic political thought was familiar with the notion of the social contract, separation of powers, and public opinion. The caliph was (ideally) supposed to be elected rather than holding a hereditary position and was a constitutional ruler rather than an absolute despot who enjoyed unlimited power (as some observers mistakenly believed, according to Sanhuri). The caliph was bound by the rules of Islamic law and could not act in any way that might contravene this law.[26] Furthermore:

The principle [in Islamic law] that the community's agreement (consensus) constitutes a source of law embodies the essence of the democratic spirit. This agreement becomes, in a way, the expression of divine will ... God's will cannot be expressed by the caliph, who does not have legislative power. It can only be expressed by the entire community, by the Muslim Nation. What could be more democratic than to affirm that the will of the Nation is the expression of God's will itself? ... within the limits of the *Quran* and the *Hadith*, constituting in a certain way a constitutional law from which one cannot derogate, the Nation alone, and not the caliph, can legislate. This is the very basis of the modern parliamentary system, with the difference, however, that in the Muslim system, the representatives of the Nation are not elected;

24 Sanhuri and Abu Sittit, *Usul al-qanun*, 138n1.

25 A. Sanhoury, *Le califat: son évolution vers une société des nations orientale* (Paris: Paul Geuthner, 1926). This work is the subject of a chapter in a forthcoming Tel Aviv University doctoral dissertation by Mary Haddad.

26 Ibid., 5–19, 53–5, 171–86.

they are self-appointed by virtue of their expertise in legal science (*ijtihad*); the Muslim government is a government of scholars.[27]

Similarly, Sanhuri's diary contained musings on the nature of Islam as a political religion (unlike Christianity); on the need to create an organization devoted to the study of Islamic international and constitutional law; and on the nature of Islamic democracy, which he viewed as superior to Western democracy.[28]

Liberalism was the dominant ideology of the Egyptian legal profession during the early decades of the twentieth century.[29] It is, therefore, not surprising to find attempts by Sanhuri to show the compatibility of Islam with liberal values. Several entries in his diary discussed the notion of equality, including statements about Islam as a religion whose essence is equality between people and nations and calls for minimizing gender inequality. Sanhuri also claimed apologetically in his diary that Islam did not seek to permit slavery and polygamy but, on the contrary, sought to restrict their scope in a world in which they were taken for granted and commonplace.[30]

Sanhuri and Abu Sittit's textbook also included discussions of Islamic law and the notion of equality, focusing specifically on gender relations. Thus, when discussing the Islamic rules regarding marriage, the textbook claimed that husbands were not permitted to "violently strike" their wives. Regarding monetary affairs, wives could freely dispose of their own property and enter into contractual relations without their husbands' consent. In this sense, the authors contended, Islamic law differed from many Western legal systems where a wife did not enjoy full legal personality and, therefore, her legal acts required her husband's permission, and where, following the marriage, the wife's property was combined with that of her husband rather than kept separate.[31]

Along with liberal values, Sanhuri's thought was influenced by socialist ideology. Like other Egyptian jurists of the time, Sanhuri believed that progressive values identified with the rise of socialism

[27] Ibid., 6–7.

[28] Sanhuri, *'Abd al-Razzaq al-Sanhuri min khilal awraqihi*, 133, 134, 167.

[29] See, e.g., Shalakany, *Izdihar*, 177.

[30] Sanhuri, *'Abd al-Razzaq al-Sanhuri min khilal awraqihi*, 60, 91, 132, 146, 262, 270.

[31] Sanhuri and Abu Sittit, *Usul al-qanun*, 312–13.

had antecedents in Islamic law.[32] Thus, his diary contained entries on the compatibility of the socialist and "Oriental" spirits.[33] Sanhuri and Abu Sittit's textbook also discussed socialism. It included an examination of the relative merits of individualism and socialism, declaring that the former, despite some advantages, was ultimately based on false premises, and the latter was the dominant approach of the modern era because the role of the state – and law – in regulating everyday life was growing.[34] While Sanhuri and Abu Sittit's book did not include explicit doctrinal reform proposals based on Islamic law, Sanhuri's doctrinal works did. In these writings, Sanhuri thoroughly discussed specific private law doctrines taken from Islamic law that, he argued, should be adopted in contemporary Egyptian law. Many of these doctrines were meant to protect weaker parties, such as debtors or peasants, and thus lessen inequality between Egypt's rich and poor.[35]

## China

Unlike India, Palestine, or Egypt, early twentieth-century China remained a formally independent state. However, beginning in the middle of the nineteenth century, Britain, along with other foreign powers, established a series of quasi-colonial enclaves in China. In these enclaves, foreigners enjoyed sweeping privileges that significantly eroded Chinese sovereignty. The earliest and most important British outpost in China was Hong Kong, which the British ruled from 1841.

Hong Kong was also a center of English culture and law in China. At the University of Hong Kong, established in 1911, a Faculty of Law was only created in 1969, but commercial and international law courses were taught at the Faculty of Arts from 1915. A course on jurisprudence was also taught from 1917 onward. Between 1924 and 1927, this course was taught by George W. Keeton, a graduate of

[32] On the argument about the compatibility of Islamic law and socialism in the thought of other interwar Egyptian jurists, see Shalakany, "Sanhuri," 177.

[33] Sanhuri, *'Abd al-Razzaq al-Sanhuri min khilal awraqihi*, 154, 299.

[34] Sanhuri and Abu Sittit, *Usul al-qanun*, 18–21.

[35] See Sanhoury, "Le droit musulman," 630–1, 635. For a detailed discussion of the link in Sanhuri's works between Islam and progressive legal reform, see Bechor, *Sanhuri Code*.

Cambridge University, who later became the Dean of the Faculty of Laws at University College London.[36]

Keeton had an ambitious and theoretically oriented vision of the role of legal education. In the inaugural issue of *Hong Kong University Law Journal*, a periodical he had helped establish together with some of his students, Keeton published a lecture in which he envisioned the creation of a "true philosophy of law," which would be based on studying and comparing Western law to Hindu and Chinese law. As the journal's table of contents attests, the articles published there were mostly theoretical, dealing with legal history, comparative law, and jurisprudence.[37]

Keeton's lectures on jurisprudence, taught to a class of "Chinese ... Hindoos, and Japanese" students, were ultimately published in 1930 as a book entitled *The Elementary Principles of Jurisprudence*. In the preface to this book, Keeton noted that it was influenced by "informal discussions" with his students about the topics he had taught them and mentioned some differences between Western and non-Western conceptions of law. According to Keeton, his students saw the notion of duty as more important than the notion of right, and custom as more important than the notion of "law as the creature of the State."[38] The book was also dotted with examples taken from Chinese law, some of which were used to critique Western jurisprudential concepts. For example, when discussing the Austinian notion of sovereignty, Keeton noted that some scholars rejected the idea that sovereignty was essential for the existence of law, arguing that law could exist even without the backing of a sovereign. In support of this proposition,

36 See Christopher Munn, *A Special Standing in the World: A History of the Faculty of Law at the University of Hong Kong* (Hong Kong: Hong Kong University Press, 2019), 1–28; A. L. Sheridan, "George Williams Keeton, 1902–1989," *Proceedings of the British Academy* 80 (1993): 333, 333–5.

37 George W. Keeton, "Legal Opportunities in China," *Hong Kong University Law Journal* 1 (1926–27): 2, 2–3. Examples of the topics covered in the journal include: "Some Leading Principles of Chinese Law Historically Considered," "Primitive and Patriarchal China," "Ancestor-Worship in Modern Chinese Society," "Hohfeld's Fundamental Juristic Conceptions," "Seventeenth Century Jottings on the Law and Administration of China," "Fascism as a Factor in Italy's Legal and Constitutional Development," and "Some Features of the Customary Law of Annam, in Relation to Chinese Law."

38 George W. Keeton, *The Elementary Principles of Jurisprudence* (London: A. & C. Black, 1930), v.

Keeton mentioned the third-century BC Chinese *Book of Lord Shang*, which, he claimed, recognized the existence of the notion of the Law of Nature.[39] In another place in his book, Keeton noted that Henry Maine believed that one of the stages through which every legal system passes is one in which law becomes associated with religion. However, he said, the Chinese never went through such a stage.[40]

Moving from Hong Kong to mainland China, the history of Westernized legal education there began during the last years of the Qing Dynasty.[41] One of the first institutions in China to offer a comprehensive program of Western-style legal education was Peiyang University, established in 1896 in Tientsin (Tianjin). The first professor of law there, James Bromley Eames, was a graduate of Oxford University, and the curriculum was therefore influenced by English legal education and included a course on "general jurisprudence." Many additional institutions were established in China in the first decade of the twentieth century, their emergence being a direct result of the legal reforms of the 1890s and 1900s, which sought to introduce a Western-style legal system, mainly inspired by Continental law, to

39 Ibid., 24. The *Book of Lord Shang* was actually a foundational text of the Chinese Legalist school, based on a positivist-like approach to law. See, e.g., Yuri Pines, "Dating a Pre-Imperial Text: The Case Study of the Book of Lord Shang," *Early China* 39 (2016): 145, 150.

40 Keeton, *Elementary Principles*, 40, 42. There were, of course, other interwar Western scholars who compared Chinese law and legal theories to Western ones. See, e.g., Jean Escarra, *Chinese Law and Comparative Jurisprudence* (Tientsin: La Libraire Française, 1926); Jean Escarra, *Le droit chinois* (Pékin: H. Vetch, 1936). On Escarra, who served as an advisor to the Chinese government and taught at the Sorbonne, see, e.g., A. F. P. Hulsewé and M. H. van der Valk, "Jean Escarra (1885–1955)," *T'oung Pao* 44 (1956): 304; Mingzhe Zhu, "La place de l'enseignement du droit français dans la modernisation chinoise: Les missions civilisatrices de quatre modernisateurs au tournant des XIXe et XXe siècles," *Cahiers Jean Moulin* 7 (2021): 21–9. For general theoretical discussions of the problems involved in using Western comparative law to study Chinese law, see, e.g., Teemu Ruskola, *Legal Orientalism: China, the United States and Modern Law* (Cambridge, MA: Harvard University Press, 2013); Kentaro Matsubara, "East, East, and West: Comparative Law and the Historical Processes of Legal Interaction in China and Japan," *American Journal of Comparative Law* 66 (2018): 769.

41 Some Chinese law students studied overseas. See, e.g., Li Chen, "Pioneers in the Fight for the Inclusion of Chinese Students in American Legal Education and Legal Profession," *Asian American Law Journal* 22 (2015): 5; Li Chen, "Early Graduate Legal Studies in America and Legal Transplantation," *Journal of Legal Education* 68 (2019): 716.

China.[42] Many of these law schools were called "schools of law and politics" since legal studies were often combined with the study of political science and economics.[43]

The first years of the Republican era, which began in 1912, were characterized by unstable political conditions, leading to the closure of some law schools. One estimate mentions sixty-four Chinese schools, colleges, and universities offering law degrees in 1912, declining to thirty-three in 1924. Another estimate mentions forty-nine law colleges in 1915 declining by half by 1921. In any event, the end of the Warlord era in 1928 saw a rise in the number of institutions and students.[44]

Many of the law schools of the Republican era were staffed by Chinese teachers who studied law in Japan, a country whose own legal system had been Westernized during the second half of the nineteenth century. As a result, the textbooks they used were mainly translated from Japanese. However, there were also law schools where European and American law teachers taught alongside Chinese professors. Two of these schools were established by Christian missionaries in Shanghai. The first was the Faculty of Law of Aurora University, a Catholic institution established by Jesuits. This law school was inaugurated in 1912, and law studies there were based on the French codes.[45]

[42] See, e.g., W. W. Blume, "Legal Education in China," *China Law Review* 1 (1923): 305; Charles S. Lobingier, "Legal Education in Twentieth Century China," *Lawyers Guild Magazine* 4(4) (July–August 1944): 1; R. St. J. Macdonald, "Legal Education in China Today," *Dalhousie Law Journal* 6 (1980): 313, 315–21; John Mo and Weidong Li, "Legal Education in the PRC," *Journal of the History of International Law* 4 (2002): 176, 182–4; Li Chen, "The Founding of Peiyang University Department of Law: Oxford Style Legal Education in China (1895–1899)," *Tsinghua China Law Review* 9 (2017): 227, 238; Halpérin, "Historical Landmarks," 57.

[43] Hugh Chan, "Modern Legal Education in China," *China Law Review* 9 (1936): 142, 144.

[44] Blume, "Legal Education in China," 307; Mo and Li, "Legal Education in the PRC," 184–7. See also R. C. W. S[heng], "Editorial," *China Law Review* 1 (1922): 67, 68.

[45] Blume, "Legal Education in China," 305, 307; Alison W. Conner, "The Comparative Law School of China," in *Understanding China's Legal System*, ed. C. Stephen Hsu (New York: New York University Press, 2003), 210, 222; Zhu, "La place de l'enseignement du droit français." See, generally, Liu Xian, "Two Universities and Two Eras of Catholicism in China: Fu Jen University and Aurora University, 1903–1937," *Christian Higher Education* 8 (2009): 405, 411; Sara Legrandjacques, "L'enseignement supérieur en Asie française et britannique: expériences croisées à l'âge des Empires (Années 1850–1930)," *Outre-Mers: Revue d'Histoire* 105 (2017): 39.

The second Shanghai law school established by Christian missionaries was Soochow University Law School, also known as the Comparative Law School of China, established in 1915. Founded by American Protestant missionaries, this school sought to provide its students with "a thorough mastery of the fundamental principles of the world's chief legal systems" and to educate students "who [could] contribute to the making of a new and better jurisprudence for China."[46] The model upon which this school was based was the Harvard model of legal education, including the use of casebooks, a requirement for prior undergraduate studies, a large law library (containing over 30,000 books), and the production of student-edited law reviews. The teachers were American lawyer-missionaries such as the first dean, Charles Rankin, French and German lawyers and judges based in Shanghai, and Chinese graduates of Chinese and foreign law schools.[47]

Many of the courses taught at Soochow were devoted to legal theory. The curriculum included courses on both Western and Chinese jurisprudence and legal philosophy, as well as courses on legal history. In addition, various comparative law courses were offered, including modern Continental law (French and German but also Japanese, Soviet, and Italian-Fascist), Roman law, and Anglo-American law. The school also offered an advanced graduate degree in law (LLM) requiring courses on Japanese, Swiss, Anglo-American, Soviet, and French law as well as a thesis. Some of the graduates of Soochow Law School also pursued advanced legal degrees outside China.[48]

The Comparative Law School was a unique institution. The fact that China's legal system was in flux during the interwar period created a niche for a school focused mainly on comparative law and legal

[46] See Chan, "Modern Legal Education," 143.

[47] Charles Y. S. Yu, "China's Law Library: Soochow University Law School Library," *Law Library Journal* 34 (1941): 65; Robert E. Tindall, "The Graduate School of Law, Soochow University, Republic of China," *International Lawyer* 7 (1973): 711; Alison W. Conner, "Training China's Early Modern Lawyers: Soochow University Law School," *Journal of Chinese Law* 8 (1994): 1; Jedidiah J. Kroncke, "Model, System, or Node?: Understanding Legal Education Reform in Twentieth-Century China and Beyond," in *American Legal Education Abroad: Critical Histories*, eds. Susan Bartie and David Sandomierski (New York: New York University Press, 2021), 162, 174–6.

[48] Chan, "Modern Legal Education," 125–8; Conner, "Training," 11–12; Conner, "Comparative Law School," 210, 216, 218, 221, 223, 238–9, 225, 244, 246.

theory rather than on the technical details of local law. The cosmopolitan nature of the legal community in interwar Shanghai and the fact that Soochow University was a place where Western and Chinese scholars interacted also contributed to the unique nature of the school. No other law school in the world at the time was comparative to such an extent.[49] However, in a certain sense, Soochow was merely a radical version of the law schools of India, Palestine, and Egypt that I previously discussed.

Turning from the history of legal education to the history of legal theory reveals a similar pattern. In the nineteenth century, articles and books by Western and Japanese scholars discussing Western jurisprudential ideas were translated into Chinese. In the first decades of the twentieth century, Chinese legal scholars began to write books and articles on jurisprudence. Indeed, hundreds of such works were written. These included books on jurisprudence, legal history, comparative law, and translations of the works of classical Western legal theorists, such as Montesquieu, and modern ones, such as Roscoe Pound.[50] Some of these works dealt with ancient Chinese law, arguing that the Chinese should be proud of their ancient law, or used Chinese legal history to critique Western theories about law – for example, by comparing the unitary Western concept of law to the more subtle Chinese distinction between the notions of *li* and *fa*.[51]

49 See Manley O. Hudson, "Address at the Inauguration Exercises," *China Law Review* 3 (1927): 148, 149. On the history of comparative law scholarship in Republican China, see Taisu Zhang, "The Development of Comparative Law in Modern China," in *The Oxford Handbook of Comparative Law*, eds. Mathias Reimann and Reinhard Zimmermann, 2nd ed. (Oxford: Oxford University Press, 2019), 228, 236–40.

50 See Qinhua He, "The Birth and Growth of Modern Jurisprudence in China," *Frontiers of Law in China* 1 (2006): 486, 486–95.

51 Ibid., 497, 498. Traditional Chinese legal and political thought distinguished between two ways of achieving social order. *Li* was a term associated with social norms (rituals, customs, and morality). *Fa* was a term associated with publicly promulgated, codified rules backed by the power of the state. See Luke T. Lee and Whalen W. Lai, "The Chinese Conceptions of Law: Confucian, Legalist, and Buddhist," Hastings Law Journal 29 (1978): 1307, 1308–10; Randall P. Peerenboom, "Law and Ritual in Chinese Philosophy," in *The Routledge Encyclopedia of Philosophy*, ed. Edward Craig (New York: Routledge, 1998), Vol. 5, 442. Thus, the Chinese translator of Montesquieu's *The Spirit of Law* was careful to note that "in Chinese, *li* refers to what is right or wrong and *fa* refers to what is legally prohibited or permitted, while in western nations *li* and *fa* are treated as the same, and what is right or wrong is equivalent to what is permitted or prohibited …." See He, "Birth," 500.

Focusing specifically on works produced at Soochow, the texts that teachers at this school wrote were, naturally, cosmopolitan and theoretical. Discussions of jurisprudence in the *China Law Review*, published at Soochow between 1922 and 1940, reflected state-of-the-art developments in Western jurisprudence. In the volumes of this law review, one could encounter articles that outlined cutting-edge Western anti-formalist ideas of thinkers such as Duguit or Pound.[52] Other late nineteenth- or early twentieth-century American proponents of anti-formalist and sociological jurisprudence, such as Oliver Wendell Holmes, Benjamin Cardozo, Felix Frankfurter, and the American Legal Realists, were also discussed.[53]

The *China Law Review* also published works on other areas of legal theory, such as comparative law and legal anthropology. A leading author of works on these topics was Charles S. Lobingier, who taught at Soochow. Lobingier had been a classmate of Roscoe Pound at the University of Nebraska in the 1880s and then served as a judge and taught law in Nebraska, the Philippines, and China. He was a prolific author who wrote extensively on legal history, legal anthropology, and comparative law, discussing in his works American law, Continental law (Roman, Spanish, French, and German), and the law of several Far Eastern countries (the Philippines, Japan, and China).[54] There were

[52] See Chang Chun Mai, "New Tendencies in the Theory of State," *China Law Review* 1 (1922): 52, 55; John C. H. Wu, "The Juristic Philosophy of Roscoe Pound," *China Law Review* 1 (1923): 360; Robert Bonnard, "The Doctrine of Duguit on 'Law' and the State," *China Law Review* 4 (1930): 193.

[53] See John C. H. Wu, "The Juristic Philosophy of Judge Cardozo," *China Law Review* 2 (1924): 109; William Timothy Kao, "Book Review: The Growth of the Law – by N. B. Cardozo," *China Law Review* 2 (1924): 346; John C. H. Wu, "Realistic Analysis of Legal Concepts: A Study in the Legal Method of Mr. Justice Holmes," *China Law Review* 5 (1932): 1; Kiang Hung-Chih, "The Pragmatic Revolt in Law," *China Law Review* 6 (1933): 93; John C. H. Wu, "The Mind of Mr. Justice Holmes," *China Law Review* 8 (1935): 77; Mangum Weeks, "Book Review: Law and the Modern Mind, by Jerome Frank," *China Law Review* 5 (1932): 238.

[54] See, e.g., Lobingier, "Legal Education," 1; Timothy G. Kearley, *Lost in Translations: Roman Law Scholarship and Translation in Early Twentieth-Century America* (Durham, NC: Carolina Academic Press, 2018), 41, 81–93. Some examples of the theoretical works that Lobingier published in the *China Law Review* are Charles S. Lobingier, "The New Science of Man and Law's Place Therein," *China Law Review* 9 (1936): 107; Charles S. Lobingier, "The Nature and Origin of Law," *China Law Review* 10 (1937): 55; Charles S. Lobingier, "The Form and Repository of Law," *China Law Review* 10 (1940): 165.

other authors, too, whose works showed a similar interest in comparative law and legal history, for example, by comparing ancient Chinese, Hindu, and Jewish law to other legal systems of the ancient world.[55]

China did not have a religious legal system equivalent to Hindu, Jewish, or Islamic law. The dominant Chinese philosophical traditions, Confucianism, Daoism, and Buddhism, did not posit a divine lawgiver or a revealed body of law to govern human affairs. Confucianism emphasized social harmony through moral cultivation rather than law. Classical Daoism, with its focus on the spontaneous natural order, tended to reject rigid legal frameworks, while Buddhism influenced broader Chinese culture primarily through its ethical notions.[56] However, these ancient philosophical traditions did provide some guidance for individual moral conduct and also for the political ordering of society, and could thus be used (in addition to the very long tradition of Chinese positivist jurisprudence) by local legal scholars seeking jurisprudential inspiration in their own national traditions.

As was the case in other non-Western countries, some late nineteenth- and early twentieth-century Chinese intellectuals sought to meld ancient Chinese traditions with new ideas from the West.[57] Similarly, some Chinese legal scholars, just like the Indian and Jewish scholars I discussed in the previous chapters, were interested in the legal aspects of these ancient traditions and, indeed, claimed that they were sometimes more "modern" than Western legal approaches. For example, Chinese scholars argued that modern notions about the non-autonomous nature

55 See R. C. W. Sheng, "The Reasons Why in the Egyptian, Babylonian, Hebrew, Hindu, and Chinese Systems, Lawyers in Our Sense of Unofficial Practitioners Apparently Did Not Exist," *China Law Review* 3(5) (July 1927): 4; Henry P. Chiu, "The Origin and Purpose of Adoption," *China Law Review* 4 (1930): 79; Henry P. Chiu, "Requisites of Adoption in Roman, Hindu and Chinese Law," *China Law Review* 4 (1930): 133, 181; Henry P. Chiu, "The Effect of Adoption in Roman, Hindu and Chinese Law," *China Law Review* 4 (1930): 277.

56 See Lee and Lai, "Chinese Conceptions of Law," 1312–25; Randall P. Peerenboom, *Law and Morality in Ancient China: The Silk Manuscripts of Huang-Lao* (Albany, NY: State University of New York Press, 1993), 171–215; Geoffrey MacCormack, *Traditional Chinese Penal Law* (Edinburgh: Edinburgh University Press, 1996), 31–2; Peerenboom, "Law and Ritual," 451; Zhuo Xinping, "Religion and Rule of Law in China Today," *Brigham Young University Law Review* (2009): 519, 520.

57 See, e.g., Edmund S. K. Fung, *The Intellectual Foundations of Chinese Modernity: Cultural and Political Thought in the Republican Era* (New York: Cambridge University Press, 2010), 4–5.

of law echoed ancient Chinese ideas about the harmonious relationship between law and the universe, describing this approach as both "typically Chinese" but also "modernistic."[58]

One of the scholars interested in blending Western and Chinese approaches to law was John C. H. Wu (Wu Jingxiong). Born in 1899, Wu began his law studies at Peiyang University, but after only one semester, he moved to the Comparative Law School to complete his law degree. There, influenced by the Bible and the fundamentalist views of the school's first dean, Charles Rankin, he converted to Christianity, becoming a Methodist and, later, a Catholic. After graduating in 1920, Wu pursued post-graduate studies, first at Michigan Law School, then at the Universities of Paris and Berlin, and finally at Harvard Law School. During his time abroad, he established academic contacts with some of the leading legal thinkers of the period, including Oliver Wendell Holmes, Benjamin Cardozo, Roscoe Pound, and John Wigmore in the United States, François Gény in France, and Rudolf Stammler in Germany. In 1924, Wu returned to China to a position at the Comparative Law School, where he taught several subjects, including jurisprudence, continuing and deepening his engagement with Western legal theory, and with Western legal scholars (see Figure 7.2). Later, he also taught in the United States – first, in 1930, at Northwestern and Harvard, then, after the Communist takeover of China in 1949 and until his retirement in 1967, at the University of Hawaii and Seton Hall Law School in New Jersey. In addition to his academic career, Wu served as a judge, lawyer, Member of the Chinese Parliament, constitutional drafter, and diplomat.[59]

58 See William Timothy Kao, "The New Way of Approaching the Law," *China Law Review* 4 (1930): 27, 29.

59 See John C. H. Wu, *Beyond East and West* (Notre Dame, IN: University of Notre Dame Press, 2018). See also Li Xiuqing, "John C. H. Wu at the University of Michigan School of Law," *Journal of Legal Education* 58 (2008): 545; Xiaomeng Zhang, "John C. H. Wu and His Comparative Law Pursuit," *International Journal of Legal Information* 41 (2013): 196; Tongxin Lu, "John C. H. Wu: A Prodigy in Synthesizing East and West and a Prophet for the Evangelization of China" (PhD diss., Catholic University of America, 2020), 18–31. On Pound's influence on, and relationship with, Chinese legal scholars, see, generally, Conner, "Comparative Law School of China," 238–9; Jedidiah J. Kroncke, *The Futility of Law and Development: China and the Dangers of Exporting American Law* (New York: Oxford University Press, 2016); William P. Alford and Xingzhong Yu, "Pound for Pound? Roscoe Pound's Adventures in China and Questions They Pose for Scholars of Contemporary China," *University of Pennsylvania Asian Law Review* 18 (2022): 1, 4–5.

FIGURE 7.2 Roscoe Pound and Chinese dignitaries sit outside the Comparative Law School, c. 1935. Pound and John C. H. Wu are seated in the middle of the front row. Photograph courtesy of Harvard Law School Library, Historical and Special Collections.

Wu's legal training and scholarly interests were as cosmopolitan as those of the Indian and Jewish scholars I discussed in the previous chapters. However, unlike most of the Indian and Jewish scholars I have analyzed (with the possible exception of Pal and Sanhuri), Wu was a well-known and internationally recognized legal theorist. One remarkable indication of his international visibility is found in an English translation of a book by the leading German legal theorist Rudolf Stammler (published by the American Modern Legal Philosophy Series in 1925). This book included two appendices discussing and critiquing Stammler's thought, one of which was written by François Gény – the leading French legal philosopher of the period, and the other by Wu. That Wu would be asked to write the other appendix is extraordinary, considering that, at twenty-six years old, he was only beginning his teaching career at Soochow.[60]

[60] John C. H. Wu, "Appendix II: Stammler and his Critics," in Rudolf Stammler, ed., *The Theory of Justice*, trans. Isaac Husik (New York: Macmillan, 1925), 555. Another example of Chinese legal scholars serving as intermediaries between

Wu was a prolific author who wrote about Catholicism, Confucianism, Daoism, Zen Buddhism, poetry, and law. His legal works included summaries and discussions of the ideas of Western scholars, which he published both in China and in the United States.[61] However, he also wrote original works on comparative law and jurisprudence, including a book on the Law of Nature and a jurisprudence textbook, which he published after moving to the United States.[62]

Many of Wu's works did not refer specifically to Chinese law.[63] However, as a young law graduate, he was interested in comparing Western and Chinese jurisprudential theories. Thus, in a 1921 article he published while still a student at Michigan Law School, he proudly noted that "China is the oldest nation that flourishes on the globe today. Her civilization had already attained a high stage of development when that of Rome was still in its cradle." Wu then argued that the jurisprudential ideas of the major Western schools – Natural Law, Positivism, and the Historical School – were all present in ancient Chinese legal thought; that Chinese legal history could provide materials for the study of the evolution of law; and that the "Chinese

German and Anglo-American law lies in the fact that the first translation of the German Civil Code to English, published in 1907, was produced by a young Chinese scholar, Chung Hui Wang (Wáng Chǒnghuì). See Chung Hui Wang, trans., *The German Civil Code* (London: Stevens, 1907); Chen, "Early Graduate Legal Studies," 717n10, 744.

61 See John C. H. Wu, "The Juristic Philosophy of Justice Holmes," *Michigan Law Review* 21 (1922–23): 523; John C. H. Wu, "The Juristic Philosophy of Roscoe Pound," *Illinois Law Review* 18 (1923–24): 285; Wu, "Juristic Philosophy of Judge Cardozo"; Wu, "Juristic Philosophy of Roscoe Pound"; Wu, "Realistic Analysis of Legal Concepts"; Wu, "Mind of Mr. Justice Holmes."

62 John C. H. Wu, *Fountain of Justice: A Study in the Natural Law* (New York: Sheed & Ward, 1955). See also John C. H. Wu, *Cases and Materials on Jurisprudence* (St. Paul, MN: West, 1958) (a textbook whose orientation is entirely Western).

63 See, e.g., John C. H. Wu, "Problem and Method of Psychological Jurisprudence," *China Law Review* 2 (1925): 214; John C. H. Wu, "Scientific Method in Judicial Process," *China Law Review* 3 (1926): 7; John C. H. Wu, "The Three Dimensions of Law," *China Law Review* 3 (1926): 126; John C. H. Wu, "Toward a Christian Philosophy of Law," *Women Lawyers Journal* 37(4) (Fall 1951): 34; John C. H. Wu, "The Natural Law and Our Common Law," *Fordham Law Review* 23 (1954): 13; John C. H. Wu, "Jurisprudence as a Cultural Study," *University of Detroit Mercy Law Review* 33 (1956): 277 (which does, briefly, mention Chinese law); John C. H. Wu, "Truth and Fiction in the Art of Justice," *University of Detroit Law Journal* 36 (1958): 130; John C. H. Wu, "Justice Holmes and the Common-Law Tradition," *Vanderbilt Law Review* 14 (1960): 221.

legal mind" was perfectly receptive to the ideas of modern sociological jurisprudence.[64]

Other works by Wu mentioned Confucianism, employed examples from Chinese legal history to prove general points about the nature of law or its history, criticized inadequate Western surveys of ancient Chinese political philosophy, and discussed Chinese legal and political thought.[65] It seems that a major driver of Wu's interest in Chinese law was his acceptance of the cultural nationalist and historicist assumptions of the German Historical School about the unique nature of the law of every nation. Wu observed:

> I do not believe, with the German jurists of the historical school, that each nation has a soul of its own called the "*Volksseele*." But I do believe that every nation has a way of living and thinking which is more or less peculiar to it, constituting, as it were, its distinctive spirit. This spirit permeates all the main channels of its activities ... [including] law ...[66]

Discussions of constitutional law in interwar China were often also informed by historicist tendencies and references to the country's unique constitutional traditions (even when these were combined with calls to Westernize Chinese governmental institutions and Chinese law). One could find them in the work of Western experts sent to China to advise on constitution-making during the Republican period – for example, in the writings of the American scholar Frank Goodnow, who taught constitutional law at Peking University and served between 1913 and 1914 as an advisor to Yuan Shikai, the second provisional President of the Republic of China. Such discussions were also evident in Roscoe Pound's 1940s works on the constitutional history of China.[67]

[64] John Wu, "Readings from Ancient Chinese Codes and Other Sources of Chinese Law and Legal Ideas," *Michigan Law Review* 19 (1920–21): 502, 502–4.

[65] See John C. H. Wu, "Book Review: Chinese Political Philosophy – by William S. A. Pott," *China Law Review* 3 (1926): 33; John C. H. Wu, "Chinese Legal and Political Philosophy," in *The Chinese Mind: Essentials of Chinese Philosophy and Culture*, ed. Charles A. Moore with the assistance of Aldyth V. Morris (Honolulu, HI: East-West Center Press, 1967), 213; John C. H. Wu, "The Status of the Individual in the Political and Legal Traditions of Old and New China," in *The Status of the Individual in East and West*, ed. Charles A. Moore with the assistance of Aldyth V. Morris (Honolulu, HI: University of Hawaii Press, 1968), 391.

[66] Wu, "Chinese Legal and Political Philosophy," 226.

[67] Kroncke, *Futility*, 145; Jedidiah J. Kroncke, "Roscoe Pound in China: A Lost Precedent for the Liabilities of American Legal Exceptionalism," *Brooklyn Journal of International Law* 38 (2012): 77, 111.

Chinese politicians, too, were influenced by the belief that ancient Chinese political philosophy and constitutional traditions were relevant to modern Chinese constitutional reform. A notable example of such an influence can be found in the constitutional thinking of Sun Yat-sen, who led the revolution that ended the rule of the Qing dynasty and established the Republic of China. Sun's constitutional ideas fused Western and Confucian political thought. One aspect of the mixed nature of Sun's approach was his rejection of Western liberal individualism in favor of a commitment to collectivism. Another manifestation of the influence of traditional Chinese political theory on his viewpoint was his suggestion that China should create a Five Powers Constitutional Government – that is, a governmental structure based on five, not three, branches of government. This approach followed the traditional Chinese structure of government, which, in addition to the legislative, executive, and judicial branches, also included "control" and "examination" branches.[68] An article published in 1924 in the *China Law Review* discussing this idea declared that "law, in order to be effective, must be able to accommodate itself to the traditional mode of life of the country in which it operates" and that, therefore, China, with its "five thousand years of civilization," should not be expected to simply adopt "a new constitution and new codes without having regard to the customary rules and mode of life of the people."[69] Further, in a way reminiscent of the scholars of India, Mandatory Palestine, and also of Egypt, Sun claimed that Western concepts such as democracy were already present in ancient Chinese political theory.[70]

The practical melding of Western and Chinese norms and political traditions was also expressed in the draft constitution produced by Wu

[68] See, e.g., Eric Chiyeung Ip, "Building Constitutional Democracy on Oriental Foundations: An Anatomy of Sun Yat-sen's Constitutionalism," *Historia Constitucional* 9 (2008): 328, 331–4, 338–9; Ngoc Son Bui, "Sun Yat-Sen's Constitutionalism," *Giornale di storia costituzionale/Journal of Constitutional History* 32(2) (2016): 157, 159, 163–8, 170–5.

[69] S. C. Ho, "Book Review: A Constitution of Five Powers (a lecture). By Dr. Sun Yat-Sen," *China Law Review* 1 (1924): 390, 391.

[70] Bui, "Sun Yat-Sen's Constitutionalism," 168–70. On arguments about the compatibility of democracy with ancient Chinese traditions, see, generally, Edmund S. K. Fung, *In Search of Chinese Democracy: Civil Opposition in Nationalist China, 1929–1949* (New York: Cambridge University Press, 2000), 22–3. On China and the Western notion of "Oriental despotism," see also Ruskola, *Legal Orientalism*.

in 1933 and in the final version of this text, the 1946 Constitution of the Republic of China (which is the basis of the current Constitution of Taiwan).[71] The 1946 Constitution adopted the very five-powers structure of government that Sun had suggested at the beginning of the twentieth century. In addition, the fusion between Western and Chinese traditions could be seen in the sections dealing with civil rights. The Constitution did contain a list of individual rights, but these could be easily infringed by the government, thus reflecting a collectivist understanding of the relationship between individuals and the state. This understanding was influenced by Chinese political traditions, which contained both proto-liberal individualist strains and also collectivist ones.[72]

The interest in ancient Chinese political and legal thought was also evident in the academic works of Chinese interwar scholars. These scholars analyzed ancient Chinese political theories.[73] They argued that liberal notions such as human rights were compatible with classical Chinese philosophy, traditions, and values.[74] They also claimed that some ancient Chinese philosophers, such as Confucius and Lao Tzu, rejected the notion of absolutism, instead viewing rulers as trustees working on behalf of the people, and subject to the Higher Law of Heaven.[75]

Finally, just as interwar Indian and Jewish scholars claimed that international law was not invented in Europe in the early modern era and sought to prove the ancient pedigree of this field of law, so, too, did

[71] The Constitution was adopted by the Chinese National Constituent Assembly on December 25, 1946, was promulgated by the National Government on January 1, 1947, and became effective as of December 25, 1947.

[72] See Wu, "Status of the Individual," 391–400 (discussing both individualist and collectivist ideas in ancient Chinese political and legal thought); Thomas E. Greiff, "The Principle of Human Rights in Nationalist China: John C. H. Wu and the Ideological Origins of the 1946 Constitution," *China Quarterly* 103 (1985): 441; "Dr. Wu's Constitution," *Harvard Law Review* 132 (2019): 2300. On different attitudes of Chinese intellectuals during the Republican era to individualism and collectivism, see, generally, Fung, *Intellectual Foundations*.

[73] See, e.g., Kuo-Cheng Wu, *Ancient Chinese Political Theories* (Shanghai: Commercial Press, 1928) (a book based on a 1926 Princeton University doctoral dissertation).

[74] See, e.g., Hans Ingvar Roth, *P. C. Chang and the Universal Declaration of Human Rights* (Philadelphia, PA: University of Pennsylvania Press, 2016); Li Chen, "A Contemporaneous Interpretation of Chung-Shu Lo's Reply to the UNESCO Human Rights Survey," *Human Rights Quarterly* 44 (2022): 168.

[75] Wu, "Chinese Legal and Political Philosophy," 214–19.

Chinese scholars. Following arguments made by the nineteenth-century American missionary W. A. P. Martin, early twentieth-century Chinese scholars wrote works on ancient Chinese international law, claiming that international law already appeared in China during the Spring and Autumn period, or, more generally, that international law originated "in the East" rather than in the West.[76]

## Conclusion

The institutional history of legal education in Egypt and China and the history of the texts produced by legal scholars in Egyptian and Chinese law schools shared many common features with the history of institutions and the texts produced in India and Palestine. Egyptian and Chinese institutions and works were cosmopolitan: they were influenced by Western theories, both Anglo-American and Continental, including anti-formalist sociological theories fashionable during the interwar period in the West. Egyptian and Chinese authors depicted their traditional legal and political systems as superior to Western law, and they referred to these traditional systems when discussing public law, specifically constitutional and international law.

There were also some differences. In colonial India, the influence of English jurisprudence was stronger than in Mandatory Palestine, Egypt, or China. The strength of this influence was due to the fact that Britain's interaction with India was longer and made a deeper impact on local legal culture. The relatively strong French influence on works produced in Egypt was due to the fact that the modern Egyptian legal system had been heavily shaped by French law since the nineteenth century. In the Chinese case, the British influence on Hong Kong was

[76] Some examples are Ma-Do-Yün, *Der eintritt des Chinesischen Reiches in den völkerrechtlichen verband* (Berlin: E. Ebering, 1907); Shih-Tsai Chen, "The Equality of States in Ancient China," *American Journal of International Law* 35 (1941): 641; Ching Cheng Shih, "International Law in the Ch'un Ch'iu Period" (PhD diss., University of Chicago, 1946). Additional works are mentioned and discussed in Ping Yi, "The Final Splendour of an Aged Empire: Chinese Thought on International Law in the Early Twentieth Century," *Journal of East Asia and International Law* 9 (2016): 29, 39–40; Li Chen, "A Forgotten Proponent of a League of Nations and His Contributions to International Law," *Leiden Journal of International Law* 35 (2022): 245, 255; Ryan Martínez Mitchell, *Recentering the World: China and the Transformation of International Law* (Cambridge: Cambridge University Press, 2023), 5, 70–1, 162.

similar in scale to that found in India. There were British law professors in mainland China too, such as James Bromley Eames of Peiyang University, but the British academic influence was weaker than that of American professors. Another distinguishing characteristic of the Chinese case was the involvement of American missionary law professors, such as Charles Rankin, the first dean of the Comparative Law School.

The differences between India, Palestine, Egypt, and China were not limited to the impact of different Western jurisprudential traditions. There were also distinctions in how local legal traditions were imagined and used. I already noted in Interlude 1 that there were almost no calls to replace British colonial laws with Hindu law in colonial India. In China, too, legal reform during the Republican era was based on a desire to Westernize Chinese law. In contrast, in Egypt, just as in Palestine, the legal revival of non-Western law was an ideal espoused by many scholars. While in Palestine, the actual impact of this ideal was ultimately negligible, in Egypt, the calls for the revival of Islamic law were implemented. Here, the study of Islamic law using Western jurisprudential tools ultimately led to the enactment of the 1949 Egyptian Civil Code, which was influenced by Islamic law. This code later served as a model for civil law codification in many other Arab countries.

To what extent can we attribute the similarities in all the places discussed in this book to mutual influence? Anti-colonial nationalist activists often interacted with one another, and anti-colonial ideas were spread through academic and ideological networks in Europe and the colonies.[77] However, it seems that the anti-colonial interaction did not expand to the realm of legal theory. One possible avenue of

[77] See, e.g., Elleke Boehmer, *Empire, the National, and the Postcolonial, 1890–1920: Resistance in Interaction* (New York: Oxford University Press, 2005); Michael Goebel, *Anti-Imperial Metropolis: Interwar Paris and the Seeds of Third World Nationalism* (New York: Cambridge University Press, 2015); Erez Manela and Heather Streets-Salter, eds., *The Anticolonial Transnational: Imaginaries, Mobilities, and Networks in the Struggle against Empire* (Cambridge: Cambridge University Press, 2023). Specifically on the interaction between Egyptian and Indian intellectuals and politicians during the interwar period, see, e.g., M. L. Roy Choudhury, *Egypt in 1945* (Calcutta: University of Calcutta Press, 1946); Noor-Aiman I. Khan, *Egyptian-Indian Nationalist Collaboration and the British Empire* (New York: Palgrave, 2011).

interaction would have been law studies in the metropole, but while many Indian law students studied in Britain, there were far fewer Chinese, Egyptian, or Palestinian law students (either Jewish or Arab) studying there.[78]

Another possible avenue of influence was through books. Were Egyptian scholars aware of the books written by Indian and Jewish scholars, and vice versa? The theoretical Indian works I analyzed in previous chapters do not appear to have been available in Egypt. The Egyptian textbooks analyzed here cited many Western works in their footnotes and bibliographies but not Indian works on either Hindu or Islamic law.[79] As for the influence of Egyptian works on Indian scholars, given that the Egyptian books I discuss were written in Arabic, scholars such as Pal, who did not read Arabic, would have found them inaccessible. Indian scholars of Islamic law were more aware of developments in the Middle East, and many of them could also read Arabic.[80] However, the early twentieth-century Islamic-Indian

[78] For example, if we focus on Indian students at the Inns of Court, between 1894 and 1947, approximately 1,500 South Asian students were admitted to one of the four inns, Lincoln's Inn, whereas only a handful of Egyptian, Chinese, or Palestinian (Jewish or Arab) students appear in the admission registers for that period. See Renu Paul (in consultation with Mitra Sharafi), "South Asians at the Inns of Court: Lincoln's Inn, 1864–1947," www.yumpu.com/en/document/view/19003915/south-asians-at-the-inns-of-court-lincolns-inn-uw-law-school; *The Records of the Honorable Society of Lincoln's Inn*, Vol. 3: *Admissions from A.D. 1894 to A.D. 1956* (London: Lincoln's Inn, 1981). On the number of South Asian students at all the Inns of Courts, see Mitra Sharafi, "South Asians at the Inns of Court: Empire, Expulsion, and Redemption circa 1900," in *In Between and Across: Legal History Without Boundaries*, eds. Kenneth W. Mack and Jacob Katz Cogan (New York: Oxford University Press, 2024), 179, 181–2.

[79] The catalog of the Federation of Egyptian Libraries, which includes the major Egyptian University Libraries, does not contain the works of the Indian scholars of Hindu law that I analyzed in Chapter 1. Works by some Indian scholars of Islamic history and theology (such as Ameer Ali's book, *Life and Teachings of Mohammed or the Spirit of Islam*), do appear in this catalog (and, as I noted in Chapter 2, Ali's *Mahommedan Law* was cited in Frederic Goadby's jurisprudence textbook). However, most of the works on Islamic law published in India in the late colonial period were written for practicing lawyers and were, therefore, surveys of contemporary Islamic personal law and not attempts to analyze the more general aspects of this legal system. Thus, they were less relevant to Egyptian works on jurisprudence. As I noted in Chapter 1, the leading theoretical Indian work on Islamic law published in interwar India was Abdur Rahim's *The Principles of Muhammadan Jurisprudence*. This book, however, was not cited in the Egyptian works I analyze in the present chapter.

[80] See Ebrahim Moosa, "Colonialism and Islamic Law," in *Islam and Modernity: Key Issues and Debates*, eds. Muhammad Khalid Masud, Armando Salvatore, and

works on jurisprudence that I discussed in Chapter 1 – for example, Abdur Rahim's book – while making use of Egyptian editions of classical Islamic texts, did not cite modern Egyptian works. As I showed in Chapter 2, Palestinian-Arab lawyers were aware of developments in Egypt. However, it does not seem that Egyptian legal scholars were aware of (or interested in) the works of Palestinian-Arab lawyers. As for the relationship between Egyptian and Jewish scholars, the language barrier would have prevented Egyptian legal scholars from reading publications in Hebrew written by the Jewish scholars of Palestine. Some Jewish scholars (Bentwich, who taught at the Cairo Law School, or Grajewsky, who studied there) might have been aware of developments in Egypt, but there is no indication in their works of Egyptian influence.

What about China? China and India have a long history of entanglement. During the first decades of the twentieth century, pan-Asian ideas reinforced the keenness among intellectuals in both countries to interact with one another.[81] Comparative law works written by Chinese scholars sometimes mentioned Hindu law.[82] However, there does not seem to have been any mutual interaction between legal scholars in places such as Soochow or Calcutta. As for the Middle East, the founder of the Comparative Law School, Charles Rankin, was a deeply religious man keen to have his students read the Old Testament.[83] As a result, some Chinese scholars teaching at Soochow became interested in Jewish law.[84] There were also scholars in interwar China who were interested in Islamic legal traditions, such as Peng Chun Chang (Zhāng Péngchūn), a philosopher, writer, and diplomat who became involved in drafting the Universal Declaration of Human Rights. Chang spent two years in Turkey in the early 1940s and wrote about the similarities and mutual influences between China

Martin van Bruinessen (Edinburgh: Edinburgh University Press, 2009), 158, 172–3. See also Sohaira Z. M. Siddiqui, *Islamic Law on Trial: Contesting Colonial Power in British India* (Oakland, CA: University of California Press, 2025), 163 (mentioning the influence of Qadri Pasha, an Egyptian legal scholar, on Indian Muslim scholars).

81 See, e.g., Tansen Sen, *India, China, and the World: A Connected History* (Lanham, MD: Rowman & Littlefield, 2017), 293–377. See also Tansen Sen and Brian Tsuie, eds., *Beyond Pan-Asianism: Connecting China and India, 1840s–1960s* (New Delhi: Oxford University Press, 2021).

82 See Zhang, "Development of Comparative Law," 236; Sheng, "Reasons."

83 See, e.g., Lobingier, "Legal Education," 2.

84 See Sheng, "Reasons."

and the Islamic world.[85] However, I did not encounter any indications of awareness among Chinese legal scholars of the works of Egyptian scholars such as Sanhuri (and vice versa), and certainly no awareness among Chinese writers of interwar Zionist legal thought.

Given the lack of mutual influence between the four places I have examined, one is left to conclude that the similarities between them were the result not of influence but of similar institutional and intellectual environments. The appearance of Western-style law schools in the late nineteenth and early twentieth centuries as a direct or indirect result of European colonialism exposed local legal scholars to Western jurisprudential theories. The legal reality in European colonies and non-Western states, and also the emergence of anti-European cultural nationalism among Indians, Jews, Egyptians, and Chinese (as well as many other non-Western societies), led local legal scholars to study local ancient legal traditions, producing works that married state-of-the-art Western jurisprudential ideas with local traditions, often in ways that were critical of Western legal theories. Together, the works that I have analyzed in this book were all part of a single interwar non-Western jurisprudential wave that appeared simultaneously in many places across the globe in the first decades of the twentieth century.

[85] Roth, *P. C. Chang*, 73–7.

# Epilogue

## *The Decline and Resurgence of Legal Nationalism in Postcolonial India and Israel*

Legal scholars in colonial India and Mandatory Palestine produced novel theoretical works that were both sophisticated and critical. They also offered unique insights into the nature of law, generally, and the nature of ancient religious systems, their norms, and their institutions, in particular. Studying the history of this forgotten episode in the development of modern legal theory is important in its own right, but also because it contains valuable lessons for contemporary political debates in India, Israel, and many other countries. To demonstrate the contemporary relevance of the story told here, I will briefly discuss the study of legal theory in post-independence India and Israel and note the surprising resurgence of political interest in Hindu and Jewish traditions and values in recent years.

India became independent in 1947. The State of Israel was born a year later. In the decade following independence in both India and Israel, the prestige of lawyers and legal scholars seems to have declined. While the respective leaders of the two new states, Jawaharlal Nehru and David Ben-Gurion, had both trained as lawyers, they held lawyers and the law in low esteem.[1]

[1] A similar trend occurred in Egypt, where Nasser's regime sought to curtail the role of lawyers in the public sphere and to replace them with doctors, engineers, and, of course, soldiers. See Amr Shalakany, "Between Identity and Redistribution: Sanhuri, Genealogy and the Will to Islamise," *Islamic Law and Society* 8 (2001): 201, 242. One might object to the argument that Nehru and Ben-Gurion held law in low esteem by pointing out that both leaders played key roles in shaping the constitutional frameworks of their respective new states. However, Nehru approached the Indian Constitution as more than a purely legal

In a speech to law students in the period immediately preceding Indian independence, Nehru did not hide his contempt for law and legal traditions. "Lawyers have had their day," he informed his audience. While they had led "public movements and public life" in the nineteenth century, they had since "faded further and further." Lawyers once used to play a "very pre-eminent" part in the Indian nationalist movement, Nehru admitted, but "to-morrow is not for the lawyers. To-morrow is for the scientists, the industrialists, and the Engineers."[2] Nor was Nehru interested in the cultural–nationalist project of studying ancient Indian culture. "India is a very ancient land," he said, but the "proud inheritance" of its traditions also constituted a disadvantage because the "long inheritance has brought dust and cobwebs of the past with it."[3] Nehru's speeches contained many other examples of a disparaging attitude toward law, lawyers, and ancient Indian legal traditions.[4]

document to be used only by lawyers. For example, in his 1946 speech in the Constituent Assembly introducing the Objective Resolution, he remarked: "Laws are made of words but this Resolution is something higher than the law. If you examine its words like lawyers you will produce only a lifeless thing." See Jawaharlal Nehru, "The Objective Resolution," *Constituent Assembly Debates* (New Delhi: Government of India, 2014), Vol. 1, 58. Ben-Gurion's approach to constitutionalism was shaped in part by a deep skepticism toward judicial review. It has been argued that his concern that a constitution might empower judges to strike down primary legislation was among the reasons he ultimately abandoned efforts to establish a formal Israeli constitution. See Shani Schnitzer, "Ben-Gurion, Bagatz veha-Hukah she-Lo Haytah," *Mishpatim* 53 (2025): 489. More broadly, the idea that constitutions are primarily legal documents is a relatively recent, American-influenced development. Historically, constitutions were often conceived as political or pedagogical texts, meant to express national ideals and guide civic life. See Assaf Likhovski, "The Rise and Demise of Constitutional Duties in Israel," *American Journal of Legal History* 61 (2021): 90, 91–2; Mila Versteeg, Adam Chilton, and Erensu Altan, "Constitutional Duties," *American Journal of Comparative Law* 72 (2024): 685.

2 Pandit Jawaharlal Nehru, "Building up of India of To-morrow," *Calcutta University Law College Magazine* 15 (1945–46): 4, 4–5. See also Alexander Williams, "Imagining the Post-Colonial Lawyer: Legal Elites and the Indian Nation-State, 1947–1967," *Asian Journal of Comparative Law* 15 (2020): 1, 8–13. Nehru's mentor, Gandhi, who was also a lawyer, shared these sentiments. See, e.g., M. K. Gandhi, *The Law and the Lawyers*, ed. S. B. Kher (Ahmedabad: Navajivan, 1981), 212, 234, 253. See also Marc Galanter, "The Aborted Restoration of 'Indigenous' Law in India," in *Law and Society in Modern India* (Delhi: Oxford University Press, 1997), 37, 39n12 (discussing Gandhi's views on the legal profession).

3 Nehru, "Building up of India of To-morrow," 6.

4 See Jagat S. Bright, ed., *Important Speeches of Jawaharlal Nehru*, 2nd ed. (Lahore: IPW, 1946), 49 ("lawyers and their petty quibbles"); 124 ("*Swaraj* [self-rule] will not be obtained by scoring lawyer's points or by forensic eloquence"); 126 ("talk, specially that of lawyers, is a harmless commodity"); 283 ("[t]he fate of nations is not decided by lawyers' arguments"); 135 ("many of us, regardless of what is happening all around us

Given this attitude, it is no wonder that the English law professor J. Duncan M. Derrett noted, following a visit to Calcutta in 1953, that "the prestige of the law degree has gone down in recent years, that fewer and less enterprising youngsters are taking up law seriously as an academic interest and that fewer students regard the law as an attractive career."[5] The decline of interest in legal education was mirrored in the condition of legal research in post-independence India. A commission examining the state of Indian universities after independence noted the neglect of the "scientific aspect" of law and an overemphasis on the professional aspect, remarking that "we have no internationally known expounders of Jurisprudence and legal studies. Our colleges of law do not hold a place of high esteem either at home or abroad, nor has law become an arena of profound scholarship and enlightened research."[6]

The life and ideas of Israel's first Prime Minister, Ben-Gurion, were, in many ways, similar to that of Nehru.[7] One similarity was Ben-Gurion's general low regard for law and lawyers. For example, in a 1949 speech, he declared:

> The question is this: Were we created for the legal principle, or was the legal principle created for us? Every jurist knows it is easy to weave legal cobwebs to

still live in the ancient past, and imagine that we can have it back again. Some want the Vedic age, others a reproduction of the early democratic days of Islam ... We forget that our ancient civilizations, great as they are, were meant for different ages and different conditions ... many of our traditions and habits and customs, our social laws, our caste system, the position we give to women, and the dogmas which religion has imposed on us, are the relics of a past, suitable in those far-off days but utterly out of joint with modern conditions"). See also Jawaharlal Nehru, *The Discovery of India* (Delhi: Oxford University Press, 1985), 87, 95, 256 (criticizing ancient Indian law and society for their rigidity and the absence of a developed notion of individual rights).

5 J. D. M. Derrett, "The Law Student and Legislation," in *Anthology of University College of Law Centenary Celebration 1909–2009* (Calcutta: Registrar of the University of Calcutta, 2010), 165. On the decline in the prestige of the Indian legal profession in the post-independence period, see also Yves Dezalay and Bryant G. Garth, *Law as Reproduction and Revolution: An Interconnected History* (Oakland, CA: University of California Press, 2021), 101–2.

6 University Education Commission, *The Report of the University Education Commission (December 1948–August 1949)*, reprint ed. (Simla: Government of India Press, 1962), Vol. 1, 224. See also Madhusudan Majumdar, "Practical versus Scientific Legal Study in India," *Calcutta University Law College Magazine* 27 (1959): xv; B. B. Misra, *The Indian Middle Classes: Their Growth in Modern Times* (London: Oxford University Press, 1961), 331.

7 See, e.g., Khinvraj Jangid, "Imagining Nations, Creating States: Nehru, Ben-Gurion and an Analogical Study of India and Israel in Post-Colonial Asia," *Israel Studies* 26 (2020): 73.

prove and disprove anything ... As a [former] law student, I know that jurists are experts at twisting every text, inventing convoluted arguments, and confusing interpretations, and the simple and straightforward approach of the layperson, who is not familiar with the many massive volumes of legal scholasticism, is preferable. Knowledge of reality and factual knowledge are required, and these should be the basis for decision-making, not legal quibbling.[8]

As for Jewish law, Ben-Gurion had little interest in the topic. While the Bible, associated with the notion of ancient Jewish sovereignty and with the universalist and humanistic messages of the prophets, played a major role in his thought, Ben-Gurion, like many secular Jews of his generation, did not view either biblical or post-biblical Jewish law as a significant part of the core of Jewish identity.[9]

While the leaders of the newly established states of India and Israel did not view law as an important aspect of their nation-building project, legal research in both places continued. Many textbooks on jurisprudence were published in postcolonial India. Some of these works argued that the Indian contribution to jurisprudence was to be found in the ability of Indians to synthesize conflicting jurisprudential approaches;[10] some talked about the spiritual nature of Indian

[8] "Mo'etset ha-Medinah ha-Zmanit: Ha-Yeshivah ha-Tesh'a-'Esreh (September 23, 1948)," in *Mo'etset ha-'Am: Yeshivot 1–4 ... : Protokol ha-Diyunim* (Tel Aviv: n.p., 1949), 17. For recent discussions of Ben-Gurion's attitude to the law, see, e.g., Nir Kedar, *David Ben-Gurion and the Foundation of Israeli Democracy* (Bloomington, IN: Indiana University Press, 2021); Schnitzer, "Ben-Gurion." Ben-Gurion's attitude toward lawyers reflected a more general desire of the new Israeli state to shape the behavior of its citizens using education and social norms rather than law. See Assaf Likhovski, *Tax Law and Social Norms in Mandatory Palestine and Israel* (New York: Cambridge University Press, 2017), 149–246.

[9] See, e.g., Gideon Katz and Nir Kedar, "Ha-Yahadut be-'Eyney Intelektu'alim Yisra'elim Hilonim," *Tarbut Demokratit* 14 (2012): 93, 123–4; Kedar, *David Ben-Gurion*, 141.

[10] The term "synthetic jurisprudence" was already used in the 1920s in Karunamy Basu's work to designate the amalgamation of various jurisprudential approaches (analytical, historical, comparative, sociological, functional, and teleological). See Karunamay Basu, *The Modern Theories of Jurisprudence* (Calcutta: University of Calcutta, 1925), Vol. 1, vii–viii; Karunamay Basu, *The Modern Theories of Jurisprudence* (Calcutta: University of Calcutta, 1929), Vol. 2, v–vi. In the post-independence period, the leading exponent of what was dubbed the "synthetic" approach was Minocher Jehangirji Sethna, the self-proclaimed "Founder and President" of the grandly named "Indian School of Synthetic Jurisprudence." See, e.g., M. J. Sethna, "Synthetic Jurisprudence," *Calcutta University Law College Magazine* 24 (1956): 16, 18; M. J. Sethna, *Jurisprudence*, revised and enlarged 2nd

jurisprudence;[11] and others suggested that the distinctive nature of Indian jurisprudence was to be found in its "Third World" or socialist nature.[12]

As for the study of Hindu law, in a lecture delivered in 1943, the legal scholar Nares Chandra Sen Gupta urged his listeners to place more emphasis on the academic rather than the practical study of law and jurisprudence, and called for the establishment of "a school for the

ed. (Girgaon: Lakhani Books, 1959). Unfortunately, "synthetic jurisprudence" turned out to be more of a slogan than a fully developed jurisprudential theory. See Rajeev Dhavan, "Means, Motives and Opportunities: Reflecting on Legal Research in India," *Modern Law Review* 50 (1987): 725, 742n73 (citing Paton's disparaging comment on Sethna's work).

[11] See B. A. Masodkar, *National Jurisprudence: Need and Approach* (Nagpur: Shree Ram Trust, 1974), 27–8 (arguing that "India's gift" to the world was the mission of "the spiritualisation of the human race," giving the world "spiritual knowledge," which was "silent" like "the dew that falls unseen and unheard, yet brings into bloom masses of roses," and, in more practical terms, translated into values such as the emphasis on social and communal norms and distributive justice); S. K. Purohit, *Ancient Indian Legal Philosophy: Its Relevance to Contemporary Jurisprudential Thought* (New Delhi: Deep & Deep, 1994), 240–1, 245 (containing a chapter entitled "A Plea for Spiritual Jurisprudence," in which the author suggested that legal theory should be rescued from the "octopus of Western influence" and "spiritualised," a process that, he argued, would lead to "integration, harmonisation and synthesis"). It might also be interesting to compare these works to post-independence Indian (or Pakistani) theoretical works on Islamic law, such as Asaf A. A. Fyzee, *Outlines of Muhammadan Law* (Calcutta: Oxford University Press, 1949).

[12] See Radhabinod Pal, *The History of Hindu Law in the Vedic Age and in Post-Vedic Times down to the Institutes of Manu* (Calcutta: University of Calcutta Press, 1958), 394–8; Masodkar, *National Jurisprudence*, 110 (calling for the creation of a jurisprudence based on "social secular spiritualism" and inspired by the "shining pilgrimage of the souls" from Manu, through Marx, to Gandhi); Purohit, *Ancient Indian Legal Philosophy*, xi (noting that "our country ... is wedded to achiev[ing] a Socialistic Pattern of Society but little do we realise that in Ancient India, the Dharmashastra had for its objective the everlasting welfare of mankind ..."); V. R. Krishna Iyer, "Towards a Third World Jurisprudence," in *Law versus Justice: Problems and Solutions* (New Delhi: Deep & Deep, 1981), 132; S. N. Dhyani, *Jurisprudence: A Study of Indian Legal Theory*, 2nd ed. (New Delhi: Metropolitan Book Co., 1985), 19–21 (mentioning "home-spun jurisprudence harmonising, reconciling and furthering the needs of the people" and making "law for little Indians"); Aakash Singh Rathore and Garima Goswamy, *Rethinking Indian Jurisprudence: An Introduction to the Philosophy of Law* (London: Routledge, 2018), 78 (mentioning Justice Krishna Iyer's "Gandhian" interpretative approach seeking to interpret laws with a view to assisting "the poorest and the weakest man whom you may have seen"). It should be noted that the term "jurisprudence" sometimes referred to case law in these works rather than legal theory, specifically designating the constitutional decisions of the Indian Supreme Court.

study of Hindu law" at the University of Calcutta. He even suggested using the Tagore Law Lectures endowment to create:

> ... a permanent school under a Professor who will work for years, so that a succession of such professors and scholars will be enabled in [the] course of time to produce a history of ancient Indian law, which by the seriousness of the research and accuracy of the results, will be able to take its place by the side of the best histories of Roman Law.[13]

However, it seems that this call went unheeded. After Indian independence, there was little interest among Indian academics, judges, and practicing lawyers in studying, researching, and teaching Hindu law.[14]

The decline in interest in the academic study of Hindu law was accompanied by legislative reforms that sought to limit the impact of this legal system on the law of India following independence. Building on proposals from the 1940s, the Indian Parliament enacted the four Hindu Code Bills, which addressed marriage; succession; minority and guardianship; and adoptions and maintenance. The four acts, passed in 1955 and 1956, standardized and modernized the personal laws of Hindus (including Sikhs, Buddhists, and Jains). They included provisions that prohibited polygamy, allowed divorce, expanded female inheritance rights, and standardized adoption procedures.[15]

A more comprehensive reform of India's personal law system was envisioned in the Indian Constitution, which includes a directive that the state shall endeavor to establish a Uniform Civil Code, aimed at replacing the diverse religious personal laws inherited from the colonial period with a single set of civil rules applicable to all citizens, regardless of religion. However, this reform has not been implemented. Segments of the Muslim minority have historically

[13] See N. C. Sengupta, "Hints on an Historical Study of Hindu Law," *Calcutta University Law College Magazine* 13 (1943): 7, 18.

[14] See Werner Menski, *Hindu Law: Beyond Tradition and Modernity* (New Delhi: Oxford University Press, 2003), 39; Werner Menski, "Hindu Law in Modern Times: How Hindu Law Continues in Modern India," in *The Oxford History of Hinduism: Modern Hinduism*, ed. Torkel Brekke (Oxford: Oxford University Press, 2019), 244, 254–5.

[15] See, e.g., Rina Verma Williams, "Hindu Law as Personal Law: State and Identity in the Hindu Code Bills Debates, 1952–1956," in *Hinduism and Law: An Introduction*, eds. Timothy Lubin, Donald R., Davis Jr., and Jayanth K. Krishnan (Cambridge and New York: Cambridge University Press, 2010), 105, 105–19.

opposed it, viewing it as a threat to religious autonomy, and in recent decades, the Uniform Civil Code has become closely associated with the political agenda of the Bharatiya Janata Party (BJP), India's current ruling party.[16]

Nevertheless, it would be wrong to assume that Hindu law does not influence the modern Indian legal system. Indeed, legal scholar Werner Menski has argued that the jurisprudential principles undergirding Hindu law – which do not accept the positivist identification of the notion of "law" with state law, reject the sharp distinction between law and morality, emphasize the importance of self-control and call for the use of social rather than legal norms, and also see custom as an important source of law – have had a *growing* influence on Indian society. Additional aspects of contemporary Indian law that, according to Menski, prove the impact of Hindu jurisprudential notions on twenty-first-century Indian law include the willingness to recognize differential statuses rather than unquestioningly accepting the abstract concept of equal citizenship or the emphasis on duties rather than on rights. Menski also mentions in this context the words of Indian Prime Minister Atal Bihari Vajpayee, one of the founders of the BJP, who argued in 2001 that Indian identity is based on ethics and morality, in contrast to the Western idea of the "rule of law."[17] These words reflect the broader desire of today's Hindu nationalists to emphasize the importance of ancient Indian history, traditions, and values, and contrast them to Western law and its values.[18]

A concrete expression of this desire to emphasize the particularist character of Indian law by connecting it to Indian traditions can be found in the realm of criminal law reforms. In 2024, India replaced its Penal Code, Evidence Act, and Code of Criminal Procedure (all of which were British enactments either created during, or derived from, the colonial era) with new legislation. While these reforms were

[16] See, e.g., Manjari Katju, "The History of Hindu Nationalism in India," in Brekke, ed., *Modern Hinduism*, 203, 211–12.

[17] Menski, *Hindu Law*, 39, 59–60, 66, 68; Menski, "Hindu Law in Modern Times," 245.

[18] See, e.g., Christophe Jaffrelot, *Modi's India: Hindu Nationalism and the Rise of Ethnic Democracy*, trans. Cynthia Schoch (New York: Columbia University Press, 2019), 169–75; Raja M. Ali Saleem, "Hinduism, Hindutva and Hindu Populism in India: An Analysis of Party Manifestos of Indian Rightwing Parties," *Religions* 12 (2021): 803.

officially presented as part of the process of modernizing the law, they were simultaneously framed as a reassertion of Indian civilizational values. In describing the reforms Amit Shah, the Indian Minister of Home Affairs (and a leading BJP politician) said that the new codes reflected the "Indian spirit." The criminal justice system, he asserted, is "becoming completely 'Swadeshi' (made-in-India)," echoing the "Indian ethos." This ethos, he explained, was based on the promotion of "nyay" (justice) instead of "dand" (punishment).[19] The Indian government also characterized the enactment of the three new codes as part of a process of "decolonizing" Indian law. Some critical scholars argue that the "deployment of the language of decolonization may be a means to consolidate … Hindu nationalism," by contrasting Western law with an essentialized (and therefore false) version of "Indian culture and tradition."[20]

The cultural nationalist ideas which are now being promoted by BJP politicians are indirectly linked to the intellectual legacy of the Indian scholars discussed in this book. The reformer of the University of Calcutta, Asutosh Mookerjee, played a pivotal role in mentoring many early twentieth-century legal scholars at the University of Calcutta and beyond. His son, Syama Prasad Mookerjee, it might be recalled, was a colleague of Radhabinod Pal at the University of Calcutta. The younger Mookerjee is also widely recognized as a key ideological forerunner of the BJP and is accordingly revered by the party and its supporters.[21] However, the body of scholarship that Asutosh Mookerjee's followers created is all but forgotten.

19 "Focus on 'Nyay' instead of 'Dand': Amit Shah Welcomes 'Swadeshi' Criminal Laws," *Economic Times Online*, July 1, 2024, https://economictimes.indiatimes.com/news/india/criminal-justice-system-becoming-completely-swadeshi-amit-shah-on-new-criminal-laws/articleshow/111399264.cms?utm_source=contentofinterest&utm_-medium=text&utm_campaign=cppst; Ministry of Home Affairs, "Union Home Minister and Minister of Cooperation Shri Amit Shah Holds a Press Conference in New Delhi on Three New Criminal Laws, Calls the Laws Victim-Centric and Justice-Oriented," July 1, 2024, www.pib.gov.in/PressReleasePage.aspx?PRID=2030088&utm.

20 See Rishika Sahgal, "Decolonizing Criminal Law in India," in *The Routledge International Handbook on Decolonizing Justice*, ed. Chris Cunneen (London: Routledge, 2023), 391, 392–3.

21 See Christophe Jaffrelot, *The Hindu Nationalist Movement in India* (New York: Columbia University Press, 1996), 51; *Dr. Syama Prasad Mookerjee: A Selfless Patriot* (New Delhi: Dr. Syama Prasad Mookerjee Research Foundation, 2017), https://spmrf.org/spmookerjee/dr-spm-a-selfless-patriot.pdf.

Turning now to Israel, the decade after 1948 saw the publication of several books on legal theory.[22] There was also some practical, scholarly, and pedagogical interest in Jewish law. In the 1950s, Israeli legislative drafters sometimes attempted to use Jewish law notions in new legislation. One of the first justices appointed to the Israeli Supreme Court, Simha Assaf, the former Rector of the Hebrew University, was an expert on Jewish law, and his appointment as a judge was seen as a way to introduce Jewish law notions to Israeli case law. Several quasi-academic and academic institutions operating in Israel in the 1950s and early 1960s were devoted to studying Jewish law. One of these institutions was the Harry Fischel Institute, established in 1932 and affiliated with the Chief Rabbinate. There was also a short-lived institute for the study of Jewish law established by the Israeli Ministry of Justice after Israeli independence. The curriculum of the newly established Faculty of Law at the Hebrew University in the 1950s contained required courses on Jewish law. In 1963, the Hebrew University established an academic Institute for the study of Jewish law. This body was headed by Menachem Elon, a Tel Aviv School of Law and Economics graduate. Elon's agenda, as an academic scholar and later as an Israeli Supreme Court justice, was to continue the Jewish legal revival project championed by the founders of the Tel Aviv School of Law and Economics. Some professors teaching at the Tel Aviv School in the 1950s, including Eisenstadt and Dikshtein, continued studying and teaching Jewish law driven by the same scholarly motivation that guided their work during the period of the British Mandate.[23]

22 See, e.g., Eliezer Malhi, *Taskir Toldot ha-Mishpat be-Erets Yisrael* (Tel Aviv: Beyt ha-Sefer ha-Gavohah le-Mishpat vele-Kalkalah, 1950); Alfred Witkon, *Mishpat ve-Hevrah* (Tel Aviv: Dvir, 1955); Gad Tedeschi, *Mavo le-Torat ha-Mishpat*, ed. Aharon Barak (Jerusalem: Mif'al ha-Shikhpul, 1958); Eliezer Malhi, *Yesodey ha-Mishpat be-Yisrael*, ed. Y. Yonah (Tel Aviv: Agudat ha-Studentim shel ha-Universitah be-Tel Aviv, 1959).

23 Y. Ofir, "Makhon Harry Fischel bi-Yerushalayim," *Herut*, June 9, 1949; "Dr. Cohen be-Rosh ha-Makhon le-Heker ha-Mishpat ha-'Ivri," *Haaretz*, January 25, 1950; Yitzhak Ahi'yosef, "Mifa'alim Talmudiyim Merkaziyim bi-Yerushalyim," *Herut*, January 25, 1955; Moshe Unna, "'Al-ma Anu Nilhamim," *Ha-Tsofeh*, 22 July 1955; "Ha-Makhon le-Heker ha-Mishpat ha-'Ivri Hehel be-'Avodato bi-Yerushalayim," *Davar*, January 6, 1963; Arye Edrei, "Madu'a Lanu Mishpat 'Ivri?" *'Iyuney Mishpat* 25 (2001): 467, 467–8, 474–5; Guy Kles, "Universitah ba-Galut: Ha-Historyah shel ha-Hinukh ha-Mishpati ba-'Asor ha-Rishon la-Medinah," *Mishpatim* 41 (2012): 605,

However, the influence of Jewish law on Israeli law remained insignificant.[24] Most Israeli politicians, government officials, and legal scholars did not identify with the ideology of Jewish legal revival. Instead, they favored a vision of the modernization and Westernization of the legal system inherited by Israel from the Ottoman and British periods. In the 1950s, the Israeli Ministry of Justice created a flagship program on comparative law: the Harvard–Brandeis Cooperative Research on Israel's Legal Development Program. This legal research project was established jointly by the State of Israel and Harvard University (joined later by Brandeis University). The program sought to provide comparative law data on the legal regimes of various modern states, data that would be used to draft new Israeli legislation. Attempts by Israel's Chief Rabbi, Isaac Herzog, and by Yeshiva University Professor, Samuel Mirsky, to participate in the program and use it as a platform for the study and codification of Jewish law were rebuffed by the officials of the Israeli Ministry of Justice.[25]

Just as in the case of India, in Israel, too, the last few decades have witnessed a resurgence of political interest in ancient religious traditions and also legal ones. This trend is associated with the decline in the political power of the secular Founding Fathers' generation that established the State of Israel, coupled with the rise in power of right-wing and religious parties. In 1977, the Likud party came to power in Israel. This party, initially secular and liberal, gradually aligned itself with the conservative and religious side of the Israeli political spectrum.

In 1980, under a Likud-led government, the Israeli Parliament enacted the "Foundations of Law Act." The origins of this Act were not rooted in deliberations about the optimal connection between Israeli and Jewish law. Instead, the Act sought to answer the technical question of which sources Israeli courts should turn to when gaps arise in existing law, instead of relying on English law as

631–3; Arye Edrei, "Lo Posek Ani?! Menachem Elon: Shofet o-Posek Halakhah," in *Halakhah u-Mishpat: Sefer ha-Zikaron le-Meanchem Elon*, eds. Arye Edrei et al. (Tsafririm: Nevo, 2018), 45, 48.

24 Arye Edrei, "Madu'a lanu," 467–8, 474–5; Arye Edrei, "Lo Posek Ani?!" 48.

25 See Assaf Likhovski, "Argonauts of the Eastern Mediterranean: Legal Transplants and Signaling," *Theoretical Inquiries in Law* 10 (2009): 619, 645–7.

they had during the British Mandate period. The vague formulation that was ultimately adopted, as a result of a compromise, stated that judges should turn to the "principles of freedom, justice, equity and peace of Israel's heritage" (rather than to "Jewish law").[26]

Since its enactment in 1980, the Foundations of Law Act has failed to significantly impact Israeli case law. The vagueness of its provisions, coupled with the fact that secular judges still dominate the Israeli judiciary, has meant that, in practice, there has been relatively little use of Jewish law in Israeli case law.[27] However, as Israeli society and its politics have become less secular in recent years, the desire among politicians in the Israeli Parliament to force the courts to turn to Jewish law has intensified. A 2018 amendment to the Foundations of Law Act, initiated by members of parliament belonging to the Likud, as well as Religious-Zionist and Ultra-Orthodox parties, amended the Act by inserting the term "Jewish law" before the vague term "Israel's heritage." Thus, the amended Act now calls on judges to use "the principles of freedom, justice, equity and peace of Jewish law and Israel's heritage" in filling gaps in the law. Notwithstanding this amendment, courts are still reluctant to turn to Jewish law.

The legislators who revised the Foundations of Law Act in 2018 are probably not familiar with the works and ideas of the interwar Jewish scholars that I discussed in this book. Nor do they seem to share a similar ideological outlook. Many of the interwar scholars were secular, Westernized, and firmly opposed to rabbinical involvement in the reform of Jewish law, whereas most contemporary legislators advocating for a greater role for Jewish law in Israeli law today hold significantly more traditional views.

Thus, in both India and Israel, the decline in interest in ancient religious traditions (including law) immediately after independence has been reversed in recent decades. In India and Israel (but also in the Islamic world and the Far East), some modern politicians and

[26] See Nir Kedar, *Law and Identity in Israel: A Century of Debate* (Cambridge: Cambridge University Press, 2019), 101–8.

[27] See, e.g., Daniel B. Sinclair, "Jewish Law in the State of Israel," *Jewish Law Annual* 11 (1996): 397, 411–15; Shimon Shetreet and Walter Homolka, *Jewish and Israeli Law: An Introduction* (Berlin: De Gruyter, 2017), 336–7; Ron Harris, "History and Sources," in *The Israeli Legal System: An Introduction*, eds. Christian Walter et al. (Baden-Baden: Nomos, 2019), 15, 24.

intellectuals claim, as part of a more general rejection of Western liberal values, that there is an inherent tension between the institutions, norms, and values of the West and local religious traditions. Interest in non-Western traditions has therefore morphed and reappeared in the early twentieth century in a new, more nationalist guise. In both India and Israel, nationalist parties such as the BJP and Likud are making political use of ancient traditions in a bid to move away from the secular and modernist legacy of the early post-independence period.[28] For example, in India, the commitment of Hindu nationalists to democracy (in the sense of majoritarian rule), and even claims that India is "the mother of democracy," are now accompanied by authoritarian impulses.[29] In Israel, in recent decades, alongside the still unsuccessful attempt to compel the courts to make greater use of Jewish law, we have witnessed the rise of new forms of illiberal Jewish fundamentalism among the Religious Zionist section of Israeli society. Some of the thinkers and politicians associated with these new forms of fundamentalism reject Western democracy and its liberal values in the name of what they (falsely) claim is Judaism.[30]

However, Hindu and Jewish traditions are not uniform and homogenous in the way that modern political ideologies often are. Ancient normative systems that have existed for thousands of years are deep, rich, and multi-vocal. They can be used to further anti-democratic and anti-liberal values and practices: to mark insiders and outsiders, friends and enemies of the nation, and to create divisive social hierarchies within national communities. One can also find in

[28] See, generally, Michael Walzer, *The Paradox of Liberation: Secular Revolutions and Religious Counterrevolutions* (New Haven, CT: Yale University Press, 2015); Sultan Tepe, Keith Simonds, and Michael C. Dirksen, "The Emergence of Religious Populism? Insights from Israel, India, and Turkey," *Populism* 5 (2022): 1.

[29] See, e.g., Suhasini Haidar, "India Is Indeed the Mother of Democracy, Says PM Modi Citing Mahabharata and Vedas," *The Hindu*, March 29, 2023, www.thehindu.com/news/national/india-mother-of-democracy-home-to-idea-of-elected-leaders-much-before-rest-of-world-pm-modi/article66675267.ece; Pratap Bhanu Mehta, "Hindu Nationalism: From Ethnic Identity to Authoritarian Repression," *Studies in Indian Politics* 10 (2022): 31, 43–5.

[30] See, e.g., Avi Ma'oz, "Kol ha-Dorot lo Halmu 'al ha-Demokratyah ha-Yehidah ba-Mizrah ha-Tikhon," *Kipa Website*, April 21, 2021; Hagi Ben Artzi, "Mi she-Rotseh Demokratyah she-Yisa' Le-ARHAV," *Srugim Website*, February 17, 2023. See also "Ze Ma'avak 'al Nishmat ha-Yahadut, Lo Rak 'al Nishmat ha-Medinah," *Musaf Calcalist*, March 23, 2023.

them universal values and humanistic messages that resonate with modern democracy and modern liberal ideas.[31]

Looking back at the works of the early twentieth-century legal scholars discussed in this book may provide a more nuanced perspective on religious legal traditions than the one currently offered by contemporary politicians and intellectuals in India and Israel who advocate authoritarian and illiberal policies. The particularism of the Indian and Jewish scholars of the early twentieth century coexisted side by side with universalist tendencies. While they were keen to study their ancient systems, this was not to highlight their difference from Western legal systems but to emphasize their compatibility with Western democratic and liberal notions. Nationalist particularism led, in the case of the early twentieth-century Indian and Jewish scholars, to a desire to embrace humanism and universalism. The scholars discussed in this book sought to reconcile modernity and tradition, Western and non-Western norms and values, depicting in their works religious legal systems not as the binary opposites of Western law and values but as its twins. Indeed, sometimes they even argued that the very origins of modern Western law and its institutions and values were to be found in ancient Hindu and Jewish law. Their ideas are, therefore, important not merely as matters of historical interest. They are vital to understanding, and influencing, debates unfolding today over the role of democratic and liberal norms, institutions, and values in India, Israel, and many other parts of the world.

[31] See, e.g., Stuart Gray, "History, the Hindu Right, and Subversion of Brahmanical-Hindu Political Thought," in *The Oxford Handbook of Comparative Political Theory*, eds. Leigh K. Jenco, Murad Idris, and Megan C. Thomas (New York: Oxford University Press, 2020), 240; Leonard J. Greenspoon, ed., *Is Judaism Democratic? Reflections from Theory and Practice Throughout the Ages* (West Lafayette, IN: Purdue University Press, 2018); James Loeffler, "A Tradition in Crisis: Human Rights and Jewish Politics Reconsidered," *Journal of the Council for Research on Religion* 6 (2025): 1. See, generally, Pauline Kollontai and Friedrich Lohmann, eds., *On the Significance of Religion for Human Rights* (London: Routledge, 2023).

# Bibliography

This bibliography includes the primary and secondary sources used in writing this book (excluding most newspaper articles and some encyclopaedia entries).

## Archives

Archive of the Association of Latvian and Estonian Jews in Israel, Shfayim
Central Zionist Archives, Jerusalem
Israel State Archives, Jerusalem
The National Archives, London
National Library of Israel
Pinchas Lavon Institute for Labour Movement Research, Tel Aviv
Tel Aviv University Archive

## Databases

The British Newspapers Archive
HeinOnline
Hiteshranjan Sanyal Memorial Archive
Ideas of India Database
Internet Archive
The National Library of Israel: Historical Jewish Press
The National Library of Israel: Jrayed Arabic Newspapers and Journals Collection

## Periodicals Not Available in Listed Databases

*He-'Avar*
*Avukah: Bit'on Agudat ha-Studentim leyad Beyt ha-Sefer ha-Gavohah le-Mishpat vele-Kalkalah Tel Aviv*
*Likud*
*Ha-Mishpat*
*Ha-Mishpat ha-'Ivri*
*Ha-Praklit*
*Shaharit: 'Iton Mukdash le-'Inyeney ha-Tse'irim bi-Tfutsot ha-Golah*
*Times of India*

## Government, University, and Other Official Publications

Benares Hindu University. *Calendar 1922–1925*. Benares: Benares Hindu University, n.d.
Calcutta University Commission 1917–1919. *Report*. 13 vols. Calcutta: Superintendent of Government Printing, 1919–20.
*Census of India 1911*. 23 vols. Calcutta: Superintendent of Government Printing India, 1911–13.
*Census of Palestine 1931*. 2 vols. Alexandria: Whitehead and Morris, 1933.
Council of Legal Studies-Jerusalem. *Provisional Program of Studies and Examination Regulations, 1922*. N.p.: Ha-Solel, n.d.
Government of Palestine. *Report on Palestine Administration, July 1920–December* 1921. London: HMSO, 1922.
Indian Universities Commission. *Report of the Indian Universities Commission, 1902*. Simla: Government Central Printing Office, 1902.
Indian Universities Commission. *University of Bombay: Part III: Written Statements*. Office of the Superintendent of Government Printing, 1902.
Indian Universities Commission. *University of Calcutta: Part II: Written Statements Presented by Witnesses*. Calcutta: Office of the Superintendent of Government Printing, 1902.
*Mo'etset ha-'Am: Yeshivot 1–4 ...: Protokol ha-Diyunim*. Tel Aviv: n.p., 1949.
United Nations Special Committee on Palestine. *Report to the General Assembly*. New York: n.p., 1947.
University of Calcutta. *The Calendar 1917*. Calcutta: Calcutta University, 1917.
University of Calcutta. *The Calendar 1922*. Calcutta: Calcutta University, 1922.
University of Calcutta. *University of Calcutta Convocation Addresses*, Vol. 5: *1915–23*. Calcutta: University of Calcutta Press, 1925.
University of Calcutta. *Regulations*. Calcutta: Calcutta University, 1927.

University of Calcutta. *The Calendar 1931*. Calcutta: Calcutta University, 1931.
University of Calcutta. *University of Calcutta Convocation Addresses*, Vol. 6: *1924–34*. Calcutta: University of Calcutta Press, 1938.
University Education Commission. *The Report of the University Education Commission (December 1948–August 1949)*. Reprint ed. Simla: Government of India Press, 1962.
The University of Leeds. *First Report 1903–4*. Leeds: McCorquodale, 1905.

## Printed Primary Sources

'Abd al-Hadi, Husni. "Muqayasat qawanin al-umam." *Al-Huquq* 1 (1924): 227.
Abdul Majid, Syed H. R. "Moslem International Law." *Law Quarterly Review* 28 (1912): 89.
Abdur Rahim. "Historical Sketch of Mohammedan Jurisprudence." *Columbia Law Review* 7 (1907): 101.
Abdur Rahim. *The Principles of Muhammadan Jurisprudence: According to the Hanafi, Maliki, Shafi'i and Hanbali Schools*. London: Luzac, 1911.
A. B.-S. [probably Anantaprasad Banerji-Sastri]. "Reviews and Notes of Books." *Journal of the Bihar and Orissa Research Society* 14 (1928): 450.
Abu al-'Afiyah, Darwish. "Al-'Awamil al-iqtisadiyyah wal-ijtima'iyyah min huduth al-jara'im." *Al-Huquq* 1 (1924): 484.
Acharyya, B. K. "Scientific Study of Law." *Calcutta Law Journal* 27 (1918): 29n.
Agarwal, Shriman Narayan. *Gandhian Constitution for Free India*. Allahabad: Kitabistan, 1946.
Agaska, B. R. and V. N. Vedak. *Summary Lecture Notes on Jurisprudence; Being a Student's Personal Book of Notes Covering the Matter Generally Required for the Paper on General Jurisprudence as Set at the First LL.B. Examination in Bombay*. Bombay: Vinaya Printing Press, 1917.
Aiyangar, K. V. Rangaswami. *Considerations on Some Aspects of Ancient Indian Polity*. Madras: S. P. C. K. Press, 1916.
Aiyangar, K. V. Rangaswami. "The Evolution of Ancient Indian Polities." In *Sir Asutosh Memorial Volume*, edited by J. N. Samaddar, 164. Patna: J. N. Samaddar, 1928.
Aiyer, Sivaswami. *Indian Constitutional Problems*. Bombay: Taraporevala, 1928.
Aiyer, P. S. Sivaswamy. *Evolution of Hindu Moral Ideals*. Calcutta: Calcutta University, 1935.
Ali, Ameer. *The Personal Law of the Mahommedans*. London: W. H. Allen, 1880.
Ali, Ameer. *The Law Relating to Gifts, Trusts and Testamentary Dispositions among the Mahommedans*. Calcutta: Thacker, Spink and Co., 1885.

Ali, Ameer. *Student's Handbook of Mahommedan Law*. 4th ed. Calcutta: Thacker, Spink and Co., 1903.
Ali, Hamid. *Custom and Law in Anglo-Muslim Jurisprudence*. Calcutta: Thacker, Spink and Co., 1938.
Allen, Carleton Kemp. *Law in the Making*. Oxford: Clarendon Press, 1927.
Altekar, A. S. *The Position of Women in Hindu Civilization from Prehistoric Times to the Present Day*. Benares: Culture Publication House, 1938.
Altekar, A. S. "A Bird's-Eye View of the Hindu Polity: What It Teaches." *Proceedings of the Indian History Congress* 10 (1947): 56.
Altekar, A. S. *State and Government in Ancient India: From Earliest Times to c. 1200 A.D.* Banaras: Motilal Banarsidass, 1949.
Amos, Sheldon. *A Primer of the English Constitution and Government*. London: Longmans, 1877.
Armour, W. S. "Customs of Warfare in Ancient India." *Transactions of the Grotius Society* 8 (1922): 71.
Assaf, Simha. *Ha-'Onshin aharey Hatimat ha-Talmud: Homer le-Toldot ha-Mishpat ha-'Ivri*. Jerusalem: n.p., 1921/22.
Assaf, Simha. *Batey ha-Din ve-Sidrehem aharey Hatimat ha-Talmud: Homer le-Toldot ha-Mishpat ha-'Ivri*. Jerusalem: Dfus ha-Po'alim, 1923/24.
Assaf, Simha. "Minuy Nashim le-Apotropsut." *Ha-Mishpat ha-'Ivri* 2 (1926/27): 75.
Austin, John. *Lectures on Jurisprudence or the Philosophy of Positive Law*. 3rd ed. London: John Murray, 1869.
Austin, John. *The Province of Jurisprudence Determined, and the Uses of the Study of Jurisprudence*. Indianapolis, IN: Hackett, 1998.
"A Vakil." *Principles of Jurisprudence: For the Use of Law Students*. 7th ed. Calcutta: Das Gupta & Co., 1926.
Ayyar, A. S. Panchapakesa. "The Contribution of Hindu Law to World Jurisprudence." Reprint from the *Madras Law Journal*, Golden Jubilee Number, 1941.
Bailey, Albert, and Charles Foster Kent. *History of the Hebrew Commonwealth*. New York: Scribner, 1920.
Balogh, Elemér. *Les sources du droit positif: Fascicule 1, Orient (Égypte, Palestine, Chine, Japon)*. Berlin: Hermann Sack, 1929.
Bandyopadhyay, Pramathanath. *International Law and Custom in Ancient India*. Calcutta: University of Calcutta Press, 1920.
Bandyopadhaya, Narayan Chandra. *Development of Hindu Polity and Political Theories*. Calcutta: Kerr, 1927.
Bandyopadhyaya, Narayan Chandra. *Kautilya: Or an Exposition of His Social Ideal and Political Theory*. Calcutta: Chuckervertty, 1927.
Banerjea, Pramathanath. *Public Administration in Ancient India*. London: Macmillan, 1916.
Banerjee, Gooroodass. *The Hindu Law of Marriage and Stridhan*. Calcutta: Thacker, Spink and Co., 1879.

Banerjee, Pramathanath, Pratulchandra Gupta, Atindranath Bose et al., eds., *Hundred Years of the University of Calcutta: A History of the University Issued in Commemoration of the Centenary Celebration.* Calcutta: University of Calcutta, 1957.

Banerjee, Sitaram. "Philosophy and Law." *Calcutta Law Journal* 26 (1917): 5n.

Banerjee, Sitaram. "Principles of Criminology." *Calcutta Law Journal* 31 (1920): 1n.

Banerji, Satish Chandra. "The Woman in Hindu Law." *Allahabad Law Journal* 11 (1913): 25.

Barak, Aharon, ed. *Mavo le-Torat ha-Mishpat 'alpi Hartsa'otav shel Professor G. Tedeschi*, Jerusalem: Mif'al ha-Shikhpul, 1958.

Barkat Ali, M. *A Handbook of Jurisprudence.* Lahore: The Observer Press, 1919.

Barnett, Lionel D. *Antiquities of India.* London: Warner, 1913.

Basu, Karunamay. *The Modern Theories of Jurisprudence*, Vol. 1. Calcutta: University of Calcutta, 1925.

Basu, Karunamay. *The Modern Theories of Jurisprudence*, Vol. 2: *The Plea for a Synthetic Philosophy of Law.* Calcutta: University of Calcutta, 1929.

Ben-Amittay, Jacob. *Torat ha-Medinah ha-Klalit.* Tel Aviv: Tkufah, 1935.

Ben-Shamai, Meir Hillel, ed. *Sefer ha-Adam veha-Medinah.* Tel Aviv: Neuman, 1947/48.

Bentwich, Norman. *Yerushalayim: 'Ir ha-Shalom.* Jerusalem: Hebrew University Press, 1932.

Bentwich, Norman. "Ha-Tanakh ke-Makor le-Diney ha-Milhamah shel he-'Amim." *Ha-Mishpat ha-'Ivri* 4 (1932/33): 147.

Bentwich, Norman. *The Religious Foundations of Internationalism: A Study in International Relations through the Ages.* London: Allen & Unwin, 1933.

Bentwich, Norman. *Ha-Mishpat ha-Beyn Leumi*, translated by Joseph Nedava. Jerusalem: Aharonson, 1945.

Bentwich, Norman. *My 77 Years: An Account of My Life and Times, 1883–1960.* Philadelphia, PA: Jewish Publication Society of America, 1961.

Bentwich, Norman de Mattos, and Helen Bentwich. *Mandate Memories, 1918–1948.* New York: Schocken, 1965.

Berman, Ya'acov. *Torat ha-Medinah be-Yisrael.* Jerusalem: Mosad ha-Rav Kook, 1944.

Berolzheimer, Fritz. *The World's Legal Philosophies*, translated by Rachel Szold Jastrow. Boston, MA: Boston Book Company, 1912.

Bhagvat, Durga N. *Early Buddhist Jurisprudence.* Poona: Oriental Book Agency, 1939.

Bhandarkar, D. R. *Lectures on the Ancient History of India on the Period from 650 to 325 B.C.* Calcutta: University of Calcutta Press, 1919.

Bhandarkar, D. R. *Some Aspects of Ancient Hindu Polity.* Benares: Benares Hindu University, 1929.

Bhandarkar, D. R. "Reminiscences." In *Professor K. V. Rangaswami Aiyangar Commemoration Volume*, lvi. Madras: G. S. Press, 1940.

Blackstone, William. *Commentaries on the Laws of England*, Vol. 1. Oxford: Clarendon Press, 1765.

Blume, W. W. "Legal Education in China." *China Law Review* 1 (1923): 305.

Bonnard, Robert. "The Doctrine of Duguit on 'Law' and the State." *China Law Review* 4 (1930): 193.

"Book Review." *Law Quarterly Review* 5 (1889): 322.

Breuer, Yitzhak. "Tokhnit le-Hukah ba-Medinah ha-Yehudit." *Yavneh* 3 (1949): 33.

Breuer, Yitzhak. *Nahali'el: Yesodot ha-Hinukh le-Mitsvot ha-Torah*. Jerusalem: Mosad ha-Rav Kook, 1982.

Breuer, Isaac. "The Philosophical Foundations of Jewish and of Modern Law." Reprinted in *Jewish Legal Theories: Writings on State, Religion, and Morality*, edited by Leora Batnitzky and Yonatan Brafman, 125. Waltham, MA: Brandeis University Press, 2018.

Bright, Jagat S., ed. *Important Speeches of Jawaharlal Nehru*. 2nd ed. Lahore: IPW, 1946.

Broida, Efraim. "Rashey Prakim 'al Hodu ve-Yisra'el." *Molad* 2(7) (October 1948): 10.

Broom, Herbert. *A Selection of Legal Maxims*. London: A. Maxwell & Son, 1845.

Chakravarti, Sures Chandra. *Studies in Jurisprudence and International Law*. Calcutta: Butterworth, 1924.

Chan, Hugh. "Modern Legal Education in China." *China Law Review* 9 (1936): 142.

Chan-Toon. *The Nature and Value of Jurisprudence, Roman Law and International Law*. London: W. Clowes & Sons, 1888.

Chan-Toon. *The Nature and Value of Jurisprudence*. 2nd enlarged ed. London: Reeves and Turner, 1889.

Chan-Toon. *The Principles of Buddhist Law: Also Containing a Translation of Important Portions of The Manu Thara Shwe Myin, with Notes*. Rangoon: Myles Standish, 1894.

Chatterjee, Atul. "Roman Law and Hindu Law: A Comparative Study." *Calcutta University Law College Magazine* 10 (1939): 37.

Chaudhury, Kiron Kumar Roy. "Hindoo Penal Law." *Calcutta University Law College Magazine* 12 (1942): 61.

Chen, Shih-Tsai. "The Equality of States in Ancient China." *American Journal of International Law* 35 (1941): 641.

Chiu, Henry P. "The Effect of Adoption in Roman, Hindu and Chinese Law." *China Law Review* 4 (1930): 277.

Chiu, Henry P. "The Origin and Purpose of Adoption." *China Law Review* 4 (1930): 79.

Chiu, Henry P. "Requisites of Adoption in Roman, Hindu and Chinese Law." *China Law Review* 4 (1930): 133.

Cohn, Haim. "De'agah le-Yom Mahar." *Ha-Praklit* 3 (1946): 38.

Das Gupta, Ramaprasad. *Crime and Punishment in Ancient India*. Calcutta: Book Company, 1930.

Davids, T. W. Rhys. *Buddhist India*. New York: Putnam, 1903.

Davids, T. W. Rhys, and Hermann Oldenberg, trans. *The Sacred Books of the East*, Vol. 13: *Vinaya Texts – Part 1*. Oxford: Clarendon Press, 1881.

Daykan, Paltiel. *Ha-Matsav ha-Mishpati shel ha-Ishah be-Yisrael*. Tel Aviv: Tversky, 1949/50.

Daykan, Paltiel. *Torat ha-Mishpat: Taktsir ha-Hartsa'ot she-Nikre'u be-Veit ha-Sefer ha-Gavohah le-Mishpat vele-Kalkalah be-Tel Aviv ba-Shanim 1942/3–1949/50*. Tel Aviv: Beyt ha-Sefer ha-Gavohah le-Mishpat vele-Kalkalah, 1949/50.

*See also* Dikshtein, Paltiel.

Dikshitar, V. R. Ramachandra. *Hindu Administrative Institutions*. Madras: University of Madras, 1929.

Dikshitar, V. R. Ramachandra. "The Social Order in Old India." *The Aryan Path* (April 1939): 182.

Dikshtein, Paltiel. *Mishpat ha-Shalom Ha-'Ivri: She'elotav le-Halakhah ule-Ma'aseh*. Tel Aviv: Hotsa'at Mishpat ha-Shalom Ha-'Ivri ha-'Elyon, 1924/25.

Dikshtein, Paltiel. "Mehir Tsedek ve-Ona'ah." *Ha-Mishpat Ha-'Ivri* 1 (1925/26): 15.

Dikshtein, Paltiel. "Ha-Universitah veha-Mishpat." *Ha-'Olam*, August 18, 1931.

Dikshtein, Paltiel. "Birkat Yovel: Shimshon Rosenbaum." *Ha-Mishpat ha-'Ivri* 4 (1932/33): 205.

Dikshtein, Paltiel. "Mishpat u-Medinah be-Yisrael." Pts. 1, 2, and 3. *Ha-Tekufah* 28 (1935): 363; 29 (1936): 245; 34–5 (1950): 664.

Dikshtein, Paltiel. "Shimshon Rosenbaum." *Ha-Mishpat Ha-'Ivri* 5 (1936/37): 278.

Dikshtein, Paltiel. "Ariyeh Karlin, ZL." *Ha-Praklit* 14 (1957): 380.

Dikshtein, Paltiel. "Hukey Moshe ve-Hukey Hammurabi." In *Professor Paltiel Daykan (Dikshtein): Mivhar Monografyot, Mehkarim u- Ma'amarim*, edited by Yitzhak Orren, 150. Tel Aviv: Yavneh, 1975.

*See also* Daykan, Paltiel.

"Al-Din wa-hurriyyat al-raay." *Al-Huquq* 2(8) (1925): 66.

Donnedieu de Vabres, Henri. *Introduction à l'étude du droit pénal international*. Paris: Sirey, 1922.

"Dr. Priya Nath Sen." *Calcutta Law Journal* 10 (1909): 37n.

Dubey, Thakur Prasad. "Hindu Jurisprudence: Its Beauties and Comparative Greatness." *Allahabad Law Journal* 42 (1944): 11.

Duguit, Léon. *Leçons de droit public général faites à la Faculté de droit de l'Université égyptienne*. Paris: E. de Boccard, 1926.
"Durar al-hukkam fi al-suhuf waal-majalat." *Al-Huquq* 2(7) (1925): 150.
Edersheim, E. W. *The Law and Polity of the Jews*. London: Religious Tract Society, 1883.
Eisenstadt, Samuel. "Di Arbayter un di Arbayter-Frage in der Alter Yidisher Geshikhte." *Di Tsukunft* 8 (1908): 762.
Eisenstadt, Samuel. "Le-Korot ha-Mishpat ha-'Ivri (Skirah Klalit)." *He-'Atid: Me'asef Sifruti Mada'i* 3 (1909–11): 194.
Eisenstadt, Samuel. "Beyt ha-Midrash ha-'Ivri." *Shaharit* 1 (1913): 69.
Eisenstadt, Samuel. "Be-Sifruteynu ha-Mishpatit." *Ha-Schiloah* 31 (1914): 181.
Eisenstadt, Samuel. "Kadmoniyot ha-Mishpat ha-Yisre'eli." Pts. 1 and 2. *Ha-'Am* (March 9, 1917): 12; (May 18, 1917), 10.
Eisenstadt, Samuel. "Le-Heker Mishpatenu ha-Pumbi." *Ha-Mishpat ha-'Ivri: Riv'on Mada'i* (1918): 8.
Eisenstadt Samuel. *Di Nevi'im: Zeyer tsayt un Zeyere Gezelshaftlekhe Ideyen*. Vilna: Klachkin, 1926.
Eisenstadt, Samuel. "'Al Hora'at ha-Mishpat ha-'Ivri be-Veyt ha-Sefer shel Memshelet Erets Yisrael." *Ha-Mishpat* 2 (1927): 209.
Eisenstadt, Samuel. *Ha-Institutsyot*. Jerusalem: Ha-Mishpat, 1929.
Eisenstadt, Samuel. *'Ein Mishpat: Sefer Shimush Bibliyografi le-Sifrut ha-Mishpat ha-'Ivri*. Jerusalem: Ha-Mishpat, 1931.
Eisenstadt, Samuel. "Ha-Po'el ha-'Ivri bi-Tkufat ha-Mishnah." *Ha-'Olam*, September 2, 1937, 1002.
Eisenstadt, Samuel. "Likrat ha-'Atsma'ut ha-Mishpatit." *Ha-'Olam*, April 14, 1938, 5.
Eisenstadt, Samuel. *Prakim be-Toldot Tnu'at ha-Po'alim ha-Yehudit*. 2 vols. Merhavyah: Sifriyat Po'alim, 1944.
Eisenstadt, Samuel. "Early History and Principles of Jewish Family Law." *Juridical Review* 60(1) (1948): 48.
Eisenstadt, Samuel. "Medinah u-Mishpat." *Ha-Praklit* 5 (1948): 113.
Eisenstadt, Samuel. *Ha-Mishpat ha-Roma'i: Toldotav ve-Torato*. Tel Aviv: Ha-Mishpat, 1953.
Eisenstadt, Samuel. *Ta'arikhim Biyografim le-Yovel ha-70 shel ha-Professor Shmuel Aizenshtadt, 20 March 1956*. Tel Aviv: n.p., 1956.
Eisenstadt, Samuel. *Rishmey Bikur be-Tsekhoslovakyah*. Tel Aviv: Likud, 1957.
Eisenstadt, Samuel. *Sefer Roza: Divrey Zikaron le-Re'ayah, le-Em, vele-Haverah*. Tel Aviv: n.p., 1959.
Eisenstadt, Samuel. *Hayehah ha-Ruhaniyim shel Roza, li-Melot Arba' Shanim le-Motah*. Tel Aviv: n.p., 1961.
Eisenstadt, Samuel. "Paralleleinblicke in das jüdische und römische Familien- und Erbrecht." *Klio* 40 (1962): 244.

Eisenstadt, Samuel. *Ha-Halutz ba-Ma'arakhah: Le-Zekher ha-Av veha-Moreh*. Tel Aviv: Likud, 1965.

Eisenstadt, Samuel. "'Al Hora'at ha-Mishpat ha-'Ivri be-Veyt ha-Sefer le-Mishpat shel Memshelet Eretz Yisrael." In *Tsiyon be-Mishpat: 'Iyunim ba-Mishpat ha-'Ivri veha-Roma'i*, 120. Tel Aviv: Ha-Mishpat, 1967.

Eisenstadt Samuel. "Beyn ha-Rashuyot: Ra'ayonot be-Diney Mishpahah be-Yisrael." In *Tsiyon be-Mishpat: 'Iyunim ba-Mishpat ha-'Ivri veha-Roma'i*, 213. Tel Aviv: Ha-Mishpat, 1967.

Eisenstadt, Samuel. "Ha-Mishpat ha-'Ivri veha-Roma'i." In *Tsiyon be-Mishpat: 'Iyunim ba-Mishpat ha-'Ivri veha-Roma'i*, 260. Tel Aviv: Ha-Mishpat, 1967.

Eisenstadt, Samuel. "He'arot le-Hatsa'at Hok Shivuy Zkhuyot ha-Ishah." In *Tsiyon be-Mishpat: 'Iyunim ba-Mishpat ha-'Ivri veha-Roma'i*, 184. Tel Aviv: Ha-Mishpat, 1967.

Eisenstadt, Samuel. "He'arot le-Sefer ha-Institutsyot shel Yustinyanus Keysar." In *Tsiyon be-Mishpat: 'Iyunim ba-Mishpat ha-'Ivri veha-Roma'i*, 71. Tel Aviv: Ha-Mishpat, 1967.

Eisenstadt, Samuel. "Hevrah Mada'it le-Hakirat ha-Mishpat ha-'Ivri: Mikhtav Galuy." In *Tsiyon be-Mishpat: 'Iyunim ba-Mishpat ha-'Ivri veha-Roma'i*, 31. Tel Aviv: Ha-Mishpat, 1967.

Eisenstadt, Samuel. "Kadmoniyot ha-Mishpat ha-'Ivri." In *Tsiyon be-Mishpat: 'Iyunim ba-Mishpat ha-'Ivri veha-Roma'i*, 291. Tel Aviv: Ha-Mishpat, 1967.

Eisenstadt, Samuel. "Kavey Yesod be-Hitpathutam shel Diney-ha-Mishpahah ha-'Ivrit ha-Kdumim." In *Tsiyon be-Mishpat: 'Iyunim ba-Mishpat ha-'Ivri veha-Roma'i*, 231. Tel Aviv: Ha-Mishpat, 1967.

Eisenstadt, Samuel. "Le-Hitpathuto shel ha-Klal be-Sifrutenu ha-Mishpatit." In *Tsiyon be-Mishpat: 'Iyunim ba-Mishpat ha-'Ivri veha-Roma'i*, 156. Tel Aviv: Ha-Mishpat, 1967.

Eisenstadt, Samuel. "Le-Matsavah ha-Mishpati shel ha-Ishah be-Ugarit." In *Tsiyon be-Mishpat: 'Iyunim ba-Mishpat ha-'Ivri veha-Roma'i*, 247. Tel Aviv: Ha-Mishpat, 1967.

Eisenstadt, Samuel. "Munahey ha-Mishpat ha-'Ivriyim, Kinusam u-Mehkaram." In *Tsiyon be-Mishpat: 'Iyunim ba-Mishpat ha-'Ivri veha-Roma'i*, 303. Tel Aviv: Ha-Mishpat, 1967.

Eisenstadt, Samuel. "Musag ha-Ishiyut ha-Mishpatit ba-Mishpatim ha-'Ivri veha-Roma'i." In *Tsiyon be-Mishpat: 'Iyunim ba-Mishpat ha-'Ivri veha-Roma'i*, 201. Tel Aviv: Ha-Mishpat, 1967.

Eisenstadt, Samuel. "Reshit Yihusav ha-Beyn Le'umim shel ha-'Am ha-Yisra'eli." In *Tsiyon be-Mishpat: 'Iyunim ba-Mishpat ha-'Ivri veha-Roma'i*, 97. Tel Aviv: Ha-Mishpat, 1967.

Eisenstadt, Samuel. *Sfatenu ha-'Ivrit ha-Hayah*. Tel Aviv: Tkumah, 1967.

Eisenstadt, Samuel. "Shiyarey ha-Poligamyah ba-Mishpat ha-'Ivri." In *Tsiyon be-Mishpat: 'Iyunim ba-Mishpat ha-'Ivri veha-Roma'i*, 150. Tel Aviv: Ha-Mishpat, 1967.

Eisenstadt, Samuel. "Sifruto shel ha-Mishpat ha-'Ivri." In *Tsiyon be-Mishpat: 'Iyunim ba-Mishpat ha-'Ivri veha-Roma'i*, 130. Tel Aviv: Ha-Mishpat, 1967.

Eisenstadt, Samuel. *Tsiyon be-Mishpat: 'Iyunim ba-Mishpat ha-'Ivri veha-Roma'i*. Tel Aviv: Ha-Mishpat, 1967.

Eisenstadt, Samuel. "Le-Toldot ha-Tsiburiyut veha-Tarbut ha-'Ivrit be-Rusyah bi-T'hilat ha-Me'ah ha-'Esrim." *He-'Avar* 16 (1968): 1.

Eisenstadt, Samuel. "Sodo shel Shim'on Dimanshtein." *He-'Avar* 15 (1968): 240.

Eisenstadt, Samuel. *'Al 'Alumim she-Nikpedu*. Jerusalem: n.p., 1969/70.

Eisenstadt, Samuel. *Pionerishe Geshtaltn*. Tel Aviv: Oyfkum, 1970.

Eisenstadt, Samuel, ed., *Sarah Patt: Lebn un Shafn*. Tel Aviv: Oyfkum, 1970.

Eisenstadt, Samuel. *The Prophets: Their Times and Their Social Ideas*, translated by Max Rosenfeld. New York: YKUF, 1971.

Eisenstadt, S. I. "Xarakter i istoricheskaia evoliutsiia evreiskogo prava." *Evreiski Student* 1(5) (1923): 11.

Escarra, Jean. *Chinese Law and Comparative Jurisprudence*. Tientsin: La Libraire Française, 1926.

Escarra, Jean. *Le droit chinois*. Pékin: H. Vetch, 1936.

Falk, Z. "Shilton ha-Mishpat." *'Alon Agudat ha-Talmidim ha-'Ivriyim be-Veyt ha-Sefer le-Mishpatim bi-Yerushalayim*. June 1946: 3.

Federbusch, Simon. *Ha-Musar veha-Mishpat be-Yisrael*. Jerusalem: Mosad ha-Rav Kook, 1947.

Federbusch, Simon. *Mishpat ha-Melukhah be-Yisrael*. Jerusalem: Mosad ha-Rav Kook, 1952.

Feinberg, Nathan. *Pirkey Hayim ve-Zikhronot*. Jerusalem: Mabat, 1985.

Feldman, S. B. *Hok ha-'Avodah ha-Kadum ba-'Olam*. Jerusalem: Ha-Va'adah le-Torah ve-Sifrut shel ha-Mo'atsah le-Ma'an ha-Shabat, 1947/48.

Findling, Moshe. *T'hukat ha-'Avodah*. Jerusalem: Schreiber, 1944/45.

Freeman, Edward A. *The Growth of the English Constitution from the Earliest Times*. London: Macmillan, 1872.

Freimann, Avraham Hayim. *Seder Kidushin ve-Nisu'in Ahare Hatimat ha-Talmud: Mehkar Histori-Dogmati be-Dine Yisra'el*. Jerusalem: Mosad ha-Rav Kook, 1944/45.

Frero, Gulilemo. "Al-Sharq waal-gharb." *Al-Huquq* 2(8) (1925): 47.

Friedlaender, Israel. "The Political Ideal of the Prophets." In *Past and Present: A Collection of Jewish Essays*, 1. Cincinnati, OH: Ark, 1919.

Friedlaender, Israel. "Were Our Ancestors Capable of Self-Government?" In *Past and Present: A Collection of Jewish Essays*, 40. Cincinnati, OH: Ark, 1919.

Friedrich, Carl J. "The Israeli Covenant." *Jewish Frontier* (January 1949): 24.

Frumkin, Gad. *Derekh Shofet bi-Yerushalayim*. Tel Aviv: Dvir, 1954.

Fyzee, Asaf A. A. *Outlines of Muhammadan Law*. Calcutta: Oxford University Press, 1949.

Gandhi, M. K. *The Law and the Lawyers*, edited by S. B. Kher. Ahmedabad: Navajivan, 1981.
Gandz, Salomon, ed. *Monumenta Talmudica*. Vol. 2: *Recht*. Vienna: Orion, 1914.
Gankin, Baruch. *Mishpat ha-Yerushah shel Brit ha-Mo'etsot*. Jerusalem: Dfus Eretz Yisrael, n.d.
Gankin, Baruch. *Shemhazai: Sipur me-Hayey ha-Externim be-Russia mi-Kets ha-Me'ah She'avrah*. Jerusalem: Dfus Raphael Haim ha-Cohen, 1944/45.
Gankin, B. *Torat ha-Mishpat*. 2 vols. Jerusalem: n.p., 1949.
Gershoni, Yehudah. *Sefer Mishpat ha-Melukhah: 'al Hilkhot Melakhim leha-Rambam, Z"L*. New York: n.p., 1949/50.
Ghorpure, J. R. *Hindu Law*. Bombay: Maruti Babaji, 1905.
Ghose, Jogendra Chunder. *The Principles of Hindu Law*, Vol. 1. 3rd ed. Calcutta: S. C. Auddy & Co, 1917.
Ghose, Jogendra Chunder. *The Principles of Hindu Law*, Vol. 2. 1st ed. Calcutta: S. B. Chatterjee & Sons, 1917.
Ghose, Nagendranath. *Comparative Administrative Law*. Calcutta: Butterworth, 1919.
Ghoshal, U. *A History of Hindu Political Theories*. London: H. Milford, 1923.
Ghoshal, U. N. *Contributions to the History of the Hindu Revenue System*. Calcutta: University of Calcutta Press, 1929.
Ghoshal, U. N. *The Beginnings of Indian Historiography and Other Essays*. Calcutta: Ramesh Ghoshal, 1944.
Ghoshal, U. N. *A History of Hindu Public Life*. Calcutta: Ramesh Ghoshal, 1945.
Ghoshal, U. N. "The Genius of Hindu Polity." In *Studies in Indian History and Culture*, 195. 2nd rev. ed. Calcutta: Orient Longmans, 1965.
Ghoshal, Upendranath. "The Brahminical Conception of the Science of Politics." In *Sir Asutosh Mookerjee Silver Jubilee Volumes*, Vol. 3.1, 53. Calcutta: Calcutta University Press, 1922.
Ghoshal, Upendra Nath. *A History of Indian Political Ideas: The Ancient Period and the Period of Transition to the Middle Ages*. Bombay: Oxford University Press, 1959.
Goadby, Frederic M. *Introduction to the Study of Law: A Handbook for the Use of Egyptian Law Students*. London: Butterworth, 1910.
Goadby, Frederic M. *Introduction to the Study of Law: A Handbook for the Use of Law Students in Egypt and Palestine*. 3rd ed. London: Butterworth, 1921.
Goadby, Frederic M. "Al-Qanun, al-haq, al-'adalah." *Al-Huquq* 3 (1926): 8.
Goadby, Frederic, M. *Al-Qanun al-duwali wa-al-millali al-khass fi filastin wa-al-sharq al-adna*. Jerusalem: Matba'at bayt al-maqdas, 1931.
Grady, Standish Grove. *A Manual of Hindu Law for the Use of Students and Practitioners*. London: Wildy and Sons, 1871.

Grajewsky, Arye L. "Ha-Medinah veha-Knesiyah, ha-Mishpat veha-Dat." In *Sugyot ba-Mishpat uva-Historyah*, edited by Yosef Kariv, 60. Jerusalem: Jerusalem Post Press, 1971/72.
Gulak, Asher. "Ha-Probleymot ha-Mamlakhtiyot be-Divrey Yemey 'Amenu." *Ha-'Am*, December 30, 1916, 20; January 13, 1917, 14; February 3, 1917, 15; February 10, 1917, 13.
Gulak, Asher. *Yesodey ha-Mishpat ha-'Ivri.* 4 vols. Berlin: Dvir, 1922.
Gulak, Asher. "Hashva'ah Klalit beyn Ru'ah Diney Mamonot ha-'Ivriyim ve-Ru'ah Diney Mamonot ha-Roma'im." *Mad'ey ha-Yahadut* 1 (1925/26): 45.
Gulak, Asher. *Le-Heker Toldot ha-Mishpat ha-'Ivri bi-Tekufat ha-Talmud.* Jerusalem: Ha-Sefer, 1928/29.
Gulak, Asher. *Das Urkundenwesen im Talmud im Lichte der griechisch-aegyptischen Papyri und des griechischen und roemischen Rechts.* Jerusalem: R. Mass, 1935.
Gupta, Atul Chandra. "The Spirit of Hindu Law." *Calcutta Law Journal* 42 (1925): 43n.
Hakkı, Babanzade İsmail. "Al-Hakimiyyah al-siyasiyyah waal-ahkam al-islamiyyah." *Al-Huquq* 1 (1924): 540.
Ha-Lishkah ha-Tsiyonit ha-Merkazit. "'Al Ve'idat ha-Universitah." *Ha-'Olam.* January 9, 1920.
Hamilton, Charles, trans. *The Hedaya, or Guide: A Commentary on the Mussulman Laws.* London: T. Bensley, 1791.
*A Hand-Book of Jurisprudence Incorporating Maine's Ancient Law.* Madras: V. Ramaswamy Sastrulu & Sons, 1929.
Hayat, Francis. *Muhadarat fi al-qanun al-tijari.* Jerusalem: Dir al-rum, 1924.
Herzog, Isaac. *The Main Institutions of Jewish Law.* 2 vols. London: Soncino Press, 1936.
Hirschensohn, Haim. *Malki ba-Kodesh: She'elot u-Tshuvot be-Hanhagat ha-Mamlakhah be-Yisrael 'al-pi Darkey ha-Halakhah.* St. Louis, MO: Moineshter, 1918/19.
Ho, S. C. "Book Review: A Constitution of Five Powers (a Lecture). By Dr. Sun Yat-Sen." *China Law Review* 1 (1924): 390.
Holland, Thomas Erskine. *The Elements of Jurisprudence.* 12th ed. New York: Oxford University Press, 1917.
Hopkins, Edward W., trans. *Hindu Polity (The Ordinances of Manu).* London: Trubner, 1884.
Hudson, Manley O. "Address at the Inauguration Exercises." *China Law Review* 3 (1927): 148.
Hung-Chih, Kiang. "The Pragmatic Revolt in Law." *China Law Review* 6 (1933): 93.
"Al-Huquq al-dawliyyah." *Al-Huquq* 1 (1924): 436.
"Hurriyyat al-adyan." *Al-Huquq* 2(1) (1925): 7.
"Hurriyyat al-fikr." *Al-Huquq* 2(5) (1925): 1.
"Hurriyyat al-sahafah." *Al-Huquq* 1 (1924): 664.

Husein, Syed Karamat. *A Treatise on Right and Duty, Their Evolution, Definition, Analysis, and Classification According to Jurisprudence, Being a Portion of the Muhammadan Law of Gifts*. Allahabad: Indian Press, 1899.

Isaacs, Nathan. "The Influence of Judaism on Western Law." In *The Legacy of Israel*, edited by George Adam Smith, Edwyn Bevan, F. C. Burkitt et al., 377. Oxford: Clarendon Press, 1927.

Jayaswal, K. P. "An Introduction to Hindu Polity." *Modern Review* 13 (1913): 535.

Jayaswal, K. P. *Hindu Polity: A Constitutional History of India in Hindu Times*. Calcutta: Butterworth, 1924.

Jayaswal, K. P. *Manu and Yâjñavalkya – A Comparison and a Contrast: A Treatise on the Basic Hindu Law*. Calcutta: Butterworth, 1930.

Jayaswal, K. P. *Hindu Polity: A Constitutional History of India in Hindu Times*. 2nd enlarged ed. Bangalore: Bangalore Printing & Publishing Co., 1943.

Jha, Ganganatha. *Hindu Law in Its Sources*. 2 vols. Allahabad: Indian Press, 1930–33.

Jhering, Rudolf von. *Ha-Ma'avak le-Mishpat*, translated by Baruch Krupnik. Tel Aviv: Mishpat u-Medinah, 1947.

"Al-Jins waal-jarimah." *Al-Huquq* 2(2) (1925): 1.

Jolly, Julius. "Über die alte politische Literatur Indiens und ihre Bearbeiter." *Zeitschrift für vergleichende Rechtswissenschaft* 41 (1925): 305.

Jolly, Julius. *Hindu Law and Custom*, translated by Batakrishna Ghosh. Calcutta: Greater Indian Society, 1928.

Joseph, Bernard. *Zkhuyot ha-Ishah 'al pi Hukey Eretz Yisrael*. Jerusalem: Hit'ahdut Nashim 'Ivriyot, 1929/30.

Kahana, Kalman. "Li-Ve'ayat Ha-Thukah ha-Toratit 'Avur ha-Medinah." *She'arim*, December 11, 1947, 2.

Kane, P. V. *History of Dharmaśāstra*. 5 vols. Poona: Bhandarkar Oriental Research Institute, 1930–62.

Kantrovitch, H. "Ha-Shi'urim le-Mishpat." *Ha-Mishpat ha-'Ivri* 1 (1925/26): 145.

Kantrovitch, H. "The Jerusalem Law Classes." *Journal of the Society of Public Teachers of Law* 1937 (1937): 46.

Kao, William Timothy. "Book Review: The Growth of the Law – by N. B. Cardozo." *China Law Review* 2 (1924): 346.

Kao, William Timothy. "The New Way of Approaching the Law." *China Law Review* 4 (1930): 27.

Keeton, George W. "Legal Opportunities in China." *Hong Kong University Law Journal* 1 (1926–27): 2.

Keeton, George W. *The Elementary Principles of Jurisprudence*. London: A. & C. Black, 1930.

Keith, Arthur Berriedale. "Hindu Constitutional Law." *Journal of Comparative Legislation and International Law* 7 (1925): 265.

Keith, Arthur Berriedale. *A Constitutional History of India 1600–1935*. London: Methuen, 1936.

Khan, Mohamed Kalandar Ally. *A Summary of the Science of Jurisprudence with an Appendix Containing Leading Cases and Examination Questions*. Hyderabad: Premier Steam Press, 1912.

Khuda Bukhsh, S. "The Islamic Conception of Sovereignty." In *Essays: Indian and Islamic*, 25. London: Probsthain, 1912.

Khuda Bukhsh, S. Foreword to *The Orient under the Caliphs* by Alfred von Kremer, xi. Translated by S. Khuda Bukhsh. Calcutta: University of Calcutta Press, 1920.

Kocourek, Albert, and John H. Wigmore, eds. *Evolution of Law: Select Readings on the Origin and Development of Legal Institutions*. 3 vols. Boston, MA: Little, Brown and Co., 1915–18.

Kohler, Josef. *Grundlagen des völkerrechts: Vergangenheit, gegenwart, zukunft*. Stuttgart: Enke, 1918.

Kohler, Josef and Leopold Wenger. *Allgemeine Rechtsgeschichte*, Vol. 1: *Orientalisches Recht und Recht der Griechen und Römer*. Leipzig: Teubner, 1914.

Kohn, Leo. "Observations on the Constitution." *Jewish Frontier*, January 1949, 10.

Kohn, Leo. "The Constitution of Israel." *India Quarterly* 9 (1953): 78.

Kohn, Yehuda Pinchas (Leo). *Hukah le-Yisrael: Hatsa'ah ve-Divrey Hesber*. Ha-Kiryah [Tel Aviv]: Mo'etset ha-Medinah, 1949.

Korngruen, P. *Hukey ha-Mizrah ha-Kadmon: Mehkar Hashva'ah be-Mishpetey Yisrael, Bavel, Ashur ve-Het*. Tel Aviv: Yavneh, 1944.

Lahiri, Sisir Chandra. *Principles of Modern Burmese Buddhist Law*. N.p.: Graduate Friends & Co., 1925.

Laserson, Max. "Power and Justice: Hobbes Versus Job." *Judaism: A Quarterly Journal of Jewish Life and Thought* 2 (1953): 52.

Laserson, Max M. *Ha-Filosofiyah ha-Mishpatit shel ha-Rambam*. Tel Aviv: Beyt ha-Sefer ha-Gavohah le-Mishpat vele-Kalkalah, 1939.

Laserson, Max M. "Hebrew Roots of International Law." *Menorah Journal* 36 (1948): 174.

*See also* Lazerson, Maxime.

Law, B. C. "The Late Professor Dr. Devadatta Ramkrishna Bhandarkar." *Annals of the Bhandarkar Oriental Research Institute* 30 (1949): 373.

Law, Narendra Nath. *Studies in Ancient Hindu Polity: Based on the Arthaśâstra of Kautilya*. London: Longmans, 1914.

Law, Narendra Nath. "The Religious Aspects of Ancient Hindu Polity." *Modern Review* (December 1917): 620.

Law, Narendra Nath. *Inter-State Relations in Ancient India*. London: Luzac, 1920.

Law, Narendra Nath. *Aspects of Ancient Hindu Polity*. Oxford: Clarendon Press, 1921.

Lazerson, Maxime. "Estestvennoe pravo v pamiatnikakh drevne-evreiskoi literatury i zakonodatelstva." *Voprosy Prava* 11 (1912): 108.

Lazerson, Maxime. "La réalité du droit et la politique juridique." In *IIe Annuaire de l'Institut International de Philosophie du Droit et de Sociologie Juridique: Travaux de la seconde session: Droit, Morale, Moeurs*, 235. Paris: Sirey, 1935–36.

Lazerson, Maxime. "La philosophie du droit de Maïmonide." *Archives de philosophie du droit et de sociologie juridique* 7 (1937): 191.

*See also* Laserson, Max.

Lee, Blewett. "A Sketch of Woman's Rights in Ancient Rome." *Northwestern Law Review* 2 (1894): 67.

Lewin, Benjamin Manasseh. *Masekhet Po'alim: Talmud Katan*. Jerusalem: Mosad ha-Rav Kook, 1942/43.

Liebenstein (Livneh), Eliezer. "Be-Fetah ha-Sefer." In *Ha-Medinah ha-'Ivrit: Yalkut Mekorot u-Firkey Mahshavah*, edited by S. Levi, 9. Tel Aviv: Be-Terem, 1946/47.

Lobingier, Charles S. "The New Science of Man and Law's Place Therein." *China Law Review* 9 (1936): 107.

Lobingier, Charles S. "The Nature and Origin of Law." *China Law Review* 10 (1937): 55.

Lobingier, Charles S. "The Form and Repository of Law." *China Law Review* 10 (1940): 165.

Lobingier, Charles S. "Legal Education in Twentieth Century China." *Lawyers Guild Magazine* 4(4) (July–August 1944): 1.

al-Ma'aluf, Issa Iskandar. "Al-Qada 'ind al-'Arab." *Al-Huquq* 3 (1926): 677.

Macaulay, T. B. "Minute by the Hon'ble T. B. Macaulay dated the 2nd February 1835." In *Selections from the Educational Records*, edited by H. Sharp, 107. Calcutta: Superintendent of Government Printing, 1920.

Macnaghten, William Hay. *Principles and Precedents of Moohummudan Law* ... Calcutta: Mission Press, 1824.

Macnaghten, William Hay. *Principles and Precedents of Hindu Law*. Calcutta: Baptist Mission Press, 1828–29.

Ma-Do-Yün. *Der eintritt des Chinesischen Reiches in den völkerrechtlichen verband*. Berlin: E. Ebering, 1907.

Mai, Chang Chun. "New Tendencies in the Theory of State." *China Law Review* 1 (1922): 52.

Maine, Henry Sumner. *Ancient Law*. London: John Murray, 1861.

Majumdar, J. "A Criticism of the Draft Hindu Code." *Calcutta University Law College Magazine* 14 (1944): 3.

Majumdar, Madhusudan. "Practical versus Scientific Legal Study in India." *Calcutta University Law College Magazine* 27 (1959): xv.

Majumdar, Ramesh Chandra. *Corporate Life in Ancient India*. Calcutta: Surendra Nath Sen, 1918.

Majumdar, Ramesh Chandra. *Corporate Life in Ancient India.* 2nd ed. Poona: Oriental Books, 1922.
Malhi, Eliezer. *Taskir Toldot ha-Mishpat be-Erets Yisrael.* Tel Aviv: Beyt ha-Sefer ha-Gavohah le-Mishpat vele-Kalkalah, 1950.
Malhi, Eliezer. *Yesodey ha-Mishpat be-Yisrael*, edited by Y. Yonah. Tel Aviv: Agudat ha-Studentim shel ha-Universitah be-Tel Aviv, 1959.
Margaliot, Reuven. *Tal T'hiyah.* Lwow: Margulies, 1921/22.
Markby, Lucy Taylor. *Memories of Sir William Markby, K.C.I.E.: By His Wife.* Oxford: Clarendon Press, 1917.
Markby, William. *Elements of Law: Considered with Reference to Principles of General Jurisprudence.* Oxford: Clarendon Press, 1871.
Markby, William. "Analytical Jurisprudence." *Law Magazine & Review and Quarterly Digest of All Reported Cases* 5th Ser. 1 (1876): 617.
Masiha, Kamil Samu'il. "Hayat al-'amilah bil-Sin." *Al-Huquq* 1 (1924): 811.
Mayne, John D. "Hindu Law in Madras." *Law Quarterly Review* 3 (1887): 446.
Mayne, John D. *A Treatise on Hindu Law and Usage.* 7th ed. Madras: Higginbotham, 1906.
Menon, K. Krishna. *Outlines of Jurisprudence.* Madras: Huxley Press, 1929.
Merchavia, Chenmelech, ed. *Herut u-Mishtar: Adam-'Am-Medinah-Ma'amad: Otsar Te'udot Historiyot u-Folitiyot.* Jerusalem: Goren, 1945.
Michell, R. B. *Jurisprudence: With Special Reference to the Law of India.* Madras: Higginbotham, 1883.
Mikliszanski, Jacques K. "Military Life among the Ancient Hebrews." *Jewish Review* 1 (1943): 169.
Mikliszanski, J. K. "Ha-Mishpat ha-Plili ha-Beyn Le'umi 'al-pi ha-Mishpat ha-'Ivri." In *Gvilin: Le-Mahshevet ha-Torah veha-'Avodah*, edited by Yehudah Yefet and Moshe Krone, 58. Warsaw: Jabne, 1937.
Mikliszanski, J. K. *Ha-Mishpat ha-Plili ha-Beyn Le'umi 'al-pi ha-Mishpat ha-'Ivri.* Warsaw: Haohela, 1938.
Mikliszanski, J. K. "J. S. Zuri." In *'Ishim u-Dmuyot be-Hohmat Yisrael be-Eropah ha-Mizrahit lifney Shki'atah*, edited by Samuel K. Misrky, 338. New York: Ha-'Ogen, 1959.
Mikliszanski, J. K. "Mishpat ha-Milhamah." In *'Arakhim ve-Ha'arakhot, 80.* Jerusalem: Neuman, 1975.
Mikliszanski, J. K. "Yesodot Beyn-Leumiyim ba-Mishpat ha-'Ivri." In *'Arakhim ve-Ha'arakhot*, 11. Jerusalem: Neuman, 1975.
Mikliszanski, Kopek. *Le droit pénal international d'après la législation polonaise.* Paris: Sirey, 1935.
Mill, John Stuart. *Considerations on Representative Government.* London: Parker, 1861.
Miraglia, Luigi. *Comparative Legal Philosophy: Applied to Legal Institutions*, translated by John Lisle. New York: Macmillan, 1921.

Mitter, Dwarka Nath. *The Position of Women in Hindu Law*. Calcutta: n.p., 1913.

Mohamad, Syed. *The Student's Holland: An Analytical Explanatory and Critical Commentary*. Allahabad: Ram Dayal Agarwala, 1912.

Mookerjee, Asutosh. "The Study of Law." In *The Judicial World of a Multi-Splendoured Genius: Sir Asutosh Mookerjee*, edited by Sudhish Pai, 143. New Delhi: Universal Law Publishing, 2014.

*See also* Mukhopadhyay, Asutosh.

Mookerjee, Syama Prasad. "Education in British India." *Annals of the American Academy of Political and Social Science* 233 (1944): 30.

Mookerjee, Syamaprasad. "Heritage of India [a Lecture Delivered in 1937 at Patna University]." In *Anthology of University College of Law Centenary Celebration 1909–2009*, 33. Calcutta: Registrar of the University of Calcutta, 2010.

Mookerji, Radhakumud. "An Introductory Essay on the Age and Authenticity of the Arthaśâstra of Kautilya." In Narendra Nath Law, *Studies in Ancient Hindu Polity: Based on the Arthaśâstra of Kautilya*, ix. London: Longmans, 1914.

Mookerji, Radhakumud. *Local Government in Ancient India*. Oxford: Clarendon Press, 1919.

Morton, Philip, ed. *Outlines of Jurisprudence*. Allahabad: Pioneer Press, 1892.

Morton, Philip. *A Preliminary Manual of Jurisprudence for the Use of Students*. Lahore: The "News" Press, 1898.

M. S. A. "[Review] Introduction to the Study of the Law: A Handbook for the use of Egyptian Law Students." *Law Quarterly Review* 27 (1911): 121.

Mukerjee, Nagendra Nath. "Indo-Aryan Penal Jurisprudence." *Calcutta Law Journal* 14 (1911): 29n.

Mukerjee, Radhakamal. *Democracies of the East: A Study in Comparative Politics*. London: P. S. King & Son, 1923.

Mukherjee, Achintya. "The Science of Hindu Polity: Some Old Ideas for the Present Situation." *The Aryan Path*, September 1934, 572.

Mukhopadhyay, Asutosh. *The Law of Perpetuities in British India*. Calcutta: Thacker, Spink and Co., 1902.

*See also* Mookerjee, Asutosh.

Mulla, Dinshah Fardunji. *Principles of Mahomedan Law*. Bombay: Thacker & Co., 1905.

Mulla, Dinshah Fardunji. *Principles of Hindu Law*. Bombay: N. M. Tripathi, 1912.

"Muqabalah bayn al-huquq al-romaniyyah waal-huquq al-islamiyyah waal-faransiyyah waal-inkliziyyah." *Al-Huquq* 1 (1924): 909.

Mursi, Muhammad Kamil, and Sayyid Mustafa. *Usul al-qawanin: ma'a tatbiqat min al-qanun al-misri wa-ba'ad al-qawanin al-ukhra*. Cairo: Al-Matba'ah al-rahmaniyyah, 1923.

Nag, Kalidas. *Les théories diplomatiques de L'Inde ancienne et l'Arthasastra*. Paris: Maisonneuve Frères, 1923.
Nag, Kalidas, and V. R. Ramachandra Dikshitar, "The Diplomatic Theories of Ancient India and the Arthashastra." *Journal of Indian History* 5 (1926): 235.
al-Nakdi, 'Arif. "Al-Qada' fi al-Islam." *Al-Huquq* 3 (1926): 656.
Nehru, Jawaharlal. "Building up of India of To-Morrow." *Calcutta University Law College Magazine* 15 (1945–46): 4.
Nehru, Jawaharlal. *The Discovery of India*. Delhi: Oxford University Press, 1985.
Nehru, Jawaharlal. "The Objective Resolution." In *Constituent Assembly Debates*, Vol. 1, 58. New Delhi: Government of India, 2014.
Nelson, J. H. *A View of Hindu Law as Administered by the High Court of Judicature at Madras*. Madras: Higginbotham, 1877.
Nelson, J. H. *A Prospectus of the Scientific Study of the Hindu Law*. London: C. Kegan Paul & Co., 1881.
Norton, John Bruce. *Topics of Jurisprudence: Or Aids to the Office of the Indian Judge*. Madras: Higginbotham, 1862.
"Notes: Kautilyan Studies in Calcutta University." *Modern Review* 84 (1948): 259.
Nurullah, Syed and J. P. Paik. *History of Education in India during the British Period*. Bombay: Macmillan & Co., 1943.
"'Orekh ha-Din S. Rosenbaum: Ha-Mishpat ha-Beyn Leumi be-Yisrael bi-Yemey Kedem." *Ha-Mishpat Ha-'Ivri* 1 (1925/26): 204.
Pokrovsky, Iosif. *Ha-Probleymot ha-Yesodiyot shel ha-Mishpat ha-Ezrahi*, translated by A. Litai. Jerusalem: Dfus ha-Po'alim, 1922/23.
Pal, Radhabinod. *The Hindu Philosophy of Law in the Vedic and Post-Vedic Times Prior to the Institutes of Manu*. Calcutta: Biswabhandar Press, n.d.
Pal, Radhabinod. *History of Hindu Law During the Vedic and Post-Vedic Ages Down to the Age of Manusmriti: Introductory Lecture (Intended for Tagore Law Lectures 1918–1919)*. Calcutta: Lily Press, 1918.
Pal, Radha Binode. *The History of the Law of Primogeniture: With Special Reference to India, Ancient and Modern (Intended for Tagore Law Lectures, 1923)*. Calcutta: Oriental Press, 1922.
Pal, Radhabinod. *The History of Hindu Law in the Vedic Age and in the Post-Vedic Times down to the Institutes of Manu (Intended for Tagore Law Lectures 1928)*. Calcutta: Biswabhandar Press, 1927.
Pal, Radhabinod. *The History of the Law of Primogeniture: With Special Reference to India, Ancient and Modern* [the Tagore Law Lectures, 1925]. Calcutta: University of Calcutta, 1929.
Pal, Radhabinod. *The Law of Limitations in British India*. Calcutta: N. M. Raychowdhury & Co., 1933.

Pal, Radhabinod. *The Law of Income Tax in British India: Being Act XI of 1922 as Amended by Act VII of 1939, with Explanatory Notes and Commentary*. 2 vols. Calcutta: Eastern Law House, 1940.

Pal, Radhabinod. "Convocation Address." *The Calcutta Review*, April 1946, 1.

Pal, Radhabinod. *Crimes in International Relations* [the Tagore Law Lectures, 1938]. Calcutta: University of Calcutta, 1955.

Pal, Radhabinod. *The History of Hindu Law in the Vedic Age and in Post-Vedic Times down to the Institutes of Manu*. Calcutta: University of Calcutta Press, 1958.

Pal, Radhabinod. *International Military Tribunal for the Far East: Dissentient Judgement of Justice Pal*. Tokyo: Kokusho Kankokai, 1999.

P[ound], R[oscoe]. "[Review] Introduction to the Study of Law: A Handbook for the Use of Egyptian Law Students by Frederic M. Goadby." *Harvard Law Review* 25 (1912): 397.

Pound, Roscoe. "Book Review." *Harvard Law Review* 29 (1916): 348.

Prasad, Beni. *Theory of Government in Ancient India (Post-Vedic)*. Allahabad: Indian Press, 1927.

Prasad, Beni. *The State in Ancient India: A Study in the Structure and Practical Working of Political Institutions in North India in Ancient Times*. Allahabad: Indian Press, 1928.

Presidency College Calcutta. *Centenary Volume, 1955*. Alipore: West Bengal Government Press, 1956.

"Al-Qada fi al-islam." *Al-Huquq* 1 (1924): 911.

Radbruch, Gustav. "Le relativisme dans la philosophie de droit." *Archives de philosophie du droit et de sociologie juridique* 4 (1934): 105.

Rambani, Haim. *Dat u-Medinah: Shitat Mahshavah be-Torat ha-Hevrah*. Jerusalem: Reuven Mass, 1942/43.

Rao, C. Hayavadana, ed. *Indian Biographical Dictionary*. Madras: Pillar & Co., 1915.

Rattigan, William H. *The Science of Jurisprudence: Chiefly Intended for Indian Law Students*. Lahore: Civil and Military Gazette Press, 1888.

Rattigan, William H. *The Science of Jurisprudence: Chiefly Intended for Indian Law Students*, 3rd ed. London: Wildy, 1899.

Rau, Benegal Narsing. "The Parliamentary System of Government in India." *Washington Law Review and State Bar Journal* 24 (1949): 91.

Rau, B. N. "The Indian Constitution." *India Quarterly* 5 (1949): 293.

Rav Tsa'ir. *See* Tchernowitz, Chaim.

Ray[chaudhuri], Hemchandra. "Was State-Socialism Known in Ancient India?" In *Sir Asutosh Mookerjee Silver Jubilee Volumes*, Vol. 3.1, 429. Calcutta: Calcutta University Press, 1922.

Raychaudhuri, Hemchandra. *Political History of Ancient India from the Accession of Parikshit to the Extinction of the Gupta Dynasty*. Calcutta: University of Calcutta Press, 1923.

*The Records of the Honorable Society of Lincoln's Inn*, Vol. 3: *Admissions from A.D. 1894 to A.D. 1956*. London: Lincoln's Inn, 1981.
"[Review] Introduction to the Study of the Law: A Handbook for the Use of Egyptian Law Students, 2nd edition, 1914." *Law Quarterly Review* 31 (1915): 123.
"Reviews." *Calcutta Law Journal* 48 (1928): 24n.
Rosenbaum, Shimshon. "Shgi'ot Mekubalot." *Ha-Mishpat ha-'Ivri* 4 (1932/33): 113.
Roy, Naresh Chandra. *The Constitutional System of India*. Calcutta: University of Calcutta Press, 1937.
Roy, Naresh Chandra. *A Critical Study of Some Aspects of Public Administration in Bengal*. Calcutta: University of Calcutta Press, 1945.
Roy, Naresh Chandra. *Main Currents of Political Thinking in India: Two Lectures Delivered at the Federation Hall*. Calcutta: Bimal Ch. Ray, 1965.
Roy, Sripati. *Customs and Customary Law in British India*. Calcutta: Hare Press, 1911.
Roy Choudhury, M. L. *Egypt in 1945*. Calcutta: University of Calcutta Press, 1946.
Saalschütz, Joseph Levin. *Das mosaische Recht: mit Berücksichtigung des spätern jüdischen*. Berlin: Heymann, 1846–48.
"Safhat min karl marx." *Al-Huquq* 2(3) (1925): 1.
Safra, B. "Ha-Kinyan ha-Prati ba-Mishpat ha-'Ivri." *Ha-Mishpat ha-'Ivri* 2 (1927): 25.
Salah, Abdel Latif. *Sharh qanun al-muhakamat al-huquqiyyah*. Jerusalem: Madrasat dar al-aytam al-islamiyyah, 1924.
Salant, E. *An Outline of the Constitutional Laws of the British Empire*. London: Sweet & Maxwell, 1934.
Salmond, John. *Jurisprudence*. 7th ed. London: Sweet & Maxwell, 1924.
Sanhoury, A. *Le califat: son évolution vers une société des nations orientale*. Paris: Paul Geuthner, 1926.
el-Sanhoury, Abd-el-Razzak Ah. "Le droit musulman comme élément de refonte du Code civil égyptien." In *Introduction à l'étude du droit comparé: recueil d'études en l'honneur d'Edouard Lambert*, Vol. 3, 621. Paris: Sirey, 1938.
al-Sanhuri, 'Abd al-Razzaq. *'Abd al-Razzaq al-Sanhuri min khilal awraqihi al-shakhsiyyah*, edited by Nadiyah al-Sanhuri and Tawfiq al-Shawi. Cairo: Al-Zahrah, 1988.
al-Sanhuri, 'Abd al-Razzaq, and Ahmad Hishmat Abu Sittit. *Usul al-qanun*. Cairo: Matba'at lajnat al-ta'lif wa-al-tarjamah wa-al-nashr, 1941.
Sarkar, Benoy Kumar. "Democratic Ideals and Republican Institutions in India." *American Political Science Review* 12 (1918): 581.
Sarkar, Benoy Kumar. *Positive Background of Hindu Sociology, Book II, Part I: Political*. Allahabad: Sudhindra Natha Vasu, 1921.

Sarkar, Benoy Kumar. *The Political Institutions and Theories of the Hindus.* Leipzig: von Markert, 1922.
Sarkar, Benoy Kumar. "The German Translation of the Kautilyan Arthasastra." *Indian Historical Quarterly* 4 (1928): 348.
Sarkar, H. B. "Obituary Notices: Ramesh Chandra Majumdar." *Annals of the Bhandarkar Oriental Research Institute* 61 (1980): 361.
Sarvadhikari, Jyoti Prasad. *A Handbook of English Constitutional Law (with a Chapter on India).* Calcutta: n.p., 1928.
Sastri, Janaki Nath Pal. "Hindu Jurisprudence." *Calcutta Law Journal* 8–9 (1908–09): 13n.
Sastri, K. A. Nilakanta. "The Place of the Arthaśāstra in the Literature of Indian Polity." *Annals of the Bhandarkar Oriental Research Institute* 28 (1947): 84.
Sastri, K. S. Ramaswami. "The Evolution of Law as a Science and as a Profession in India." *Hindu Law Journal* 5(10) (April 1923): 1.
Sastri, R. Shama. *Evolution of Indian Polity.* Calcutta: University of Calcutta, 1920.
Savigny, F. C. von. *Of the Vocation of Our Age for Legislation and Jurisprudence*, translated by Abraham Hayward. London: Littlewood, 1831.
Sciaky, Yitzhak. *Pirkey Mavo le-Mada' ha-Medinah.* Tel Aviv: Mishpat u-Medinah, 1951/52.
Sen, Asoke. "The Relation between Law and Morality." *Calcutta University Law College Magazine* 12 (1942): 75.
Sen, P. C. *A Summary of Holland's Jurisprudence.* Konnagar near Calcutta: J. M. Sen & Co., 1896.
Sen, Priyanath. *The General Principles of Hindu Law.* Calcutta: University of Calcutta Press, 1918.
Sen, Priya Nath. *Philosophy of the Vedanta.* Calcutta: Oriental Publishing House, 1900.
Sen, Surendra Nath. *An Essay on Hindu Jurisprudence.* Allahabad: Indian Press, 1911.
Sen Gupta, Nares Chandra. *Sources of Law and Society in Ancient India.* Calcutta: Art Press, 1914.
Sen Gupta, Nares Chandra. *The Evolution of Law.* Calcutta: University of Calcutta Press, 1925.
Sengupta, N. C. "Hints on an Historical Study of Hindu Law." *Calcutta University Law College Magazine* 13 (1943): 7.
Setlur, S. S. "Origin and Development of the Bengal School of Hindu Law." *Law Quarterly Review* 23 (1907): 202.
S[heng]. R. C. W. "Editorial." *China Law Review* 1 (1922): 67.
Sheng, R. C. W. "The Reasons Why in the Egyptian, Babylonian, Hebrew, Hindu, and Chinese Systems, Lawyers in Our Sense of Unofficial

Practitioners Apparently Did Not Exist." *China Law Review* 3(5) (July 1927): 4.

Shih, Ching Cheng. "International Law in the Ch'un Ch'iu Period." PhD dissertation, University of Chicago, 1946.

"Shimshon Rosenbaum Z"L." *Ha-Mishpat* 5(5) (1935): 1.

Sidhanta, N. K., B. C. Law, C. D. Chatterjee et al., eds., *Bharata-Kaumudi: Studies in Indology in Honour of Dr Radha Kumud Mookerji*. Allahabad: Indian Press, 1945.

Silver, Abba Hillel. *The Democratic Impulse in Jewish History*. New York: Bloch, 1928.

Silver, Abba Hillel. *Where Judaism Differed: An Inquiry into the Distinctiveness of Judaism*. New York: Macmillan, 1956.

Silving, Helen. "The State Contract in the Old Testament." *Journal of Religion* 24 (1944): 17.

Silving, Helen. "The Jurisprudence of the Old Testament." *New York University Law Review* 28 (1953): 1129.

Silving, Helen. "Torat ha-Mishpat sheba-Tanakh." *Ha-Praklit* 13 (1956/57): 49.

Silving, Helen. "The Origins of the Magnae Cartae." *Harvard Journal on Legislation* 3 (1965): 117.

Silving, Helen. *Helen Silving: Memoirs*. New York: Vantage, 1988.

*Sir Asutosh Mookerjee Silver Jubilee Volumes*. Calcutta: University of Calcutta Press, 1921–22.

"The Society and the Law (Psychical Theory of Society)." *Calcutta Law Journal* 28 (1918): 5.

Srinivasan, N. "The Juristic and Political Ideas of Duguit." *Indian Journal of Political Science* 1 (1939): 1.

Strange, Thomas. *Hindu Law* ... London: Parbury, Allen, 1830.

Stubbs, William. *The Constitutional History of England: In Its Origins and Development*. 3 vols. Oxford: Clarendon Press, 1874–78.

Sulzberger, Mayer. *The Am Ha-Aretz: The Ancient Hebrew Parliament: A Chapter in the Constitutional History of Ancient Israel*. Philadelphia, PA: Greenstone, 1910.

Sulzberger, Mayer. *The Polity of the Ancient Hebrews*. Philadelphia, PA: Greenstone, 1912.

Swindlehurst, Albert. "Hindu Law and Its Influence." *Yale Law Journal* 27 (1918): 857.

"Al-Talaq waal-zawaj wa-ikhtilaf al-nazr fi-hima' bayn al-sharq waal-gharb." *Al-Huquq* 2(4) (1925): 21.

Tchernowitz, Chaim. "'Al ha-Historiyah shel ha- Ha-Mishpat Ha-'Ivri." *Ha-Mishpat Ha-'Ivri* 1 (1925/26): 1.

Tchernowitz, Chaim. "Reshimot ve-He'arot." *Ha-Mishpat* 2 (1927): 44.

Tchernowitz, Chaim [Rav Tsa'ir, pseud.]. "Ha-Dat veha-Medinah." In *Sha'arey Tsiyon* (New York: n.p., 1936), 162.

Tedeschi, Guido (Gad). "Su lo Studio dell'applicazione del Diritto civile." *Annuario di diritto comparato e di studi legislativi* 7(1) (1932): 2.

Tedeschi, Guido (Gad). *Mehkarim be-Mishpat Artsenu*. Jerusalem: Magnes Press, 1951.

Tedeschi, Guido (Gad). *Mavo le-Torat ha-Mishpat*, edited by Aharon Barak. Jerusalem: Mif'al ha-Shikhpul, 1958.

Tedeschi, Guido (Gad). "On the Inductive Study of Law." In *Studies in Israel Law*, 1. Jerusalem: Mif'al ha-Shikhpul, 1960.

Tedeschi, Guido (Gad). "Ha-Minhag be-Mishpatenu ha-Noheg veha-'Atiti." *Mishpatim* 5 (1973): 9.

Teplicki, J. "Diney Mamonot." *Ha-Mishpat ha-'Ivri: Riv'on Mada'i* (1918): 77.

"Te'udatenu." *Ha-Mishpat ha-'Ivri: Riv'on Mada'i* (1918): 3.

Thakur, Amareswar. *Hindu Law of Evidence: Or a Comparative Study of the Law of Evidence According to the Smrtis*. Calcutta: University of Calcutta Press, 1933.

Tupper, C. L. "English Jurisprudence and Indian Studies in Law." *Journal of the Society of Comparative Legislation* 3 (1901): 84.

Tyabji, Faiz Badruddin. *Principles of Muhammadan Law: An Essay at a Complete Statement of the Personal Law Applicable to Muslims in British India*. 2nd ed. Calcutta: Butterworth, 1919.

Urbach, Ephraim. "Ha-Shimush be-Sifrutenu ha-Masortit le-Hinukho shel ha-Ezrah." In *'Al Hinukh ha-Ezrah*, edited by H. Y. Roth, 91. Jerusalem: Magnes Press, 1949/50.

Ussishkin, Shmuel. *Prakim ba-Mishpat ha-Konstitutsyoni ha-Angli*. Jerusalem: Dfus ha-Po'alim, 1927.

Ussishkin, Shmuel. *Shitat ha-Shilton ba-Keysarut ha-Britit*. Tel Aviv: Mitzpeh, 1937.

Ussishkin, Shmuel. *Ha-Mishtar ha-Medini be-Britanyah*. Tel Aviv: Umah u-Moledet, 1945/46.

"Al-Ustaz dugi: 'amid kulliyyat al-huquq al-jadid bil-qahirah." *Al-Huquq* 2(10) (1925): 1.

Varadachariar, S. *The Hindu Judicial System*. Lucknow: Lucknow University, 1946.

Vesey-FitzGerald, S. G. "The Place of Hindu Law in Comparative Jurisprudence." *Law Quarterly Review* 39 (1923): 357.

Vinogradoff, Paul. *Outlines of Historical Jurisprudence*, Vol. 1: *Introduction – Tribal Law*. London: Oxford University Press, 1920.

Viswanatha, S. V. *International Law in Ancient India*. Bombay: Longmans, 1925.

Wang, Chung Hui, trans. *The German Civil Code*, London: Stevens, 1907.

Wasti, Syed Razi, ed. *Memoirs and Other Writings of Syed Ameer Ali*. Lahore: People's Publishing House, 1968.

W. D. T. "Book Review." *American Law Review* 23 (1889): 461.

Weeks, Mangum. "Book Review: Law and the Modern Mind, by Jerome Frank." *China Law Review* 5 (1932): 238.

Witkon, Alfred. *Mishpat ve-Hevrah*. Tel Aviv: Dvir, 1955.

Wu, John. "Readings from Ancient Chinese Codes and Other Sources of Chinese Law and Legal Ideas." *Michigan Law Review* 19 (1920–21): 502.

Wu, John C. H. "The Juristic Philosophy of Justice Holmes." *Michigan Law Review* 21 (1922–23): 523.

Wu, John C. H. "The Juristic Philosophy of Roscoe Pound." *China Law Review* 1 (1923): 360.

Wu, John C. H. "The Juristic Philosophy of Roscoe Pound." *Illinois Law Review* 18 (1923–24): 285.

Wu, John C. H. "The Juristic Philosophy of Judge Cardozo." *China Law Review* 2 (1924): 109.

Wu, John C. H. "Appendix II: Stammler and His Critics." In Rudolf Stammler, *The Theory of Justice*, translated by Isaac Husik, 555. New York: Macmillan, 1925.

Wu, John C. H. "Problem and Method of Psychological Jurisprudence." *China Law Review* 2 (1925): 214.

Wu, John C. H. "Book Review: Chinese Political Philosophy – by William S. A. Pott." *China Law Review* 3 (1926): 33.

Wu, John C. H. "Scientific Method in Judicial Process." *China Law Review* 3 (1926): 7.

Wu, John C. H. "The Three Dimensions of Law." *China Law Review* 3 (1926): 126.

Wu, John C. H. "Realistic Analysis of Legal Concepts: A Study in the Legal Method of Mr. Justice Holmes." *China Law Review* 5 (1932): 1.

Wu, John C. H. "The Mind of Mr. Justice Holmes." *China Law Review* 8 (1935): 77.

Wu, John C. H. "Toward a Christian Philosophy of Law." *Women Lawyers Journal* 37(4) (Fall 1951): 34.

Wu, John C. H. "The Natural Law and Our Common Law." *Fordham Law Review* 23 (1954): 13.

Wu, John C. H. *Fountain of Justice: A Study in the Natural Law*. New York: Sheed & Ward, 1955.

Wu, John C. H. "Jurisprudence as a Cultural Study." *University of Detroit Mercy Law Review* 33 (1956): 277.

Wu, John C. H. *Cases and Materials on Jurisprudence*. St. Paul, MN: West, 1958.

Wu, John C. H. "Truth and Fiction in the Art of Justice." *University of Detroit Law Journal* 36 (1958): 130.

Wu, John C. H. "Justice Holmes and the Common-Law Tradition." *Vanderbilt Law Review* 14 (1960): 221.

Wu, John C. H. "Chinese Legal and Political Philosophy." In *The Chinese Mind: Essentials of Chinese Philosophy and Culture*, edited by Charles

A. Moore with the assistance of Aldyth V. Morris, 213. Honolulu, HI: East-West Center Press, 1967.

Wu, John C. H. "The Status of the Individual in the Political and Legal Traditions of Old and New China." In *The Status of the Individual in East and West*, edited by Charles A. Moore with the assistance of Aldyth V. Morris, 391. Honolulu, HI: University of Hawaii Press, 1968.

Wu, John C. H. *Beyond East and West*. Notre Dame, IN: University of Notre Dame Press, 2018.

Wu, Kuo-Cheng. *Ancient Chinese Political Theories*. Shanghai: Commercial Press, 1928.

Yehoshafat, Y. "Shilton ha-Hok." *Ha-Mishpat ha-'Ivri* 3 (1928/29): 1.

Yu, Charles Y. S. "China's Law Library: Soochow University Law School Library." *Law Library Journal* 34 (1941): 65.

Zeitlin, Hillel. "Kdushat ha-Kinyan be-Mamlakhah Toratit." In *Gvilin: Le-Mahshevet ha-Torah veha-'Avodah*, edited by Yehudah Yefet and Moshe Krone, 13. Warsaw: Jabne, 1937.

Zuri-Rzezak, J. S. *Mishpat ha-Talmud*, Vol. 8: *Mishpat ha-Medinah*. Warsaw: Merkaz: 1922.

Zuri, Jacob. *Toldot ha-Mishpat ha-Tsiburi ha-'Ivri*. 6 vols. Paris, London, Tel Aviv: Voltaire, Urim, Mitspeh, 1930/31–38.

## Secondary Sources

Abiri, Gilad. "Intimate Rivals: The Freedom of Religious Nationalism." *Asian Journal of Law and Society* 8 (2021): 19.

Acevedo, Deepa Das. "Developments in Hindu Law from the Colonial to the Present." *Religion Compass* 7 (2013): 252.

Aggarwal, Arjun P. "Legal Education in India." *Journal of Legal Education* 12 (1959–60): 231.

Agrawala, Rajkumari. "Indian Legal Research: An Evolutionary and Perspective Analysis." *Journal of the Indian Law Institute* 24 (1982): 470.

Ahmed, Faiz. *Afghanistan Rising: Islamic Law and Statecraft between the Ottoman and British Empires*. Cambridge, MA. Harvard University Press, 2017.

Albeck, Shalom. "Ha-Mishpat ha-'Ivri u-Mada'ey ha-Yahadut." In *Heker ha-Torah shebe-'Alpeh be-Hamishim Shnot ha-Medinah*, edited by Zvi Arieh Steinfeld, 15. Jerusalem: Orkhot, 2001/02.

Alexandrowicz, Charles Henry. *A Bibliography of Indian Law*. Madras: Oxford University Press, 1958.

Alexandrowicz, C. H. "Kautilyan Principles and the Law of Nations." In *The Law of Nations in Global History*, edited by David Armitage and Jennifer Pitts, 35. Oxford: Oxford University Press, 2017.

Alford, William P., and Xingzhong Yu. "Pound for Pound? Roscoe Pound's Adventures in China and Questions They Pose for Scholars of

Contemporary China." *University of Pennsylvania Asian Law Review* 18 (2022): 1.

Altman, Amnon. *Tracing the Earliest Recorded Concepts of International Law: The Ancient Near East (2500–330 BCE)*. Leiden: Martinus Nijhoff, 2012.

Ambastha, Gadadhar Prasad. "Dr. K. P. Jayaswal: A Memoir." in K. P. Jayaswal, *Hindu Polity: A Constitutional History of India in Hindu Times*, xxiii. 2nd enlarged ed. Bangalore: Bangalore Printing & Publishing Co., 1943.

Amir, Gal, and Na'ama Ben-Ze'ev. "Lawyers in Transition: Palestinian Arab Lawyers in the First Decade of the Jewish State." *Continuity and Change* 35 (2020): 371.

Anderson, Michael R. "Islamic Law and the Colonial Encounter in British India." In *Institutions and Ideologies: A SOAS South Asian Reader*, eds. David Arnold and Peter Robb, 165. London: Routledge, 1993.

Aoki, Hitoshi. "Nobushige Hozumi: A Skillful Transplanter of Western Legal Thought into Japanese Soil." In *Rethinking the Masters of Comparative Law*, edited by Annelise Riles, 129. Oxford: Hart, 2001.

Armitage, David, and Jennifer Pitts. "'This Modern Grotius': An Introduction to the Life and Thought of C. H. Alexandrowicz." In *The Law of Nations in Global History: C. H. Alexandrowicz*, edited by David Armitage and Jennifer Pitts, 1. Oxford: Oxford University Press, 2017.

Armitage, David, and Ignacio de la Rasilla, "'The Most Neglected Province': British Historiography of International Law." In *The Cambridge History of International Law*, Vol. 1: *The Historiography of International Law*, eds. Randall Lesaffer and Anne Peters, 293. Cambridge: Cambridge University Press, 2024.

Arvidsson, Stefan. *Aryan Idols: Indo-European Mythology as Ideology and Science*, translated by Sonia Wichmann. Chicago, IL: University of Chicago Press, 2006.

Ashby, Eric, with Mary Anderson. *Universities: British, Indian, African: A Study in the Ecology of Higher Education*. London: Weidenfeld and Nicolson, 1966.

Al-'Asli, Kamil. "Al-Fikr al-dini: al-'ulum al-islamiyyah fi Filastin." In *Al-Mawsu'ah al-filastiniyyah*, Vol. 3, 443. Beirut: n.p, 1990.

Auer, Marietta. "What Is Legal Theory?" *Rg (Rechtsgeschichte)* 29 (2021): 30.

Austin, Granville. *The Indian Constitution: Cornerstone of a Nation*. Oxford: Clarendon Press, 1966.

Avenarius, Martin. "Osnovnyia Problemy Grazhdanskago Prava (Basic Problems of Private Law), 1917, Iosif Alekseevich Pokrovsky (1868–1920)." In *The Formation and Transmission of Western Legal Culture: 150 Books That Made the Law in the Age of Printing*, edited by Serge Dauchy, Georges Martyn, Anthony Musson et al., 438. Cham: Springer, 2016.

Ayalon, Ami. *Reading Palestine: Printing and Literacy, 1900–1948*. Austin, TX: University of Texas Press, 2004.

Aydin, Cemil. *The Politics of Anti-Westernism in Asia: Visions of World Order in Pan-Islamic and Pan-Asian Thought*. New York: Columbia University Press, 2007.

Babie, Paul, and Jessica Viven-Wilksch, eds. *Léon Duguit and the Social Obligation Norm of Property: A Translation and Global Exploration*. Singapore: Springer, 2019.

Bachi, Roberto. "Divrey Roberto Bachi." In *Le-Zikhro shel Gad Tedeschi: Davrim she-Ne'emru bi-Mlot Shloshim le-Moto*, 10. Jerusalem: Ha-Akademyah ha-Yisre'elit le-Mada'im, 1995.

Baker, G. Blaine. "The Reconstitution of Upper Canadian Legal Thought in the Late-Victorian Empire." *Law and History Review* 3 (1985): 219.

Baker, G. Blaine. "Popularizing the Rule of Law: Sheldon Amos and the International Scientific Series, 1874 to 1909." *Journal of Legal History* 33 (2012): 151.

Banerjee, Milinda. "Does International Criminal Justice Require a Sovereign? Historicising Radhabinod Pal's Tokyo Judgment in Light of His 'Indian' Legal Philosophy." In *Historical Origins of International Criminal Law*, edited by Morten Bergsmo, Wui Ling Cheah, and Ping Yi, Vol. 2, 69. Brussels: Torkel Opsahl Academic EPublisher, 2014.

Banerjee, Milinda. *The Mortal God: Imagining the Sovereign in Colonial India*. Cambridge: Cambridge University Press, 2018.

Banerjee, Milinda. "Sovereignty as a Motor of Global Conceptual Travel: Sanskritic Equivalents of 'Law' in Bengali Discursive Production." *Modern Intellectual History* 17 (2020): 487.

Banerjee, P. N. "Foundation of the University Law College." *Calcutta University Law College Magazine* 27 (1959): ix.

*Banglapedia: National Encyclopedia of Bangladesh*, https://en.banglapedia.org.

Bapu, Prabhu. *Hindu Mahasabha in Colonial North India,1915–1930: Constructing Nation and History*. New York: Routledge, 2013.

Barak-Erez, Daphne. "Symbolic Constitutionalism: On Sacred Cows and Abominable Pigs." *Law, Culture and the Humanities* 6 (2010): 420.

Bartie, Susan, and David Sandomierski, eds. *American Legal Education Abroad: Critical Histories*. New York: New York University Press, 2021.

Bar-Yosef, Eitan, ed. "Hodu/Yisrael." Special issue, *Teorya u-Vikoret* 44 (2015).

Bass, Gary J. *Judgment at Tokyo: World War II on Trial and the Making of Modern Asia*. New York: Knopf, 2023.

Basu, Shamita. *Religious Revivalism as Nationalist Discourse: Swami Vivekananda and New Hinduism in Nineteenth-Century Bengal*. New Delhi: Oxford University Press, 2002.

Batnitkzy, Leora. "From Politics to Law: Modern Jewish Thought and the Invention of Jewish Law." *Diné Israel* 26 (2008–10): 7.

Batnitzky, Leora. *How Judaism Became a Religion*. Princeton, NJ: Princeton University Press, 2011.

Batnitzky, Leora. "Between Ancestry and Belief: 'Judaism' and 'Hinduism' in the Nineteenth Century." *Modern Judaism* 41 (2021): 194.

Batnitzky, Leora, and Yonatan Brafman, eds. *Jewish Legal Theories: Writings on State, Religion, and Morality*. Waltham, MA: Brandeis University Press, 2018.

Baxi, Upendra. "Understanding the Traffic of Ideas in 'Law' between America and India." In *Traffic of Ideas between India and America*, edited by Robert M. Crunden, 319. Delhi: Chanakya Press, 1985.

Baxi, Upendra. "People's Law in India – the Hindu Society." In *Asian Indigenous Law: In Interaction with Received Law*, edited by Masaji Chiba, 215. London: KPI, 1986.

Bayly, C. A. *Recovering Liberties: Indian Thought in the Age of Liberalism and Empire*. Cambridge: Cambridge University Press, 2012.

Bayly, Martin J. "Lineages of Indian International Relations: The Indian Council on World Affairs, the League of Nations, and the Pedagogy of Internationalism." *International History Review* 44 (2022): 819.

Bayly, Susan. "Imagining 'Greater India': French and Indian Visions of Colonialism in the Indic Mode." *Modern Asian Studies* 38 (2004): 703.

Bechor, Guy. *The Sanhuri Code, and the Emergence of Modern Arab Civil Law (1932 to 1949)*. Leiden: Brill, 2007.

Ben-Bassat, Yuval. *Petitioning the Sultan: Protests and Justice in Late Ottoman Palestine*. London: I. B. Tauris, 2013.

Bendikaitė, Eglė. "Intermediary between Worlds: Shimshon Rosenbaum: Lawyer, Zionist, and Politician." *Osteuropa: Impulses for Europe* 2008 (8–10) (2008): 171.

Bendikaitė, Eglė. "One Man's Struggle: The Politics of Shimshon Rosenbaum." *Jahrbuch des Simon-Dubnow-Instituts* 13 (2014): 87.

Bendikaitė, Eglė. "Interwar Lithuania as a Laboratory of International Law." *Jus Gentium* 2 (2017): 555.

Ben-Menahem, Hanina. "Is Talmudic Law a Religious Legal System? A Provisional Analysis." *Journal of Law and Religion* 24 (2008–09): 379.

Ben-Menahem, Yemima. "Havnayah Ratsyonalit." *Diné Yisrael* 35–6 (2022): 13.

Berda, Yael. *Colonial Bureaucracy and Contemporary Citizenship: Legacies of Race and Emergency in the Former British Empire*. Cambridge: Cambridge University Press, 2023.

Bhatt, Chetan. *Hindu Nationalism: Origins, Ideologies and Modern Myths*. Oxford: Berg, 2001.

Bhattacharya, Neeladri. "Remaking Custom: The Discourse and Practice of Colonial Codification." In *Tradition, Dissent and Ideology: Essays in*

*Honour of Romila Thapar*, edited by R. Champakalakshmi and S. Gopal, 20. New Delhi: Oxford University Press, 1996.
Bhattacharyya, Kankan. "Sir Asutosh and Rise of Modern Science in India." *Indian Journal of History of Science* 50 (2015): 420.
Bhattacharyya-Panda, Nandini. *Appropriation and Invention of Tradition: The East India Company and Hindu Law in Early Colonial Bengal*. Oxford: Oxford University Press, 2008.
Biale, David. "Between Polemics and Apologetics: Jewish Studies in the Age of Multiculturalism." *Jewish Studies Quarterly* 3 (1996): 174.
Birnbaum, Maria. "Entangled Empire: Religion and the Transnational History of Pakistan and Israel." *Millennium: Journal of International Studies* 50 (2022): 561.
Blidstein, Gerald J. *'Ekronot Mediniyim be-Mishnat ha-Rambam: 'Iyunim be-Mishnato ha-Hilkhatit*. Ramat Gan: Bar Ilan University Press, 1983.
Boehmer, Elleke. *Empire, the National, and the Postcolonial, 1890–1920: Resistance in Interaction*. New York: Oxford University Press, 2005.
Boon, Andrew, and Julian Webb, "Legal Education and Training in England and Wales: Back to the Future." *Journal of Legal Education* 58 (2008): 79.
Brandes, Yehuda. *Yahadut ve-Zkhuyot Ezrah: Ha-Masoret ha-Ezrahit be-Yisrael*. Jerusalem: IDI Press, 2019.
Brook, Timothy. "Radhabinod Pal on the Rape of Nanking: The Tokyo Judgment and the Guilt of History." In *The Nanking Atrocity 1937–38: Complicating the Picture*, edited by Bob Tadashi Wakabayashi, 2nd ed., 149. New York: Berghahn Books, 2017.
Brown, D. Mackenzie. *The White Umbrella: Indian Political Thought from Manu to Gandhi* Berkeley, CA: University of California Press, 1953.
Browning, Gary. "Agency and Influence in the History of Political Thought: The Agency of Influence and the Influence of Agency." *History of Political Thought* 31 (2010): 345.
Brun, Nathan. *Shoftim u-Mishpetanim be-Erets Yisrael: Beyn Kushta li-Yerushalayim, 1900–1930*. Jerusalem: Magnes Press, 2008.
Bryant, Edwin F. *The Quest for the Origins of Vedic Culture: The Indo-Aryan Migration Debate*. New York: Oxford University Press, 2001.
Bui, Ngoc Son. "Sun Yat-Sen's Constitutionalism." *Giornale Di Storia Costituzionale/Journal of Constitutional History* 32(2) (2016): 157.
Burset, Christian R. *An Empire of Laws: Legal Pluralism in British Colonial Policy*. New Haven, CT: Yale University Press, 2023.
Butkevych, Olga V. "History of Ancient International Law: Challenges and Prospects." *Journal of the History of International Law* 5 (2003): 189.
Cairns, John W. "Development of Comparative Law in Great Britain." In *The Oxford Handbook of Comparative Law*, edited by Mathias Reimann and Reinhard Zimmermann, 2nd ed., 111. Oxford: Oxford University Press, 2019.

Cannon, Byron D. "Social Tensions and the Teaching of European Law in Egypt before 1900." *History of Education Quarterly* 15 (1975): 299.
Casolari, Marzia. *In the Shadow of the Swastika: The Relationships between Indian Radical Nationalism, Italian Fascism and Nazism*. London: Routledge, 2020.
Chacko, C. Joseph. "India's Contribution to the Field of International Law Concepts." *Recueil des Cours de l'Academie de Droit International* 93 (1958): 121.
Chandrasekharan, K. *P. S. Sivaswami Aiyer*. 2nd reprint. New Delhi: Publication Division of the Government of India, 2000.
Charsley, Simon. "Sanskritization: The Career of an Anthropological Theory." *Contributions to Indian Sociology (n.s.)* 32 (1998): 527.
Chatterjee, Indrani. *Gender, Slavery and Law in Colonial India*. New Delhi: Oxford University Press, 1999.
Chatterjee, Margaret. *Studies in Modern Jewish and Hindu Thought*. New York: St. Martin's Press, 1997.
Chatterjee, Nandini. "Law, Culture and History: Amir Ali's Interpretation of Islamic Tradition." In *Legal Histories of the British Empire: Laws, Engagements and Legacies*, edited by Shaunnagh Dorsett and John McLaren, 45. London: Routledge, 2014.
Chatterjee, Partha. *Nationalist Thought and the Colonial World: Derivative Discourse?* London: Zed Books, 1993.
Chatterjee, Partha. *I Am the People: Reflections of Popular Sovereignty Today*. New York: Columbia University Press, 2020.
Chattopadhyay, Indranil. "Quit India Movement in Northern Bengal: A Study of Socio-Economic Perspective." PhD dissertation, University of North Bengal University, 2009.
Chaudhry, Faisal. *South Asia, the British Empire, and the Rise of Classical Legal Thought: Toward a Historical Ontology of the Law*. Oxford: Oxford University Press, 2024.
Cheema, Shahbaz Ahmad. "Tagore Law Lecturer's [Sic] Contribution to Islamic Legal Scholarship in British India." *Al-Qalam*, December 2013.
Cheema, Shahbaz Ahmad. "Mulla's Principles of Mahomedan Law in Pakistani Courts: Undoing/Unraveling the Colonial Enterprise?" *Lahore University of Management Sciences Law Journal* 4 (2017): 56.
Cheema, Shahbaz Ahmad, and Samee Ozair Khan. "Genealogical Analysis of Islamic Law Books Relied on in the Courts of Pakistan." *Al-Adwa* 28(40) (2013): 23.
Chen, Li. "Pioneers in the Fight for the Inclusion of Chinese Students in American Legal Education and Legal Profession." *Asian American Law Journal* 22 (2015): 5.
Chen, Li. "The Founding of Peiyang University Department of Law: Oxford Style Legal Education in China (1895–1899)." *Tsinghua China Law Review* 9 (2017): 227.

Chen, Li. "Early Graduate Legal Studies in America and Legal Transplantation." *Journal of Legal Education* 68 (2019): 716.

Chen, Li. "A Contemporaneous Interpretation of Chung-Shu Lo's Reply to the UNESCO Human Rights Survey." *Human Rights Quarterly* 44 (2022): 168.

Chen, Li. "A Forgotten Proponent of a League of Nations and His Contributions to International Law." *Leiden Journal of International Law* 35 (2022): 245.

Chen, Ofer. *Hemshekhiyut u-Mifneh: Mi-Germanyah le-Eretz Yisrael: Ha-Ortodoxyah ha-Modernit le-Nokhah ha-Etgar ha-Tsiyoni*. Tel Aviv: Ha-Kibuts ha-Meuhad, 2015.

Chew, Dolores F. "Of 'Unchaste' Widows and Tenants-for-Life: Legal Constructions of Gender and Property in Nineteenth Century Bengal." PhD dissertation, University of Calcutta, 1994. http://shodhganga.inflibnet.ac.in/handle/10603/164657.

Chimni, B. S. "International Law Scholarship in Post-Colonial India: Coping with Dualism." *Leiden Journal of International Law* 23 (2010): 23.

Choudhary, Radhakrishna. *Kautilya's Political Ideas and Institutions*. Varanasi: Chowkhamba Sanskrit Series Office, 1971.

Clark, David S. "The Modern Development of American Comparative Law, 1904–1945." *American Journal of Comparative Law* 55 (2007): 587.

Cocks, Raymond. *Sir Henry Maine: A Study in Victorian Jurisprudence*. Cambridge: Cambridge University Press, 2004.

Cocks, Raymond. "'Sustaining the Character of a Judge': Conflict Within the Legal Thought of British India." *Journal of Legal History* 35 (2014): 44.

Coffey, Donal K. "Constitutional Law and Empire in Interwar Britain: Universities, Liberty, Nationality and Parliamentary Supremacy." *Northern Ireland Legal Quarterly* 71 (2020): 193.

Cohen, Asher. *Ha-Talit veha-Degel: Ha-Tsiyonut ha-Datit ve-Hazon Medinat ha-Torah bi-Yemey Reshit ha-Medinah*. Jerusalem: Yad Ben-Zvi, 1998.

Cohen, Uri. "Ha-Mirdaf Ahar Legitimatsyah Akademit: Beyt ha-Sefer ha-Gavohah le-Mishpat vele-Kalkalah." *Mehkarey Mishpat* 25 (2009): 179.

Cohn, Bernard S. *Colonialism and Its Forms of Knowledge: The British in India*. Princeton, NJ: Princeton University Press, 1996.

Colley, Linda. *The Gun, the Ship, and the Pen: Warfare, Constitutions, and the Making of the Modern World*. New York: Liveright, 2021.

Conner, Alison W. "Training China's Early Modern Lawyers: Soochow University Law School." *Journal of Chinese Law* 8 (1994): 1.

Conner, Alison W. "The Comparative Law School of China." In *Understanding China's Legal System*, edited by C. Stephen Hsu, 210. New York: New York University Press, 2003.

Cornish, William, Michael Lobban, and Keith Smith. "Theories of Law and Government." In *The Oxford History of the Laws of England*, edited by

William Cornish, J. Stuart Anderson, Ray Cocks et al. Vol. 11: *1820–1914, English Legal System*, 72. Oxford: Oxford University Press, 2010.

Cotterrell, Roger. "Ehrlich at the Edge of Empire: Centres and Peripheries in Legal Studies." In *Living Law: Reconsidering Eugen Ehrlich*, edited by Marc Hertogh, 75. Oxford: Hart, 2008.

Cotterrell, Roger. *Sociological Jurisprudence: Juristic Thought and Social Inquiry*. Abingdon: Routledge, 2017.

Cover, Robert C. "Foreword: The Supreme Court: 1982 Term [Nomos and Narrative]." *Harvard Law Review* 97 (1983): 1.

Dalmia, Vasudha. "Sanskrit Scholars and Pandits of the Old School: The Benares Sanskrit College and the Constitution of Authority in the Late Nineteenth Century." *Journal of Indian Philosophy* 24 (1996): 321.

Dann, Philipp. "Southern Turn, Northern Implications: Rethinking the Meaning of Colonial Legacies for Comparative Constitutional Studies." *Comparative Constitutional Studies* 1 (2023): 174.

Datta, Surja. *A History of the Indian University System: Emerging from the Shadows of the Past*. London: Palgrave Macmillan, 2017.

Davis, Donald R., Jr. *The Spirit of Hindu Law*. Cambridge: Cambridge University Press, 2010.

Davis, Donald R., Jr., and Timothy Lubin. "Hinduism and Colonial Law." In *Hinduism in the Modern World*, edited by Brian A. Hatcher, 96. New York: Routledge, 2016.

Dayal, S. "Legal Profession and Legal Education." In *The Indian Legal System*, edited by Joseph Minattur, 148. New Delhi: Indian Law Institute, 1978.

De, Rohit. "Constitutional Antecedents." In *The Oxford Handbook of the Indian Constitution*, edited by Sujit Choudhary, Madhav Khosla and Pratap Bhanu Mehta, 17. Oxford: Oxford University Press, 2016.

De, Rohit. *A People's Constitution: The Everyday Life of Law in the Indian Republic*. Princeton, NJ: Princeton University Press, 2018.

De, Rohit, and Ornit Shani, *Assembling India's Constitution: A New Democratic History*. Cambridge: Cambridge University Press, 2025.

Debs, Richard A. *Islamic Law and Civil Code: The Law of Property in Egypt*. New York: Columbia University Press, 2010.

Dedek, Helge. "The Tradition of Comparative Law: Comparison and its Colonial Legacies." In *The Cambridge Handbook of Comparative Law*, edited by Mathias Siems and Po Jen Yap, 32. New York: Cambridge University Press, 2024.

Derrett, J. Duncan M. "The Role of Roman Law and Continental Laws in India." *Zeitschrift für ausländisches und internationales Privatrecht* 24 (1959): 657.

Derrett, J. D. M. "J. H. Nelson: A Forgotten Administrator-Historian of India." In *Historians of India, Pakistan and Ceylon*, edited by C. H. Philips, 354. London: Oxford University Press, 1961.

Derrett, J. D. M. "The Law Student and Legislation." In *Anthology of University College of Law Centenary Celebration 1909–2009*, 165. Calcutta: Registrar of the University of Calcutta, 2010.

Deshpande, Madhav M. "Efforts to Vernacularize Sanskrit: Degree of Success and Failure." In *Handbook of Languages and Ethnic Identity*, edited by Joshua A. Fishman and Ofelia García, Volume 2, 218. Oxford: Oxford University Press, 2011.

Devji, Faisal. "Apologetic Modernity." *Modern Intellectual History* 4 (2007): 61.

Devji, Faisal. *Muslim Zion: Pakistan as a Political Idea*. Cambridge, MA: Harvard University, 2013.

Devnath, Samaresh. "Sengupta, Naresh Chandra." In *Banglapedia: National Encyclopedia of Bangladesh*, Volume 9, 168. Dhaka: Asiatic Society of Bangladesh, 2003.

Dezalay, Yves, and Bryant G. Garth. *Law as Reproduction and Revolution: An Interconnected History*. Oakland, CA: University of California Press, 2021.

Dhavan, Rajeev. "Borrowed Ideas: On the Impact of America Scholarship on Indian Law." *American Journal of Comparative Law* 33 (1985): 505.

Dhavan, Rajeev. "Legal Research in India: The Role of the Indian Law Institute." *American Journal of Comparative Law* 34 (1986): 527.

Dhavan, Rajeev. "Means, Motives and Opportunities: Reflecting on Legal Research in India." *Modern Law Review* 50 (1987): 725.

Dhyani, S. N. *Jurisprudence: A Study of Indian Legal Theory*. 2nd ed. New Delhi: Metropolitan Book Co., 1985.

Diament, Nathan J. "Judaism and the Death penalty: Of Two Minds but One Heart." *Tradition: A Journal of Orthodox Jewish Thought* 38 (2004): 76.

Dirks, Nicholas B. *Castes of Mind: Colonialism and the Making of Modern India*. Princeton, NJ: Princeton University Press, 2001.

Djalins, Upik. "Re-Examining Subject Making in the Netherlands East Indies Legal Education: Pedagogy, Curriculum, and Colonial State Formation." *Itinerario* 37(2) (August 2013): 121.

Donlan, Seán Patrick. "Comparative? Legal? History? Crossing Boundaries." In *Comparative Legal History*, edited by Olivier Moréteau, Aniceto Masferrer, and Kjell A. Modéer, 78. Cheltenham: Edward Elgar, 2019.

*Dr. Syama Prasad Mookerjee: A Selfless Patriot*. New Delhi: Dr. Syama Prasad Mookerjee Research Foundation, 2017. https://spmrf.org/spmookerjee/dr-spm-a-selfless-patriot.pdf.

"Dr. Wu's Constitution." *Harvard Law Review* 132 (2019): 2300.

Duara, Prasenjit. "The Discourse of Civilization and Pan-Asianism." *Journal of World History* 12 (2001): 99.

Dubnov, Arie. "Notes on the Zionist Passage to India, or: The Analogical Imagination and its Boundaries." *Journal of Israeli History* 35 (2016): 177.

Dumézil, Georges. *Mitra-Varuna: An Essay on Two Indo-European Representations of Sovereignty*, translated by Derek Coltman. New York: Zone Books, 1988.

Dupret, Baudouin, and Jean-Louis Halpérin eds. *State Law and Legal Positivism: The Global Rise of a New Paradigm*. Leiden: Brill, 2022.

Dupret, Baudouin, and Gianluca Parolin. "The Great Divide in Legal Discourse." In *State Law and Legal Positivism: The Global Rise of a New Paradigm*, edited by Baudouin Dupret and Jean-Louis Halpérin, 5. Leiden: Brill, 2022.

Duve, Thomas, ed. *Entanglements in Legal History: Conceptual Approaches*. Frankfurt am Main: Max Planck Institute for European Legal History, 2014.

Duve, Thomas. "What Is Global Legal History?" *Comparative Legal History* 8 (2020): 73.

Duxbury, Neil. *Jurists and Judges: An Essay on Influence*. Oxford: Hart, 2001.

Duxbury, Neil. "English Jurisprudence between Austin and Hart." *Virginia Law Review* 91 (2005): 1.

Edrei, Arye. "Madu'a Lanu Mishpat 'Ivri?" *'Iyuney Mishpat* 25 (2001): 467.

Edrei, Ayre. "Law, Interpretation, and Ideology: The Renewal of the Jewish Laws of War in the State of Israel." *Cardozo Law Review* 28 (2006): 187.

Edrei, Arye. "Lo Posek Ani?! Menachem Elon: Shofet o-Posek Halakhah." In *Halakhah u-Mishpat: Sefer ha-Zikaron le-Meanchem Elon*, edited by Arye Edrei, David Gliksberg, Aviad Hacohen et al., 45. Tsafririm: Nevo, 2018.

Edrei, Arye. "Menachem Elon veha-Mishpat ha-'Ivri: Tsiyuney Derekh." In *Halakhah u-Mishpat: Sefer ha-Zikaron le-Menachem Elon*, edited by Arye Edrei, David Gliksberg, Aviad Hacohen et al., 13. Tsafririm: Nevo, 2018.

Edrei, Arye. "Rav-Tarbutiyut be-Girsah Haredit Mukdement: Yitzhak Breuer mi-Medinat ha-Torah le-Kehilat ha-Torah." *Diné Israel* 32 (2018): 187.

Edrei, Arye. "A Religious Zionist Dream: Rabbi Herzog's Vision of Israeli Law." *Jewish Quarterly Review* 112 (2022): 620.

Edrei, Arye. "Halom ha-Mishpat: Ha-Rav Herzog veha-Rav Goren 'al Yahasey Mishpat ve-Halakhah be-Yisrael." *Diné Israel* 35–6 (2022): 31.

Edrei, Arye, and Anver M. Emon. "Sovereignty, Law, and the Pedagogy of Historical Fantasy: On the Halakha on the Laws of War and the Fiqh on Dhimmis." In *Islamic and Jewish Legal Reasoning: Encountering our Legal Other*, edited by Anver M. Emon, 155. London: Oneworld, 2016.

Egorova, Yulia. *Jews and India: History, Image, Perceptions*. Milton Park and New York: Routledge, 2006.

Elhalaby, Esmat. "Empire and Arab Indology." *Modern Intellectual History* 19 (2022): 1081.

Elias, Mohamed. "A. S. Panchapakesa Ayyar." In *Encyclopedia of Post-Colonial Literatures in English*, edited by Eugene Benson and L. W. Conolly, 2nd ed., Vol. 1, 91. London: Routledge, 2005.

Elst, Koenraad. "Manu as a Weapon against Egalitarianism: Nietzsche and Hindu Political Philosophy." In *Nietzsche, Power and Politics: Rethinking Nietzsche's Legacy for Political Thought*, edited by Herman W. Siemens and Vasti Roodt, 543. Berlin: Walter de Gruyter, 2008.

*Eminent Mussalmans*. Madras: G. A. Natesan & Co., 1926.

Erlich, Haggai. *Students and University in 20th Century Egyptian Politics*. London: F. Cass, 1989.

Esmeir, Samera. *Juridical Humanity: A Colonial History*. Stanford, CA: Stanford University Press, 2012.

Esmeir, Samera. "On the Coloniality of Modern Law." *Critical Analysis of Law* 2 (2015): 19.

Fadel, Mohammad. "Sovereignty, Territoriality, and Private International Law in Classical Muslim International Law." *American Journal of Comparative Law* 71 (2023): 853.

"Federbusch, Simon." In *Universal Jewish Encyclopedia*, Vol. 4, 622. New York: Ktav, 1969.

Fekete, Balázs. *Paradigms in Modern European Comparative Law: A History*. Oxford: Hart, 2021.

Fernandez, Angela, and Markus Dubber. "Introduction: Putting the Legal Treatise in Its Place." In *Law Books in Action: Essays on the Anglo-American Legal Treatise*, edited by Markus Dubber and Angela Fernandez, 1. Oxford: Hart, 2012.

Ferrara, Antonio. "Eugene Kulischer, Joseph Schechtman and the Historiography of European Forced Migrations." *Journal of Contemporary History* 46 (2011): 715.

Fillon, Catherine. "L'enseignement du droit, instrument et enjeu de la diplomatie culturelle française: L'exemple de l'Égypte au début du XXe siècle." *Mil neuf cent: Revue d'histoire intellectuelle* 29 (2011): 123.

Fillon, Catherine, Florence Renucci, Silvia Falconieri, and Laetitia Guerlain, eds., "Enseigner le droit hors des frontières nationales (XIXe–XXe siècles): Deuxième partie." Numéro spécial, *Cahiers Jean Moulin* 9 (2023). https://journals.openedition.org/cjm/2051.

Flaks, Samuel. "Law, Religion, and Pluralism: The Thought and Experiences of Nathan Isaacs (1886–1941)." *Touro Law Review* 29 (2013): 307.

Flatto, David C., and Benjamin Porat. *Law as Religion, Religion as Law*. Cambridge: Cambridge University Press, 2022.

Frankenberg, Günter. "Critical Histories of Comparative Law." In *The Oxford Handbook of Legal History*, edited by Markus Dubber and Christopher Tomlins, 43. Oxford: Oxford University Press, 2018.

Friedman, Shuki, and Amihai Radzyner. *Hukah shelo Ktuvah ba-Torah*. Jerusalem: IDI Press, 2006.

Fung, Edmund S. K. *In Search of Chinese Democracy: Civil Opposition in Nationalist China, 1929–1949*. New York: Cambridge University Press, 2000.
Fung, Edmund S. K. *The Intellectual Foundations of Chinese Modernity: Cultural and Political Thought in the Republican Era*. New York: Cambridge University Press, 2010.
Furas, Yoni. *Educating Palestine: Teaching and Learning History under the Mandate*. Oxford: Oxford University Press, 2020.
Furstenberg, Yair. "Imperialism and the Creation of Local Law: The Case of Rabbinic Law." In *Legal Engagement: The Reception of Roman Law and Tribunals by Jews and Other Inhabitants of the Empire*, edited by Katell Bertholet, Natalie Dohrmann, and Capucine Nemo-Peckelman, 271. Rome: École française de Rome, 2021.
Galanter, Marc. "The Displacement of Traditional Law in Modern India." *Journal of Social Issues* 24 (1968): 65.
Galanter, Marc. "The Aborted Restoration of 'Indigenous' Law in India." In *Law and Society in Modern India*, 37. Delhi: Oxford University Press, 1997.
Galili, Ziva. "The Soviet Experience of Zionism: Importing Soviet Political Culture to Palestine." *Journal of Israeli History* 24 (2005): 1.
Gassner, Miriam. "The Distaff Side? Hans Kelsen's Viennese Female Students." *Journal on European History of Law* 15(1) (2024): 2.
G. C. B. "John Bruce Norton (1815–1883)." In *Dictionary of National Biography*, edited by Sidney Lee, Vol. 41, 216. New York: Macmillan & Co., 1895.
Gelber, Yoav. "Is Zionism Colonialism?" In *The British Mandate in Palestine: A Centenary Volume, 1920–2020*, edited by Michael J. Cohen, 221. New York: Routledge, 2020.
Giaro, Tomasz. "A Purely Western Tradition: The 100th Anniversary of the Orientalisation Debate." In *The Grand Strategy of Comparative Law: Themes, Methods, Developments*, edited by Luca Siliquini-Cinelli, Davide Gianti, and Mauro Balestrieri, 253. New York: Routledge, 2024.
Giladi, Rotem. *Jews, Sovereignty, and International Law: Ideology, Identity, and Ambivalence in Early Israeli Diplomacy*. Oxford: Oxford University Press, 2021.
Giunchi, Elisa. "The Reinvention of Sharia under the British Raj: In Search of Authenticity and Certainty." *Journal of Asian Studies* 69 (2010): 1119.
Giurato, Rocco. "Constitutional History Teaching in Britain (19th–20th Centuries)." *Giornale Di Storia Costituzionale / Journal of Constitutional History* 47 (2024): 85.
Goebel, Michael. *Anti-Imperial Metropolis: Interwar Paris and the Seeds of Third World Nationalism*. New York: Cambridge University Press, 2015.
Goldsworthy, Jeffrey. "Constitutional Theory and Thought." In *The Cambridge Constitutional History of the United Kingdom*, edited by

Peter Cane and H. Kumarasingham, 254. Cambridge: Cambridge University Press, 2023.

Gray, Stuart. "History, the Hindu Right, and Subversion of Brahmanical-Hindu Political Thought." In *The Oxford Handbook of Comparative Political Theory*, edited by Leigh K. Jenco, Murad Idris, and Megan C. Thomas, 240. New York: Oxford University Press, 2020.

Greenspoon, Leonard J., ed. *Is Judaism Democratic? Reflections from Theory and Practice Throughout the Ages*. West Lafayette, IN: Purdue University Press, 2018.

Greiff, Thomas E. "The Principle of Human Rights in Nationalist China: John C. H. Wu and the Ideological Origins of the 1946 Constitution." *China Quarterly* 103 (1985): 441.

Gross, Nahum. "Mada'i ha-Hevrah ba-Universitah ha-'Ivrit 'ad 1948/9: Tokhniyot ve-Hathalot." In *Toldot ha-Universitah ha-'Ivrit: Hitbasesut u-Tsmihah*, edited by Hagit Lavsky, 503. Jerusalem: Magnes Press, 2005.

Guenther, Alan M. "Syed Mahmood and the Transformation of Muslim Law in British India." PhD dissertation, McGill University, 2004.

Guerlain, Laetitia, and Florence Renucci. "L'École de droit de Pondichéry (1838–1960): Étude exploratoire d'un établissement d'enseignement supérieur colonial." *Cahiers Jean Moulin* 7 (2021). https://doi.org/10.4000/cjm.1278.

Guerlain, Laetitia, Catherine Fillon, Florence Renucci et al., eds., "Enseigner le droit hors des frontières nationales (XIXe–XXe siècles)." Numéro spécial, *Cahiers Jean Moulin* 7 (2021). https://journals.openedition.org/cjm/1253.

Guerlain, Laetitia, Catherine Fillon, Florence Renucci et al. "Pour une histoire de l'enseignement du droit hors des frontières nationales (XIXe–XXe siècle." *Cahiers Jean Moulin* 7 (2021). https://doi.org/10.4000/cjm.1258.

Guha, Ranajit. *An Indian Historiography of India: A Nineteenth-Century Agenda and Its Implications*. Calcutta: K. P. Bagchi, 1988.

Hakim, Nader. "Droit naturel et histoire chez François Gény." *Clio@Themis* 9 (2015). https://doi.org/10.35562/cliothemis.1534.

Hakim, Nader, and Fabrice Melleray, eds. *Le renouveau de la doctrine française: Les grands auteurs de la pensée juridique au tournant du XXe siècle*. Paris: Dalloz, 2009.

Halevi, Leor. *Modern Things on Trial: Islam's Global and Material Reformation in the Age of Rida, 1865–1935*. New York: Columbia University Press, 2019.

Hallaq, Wael B. *The Impossible State: Islam, Politics, and Modernity's Moral Predicament*. New York: Columbia University Press, 2013.

Halpérin, Jean-Louis. *Profils des mondialisations du droit*. Paris: Dalloz, 2009.

Halpérin, Jean-Louis. "Western Legal Transplants and India." *Jindal Global Law Review* 2 (2010): 14.

Halpérin, Jean-Louis. *Five Legal Revolutions Since the 17th Century: An Analysis of a Global Legal History*. Cham: Springer, 2014.

Halpérin, Jean-Louis. "Historical Landmarks in Mapping the Spread of Positive Law Teaching." In *State Law and Legal Positivism: The Global Rise of a New Paradigm*, edited by Baudouin Dupret and Jean-Louis Halpérin, 34. Leiden: Brill, 2022.

Halpérin, Jean-Louis. "Historical-Jurisprudential Methods." In *The Cambridge Handbook of Comparative Law*, edited by Mathias Siems and Po Jen Yap, 32. New York: Cambridge University Press, 2024.

Hannaford, Ivan. *Race: The History of an Idea in the West*. Washington, DC: Woodrow Wilson Center Press; Baltimore, MD: Johns Hopkins University Press, 1996.

Harel-Shalev, Ayelet. *The Challenge of Sustaining Democracy in Deeply Divided Societies: Citizenship, Rights, and Ethnic Conflicts in India and Israel*. Lanham, MD: Lexington Press, 2010.

Harif, Hanan. *Anashim Ahim Anahnu: Ha-Pniyah Mizrahah ba-Hagut ha-Tsiyonit*. Jerusalem: Shazar, 2019.

Harris, Ron. "History and Sources." In *The Israeli Legal System: An Introduction*, edited by Christian Walter, Barak Medina, Lothar Scholz et al., 15. Baden-Baden: Nomos, 2019.

Hayward, J. E. S. "Solidarity: The Social History of an Idea in Nineteenth Century France." *International Review of Social History* 4 (1959): 261.

He, Qinhua. "The Birth and Growth of Modern Jurisprudence in China." *Frontiers of Law in China* 1 (2006): 486.

Heehs, Peter. "Aurobindo Ghose and Revolutionary Terrorism." *South Asia* 15 (1992): 47.

Hellinger, Moshe, ed. *Ha-Masoret ha-Politit ha-Yehudit le-Dorotehah*. Ramat Gan: Bar Ilan University Press, 2010.

Herget, James E., and Stephen Wallace. "The German Free Law Movement as the Source of American Legal Realism." *Virginia Law Review* 73 (1987): 399.

Hill, Enid. *Al-Sanhuri and Islamic Law: The Place and Significance of Islamic Law in the Life and Work of 'Abd al-Razzaq Ahmad al-Sanhuri, Egyptian Jurist and Scholar, 1895–1971*. Cairo: American University in Cairo Press, 1987.

Hill, Enid. "Islamic Law as a Source for the Development of a Comparative Jurisprudence, the 'Modern Science of Codification': Theory and Practice in the Life and Work of 'Abd al-Razzaq Ahmad al-Sanhuri (1895–1971)." In *Islamic Law: Social and Historical Contexts*, edited by Aziz al-Azmeh, 145. London: Routledge, 1988.

Al-Hout, Bayan Nuweihid. "The Palestinian Political Elite During the Mandate Period." *Journal of Palestine Studies* 9 (1979): 85.

Hroch, Miroslav. *Social Preconditions of National Revival in Europe: A Comparative Analysis of the Social Composition of Patriotic Groups among the Smaller European Nations*. Cambridge: Cambridge University Press, 1985.

Hulsewé, A. F. P., and M. H. Valk. "Jean Escarra (1885–1955)." *T'oung Pao* 44 (1956): 304.

Hussain, Adeel. *Law and Muslim Political Thought in Late Colonial North India*. Oxford: Oxford University Press, 2022.

Hussein, Mostafa. *Hebrew Orientalism: Jewish Engagement with Arabo-Islamic Culture in Late Ottoman and British Palestine*. Princeton, NJ: Princeton University Press, 2026.

Hussin, Iza R. *The Politics of Islamic Law: Local Elites, Colonial Authority, and the Making of the Muslim State*. Chicago, IL: University of Chicago Press, 2016.

Huxley, Andrew. "Positivists and Buddhists: The Rise and Fall of Anglo-Burmese Ecclesiastical Law." *Law and Social Inquiry* 26 (2001): 113.

Inden, Ronald B. *Imagining India*. Bloomington, IN: Indiana University Press, 2000.

International Commission of Jurists, *Under False Colours: A Report on the Character of the International Association of Democratic Lawyers*. The Hague: n.p., 1955.

Ip, Eric Chiyeung. "Building Constitutional Democracy on Oriental Foundations: An Anatomy of Sun Yat-sen's Constitutionalism." *Historia Constitucional* 9 (2008): 328.

Israel-Vleeschhouwer, Amos. "Yahas ha-Halakhah la-Mishpat ha-Beyn Leumi: Nitu'ah ha-Psikah ve-Nituah Tahalikhi." PhD dissertation, Tel Aviv University Faculty of Law, 2012.

Iyer, V. R. Krishna. "Towards a Third World Jurisprudence." In *Law versus Justice: Problems and Solutions*, 132. New Delhi: Deep & Deep, 1981.

Jaffe, James. *Ironies of Colonial Governance: Law, Custom and Justice in Colonial India*. Cambridge: Cambridge University Press, 2015.

Jaffe, James. "Gandhi, Lawyers, and the Courts' Boycott During the Non-Cooperation Movement." *Modern Asian Studies* 51 (2017): 1340.

Jaffrelot, Christophe. *The Hindu Nationalist Movement in India*. New York: Columbia University Press, 1996.

Jaffrelot, Christophe. *Modi's India: Hindu Nationalism and the Rise of Ethnic Democracy*, translated by Cynthia Schoch. New York: Columbia University Press, 2019.

Jain, M. P. *Outlines of Indian Legal and Constitutional History*. 7th ed. Gurgaon: Lexis Nexis, 2016.

Jain, Naresh Kumar, ed. *Muslims in India: A Biographical Dictionary*. New Delhi: Manohar, 1979.

Jain, Subhash C. "French Legal System in Pondicherry: An Introduction." *Journal of the Indian Law Institute* 12 (1970): 573.

Jangid, Khinvraj. "Imagining Nations, Creating States: Nehru, Ben-Gurion and an Analogical Study of India and Israel in Post-Colonial Asia." *Israel Studies* 26 (2020): 73.

Jha, J. S., ed., *K. P. Jayaswal Commemoration Volume*. Patna: K. P. Jayaswal Research Institute, 1981.

Jones, Colin Philip Charles. "Living Law in Japan: Social Jurisprudence in the Interwar Period." PhD dissertation, Columbia University, 2017.

Jones, Kenneth W. *Socio-Religious Reform Movements in British India*. Cambridge: Cambridge University Press, 1989.

Judson, Daniel. "A Home for Jewish Learning in 'The City on the Hill': The History of Hebrew College." In *Hiddushim: Celebrating Hebrew College's Centennial*, edited by Jonathan D. Sarna, Arthur Green, and Michael Fishbane, 11. Boston, MA: Academic Studies Press, 2022.

Kabha, Mustafa. *Ha-'Itonut ha-'Aravit ha-Falastinit bi-Tkufat ha-Mandat ha-Briti 'al Erets-Yisrael*, 29. Jerusalem: Yad Ben Zvi, 2004.

Kahn-Freund, Otto. "On Uses and Misuses of Comparative Law." *Modern Law Review* 37 (1974): 1.

Kalmbach, Hilary. *Islamic Knowledge and the Making of Modern Egypt*. Cambridge: Cambridge University Press, 2020.

Kannan, K. S., ed., *Western Indology & Its Quest for Power: Proceedings of Swadeshi Indology Conference Series*. Chennai: Infinity Foundation India, 2017.

Katju, Manjari. "The History of Hindu Nationalism in India." In *The Oxford History of Hinduism: Modern Hinduism*, edited by Torkel Brekke, 203. Oxford: Oxford University Press, 2019.

Katz, Ethan, Lisa Moses Leff, and Maud S. Mandel. "Introduction: Engaging Colonial History and Jewish History." In *Colonialism and the Jews*, edited by Ethan Katz, Lisa Moses Leff, and Maud S. Mandel, 1. Bloomington, IN: Indiana University Press, 2017.

Katz, Gideon, and Nir Kedar. "Ha-Yahadut be-'Eyney Intelektu'alim Yisra'elim Hilonim." *Tarbut Demokratit* 14 (2012): 93.

Kaye, Alexander. *The Invention of Jewish Theocracy: The Struggle for Legal Authority in Modern Israel*. New York: Oxford University Press, 2020.

Kearley, Timothy G. *Lost in Translations: Roman Law Scholarship and Translation in Early Twentieth-Century America*. Durham, NC: Carolina Academic Press, 2018.

Kedar, Alexandre (Sandy). "Expanding Legal Geographies: A Call for a Critical Comparative Approach." In *The Expanding Spaces of Law: A Timely Legal Geography*, edited by Irus Braverman, Nicholas Blomley, David Delaney et al., 97. Stanford, CA: Stanford University Press, 2014.

Kedar, Nir. *Law and Identity in Israel: A Century of Debate*. Cambridge: Cambridge University Press, 2019.

Kedar, Nir. *David Ben-Gurion and the Foundation of Israeli Democracy*. Bloomington, IN: Indiana University Press, 2021.

Kemp, Sandra, Charlotte Mitchell, and David Trotter, eds. "Chan-Toon, Mrs. M.: Mabel Mary Agnes Cosgrove." In *Edwardian Fiction: An Oxford Companion*, 62. Oxford: Oxford University Press, 1997.

Kennedy, Duncan. "Three Globalizations of Law and Legal Thought: 1850–2000." In *The New Law and Economic Development: A Critical Appraisal*, edited by David M. Trubek and Alvaro Santos, 19. New York: Cambridge University Press, 2006.

Khan, Noor-Aiman I. *Egyptian-Indian Nationalist Collaboration and the British Empire*. New York: Palgrave, 2011.

Kles, Guy. "Universitah ba-Galut: Ha-Historyah shel ha-Hinukh ha-Mishpati ba-'Asor ha-Rishon la-Medinah." *Mishpatim* 41 (2012): 605.

Kollontai, Pauline, and Friedrich Lohmann, eds. *On the Significance of Religion for Human Rights*. London: Routledge, 2023.

Koskenniemi, Martti. "Histories of International Law: Dealing with Eurocentrism." *Rechtsgeschichte* 19 (2011): 152.

Koskenniemi, Martti, and Ville Kari. "A More Elevated Patriotism: The Emergence of International and Comparative Law (Nineteenth Century)." In *The Oxford Handbook of European Legal History*, edited by Heikki Pihlajamäki, Markus D. Dubber, and Mark Godfrey, 974. Oxford: Oxford University Press, 2018.

Kozlowski, Gregory C. *Muslim Endowments and Society in British India*. Cambridge: Cambridge University Press, 1985.

Kresin, Oleksii V. *Comparative Legal Studies 1750–1835: Approaches to Conceptualization*, edited and translated by William E. Butler. London: Wildy, Simmonds and Hill, 2019.

Krishnan, Jayanth K. "Professor Kingsfield Goes to Delhi: American Academics, the Ford Foundation, and the Development of Legal Education in India." *American Journal of Legal History* 47 (2003): 447.

Krishnan, Jayanth K. "From the ALI to the ILI: The Efforts to Export an American Legal Institution." *Vanderbilt Journal of Transnational Law* 38 (2005): 1255.

Kroncke, Jedidiah J. "Roscoe Pound in China: A Lost Precedent for the Liabilities of American Legal Exceptionalism." *Brooklyn Journal of International Law* 38 (2012): 77.

Kroncke, Jedidiah J. *The Futility of Law and Development: China and the Dangers of Exporting American Law*. New York: Oxford University Press, 2016.

Kroncke, Jedidiah J. "Model, System, or Node? Understanding Legal Education Reform in Twentieth-Century China and Beyond." In *American Legal Education Abroad: Critical Histories*, edited by Susan Bartie and David Sandomierski, 162. New York: New York University Press, 2021.

Kugle, Scott Alan. "Framed, Blamed and Renamed: The Recasting of Islamic Jurisprudence in Colonial South Asia." *Modern Asian Studies* 35 (2001): 257.

Kumarasingham, H. "Written Differently: A Survey of Commonwealth Constitutional History in the Age of Decolonisation." *Journal of Imperial and Commonwealth History* 46 (2018): 874.

Kupferschmidt, Uri. *The Supreme Muslim Council: Islam under the British Mandate for Palestine*. Leiden: Brill, 1987.

Lal, Ratan. *Kashi Prasad Jayaswal: The Making of a "Nationalist" Historian*. Delhi: Aakar Books, 2018.

Landauer, Carl. "Passage from India: Nagendra Singh's India and International Law." *Indian Journal of International Law* 56 (2016): 265.

Landauer, Carl. "The Polish Rider: CH Alexandrowicz and the Reorientation of International Law, Part I: Madras Studies." *London Review of International Law* 7 (2019): 321.

Landauer, Carl. "C. H. Alexandrowicz's India and the Kautilyan Moment." *Asian Journal of International Law* 15 (2025): 107.

Last Stone, Suzanne. "Sinaitic and Noahide Law: Legal Pluralism in Jewish Law." *Cardozo Law Review* 12 (1991): 1157.

Lawson, F. H. *The Oxford Law School 1850–1965*. Oxford: Clarendon Press, 1968.

Lee, Luke T., and Whalen W. Lai. "The Chinese Conceptions of Law: Confucian, Legalist, and Buddhist." *Hastings Law Journal* 29 (1978): 1307.

Legrandjacques, Sara. "L'enseignement supérieur en Asie française et britannique: expériences croisées à l'âge des Empires (Années 1850–1930)." *Outre-Mers: Revue d'Histoire* 105 (2017): 39.

Legrandjacques, Sara. "Global Students? The International Mobility and Identity of Students from Colonial India and Indochina, 1880s–1945." *Global Histories* 4(2) (October 2018): 46.

Legrandjacques, Sara. "Inégaux en droit: approche comparée de l'enseignement juridique en Inde britannique et en Indochine française XIXe–XXe siècle." *Cahiers Jean Moulin* 7 (2021). https://doi.org/10.4000/cjm.1334.

Legrandjacques, Sara. "Law of the Strongest? A Global Approach of Access to Law Studies and Its Social and Professional Impact in British India (1850s–1940s)." *Social Sciences* 10 (2021): 113.

Lerner, Hanna. *Making Constitutions in Deeply Divided Societies*. Cambridge: Cambridge University Press, 2011.

Lerner, Pablo. "Leaving Home, Transplanting Law: Guido Tedeschi and Other Jewish Émigrés from Europe." *Studi Senesi* 130 (2018): 229.

Lev, Shimon. *Nehirin lanu Shevilin de-Hodu: Ha-Mifgash beyn ha-'Olam ha-Yehudi-Tsiyoni le-Hodu ve-Tarbutah 'al Rek'a Tsmihat ha-Tnu'ot ha-Leumiyot*. Tel Aviv: Gama, 2018.

Levine, Norman. "The German Historical School of Law and the Origins of Historical Materialism." *Journal of the History of Ideas* 48 (1987): 431.

Levitt, Jeremy I. "The African Origins of International Law: Myth or Reality." *UCLA Journal of International Law and Foreign Affairs* 19 (2015): 113.

Levy, Amit. *A New Orient: From German Scholarship to Middle Eastern Studies in Israel*. Waltham, MA: Brandeis University Press, 2024.

Lewis, Bernard. *The Emergence of Modern Turkey*. 2nd ed. London: Oxford University Press, 1968.

Likhovski, Assaf. "The Invention of 'Hebrew Law' in Mandatory Palestine." *American Journal of Comparative Law* 46 (1998): 339.

Likhovski, Assaf. "Colonialism, Nationalism and Legal Education: The Case of Mandatory Palestine." In *The History of Law in a Multicultural Society: Israel 1917–1967*, edited by Ron Harris, Alexandre Kedar, Pnina Lahav et al., 75. Dartmouth: Ashgate, 2002.

Likhovski, Assaf. "Czernowitz, Lincoln, Jerusalem, and the Comparative History of American Jurisprudence." *Theoretical Inquiries in Law* 4 (2003): 621.

Likhovski, Assaf. "Limudey ha-Mishpatim ba-Universitah ha-'Ivrit bi-Tkufat ha-Mandat." In *Toldot ha-Universitah ha-'Ivrit bi-Yerushalayim: Hitbasesut u-Tsmihah*, edited by Hagit Lavsky, 543. Jerusalem: Magnes Press, 2005.

Likhovski, Assaf. *Law and Identity in Mandate Palestine*. Chapel Hill, NC: University of North Carolina Press, 2006.

Likhovski, Assaf. "Le droit comme objet de conflit culturel anglo-français dans la Palestine mandataire." In *De Balfour à Ben Gourion: Les puissances européennes et la Palestine 1917–1948*, edited by Dominique Trimbur and Ran Aaronsohn, 201. Paris: CNRS, 2008.

Likhovski, Assaf. "Argonauts of the Eastern Mediterranean: Legal Transplants and Signaling." *Theoretical Inquiries in Law* 10 (2009): 619.

Likhovski, Assaf. "History of British Legal Education in Mandatory Palestine." In *Experimental Legal Education in a Globalized World: The Middle East and Beyond*, eds. Mutaz M. Qafisheh and Stephen A. Rosenbaum, 177. Newcastle upon Tyne: Cambridge Scholars Publishing, 2016.

Likhovski, Assaf. *Tax Law and Social Norms in Mandatory Palestine and Israel*. New York: Cambridge University Press, 2017.

Likhovski, Assaf. "The Eagle and the Dove: Jewish Law Scholars and Roman Law During the Interwar Period." In *Pensiero giuridico occidentale e giuristi romani: Eredità e genealogie*, edited by Pierre Bonin, Nader Hakim, Fara Nasti et al., 267. Turin: G. Giappichelli, 2019.

Likhovski, Assaf. "The Rise and Demise of Constitutional Duties in Israel." *American Journal of Legal History* 61 (2021): 90.

Likhovski, Assaf. "The Many Exiles of Max Laserson." *Clio@Themis* 22 (2022). http://journals.openedition.org/cliothemis/2087.

Likhovski, Assaf. "Jurisprudence and Nationalism in the British Empire in the Early Twentieth Century: India, Egypt, and Palestine Compared." *English Historical Review*. Forthcoming.

Likhovski, Assaf, and Aviram Shahal. "Israeli Pre-State Constitutionalism." In *The Oxford Handbook of the Israeli Constitution*, edited by Aharon Barak, Barak Medina, and Yaniv Roznai. Oxford University Press. Forthcoming.

Lobban, Michael. "Was There a Nineteenth Century 'English School of Jurisprudence'?" *Journal of Legal History* 16 (1995): 34.

Lobban, Michael. "Legal Theory and Judge-Made Law in England, 1850–1920." *Quaderni Fiorentini* 40 (2011): 553.

Loeffler, James. "The Religions of Human Rights." *Harvard Theological Review* 116 (2023): 147.

Loeffler, James. "A Tradition in Crisis: Human Rights and Jewish Politics Reconsidered." *Journal of the Council for Research on Religion* 6 (2025): 1.

Lorberbaum, Menachem. *Politics and the Limits of Law: Secularizing the Political in Medieval Jewish Thought*. Stanford, CA: Stanford University Press, 2001.

Lorca, Arnulf Becker. *Mestizo International Law: A Global Intellectual History 1842–1933*. Cambridge: Cambridge University Press, 2014.

Lu, Tongxin. "John C. H. Wu: A Prodigy in Synthesizing East and West and a Prophet for the Evangelization of China." PhD dissertation, Catholic University of America, 2020.

Lubin, Timothy, Donald R. Davis, Jr., and Jayanth K. Krishnan, eds., *Hinduism and Law: An Introduction*. Cambridge and New York: Cambridge University Press, 2010.

Lubin, Timothy Jr., Donald R. Davis, and Jayanth K. Krishnan. "Introduction." In *Hinduism and Law: An Introduction*, edited by Timothy Lubin Jr., Donald R. Davis, and Jayanth K. Krishnan, 1. Cambridge and New York: Cambridge University Press, 2010.

MacCormack, Geoffrey. *Traditional Chinese Penal Law*. Edinburgh: Edinburgh University Press, 1996.

Macdonald, R. St. J. "Legal Education in China Today." *Dalhousie Law Journal* 6 (1980): 313.

Mackie, Gregory. "Forging Oscar Wilde: Mrs. Chan-Toon and for Love of the King." *English Literature in Transition, 1880–1920* 54 (2011): 267.

Manela, Erez, and Heather Streets-Salter, eds. *The Anticolonial Transnational: Imaginaries, Mobilities, and Networks in the Struggle against Empire*. Cambridge: Cambridge University Press, 2023.

Manjapra, Kris. "From Imperial to International Horizons: A Hermeneutic Study of Bengali Modernism." *Modern Intellectual History* 8 (2011): 327.

Manjapra, Kris. "Knowledgeable Internationalism and the Swadeshi Movement, 1903–1921." *Economic and Political Weekly* 47(42) (October 2012): 53.

Manjapra, Kris. *Age of Entanglement: German and Indian Intellectuals across Europe*. Cambridge, MA: Harvard University Press, 2014.

Mantena, Karuna. *Alibis of Empire: Henry Maine and the Ends of Liberal Imperialism*. Princeton, NJ: Princeton University Press, 2010.

March, Andrew F. *The Caliphate of Men: Popular Sovereignty in Modern Islamic Thought*. Cambridge, MA: Harvard University Press, 2019.

Marchand, Suzanne. "Has the History of the Disciplines Had Its Day?" In *Rethinking Modern European Intellectual History*, edited by Darrin M. McMahon and Samuel Moyn, 130. New York: Oxford University Press, 2014.
Martin, Terry. *The Affirmative Action Empire: Nations and Nationalism in the USSR, 1923–1939*. Ithaca, NY: Cornell University Press, 2001.
Masé, Aline. "Student Migration of Jews from Tsarist Russia to the Universities of Bern and Zürich, 1865–1914." Master's thesis, Utrecht University, 2012.
Masodkar, B. A. *National Jurisprudence: Need and Approach*. Nagpur: Shree Ram Trust, 1974.
Matsubara, Kentaro. "East, East, and West: Comparative Law and the Historical Processes of Legal Interaction in China and Japan." *American Journal of Comparative Law* 66 (2018): 769.
McClish, Mark. *The History of the Arthaśāstra: Sovereignty and Sacred Law in Ancient India*. Cambridge: Cambridge University Press, 2019.
Mehta, Pratap Bhanu. "Hindu Nationalism: From Ethnic Identity to Authoritarian Repression." *Studies in Indian Politics* 10 (2022): 31.
Mendes-Flohr, Paul. *Divided Passions: Jewish Intellectuals and the Experience of Modernity*. Detroit, MI: Wayne State University Press, 1991.
Menski, Werner. *Hindu Law: Beyond Tradition and Modernity*. New Delhi: Oxford University Press, 2003.
Menski, Werner. *Comparative Law in a Global Context: The Legal Systems of Asia and Africa*. 2nd ed. Cambridge: Cambridge University Press, 2006.
Menski, Werner. "Hindu Law in Modern Times: How Hindu Law Continues in Modern India." In *The Oxford History of Hinduism: Modern Hinduism*, edited by Torkel Brekke, 244. Oxford: Oxford University Press, 2019.
Metcalf, Barbara D., and Thomas R. Metcalf. *A Concise History of Modern India*. 2nd ed. New York: Cambridge University Press, 2006.
Michaels, Axel. "The Practice of Classical Hindu Law." In *Hinduism and Law: An Introduction*, eds. Timothy Lubin, Donald R. Davis, Jr., and Jayanth K. Krishnan, 58. Cambridge and New York: Cambridge University Press, 2010.
Michaels, Ralf. "How Asian Should Asian Law Be?" In *Convergence and Divergence of Private Law in Asia*, edited by Gary Low, 227. Cambridge: Cambridge University Press, 2022.
Minault, Gail. *The Khilafat Movement: Religious Symbolism and Political Mobilization in India*. New York: Columbia University Press, 1982.
Misra, B. B. *The Indian Middle Classes: Their Growth in Modern Times*. London: Oxford University Press, 1961.
Misra, Maria. "The Indian Machiavelli: Pragmatism versus Morality, and the Reception of the *Arthasastra* in India, 1905–2014." *Modern Asian Studies* 50 (2016): 310.

Mitchell, Ryan Martínez. *Recentering the World: China and the Transformation of International Law*. Cambridge: Cambridge University Press, 2023.

Mittleman, Alan. "Mishpat Hamelukhah and the Jewish Political Tradition in the Thought of R. Shimon Federbush." *Jewish Political Studies Review* 10 (1998): 67.

Mo, John, and Weidong Li. "Legal Education in the PRC." *Journal of the History of International Law* 4 (2002): 176.

Monateri, Pier Giuseppe. "Black Gaius: A Quest for the Multicultural Origin of the Western Legal Tradition." *Hastings Law Journal* 51 (2000): 479.

Monti, Annamaria. "Professeurs italiens enseignant à l'étranger (XIXe–XXe siècle): Pour une mise en perspective des trajectoires individuelles." *Cahiers Jean Moulin* 9 (2023). https://doi.org/10.4000/cjm.2233.

Mookherjee, Dr. Dilip. "Acharya Pramatha Nath Banerjea, Oration at Federation Hall Society Auditorium." July 6, 2019. Photocopy in the author's possession.

Moosa, Ebrahim. "Colonialism and Islamic Law." In *Islam and Modernity: Key Issues and Debates*, edited by Muhammad Khalid Masud, Armando Salvatore, and Martin van Bruinessen, 158. Edinburgh: Edinburgh University Press, 2009.

Morgan, Jason. *Law and Society in Imperial Japan: Suehiro Izutarō and the Search for Equity*. Amherst, NY: Cambria Press, 2020.

Morse, Robin. "Dower, Dogma and Grand Designs: Law at King's Nineteenth Century Style." In *King's College London: In the Service of Society*, edited by Christine Kenyon Jones, 60. London: King's College, 2004.

Moss, Kenneth B. *Jewish Renaissance in the Russian Revolution*. Cambridge, MA: Harvard University Press, 2009.

Mousourakis, George. *Comparative Law and Legal Traditions: Historical and Contemporary Perspectives*. Cham: Springer, 2019.

Mukharji, Projit Bihari, *Brown Skins, White Coats: Race Science in India, 1920–66*. Chicago, IL: University of Chicago Press, 2020.

Mukherjee, Mithi. *India in the Shadows of Empire: A Legal and Political History, 1774–1950*. Oxford: Oxford University Press, 2010.

Mulvagh, Conor. *Irish Days, Indian Memories: V. V. Giri and Indian Law Students at University College Dublin, 1913–1916*. Sallins: Irish Academic Press, 2016.

Munn, Christopher. *A Special Standing in the World: A History of the Faculty of Law at the University of Hong Kong*. Hong Kong: Hong Kong University Press, 2019.

Murayama, Masayuki. "Kawashima and the Changing Focus on Japanese Legal Consciousness: A Selective History of the Sociology of Law in Japan." *International Journal of Law in Context* 9 (2013): 565.

Mutua, Makau. "What Is TWAIL?" *Proceedings of the Annual Meeting (American Society of International Law)* 94 (2000): 31.

Myers, David N. *Re-inventing the Jewish Past: European Jewish Intellectuals and the Zionist Return to History*. New York: Oxford University Press, 1995.

Nakazato, Nariaki. *Neonationalist Mythology in Postwar Japan: Pal's Dissenting Judgment at the Tokyo War Crimes Tribunal*. Lanham, MD: Lexington Books, 2016.

Nandy, Ashis. "The Other Within: The Strange Case of Radhabinod Pal's Judgment on Culpability." *New Literary History* 23 (1992): 45.

Narain, A. K. "Professor Anant Sadashiv Altekar." *Journal of the Numismatic Society of India* 22 (1960): xxvii.

Narula, Smita. "Law and Hindu Nationalist Movements." In *Hinduism and Law: An Introduction*, eds. Timothy Lubin, Donald R. Davis, Jr., and Jayanth K. Krishnan, 234. Cambridge and New York: Cambridge University Press, 2010.

Nathans, Benjamin. *Beyond the Pale: The Jewish Encounter with Late Imperial Russia*. Berkeley, CA: University of California Press, 2004.

Neis, Rachel Rafael. "The Seduction of Law: Rethinking Legal Studies in Jewish Studies." *Jewish Quarterly Review* 109 (2019): 119.

Nelson, Eric. *The Hebrew Republic: Jewish Sources and the Transformation of European Political Thought*. Cambridge, MA: Harvard University Press, 2010.

Newbigin, Eleanor. *The Hindu Family and the Emergence of Modern India: Law, Citizenship and Community*. Cambridge: Cambridge University Press, 2013.

Nirenberg, David. *Anti-Judaism: The Western Tradition*. New York: Norton, 2013.

Nordbruch, Götz. "Arab Scholars at the Institut de Droit Comparé in Lyon: Rereading the History of Arab-European Intellectual Encounters in the Interwar Period." In *Transnational Islam in Interwar Europe: Muslim Activists and Thinkers*, edited by Götz Nordbruch and Umar Ryad, 89. New York: Palgrave Macmillan, 2014.

Nygård, Stefan, Johan Strang, and Marja Jalava. "At the Periphery of European Intellectual Space." In *Decentering European Intellectual Space*, edited by Marja Jalava, Stefan Nygård, and Johan Strang, 1. Leiden: Brill, 2018.

Obregón, Liliana. "Peripheral Histories of International Law." *Annual Review of Law and Social Science* 15 (2019): 437.

Oddie, Geoffrey A. *Imagined Hinduism: British Protestant Missionary Constructions of Hinduism, 1793–1900*. New Delhi: Sage, 2006.

Ofer, Pinhas. "A Scheme for the Establishment of a British University in Jerusalem in the Late 1920s." *Middle Eastern Studies* 22 (1986): 274.

Ofer, Tehila. *Ish Hazon u-Ma'as: Hayav u-Fo'alo shel Prof. Shmuel Aizenshtadt*. Petah Tikvah: Dfus Havatselet, 1999.

Oldmeadow, Harry. “Ex Oriente Lux: Eastern Religions, Western Writers.” *Literature & Aesthetics* 21 (2011): 23.

Olivelle, Patrick, trans. *King, Governance, and Law in Ancient India: Kautilya’s Arthaśāstra*. Oxford: Oxford University Press, 2012.

Ophir, Adi, and Ishay Rosen-Zvi. *Goy: Israel’s Multiple Others and the Birth of the Gentile*. Oxford: Oxford University Press, 2018.

Oron, S. “Kibud Av.” *He-‘Avar* 13 (1966): 196.

Orren, Yitzhak. “Kenes Yovel ha-50 le-Veyt ha-Sefer le-Mishpat be-Tel Aviv: Divrey Ptihah.” *‘Iyuney Mishpat* 11 (1985/86): 5.

Orren, Yitzhak, ed. *Professor Paltiel Daykan (Dikshtein): Mivhar Monografyot, Mehkarim u- Ma’amarim*. Tel Aviv: Yavneh, 1975.

Osterhammel, Jürgen. *Unfabling the East: The Enlightenment’s Encounter with Asia*, translated by Robert Savage. Princeton, NJ: Princeton University Press, 2018.

Overstreet, Gene D., and Marshall Windmiller. *Communism in India*. Berkeley, CA: University of California Press, 1959.

Owen, Nicholas. “Democratisation and the British Empire.” *Journal of Imperial and Commonwealth History* 47 (2019): 974.

*Oxford Dictionary of National Biography*. 60 vols. Oxford: Oxford University Press, 2004.

Pal, Somnath, *Justice Dr. Radhabinod Pal: A Phenomenal & Inspirational Life’s Journey*, translated by Asok Kumar Ray. New Delhi: Akansha Publishing House, 2020.

Palabıyık, Mustafa Serdar. “International Law for Survival: Teaching International Law in the Late Ottoman Empire (1859–1922).” *Bulletin of SOAS* 78 (2015): 271.

Pant, Apa. *An Unusual Raja: Mahatma Gandhi and the Aundh Experiment*. Hyderabad: Sangam Books, 1989.

Pappé, Ilan. “Why Only a Hebrew University? The Tale of the Arab University in Mandatory Jerusalem.” *Jerusalem Quarterly* 92 (2022): 102.

Parasher, Tejas. *Radical Democracy in Modern Indian Political Thought*. Cambridge: Cambridge University Press, 2023.

Pargendler, Mariana. “The Rise and Decline of Legal Families.” *American Journal of Comparative Law* 60 (2012): 1043.

Pattaro, Enrico, ed., *A Treatise of Legal Philosophy and General Jurisprudence*. 12 vols. Dordrecht: Springer, 2005–16.

Pattaro, Enrico, ed. *A Treatise of Legal Philosophy and General Jurisprudence*, Vol. 8: *A History of the Philosophy of Law in the Common Law World, 1600–1900*. Dordrecht: Springer, 2007.

Paul, John J. *The Legal Profession in Colonial South India*. Bombay: Oxford University Press, 1991.

Paul, Renu (in consultation with Mitra Sharafi). “South Asians at the Inns of Court: Lincoln’s Inn, 1864–1947.” www.yumpu.com/en/document/view/19003915/south-asians-at-the-inns-of-court-lincolns-inn-uw-law-school.

Paz, Reut Yael. "A Forgotten Kelsenian? The Story of Helen Silving-Ryu (1906–1993)." *European Journal of International Law* 25 (2014): 1123.

Peerenboom, Randall P. *Law and Morality in Ancient China: The Silk Manuscripts of Huang-Lao*. Albany, NY: State University of New York Press, 1993.

Peerenboom, Randall P. "Law and Ritual in Chinese Philosophy." In *The Routledge Encyclopedia of Philosophy*, edited by Edward Craig, Vol. 5, 442. New York: Routledge, 1998.

Pennington, Brian K. *Was Hinduism Invented? Britons, Indians, and the Colonial Construction of Religion*. New York: Oxford University Press, 2005.

Penslar, Derek J. *Zionism: An Emotional State*. New Brunswick, NJ: Rutgers University Press, 2023.

Pérez-Perdomo, Rogelio. *Legal Education in the Western World: A Cultural and Comparative History*, translated by Anapaula Pérez and Rosa Meléndez. Stanford, CA: Stanford University Press, 2024.

Pillai, Sarath. "German Lessons: Comparative Constitutionalism, States' Rights, and Federalist Imaginaries in Interwar India." *Comparative Studies in Society and History* 65 (2023): 801.

Pines, Yuri. "Dating a Pre-Imperial Text: The Case Study of the Book of Lord Shang." *Early China* 39 (2016): 145.

Pinto, Vincenzo. "Between Imago and Res: The Revisionist-Zionist Movement's Relationship with Fascist Italy, 1922–1938." *Israel Affairs* 10 (2004): 90.

Pirbhai, M. Reza. "Demons in Hindutva: Writing a Theology for Hindu Nationalism." *Modern Intellectual History* 5 (2008): 27.

Polden, Patrick. "The Education of Lawyers." In *The Oxford History of the Laws of England*, edited by William Cornish, J. Stuart Anderson, Ray Cocks et al., Vol. 11: *1820–1914, English Legal System*, 1175. Oxford: Oxford University Press, 2010.

Pollock, Sheldon. "The Death of Sanskrit." *Comparative Studies in Society and History* 43 (2001): 392.

Porat, Beni, ed. *Mahshavot 'al Demokratyah Yehudit*. Jerusalem: IDI Press, 2010.

Portemer, Jean and Jean-Marie Carbasse, eds., "L'influence des Facultés françaises de droit Outre-Mer et à l'étranger." Numéro spécial, *Revue d'histoire des facultés de droit et de la science juridique* 15 (1994).

*Professor K. V. Rangaswami Aiyangar Commemoration Volume*. Madras: G. S. Press, 1940.

Provence, Michael. *The Last Ottoman Generation and the Making of the Modern Middle East*. New York: Cambridge University Press, 2017.

Pue, W. Wesley. "Guild Training vs. Professional Education: The Committee on Legal Education and the Law Department of Queen's College,

Birmingham in the 1850s." *American Journal of Legal History* 33 (1989): 241.
Purohit, S. K. *Ancient Indian Legal Philosophy: Its Relevance to Contemporary Jurisprudential Thought*. New Delhi: Deep & Deep, 1994.
Qureshi, Naeem. *Pan-Islam in British Indian Politics: A Study of the Khilafat Movement, 1918–1924*. Leiden: Brill, 1999.
Rabban, David. *Law's History: American Legal Thought and the Transatlantic Turn to History*. New York: Cambridge University Press, 2013.
Radzyner, Amihai. "Talmid Haham shelo Nispad Ka-Halakhah: Yaacov Shmuel Zuri u-Mehkarav ba-Mishpat ha-'Ivri 'al Reka Toldot Mehkar T'hum Ze." *Shenaton ha-Mishpat ha-'Ivri* 23 (2004/05): 253.
Radzyner, Amihai. "A Constitution for Israel: The Design of the Leo Kohn Proposal, 1948." *Israel Studies* 15 (2010): 1.
Radzyner, Amihai. "Ha-Mishpat ha-'Ivri beyn Leumi le-Dati: Ha-Dilemah shel ha-Tnu'ah ha-Datit Leumit." *Mekhkarey Mishpat* 26 (2010): 91.
Radzyner, Amihai. "Jewish Law in London: Between Two Societies." *Jewish Law Annual* 18 (2010): 81.
Radzyner, Amihai. "The Irish Influence on the Israeli Constitution Proposal, 1948." In *The Irish Constitution: Perspectives and Prospects*, edited by Eoin Carolan, 69. Haywards Heath: Bloomsbury, 2012.
Radzyner, Amihai. "Judaism and Jewish Law in Pre-State Palestine." In *The Cambridge Companion to Judaism and Law*, edited by Christine Hayes, 317. New York: Cambridge University Press, 2017.
Radzyner, Amihai, and Rivka Brot. "Masa' u-Masa le-Vitul 'Onesh ha-Mavet 'al 'Averat ha-Retsah." *'Iyuney Mishpat* 47 (2024): 475.
Ramnath, Kalyani. "Intertwined Itineraries: Debt, Decolonization, and International Law in Post-World War II South Asia." *Law and History Review* 38 (2020): 1.
Rasilla, Ignacio de la. "Looking Forward Through and Beyond the Western Classics of International Law." *Asian Journal of International Law* 13 (2023): 146.
Rasilla, Ignacio de la, and Ayesha Shahid, eds. *International Law and Islam: Historical Explorations*. Leiden: Brill, 2019.
Rathore, Aakash Singh, and Garima Goswamy. *Rethinking Indian Jurisprudence: An Introduction to the Philosophy of Law*. London: Routledge, 2018.
Raychaudhuri, Tapan. *Europe Reconsidered: Perceptions of the West in Nineteenth-Century Bengal*. Delhi: Oxford University Press, 1988.
Reid, Donald M. *Lawyers and Politics in the Arab World, 1880–1960*. Minneapolis, MN: Bibliotheca Islamica, 1981.
Reid, Donald Malcolm. *Cairo University and the Making of Modern Egypt*. Cambridge: Cambridge University Press, 1990.

Renold, Leah. *A Hindu Education: Early Years of the Banaras Hindu University*. Delhi: Oxford University Press, 2005.

Rice, William G. "A Quick Look at Legal Education in India and Pakistan." *Journal of Legal Education* 11 (1958): 364.

Riles, Annelise, ed. *Rethinking the Masters of Comparative Law*. Oxford: Hart, 2004.

Roberts, Anthea. *Is International Law International?* New York: Oxford University Press, 2017.

Roberts, Geoffrey. "Averting Armageddon: The Communist Peace Movement, 1948–1956." In *The Oxford Handbook of the History of Communism*, edited by Stephen A. Smith, 322. Oxford: Oxford University Press, 2014.

Roth, Hans Ingvar. *P. C. Chang and the Universal Declaration of Human Rights*. Philadelphia, PA: University of Pennsylvania Press, 2016.

Roy, Tirthankar, and Anand V. Swamy. *Law and the Economy in Colonial India*. Chicago, IL: University of Chicago Press, 2016.

Rozin, Orit. *A Home for All Jews: Citizenship, Rights and National Identity in the New Israeli State*. Waltham, MA: Brandeis University Press, 2016.

Rubin, Avi. *Ottoman Nizamiye Courts: Law and Modernity*. New York: Palgrave Macmillan, 2011.

Rudolph, Lloyd I., and Susanne Hoeber Rudolph. "Barristers and Brahmans in India: Legal Cultures and Social Change." *Comparative Studies in Society and History* 8 (1965): 24.

Rumble, Wilfrid E., *Doing Austin Justice: The Reception of John Austin's Philosophy of Law in Nineteenth-Century England*. London: Continuum, 2005.

Ruskola, Teemu. *Legal Orientalism: China, the United States and Modern Law*. Cambridge, MA: Harvard University Press, 2013.

Sagy, Yosef. "Re'ayon 'im Profesor Gad Tedeschi." In *Sefer Zikaron le-Gad Tedeschi*, edited by Izhak Englard, Aharon Barak, Mordechai A. Rabello et al., 23. Jerusalem: Harry Sacher Institute, 1995.

Saha, Suhrita. "Benoy Kumar Sarkar (1887–1949): A Tryst with Destiny." *Sociological Bulletin* 62 (2013): 4.

Sahgal, Rishika. "Decolonizing Criminal Law in India." In *The Routledge International Handbook on Decolonizing Justice*, edited by Chris Cunneen, 391. London: Routledge, 2023.

Said, Edward W. *Orientalism*. New York: Vintage, 1979.

Saleem, Raja M. Ali. "Hinduism, Hindutva and Hindu Populism in India: An Analysis of Party Manifestos of Indian Rightwing Parties." *Religions* 12 (2021): 803.

Saletore, B. A., *Ancient Indian Political Thought and Institutions*. Bombay: Asia Publishing, 1963.

Saposnik, Arieh B. *Becoming Hebrew: The Creation of a Jewish National Culture in Ottoman Palestine*. New York: Oxford University Press, 2008.

Sarkar, Sumit. *The Swadeshi Movement in Bengal*. New ed. Ranikhet: Permanent Black, 2010.

Sartori, Andrew. *Bengal in Global Concept History: Culturalism in the Age of Capital*. Chicago, IL: University of Chicago Press, 2008.

Sartori, Andrew. "A Liberal Discourse of Custom in Colonial Bengal." *Past and Present* 212 (2011): 163.

Sartori, Paolo. "What Went Wrong? The Failure of Soviet Policy on Shari'a Courts in Turkestan, 1917–1923." *Die Welt des Islams* 50 (2010): 397.

Schmidt, Katharina Isabel. "Law, Modernity, Crisis: German Free Lawyers, American Legal Realists, and the Transatlantic Turn to 'Life,' 1903–1933." *German Studies Review* 39 (2016): 121.

Schmitthener [Schmitthenner], Samuel. "A Sketch of the Development of the Legal Profession in India." *Law and Society Review* 3 (1968/69): 337.

Schneider, Suzanne. *Mandatory Separation: Religion, Education, and Mass Politics in Palestine*. Stanford, CA: Stanford University Press, 2018.

Schnitzer, Shani. "Ben-Gurion, Bagatz veha-Hukah she-Lo Haytah." *Mishpatim* 53 (2025): 489.

Schochet, Gordon, Fania Oz-Salzberger, and Meirav Jones, eds. *Political Hebraism: Judaic Sources in Early Modern Political Thought*. Jerusalem: Shalem Press, 2008.

Schweid, Eliezer. *Democracy and Halakhah*. Lanham, MD: University Press of America, 1994.

Sebba, Leslie. "Professor Tedeschi ve-'Torat ha-Hakikah' – Kol Kore ba-Midbar." In *Sefer Zikaron le-Gad Tedeschi*, edited by Izhak Englard, Aharon Barak, Mordechai A. Rabello et al., 535. Jerusalem: Harry Sacher Institute, 1995.

Sebba, Leslie. "Law and Society in Israel: An Emerging Agenda." *Israel Studies Forum* 17 (2001): 83.

Sen, Rohini, and Rashmi Raman. "Retelling Radha Binod Pal: The Outsider and the Native." In *The Dawn of a Discipline: International Criminal Justice and Its Early Exponents*, edited by Frédéric Mégret and Immi Tallgren, 230. Cambridge: Cambridge University Press, 2020.

Sen, Satadru, *Benoy Kumar Sarkar: Restoring the Nation to the World*. New Delhi: Routledge, 2015.

Sen, Tansen. *India, China, and the World: A Connected History*. Lanham, MD: Rowman & Littlefield, 2017.

Sen, Tansen, and Brian Tsui, eds. *Beyond Pan-Asianism: Connecting China and India, 1840s–1960s*. New Delhi: Oxford University Press, 2021.

Seppänen, Samuli. *Ideological Conflict and the Rule of Law in Contemporary China*. Cambridge: Cambridge University Press, 2016.

Seppänen, Samuli. "Anti-Formalism and the Preordained Birth of Chinese Jurisprudence." *China Perspectives* 2018(4) (2018): 31.

Seth, Sanjay. *Subject Lessons: The Western Education of Colonial India*. Durham, NC: Duke University Press, 2007.

Sethna, M. J. "Synthetic Jurisprudence." *Calcutta University Law College Magazine* 24 (1956): 16.
Sethna, M. J. *Jurisprudence*. Revised and enlarged 2nd ed. Girgaon: Lakhani Books, 1959.
Sezgin, Yüksel. *Human Rights under State-Enforced Religious Family Laws in Israel, Egypt, and India*. Cambridge: Cambridge University Press, 2013.
Shahal, Aviram. "Ha-Hukah she-Nishkehah: Hatsa'at ha-Hukah shel Leo Kohn veha-Be'ayah ha-'Arvit." LLM thesis, Tel Aviv University, 2014.
Shalakany, Amr. "Between Identity and Redistribution: Sanhuri, Genealogy and the Will to Islamise." *Islamic Law and Society* 8 (2001): 201.
Shalakany, Amr. "Sanhuri, and the Historical Origins of Comparative Law in the Arab World (Or How Sometimes Losing Your *Asalah* Can Be Good for You)." In *Rethinking the Masters of Comparative Law*, edited by Annelise Riles, 152. Oxford: Hart, 2001.
Shalakany, Amr. *Izdihar wa-inhiyar al-nukhbah al-qanuniyyah al-misriyyah, 1805–2005*. Cairo: Dar al-shuruq, 2013.
Shamir, Ronen. *The Colonies of Law: Colonialism, Zionism and Law in Early Mandate Palestine*. New York: Cambridge University Press, 2000.
Sharafi, Mitra. "A New History of Colonial Lawyering: Likhovski and Legal Identities in the British Empire." *Law and Social Inquiry* 32 (2007): 1059.
Sharafi, Mitra. *Law and Identity in Colonial South Asia: Parsi Legal Culture, 1772–1947*. New York: Cambridge University Press, 2014.
Sharafi, Mitra. "South Asian Legal History." *Annual Review of Law and Social Science* 11 (2015): 309.
Sharafi, Mitra. "South Asians at the Inns of Court: Empire, Expulsion, and Redemption circa 1900." In *Between and Across: Legal History Without Boundaries*, edited by Kenneth W. Mack and Jacob Katz Cogan, 179. New York: Oxford University Press, 2024.
Sharanjit, Amanjit Kaur. "La colonisation et la transposition des concepts juridiques: L'exemple du droit coutumier au Punjab (Inde)." *Cahiers Jean Moulin* 6 (2020). https://doi.org/10.4000/cjm.1118.
Sharma, G. S. "Some Reflections on the Teaching of Jurisprudence in India." In *Studies in Law: An Anthology of Essays in Municipal and International Law*, edited by V. V. Deshpande, 39. Bombay: Asia Publishing, 1961.
Sharma, K. M. "Civil Law in India." *Washington University Law Quarterly* 1 (1969): 1.
Sharma, Ram Sharan. *Aspects of Political Ideas and Institutions in Ancient India*, 2nd rev. ed. Delhi: Motilal Banarsidass, 1968.
Shavit, Yaacov. *Ha-Yahadut bi-Re'i ha-Yevanut*. Tel Aviv: 'Am 'Oved, 1992.
She'altiel, Eli. *Tamid be-Meri: Moshe Sne, Biyografyah, 1909–1948*. Tel Aviv: 'Am 'Oved, 2000.
Shechter, Relli. *The Egyptian Social Contract: A History of State–Middle Class Relations*. Edinburgh: Edinburgh University Press, 2023.

Sheridan, A. L. "George Williams Keeton, 1902–1989." *Proceedings of the British Academy* 80 (1993): 333.

Shetreet, Shimon, and Walter Homolka. *Jewish and Israeli Law: An Introduction*. Berlin: De Gruyter, 2017.

Sicker, Martin. "Democracy and Judaism: The Question of Equality." *Jewish Political Studies Review* 5 (1993): 57.

Siddiqui, Sohaira. "Navigating Colonial Power: Challenging Precedents and the Limitation of Local Elites." *Islamic Law and Society* 26 (2019): 272.

Siddiqui, Sohaira Z. M. *Islamic Law on Trial: Contesting Colonial Power in British India*. Oakland, CA: University of California Press, 2025.

Siegel, Benjamin. "The Kibbutz and the Ashram: Sarvodaya Agriculture, Israeli Aid, and the Global Imaginaries of Indian Development." *American Historical Review* 125 (2020): 1175.

Simpson, A. W. B. "The Rise and Fall of the Legal Treatise: Legal Principles and the Forms of Legal Literature." *University of Chicago Law Review* 48 (1981): 632.

Simpson, A. W. B. "The Salmond Lecture." *Victoria University of Wellington Law Review* 38 (2007): 669.

Sinclair, Daniel B. "Jewish Law in the State of Israel." *Jewish Law Annual* 11 (1996): 397.

Sinha, Narendra Krishna. *Asutosh Mookerjee: A Biographical Study*. Calcutta: Asutosh Mookerjee Centenary Committee, 1966.

Skinner, Quentin. "The Limits of Historical Explanation." *Philosophy* 41 (1966): 203.

Slezkine, Yuri. "The USSR as a Communal Apartment, or How a Socialist State Promoted Ethnic Particularism." *Slavic Review* 53 (1994): 414.

Somos, Mark. "Political Thought and the Historiography of International Law." In *The Cambridge History of International Law*, edited by Randall Lesaffer and Anne Peters, Vol. 1, 107. Cambridge: Cambridge University Press, 2024.

Srikantan, Geetanjali. *Identifying and Regulating Religion in India: Law, History and the Place of Worship*. Cambridge: Cambridge University Press, 2020.

Stasavage, David. *The Decline and Rise of Democracy: A Global History from Antiquity to Today*. Princeton, NJ: Princeton University Press, 2020.

Steller, Verena. "The 'Rule of Law' in British India, or a Rule of Lawyers? Indian Barristers vs the Colonial State." *Comparativ: Zeitschrift für Globalgeschichte und Vergleichende Gesellschaftsforschung* 24(5) (2014): 78.

Stephens, Julia. *Governing Islam: Law, Empire, and Secularism in South Asia*. Cambridge: Cambridge University Press, 2018.

Stern, Rephael G. "Uncertain Comparisons: Zionist and Israeli Links to India and Pakistan in the Age of Partition and Decolonization." *Law and History Review* 39 (2021): 451.

Stern, Rephael G., and Arie M. Dubnov. "A Part of Asia or Apart from Asia? Zionist Perceptions of Asia, 1947–1956." In *Unacknowledged Kinships: Postcolonial Studies and the Historiography of Zionism*, edited by Stefan Vogt, Derek Penslar, and Arieh Saposnik, 233. Waltham, MA: Brandeis University Press, 2023.

Stolte, Carolien, and Harald Fischer-Tiné. "Imagining Asia in India: Nationalism and Internationalism (ca. 1905–1940)." *Comparative Studies in Society and History* 54 (2012): 65.

Strassman, Gabriel. *'Otey ha-Glimah: Toldot 'Arikhat ha-Din be-Erets Yisra'el*. Tel Aviv: Lishkat 'Orkhey ha-Din be-Yisra'el, 1984.

Strawson, John. "Islamic Law and English Texts." *Law and Critique* 6 (1995): 21.

Strawson, John. "Orientalism and Legal Education in the Middle East: Reading Frederic Goadby's Introduction to the Study of Law." *Legal Studies* 21 (2001): 663.

Strawson, John. "Revisiting Islamic Law: Marginal Notes from Colonial History." *Griffith Law Review* 12 (2003): 362.

Sturman, Rachel. *The Government of Social Life in Colonial India: Liberalism, Religious Law and Women's Rights*. Cambridge: Cambridge University Press, 2012.

Sugarman, David. "Legal Theory, the Common Law Mind and the Making of the Textbook Tradition." In *Legal Theory and Common Law*, edited by William Twining, 26. Oxford: Blackwell, 1986.

Sugarman, David. "'A Hatred of Disorder': Legal Science, Liberalism and Imperialism." In *Dangerous Supplements: Resistance and Renewal in Jurisprudence*, edited by Peter Fitzpatrick, 34. London: Pluto Press, 1991.

Sugarman, David. "A Special Relationship? American Influences on English Legal Education, c. 1870–1965." *International Journal of the Legal Profession* 18 (2011): 7.

Sultan, Nazmul S. "Between the Many and the One: Anticolonial Federalism and Popular Sovereignty." *Political Theory* 50 (2022): 247.

Suman, Amit Kumar. "Colonial State and Indigenous Islamic Learning: A Case Study of Calcutta Madrasa." *Paedagogica Historica* 58 (2022): 486.

Tamanaha, Brian Z. "Sociological Jurisprudence Past and Present." *Law and Social Inquiry* 45 (2020): 493.

Tamir, Dan. *Hebrew Fascism in Palestine, 1922–1942*. Cham: Palgrave Macmillan, 2018.

Tepe, Sultan, Keith Simonds, and Michael C. Dirksen. "The Emergence of Religious Populism? Insights from Israel, India, and Turkey." *Populism* 5 (2022): 1.

Thapar, Romila. "The Theory of the Aryan Race and the Origins of the South Asian Civilisation." *Social Scientist* 24 (1996): 3.

Tidhar, David, ed. *Entsiklopediyah le-Halutsey ha-Yishuv u-Vonav*. 19 vols. Tel Aviv: Sifriyat Rishonim, 1947–71.

Timoshina, Elena V., G. Lorini, and W. Żełaniec. "Other Russian or Polish Legal Realists." In *A Treatise of Legal Philosophy and General Jurisprudence*, edited by Enrico Pattaro and Corrado Roversi, Vol. 12.2, 527. Dordrecht: Springer, 2016.

Tindall, Robert E. "The Graduate School of Law, Soochow University, Republic of China." *International Lawyer* 7 (1973): 711.

Tolley, Howard B., Jr. *The International Commission of Jurists: Global Advocates for Human Rights*. Philadelphia, PA: University of Pennsylvania Press, 2010.

Tomlins, Christopher. "Literature Review Article: Comparative Legal History." In *Comparative Legal History*, edited by Christopher Tomlins and Elizabeth Josselyn Boalt, 1. Cheltenham: Edward Elgar, 2021.

Trautmann, Thomas R. *Aryans in British India*. Berkeley, CA: University of California Press, 1997.

Twining, W. L. "Laws." In *The University of London and the World of Learning, 1836–1986*, edited by F. M. L. Thompson, 82. London: Hambledon Press, 1990.

Twining, William. *Blackstone's Tower: The English Law School*. London: Stevens, 1994.

Twining, William. *General Jurisprudence: Understanding Law from a Global Perspective*. Cambridge: Cambridge University Press, 2009.

Twining, William. *Jurist in Context: A Memoir*. Cambridge: Cambridge University Press, 2019.

Tzoreff, Avi-ram. *Kedmah Mizrahah: R. Binyamin, du-Le'umiyut ve-Tsiyonut sheke-Neged*. Jerusalem: Shazar, 2023.

Varma, Vishwanath Prasad. *Studies in Hindu Political Thought and Its Metaphysical Foundations*. Delhi: Motilal Banarsidass, 1959.

Veidlinger, Jeffrey. *Jewish Public Culture in the Late Russian Empire*. Bloomington, IN: Indiana University Press, 2009.

Venturi, Franco. "Oriental Despotism." *Journal of the History of Ideas* 24 (1963): 133.

Versteeg, Mila, Adam Chilton, and Erensu Altan. "Constitutional Duties." *American Journal of Comparative Law* 72 (2024): 685.

Viola, Francesco. "Introduction: Natural Law Theories in the Twentieth Century." In *A Treatise of Legal Philosophy and General Jurisprudence*, edited by Enrico Pattaro and Corrado Roversi, Vol. 12.2, 3. Dordrecht: Springer, 2016.

Vishwanathan, Gauri. "Colonialism and the Construction of Hinduism." In *The Blackwell Companion to Hinduism*, edited by Gavin Flood, 23. Oxford: Blackwell, 2003.

Vogenauer, Stefan. "An Empire of Light? Learning and Lawmaking in the History of German Law." *Cambridge Law Journal* 64 (2005): 481.

Vogt, Stefan, Derek Penslar, and Arieh Saposnik. "Introduction: Unacknowledged Kinships." In *Unacknowledged Kinships: Postcolonial*

*Studies and the Historiography of Zionism*, edited by Stefan Vogt, Derek Penslar, and Arieh Saposnik, 1. Waltham, MA: Brandeis University Press, 2023.

Walicki, Andrzej. *Legal Philosophies of Russian Liberalism*. Notre Dame, IN: University of Notre Dame Press, 1992.

Walzer, Michael. *The Paradox of Liberation: Secular Revolutions and Religious Counterrevolutions*. New Haven, CT: Yale University Press, 2015.

Walzer, Michael, Menachem Lorberbaum, and Noam J. Zohar, eds. *The Jewish Political Tradition*. 3 vols. New Haven, CT: Yale University Press, 2000–18.

Watkin, T. G. "Sir William Markby (1829–1914)." In *Oxford Dictionary of National Biography*. Oxford: Oxford University Press, 2004. https://doi.org/10.1093/ref:odnb/50590.

Watson, Andrew. "The Legal Education Revolution that Failed: Attempts to Establish a Legal University in Victorian Britain." *Journal on European History of Law* 14 (2023): 28.

Weeramantry, C. G. *Islamic Jurisprudence: An International Perspective*. New York: St. Martin's Press, 1988.

Weller, R. Charles. *Moses, Muhammad and Nature's God in Early American Religious-Legal History, 1640–1830: A Global Crosscultural Perspective*. Cham: Palgrave Macmillan, 2024.

Werner, Michael, and Bénédicte Zimmermann. "Beyond Comparison: Histoire Croisée and the Challenge of Reflexivity." *History and Theory* 45 (2006): 30.

Wilf, Steven Robert. *The Law before the Law*. Lanham, MD: Lexington Books, 2008.

Wilf, Steven. "Legal Treatise." In *The Oxford Handbook of Law and Humanities*, edited by Simon Stern, Maksymilian Del Mar, and Bernadette Meyler, 687. New York: Oxford University Press, 2020.

Williams, Alexander. "Imagining the Post-Colonial Lawyer: Legal Elites and the Indian Nation-State, 1947–1967." *Asian Journal of Comparative Law* 15 (2020): 1.

Williams, E. T. "Allen, Sir Carleton Kemp." In *Oxford Dictionary of National Biography*. Oxford: Oxford University Press, 2004. https://doi.org/10.1093/ref:odnb/30383.

Williams, Rina Verma. "Hindu Law as Personal Law: State and Identity in the Hindu Code Bills Debates, 1952–1956." In *Hinduism and Law: An Introduction*, edited by Timothy Lubin, Donald R. Davis Jr., and Jayanth K. Krishnan, 105. Cambridge and New York: Cambridge University Press, 2010.

Wood, Leonard. *Islamic Legal Revival: Reception of European Law and Transformations in Islamic Legal Thought in Egypt, 1875–1952*. Oxford: Oxford University Press, 2016.

Xavier, Sujith. "Locating and Situating Justice Pal: TWAIL, International Criminal Tribunals, and Judicial Powers." *Asian Journal of International Law* 12 (2022): 292.

Xian, Liu. "Two Universities and Two Eras of Catholicism in China: Fu Jen University and Aurora University, 1903–1937." *Christian Higher Education* 8 (2009): 405.

Xinping, Zhuo. "Religion and Rule of Law in China Today." *Brigham Young University Law Review* (2009): 519.

Xiuqing, Li. "John C. H. Wu at the University of Michigan School of Law." *Journal of Legal Education* 58 (2008): 545.

Yedidya, Asaf. *Halakha and the Challenge of Israeli Sovereignty*. Lanham, MD: Lexington Books, 2019.

Yelle, Robert A. "The Hindu Moses: Christian Polemics against Jewish Ritual and the Secularization of Hindu Law under Colonialism." *History of Religions* 49 (2011): 141.

Yi, Ping. "The Final Splendour of an Aged Empire: Chinese Thought on International Law in the Early Twentieth Century." *Journal of East Asia and International Law* 9 (2016): 29.

Zabarskaitė, Jolita. *"Greater India" and the Indian Expansionist Imagination, c. 1885–1965: The Rise and Decline of the Idea of a Lost Hindu Empire*. Munich: De Gruyter, 2022.

Zalkin, Mordechai. "The 'Hebrew Law Society' and the Emergence of Hebrew-Nationalism in the Early 20th-Century Russian Empire." *Diné Israel* 33 (2019): 137*.

Zhang, Taisu. "The Development of Comparative Law in Modern China." In *The Oxford Handbook of Comparative Law*, edited by Mathias Reimann and Reinhard Zimmermann, 2nd ed., 228. Oxford: Oxford University Press, 2019.

Zhang, Xiaomeng. "John C. H. Wu and His Comparative Law Pursuit." *International Journal of Legal Information* 41 (2013): 196.

Zhu, Mingzhe. "La place de l'enseignement du droit français dans la modernisation chinoise: Les missions civilisatrices de quatre modernisateurs au tournant des XIXe et XXe siècles." *Cahiers Jean Moulin* 7 (2021). https://doi.org/10.4000/cjm.1454.

Ziadeh, Farhat Jacob. *Lawyers, the Rule of Law and Liberalism in Modern Egypt*. Stanford, CA: Stanford University Press, 1968.

"Zikhron le-Rishonim: Hayim Yehudah Roth." *Katarsis* 11 (2009): 196.

al-Zirikli, Khayr al-Din. *al-A'lam: qamus tarajim li-ashhar al-rijal wa-al-nisa min al-'Arab wa-al-musta'ribin wa-al-mustashriqin*. 15th ed., 7 vols. Beirut: Dar al-'ilm lil-malayin, 2002.

Zohar, David. *Mehuyavut Yehudit be-'Olam Moderni: Ha-Rav Hayim Hirshenzon ve-Yahaso el ha-Modernah*. Tel Aviv: Ha-Kibuts ha-Me'uhad, 2003.

# Index

For EU product safety concerns, contact us at Calle de José Abascal, 56–1°, 28003 Madrid, Spain or eugpsr@cambridge.org.

www.ingramcontent.com/pod-product-compliance
Ingram Content Group UK Ltd.
Pitfield, Milton Keynes, MK11 3LW, UK
UKHW040017280926
476049UK00001B/8

* 9 7 8 1 0 0 9 6 9 9 8 8 4 *